New Hampshire

New Hampshire

Christina Tree & Christine Hamm
with photographs by the authors

The Countryman Press ✳ Woodstock, Vermont

SEVENTH EDITION

For William A. Davis.
  —Christina Tree

For friends and family whose extra eyes have
made these explorations an excellent adventure.
  —Christine Hamm

We welcome your comments and suggestions. Please contact Explorer's Guide
Editor, The Countryman Press, P.O. Box 748, Woodstock, Vermont 05091; e-mail
ctree@traveltree.net or countrymanpress@wwnorton.com.

Seventh Edition

New Hampshire: An Explorer's Guide

ISBN 978-0-88150-841-3

Maps by XNR Productions, © 2006 The Countryman Press
Book design by Bodenweber Design
Text composition by PerfecType, Nashville, TN
Cover photograph, © Robert J. Kozlow. To see more of his work, please visit
robertkozlow.com.

Published by The Countryman Press, P.O. Box 748, Woodstock, Vermont 05091

Distributed by W. W. Norton & Company, Inc., 500 Fifth Avenue, New York, NY
10110

Printed in the United States of America

10 9 8 7 6 5 4 3 2 1

EXPLORE WITH US!

Welcome to the most widely used and comprehensive travel guide to the Granite State. All inclusions—attractions, inns, and restaurants—are chosen on the basis of personal experience, not paid advertising.

The following points will help to get you started on your way.

WHAT'S WHERE

In the beginning of the book you'll find an alphabetical listing of highlights and important information that you may want to reference quickly.

LODGING

Prices: Please don't hold us or the respective innkeepers responsible for the rates listed as of press time in 2010. Some changes are inevitable. The state rooms and meals tax is 9 percent as of this writing, but that also may change. The following codes are used: **EP:** lodging only; **MAP:** lodging, breakfast, and dinner; **B&B:** lodging and breakfast; **AP:** lodging and three meals.

RESTAURANTS

In most sections, please note a distinction between *Dining Out* and *Eating Out*. Restaurants in the *Eating Out* group are generally inexpensive.

KEY TO SYMBOLS

  ⊚ **Weddings.** The wedding-ring symbol appears next to properties that specialize in weddings.

  ❦ **Special value.** The blue-ribbon symbol appears next to selected lodging and restaurants that combine quality and moderate prices.

  🐾 **Pets.** The dog-paw symbol appears next to venues that accept pets (usually with prior notice).

  ✐ **Child-friendly.** The crayon symbol appears next to lodging, restaurants, activities, and shops of special interest or appeal to youngsters.

  ♿ **Handicapped access.** The wheelchair symbol appears next to lodging, restaurants, and attractions that are partially or completely handicapped accessible.

  ("T") **Wireless Internet.** The wireless symbol appears next to lodging, restaurants, and attractions that offer wireless Internet access.

  ✪ **Authors' favorites.** These are the places we think have the best to offer in each region, whether that means great food, outstanding rooms, beautiful scenery, or overall appeal.

We would appreciate your comments and corrections about places you visit or know well in the state. Please address your correspondence to Explorer's Guide Editor, The Countryman Press, P.O. Box 748, Woodstock, VT 05091, or via email at countrymanpress@wwnorton.com. You can also e-mail Chris Tree: ctree@traveltree.net.

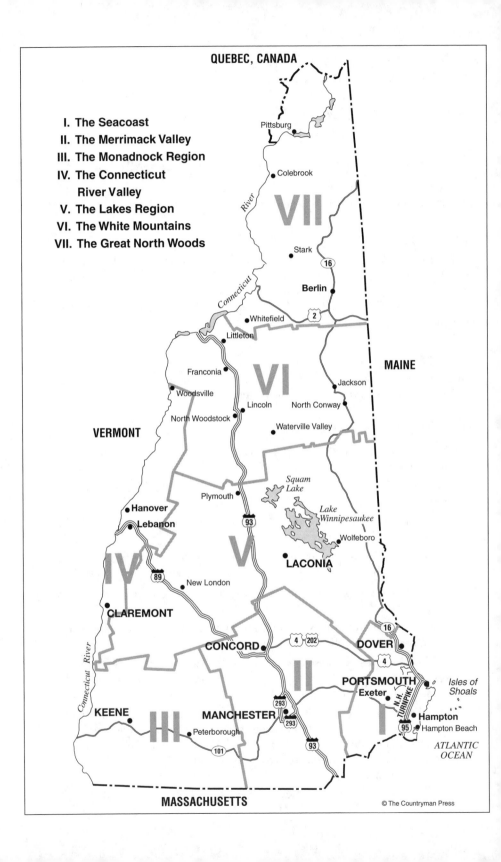

CONTENTS

7 The Great North Woods / 457

INTRODUCTION

Welcome to the seventh edition of New Hampshire's most comprehensive travel guide. We hope that residents as well as visitors will find it useful.

Each chapter focuses on a different region, beginning with a verbal snapshot of the landscape and historical background. Sources of information, how to get around, and descriptions of everything to see and do, from winter sports to places to swim and picnic, follow. Then come capsule descriptions of places to stay. Our focus is on inns and bed & breakfasts, but other lodging ranges from family-run motels to Appalachian Mountain Club huts and lodges. We have personally visited more than 90 percent of the lodgings described; the other 10 percent have come highly recommended. Nobody has paid to be included.

We generally include prices because categories like "moderate" and "expensive" can be misleading, depending on what they include. Please allow for inflation. Most lodging places add the 9 percent New Hampshire room and meals tax, and some also add a service charge; be sure to inquire. After lodging come critiques of local upscale restaurants (*Dining Out*) and more casual options (*Eating Out*). We also describe shops and farms worth seeking out and the special events of that area.

Our regions reflect those accepted by the people who live in them. Generally they mirror the way into which the New Hampshire Department of Travel and Tourism divides the state, but there are differences. Crossing the border from Massachusetts, visitors enter the part of the state we've called "The Merrimack Valley." Following the Merrimack River north, I-93 passes by Manchester, a city well worth a stop for its Currier Museum of Art, one of the best small museums in the country. A few minutes beyond is Concord, home of the nation's oldest state capitol building in continuous use as well as of the McAuliffe-Shepard Discovery Center, a world-renowned planetarium named for New Hampshire's very own space pioneers, Christa McAuliffe and Alan Shepard. Other attractions in this sometimes overlooked area include white clapboard villages, the Derry home of poet Robert Frost, and Canterbury Shaker Village.

The scattering of lakes across the width of the state we term simply "The Lakes Region." We divide our chapter, as I-93 does, into "The Lake Winnipesaukee Region" and "Ossipee Valley" east of the interstate and "the Sunapee/Newfound Lakes Region" to the west.

Lake Winnipesaukee, the state's largest lake, remains the popular tourist destination that it's been for more than a century. Still, there are quiet corners such as

Squam Lake and the hills around Center Sandwich. Wolfeboro, billed as America's first summer resort, remains a lively and visitor-friendly magnet. The neighboring Ossipee Valley, flanking Rt. 16, harbors both lakes and mountains, also the gem-like villages of Tamworth and Eaton Center. West of I-93 the open, rolling countryside from Newfound Lake to Lake Sunapee is spotted with lakes big and small, most with a view of one of the area's three mighty mountains, Sunapee, Kearsarge, and Cardigan.

Our "Upper Valley Towns" chapter includes both the Vermont and New Hampshire banks of the Connecticut River for some 20 miles north and south of Dartmouth College, an area at the heart of the "Connecticut River National Scenic Byway." Here you can enjoy a picnic and chamber music concert on the lawns of the Saint-Gaudens National Historic Site in Cornish, New Hampshire, overlooking Mount Ascutney in Vermont. The country's longest historic covered bridge links the two. The interstate (I-91) on the Vermont side of the river is the area's prime access. Essentially rural, this is also one of New England's most distinctive regions and one of its most sophisticated corridors, with outstanding museums, dining, and lodging.

South of the Upper Valley several communities, notably Walpole, are part of both this corridor and the Monadnock Region. Mount Monadnock towers above the surrounding roll of southwestern New Hampshire and is visible from an amazing number of the 40 towns in this region, most characterized by narrow roads and quintessential New England villages. Monadnock itself is one of the world's most heavily hiked mountains but—fortunately for those who have discovered the area's exceptional small inns, winter skiing, summer swimming holes, and cultural calendar—most of these hikers day-trip.

Serious hikers head for the White Mountains, which form a ragged line, beginning near the Connecticut River with Mount Moosilauke and marching diagonally northeast across New Hampshire. Mount Washington, literally the high point of New England, has been the state's top tourist attraction for more than 150 years. Accessible by cog railway and car or "stage" as well as by spectacular hiking trails from all directions, it remains magnificent and untamed. This region has loomed large on the national ski map since the birth of alpine skiing here. It presently offers a choice of varied ski resorts and hundreds of miles of snowshoeing and cross-country ski trails. During summer and fall it is a mecca for hikers and technical climbers as well as a great family destination, offering an easy entrée to both natural and human-made attractions. It also represents one of New Hampshire's largest concentrations of lodging places, dining, and shopping.

We divide this high-mountain region into "Mount Washington and Its Valleys" and the "Western Whites," a rugged region largely within the White Mountain National Forest that includes Loon Mountain and Waterville Valley, both founded as ski areas but now full-fledged year-round resorts. This area is an especially good bet for families, offering varied activities and condo-based lodging. It includes dramatic Franconia Notch and the old resort communities of Franconia, Sugar Hill, and Bethlehem.

North of "the Whites" lies the least touristed section of the state, the Great North Woods. This vast forested area includes the northern White Mountains, the headwaters of the Connecticut River, and the mighty Androscoggin. Here moose graze beside the roads, and you can find wilderness campsites and fall asleep to the call of loons. You can also stay in The Balsams and the Mountain View Grand

Resort and Spa, two surviving grand hotels, or in a surprisingly wide choice of

sporting camps and lodges.

The area around New Hampshire's 18 miles of Seacoast combines historic charm, urbane sophistication, and numerous coastal digressions—everything from historic hotels, lighthouses, and forts to mansions, gardens, and natural seascapes. Portsmouth's Market Square epitomizes the city's blend of old and new with North Church's vaulting spire, sidewalk cafes, and funky and fine boutiques all sharing the landscape. Allow enough time to sample the region's many fine restaurants, theaters, museums, boat excursions, and beaches.

The first edition of *New Hampshire, An Explorer's Guide* appeared in 1991 and has been thoroughly updated regularly since. To our knowledge the *Explorer Guides* were the first practical guidebooks (detailing lodging, dining, and shopping as well as attractions) to individual New England states. This isn't to discount the magnificent 1930s WPA guides or the many 19th-century guides published by railroads. The post–Civil War decades brought an explosion of illustrated guides, which continued to multiply through the 1880s and '90s, and also early-20th-century "motoring guides." Current guidebooks cover seemingly every aspect of travel— from dog-friendly inns to birding, biking, wedding venues, and, of course, hiking. Still, we see a need—more than ever with the explosion of narrowly targeted pieces of information both in print and online—for a general guide that puts the pieces together, offering an overview as well as details and depth. We look forward to the day when this book will be interactive and all the listed websites become live links. In the meantime please don't hesitate to email us (ctree@traveltree.net).

One author of this book is a "visitor," the other a longtime resident.

Cambridge, Massachusetts–based Chris Tree has written more than 100 New England stories for the *Boston Globe* Sunday travel section and contributes regularly to *Yankee* magazine. She is the author of *How New England Happened* (a historical guide to the region) and launched the *Explorer's Guides* series, co-authoring those to Maine, Vermont, and Western Massachusetts as well as New Hampshire.

Christine Hamm moved in 1972 to Hopkinton, New Hampshire, where she now lives in one of the state's classic white-clapboard villages within earshot of a Paul Revere bell. In addition to many years of writing for the *Concord Monitor*'s arts and entertainment section, Chris has contributed articles to the *New York Post*, *Yankee Magazine's New England Travel Guide*, and numerous statewide publications. She is currently a member of the New Hampshire State Legislature.

The authors wish to thank Peter Randall, original coauthor of the book, who contributed hugely to its first two editions. We also owe thanks to numerous local chambers of commerce, innkeepers, and friends who helped provide and check information for the book.

For their kind support Chris Tree would like to thank chambers of commerce staffers, especially Susan Cerutti of Meredith, Jack Burnett of Peterborough, Rob Bryant of New London, and Erica Fairhurst of Hanover. Also special thanks to Deb Moore of Waterville Valley, Stacy Lopes of Loon Mountain, and Jayne O'Conner of the White Mountains Visitors Bureau, Ryan Triffit of the Mount Washington Auto Road, Rob Burbank of the Appalachian Mountain Club, Amy Bassett at the New Hampshire Division of Parks and Recreation, Sharon Francis of the Connecticut River Joint Commissions, and Steve Smith, the Mountain Wanderer of Lincoln. Thanks, too, to those innkeepers who offered help as well as hospitality:

NEW HAMPSHIRE'S TOURISM HISTORY

New Hampshire probably hosts fewer summer visitors today than it did a century ago. Certainly its market share of the country's travelers was far larger in 1910 than it is now. At the turn of the 20th century, New Hampshire's White Mountains were home to the greatest concentration of grand hotels in America, and the state in general offered hundreds of now-vanished summer inns and hotels.

Courtesy, Mt. Washington Auto Road

A 19TH-CENTURY MOUNTAIN WAGON AT THE HALF WAY HOUSE ON THE MOUNT WASHINGTON CARRIAGE ROAD

Tourism has always been driven by images. As early as the 1820s artist Thomas Cole visited New Hampshire, depicting a landscape that he called "a union of the picturesque, the sublime, and the magnificent." Other artists followed. Thoreau, Emerson, Hawthorne, and Whittier touted the White Mountains in prose and poetry. In the 1830s Starr King's *The Great White Hills*, first serialized with illustrations in the *Boston Transcript*, drew droves of city dwellers to these mountains.

Amazingly early on, Mount Washington itself became literally the high point of every visitor's New Hampshire expedition. By 1819 the pioneer father and son Abel and Ethan Crawford had cut a way to the summit for tourists (the Crawford Path is now America's oldest continually used hiking trail). In the 1850s both a Summit House and rival Tiptop House were built 6,288 feet high on the mountain's bald pate.

After the Civil War, the White Mountains became easily accessible via steamboat and train from every city in the East. More than 50 trains a day deposited visitors at Crawford Notch hotels at the western base of Mount Washington—from which they could board the world's very first mountain-climbing cog railway to the top. It competed with the 8-mile-long Mount Washington Carriage Road, completed to the summit in 1861.

Travelers flocked to vast wooden summer hotels, built to accommodate city dwellers who wanted a sanitized version of the wilderness, a kind of eastern dude ranch in which families could ride in the relative comfort of a stagecoach to view the Flume, Echo Lake, and the Old Man of the Mountain. In late afternoon parents and grandparents could retire to a rocking chair, sip a glass of claret, and view the peaks of the Presidentials from the cloister of a sweeping, colonnaded porch. This curious mix of wilderness and civility made the area an ideal destination. Most tourists stayed at one hotel for a week, a month, or for the entire summer season. Far enough away but not so dangerously distant as the still wild-seeming West, the towering waterfalls, emerald hills, and placid ponds of New Hampshire offered an escape to another world. Or almost.

The more city folk explored the high country, the more outraged they became about the ugly gashes and clogged streams caused by lumbering. The new idea that forest cover influenced rainfall was also widely discussed. Since 1810 New Hampshire had been selling off its wild lands, and by 1867 the last swath—172 acres that included Mount Washington itself—had been auctioned for $25,000. Six major lumber companies were methodically stripping and burning.

The Appalachian Mountain Club (AMC), America's first hiking group, had begun surveying trails and building mountain huts to accommodate foot traffic in 1876, thus further increasing awareness of the devastation. In 1910 a group of Boston financiers and New Hampshire politicians founded the Society for the Protection of New Hampshire Forests (SPNHF), which lobbied to get sponsored and passed a bill that enabled the 1918 creation of White Mountain National Forest (currently 800,000 acres).

Throughout the late 19th century New Hampshire's accessibility and popularity was far from limited to the White Mountains. Train lines webbed the state and small country households throughout New Hampshire opened their doors while major entrepreneurs were invested in the new business of

MR. AND MRS. F. O. STANLEY IN THEIR STANLEY STEAMER, THE FIRST MOTOR CAR TO ASCEND MOUNT WASHINGTON, AUG. 25, 1899

Courtesy, Mt. Washington Auto Road

The Mt. Washington at Bretton Woods, N. H.
The Presidential Range in distance.

Courtesy, Omni Mount Washington Resort

MOUNT WASHINGTON HOTEL IN THE AGE OF AUTO TOURING

tourism. Mark Twain, who summered in the Monadnock Region, reported that "the atmosphere of the New Hampshire highlands is exceptionally bracing and stimulating, and a fine aid to hard and continuous work." Louisa May Alcott summered in Walpole, and Emily Dickinson visited. Artists like Childe Hassam gathered around poet and innkeeper Celia Thaxter on Appledore Island in the Isles of Shoals off Portsmouth.

According to conventional wisdom, it was the automobile that put an end to grand hotels and the way of summer life they represented, but that wasn't the only factor. Initially auto touring added to the adventure of exploring the region, even to climbing Mount Washington. The Mount Washington Hotel itself was built during this early auto-crazed era. Then there was World War I.

After the war many of the big, wooden hotels were destroyed by fire, while others were razed, unable to compete with the more economical cabin colonies and camping areas that mushroomed in the 1920s and '30s—an era that also saw the advent of a new breed of visitor: the skier. The nation's first ski school opened at Peckett's-on-Sugar-Hill in 1929 in Franconia; competing ski tows and schools quickly followed in Jackson. In 1938 the ground-hugging "Skimobile" began ferrying skiers up the slopes of Mount Cranmore in North Conway, carrying patrons, most of whom had arrived by ski trains. By the 1940s ski hills were more numerous than they are today. Special ski trains ran to Warner and the foot of Mount Kearsarge while the AMC carved trails on the eastern flank of Mount Cardigan, building a lodge at the base.

The decades after World War II saw New Hampshire's visitors following tourist trails up Rt. 3 or Rt. 16 to and around through the White Mountains. They stayed in campgrounds and motels, visiting popular sites within state parks and human-made "attractions." In 1958 the White Mountains Attractions Association began promoting the region along with its members, ranging from the Cog Railroad to Clark's Trading Post and Story Land.

In the late 1960s, when this writer (Chris Tree) began traveling New Hampshire for the *Boston Globe*, I-93 was inching its way north from Boston. In Waterville Valley, a low-key 19th century summer haven along its path, ex-

Olympian Tom Corcoran was creating the state's first self-contained ski resort. Farther along, ex-governor Sherman Adams was transforming Lincoln from mill town to ski town, with his Loon Mountain at its center.

At the time, motor inns with indoor pools and all the AAA-rated comforts represented the height of luxury. The wooden bones of long-closed hotels still littered old White Mountains resort towns like Jackson and Bethlehem. Around the time of America's bicentennial (1975), however, country inns once more gained cachet as romantic alternatives to the predictability of motels, and finding them meant heading back up old roads and into villages far off the tourist trail. In the 1980s and '90s bed & breakfasts expanded these alternatives and in the process reopened many of the state's beautiful, less touristed corners to visitors.

The clutch of grand old hotels that have survived——The Omni Mount Washington in Bretton Woods, the Grand View in Whitefield, and The Balsams up in Dixville Notch—have since been revitalized and then some. The historic cores of both The Wentworth in Jackson and Wentworth-by-the-Sea in Portsmouth have been preserved. Eagle Mountain House in Jackson and several more smaller vintage inns have been beautifully preserved; two low-key family-style summer resorts—Twin Lake Village on Little Sunapee Lake in New London and Rockywold-Deephaven Camps on Squam Lake in Holderness—have changed little over the century.

New Hampshire's prime appeal continues to be its natural beauty, now more accessible than ever. Mount Washington remains its literal high point (winter snow coaches supplement the seasonal cog and Auto Road traffic), and many of the more than 20 major ski areas offer summer attractions ranging from gondolas and lift-assisted mountain biking to alpine slides and ziplines. Add to this magnificent cross-country skiing networks and the ever-growing popularity of kayaking, mountain and long-distance biking (utilizing the state's splendid system of rail-trails), not to mention rock and ice climbing. Hiking, of course, remains not just the oldest but still the most popular way into the mountains, thanks in good part to the ever-service-geared AMC.

THE BRIDLE PATH, WHITE MOUNTAINS BY WINSLOW HOMER, 1868

Sterling and Francine Clark Art Institute, Williamstown, Massachusetts

Carol and Ken Beckwith of the Ashburn House in Fitzwilliam, Kay and Peter Shumway of Moose Mountain Lodge in Etna, Mike and Meri Hern of Hilltop House in Sugar Hill, Jacqueline Caserta of the Inn at Valley Farms in Walpole, Bill and Bonnie Webb at The Inn on Golden Pond in Holderness, Andrea Damato of Ferry Point House on Lake Winnisquam, and Don Bilger of Whitney's Inn in Jackson. Thanks are also due to our friend Ann Keefe of Peterborough and to *Yankee* magazine editor Mel Allen, whose assignment (and deadline) to select New Hampshire "Bests" kept her snooping through the seasons. Most all, thank you to former *Boston Globe* travel editor Bill Davis, her long-suffering husband, who cheered her on over icy winter roads.

Chris Hamm wants to acknowledge those chamber of commerce staff members who helped lighten the load with their editorial comments and enthusiasm for the project. She extends particular thanks to chamber members Gloria Bunnell from Colebrook, Carolyn O'Brien from Concord, Aaron Wensley from Dover, Molly Palmer from Exeter, Sherrill Ayles from Hampton, Charlene Courtemanche from Manchester, Mary-Ellen Marcouillier from Nashua, and Valerie Rochon from Portsmouth. Others who were particularly helpful by providing hospitality along the way include Nancy Spaulding at the Stark Village Inn, Rick McCarten at the Mountain View Grand Resort in Lancaster, Jeff McIver at The Balsams Grand Resort Hotel in Dixville Notch, the Caron family at Tall Timber Lodge in Pittsburg, Ann and Larry Leger at the Philbrook Farm Inn in Shelburne, Douglas Palardy and Kara Nichols at the Ale House Inn in Portsmouth, and Lynn Spann Bowditch of the Portsmouth Harbor Inn and Spa in Kittery, Maine.

Thanks especially to our editors, Lisa Sacks and Laura Jorstad, and to Kermit Hummel at The Countryman Press, for their support and exceptional patience during the two years it took to birth this book.

WHAT'S WHERE IN NEW HAMPSHIRE

AREA CODE 603 covers all of New Hampshire.

AGRICULTURAL FAIRS Since the 19th century, the country fair has been the place where farm families meet their friends and exhibit their best home-canned and fresh vegetables, livestock, and handwork such as quilts, baked goods, and needlework. Horse and cattle pulling, 4-H competitions, horse shows, and woodsmen's competitions are joined by midways, food stalls, and exhibits of farm implements, home furnishings, and a host of other items. The largest fair is Deerfield, held annually in fall, but other popular fairs include North Haverhill in late July, Cornish in August, and Hopkinton and Lancaster, both held on Labor Day weekend; the

last and one of the most colorful is in Sandwich, Columbus Day weekend. For current dates, check nhfairs.com.

AIR SERVICE Manchester/Boston Regional Airport (603-624-6556; flymanchester.com) is northern New England's major gateway, with connections to all parts of the country and Canada. It's served by United/United Express, US Airways and US Airways Express, Continental/Continental Express, Air Canada, Delta Air Lines, and Southwest Airlines; also by national rental car companies, limo services, taxis, and bus lines. **Lebanon Municipal Airport** (603-298-8878; flyleb .com), just off I-89 in West Lebanon, is served by Cape Air with frequent flights to and from Boston and New York/White Plains. Boston's **Logan International Airport** (mass

NEW HAMPSHIRE DIVISION OF TRAVEL AND TOURISM

port.com/logan) and the **Portland (Maine) International Jetport** (portlandjetport.org) are also major gateways for New Hampshire. In addition, the state offers more than 20 airfields without scheduled service. For details contact the **New Hampshire Bureau of Aeronautics** (603-271-2551), 65 Airport Rd., Concord.

AMTRAK New Hampshire enjoys daily service to New York and Montreal, albeit on the *Vermonter* (800-872-7245; amtrak.com), which stops at **Claremont** and **White River Junction, Vermont**.

ANTIQUARIAN BOOKSHOPS It's hard to resist a good old book, and New Hampshire has enough dealers in used, rare, and antiquarian books to keep any bibliophile busy. Among the specialty dealers are shops selling first editions and books related to espionage, gardening, the White Mountains, hot-air ballooning, and women's studies. Members of the **New Hampshire Antiquarian Booksellers Association** are listed at **nhaba.org**; a brochure version of the listing can be found at most antiquarian bookstores. Check the website for the date and location of the annual book fair.

ANTIQUES The **New Hampshire Antiques Dealers Association** (nhada.org). Dealers are scattered from the seacoast to the Connecticut River Valley and from the Monadnock region to the Great North Woods. Perhaps the largest concentration of shops is along Rt. 4 in Northwood and Epsom, but Concord and environs has nearly as many shops. Meredith, Center Harbor, and Center Sandwich also have many, as do Hillsboro, Peterborough, Fitzwilliam, and Rt. 1 in the seacoast area. Check the website for the current date of NHADA's annual August show in Manchester and the Canterbury Shaker Village Antiques Show in September. Within each chapter we describe outstanding and multidealer shops in *Selective Shopping* under *Antiques*.

APPALACHIAN MOUNTAIN CLUB Founded (outdoors.org) in 1876 to blaze and map hiking trails through the White Mountains, the AMC was a crucial lobbying group for the passage of the Weeks Act, which enabled the creation of the eastern national forest system, of which the White Mountain National Forest was the first. Today it continues to support land conservation and environmental causes and cater to hikers, maintaining hundreds of miles of trails and feeding and sheltering hikers in a chain of eight "high huts" in the White Mountains, each a day's hike apart. **Pinkham Notch Visitor Center** in Gorham, a comfortable complex at the eastern base of Mount Washington, and the luxurious (by hiker's norms) Highland Lodge, part of the **Highland Center at Crawford Notch** at the western base of Mount Washington, are the venues for a wide variety of year-round workshops in such subjects as camping, snowshoeing, wilderness medicine, and mountaineering. The Highland Center also offers low-cost lodging for hikers in the Shapleigh Bunkhouse. The AMC maintains a hostel-like camping and lodging facility at **Mount Cardi-**

Courtesy, AMC

gan, runs shuttle buses for hikers in the White Mountains, and much more. Their guidebooks (see *Canoeing and Kayaking* and *Hiking*) remain the best of their kind. For more information contact AMC headquarters at 5 Joy St., Boston, MA 02108 (617-523-0636).

APPLE AND FRUIT PICKING
New Hampshire has many orchards and farms offering PYO (pick your own) apples, pears, peaches, and berries. The vegetable- and fruit-picking season begins in early summer, while apples and other tree fruits ripen as fall begins. Many orchards have weekend festivals with fresh-baked apple pies, doughnuts and cider, pumpkins, tractor-pulled wagon rides, music, and other activities aimed at making a perfect family outing. Don't forget to visit the orchards in spring when the trees are blossoming. From the **New Hampshire Department of Agriculture** (603-271-3788; agriculture.nh.gov), request the *Experience Rural New Hampshire* and *Harvest New Hampshire* pamphlets. At the **New Hampshire Virtual Farmers Marketplace** (nhfarms.com), farms can be located by product as well as name.

ART MUSEUMS AND GALLERIES
New Hampshire's two major art museums are the **Currier Museum of Art** (currier.org) in Manchester and the **Hood Museum of Art** (hoodmuseum.dartmouth.edu) at Dartmouth College. The Currier's collection includes some outstanding 19th- and 20th-century European and American works, and the museum is a departure point for tours to the Zimmerman House, designed by Frank Lloyd Wright. The Hood Museum's permanent collection ranges from some outstanding ancient Assyrian bas-reliefs to Picasso and Frank Stella. Both museums stage changing exhibits. (See "The Manchester/Nashua Area" and "Upper Valley Towns" for descriptions of each museum.) Within each chapter we describe art galleries under *Selective Shopping*.

BANDS
Town bands are still popular in New Hampshire, and many hold summer concerts in outdoor bandstands. Schedules change yearly, so check with local chambers of commerce. Conway, North Conway, Alton, Wolfeboro, Exeter, Hopkinton, New London, Newport, Amherst, Hollis, and Hampton Beach are among the places with regular band concerts. The Temple Band claims to be the oldest town band in the country.

BED & BREAKFASTS
B&Bs appear under their own listing within the *Lodging* section of each chapter. We don't list every one, but we physically check out every B&B we can find. Our selection ranges from two-guest-room private homes to ski lodges to elegant mansions with up to a dozen rooms but serving only breakfast. B&B rates in this book are for two people (unless otherwise specified).

BICYCLING
The Monadnock region is particularly popular with touring bikes (see "Peterborough" for rentals). For mountain biking check Waterville Valley and Loon Mountain in "The Western Whites"; Mount Sunapee and Gunstock in "The Lakes Region"; Great Glen Trails; and Attitash Bear Peak in Bartlett. Other popular venues include **Bear Brook State Park** in Allentown (603-485-9869), **Pawtuckaway State Park** in Raymond (603-895-3031), and **Pisgah State Park** in Winchester (603-239-8153). Maps for the White Mountain National Forest can be obtained by calling 603-528-8721. The

Granite State Wheelmen (granitestatewheelmen.org) schedule frequent rides throughout the state for resident bicycling enthusiasts. Request copies of New Hampshire Regional Bicycle Maps from the Department of Transportation (603-271-3734). The website **nhoutdoors.com** lists popular venues throughout the state. **Inn-to-inn bicycle tours** are offered in the North Conway area (**bikethewhites .com**) and in the Lake Sunapee Area (**granitestatevacations.com**). Also see *Rail-Trails*.

BIRDING In the course of the book we have described many of the more than 40 properties and centers maintained by **New Hampshire Audubon** (603-224-9909; nhaudubon.org). Regional Audubon chapters offer bird walks throughout the year. **The McLane Center**, the society's headquarters (84 Silk Rd., Concord, just off I-89 Exit 2), includes an information center and Nature Store and walking trails around Great Turkey Pond. The **Massabesic Audubon Center** in Auburn near Manchester offers a variety of birding opportunities with bluebirds and swallows nesting in the fields, and trails through the woodlands to Massabesic Lake with its nesting loons. **Newfound Audubon**

Center with its **Paradise Point Nature Center** on Newfound Lake is another birding base well worth finding. A recent report notes that there are 186 species of breeding birds in the state. More than 230 species have been recorded at **Pondicherry National Wildlife Refuge** in Whitefield. With its Big and Little Cherry Ponds and extensive wetland, Pondicherry is well known to New England birders. It's also a haven for butterflies, dragonflies, and moose; the adjacent grasslands around the Whitefield Airport are a prime birding area as well. Another favorite venue is coastal Rt. 1A from Seabrook to New Castle, which provides numerous ocean, harbor, and salt-marsh vantage points for observing shorebirds and sea fowl of all types, as well as various ducks and larger wading birds, especially in summer when snowy egrets, great and little blue herons, glossy ibises, and black-crowned night herons are common. **Umbagog Lake**, described in "Northern White Mountains," has nesting eagles and ospreys, loons, and other freshwater birds. Also check out the **Tin Mountain Conservation Center** (tinmountain.org) in Albany (near Conway) and Jackson and at **Prescott Farm** (prescottfarm.org) in Laconia.

BOATING New Hampshire law requires all boats used in fresh water to be registered, a formality that most marinas can provide. Otherwise contact the **New Hampshire Department of Safety, Motor Vehicle Division** (603-271-2251; nh.gov), Hazen Dr., Concord. In the Lake Winnipesaukee area, in emergencies contact the **Safety Services Marine Division** (603-293-2037), Rt. 11, Glendale. Boats used in tidal waters must be registered with the US Coast

Guard. Contact the **USCG Portsmouth Harbor Station** (603-436-4415), New Castle 03854, or the **New Hampshire Port Authority** (603-436-8500; portofnh.org). Also see *Canoeing and Kayaking*. Request the excellent New Hampshire Boating and Fishing Public Access Map from the **New Hampshire Fish and Game Department** (603-271-2224; wildlife .state.nh.us).

BOOKS The **Mountain Wanderer Map & Book Store** in Lincoln (603-745-2594; 800-745-2707; mountain wanderer.com) is devoted to New Hampshire maps and guidebooks; author-owner Steve Smith, himself an authority on the state's history, hiking, and snowshoeing, offers the following recommendations:

Michael J. Caduto's *A Time Before New Hampshire* (University Press of New England) is a fascinating chronicle of the state's geological origins and the life of its Native American peoples. *It Happened in New Hampshire*, by Stillman Rogers (Globe Pequot Press), describes 31 landmark events in the state's history, and *The New Hampshire Century*, edited by Felice Belman and Mike Pride (University Press of New England), is an illustrated account of 100 people who shaped the state during the 20th century. *Classic New Hampshire*, by Linda Landry (University Press of New England), profiles 15 unique New Hampshire institutions. *New Hampshire Architecture: An Illustrated Guide*, by Bryant F. Tolles Jr. (University Press of New England), is an invaluable guide to the rich architectural heritage of the state. *The White Mountains: Alps of New England*, by Randall H. Bennett (Arcadia Publishing), is an excellent history of that region. *This Grand & Magnificent Place*, by Christopher Johnson, is a fine environmental history of the White Mountains (University of New Hampshire Press). *More Than Petticoats: Remarkable New Hampshire Women*, by Gail Underwood Parker (Globe Pequot Press), and *They Paved the Way: A History of New Hampshire Women*, by Olive Tardiff (Publishing Works), profile notable women in the state's history. Out-of-print classics that may be available at your local library or through interlibrary loan include *New Hampshire*, by Elting and Elizabeth Morison, Jere Daniell's *Colonial New Hampshire: A History*, and *New Hampshire: Portrait of the Land and Its People*. Peter Randall's *New Hampshire: A Living Landscape* (University Press of New England) is a collection of panoramic photographs. The photographs of Dick Hamilton, the state's now retired "Mr. White Mountains," are displayed in *New Hampshire: Scenes and Seasons* (New England Press).

The *New Hampshire Atlas & Gazetteer* (DeLorme) has topographic maps that cover the entire state, plus detailed maps of all major communities. The most detailed maps for the state are found in the *New Hampshire Road Atlas* (Jimapco). The waterproof New Hampshire Outdoor Travel Map (Topaz Maps) is a useful resource. The Appalachian Mountain Club publishes the definitive guidebooks to outdoor recreation in New Hampshire (800-262-4455; outdoors.org). Also be sure to check with independent bookstores, most of which have strong local book sections and may carry titles unavailable elsewhere.

BUS SERVICE Concord Coach Lines (800-639-3317; concordcoach lines.com) serves the Merrimack Valley and north on the one hand to the Lake Winnipesaukee region, and on the other to Franconia, North Conway, and Jackson in the White Mountains and north to Berlin. Its Dartmouth Coach (dartmouthcoach.com) offers frequent service between Hanover and Boston/Logan International Airport, also to Stanford, Connecticut, and New York City. **Greyhound Lines** (800-552-8737; greyhound.com) stops in Keene. **C&J** (ridecj.com) covers Dover, Durham, and Portsmouth, and goes to Boston and Logan. Boston Express (bostonexpressbus.com) provides similar service from Concord, Manchester, Londonderry, Salem, and Nashua.

CAMPGROUNDS New Hampshire camping opportunities range from primitive sites with few amenities to full-service areas with water and sewer hookups, electricity, TV, stores, recreation buildings, playgrounds, swimming pools, and boat launching. The most complete information about private campgrounds is available from the **New Hampshire Campground Owners' Association** (603-736-5540; 800-822-6764; ucampnh.com). **New Hampshire State Parks** (nhstate

parks.org) offers 19 parks with camping facilities varying from primitive to full-service RV hookups and cabin rentals. Camping reservations are made through ReserveAmerica, either online or through their call center: 877-NH-PARKS (647-2757); before Memorial and after Columbus Day, contact the parks directly. We describe each state park as it appears geographically within respective chapter.

The **White Mountain National Forest** (WMNF) operates 23 campgrounds ranging in size from 7 to 176 sites. No electrical, water, or sewer connections, no camp stores, no playgrounds. Toilets, water, tables, and fireplaces are provided. The sites were designed for tent camping, although trailers and RVs can be accommodated. Most of the campgrounds are open mid-May–mid-Oct., with a few opening earlier and closing later; several are open all winter, though the roads are not plowed. The daily fees range from $10 for a tent site to $30 for a cabin. For reservations call 877-444-6777 or visit recreation.gov. For details about specific campgrounds see "White Mountain National Forest" and the entry at the end of this chapter.

CANOEING AND KAYAKING New Hampshire offers many miles of flatwater and whitewater canoeing opportunities. The Androscoggin, Connecticut, Saco, and Merrimack Rivers are the most popular waters for canoeing, but there are many other smaller rivers as well. Many folks also like to paddle the numerous lakes and ponds. Since spring runoffs have an impact on the degree of paddling difficulty, make sure you know what your river offers before heading downstream. The best source of information is the *AMC River Guide: New Hampshire and Vermont*, published by the

Appalachian Mountain Club, 5 Joy St., Boston, MA 02108. Also see *Canoe Camping Vermont and New Hampshire Rivers* (Backcountry Publications). Contact the **Merrimack River Watershed Council** (978-275-0130; merrimack.org) for information on the Merrimack River. Canoe and kayak rentals have, happily, become too numerous to list here. Check every chapter. Outstanding outfitters include **North Star Livery** (603-542-6929; kayak-canoe.com) in Cornish, which will shuttle patrons to put-ins farther up the Connecticut River and to campsites in Wilgus State Park on the Vermont bank; and **Northern Waters Outfitters** (603-482-3817; beoutside .com) in Errol. In the Sunapee area **Kayak Country** (kayakcountry.com) offers guided trips as well as rentals; on Newfound Lake kayaks can be rented at the **Paradise Point Nature Center** (603-744-3516), and on Squam Lake from the **Squam Lakes Association** (603-968-7336). In Center Harbor on Lake Winnipesaukee the rental source is **Wild Meadow Canoes and Kayaks** (wildmeadow canoes.com).

CHILDREN, ESPECIALLY FOR

Throughout the book, the *❧* symbol indicates restaurants, lodgings, and attractions that are appropriate for children and families. Founded on the New Hampshire side of the river and expanded on the Vermont side (just across the bridge from Hanover) and combining both states in its name, the **Montshire Museum of Science** (montshire.org) gets our vote for the most stimulating museum geared to children, both inside and out. The **Squam Lakes Natural Science Center** (nhnature.org) is the best place to connect with endemic wildlife. Wooded paths lead to species ranging from otters to black bear and mountain lions. These are viewed safely but frequently up close, in ways wonderfully geared to kids. The **Children's Museum of New Hampshire** in Dover (childrens-museum.org) is newly expanded and very stimulating. Kids and families can dig up dinosaur fossils and navigate both a spaceship and a submarine. **The Remick Country Doctor Museum and Farm** (remick museum.org) offers frequent workshops and special events for children as well as the chance to visit with farm animals. The **White Mountain Attractions** (visitwhitemountains.com) add up to the state's single largest family-geared magnet. Members range from natural phenomena like **Lost River** (in North Woodstock) to theme parks like **Story Land** (in Glen) and **Six Gun City** and **Santa's Village** (both in Jefferson). This is a highly organized promotional association with a helpful visitors center just off Exit 32, I-93, in North Woodstock (603-745-8720; 800-FIND-MTS).

CHILDREN'S SUMMER CAMPS

More than 100 summer camps are located in New Hampshire. For a free brochure contact the **New Hampshire Camp Directors' Association** (800-549-2267; nhcamps.org).

CHRISTMAS TREES Plantation-grown trees can be harvested at about 10 years of age. Some growers allow you to come early in the season to tag your own tree, which you can cut at a later time; others allow choose-and-cut only in December. Contact the **Department of Agriculture** (603-271-3551; nhfarms.org).

COLLEGES AND UNIVERSITIES Higher-education opportunities range from two-year schools to the highly regarded University of New Hampshire and Dartmouth College. For information contact the **New Hampshire College and University Council** (603-225-4199; nhcuc.org), 2321 Elm St., Manchester 03104.

CLIMBING The White Mountains draw many rock and ice climbers. In North Conway, **Eastern Mountain Sports Climbing School** (emsclimb.com) and **International Mountain Equipment Climbing School** (ime-usa.com) both offer stores with extensive technical climbing equipment as well as programs. Cathedral Ledge, also in town, is one of New England's most popular climbing spots. The

Ct. River Joint Commissions

Appalachian Mountain Club (oudoors.org) also offers climbing programs from its center in Pinkham Notch.

CONSERVATION GROUPS Elsewhere in this section, see the **Appalachian Mountain Club,** the **Society for the Protection of New Hampshire Forests** (SPNHF), and the **Audubon Society of New Hampshire** (under *Birding*). **The Nature Conservancy** (603-224-5853; nature.org), a national organization with state holdings, publishes its own list.

COVERED BRIDGES New Hampshire harbors 64 covered bridges. These are marked on the official state highway map, and we have tried to describe them within each chapter. The country's longest historical covered bridge connects Cornish with Windsor, Vermont (technically the New Hampshire line runs to the Vermont shore, so it's all in New Hampshire). The state's oldest authenticated covered bridge (1827) links Haverhill and Bath. The Swanzey area near Keene boasts the state's greatest concentration of covered bridges: five within little more than a dozen miles.

Courtesy, AMC

CRAFTS The **League of New Hampshire Craftsmen** (603-224-3375; nhcrafts.org), with headquarters at 205 N. Main St., Concord, is one of the country's oldest, most effective statewide craft groups. It maintains seven retail galleries displaying work by members and sponsors the outstanding annual **Craftsmen's Fair** in early August at Mount Sunapee State Park in Newbury. In the Monadnock region the **Sharon Arts Center** in Peterborough (603-924-2787; sharon arts.org) offers destination craft shopping. Many other outstanding craft galleries are described as they appear within each chapter under *Selective Shopping*.

CRUISES New Hampshire has many trips available, from the ocean to the lakes. The two most popular cruises are the M/V *Thomas Laighton* (Isles of Shoals Steamship Company), which sails several times daily from Portsmouth to the offshore Isles of Shoals, and the M/S *Mount Washington* on Lake Winnipesaukee. On Squam Lake a Golden Pond Tour (nhnature.org) evokes the 1980s film and also offers naturalist-led cruises. Lake Sunapee offers both daytime and dinner cruises (sunapeecruises.com). For details see *To Do—Boat Excursions* in the relevant chapters.

Chris Tree

Chris Tree

EMERGENCIES The statewide emergency number is 800-525-5555; **911** also now covers the state.

EVENTS In each chapter we have listed special events that occur year after year (see *Special Events*). Special events are also listed on the state's visitors information website (visitnh.gov). Seasonal guides are also available by calling the state's tourism office at 603-271-2665.

FACTORY OUTLETS New Hampshire charges no sales tax. Its best-known shopping mecca is **North Conway**, with more than 200 shops, discount stores, and factory outlets. North Hampton also has a large outlet shopping complex, but seacoast shoppers also drive across the Piscataqua River to Kittery, Maine, where outlets line Rt. 1. In the Winnipesaukee area more than 50 outlets are grouped in the **Lakes Region Factory Stores** just off I-93 Exit 20 at **Tilton**.

FARM STANDS AND FARMER'S MARKETS One day each week, mainly from late June through Columbus Day, more than 75 New Hampshire towns host farmer's markets, gatherings of farmers and craftspeople, frequently musicians too. The day for each differs; for current times and venues check out nhfma.org.

Hillsboro Chamber of Commerce

FISHING Freshwater fishing requires a license for anyone age 16 and older. Some 450 sporting goods and country stores sell licenses, or you can buy one online from the **New Hampshire Fish and Game Department** (603-271-3211; nhfg.net), 11 Hazen Dr., Concord. Request a copy of the New Hampshire Boating and Fishing Public Access Map. Party boats leave several times daily April until October from docks at Rye, Hampton, and Seabrook harbors. Most of these boats have full tackle for rent. Fishing guides and outfitters are listed in the "Great North Woods" chapters.

New Hampshire State Parks

FOLIAGE Color first appears on hillsides in the North Country in mid-September, and by the end of that month Franconia, Crawford, and Pinkham Notches are usually spectacular. The colors spread south and through lower elevations during the first two weeks in October. Columbus Day weekend is traditionally the time New England residents come "leaf-peeping," and it's the period we suggest you avoid, if possible. At least avoid the traditional foliage routes—the Kancamagus Highway, Rt. 3 through Franconia Notch, and Rt. 16 to North Conway—on those three days. Come a week earlier instead and try to get off the road entirely. This is prime hiking weather—no bugs. The state maintains a **Fall Foliage Hotline** (800-258-3608) with "conditions" updated regularly; their website keeps a visual tab on what's going on: visitnh .gov. Weekend lodging reservations are advised well in advance for this period.

GOLF New Hampshire is home to more than 90 public and semi-private golf courses. Within this book they are listed within individual chapters; also check the state tourism website **visitnh.gov**.

HANDICAPPED ACCESS Throughout this book, the wheelchair symbol & indicates restaurants, lodgings, and attractions that are handicapped accessible.

HIGH HUTS OF THE WHITE MOUNTAINS The most unusual lodging opportunities in the state are found in the White Mountains, where the **Appalachian Mountain Club** (outdoors.org) operates eight full-service high-mountain huts. Generally the huts are open from June through Labor Day, but several welcome hikers

Chris Tree

through September and two are open all year on a self-serve, caretaker basis. Guests hike to the huts, most of which are located a day's walk apart so that you can walk for several days and stay in a different hut each night. You sleep in coed bunk rooms equipped with mattresses and blankets. Meals are huge and varied. Reservations are required. A shuttle service allows you to park at the trailhead for one hut, then ride back to your vehicle after your hike. Contact the **Appalachian Mountain Club Pinkham Notch Camp** (603-466-2727; outdoors.org) for overnight or workshop reservations. See "Mount Washington."

HIKING New Hampshire offers the most diverse hiking in New England.

Michael Kautz, courtesy of AMC

The **White Mountain National Forest** alone has some 1,200 miles of hiking trails, and there are additional miles in state parks. A long, difficult section of the **Appalachian Trail** cuts through New Hampshire, entering the state near Hanover, crossing the highest peaks, including Mount Washington, and exiting along the rugged Mahoosuc Range on the Maine border. The most spectacular White Mountains climbs are on the Franconia Ridge and over the Presidential Range, which includes **Mount Washington,** at 6,288 feet the highest peak in the Northeast. Although relatively low compared with the Rockies, Mount Washington records the worst weather for any surface station outside the polar regions. Hikers are urged to use caution and to consult weather forecasts before venturing onto the exposed areas above tree line. More than 110 people have died on Mount Washington, some of them in summer when caught unprepared by sudden, extreme changes in weather conditions. For current conditions at the top check mountwashington.org. The **Appalachian Mountain Club** (603-466-2727; outdoors.org) offers hikers year-round meals, lodging, equipment, and workshops at both its Pinkham Notch and its Highland Center facilities. The **White Mountain National Forest** desk at the **White Mountains Gateway Visitors Center** (603-745-3816) in North Woodstock offers daily weather updates.

Mount Monadnock in southern New Hampshire is one of the most heavily climbed peaks in the world, and **Kearsarge** in central New Hampshire offers a relatively easy walk to its summit and 360-degree views. Several lower mountains in the Lake Winnipesaukee area are easily climbed. **Mount Major**, in particular, is easy

Chris Tree

and has a fine view across the lake. These hikes are noted within their respective chapters, but for detailed descriptions pick up the *AMC White Mountain Guide* (the serious hiker's bible). Also see *50 Hikes in the White Mountains* and *50 More Hikes in New Hampshire* and *Waterfalls of the White Mountains* (Countryman Press).

HISTORIC MUSEUMS, HOMES, AND SITES Most New Hampshire communities have historical societies, and throughout the state many historic buildings and sites are open to the public; most are listed in this guide. The **Association of Historical Societies of New Hampshire** (historical societiesnh.org) offers an online guide.

Bill Davis

The largest concentration of historical houses is in Portsmouth, home of **Strawbery Banke** (603-433-1100; strawberybanke.org) and eight other houses open to the public. Along New Hampshire highways, roadside markers recount short tidbits of local history. *New Hampshire Architecture* (University Press of New England) is a fine guide to historical and significant buildings. The New Hampshire Historical Society's **Museum of New Hampshire History** (603-662-7531; nhhistory.org) in Concord is well worth checking out, as are the **New Hampshire State House** (the nation's oldest state capitol in which a legislature still meets in its original chambers) and Manchester's **Millyard Museum** (603-662-7531; manchesterhistoric.org), which offers a glimpse into the area's onetime predominance as the world's leading textile center. The state's other major historical museum is **Canterbury Shaker Village** (603-783-9511; shakers.org) in the same chapter. Many more are described as they appear regionally.

HONEY More than 200 members of the New Hampshire Beekeepers Association (nhbeekeepers.org) have hives throughout the state, and their honey is usually for sale at farmer's markets, some country stores, and roadside stands.

HORSEBACK RIDING Rising insurance costs are narrowing trail-riding options, but you can still ride a horse through the woods at several places in the state, including **Inn at East Hill Farm** (east-hill-farm.com) and **Peep-Willow Farm Bed & Breakfast** (peepwillowfarm.com) in the Monadnock Region, **Rocky Ridge Ranch** (rocky-ridge-ranch.com) in the Waterville Valley area, the **Gunstock**

Cobble Mountain Stables in Gilford, Loon Mountain and the Franconia Inn in the Western Whites, the Omni Mount Washington Hotel (mountwashingonhotel.com), Farm by the River (farmbytheriver.com), and Black Mountain (blackmt.com).

HUNTING New Hampshire has long been a popular state for hunting. Licenses are required and are available from some 450 sporting goods and country stores, or online from the New Hampshire Fish and Game Department (603-271-3421; nhfg .net), Concord.

ICE CREAM It's hard to beat Annabelle's Ice Cream, located on Ceres Street in Portsmouth and Rt. 125 in Barrington, open from spring through late fall. Another popular homemade brand of ice cream is served at Lagos' Lone Oak Dairy Bars on old Rt. 16 in Rochester and Rt. 1 in Rye. In the Lake Winnipe-saukee Region, Kellerhaus near Weirs Beach and Bailey's Bubble in Wolfe-boro are the big names; Sandwich Creamery in Center Sandwich and Jordan's Ice Creamery in Belmont are the insider's picks. Beech Hill Farm, just off Rts. 9, 202, and 103 between Concord and Hopkinton, has been owned by the Kimball family since 1776. The old dairy farm remains the place to go for a scoop of history along with make-your-own sundaes. In Lit-tleton look for Bishop's Homemade Ice Cream, in Bethlehem for Ren-nell's Ice Cream; Udderly Deli-cious is in Lincoln. In the Connecticut River Valley notable scoop shops include the Walpole Creamery in Walpole, Wade's Ice Cream in Clare-mont, and Whippi Dip in Fairlee, Vermont. Look for details on each of these in their respective chapters.

INFORMATION We describe regional information sources at the head of each chapter. The New Hampshire Division of Travel and Tourism Development maintains an excellent toll-free hotline (800-258-3608) with recorded info on fall foliage; or check their website (visitnh.gov). You can also call (603-271-2665; 800-386-4664) or write to the office for a copy of the *Official New Hampshire Visitors Guide* and a highway map. The guide includes year-round listings of the basics: lodging and dining, shopping, historic sites, museums, alpine and cross-country ski areas, covered bridges, scenic drives, fish and game rules, state parks, and state liquor stores. It also includes paid dining and lodging listings. The department offers a seasonal events guide as well. Maps and pamphlets are available in the state's 17 full-service highway rest areas. These range from spacious welcome centers in Seabrook on I-95, Salem on I-93, and Springfield on I-89 to classic clapboard Capes welcoming travelers in cooler seasons with a crackling wood fire and friendly staff as well as facilities and printed material. Look for these along I-89 southbound in Lebanon and Sutton and on I-93 in Canterbury. There are also facilities attached to the state liquor

Chris Tree

stores in Hooksett (I-93 northbound and southbound). Also worth noting: On I-89 the Springfield rest area is worth a stop just for the view, while the Colebrook rest area (603-237-2390), north of town on Rt. 3, is your key to the state's northernmost North Country. All areas with current open times are listed at visitnh.gov. Within this book local chambers and other information sources are listed at the beginning of each chapter under *Guidance*.

LAKES Central New Hampshire is open, rolling country, spotted with lakes. **Winnipesaukee** is by far the state's largest, most visitor-oriented lake, and it is surrounded by smaller lakes: **Winnisquam**, **Squam**, **Wentworth**, **Ossipee**. Traditionally this has been New Hampshire's Lakes Region, but west of I-93 we've added the **Sunapee/Newfound Lakes Region**, which also includes **Little Sunapee**, **Massasecum**, **Pleasant**, **Highland**, and **Webster** Lakes. Outdoorsmen are also well aware of the grand expanses of **Umbagog Lake** and the **Connecticut Lakes** in New Hampshire's Great North Woods.

LIBRARIES Every New Hampshire city and town has a public library, and there are many college and private libraries as well. On the seacoast, the **Portsmouth Public Library** and the **Portsmouth Athenaeum** and the **Exeter Public Library** and **Exeter Historical Society** are centers for regional history and genealogical research. The **University of New Hampshire's Dimond Library** has an extensive New Hampshire special collections section and all of the resources you would expect to find in a major educational institution. In Concord the **State Library**—with its

Political Library (603-225-4617; politicallibrary.org) devoted to New Hampshire's half-century history as host to the first-in-the-nation primary— and the **New Hampshire Historical Society**, located side by side on Park Street, are centers for New Hampshire research. **Peterborough's Public Library** was the first in New Hampshire, and it and the nearby **Peterborough Historical Society Library** have important regional collections. In Keene the **Historical Society of Cheshire County Archive Center** and the **Keene State Library** are the best sources for local research. **Baker Library at Dartmouth College** is one of the finest institutions in the East. Among its many resources is an extensive White Mountains collection.

LOTTERY New Hampshire's is the oldest legal lottery (nhlottery.org) in the country. Since 1964 it has provided more than $1.3 billion in aid to local education.

MAGAZINES AND NEWSPAPERS The *New Hampshire Union Leader* (theunionleader.com) is the only statewide daily, and its strong conservative editorial policy has made it well known throughout the country. It is the best source of statewide news, but there are also dailies in Portsmouth, Dover, Laconia, Conway, Claremont, Lebanon, Keene, Nashua, and Concord. Many of the larger towns also have weekly newspapers. An alternative Manchester/Nashua weekly, *The Hippo Press* (hippopress.com), is reputed to have the state's second highest circulation. *New Hampshire Magazine* (nhmagazine.com) is the state's popular monthly. *Yankee* (yankeemagazine.com), New England's premier regionwide magazine, is based in Dublin.

MAPLE SUGARING When cool nights and warm days during late February through April start the sap running in maple trees, maple syrup producers fire up their evaporators to begin making the sweet natural treat. Most producers welcome visitors, and many offer tours, sugar-on-snow parties, and breakfast (pancakes with maple syrup, of course). For a list of maple syrup producers, contact the **New Hampshire Maple Producers** (603-225-3757; nhmapleproducers .com). During Maple Weekend, usually the last weekend in March, some 60 sugarhouses throughout the state hold open house and stage special events. A **New Hampshire Maple Museum**, housed in a former sawmill at the Rocks Estate (the rocks.org) in Bethlehem, just off I-93 Exit 40, is open June–Columbus Day and during sugaring season (mid-March to early April); special programs include a horse-drawn ride and tree tapping.

MOOSE AND MOOSE TOURS The state's largest animal is becoming more common and is often seen along roadsides, especially in the mountainous northern half of New Hampshire. Stay very alert when driving, since moose may unexpectedly walk into the road

Robert Kozlow

without looking. The state has about 4,500 moose and averages around 200 vehicle-and-moose collisions annually. A colorful annual **North Country Moose Festival**, based in the town of Colebrook, is staged annually the last weekend in August. See the "Great North Woods" introduction for a full description of this noble beast. The state's most popular organized moose tours are based in Gorham, described in "Northern White Mountains." **Dan's Scenic Moose Tours** (dansscenic moosetours.com) are based in Gorham. Also see **Pemi Valley Excursions** (603-745-2744), Lincoln, for morning and evening guided Moose Tours.

MOUNTAINTOPS The summits of some New Hampshire mountains are more popular than others mainly because they offer better views, great hiking trails, or ways to ride to the top. The most popular, of course, is Mount Washington, at 6,288 feet the highest peak in the Northeast. The **Mount Washington Auto Road** (mountwash ingtonautoroad.com; 603-466-3988) is an 8-mile graded road on which you can drive your own car or opt for a "stage"; in winter modified vans also offer rides a ways up the mountain. The **Mount Washington Cog Railway** (thecog.com), the world's oldest mountain-climbing railway, is still steam powered, carrying passengers all the way to the summit in-season and a portion of the way up, permitting them to ski or snowshoe down, in winter. Across Rt. 16 from Mount Washington, the **Wildcat Mountain gondolas** (skiwildcat.com) whisk you to the top of that wooded peak for a spectacular view of the Presidential Range, and at **Attitash** (attitash.com) in Bartlett you can ride to the top of the mountain on the chairlift; slide down the curving, bowed, 0.75-mile **Alpine Slide** on a self-controlled sled; then cool off in the Aquaboggan Waterslide. At the **Loon Mountain Skyride** (loonmt .com) gondolas hoist you to a summit complete with cafeteria, cave walk, and hiking trails. Both here and at **Mount Sunapee** (where a chairlift hoists you to the summit), cookout-style suppers are offered throughout summer. The **Cannon Mountain Tramway** (cannonmt.com) in Franconia offers its riders a view of the Franconia Range, the state's second highest group of mountains. Although not a mountaintop, **Castle in the Clouds** (castleinthe clouds.org) gives nonhikers the best view of Lake Winnipesaukee. For purist hikers **Mount Lafayette** is the favored summit in Franconia Notch. **Mount Moosilauke**, westernmost of the White Mountains, is also a spectacular summit. Lower mountains can nonetheless provide worthy views: **Mount Chocorua** rises beside Rt. 16 in Tamworth; although only 3,400 feet high, it is a challenging hike with a great vista from its summit. **Mount Major** (Rt. 11, Alton) and **Mount Kearsarge** in Warner offer easy walks to relatively open summits. **Mount Monadnock** dominates the view throughout southwestern New Hampshire, but if you're not up to the hike, drive to the top of nearby **Pack Monadnock** (Miller State Park), Rt. 101, Peterborough. For those who like a challenge, the **Appalachian Mountain Club** (outdoors.org) has an informal Four Thousand Footer Club; become a member by climbing all 48 New Hampshire mountains higher than 4,000 feet in elevation. The peaks are listed in the *AMC White Mountain Guide.* Some rugged folks have climbed all 48 in winter; others have done them all twice, or with their dogs, or some other unique way.

MUSEUMS The **New Hampshire Farm Museum** (farmmuseum.org) in Milton tells the history of farming in the state. The **Montshire Museum of Science** (montshire.org) in Norwich, Vermont (just across the river from Hanover, New Hampshire, where it began), is the most highly regarded science museum in northern New England, worth a stop for inquiring minds of all ages. The **McAuliffe-Shepard Discovery Center** in Concord (starhop.com), named for the state's two pioneer astronauts, has recently quadrupled in size to become a premier science center in New England with a state-of-the-art planetarium theater, high-tech observatory, and innovative, interactive exhibits. The **Mount Kearsarge Indian Museum** (indian museum.org) in Warner is also well worth checking out, and don't miss the fascinating **New Hampshire Telephone Museum**, also in Warner. **Canterbury Shaker Museum** (shakers .org) in Canterbury (see "The Concord Area") is an outstanding museum village, while the **Enfield Shaker Museum** (shakermuseum.org) also evokes the distinctive life as lived by creative utopian community. Frequent programs are offered with meals and lodging in its centerpiece Great Stone Dwelling. We have described the state's historical museums and houses region by region. Also see *Art Museums and Galleries* and *Children, Especially For*.

MUSIC Music festivals are described under *Entertainment* and/or *Special Events* in each chapter. Check out the **New Hampshire Music Festival** (nhmf.org) in Plymouth, year-round performances at the **North Country Center for the Arts** in Lincoln, summer concerts at the **Great Waters Music Festival** in Wolfeboro (great waters.org), **Meadowbrook Farm** (meadowbrookfarm.net) in Gilford, and the **Prescott Park Festival** (prescottpark.org) in Portsmouth. The Monadnock Region is a traditional center for outstanding classical music; **Monadnock Music** (monadnock music.org) is a series of two dozen summer concerts, operas, and orchestra performances (many of them free) staged in town halls, churches, and schools, and the **Apple Hill Chamber Players** (applehill.org) in Nelson offers free faculty concerts. Band music is another sound of summer in New Hampshire. The **Temple Band**, also based in the Monadnock Region, claims to be the oldest town band in the country. **Saint-Gaudens National Historic Site** (sgnhs.org) in Cornish is the setting for a series of free Sunday-afternoon concerts. It's a glorious setting with Mount Ascutney in the background and picnic-packing patrons spread out across the estate's wide lawn.

NATIONAL PUBLIC RADIO New Hampshire Public Radio is excellent; check out nhpr.org for an overview of what's offered. For (FM) commercial-free news and music turn to 103.9 in Portsmouth, 89.1 in Concord and southern New Hampshire, 88.3 in Nashua, 104.3 in Dover, 91.3 in the Upper Valley, 90.7 in the Monadnock Region, 99.5 in the Mount Washington Valley, and 107.1 in Berlin. You can also pick up Vermont Public Radio (VPR) at 89.5 in the western part of the state, and WGBH (Boston Public Radio) at 89.7 as you near the Massachusetts border.

PARKS The **New Hampshire Division of Parks and Recreation** (603-271-3556; nhstateparks.org) is one of the oldest and best state park systems

in the country. There are around 70 parks and historical sites with activities that include swimming, fishing, picnicking, camping, and hiking. A map/guide to the parks and campgrounds is available at most information centers. A commercial site—nhstateparks.com—offers helpful details often not available on the state site, but the official folks warn us to double-check the information. Almost all cities and towns have parks, many of which include tennis courts open to the public. Also see *Campgrounds*.

PETS, TRAVELING WITH The dog-paw symbol 🐾 indicates lodgings that accept pets as of press time. Most require prior notice and a reservation; many also require an additional fee. But don't take our word for it; always call ahead to confirm an establishment's policy when traveling with your pet.

RAIL EXCURSIONS The **Mount Washington Cog Railway** (603-278-5830; thecog.com), the country's oldest railroad excursion, takes nonhikers on a steam locomotive trip to the top of the highest mountain in the Northeast (see "Mount Washington and Its Valleys"). Less hair-raising but just as appealing is the **Conway Scenic Railroad** (603-356-5281; conwayscenic.com), which journeys through historic Crawford Notch. Also see the **Hobo Railroad** (603-745-2135; hoborr.com) in Lincoln, which also operates the **Winnipesaukee Railroad** based in Weirs Beach.

RAIL-TRAILS The **New Hampshire Bureau of Trails** (nhtrails.org), part of the NH Division of Parks and Recreation, administers some 300 miles of recreational trails, the legacy of railroads that once webbed the state. The website maps 24 trails currently in use around the state, from the 8.9-mile Fort Hill trails beginning in Hinsdale in the southeastern corner of the state to the 10.5-mile Colebrook to Beecher Falls (Vermont) trails in Upper Coos. The longest (and almost complete) is the Northern Line, running 49.3 miles from Lebanon southwest to Boscawen, with many access points to scenic stretches along the way. We have described a few of these trails within their respective chapters, but check this website for the full picture and details. *Rail-Trails, New England* (Wilderness Press, 2007) is slightly outdated but otherwise helpful.

RENTAL COTTAGES, CONDO-MINIUMS Cottages are particularly plentiful and available in the **Lake Winnipesaukee** and **Sunapee/Newfound Lakes** areas (contact the local chambers). Condominiums at the state's self-contained ski resorts like Waterville Valley, Loon Mountain, Cranmore, and Attitash Bear Peak are good-value family summer rentals, with golf, horseback riding, hiking, and a variety of other activities. The **Mount Washington Valley Chamber of Commerce** (603-356-3171; 800-367-3364; mtwashingtonvalley.org)

Kim Grant

also keeps year-round tabs on condominiums and other family lodging. In the seacoast region, contact the **Hampton Beach Chamber of Commerce** (603-926-8718; 800-GET-A-TAN hamptonbeach.org) for information about condo and cottage rentals.

ROCKHOUNDING Ruggles Mine in Grafton (rugglesmine.com) is said to offer 150 kinds of minerals and gemstones. Commercial production of mica began here in 1803, and it's an eerie, interesting place that has gotten many a rockhound hooked.

SALES TAX New Hampshire has no sales tax, making it a destination for shoppers from throughout the Northeast.

SKIING, CROSS-COUNTRY New Hampshire offers more than 1,300 kilometers of trails. The **Jackson Ski Touring Foundation** (jacksonxc.org) is the state's largest, with more than 140km of varied superbly groomed trails, the most extensive in the East, ranging from 755 to 4,000 feet in altitude. Three of the state's surviving grand hotels offer substantial touring systems: **The Balsams** (thebalsams.com) up in Dixville Notch with 95km has reliable snow cover as well as grooming; **Bretton Woods Nordic Ski Center** (brettonwoods.com) features a run from the top of its alpine area and a total of 100km of trails as well as a full-service center at the **Omni Mount Washington Hotel**; and **Mountain View** (mountainviewgrand.com) in Whitefield offers 27km. The **Mount Washington Valley Ski Touring & Snowshoe Center** (crosscountryskinh.com) has another 65km, while the **Appalachian Mountain Club** (outdoors.org) in Pinkham Notch and at the **Highland Center** in Crawford Notch offers cross-country workshops and guided tours on national forest trails. **Bear Notch Ski Touring Center** (bearnotchski.com) in Bartlett also offers 70km of pet-friendly trails. **Great Glen Trails Outdoor Center** (greatglentrails.com) in Pinkham Notch boasts 50km of trails as well as a run down the lower portion of the auto road.

Farther south both **Loon Mountain** and **Waterville Valley** offer cross-country centers that tie into national forest trails. Less well known is the fact that the Lake Sunapee area town of New London, given its high elevation, is usually a snow pocket with 22 well-groomed, mostly wooded trails at **Pine Hill XC Ski Club** (pinehillskiclub.com) and 20 more at **Dexter's Inn** (dextersnh.com). **Nordic Skier** (wolfeboroxc.org) skate-grooms and tracks 30km in Wolfeboro. **Windblown Ski Touring Center** (windblownxc.com) with 40km of splendidly groomed trails in New Ipswich is favored by Bostonians; it's high, handy, and quite beautiful with snow we happily tested this very week (March 20, 2010). The New Hampshire **cross-country snow report** line is 800-887-5464. The centers are described region by region within this book. Information on these and all the state's ski-touring centers is available from **Ski New Hampshire** (skinh.com).

SKIING, DOWNHILL New Hampshire boasts 17 major downhill ski areas and one of the world's largest concentrations of snowmaking. The quality of the snowmaking varies, but most of the state's alpine slopes are now dependably white from Christmas through Easter. **Ski New Hampshire** (skinh.com) is the prime source for all areas, big and small, and their snow

Thom Perkins, Jackson Ski Touring Foundation Photo

phone (800-887-5464) is a quick way to check conditions on any given day. On weekends the proximity to Boston puts Granite State lifts at a real premium, but on weekdays they tend to be empty. **Cannon Mountain** (cannonmt.com; snow phone 603-823-7771) in Franconia Notch—home of the **New England Ski Museum** (skimuseum.org)—offers some of the most challenging skiing around. **Loon Mountain** (loonmt.com) in Lincoln and **Waterville Valley** (waterville.com), also in "The Western Whites," is a major self-contained, condo-based resort. **Cranmore Mountain Resort** (cranmore.com), one of the country's oldest ski hills, right in the village of North Conway maintains an enthusiastic family following. **Attitash** (snow phone 877-677-7669; attitash.com),

NEW HAMPSHIRE DIVISION OF TRAVEL AND TOURISM

Wildcat Mountain (skiwildcat.com), and **Bretton Woods Mountain Resort** (brettonwoods.com) are all major ski mountains described in "Mount Washington and Its Valleys." **Mount Sunapee Ski Resort** (603-763-3500; snow phone 603-763-4020; mountsunapee.com) in "Sunapee/ Newfound Lakes," a state-owned resort now leased to and expanded by the owners of Okemo Mountain in Vermont and Crested Butte in Colorado, draws loyal regulars from Boston and Rhode Island. **Crotched Mountain** (crotchedmountain.com) in Francestown is smaller but recently revived and a solid family ski hill within an hour's drive of Boston. **Pats Peak** in Henniker (888-728-7732; pats peak.com) is also easily accessible and surprisingly challenging. Among half a dozen other small but beloved mountains, Danbury's **Ragged Mountain Resort** (603-768-3600; 827-407-5476; raggedmountainresort.com;) in the Lakes Region stands out thanks to recent improvements in lifts, lodge, and trails. For details on these and more, check skinh.com.

SLED DOG RACES The world championships are in Laconia in February, but earlier in the winter there are local races in Tamworth and Meredith. Snow conditions often determine whether or not races are held. The New Hampshire–based **New England Sled Dog Club** (978-815-1861; nesdc.org) was founded in 1924.

SNOWMOBILING Some 6,800 miles of trails are maintained by the 115 local clubs that are members of the **New Hampshire Snowmobile Association** (603-224-8906; nhsa.com). Large portions of the White Mountain National Forest are off-limits to snowmobiling, but most state parks do permit off-road vehicles on marked trails. For a current map of the 24 long-distance snowmobile corridor trails and regulations as well as rental outlets, contact the **New Hampshire Bureau of Trails** (603-271-3254; nhtrails.org); for trail reports check out nhtrails.org. Given its reliable snow cover, the Great North Woods area is a favorite destination; winter lodging and dining options have increased in response to the demand.

SOCIETY FOR THE PROTECTION OF NEW HAMPSHIRE FORESTS (SPNHF) Founded in 1901 to fight the systematic leveling of the state's forests by lumber firms, SPNHF was instrumental in securing passage of the 1911 Weeks Act, authorizing (for the first time) the federal purchase of lands to create national forests. One direct result is the 800,000-acre White Mountain National Forest. The group is also largely responsible for Mount Monadnock's current public status, and it now holds 160 reservations totaling more than 48,000 acres. Many are described within this book, especially within the Monadnock Region, which harbors a large percentage. Check the website (**spnhf.org**) and stop by the LEED-certified SPNHF **Conservation Center** in Concord, just off I-93 Exit 15, open for tours. If you are a hiker, angler, or cross-country skier, SPNHF reservations are valuable keys to real treasure. The **Rocks Estate** (therocks.org) in Bethlehem, just off I-93 Exit 40, is the society's **North Country Conservation and Education Center**.

SUMMER THEATER New Hampshire offers some outstanding summer theater. The **Barnstormers** (barn stormers.com) in Tamworth, the **Peterborough Players** (peterborough players.org) in Peterborough, and the **New London Barn Playhouse** (nlbarn.org) in New London all rank among New England's oldest, best-respected "straw hat" theaters. The **Weathervane Theatre** (weathervane theatre.org) has been staging summer theater in Whitefield for 45 years. In the Lake Winnipesaukee area **Summer Theater in Meredith Village** (interlakentheatre.com) features upbeat Broadway-type plays, and the **Winnipesaukee Playhouse** (winni playhouse.com) stages off-Broadway-type productions. **Hopkins Center** at Dartmouth College in Hanover, the **Arts Center at Brickyard Pond** in Keene, and the **Prescott Art Festival** in Portsmouth also stage lively summer productions. The **Seacoast Repertory Theatre** (seacoastrep.org) in Portsmouth stages professional productions year-round. This is a sampling from *Entertainment* described in each region.

TRAILS, LONG-DISTANCE New Hampshire from the road is beautiful, but unless you see its panoramas from a high hiking trail, you miss its real magnificence. Long-distance hiking trails now crisscross the state. The longest, most spectacular, and most famous, the **Appalachian Trail**, cuts diagonally across the White Mountains, entering the state in Hanover on the west and traversing Franconia Notch, Mount Washington, and Pinkham Notch on its way into Maine. Detailed maps and guides as well as a free pamphlet guide, *The Appalachian Trail in New Hampshire and the White Mountains*, are available from the **Appalachian Mountain Club** (out doors.org). The **Metacomet Trail**, running 14 miles south from Little Monadnock; the **Wapack Trail**, which heads south along ridges from North

Pack Monadnock; the **Monadnock-Sunapee Trail**, a 47-mile footpath; and the 75-mile emerald necklace of hiking trails known as the **Sunapee-Ragged-Kearsarge Greenway** (srkg .com) are also well mapped. (Also see *Hiking* within each region.) The newest long-distance trail links existing paths, railbeds, and logging roads into one continuous trail from Bartlett down in the Mount Washington Valley to the Canadian border in Pittsburg. See cohostrail.org for details.

WATERFALLS The White Mountains have the best waterfalls to view. All are described in *Waterfalls of the White Mountains* (Countryman Press), which lists 30 trips to some 100 waterfalls.

WEDDINGS Within this book we indicate lodging places and venues that specialize in weddings with the ∞ symbol. Also see the Department of Travel and Tourism's wedding planning website: weddings.visitnh.gov.

WHITE MOUNTAIN NATIONAL FOREST (WMNF) The 800,000-acre **White Mountain National Forest**

Robert J. Kozlow

(fs.fed.us/r9/white) is the largest national forest in the East. It is managed for multiple-use activities including lumbering as well as recreation. The **White Mountains Gateway Visitors Center** in Lincoln (I-93 Exit 32), open daily 8:30–5, July–Labor Day until 6, includes interactive displays about wildlife-watching and the history and mandate of the White Mountain National Forest. A staffed WMNF desk here (603-745-3816) is stocked with hiking, biking, and cross-country maps, as well as information about biking trails, fishing, and camping. It's also a source for the **recreation passes required within the forest**. This is a great location, handy both to the 34-mile long east–west **Kancamagus National Scenic Byway** through the heart of the national forest and to Franconia Notch with its many trails, just to the north.

Information is also available from **WMNF headquarters** (603-536-6100), 71 White Mountain Dr., Campton. Contact them, especially in the off-season, for details of campgrounds, fishing, hiking, or other activities. Visitors services and restrooms are open Mon.–Sat.8–4:30 daily (weekends are seasonal). Office hours weekdays 8–4:30. Details about other ranger stations can be found in "White Mountain National Forest."

WHITEWATER RAFTING North Woods Rafting (northwoodsrafting .com) in Milan offers whitewater rafting and kayaking on the Androscoggin River for young and old, brave and timid.

WINE AND CHEESE TRAILS
Check nhwineryassociation.com for a listing of more than a dozen wine,

cider, and mead producers in the state. The list is quickly growing as vintners discover hardy blends and fruit wines become more widely accepted. We are particularly intrigued with the rediscovery of quality hard ciders (see farnumhillciders.com), New England's original tavern drink. Half a dozen cheese producers are listed at nhdairypromo.org. The "trail" linking vineyards and barnyards is found at visitnh.gov and in a handy pamphlet guide available at visitors centers and by request (see *Information*).

ZIP LINES Scooting along at 50 miles an hour while dangling from a wire hundreds of feet above the trees is New Hampshire's newest attraction. Within their respective chapters check out **Alpine Adventures Outdoor Recreation** (alpinezipline.com) in Lincoln, **Bretton Woods Canopy Tour** (mountwashingtonresort.com), the **Ziprider at Wildcat Mountain** (skiwildcat.com) in Pinkham Notch, and **Adventure Gorge Zip Line Canopy Tour** (whitemountain exploration.com), Tenney.

Brooks Dodge, courtesy Wildcat

The Seacoast 1

PORTSMOUTH AND VICINITY

HAMPTON, HAMPTON BEACH,
EXETER, AND VICINITY

DOVER, DURHAM, AND VICINITY

Robert J. Kozlow

INTRODUCTION

With only 18 miles of oceanfront, New Hampshire's seacoast is often overlooked by visitors, who are more impressed with neighboring Maine's more than 2,500 miles of coastline. In its small coastal area, however, New Hampshire has more than enough historical sites, beaches, restaurants, and events and attractions to keep her guests busy for many days and returning again and again for more.

At opposite ends of the seacoast are Portsmouth and Hampton Beach, near to each other in mileage but much farther apart in ambience and style.

Settled in 1623, Portsmouth was the colonial capital and an important seaport during the Georgian and Federal eras, periods that have given the city its distinctive architectural character. With fine inns and restaurants, a number of original and restored historical houses open to the public, theater, dance, music, and a superb waterfront park, Portsmouth is New Hampshire's most delightful and interesting city, loved and appreciated by its residents and visitors alike.

Hampton Beach has been one of New England's most popular seaside resorts since the development of the electric trolley at the turn of the 20th century. Too bad the trolleys don't operate anymore, since the automobile traffic, especially on weekends, is one long snarl. Sand and sun, pizza and fried dough, and lively entertainment characterize Hampton Beach, where more than 200,000 people can be found on a summer holiday weekend. For many people, a week at Hampton Beach has been an annual family tradition for half a century or more.

Between these two extremes are mostly small towns (with populations ranging from less than 1,000 up to 12,000) with white churches, town commons, Colonial architecture, and an ambience that is attracting many new residents and straining the capacity of these towns to manage the growth that has characterized this area since the end of World War II. Onetime Pease Air Force Base is now an industrial park and airport. The seacoast's superb location and abundant educational, cultural, physical, and human resources seem to be more than adequate to continue the region's reputation as one of the top places in the country to live and work (and vacation).

GETTING THERE *By plane:* Boston's Logan Airport, Portland's Jetport, and the Manchester Airport are each an hour's drive from the seacoast.

By car: I-95, the state's first superhighway, built in the 1950s, bisects the seacoast, connecting New Hampshire to the seacoast regions of Massachusetts and Maine.

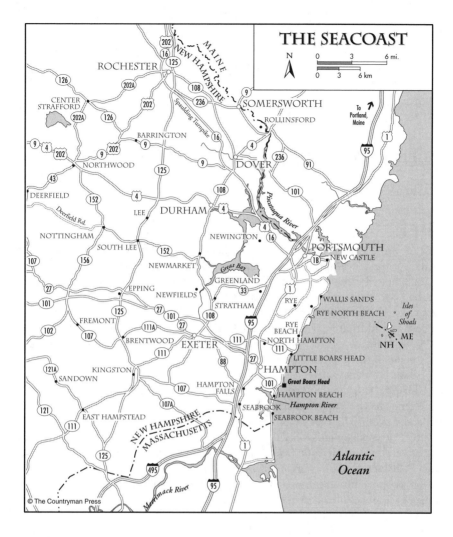

THE SEACOAST

From the west, Rts. 4 and 101 connect the seacoast with the central regions of the state, while Rt. 16 is the road from the mountains.

By bus: **Greyhound Bus Lines** (603-436-0163; greyhound.com) stops daily on Hanover St. at the Bus Stop connecting the seacoast with nationwide bus service. **Coach Company** (603-431-0163; 800-874-3377; coachco.com) has twice-daily trips to Boston. **C&J Transportation** (603-439-1100; 603-742-2990; ridecj.com) provides many trips daily, connecting Logan Airport and downtown Boston with Dover, Durham, and Portsmouth (Pease), New Hampshire; and Newburyport, Massachusetts. **Hampton Shuttle** (603-659-9893; outside New Hampshire 800-225-6426), a reservation-only shuttle service, makes eight trips daily from Hampton, Exeter, and Seabrook to Logan Airport.

By train: **Amtrak** (800-USA-RAIL; amtrakdowneaster.com). Slide down the Maine and New Hampshire coasts with ease on the Downeaster, a commuter train that links Portland and Boston. The train runs year-round. On the seacoast it stops at Dover, Durham, and Exeter.

PORTSMOUTH AND VICINITY

For more than 400 years the seacoast's largest community has been influenced by its maritime location. "We came to fish," announced Portsmouth's first residents in 1623, but shortly the community (first called Strawbery Banke) became a center for the mast trade, supplying long, straight timbers for the Royal Navy. Portsmouth's captains and crews soon roamed the entire world in locally built vessels, hauling cargoes to and from New England, the Caribbean, Europe, and the Far East. In the years before and after the Revolutionary War, wealthy captains and merchants built many of the fine homes and commercial buildings that characterize Portsmouth today.

Unhappy with the demands of the British government, Portsmouth residents were quick to voice opposition to the Crown. Before Paul Revere rode to Lexington and Concord, he first galloped to Portsmouth, warning the patriots to raid nearby Fort William and Mary (now Fort Constitution) and remove the gunpowder before the British came from Boston to strengthen the undermanned fort. John Paul Jones lived in Portsmouth while overseeing the construction of two major warships during the Revolution. Built on the banks of the Piscataqua River were 28 clippers, unrivaled in construction, beauty, and speed as they hauled passengers and merchandise around the world.

The Portsmouth Naval Shipyard, founded in 1800, has long been associated with submarines, turning out 100 vessels to aid the Allied cause in World War II. Portsmouth's red and green tugboats symbolize the city's current maritime activity. Oil tankers and bulk cargo vessels continue to ply the river, halting traffic as they pass through bridges, creating a bustle of activity now missing from so many other old New England seaports, which have lost their commercial ship traffic.

The result of this 400-year maritime heritage is present in the city's architecture; in its active waterfront, which is used for international, commercial, and recreational boating; and in the many cultural activities that involve its riverfront location. Once an old swabbie town, complete with rundown bars and a decaying city center and surrounding neighborhoods, Portsmouth has been transformed into an exciting city as its residents have begun to appreciate its historical traditions and classic architecture. Portsmouth's renaissance continues, fueled by fine restaurants (the best north of Boston, and some would say "including" Boston), inns, music, dance, theater, and, seemingly, a festival every month of the year.

The Piscataqua River, one of the fastest-flowing navigable rivers in the world, separates New Castle, Portsmouth, and Newington, New Hampshire, from Kittery

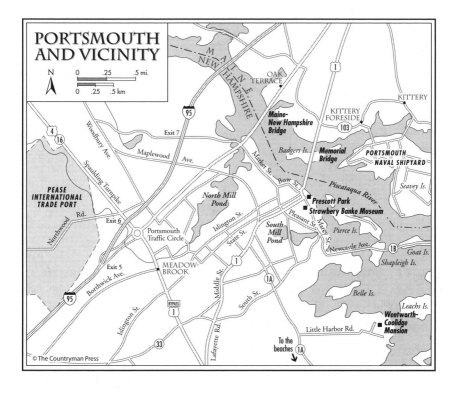

PORTSMOUTH AND VICINITY

N 0 .25 .5 mi.
0 .25 .5 km

MAINE / NEW HAMPSHIRE

OAK TERRACE

KITTERY

Maine-New Hampshire Bridge

KITTERY FORESIDE 103

95

Exit 7

Maplewood Ave.

Woodbury Ave.

4 16

Spaulding Turnpike

Market St.

Badgers Is. Memorial Bridge

PORTSMOUTH NAVAL SHIPYARD

Bow St.

Piscataqua River

Seavey Is.

PEASE INTERNATIONAL TRADE PORT

Northwood Rd.

Exit 6

North Mill Pond

Portsmouth Traffic Circle

Islington St.

State St.

Pleasant St.

South Mill Pond

St. Mary's St.

Pierce Is.

Newcastle Ave.

1B Goat Is.

Shapleigh Is.

Exit 5

MEADOW-BROOK

Borthwick Ave.

Middle St.

South St.

1

1A

Belle Is.

95

Islington St.

BYPASS 1

Lafayette Rd.

33

Little Harbor Rd.

Leachs Is.

Wentworth-Coolidge Mansion

To the beaches 1A

© The Countryman Press

and Eliot, Maine. It is crossed by three main bridges. The lowest is Memorial Bridge, near the center of town, which raises its draw many times daily for commercial and recreational vessels. Residents and visitors alike usually stop to watch as the little tugs shepherd huge oceangoing vessels past this bridge. Next upstream is the Sarah Mildred Long Bridge, once the busiest bridge for motor vehicles but no longer now that the I-95 bridge just upriver carries most of the through traffic. The Piscataqua drains Great Bay, a large, relatively shallow tidal bay known for its wildlife and winter ice fishing.

GUIDANCE Greater Portsmouth Chamber of Commerce (603-436-3988); portsmouthchamber.org), 500 Market St., Box 239, Portsmouth 03802-0239. A busy and active promoter of local tourism, the chamber has a year-round information center on Market St., a short walk west of downtown. It serves Portsmouth and adjacent communities on both sides of the Piscataqua River. There is also a summer information kiosk, open late May–Oct. 12, in Market Square.

GETTING AROUND *By taxi:* **Blue Star Taxi** (603-436-2774) is available by phone.

By bus: **COAST** (Cooperative Alliance for Seacoast Transportation) (603-743-5777; coastbus.org), the local bus transportation, connects Portsmouth and major outlying shopping centers with Durham, Dover, Newmarket, Rochester, and Somersworth, New Hampshire, and Berwick, Maine. A main stop is in Market Square. Fares range from 75¢ to $1.75; children under 5 ride free. From June to

Labor Day, the Downtown Trolley Loop takes visitors around town; 10:30–5:30 daily for 50 cents. A three-day pass can be purchased for $2. Hop on, hop off. What a bargain!

By car: When traveling on I-95, take Exit 7, then turn right onto Market St., which leads directly downtown, past the Chamber of Commerce Information Center to Market Square.

PARKING Although Portsmouth's traffic is no worse than any other city's, it does have limited on-street parking, and its meter attendants will often issue a ticket within moments of your parking meter's expiration. Metered parking (daily except Sun.) is limited to two hours, so seek out the 75¢ per hour parking garage, situated just off Market Square in the middle of town, or the large lot off Pleasant St., adjacent to the South Mill Pond. All of Portsmouth's points of interest and finest restaurants are within an easy walk of both places. Portsmouth is best enjoyed on foot anyway.

MEDICAL EMERGENCY Portsmouth Regional Hospital (603-436-5110; 800-685-8282), 333 Borthwick Ave., Portsmouth. The hospital offers 24-hour emergency walk-in service.

Careplus Ambulance Service (800-633-3590).

✹ Villages

Portsmouth is surrounded by four small towns: Newington, Greenland, New Castle, and Rye. **Newington**, upriver from Portsmouth, is the commercial and industrial center of the region. It has two major shopping malls and many other shops, plus a large power plant, oil storage tanks, and other industries. Most of this commercial-industrial complex is located between the river and the Spaulding Turnpike (Rt. 4/16). The residential area and village are south of the turnpike, by the former Pease Air Force Base, whose construction in the 1950s cut the town of Newington in half. **Greenland** is south of Newington, another residential town with a picturesque village green. East along the Piscataqua is the small island village of **New Castle**. Winding, narrow streets lined with 18th- and 19th-century homes combine to give New Castle the appearance of a town unchanged since the turn of the 20th century. The historic Wentworth-by-the-Sea Hotel recalls the area's maritime glory and, along with the adjacent large marina, keeps the town's tourist image alive. Next to New Castle is the largest of the four towns, **Rye**, once a popular summer retreat when it had several large hotels. Those old structures are gone now, and its summer

NORTH CHURCH AND TROLLEY, DOWNTOWN PORTSMOUTH
Tom Cocchiaro, courtesy of Portsmouth Chamber of Commerce

residents live in oceanfront cottages. Several of the finest residential developments have been built in Rye, and it is a popular address for many seacoast executives. Rt. 1A along the coast of Rye is a fine bike route, passing several state parks, restaurants, and a few motels.

Also not to be missed is the **Isles of Shoals**, a historic nine-island group off the coast, and visible from Rt. 1A. Summer ferry service by Isles of Shoals Steamship Co. (603-431-5500) and Portsmouth Harbor Cruise (603-436-8084) provides tours around the islands.

Chris Tree

BUSTLING MARKET SQUARE, PORTSMOUTH

✳ To See

St. John's Episcopal Church (603-436-8283; stjohnsnh.org), 101 Chapel St., Portsmouth. Open Sun. and other times by applying at the church office in the adjacent building. Built in 1732, this church is a prominent city landmark located beside the river. Its classic interior has trompe l'oeil art, religious objects, and interesting plaques. Its adjacent 1754 graveyard is the resting place of many of the city's colonial leaders, including Benning Wentworth, royal governor 1741–1766.

Little Harbor Chapel (603-436-4902), Little Harbor Rd., Portsmouth. Tucked behind tall pines and a crop of rhododendrons, this 1902 redbrick, Colonial Revival chapel is a charming site on the road to the Wentworth-Coolidge Mansion.

Newington Historical Society (603-649-7420), Nimble Hill Rd., Newington. Open Thu. 2–4 PM in July and Aug. The Old Parsonage, built in 1710, has local artifacts and a special children's room with antique toys. Across the street is the 1712 Old Meetinghouse, in continuous use since that time but structurally altered, and nearby is the Langdon Library, with an extensive genealogical collection.

Albacore Park (603-436-3680), 600 Market St., Portsmouth. Take Exit 7 off I-95, drive 0.2 mile east, and turn right off Market St. Open daily 9:30–5:30, Memorial Day–Columbus Day; 9:30–4:30 every day but Tue. and Wed. the rest of the year. Closed Jan. 12–Feb. 18. $5 adults, $4 military, $3 ages 7–17; under 7 free. Tour the USS *Albacore*, an important experimental submarine built in the 1950s at the nearby Portsmouth Naval Shipyard. Once the world's fastest submarine, this 55-person vessel was used for 20 years as the design model for the contemporary US nuclear fleet. The tour includes a memorial park and gardens, a short film, a picnic area, a gift shop, and the submarine.

Portsmouth Harbor Lighthouse (603-431-9155; portsmouthharborlighthouse .org), off Rt. 1B adjacent to Fort Constitution and the US Coast Guard Station, New Castle. Also known as Fort Point Lighthouse, New Castle Lighthouse, and Fort Constitution Lighthouse, this was the first light station north of Boston in the American colonies. Today's 48-foot tower was built in 1877. A preservation organization offers tours every Sat. 1–5 PM, May–Oct.

Portsmouth Athenaeum (603-431-2538), 9 Market Square, Portsmouth. Research library open Tue. and Thu. 1–4, Sat. 10–4, and by appointment. Reading Room open to the public for tours Thu. 1–4. Free. This three-story brick Federal building, with its four white pilasters, is the architectural anchor for Market Square. Built in 1805, after one of Portsmouth's disastrous fires, the building has, since 1823, been the home of the Athenaeum, a private library and museum. Genealogy, maritime history, biographies, and Civil War memorabilia are among its important holdings. Throughout the building are fully rigged ship models, half models, and paintings.

Portsmouth Museum of Fine Art (603-436-0332), 1 Harbour Place, corner of Bow and Daniel Sts., Portsmouth. Open 9:30–5:30 Wed.–Fri., 11–6 Sat., noon–5 Sun. Spearheaded by a local resident, this handsome 4,200-square-foot venue opened in June 2009 with 100 works of art, many by well-known pop artists, including Andy Warhol. Plans for educational programs and future exhibits were in the works as we went to press.

Redhook Ale Brewery (603-430-8600), 35 Corporate Dr., Pease International Tradeport, Portsmouth. Open daily. Founded in Seattle in 1981, the Redhook Brewery was an innovator in America's craft beer movement. Its Portsmouth facility has Bavarian-inspired rooflines. Inside, the equipment is state of the art. Brewery tours $1. Gift shop.

Star Island (603-430-6272; starisland.org), Isles of Shoals. One of the nine Isles of Shoals off the coast of Portsmouth, Star Island has an eclectic history that includes sojourns by pirates, writers, fishermen, artists, and naturalists. Today the old Oceanic Hotel offers summer conferences and retreats sponsored by the Unitarian Universalist Church. Day-trippers, arriving by chartered or private boat, are welcome to explore the circa-1800 stone chapel, visit an exhibit of poet Celia Thaxter memorabilia, or sit and enjoy the view from the sprawling hotel porch. There's a snack bar, bookstore, and gift shop, plus plenty of sea air, windswept scenery, wildflower paths, and inspiring picnic opportunities.

STRAWBERY BANKE INN PORTSMOUTH
Robert J. Kozlow

Strawbery Banke (603-433-1100; strawberybanke.org), ticket office off Marcy St., Portsmouth. Open May 1–Oct. 31, 10–5 daily, weekends only in Nov.; Holiday House tours on weekdays, 10–2 in Dec. There are also Candlelight Strolls 4–9 several evenings in December. Closed Dec. 24, 25, and 31. $15 adults, $10 ages 5–17, 4 years and under free. Family rate (two adults and youths 5–17) $40. In the 1950s the Puddle Dock neighborhood that is now this nationally known and respected restoration was supposed to be razed for an urban renewal project. Local protests stopped the demolition, saving more than 30 historically significant buildings. The museum, sited on 10 acres, now has 10 furnished houses and more than 40 historic buildings, including several moved to this site to protect them from demolition elsewhere in the city. Most of the buildings are on their original foundations, which makes this a unique project compared with other historical restorations composed of new re-creations or buildings assembled from many places. As the location of Portsmouth's first settlement in 1630 and a residential area until the early 1960s, Strawbery Banke reflects the living 375-year history of this neighborhood, not just one era. Furnished houses have rooms reflecting life from the 17th through the mid-20th centuries, depicting a variety of lifestyles, from wealthy merchants and professional people to sea captains, poor widows, and ordinary working families. Other houses have exhibits, displays, and craftspeople who offer their work for sale. The December candlelight stroll is a popular holiday attraction, and there are other special events throughout the year, including militia musters, horticulture and fabric workshops, and small-craft displays—the latter complementing the institution's wooden boat shop. Extensive 18th- and 19th-century gardens enhance the grounds. The **Museum Shop** (603-433-1114), offering books and gifts, is open during museum hours and for holiday shopping. The **Café on the Banke** (603-373-6112) is one of the city's best spots for full-service lunch and elegant dinner fare. Strawbery Alley is open seasonally for ice cream.

Also see *Green Space.*

HISTORIC HOMES Beginning at the kiosk in Market Square, knowledgeable **Portsmouth Harbor trail guides** (603-436-3988) offer a wealth of background about the city's early settlers, patriots, ship captains, and industrialists on scheduled tours July–mid-Oct. Private group walking tours and step-on guide service for bus tours are available year-round by appointment. There is also a 32-page, self-guided trail map and guide, available for a nominal fee from many area shops and hotels (also the chamber of commerce), which highlights several different routes through the city's waterfront and downtown. $10 adults, $8 students and seniors, $5 ages 8–14; under 8, free. Reservations recommended but not required.

John Paul Jones House (603-436-8420; portsmouthhistory.org), 43 Middle St., Portsmouth. Open mid-May–Oct. 31, 11–5 daily. $6 adults, $5 seniors, children free with an adult. The museum house of the Portsmouth Historical Society, this home was the residence of Captain John Paul Jones when he lived in Portsmouth overseeing the construction of two Revolutionary War frigates, the *Ranger* and the *America*. A traditional Georgian house built in 1758, it has furnished period rooms and a small museum.

Governor John Langdon Memorial (603-436-3205; spnea.org/visit/homes/landon.htm), 143 Pleasant St., Portsmouth. Open June–mid-Oct. Tours on the hour Fri.–Sun. 11–4. Admission $6. One of New England's finest Georgian mansions, this house was built in 1784 by John Langdon, a wealthy merchant who was an important figure in the Revolution and later a US senator and governor of New Hampshire. George Washington was entertained in this house, which is now owned by the Society for the Preservation of New England Antiquities. Extensive gardens are behind the house.

Moffatt-Ladd House (603-436-8221; moffattladd.org), 154 Market St., Portsmouth. Open mid-June–mid-Oct., Mon.–Sat. 11–5, Sun. 1–5. Guided tours. $6 adults, $2 children; garden only $2. Built in 1763, this house was the residence of wealthy 18th-century shipowners and merchants and is furnished in that period to reflect the family's lifestyle. William Whipple, a signer of the Declaration of Independence, lived here. Its great hall is a masterpiece of detailed woodworking. Internationally famous gardens fill the backyard, and don't miss the summerlong book sale in the carriage house. Owned by the Society of Colonial Dames.

Rundlet-May House (603-436-3205; spnea.org), 364 Middle St., Portsmouth. Open 11–4, first and third Sat. of the month, June 1–Oct. 15. Admission $6. Built in 1807, this Federal mansion remained in the builder's family until just a few years ago, when it was acquired by the Society for the Preservation of New England Antiquities. Although it has many fine Federal pieces built especially for the house, it does reflect the continuous ownership of successive generations of a family who valued the original features of the house and adapted their lifestyle with an appreciation for the past. The stable is impressive, as are the extensive gardens and grounds, which retain much of their original layout.

Warner House (603-436-5909; warnerhouse.org), 150 Daniel St., Portsmouth. Open mid-June–mid-Oct., Mon.–Sat. 11–4, Sun. noon–4; closed Wed. $5 per adult, $4 senior/student/AAA, $2.50 ages 7–12; under 7 and museum professionals, free. The finest New England example of an 18th-century, urban brick dwelling, this house was built in 1716 and, during its early years, was the home of leading merchants and officials of the royal provincial government. It has outstanding murals painted on the staircase walls, splendid paneling, and period furnishings. Benjamin Franklin is said to have installed the lightning rod on the west wall.

Wentworth-Gardner and Tobias Lear Houses (603-436-4406; wentworth gardnerandlear.org, Gardner and Mechanic Sts., Portsmouth. The Wentworth-Gardner House is open mid-June–mid-Oct., Wed.–Sun. noon–4; the Lear House is open Wed. 1–4. $5 adults, $2 children. Built in 1760, the Wentworth-Gardner House is one of the most perfect examples of Georgian architecture found in America. Built by Elizabeth (Rindge) and Mark Hunking Wentworth as a gift to their son Thomas (brother of the last royal governor), its exquisite carving took 14 months to complete. At one time the Metropolitan Museum planned to move it to New York's Central Park; then a group of Portsmouth citizens repurchased the building, and restored and furnished it as it is today. Adjacent is the **Tobias Lear House**, built in 1740, the childhood home of George Washington's private secretary. The president enjoyed tea in the parlor in 1789. Part of the property includes an 18th-century post-and-beam warehouse, one of the few remaining buildings of its style in the area.

Richard Jackson House (603-436-3205), 76 Northwest St., Portsmouth. Open 11–4 the first and third Sat. of every month June–mid-Oct. Tours on the hour, 11–4. Admission $5; Portsmouth residents free. This is New Hampshire's oldest house, built in 1664 with later additions. It has few furnishings and is of interest primarily for its 17th-century architectural details. It is most picturesque in May when its apple orchard is in bloom. Owned by the Society for the Preservation of New England Antiquities.

Wentworth-Coolidge Mansion Historic Site (603-436-6607; wentworth coolidge.org), 375 Little Harbor Rd. (off Rt. 1A), Portsmouth. Mansion tours daily mid-June–Labor Day, Fri.–Sun Sept. 5–Oct. 13. Admission free for New Hampshire residents; other admission is $7 for adults, $3 for ages 6–11, under 6 free.

Kim Grant

WENTWORTH-COOLIDGE MANSION

Best to call in advance to confirm hours. Owned by the state, this rambling 40-room mansion is one of the most interesting and historic buildings in New Hampshire. It was the home of Royal Governor Benning Wentworth, whose term from 1741 until 1766 was the longest of any royal governor in America. Council meetings were held in an ornately paneled room overlooking the channel between Portsmouth and Little Harbors. Its lilacs, which bloom in late May, are said to be the first planted in America. Although the house is not furnished, its extensive woodwork is an exquisite display of the prowess of Portsmouth craftsmen of the period. The adjoining art gallery, managed by McGowan Fine Arts, is free and open Wed.–Sun. mid-May–Sept. Picnicking on the grounds is welcomed, although pets are prohibited. Restrooms are available in the carriage house.

FOR FAMILIES *Water Country* (603-427-1111; watercountry.com), Rt. 1, 3 miles south of Exit 5 off Rt. 95, Portsmouth. Open June–Labor Day, 9:30–6:30 during the height of the season; otherwise 10 AM to 5 or 6. Called New England's largest water park, this complex has multiple large waterslides, a huge wave pool, a Racing Rapids ride and plunge, plus an Adventure River ride, bumper boats, fountains, and a kiddie pool. Tickets may be purchased online. One admission covers all day for all rides; tube and boat rentals are additional.

Seacoast Science Center (603-436-8043; seacoastsciencecenter.org), Rt. 1A at Odiorne State Park, 570 Ocean Blvd., Rye. Open daily Apr.–Oct., 10–5; Sat., Mon., and school vacation days Nov.–Mar. $4 adults, $2 ages 3–12; members and kids under 3, free. A facility of the Audubon Society of New Hampshire, this handsome environmental center is right on the rocky shore and offers marine exhibits and aquariums (Tofu the Whale is a special treat), a museum shop, children's workshops, tidepooling and marsh walks, and occasional lectures. Programs and exhibits appeal to a wide range of ages and interests. There's a Music-by-the-Sea concert series with local bands, grilled food, and optional dancing held on Thursday evening in summer. Fee charged.

Rye Airfield Skate Park (603-964-2800; ryeairfield.com), 6 Airfield Dr. (Lafayette Rd./Rt. 1), Rye. Open Tue.–Fri 3–9 PM, Sat from 9 (from noon during summer), Sun until 6. "Ramp Camp" offers equipment rentals plus coaching, video analysis, games, and private and group lessons at a 50,000-square-foot indoor skate park.

⚓ **Prescott Park** (603-436-2848; prescottpark.org), Marcy St., Portsmouth. Located on the waterfront directly across from Strawbery Banke, this city park offers lovely gardens and a full schedule of attractions from early June into Oct. Locals and tourists alike fill the lawn with blankets and picnics to enjoy Wed.-night concerts, jazz and folk festivals, an annual art show, dance series, kids' programs, Broadway musicals, Shakespeare under the stars, and a chowder fest and chili cook-off. Admission is amazingly free, although a $5 donation is suggested.

Historic Cemeteries North Cemetery, Maplewood Ave., Portsmouth. Dating from 1753, this cemetery holds the remains of prominent people from the Revolutionary War to the War of 1812. Diverse headstones reveal the skill of early stone-cutters.

Point of Graves Cemetery, off Marcy St., Portsmouth. Adjacent to Prescott Park, this old cemetery was established in 1671. Although most of the oldest stones have sunk from sight, many old and uniquely carved stones remain.

✳ To Do

BOAT EXCURSIONS ⚓ **Isles of Shoals Steamship Company** (603-431-5500; 800-441-4620; islesofshoals.com), Barker Wharf, 315 Market St., Portsmouth 03801. Open daily mid-June–Labor Day; additional spring and fall schedule dependent on Mother Nature. This is the Isles of Shoals ferry, hauling passengers and freight to Star Island and providing one of New England's finest narrated tours. The 90-foot *Thomas Laighton* is a replica of a turn-of-the-20th-century steamship, the type of vessel used when the islands were the leading New England summer colony, attracting the era's most famous artists, writers, poets, and musicians. The boat docks at Star Island, home of the Star Island Conference Center, a summer religious institution meeting here since the turn of the 20th century. Some morning trips allow passengers to leave the *Laighton* for a stopover, returning to the mainland in the late afternoon. Buy tickets early—they sometimes sell out. Bring your picnic lunch and camera. Since the *Laighton* is the supply line for the conference center, delivering food, drinking water, supplies, mail, and oil for the island's generators, it operates rain or shine. The trip to the islands takes about an hour; the roundtrip, about three hours. In addition to the daily Isles of Shoals cruises, the *Laighton* is used for dinner cruises, including clambakes and big-band dance cruises. The 71-foot *Oceanic* is used for whale-watching (an all-day, offshore trip), special lighthouse cruises, the nightly sunset cruise to the islands, and weekend cocktail and dance cruises. Reservations may be made by phone or online. Parking at the dock is $5 per vehicle.

⚓ **Portsmouth Harbor Cruises** (603-436-8084; 800-776-0915; portsmouthharbor .com), Ceres St. Dock, Portsmouth. Open weekends from early May, daily mid-June–late Oct. The 49-passenger *Heritage* offers a variety of narrated cruises, which, depending on the tide and the season, tour the harbor and wend down the Piscataqua, past the two lighthouses, around New Castle Island, through Little Harbor, and back to the dock. Several trips circle the Isles of Shoals, and fall foliage trips travel the winding rivers and expanse of Great Bay. Our favorite is the 5:45 evening hour cruise—no narration, just a cool drink and a quiet ride after a hot summer day. Several trips regularly sell out, so buy tickets early. Also available is a large sailboat for single-day or overnight charters.

Shoals Marine Laboratory (603-430-5220; sml.cornell.edu), 400 Little Harbor Rd., Portsmouth. Poet and writer Celia Thaxter's 1893 garden on Appledore Island is still lovingly maintained for visitors lucky enough to take one of the daylong tours offered on Thu. late June–late Aug. Reservations aboard the Portsmouth Harbor Cruise ship M/V *Heritage* are $97, including lunch, and are limited to 46 passengers per trip. All tour participants must be 18 years of age or older and should be in good physical condition. The majority of the day is spent walking the island's lovely but rugged landscape.

Island Cruises Inc. (603-964-6446; ryeharborcruises.com), Rye Harbor State Marina, Rt. 1A, Ocean Blvd., Rye. Open weekends in spring and fall, daily late June–late Aug. *Uncle Oscar*, a 20-passenger Maine-built lobster boat, ferries folks on a one-hour lobster trip, a two-hour tour of the Isles of Shoals, or a three-hour trip with a stopover and the possibility of eating dinner at the Oceanic Hotel on Star Island. Since Rye Harbor is the closest mainland port to the islands, fares are a little less than from Portsmouth.

Tug Alley Too (603-430-9556; tugboatalley.com), 2 Ceres St., Portsmouth. *Tommie the Tugboat*, aka *Tug Alley Too*, is available for charter excursions of Portsmouth Harbor and the Piscataqua River. Pack your own picnic or skippers Bob and Natalie Hassold (who own the retail shop Tugboat Alley) will provide one. They'll also provide a justice of the peace in case you want to get married or renew your vows while cruisin' down the river. Accommodates up to six passengers.

❧ **Granite State Whale Watch** (603-964-5545; 603-382-6743; whales-rye.com), Rye Harbor State Marina, Rt. 1A, Box 232, Rye. Open daily mid-June–Labor Day; weekend whale-watches May, June, Sept., and Oct. Ride the 150-person-capacity *Granite State* for a six-hour whale-watch or a two-hour cruise around the Isles of Shoals.

Atlantic Fishing and Whalewatching (603-964-5220; 800-WHALE-NH; atlanticwhalewatch.com), Rye Harbor Marina, Rt. 1A, Box 678, Rye. Open weekends mid-Apr.–May for all-day fishing; daily through Labor Day weekend for whale-watch tours and half-day fishing excursions; reduced schedule through mid-Oct. The speedy, 70-foot *Atlantic Queen II* is designed for all-weather ocean fishing. Offshore trips seek cod, cusk, pollack, haddock, mackerel, striped bass, and bluefish. Marine biologists from the Blue Ocean Society for Marine Conservation serve as naturalists. Reservations strongly recommended.

New England Lighthouse Tours (603-431-9155; newenglandlighthousetours .com). Lighthouse historian Jeremy D'Entremont offers full- and half-day motor coach tours of area lighthouses in both New Hampshire and Maine. Reservations required. Tours leave from in front of the High-Hanover Garage at 34 Hanover St., Portsmouth.

Portsmouth Kayak Adventures (603-559-1000; portsmouthkayak.com), Witch Cove Marina, 185 Wentworth Rd. (Rt. 1B), Portsmouth. Open Mon.–Fri. 9–5, Sat. and Sun. 8:30–6. Certified guides are available to instruct paddlers in the basics of the sport and escort them to the Piscataqua River Basin and its tributaries. The area is rich in nautical history and natural beauty, a favorite spot for great blue herons— sometimes even harbor seals. Half-day kayak rentals start at 9 AM and 1 PM.

Portsmouth Rent & Ride (603-43306777; portsmouthrentandride.com), 37 Hanover St., Suite 2, Portsmouth. Open daily 9–5, though times may vary with the season. This outdoor recreation outfitter rents and sells bikes, kayaks, snowshoes, cross-country skis, and all-terrain skates. Guided tours available.

Papa Wheelies Bicycle Shop (papa-wheelies.com), 653 Islington St., Portsmouth. Owned and operated by enthusiastic cyclists with knowledge of the area's best rides and trails for beginners to pros.

Saboutime Sailing, LLC (207-475-6248; saboutimesailing.com), Pepperell Cove Town Dock, Kittery Point, Me. (just across Memorial Bridge from downtown Portsmouth). Open mid-May–mid-Oct., Mon.–Sat. Three-hour morning or afternoon sails, plus evening cruises. A range of lessons and customized tours are also available.

Amaryllis Sailing (603-205-0630; sailamaryllis.com), Badgers Island Marina, Portsmouth Harbor. This 45-foot luxury catamaran can accommodate up to six passengers for a day sail, sunset dinner cruise, or offshore B&B charter to the Isles of Shoals. If desired, guests can join the crew to help hoist and trim the sails. Reservations recommended.

GOLF Breakfast Hill Golf Club (603-426-5001; breakfasthill.com), 339 Breakfast Hill Rd., Greenland. An 18-hole championship public golf course on 170 acres of rolling fairways and contoured greens. Pro shop, driving range, practice green, a full-service restaurant and on-course beverage cart.

Pease Golf Club (603-433-1331; peasegolfcourse.com), 200 Grafton Rd., Portsmouth. A 27-hole regulation course open to the public daily spring–Nov. Tee times available seven days in advance. Pro shop, cafeteria, golf and pull cart rentals, and driving and practice ranges.

Portsmouth Country Club (603-436-9719), Country Club Dr. (off Rt. 101 south of Portsmouth), Greenland. Open mid-Apr.–mid-Nov. Designed by Robert Trent Jones; 18 holes, the longest course in New Hampshire, with several holes sited on the shores of Great Bay. Cart rentals, full bar and food service, and pro shop. Call for starting times.

WALKING TOURS Art 'Round Town (603-431-4230; artroundtown.org), 136 State St., Portsmouth. A gallery walk of 10 local art spaces, more than 100 artists. May–Dec., the first Fri. of the month, 5–8 PM. Sponsored by the New Hampshire Art Association–Kennedy Studios.

Portsmouth Black Heritage Trail (603-431-2768; seacoastnh.com/blackhistory; friendsofthepearl.org). A self-guided walking tour of 24 sites relating the story of early African Americans and their descendants in this port city. Tour brochures are available at the Strawbery Banke Museum Visitor Center, across Marcy Street from the start of the trail in Prescott Park, as well as at the Strawbery Banke Museum Shop and the Greater Portsmouth Chamber of Commerce, Market Street Extension.

✸ Green Space

PARKS ✿ ✍ **Prescott Park**, Marcy St., Portsmouth. Open year-round. Marcy Street was once an area of bawdy houses, bars, and run-down businesses. The Prescott sisters, who were born in this section of the city, inherited millions of dollars and sought to clean up the waterfront by creating a park, which they gave to the city. Supported by a substantial trust fund, the park is famous for its beautiful gardens, but it also includes boat wharves, an amphitheater, picnic areas, sculpture, fountains, and the historic 1705 Sheafe Warehouse with exhibits. During the summer it is the location of the daily Prescott Park Arts Festival (donation requested), offering outdoor summer theater, varied musical performances, an art exhibit, and children's theater and art programs. At the eastern end of the park, cross the bridge to adjacent Peirce Island, home of the state's commercial fishing pier, and walk out to Four Tree Island, a picnic ground nearly in the middle of the river.

🦆 **Urban Forestry Center** (603-431-6774), Elwyn Rd., off Rt. 1 south of Portsmouth. Open year-round; summer 8–8, winter 8–4; office hours Mon.–Fri. 8–4. Free. Bordering tidal Sagamore Creek, this site has nature trails, herb gardens, hiking, cross-country skiing, and snowshoeing, and offers environmental programs throughout the year.

🦆 ✒ **Fort Constitution**, off Rt. 1A, New Castle. Open year-round 10–5. Turn in at the US Coast Guard Station and park where indicated. Free. This historic site was first used for fortifications in the early 1600s, but today it reflects the Revolutionary and Civil War periods. In December 1774, after being alerted by Paul Revere, local patriots raided what was then called Fort William and Mary, overwhelmed its few defenders, and removed its powder and some weapons before British warships from Boston could reinforce the garrison. This is considered to be the first overt act against the king and predated the war's outbreak by some four months. The powder was used against the British at the Battle of Bunker Hill. The last royal governor, John Wentworth, and his family fled their home in the city and remained in the fort before leaving the rebellious province. Restored and maintained by the state, the fort's entrance portcullis reflects the colonial period, while the fortifications along the water date from the Civil War, although there were no battles here. Adjacent to the fort is the picturesque and still-important Fort Point lighthouse, and just offshore is the Whaleback lighthouse. Ten miles at sea the Isles of Shoals are visible.

Fort Stark, Wild Rose Lane, off Rt. 1A, New Castle. Open May–Oct., weekends and holidays 10–5. Free. To protect the important Portsmouth Naval Shipyard during World War II, the military occupied several points at the mouth of the river. One was Fort Foster, across the river from Fort Constitution, and Fort Stark was another. Although used as a fort from 1746, the site today reflects its World War II service.

✒ **New Castle Great Common**, Rt. 1A, New Castle. Open year-round; a small fee is charged to nonresidents during summer. Another World War II site, this was Camp Langdon, an army base. It was acquired by the town of New Castle as a recreation area and the site for a new office complex. There are restrooms, picnic tables, a small beach, and a pier for fishing. Overlooking the mouth of the river and its two lighthouses, this area is one of the scenic highlights along the coast.

✒ ♿ **Odiorne Point State Park** (603-436-7406), Rt. 1A, Rye. Open year-round; a park fee is charged in the main season, June–Sept. This 137-acre oceanfront park was the site of the first settlement in New Hampshire in 1623. Later, fine mansions were built here; then the site was taken over during World War II and named Fort Dearborn, with huge guns placed in concrete bunkers. As a park it has handicapped-accessible nature trails, a boat-launching ramp, picnic tables, and a fine nature center—open late June–late Aug.—operated by the University of New Hampshire. The center has exhibits and offers varied daily nature programs using

Greater Portsmouth Chamber of Commerce

MORAN TUGBOATS, A MODERN PART OF THE CITY'S 400-YEAR MARITIME HISTORY

the park, its nearby marsh, and the ocean's intertidal zone. No swimming. Also see the Seacoast Science Center in *For Families*.

Rye Harbor State Park and Marina (603-436-5294), Rt. 1A, Rye. Open year-round; a fee is charged in the summer season for the park and boat launching. New Hampshire's smallest state park, this jewel occupies an ocean point just south of Rye Harbor. It has picnic tables, a playground, a jetty for fishing, a view of the picturesque harbor, and cooling ocean breezes on hot summer days. Around the corner is the **Rye Harbor State Marina** with a launching ramp and wharves, where you can buy tickets for deep-sea fishing, whale-watches, or sightseeing boat rides.

BEACHES Wallis Sands State Park (603-436-9404), Rt. 1A, Rye. Open weekends mid-May–late June, then daily until Labor Day. A large, sandy beach with lifeguards, restrooms, parking, and a snack bar. Fee charged.

Jenness State Beach, Rt. 1A, Rye. Another large, sandy beach with lifeguards, restrooms, and parking meters. A snack bar is across the street.

New Castle State Park, Rt. 1A, New Castle. Grills, parking, restrooms, sandy beach. Fee charged.

✳ Lodging

RESORT Wentworth by the Sea (603-422-7322; wentworth.com), 588 Wentworth Rd., New Castle 03854. One of New Hampshire's historic "Grand Hotels." In 1905 this seaside superstructure was the site of the peace talks that ended the Russo-Japanese War. Although it once hosted socialites, film stars, and presidents, in recent years the formerly opulent hotel had grown faded and stood empty until 2003, when the Marriott Hotel chain invested millions to perform a miracle. Perched high atop a bluff overlooking the Atlantic Ocean, the hotel, originally built in 1874, now boasts 161 rooms, two restaurants, lavish gardens, indoor and outdoor pools, state-of-the-art meeting space, and a full-service spa. There's also golf, tennis, and a marina for guests who arrive by "yacht," available at the nearby Wentworth-by-the-Sea Country Club. Call for rates.

BED & BREAKFASTS ⁰ɪ⁰ Ale

House Inn (603-431-7760; alehouse inn.com, 121 Bow St., Portsmouth 03801. Open all year. Overlooking the waterfront in the heart of the downtown restaurant/shopping area, this converted brick brewery has a cosmopolitan feel with the Seacoast Repertory Theatre on the main floor; the inn is an elevator's ride above. Recently updated by new owners, the lobby/library/living room and 10 guest rooms have a loft-like, urban feel that captures the city's air of laid-back sophistication. With your choice of queen or king bed, private bath, coffeemaker, refrigerator/freezer, flat-screen HDTV, WiFi, air-conditioning, and iPod docking station, you may want to move in to stay. $129–199 Nov.–May; $179–279 in high season.

The Arbor Inn (603-431-7010; arborinn.com), 400 Brackett Rd., Rye 03870. Located within walking distance of Wallis Sands Beach, this reproduction Colonial offers all the comforts of home and then some. You can rent the luxuriously furnished, four-bedroom house for $3,000 per week in June and Sept.; $3,500 in July and Aug. The rest of the year it's a B&B with rooms available for $125–245, depending on season. Gourmet breakfast prepared by Joanne, an award-winning baker.

The Governor's House (603-427-5140; governors-house.com), 32 Miller Ave., Portsmouth 03801. Once the home of a former New Hampshire governor, this stately Colonial Revival home offers four guest rooms, each with private bath, queen-sized bed, cable TV and DVD player, air-conditioning, and high-speed Internet access. There's an outdoor hot tub,

lighted tennis court, library, and game room, all within a 10-minute walk from downtown. Or you can catch the coast trolley at the door. The $159–239 rate (depending on season and accommodations) includes pampering—Italian linens and robes, evening wine and cheese, and a continental breakfast with fresh fruit and freshly baked breads served in your room, on the porch, or in the handsome dining room. Massages and tennis lessons available for an additional fee.

The Inn at Strawbery Banke (603-436-7242; 800-428-3933; innatstraw berybanke.com), 314 Court St., Portsmouth 03801. Around the corner from Strawbery Banke and two blocks from Market Square, Sarah Glover O'Donnell's homey B&B has location, location, location! It also boasts seven bright, comfortable rooms that meander through the circa-1800 home and a more recent addition. All have updated private bath. Some rooms have queen-sized beds; others, a queen and a single. Upstairs and down, common rooms offer TV and travel books. A skylit breakfast room overlooks gardens, a strawberry patch, and bird feeders, assuring a sunny start to your day. Full breakfast. Rates are $160–170 high season, $100–115 off-season.

WENTWORTH BY THE SEA, NEW CASTLE

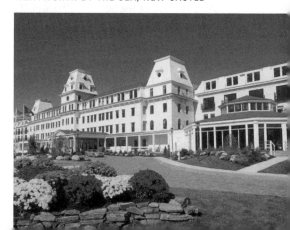

¹ Martin Hill Inn (603-436-2287; martinhillinn.com), 404 Islington St., Portsmouth 03801. Open year-round. From the street this yellow-clapboard inn with its white picket fence looks cheery, chic, and neat as a pin. Inside, the elegance of early Portsmouth comes alive. Adjacent 1820 and 1850 houses are joined by a brick garden path overlooking a courtyard and water garden. The main inn has three guest rooms with period furnishings and canopy or four-poster beds. The Guest House has four rooms, three of which are suites, one with an attached sunroom. All rooms have private bath, air-conditioning, writing tables, sofa, or separate sitting area. A no-smoking inn. New owner Margot Doering has added free WiFi and invested this award-winning B&B—the city's first—with her love of antiques and talent for gardening. Full breakfast is served in the elegant, mahogany-furnished dining room. Rates are $160–200 May–Oct.; $105– 144 the rest of the year. Packages available.

✪ The Portsmouth Harbor Inn and Spa (207-439-4040; innatportsmouth .com), 6 Water St., Kittery, ME 03904. Open year-round. Lynn Bowditch maintains this 1879 redbrick inn just off the Kittery green, across from the Piscataqua River and within walking distance (across the bridge) of theater and the many shops and restaurants of downtown Portsmouth. Common rooms are cheerful and spacious, and the six guest rooms are carefully, imaginatively furnished; all have private bath (some with claw-foot tub), air-conditioning, ceiling fan, phone, and cable TV/VCR (there's an extensive video library). Minx has a gorgeous bathroom. Add to all this a full-service day spa in the carriage house, and an exceptional list of great stuff to do in the area, e-mailed to guests before they arrive. $145–200 in-season includes a full breakfast. From $100 off-season.

Sise Inn (603-433-1200; 800-267-0525; siseinn.com), 40 Court St., Portsmouth 03801. Open year-round. An easy walk from Portsmouth's "happening" Market Square, the Sise Inn offers hotel amenities in a handsomely restored Victorian stick-style home and addition. The 34 rooms, including several suites, have private bath, mostly queen-sized beds, TV, VCR, telephone, alarm clock, radio, table, and comfortable chairs. Many also have CD player and whirlpool baths; one, a skylight and private staircase. With several meeting rooms, the inn was designed for the business traveler, but vacationers are welcome to share the Victorian luxury as well. A light breakfast is served. Rates $119– 279, depending on season and accommodation. Midweek specials available.

Downtown on Market Street (Exit 7 off I-95) is the full-service Sheraton Harborside Portsmouth Hotel and Conference Center (603-431-2300) with 205 rooms, restaurant, and lounge, within walking distance of everything. Condo suites available for longer stays. Additional accommodations are available in nearby Kittery and Eliot, Maine, just across Memorial Bridge. In addition to **Portsmouth Harbor Inn & Spa** listed above, these include **Enchanted Nights B&B** (207-439-1489) in Kittery, and **Farmstead Bed and Breakfast** (207-748-3145; far stead.qpg.com) in Eliot.

MOTELS Portsmouth is well supplied with motels, most of which are located southon Rt. 1 and at the traffic circle intersection of I-95, Rt. 1 bypass, and Rt. 4/16 (Spaulding Turnpike). Among these are the **Anchorage Inn** (603-431-8111), **Comfort Inn** (603-433-3338), **Courtyard by Marriott** (603-436-2121), **Hampton Inn** (603-431-6111), **Holiday Inn** (603-431-8000), **Wren's Nest Village Inn** (603- 436-2481), **Howard Johnson Hotel** (603-436-7600, and **Best Western** (603-436-7600).

✳ Where to Eat

Portsmouth is famous for its numerous quality restaurants, the best collection of fine dining north of Boston. Several of the top restaurants are located in the Old Harbor area where Bow, Ceres, and Market Sts. intersect. Here six-story warehouses, the largest structures north of Boston when built in the early 1800s, have been remodeled as restaurants and shops. A treat for summer and early-fall visitors are the numerous outdoor decks located on the waterfront, open for lunch and late into the evening (until the legal closing for serving liquor). Everything from snacks to sandwiches and full dinners is available on the decks. View the tugboats and watch large oceangoing ships pass, seemingly within an arm's length.

DINING OUT ⅋ **Ristorante Massimo** (603-436-4000; ristorantemassimo .com), 59 Penhallow St., Portsmouth. Dinner daily from 5; closed Sun. in summer. Tucked along a picturesque side street, this romantic basement restaurant features elegantly prepared northern and southern Italian cuisine in a grotto-like setting. The pastas are homemade, with interesting selections such as pappardelle with braised rabbit, fettuccine with shrimp, or cappellini topped with scallops and prosciutto; the antipasti and entrées are a mix of creative and classic specialties. Olive-marinated filet mignon, grilled rack of lamb, and seared salmon with beet-encrusted scallops are among the good choices. Fresh seafood specials change daily. Entrées $18.95–26.95.

Blue Mermaid (603-427-2583; blue mermaid.com), The Hill, Portsmouth. Open all year, Sun. 10 AM–9 PM, Mon.–Thu. 11:30–9, Fri.–Sat. 11:30–10. Lunch served till 5 PM. This eclectic and lively restaurant offers a diverse, flavorful menu that covers the globe. The kitchen pays homage to its coastal proximity with appetizers such as lobster and corn chowder or a Caesar salad topped with grilled shrimp; this trend carries over to the main dishes, where you can take your pick from a variety of seafood and have it tossed on the wood grill. Land-based dishes are easy to come by, too: Barbecued ribs, lamb on a skewer, and pad Thai make ordering a challenge for the daring diner. Light eaters can order from the small tapas-style menu—it features the likes of yucca fritta with cilantro adobo or a lobster quesadilla—and interesting side dishes such as plantains also pop up here and there. Eating here is definitely a unique adventure, and you may also be treated to an evening of live music if you visit on the weekend. Small plates around $10. Double that for dinner-sized specials.

Brazo (603-431-0050; portsmouthnh .com), 75 Pleasant St., Portsmouth. Open 5–9 Mon.–Tue., 5–9:30 Wed.–Thu., 5–10 Fri.–Sat. Whether winter or summer, this kind of tropical heat is a welcome addition to Portsmouth's dining scene. Fresh seafood, grilled meats, exotic fruits and local veggies, all very hip, upscale, and Latin. The almond-encrusted soft-shell crab appetizer ($13) gets raves, both in and out of season, for its size and freshness. The Brazilian churrasco topped with Argentinian chimichurri is $25; the Mexican chiles-rellenos-stuffed Cuban rice, roasted corn salsa, and goat cheese with an intense, smoky chipotle crema is $18. Leave room for the banana chocolate bread pudding ($8).

Café Mirabelle and La Crêperie (603-430-9301; cafemirabelle.com), 64 Bridge St., Portsmouth. Open Wed.–Sun. for dinner from 5:15 and Sunday 11–2 for a special menu of sweet and savory crêpes. A cozy place with many plants and large windows, this restaurant offers authentic country French dining (the chef-owner hails from France) in a romantic setting. Entrées are $18.95–24.95. Desserts are equally French—profiteroles, mousses, soufflés, clafoutis, and crème brûlée.

The Carriage House (603-964-8251; carriagehouserye.com), 2263 Ocean Blvd., Rye Beach. Open year round, daily at 5 PM. Built as a restaurant in the 1920s, the Carriage House has been a favorite gourmet eatery for more than two decades, offering quality Continental cuisine at reasonable prices. Specialties might include a Madras curry of the day; a navarin of lobster pan-roasted with big juicy sea scallops and vegetables and flamed with Pernod; or the frutti di mare fra diavolo, which features shrimp, scallops, mussels, squid, and fish all sautéed in Chablis, garlic, and lemon and tossed with spicy marinara sauce—then served over linguine! There are several pasta entrées, salmon poached with Chablis in parchment, sole Oscar, roast duckling, and steaks. Many selections offer both large and small portions. Entrées $19–32.

The Dolphin Striker (603-431-5222; dolphinstriker.com), 15 Bow St., Portsmouth. Lunch 11:30–2 on weekends, dinner daily from 5 PM. On the waterfront in a restored warehouse, this is an old favorite with a new menu that features creatively prepared food from local sources. The seafood is popular, but the menu also boasts innovative New England comfort cuisine, including shrimp and scallop hot pot and veal saltimbuca. On the lower level is the **Spring Hill Tavern**, offering free nightly entertainment amid a collection of memorabilia that celebrates the city's maritime heritage. Entrées $20–25.

Four (603-319-1547; fouronstate .com), 96 State St., Portsmouth. A handsome restaurant with old brick walls and fresh ideas for presenting steak and other grilled items on its SteakHouse menu. A second, fixed price alternative, offers four courses for $40.

Jumpin' Jay's Fish Café (603-766-FISH; jumpinjays.com), 150 Congress St., Portsmouth. Open Mon.–Thu. 5:30–9:30 PM, Fri. and Sat. 5–10, Sun. 5–9. The red-snapper-painted walls lined with contemporary fish prints set the mood for this casually hip fish house. Often there are people lined up around the corner waiting to catch the fun. You have a choice of 10 catches of the day served with your choice of half a dozen sauces, ranging from $19–24. Raw bar, hot and cold appetizers, salads, and several fish and pasta dishes round out the menu.

Cava (603-319-1575; cavatapasand winebar.com), 10 Commercial Alley, Portsmouth. Open daily 3:30–9, Fri.–Sat. until 10. Just up our alley, Commercial Alley that is, in the heart of the state's most cosmopolitan area. If the locale is cool, the menu's equally so. Chef Gregg Sessler brings the cachet of the California wine country to the table; co-host John Akar, a rich career in the local culinary scene. Modern and classic Mediterranean tapas, serious wine bar, outdoor dining in-season.

The Library (603-431-5202; library restaurant.com), 401 State St., Portsmouth. Open for lunch Mon.– Sat. 11:30–3, dinner Sun.–Thu. 5–9:30, Fri. and Sat. until 10. Sunday brunch 11:30–3. The dark paneled walls and ceilings of the old Rockingham Hotel, once Portsmouth's finest hostelry, give this restaurant its name. The menu features steaks plus traditional favorites with contemporary flair. Salmon Benedict is a Sunday brunch favorite. In the English-style pub, the hotel's original front desk makes an impressive backdrop for a nightcap or cigar. $35 for a 16-ounce steak; $25 for 8 ounces. Or splurge with the Kobe (Wagyu) sirloin steak for $58.

Black Trumpet (603-431-0887; black trumpetbistro.com), 29 Ceres St., Portsmouth. Open Sun.–Thu. 5:30– 9 PM, Fri.–Sat. until 10. Brick walls and understated elegance in both food and atmosphere at this bistro and wine bar, formerly incarnated as the Blue Strawberry and Lindbergh's Crossing. Chef Evan Mallett's menu evokes French, Iberian, and Moroccan influences, and includes soups, salads, and cheeses; small and medium dishes; plus main courses that run from $19 for a trio of gnocchis sautéed with chard and squash over a tangy avgolemono sauce to $32 for a bronzed filet mignon topped with fried oysters and whipped béarnaise. On weeknights, there's a three-course prix fixe menu for $21.

♿ **Rudi's** (603-436-0521; rudisports mouth.com), 20 High St., Portsmouth. Open daily for lunch and dinner, 11:30–closing. Located just off Market Square, this is one of the city's most elegant restaurants, with rich paneling and a brass rail in the bar . . . *très* belle epoque. Handicapped accessible, parking adjacent. Entrées from $16 for a salmon burger with onion-basil mayonnaise to $28 for rack of lamb with cranberry-mint demiglaze. Fri. and Sat. are jazz nights (no cover), and there's a Sunday jazz brunch 11–3. The crab Benedict with two poached eggs over roasted red pepper lump crab meat and an English muffin topped with homemade hollandaise sauce is rhapsodic.

Oar House (603-436-4025; ports mouthnh.com/oarhouse), 55 Ceres St.,

Portsmouth. Lunch Mon.–Sat. 11:30–3, also Sun. brunch; dinner Mon.–Sat. 5–9:30, Sun 5–9. Valet parking. Located in a remodeled warehouse, this is another longtime favorite on the waterfront and our choice for chowder. Seafood is featured and varies from bouillabaisse and baked stuffed lobster to broiled scallops and Oar House Delight, a sautéed combination of shrimp, scallops, and fresh fish topped with sour cream and crumbs baked in the oven. Sirloin with peppercorn sauce, rack of lamb, and a chef's chicken, varied daily, are also offered. The Oar House deck, open Memorial Day–early autumn, is our favorite for picturesque riverside relaxing and dining. Entrées $21–38.

Pesce (603-430-7766; pesceblue.com), 103 Congress St., Portsmouth. Open Tue.–Sun., serving lunch, dinner, and Sun. brunch. Seasonal patio dining. The loft-like ceilings, chrome bar, and sleek blue mosaic tiles add up to a cool urban look much appreciated by the local and tourist clientele as well as the regional media. Those coming north from Boston also appreciate the prices. The Italian-inspired, simply prepared meat and fish are complemented by subtle sauces to bring out the flavor. Excellent assortment of vegetables, pasta, and small plate antipasti. Entrées $17–25.

Portsmouth Gas Light Company (603-431-9122; portsmouthgaslight .com), 64 Market St. (or enter through Attrezzi), Portsmouth. Open weekdays from 11:30 AM, weekends from 11. Home of Portsmouth's first utility, now the city's popular brewpub. Traditional pub items, including homemade clam chowder and more substantial fare, plus locally brewed and national brand beers on draft and a boutique wine selection. The deck is open, weather permitting, and there's brick-oven pizza downstairs. On the third floor, a nonsmoking nightclub offers a multicolored light show, circular bar, music, and dancing for the 21–35 age group 9 PM–1 AM on weekends.

Radici Ristorante (603-373-6464; radicirestaurant.com), 142 Congress St., Portsmouth. Open Mon.–Thu. 5–9 PM, Fri.–Sat. 5–11:30, Sun. brunch 10–2, dinner 5–9. Rated one of the top 10 restaurants north of Boston by the *Boston Globe*, which said its pasta dishes "fit nicely in one's stomach." *Radici* means "roots," and here that means Italian carried to the next generation. Vegetarian, pasta, and house specialties come in two sizes and range $12–27. Try osso buco (braised veal shanks) in a mushroom Madeira demiglaze served with mashed potatoes and house vegetable for $25.

Sake Japanese Restaurant (603-431-1822), 141 Congress St., Portsmouth. Open Mon.–Thu. 11:30 AM–10 PM, Fri.–Sat. 11:30–11, Sun. 12:30–10. A large, modern, open room with a long sushi bar and lots of sushi selections. Luncheon and dinner specials include mushi mono (fresh fish fillets steamed with scallion and ginger soy sauce), tepan yaki (chunks of seafood and meat with seasonal vegetables and noodles in a light sauce), and yaki zakana (lightly seasoned broiled fish with citrus dipping sauce), as well as the more traditional tempura and teriyaki. Prices are moderate.

Sakurabana (603-431-2721; sakura bananh.com), 40 Pleasant St., Portsmouth. Lunch Tue.–Fri. 11:30–2:30, dinner weekdays and Sun. 5–9, Fri. and Sat. until 10:30. This longtime Portsmouth establishment with a new name offers fine Japanese dining with a long sushi bar where you can watch the chefs prepare creative and tasty portions of sushi and sashimi. We like the dinner box (the meal is actually served in a portioned box) with miso soup, rice, salad, and a choice of two portions of sushi, sashimi, tempura, teriyaki, and other specialties. Although fish is featured, there is beef and chicken teriyaki and sukiyaki (slices of beef and vegetables with soup and rice). For a special occasion, try "Heaven"—12 pieces of sushi and two rolls with 10 pieces of sashimi. Japanese beer, sake, and plum wine also served. Entrées are moderately priced; dinner box $16.50.

Saunders at Rye Harbor (603-964-6466; saundersatryeharbor.com), off Rt. 1A at Rye Harbor, Rye. Open all year, daily from noon. This well-known restaurant started in the 1920s selling fish from the dock. The specialty is lobster (boiled, baked, or broiled stuffed) served fresh from saltwater tanks, but the diverse menu also includes chicken with lemon and herbs, Saunders jambalaya (lobster, crab, scallops, shrimp, sausage, vegetables, and Creole sauce over rice), a variety of fresh fish, and land 'n' sea (prime rib with shrimp, scallops, or sautéed lobster). Saunders's deck overlooking picturesque Rye Harbor is one of the best spots on the seacoast for a relaxing lunch or beverage. Music and dancing some weekend evenings. Dinner prices $12.95–25.95; lobster dishes, including lobster cooked with ginger and macademia nuts, at market price.

The Wellington Room (603-431-2989; thewellingtonroom.com), upstairs at 67 Bow St., Portsmouth. Open for dinner Wed.–Sun. from 5. An intimate and elegant dining room with great views and an acclaimed menu prepared by chef-owners Matt and Karen Sharlot. Entrées include fresh local cod simmered in a coconut green curry broth over jasmine rice ($24), pan-roasted duck breast with dried cherry compote ($26), and shellfish bouillabaisse ($29).

EATING OUT **The Blue Claw** (603-427-2529; theblueclaw.com), 58 Ceres St., Portsmouth. Open daily, weather permitting, from 11 AM. Not exactly inexpensive but less upscale than some of its neighbors, this waterfront restaurant features a large deck with a view of the harbor and tugboat landing. It specializes in lobster rolls and steamed lobster dinners, prices subject to change with the market. Other specialties are Redhook beer-battered shrimp or fish-and-chips, with your choice of a side dish. Take-out available.

Celebrity Sandwich (603-433-7009; hotline for daily specials 603-433-2277; portsmouthnh.com), 171 Islington St., Portsmouth. Open Mon.–Fri. 7–5; Sat. 9–3. More than 125 sandwiches, each named for a different celebrity, served in an art deco dining room. Box lunches, soups, salads, and desserts, too. Eat in or take out. All sandwiches $5.95 whole, $3.25 half.

Currents (603-427-5427; currents bistro.com), 23 Market St., Portsmouth. Open Mon.–Fri. 11–3, Sat. 11:30–2:30 for lunch; Wed.–Sat. 5–9 for dinner; Sun. 8–2 for brunch; and Sat. 8–11:30 for breakfast. A Mediterranean bistro offering full-service dining or yummy take-out soups, salads, and sandwiches.

The Ferry Landing (603-431-5510; ferrylanding@portsmouthnh.com), 10 Ceres St., Portsmouth. Open Apr. 15–Sept., daily from 11:30 AM. Light seafood dishes of many varieties, sandwiches, chowder, and burgers are served in this 100-year-old building, which was the original ferry landing before the bridges were built. Hanging out over the river, right beside the tugboats, the place is mostly a deck. It is always busy (especially the bar on weekends) during its summer season. Lobster roll $19.95; in the rough $26.95.

✔ **Friendly Toast** (603-430-2154), 121 Congress St., Portsmouth. Open Mon.–Thu. 7 AM–noon; Fri. and Sat. open 24 hours; Sun. 7 AM–9 PM. This popular kitsch-a-thon features great breakfasts and lunches that scream diversity. Pick from unusual combinations like orange French toast, green eggs and ham, Almond Joy pancakes (buttermilk pancakes with chocolate chips, coconut, and almonds), omelets, egg scrambles, and a whopping list of sides including Cuban beans, vegetarian "soysage," and home fries. Lunch is slightly tamer, and you can get old-time faves like BLTs, club sandwiches, and grilled cheese sandwiches along with late-20th-century newcomers such as hummus or nachos. Be prepared for wait staff sporting unique tattoos, piercings, and a doin'-my-own-thing attitude. The room appears to have been furnished by a *Leave It to Beaver* set decorator gone bad, with Formica tables and clown paintings clashing with folk art touches. Most items under $10.

Geno's Chowder and Sandwich Shop (603-427-2070), 177 Mechanic St., Portsmouth. Open Mon.–Fri. 8:30 AM–4 PM, Sat. until 3 PM. Good food is its own reward—fresh lobster rolls, New England chowders, and homemade desserts—and the waterfront deck view is there to remind you that before it was a tourist destination, Portsmouth was indeed a port city.

Gilley's Diner (603-744-2321), 149 Fleet St., Portsmouth. Open 11:30 AM–2:30 AM. An urban legend for sure, this diner managed to accumulate 5,000 unpaid parking tickets before it was moved in the 1970s from its original location in Market Square. The original truck is still attached but going nowhere. Burgers, hot dogs, chili, fries, and beer.

Henrys' Market Café (603-430-2008), 52 Main St. (Rt. 1B), New Castle. Open Mon.–Fri. 8–5, Sat. 9–3, Sun. 9–1. The blue-and-yellow-striped awning tells you you're there, at the best and only way stop in this picture-postcard town. Whether you're after wine, pâté, dog food, or note cards by some local artists—or even hankering for a savory tuna melt seasoned with fresh herbs—this mini restaurant and grocery will serve you in style.

The Ice House (603-431-3086), Wentworth Rd., Rye. Open for lunch and dinner. A popular local take-out and eat-in place since 1952. The decor, recently redone, features bleached knotty-pine walls hung with license plates. The extensive menu has hot and cold sandwiches, burgers, chicken, and all kinds of fish—baked, broiled, and fried.

Me & Ollie's Café (603-436-7777), 10 Pleasant St., Market Square, Portsmouth. Open daily 7 AM–8 PM. Great central location makes this a good stop for a satisfying sandwich, either traditional or grilled panini. A half sandwich and cup of soup (all vegetarian) or small salad runs $6.25. No wonder they call it "Honest Food."

Muddy River Smokehouse (603-430-9582; muddyriver.com), 21 Congress St., Portsmouth. Open daily 11–9 PM; till 10:30 on Fri. and Sat. Just what it sounds like, a barbecue and blues joint, considered one of the best this side of the Mason-Dixon. Forget pretension. With barnboard on the walls and paper towels on the tables, this is all about down-and-dirty eating. Ribs, pulled pork, chili, Tex-Mex, and all-around backwoods grub. Moderate.

Poco's Bow Street Cantina (603-431-5967; portsmouthnh.com), 37 Bow St., Portsmouth. Open daily 11:30 AM–9 PM, Fri. and Sat. until 11. A popular Mexican restaurant with big bay windows overlooking the tugboats and the river; local art covers the walls. Almost

BOW STREET   Greater Portsmouth Chamber of Commerce

any Mexican item you can imagine is here (sizzling fajitas a specialty), plus Mexican beer, sangria, Cuban drinks, and the best margaritas in the city. The riverside deck opens as early as April and closes when it's too cool to use it (usually mid-Oct.). Sun. brunch served when the deck is closed. Lighter menus served in the downstairs bar and on the deck. Moderate.

The Portsmouth Brewery (603-431-1115), 56 Market St., Portsmouth. Open daily 11:30 AM–midnight. A lively spot best known for its microbrewery, which has been producing the city's signature beers, including Old Brown Dog, Pale Ale, Amber Lager, and Black Cat Stout, since 1991. A downstairs lounge features comfortable seating with a pool table, shuffleboard, and a jukebox. The menu is varied and includes soups, salads, chili, pizza, hot and cold super-sandwiches, and nine dinner entrées. Special dishes, changing monthly, might include spicy poached salmon or Thai curry chicken; nightly specials, too. Inexpensive to moderate. Brewery store on premises.

The Press Room (603-431-5186), 77 Daniel St., Portsmouth. Open with live music seven nights a week: Mon., 5 PM–1 AM, with the kitchen open until 10; Tue.–Sun. from 4 with the kitchen open until 11 PM. This Irish-style pub has been the place to go since 1976 for the best jazz, blues, and folk music in the city. Inexpensive, light meals, nachos, pizza, salads, soups, and sandwiches. The food is good and served with draft beer. Tuesday "hoot nights" start at 7:30; see *Entertainment*.

Ray's Seafood Restaurant (603-436-2280; raysseafoodrestaurant.com), 1677 Ocean Blvd., Rye. Open daily except Tue. from 11:30 AM. For more than 40 years a family-style seacoast favorite specializing in fresh fried seafood, lobsters, and steamers. Views of the ocean and Rye harbor from the upstairs dining room and lounge. Dinners and lobsters cooked to go. Moderate.

The River House (603-431-2600; riverhouse53bow.com), 53 Bow St., Portsmouth. Open daily 11 AM–10 PM; 11 PM Fri.–Sat. This has been a local waterfront favorite since it opened as The Stockpot in 1982. This new incarnation boasts award-winning chowder, great salads and sandwiches; entrées, some with Asian and Cajun twists, are in the $20 range. Wheat- and gluten-free options. Full bar. A small deck, open whenever it's warm enough to use it, offers relaxing dining with views past the tugboats and up the river.

LOBSTER Lobsters are a seacoast specialty, and almost every restaurant has a lobster dish. Live or cooked lobsters to go are available at several places. **Sanders Lobster Pound** is the largest local dealer. Their main lobster pound is at 54 Pray St. (603-436-3716; 800-235-3716; sanders lobster.com), open Mon.–Sat. 8 AM–5 PM, Sun. 10–5; and they own the **Olde Mill Fish Market** (603-436-4568) nearby at 367 Marcy St., open daily 9–6. The latter shop has all kinds of fresh fish in addition to live or cooked-to-order lobsters. Sanders can ship a mini clambake anywhere in the country.

Bakery (603-436-6518; ceresbakery .com), 51 Penhallow St., Portsmouth. Open 7 AM–5 PM, Sat. 7–4, Sun. 8–2. One of Portsmouth's old standbys, which is perennially our favorite bakery. Has the best bran muffins anywhere but also brioches, croissants, cookies, and a host of breads, cakes, and other diet busters. A few mostly vegetarian soups, quiches, and salads are served for lunch; daily specials. Many local restaurants serve Ceres Bakery breads.

Breaking New Grounds (603-436-9555), 14 Market Square, Portsmouth. Open daily 6:30 AM–11 PM, midnight in summer. The ambience is friendly with breads and sweets, homemade soups, salads, a variety of sandwiches, plus espresso and cappuccino. Especially popular in warm weather, when the outdoor tables and street performers lend a European-plaza atmosphere. Not to be missed as it is definitely the center of bustling Market Square.

Annabelle's (603-436-3400; annabelles icecream.com), 49 Ceres St., Portsmouth. The landmark original site of this regionally popular regional ice cream brand is open for lunch until late in the evening; closed in winter. Their red, white, and blueberry ice cream even made the White House menu one year for the Fourth of July—but our preference is the Mint Summer's Night Dream (mint chocolate ice cream with dark and white chocolate chunks). Sandwiches and soups are secondary to the sundaes, sodas, banana splits, and hand-scooped cones.

The Juicery (603-431-0693; portsmouthjuicery.com), 51 Hanover St., Portsmouth. Open Sun.–Thu. 10–6, Fri.–Sat. until 7; earlier and later during summer months. This juice and smoothie bar has been a local favorite since the mid-1990s. Added wheatgrass shots give the nutritional equivalent of 4 pounds of fresh veggies. Also offers organic veggie wraps.

✳ Entertainment

Portsmouth's busiest performance season is Sept.–May, except for the Prescott Park Arts Festival, which features theater and music outdoors July–mid-Aug. The night scene is active all year with nearly a dozen restaurants and lounges offering live music on weekends and several other nights: jazz, blues, big-band, folk, and country music.

Seacoast Repertory Theatre (603-433-4472; 800-639-7650; seacoastrep .org), 125 Bow St., Portsmouth. Professional theater with wide regional draw. Several different plays, from original scripts to traditional favorites, are performed Sept.–early June. Also presents a full docket of weekend youth theater.

The Music Hall (603-436-2400; the musichall.org), 28 Chestnut St., Portsmouth. Built in 1878 as a stage theater, this ornately restored hall is operated as a nonprofit and offers a variety of dance, theater, and musical performances throughout the year. International classical music, and national entertainment including magic shows, bluegrass, and jazz are among the regular offerings. Also frequent screenings of independent and classic films. Tours of the historic theater are available.

& **New Hampshire Theatre Project** (603-431-6644; nhtheatreproject.org), 959 Islington St., Portsmouth. Three productions annually of classic and contemporary drama plus educational programs and thought-provoking theater presented by the New Hampshire Youth Repertory Company. Free parking, handicapped accessible.

Pontine Movement Theatre (603-436-6660; pontine.org), 135 McDonough St., Portsmouth. This nationally known company with guest performers offers four productions between fall and spring.

The Players' Ring (603-436-8123; playersring.org), 105 Marcy St., Portsmouth. Attend a variety of theatrical and musical performances at this attractive and historic venue.

The Press Room (603-431-5186), 77 Daniel St., Portsmouth. Music seven nights a week. This Irish-style pub/restaurant has been a Portsmouth music lovers' tradition for decades. Acoustic guitar, folk, Irish, blues, and country sounds in an informal atmosphere make this a perennially popular spot. Often nationally known performers sit in with local favorites. Open mike on Tue.; Sat. jazz lunch.

✳ Selective Shopping

Portsmouth is filled with small shops, especially in the waterfront area bounded by Market, Bow, and Ceres Sts. Here rows of mostly Federal-era brick buildings have been remodeled and restored to offer the shopper everything from upscale clothing and antiques to natural foods, candles, secondhand clothing, jewelry, a fine children's shop, and even a Christmas shop. With several of the city's best restaurants and five waterfront decks, this is a busy and lively place until late in the evening—several shops are open until 11.

Attrezzi (603-427-1667; attrezzinh .com), 78 Market St., Portsmouth. Handsome store featuring cooking, dining, and garden accessories as well as occasional complimentary wine tastings and cooking demonstrations.

Celtic Crossing (603-436-0200; celticcrossing.com), 112 Congress St., Portsmouth. Ireland, Scotland, and Wales are the source for an extensive collection of gifts, wedding bands, and Highland kilt attire.

The Flower Kiosk (603-436-1234; flowerkiosk.com), 61 Market St., Portsmouth. Open Mon.–Thu. 9–5:30, Fri until 6 and Sat until 5, Sun. seasonally. New ideas for fresh and silk flower arrangements along with fruit and flower baskets.

Kittery Outlets (888-548-8379; thekitteryoutlets.com), Exit 3 off Rt. 95 north, Rt. 1, Kittery, Me. Open Jan. 2–Apr., Sun.–Thu. 10–6, Fri.–Sat. 10–8; May–Jan. 1, Mon.–Sat. 9–8, Sun. 10–6. Just minutes from downtown Portsmouth, this shopping mecca provides visitors with 120 factory outlet stores (Banana Republic, Coach, Coldwater Creek, J. Crew, Harry & David, Waterford Wedgwood, and 114 more), all in a single location.

Lollipop Tree (800-842-6691; lollipop tree.com), 319 Vaughan St., Portsmouth. Open Mon.–Fri. 8:30–5:30, Sat. 10–1. Gift collections and baskets of salad dressings, grilling sauces, jams, and specialty baking mixes at factory store prices. Daily samplings.

Nahcotta (603-433-1705; nahcotta .com), 110 Congress St., Portsmouth. Handcrafted furniture and rotating exhibitions of contemporary paintings by some of the region's up-and-coming artists.

Somnia (603-433-7600; somnia.net), 107 Congress St., Portsmouth. Luxurious linens, furnishings, and accessories for bedroom and bath.

Stonewall Kitchen (800-207-5267; stonewallkitchen.com), 10 Pleasant St., Portsmouth. One of several shops throughout Maine and New Hampshire representing this specialty food label—well known in New England and beyond for fine jams, mustards, sauces, and baking mixes.

Ed Weissman, Antiquarian (603-431-7575), 110 Chapel St., Portsmouth. Open June–Nov. by appointment only. A careful selection of 18th- and 19th-century furnishings, paintings, and accessories, two blocks from Market Square.

Upscale Resale (603-431-2969), 278 State St., Portsmouth. Open daily Apr.–Jan., Fri.–Sun. Feb. and Mar. Designer label reruns stylishly displayed.

Art Galleries New Hampshire Art Association–Robert Levy Gallery (603-431-4230; nhartassociation.org), 136 State St., Portsmouth. Open all year, Wed.–Sat. 10–5, Sun noon–4. Members exhibit oils, watercolors, acrylics, photographs, prints, and sculpture. Also sponsors Art 'Round Town (artroundtown.org), a gallery walk of 10 local art spaces, more than 100 artists, 5–8 PM, the second Fri. of the month, May–Dec.

Coolidge Center for the Arts (603-436-6607), 375 Little Harbor Rd., Portsmouth. Open Wed.–Sat. 10–4, Sun. 1–5 or by appointment. Located in the Wentworth-Coolidge Mansion, this gallery provides a classical setting for artists to display their work, which changes monthly.

Welcome to My Home Gallery (608-431-8726; alanawatercolors.com), 58 Cranfield St., Rt. 1B, New Castle. Maddie Alana operates a gallery and studio in her pretty village home. Fine art commissions of seascapes, florals, pets, homes, boats, and more, including custom tile painting, since 1986.

BOOKSTORES Two great bookshops are located in downtown Portsmouth:

RiverRun Bookstore (603-431-2100; riverrun.booksense.com), 7 Commercial Alley (ground floor). Open Mon.–Sat. 9–8, Sun. until 6. Portsmouth's only downtown full-service bookstore, offering new books as well as fast and easy special orders.

Gulliver's (603-431-5556; gullivers books.com), 7 Commercial Alley (basement). Open Mon.–Sat. 10–5, Sun. noon–5. Claims to offer everything for travel but the tickets, with the largest selection of travel books, maps, globes, language guides, and travel video rentals north of Boston.

FARMER'S MARKET Farmer's Market (603-332-9029; seacoast growers.org), Parrott Ave., Portsmouth. June–mid-Oct., Sat. 9–1. Fresh, locally grown veggies and fruits in-season, home-baked goods, and crafts. Seacoast Growers' Association. Also markets in Dover, Durham, Exeter, Hampton, Kingston, and Stratham.

✹ Special Events

Summer on the seacoast offers a nearly unlimited number of special events and activities for people of all ages. Check with local chambers of commerce, the Portsmouth Children's Museum, and Strawbery Banke for varied activities.

February: **Annual African-American Heritage Festival** (603-929-0654), seacoast-wide. Various organizations sponsor a variety of musical, art, theater, and other events in several seacoast locations. Coordinated by the Blues Bank Collective.

April: **New England Blues Conference** (603-929-0654), Portsmouth. Blues workshops, conferences, and concerts.

Early June: **Prescott Park Chowder Festival** (artfest.org). For $7 adults or $5 children, sample the city's best restaurant chowders. Portsmouth is closed to traffic, and the streets are lined with booths selling food, crafts, and more; as many as four stages provide continuous entertainment. More than 30,000 people jam the city for this free event. A popular clambake is held the night before at the Port Authority; purchase tickets in advance.

Second Saturday in June: **Market Square Day Festival**. A spirited day as arts and crafts, music, food, and a 10K road race converge in the heart of the city.

Mid-June: **Blessing of the Fleet**, Prescott Park. The Piscataqua River's commercial fishing fleet, with all boats decorated, converges for a water parade and traditional blessing for safety at sea.

Third weekend in June: **Harbor Arts Jazz Night**.

Last weekend in June: **Pocket Gardens of Portsmouth**.

Early July: **Seacoast Jazz Festival** (artfest.org), Prescott Park. The show runs noon–6 PM. Top jazz artists from across the country join local musicians for a musical blast. A $5 donation is requested.

First week of July: **Sanderson Airfield Ultralight Fly-In**, off Rt. 151 in Greenland.

✍ *Early July–late August:* **Prescott Park Arts Festival** (artfest.org), on the waterfront, Portsmouth. A daily variety of outdoor theater and musical events beginning late in the afternoon. Come early, bring a picnic basket, and spend a few enjoyable hours at one of New England's most popular summer festivals. A $5 donation is requested. There are also art shows and art classes for kids.

Mid-July: **Bow Street Fair** (603-433-4793). A colorful weekend street fair with music and booths selling food and crafts. Affiliated with the Seacoast Repertory Theatre.

Third Sunday in July: **Rye Horse Show** at Parson's Field in Rye.

Late July: **Chautauqua** (603-224-4071; nhhc.org), Marcy St. at Straw-

Courtesy Greater Portsmouth Chamber of Commerce

THE SQUARE IS PACKED DURING THE MARKET SQUARE DAY FESTIVAL

bery Banke, Portsmouth. History comes alive during this annual four-day happening, usually the last week in July. The New Hampshire Humanities Council–sponsored event features workshops, reading discussions, musical performances, and reincarnations of historical figures, all under a giant tent.

Mid-August: **Candlelight house tour** (603-436-1118). An evening tour of Portsmouth's historic houses, all lit by candles. **Blues Festival** (603-929-0654; bluesbankcollective.org), Harbor Place, Portsmouth. Blues on an outdoor, waterfront stage, and in several bars, along with a gospel blues church service. Starts at 11 AM and runs until sunset.

Late August: **Prescott Park Folk and Acoustic Festival** (603-436-2848). Seacoast folkies congregate in this spacious and attractive park 3–9 PM to appreciate a variety of folk and world music—Celtic and African drumming among the offerings. Also **Portsmouth Blues Fest**.

Late September: **Grand Old Portsmouth Brewers' Festival**. This annual Strawbery Banke event celebrates the history of brewing in Portsmouth. **Chili Cook-Off** (artfest .org), Prescott Park. Sample the culinary skills of the city's best chili cooks. A $7 donation is requested. The third Sunday of the month, the **Rye Lions Car Show** is held at Parson's Field in Rye.

First Saturday in October: **Annual Chili Cookoff in** Prescott Park.

Weekend before Thanksgiving: **Portsmouth Holiday Arts Tour**.

First weekend in December: **Button Factory Artists' Open House**.

The first three weekends in December: **Vintage Christmas and Candlelight Stroll** (603-433-1100), Strawbery Banke. See Strawbery Banke's historic houses by candlelight.

✆ *December 31:* **First Night** (603-436-5388). A nonalcoholic, family-oriented New Year's Eve celebration held annually in Portsmouth, late afternoon to midnight, with a wide variety of musical performances and other entertainment. Most events are held in downtown churches.

HAMPTON, HAMPTON BEACH, EXETER, AND VICINITY

The two large towns of Hampton and Exeter were founded in 1638, but while Hampton has retained little of its architectural heritage, Exeter's streets are lined with old houses and buildings.

Hampton was mostly a farming town with a small, beachside tourist community until the beginning of the 20th century, when trolley lines connected the town and its beach with the large cities of the Merrimack Valley and cities in Massachusetts and central New Hampshire. The low-cost trolley transportation made the beach an inexpensive and accessible place for urban workers to bring their families for a day or a week. A large casino was built to provide these visitors with games to play, lunches, and ballroom dancing—though not on Sunday. Hampton is now a fast-growing residential community. After World War II the population was about 2,300; now it is 12,000 people, and much of its open space has been developed except for large family holdings west of I-95. Hampton has a small shopping district, a movie complex, and several good restaurants.

Though Hampton village was small, Hampton Beach boomed and became one of the leading family vacation centers in New England. Now, during peak summer weekends, more than 200,000 people jam the beach, nearly covering the long, sandy oceanfront from one end to the other with blankets. Young people seem to predominate, but there are plenty of older folks who would not consider any other place to spend their summer free time. The center of the beach is still the 90-year-old Casino, complete with restaurants, shops, penny arcades, and a nightclub offering nationally known entertainment.

Often overlooked by residents and visitors alike is the Hampton River. Here three family-owned fishing-party businesses have been serving the public for more than 50 years, recently expanding to include whale-watches and some sightseeing cruises. Surrounding the harbor is the state's largest salt marsh, once thought of as a swamp and earmarked to be dredged and filled to create a lagoon-style seasonal home development. Although Hampton Beach development has pushed into the fringes of this 1,300-acre marsh, people now know the importance of the tidal wetlands as a source of nutrients for a wide variety of marine life, and the marshes are protected from development by state and local laws. As a green space, the marsh is used by anglers, boaters, and bird-watchers; it is perhaps the only piece of ground left on the seacoast that still looks today about the way it did when settlers arrived in the 1600s. South of the Hampton River bridge in Seabrook, bordering the marsh, is a recently protected sand dunes natural area.

West of Hampton is Exeter, with a much larger commercial area and one of the country's premier college preparatory schools. Its marvelous architectural diversity reflects its past as the state capital during the American Revolution, as well as its prominence as an industrial and educational center. Today Exeter has about 12,000 people, although its growth has been slower than Hampton's. Several historic houses open to the public date from the Revolution. The falls on the Squamscott River helped power textile mills, giving the community an important economic base.

Phillips Exeter Academy, one of America's leading preparatory schools, has a list of alumni who have achieved the highest levels of prominence in literature, business, and government service. Distinguished visiting lecturers in all fields, who often speak or perform for the public, and a fine art gallery contribute to the cultural and educational atmosphere of the town and the area. The academy's buildings reflect nearly three centuries of architectural design, contributing to the great diversity of Exeter's cityscape. The academy is in the center of the Front Street Historic District, where the wide variety of architectural styles ranges from colonial residences of the 1700s to 20th-century institutional buildings. Notable are the First Parish Meetinghouse, a variety of Victorian buildings, and the contemporary Phillips Exeter Academy Library designed by Louis Kahn, featured in the recent documentary *My Father, the Architect.*

Historic Rt. 1 bisects the seacoast from south to north. On the Massachusetts border is Seabrook, home of NextEra Energy Seabrook Station, a huge facility that pays most of the town's taxes, giving Seabrook one of the lowest property tax rates in the state. The low property tax, combined with the state's lack of a sales tax, has fueled commercial development in Seabrook; most of the retail shoppers come from heavily taxed Massachusetts. Seabrook Beach is a heavily developed residential area with little public access to the ocean since parking is limited, but many summer homes here are available for weekly rentals.

Seabrook's unplanned growth is in contrast with neighboring Hampton Falls, a residential community whose many farms are now being subdivided into exclusive home developments. North of Hampton along Rt. 1 is North Hampton, also primarily a residential community but with a large colony of summer mansions along the coast in the section called Little Boars Head.

Adjacent to Exeter, and extending west to the Merrimack Valley, are mostly small towns, once farming communities, now being heavily developed with residential subdivisions. Among these towns are Stratham, Kensington,

BELL TOWER AT PHILLIPS EXETER ACADEMY

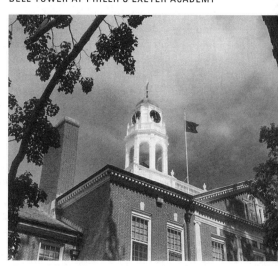

Epping, Newfields, Brentwood, Fremont, Danville, Hampstead, the Kingstons, and Nottingham. Since New Hampshire has no sales or income taxes, and once had low property taxes, the seacoast-area towns have been rapidly growing into popular bedroom communities for people who work in the Boston area, many of whom grew up in Massachusetts but moved north to escape the congestion of urban life for the peaceful countryside. The attractions of the seacoast and its proximity to metropolitan Boston have made the area a magnet for new residents and for visiting tourists.

GUIDANCE **Hampton Area Chamber of Commerce** (603-926-8718; outside New Hampshire 800-GET-A-TAN; hamptonchamber.org), 1 Lafayette Rd., Hampton 03842. A seasonal information center is open daily at the state park complex in the middle of Hampton Beach. The chamber runs daily summer events at the beach and seasonal programs in Hampton village, and publishes a free accommodations and things-to-do guide.

Exeter Area Chamber of Commerce (603-772-2411; exeterarea.org), 24 Front St., Suite 101, Exeter 03833. The chamber is open Mon.–Fri. 8:30–4:30 and offers Exeter-area maps, Historic Walking Tour maps, Exeter-area gift certificates, and more.

GETTING AROUND *By car:* Rt. 1 (Lafayette Rd.) between Seabrook and Portsmouth is lined with strip development and on summer weekends is especially snarled with traffic. If you want to go to Hampton Beach just to see the sights and the latest bathing suits, we do not recommend the weekend, when traffic entering the beach from I-95 or Rt. 1A south may be backed up for several miles.

By taxi: **Academy Taxi** (603-658-TAXI) in Exeter and **Green Rides USA** (603-642-6001) in Kingston offer area service, including trips to and from Boston's and Manchester's airports. **Reprise Limousine** (603-770-9091), a local, women-owned business, offers service around the seacoast, as well as to Logan International Airport.

By bus: **COAST** (603-743-5777; coastbus.org) provides regular bus service throughout 11 communities in the seacoast New Hampshire region.

By train: **Amtrak** (207-780-1000; 800-USA-RAIL; amtrakdowneaster.com) stops in Dover and Exeter with service between Boston and Portland, Maine. Reservations are available online, at any Amtrak station, or from the Quik-Trak ticketing machines in Portland and Wells, Maine; Woburn and Boston, Massachusetts; and Dover, Durham, and Exeter, New Hampshire.

PARKING Municipal and private parking lots behind Hampton's main beach, just a short walk to the sand, are the best places to park if you are not staying at beach lodgings. The parking meters are part of the state park and are closely monitored, so keep them filled with quarters. The main beach area now uses the prepay system; you can pay by credit card for the number of hours desired to avoid an expensive ticket. There is usually plenty of street parking on Exeter's main drag; also a municipal lot near the Szechuan Taste restaurant.

MEDICAL EMERGENCY **Exeter Hospital** (603-778-7311), 5 Alumni Dr., Exeter, offers 24-hour emergency walk-in service. **Exeter ambulance:** 603-772-1212. **Hampton ambulance:** 603-926-3315.

Fuller Gardens (603-964-5414; fullergardens.org), 10 Willow Ave., Little Boars Head, North Hampton. Open early May–mid-Oct., 10–5:30. One of the few remaining estate gardens of the early 20th century, this beautiful spot was designed in the 1920s for Massachusetts governor Alvin T. Fuller, whose family members still live in many of the surrounding mansions. There is an ever-changing display here as flowers bloom throughout the season. Among the highlights are 1,500 rosebushes, extensive annuals, a Japanese garden, and a conservatory of tropical and desert plants. Nominal fee charged.

✔ **The Science and Nature Center at NextEra Energy Seabrook Station** (800-338-7482), Rt. 1, Seabrook. Open Mar.–Thanksgiving, Mon.–Sat. 10–4; Mon.–Fri. the rest of the year. Free admission. NextEra Energy Seabrook Station began producing power in 1990, and its educational center was the first permanent facility on site. There are a variety of exhibits about electricity and nuclear power, including a stationary "elevator" that simulates a 260-foot descent into bedrock to the level of the cooling water tunnels. Kids can pedal a bicycle to light up a bulb, and touch-screen games calculate kilowatts needed to watch TV and run a dishwasher. The mile-long Owascoag Nature Trail winds through woodlands and marshes via boardwalk while a touch pool lets visitors handle sea anemones, barnacles, snails, and sponges. A giant blue lobster named Chilly Willy could give fuel to anti-nuclear visitors but they're told his color is a natural mutation that has nothing to do with the plant. The best off-site view is from Rt. 1A at the Hampton River, where the plant rises above the marsh on the western shore of the estuary. Pets are allowed on the site, but they must remain in your vehicle.

✔ **Tuck Memorial Museum** (603-929-0781; hamptonhistoricalsociety.org), 40 Park Ave., Hampton. Open mid-June–mid-Sept., Wed., Fri., and Sun. 1–4. The museum of the Hampton Historical Society has local memorabilia, especially related to early families, the trolley era, and Hampton Beach. Adjacent is the **Hampton Firefighter's Museum** with a hand engine, other equipment, and a district schoolhouse, all restored. Free admission.

Atkinson Historical Society (603-362-9317), 3 Academy Ave., Atkinson. Open Wed. 2–4 and the first Sat. of the month 10–2. The Kimball-Peabody Mansion houses a collection of local artifacts plus extensive genealogical materials.

Exeter Historical Society (603-778-2335; info@exeterhistory.org), 47 Front St., Exeter. Open Tue., Thu., and Sat. 9:30–noon. Located in the former 1894 town library, this society has research materials for local history and genealogy, artifacts, photographs, maps, and changing exhibits.

Fremont Historical Society (603-895-4032), 225 South Rd., Rt. 107, Fremont. Open by appointment. The museum was the town library, built in 1894 and measuring only 20 by 14 feet. From 1965 until 1981 it was a first-aid society, lending its rural residents hospital equipment.

Hampton Historical Society & Tuck Museum (603-929-0781), 40 Park Ave., Hampton. Call ahead for hours. The adjoining Pine Grove Cemetery, circa 1654, is the oldest public cemetery in the state.

♿ **Sandown Historical Society and Museum** (603-887-6100; sandownnh.org), Depot Rd., Box 300, Sandown. Open May–Oct., Sat.–Sun. 1–5. Local history and railroad artifacts; wheelchair access plus restrooms, picnic tables, and a nearby public swimming beach.

Stratham Historical Society (603-778-0434; 603-778-1347; strathamhistorical society.org), 158 Portsmouth Ave. (corner of Winnicutt Rd.), Stratham. Open Tue. 9–11:30, Thu. 2–4, and the first Sun. of each month 2–4. The former Wiggin Library has recently been acquired by the historical society. Local artifacts and some genealogical materials.

HISTORIC HOMES ✐ **American Independence Museum** (603-772-2622; independencemuseum.org), 1 Governor's Lane, Exeter. Open May–Oct., Wed.– Sat. 10–4; last tour at 3. $5 adults, $3 children over 6; under 6 free. Also known as Cincinnati Hall, and one of New Hampshire's most historic buildings, part of this place was constructed in 1721. It served as the state treasury from 1775 to 1789 and as governor's mansion during the 14-year term of John Taylor Gilman. The Gilman family members were political and military leaders during the Revolutionary War, when Exeter served as the revolutionary capital. The house has recently been restored, and its diverse exhibits, including an original Dunlop broadside of the Declaration of Independence, revitalized.

Gilman Garrison House (603-436-3205; spnea.org), 12 Water St., Exeter. Open selected Saturdays in summer with tours on the hour 11–4. Fee charged. A portion of this house was constructed of logs in 1660 as a garrison, but most of the building reflects the 18th century with fine paneling, especially in the governor's council meeting room. A National Historic Landmark owned by the Society for the Preservation of New England Antiquities. Group tours available with reservations.

HISTORIC SITES **Fremont Meetinghouse and Hearse House**, Rt. 107, Fremont. Open May 30 and the third Sun. in Aug. or by appointment; inquire locally. Built in 1800, this unique meetinghouse, unaltered since it was built, contains an early choir stall, slave pews, and twin porches. The Hearse House, built in 1849, has a hand engine built in that same year.

Sandown Meeting House (603-887-3946), Fremont Rd., Sandown. Owned by the Old Meeting House Association, this is the finest meetinghouse of its type in New Hampshire, unaltered since it was built in 1774. Its craftsmanship and architectural details are nationally recognized. You can easily imagine our colonial ancestors listening to a fire-and-brimstone sermon from the preacher standing in the wineglass pulpit. Service at 11 AM, second Sun. in Aug. Open by appointment; inquire locally for the caretaker.

Old South Meetinghouse (Rt. 1) and **Boyd School** (Washington St.), Seabrook. School opens the third Sun. in Aug. The old school has exhibits and local artifacts relating to salt-hay farming, shoemaking, and decoys used for bird hunting. The church is open by appointment only; inquire locally. Built in 1758, it has been altered inside.

Scenic Drives Follow Rt. 1B through New Castle, passing by Forts Constitution and Stark, and the Wentworth Hotel. Then connect with Rt. 1A through Rye, North Hampton, and Hampton Beach to the Massachusetts border. The ocean is in view most of the way, and there are several restaurants and beaches, including Jenness Beach State Park just south of the receiving station for the first Atlantic cable (on Old Beach Rd.). Coastal marshes and fish houses dot the route. About midway you'll see Little Boars Head, once called the showplace of eastern New Hampshire for its fine seaside mansions. This drive is also popular with bicyclists.

The American Independence Byway is a 29-mile cultural and historic loop that winds through the heart of two of New Hampshire's four original towns—Exeter and Hampton—and Hampton Falls and Kensington, both once part of Hampton. A map and description is available at area tourist centers and attractions, or by calling 603-778-0885.

✷ To Do

Exeter Bandstand. The Exeter Brass Band, the oldest in the country, performs at the bandstand in the center of town Mon. nights in July.

Hampton Airfield (603-964-6749; hampton-airfield.com), Rt. 1, North Hampton. Open-cockpit thrill rides.

✍ **Hampton Beach** is an attraction by itself, considered one of the five cleanest beaches in the United States. The center of activity is the Casino, a historic, rambling complex with arcades, gifts, specialty shops, and the Casino Ballroom, featuring a string of big-name entertainers mid-June–Columbus Day. Adjacent is the Casino Cascade Water Slide. Nearby, along the 0.5-mile business district, is the first seasonal McDonald's plus other fast-food take-outs, more arcades, shops, gift and clothing stores, and miniature golf. Across the street from the Casino are the ocean and the state park complex (the latter scheduled for a multimillion-dollar renovation as we go to press) with the chamber of commerce information center, restrooms, a first-aid room, and the bandstand, which offers free concerts and talent shows throughout the summer, including two free concerts nightly at the Sea Shell Stage. There is a sand sculpture contest in June and fireworks on the Fourth of July and every Wed. night at 9:30 during July and Aug., the heart of the season; but many places are open weekends beginning in Apr., then daily in June. Another major event takes place the weekend after Labor Day when the annual seafood festival features culinary demonstrations, art and craft vendors, and continuous entertainment, including skydiving and more spectacular fireworks, on three stages. A few of the newer, larger hotels are open year-round, and some have restaurants and lounges.

Platypus Tours (603-929-4696), west side of Hampton State Park, Hampton Beach. Open May–Oct. 10. Tours start every 90 minutes 9–6, June 29–Labor Day; limited hours rest of season. Amphibious vehicles once owned by the US Coast Guard provide a land-and-sea tour of Hampton Beach's historic homes and landmark buildings. Tickets also available at the Hatch Shell on Ocean Blvd.

Seacoast Fun Rides, Inc. (603-772-9041; 603-770-5972; seacoastfunrides.com), Hampton Falls. New Hampshire native Dean Kamen invented the Segway, a self-propelled machine that can make you look as if you're standing astride a rotary lawn mower. Seacoast Fun Rides will deliver your rental Segway, then show you all the moves before you glide away to explore the coastal terrain.

Boat Excursions Smith and Gilmore Fishing Parties (603-926-3503; 877-272-4005), Rt. 1A, Hampton Harbor, Hampton 03842. All-day fishing on Wed. and weekends Apr.–Columbus Day; daily half-day trips May–Sept.; night fishing June–Aug.; weekend evening whale-watches July and Aug.; Wed. fireworks cruises

July–Aug. Two modern vessels provide a variety of fishing experiences for this longtime family-operated business. Also a bait-and-tackle shop, rowboats to rent for Hampton Harbor flounder fishing, and a restaurant. Family operated since 1929.

Al Gauron Deep Sea Fishing (603-926-2469; 800-905-7820; algauron.com), State Pier, Hampton Beach 03842. All-day and half-day fishing trips daily throughout the summer; also evening fishing, whale-watches, and Wed.-night fireworks cruises. Four vessels including the 90-foot *Northern Star*. Family owned and operated for more than half a century. Check website for spring and fall schedules.

Eastman's Fishing Fleet (603-474-3461; eastmansdocks.com), River St., Rt. 1A, Seabrook. Open Apr.–Oct. Whale-watching July–Aug., daily 1:30–6. $24 adults, $16 children, under 5 free, and a special Mon.–Fri. senior rate for those 62 and above: $18. The oldest of the family-operated fishing businesses on the seacoast. The Lucky Lady fleet has three modern vessels with a variety of fishing forays available and a Wed.-night fireworks cruise ($14 adult, $12 child) during July and Aug. Tackle-and-bait shops plus a full restaurant and pub with patio dining overlooking the harbor.

Seacoast Sailing (877-899-9696; seacoastsailing.com), New Castle. Two-hour sails during the day and at sunset; also private charters on an hourly, daily, or weekly basis for individuals or events on a 60-foot, 49-passenger motorsailer. All cruises depart from "E" dock at the marina adjacent to the Wentworth-by-the-Sea Hotel.

Golf Apple Hill Country Club (603-642-4414), Rt. 107, East Kingston. Open whenever weather conditions permit; 18 holes, cart rentals, snack bar.

Captain's Cove Adventure Golf (603-926-5011; covegolf.com), Rt. 1, 812 Lafayette Rd., Hampton. Open Memorial Day–Labor Day, daily 10–10, weather permitting. An 18-hole mini golf adventure with a nautical theme.

Exeter Country Club (603-772-4752), Jady Hill Rd. (off Portsmouth Ave.), Exeter. Open May–Oct.; 18 holes, cart rentals, full bar, and food service.

Sagamore-Hampton Golf Course (603-964-8322), North Rd. (off Rt. 1), North Hampton. Open mid-Apr.–mid-Dec.; 18 holes, no motorized carts allowed, pro shop, light food, and beverages. A busy recreational course, inexpensive.

✳ Green Space

✐ **North Hampton State Beach**, Rt. 1A, North Hampton. A long, sandy beach with lifeguards, parking meters, and restrooms. A small take-out food stand is across the street. For one of the area's most scenic walks, park here, then proceed north past the old fish houses, which are now summer cottages, and a beautiful garden maintained by the Little Boars Head Garden Club. A sidewalk follows the coast for about 2 miles to the Rye Beach Club.

✐ **Hampton Central Beach**, Rt. 1A, Hampton. From the intersection of High St. and Rt. 1A, south through the main section of Hampton Beach, is a state park with lifeguards, metered parking, and restrooms. North of Hampton's Great Boars Head the beach is much less crowded, but at high tides has limited sand area. South of Great Boars Head the beach is opposite the business and touristy area. At the main beach are an information center, a first-aid room, and restrooms. Opposite the Ashworth Hotel is the **New Hampshire Marine Memorial**, a large stat-

Robert J. Kroslow

HAMPTON BEACH

ue and plaque dedicated to state residents in the merchant marine service who were lost at sea during World War II.

𝒮 **Hampton Beach State Park and Harbor** (603-925-3784), Rt. 1A, Hampton. Fees charged for the beach and boat launching in-season. At the mouth of the Hampton River is this long, sandy beach with some of the state's last oceanfront sand dunes. There is a bathhouse with dressing rooms, restrooms, and snack bar. Twenty RV sites with full hookups are available on a first-come, first-served basis. Across Rt. 1A is the harbor, with a boat-launching ramp and the state pier.

𝒮 **Swasey Parkway**, off Water St., Exeter. A small park beside the Squamscott River in downtown Exeter. Picnic area and playground. Free concerts on Thu. nights in summer.

𝒮 **Sandy Point Discovery Center** (603-778-0015; greatbay.org), 89 Depot Rd., just off Rt. 101, Stratham. Part of the Great Bay National Estuarine Research Reserve, this new education center is set up primarily for school groups, but it offers great bird-watching on self-guided nature trails through wooded uplands and over a 1,600-foot boardwalk on the tidal marsh. The grounds are available all year during daylight hours. The building, with interpretive exhibits on the ecology of an estuary, is open 10–4 on weekends in May, and Wed.–Sun., June–Oct. There is a launch ramp for cartop boats.

Kingston State Beach, off Rt. 125, Kingston. Open weekends beginning Memorial Day, daily late June–Labor Day. A small state facility on Great Pond, this park has a long, sandy beach, picnic groves, and a bathhouse. Fee charged.

Hampton and Hampton Beach offer a nearly unlimited number of rooms for tourists, especially at the beach and along Rt. 1 between Hampton Falls and North Hampton. The Hampton Area Chamber of Commerce provides a guide to most of the motels, but we have listed a few lodgings below. Both Hampton and Seabrook Beaches have numerous cottages to rent by the week, and Hampton also has many condo units. Seabrook Beach is just residential and thus quieter than Hampton, and its beach is uncrowded. For information try **Harris Real Estate** (603-926-3400), **Preston Real Estate** (603-474-3453; 603-926-2604), or **Oceanside Real Estate** (603-926-3542).

BED & BREAKFASTS The Inn by the Bandstand (603-772-6352; innbythebandstand.com), 6 Front St., Exeter 03833. Open all year. Listed on the National Register of Historic Places, this stylish 1809 golden yellow Federal-style town house, run by James and Victoria Lane, is in downtown Exeter overlooking the historic bandstand, close to movies, restaurants, and shopping. There are nine cleverly decorated rooms, including one honeymoon suite with a Jacuzzi, CD player, kitchenette, and living room, and two other family-style suites. All rooms are furnished with antiques plus pizzazz. Working fireplaces and canopy or four-poster queen beds (one room with twins) reside harmoniously with more contemporary amenities such as air-conditioning, wireless Internet, cable TV, and refrigerator. Breakfast is full and described by the owners as "fun." There's also a fax and copier machine on site, and active types can rent kayaks, canoes, or bikes. Rates for double occupancy are $139–229 weekdays;

weekends run an additional $10; extra-person charge is $30.

✄ **Stillmeadow B&B** (603-329-8381; still-meadow.com), 545 Main St., Hampstead 03841. Open all year. After a couple of decades as members of the British Institute of Innkeeping, the Mitchells moved from Scotland to southern New Hampshire and took over this Italianate home built as a honeymoon house in 1850 by one of the area's leading families. Centrally air-conditioned, the inn offers three rooms, one with an adjoining sitting area, fireplace, and mini kitchen. There's a full breakfast (which could include venison sausage, Margaret's breakfast loaf, and porridge made the Scottish way) served in the formal dining room. Ask about the possibility of packing leftovers for a brown-bag lunch. Not far away you'll find the Robert Frost Farm, the Zorvino Vineyard, and several other attractions. $135–165.

The Victoria Inn and Annex at Hampton (603-929-1437; thevictoria inn.com), 430 High St., Hampton 03842. Open year-round. Once the carriage house of former New Hampshire governor George Ashworth, this spacious inn has six king- or queen-bedded guest rooms, most with private bath. All have air-conditioning, multi-speed Casablanca ceiling fans, cozy central heating, color cable TV with remote, and in-room phone. There are two sitting rooms, one with TV, and a glassed-in porch where a full gourmet breakfast is served. Lovely grounds with a Victorian gazebo, 0.5 mile from the beach. Rates range from $99 on a weeknight off-season up to $229 for the Hydrangea Suite in midsummer. Nonsmoking.

HOTELS ⅄ **Ashworth by the Sea** (603-926-6762; 800-345-6736; ash worthbythesea.com), 295 Ocean Blvd., Hampton 03842. The only full-service oceanfront hotel has been a beach landmark and the finest beach lodging since the early 1900s. With the addition of a modern new wing and remodeling of the original hotel, it is now open year-round. All 105 rooms have queen- or king-sized bed, some with two queens, others with pullout sofa. Some handicapped-accessible rooms. There is a lounge with nightly entertainment, three restaurants (see *Dining Out*), an indoor pool, and private sundecks overlooking the ocean. Summer rates are $169–369; off-season Oct.–Mar. is $79–229; package rates and discounts for multinight stays.

D. W.'s Oceanside Inn (603-926-3542; 866-OCEAN-SI; info@ocean sideinn.com), 365 Ocean Blvd., Hampton Beach 03842. Open Memorial Day–Columbus Day weekend. This turn-of-the-20th-century summer home, located across the street from the ocean, has undergone many changes, but its interior has been maintained and tastefully furnished to reflect its Victorian beginnings. Innkeepers Duane "Skip" and Debbie Windemiller have fulfilled their dream of providing a luxurious and restful oceanside escape; returning guests tell them it's a place they dream of the rest of the year. This is not typical Hampton Beach lodging. There are nine rooms, all with private bath, all distinctively decorated, many with antiques and period pieces, including two with canopy bed; a lovely Victorian common room; and two porches. Midsummer rates (late June–Labor Day) are $200–250; off-season, 10 percent less. Discounts for multinight stays. Breakfast included. No smoking.

&. ⁕♪⁕ **The Inn of Exeter** (603-772-5901; 800-782-8444; theexeterinn .com), 90 Front St., Exeter 03833.

Open year-round. On the campus of Phillips Exeter Academy but no longer owned by the private school, this three-story, Georgian-style inn with restaurant was originally intended to accommodate visiting dignitaries and students' families. Now the inn serves a wide clientele of tourist and business travelers. Reopened in June 2008 after a multimillion-dollar renovation, the 46 rooms, including 5 suites, reflect their illustrious pedigree with classic sophistication and such modern amenities as complimentary in-room WiFi. Some have fireplace; those with views of the back lawn are favorites. The public spaces are similarly civilized. Enjoy a glass of wine, quiet conversation, maybe even a Kobe beef appetizer by the living room fireplace. The fine restaurant serves three meals daily and an award-winning Sunday brunch (see *Dining Out*). Handicapped accessible. Rates for two: $169–239.

⁕♪⁕ **Lamie's Inn & Tavern** (603-926-0330; 800-805-5050; lamiesinn.com), 490 Lafayette Rd. (corner of Rts. 1 and 27), Hampton 03842. While the old homestead dates to the 1740s, and the inn and tavern to 1928, historic credentials are only part of this inn's draw. Since acquiring the property in 1999, the Higgins family has renovated. The 32 rooms offer Colonial styling with 21st-century amenities . . . private bath, phone, air-conditioning, WiFi, fridge, microwave, and cable TV with HBO. Rates (which include a continental breakfast) May–mid-Oct. $109–155; $99 the rest of the year. There are also theater, dining, golf, and ski packages.

Housekeeping Units ⌀ Seaside Village Resort (603-964-8204; seaside villageresort.com), 1 Ocean Blvd., North Hampton 03862. Open May–Sept., weather permitting. Part of the scene for more than 75 years, this is the only resort in New Hampshire to offer lodging right on the beach, with no street to cross. There are beach cabanas, town houses, rustic "original" units, a cottage, and an apartment that sleeps up to six. All are full housekeeping: Guests bring towels and linens and rent Sat.–Sat. Outdoor gas grills are available. Many of the units are rented by the end of one season for the season to come. Most range $1,100–1,500 per week, depending on size and number of guests. Six "original" units rent for $121–156 with a four-night minimum stay.

✳ Where to Eat

DINING OUT Breakers at Ashworth by the Sea (603-926-6762; 800-345-6736; ashworthhotel.com), 295 Ocean Blvd., Hampton. Open year-round. Breakfast from 6:30 AM; café lounge 11:45 AM–1 AM; dinner in Ashworth dining room 5–9 PM. A full-service, oceanfront hotel, the Ashworth is a beach landmark, and its restaurant is among the best on the main beach. Several lobster entrées, baked and broiled seafood, and steaks are menu features (dinners from $15.95).

11 Water Street (603-773-5930; 11waterstreet.com), 11 Water St., Exeter. Open Tue.–Sun. for lunch from 11:30 AM, dinner 5:30–9:30 PM. One of this town's several fine-dining establishments with a view of the Squamscott River, this one with lunch options from macaroni and cheese or fish-and-chips to chilled couscous salad with scallops, or shrimp and penne with fresh basil and tomatoes. For dinner, try eggplant napoleon for $16 or a 14-ounce New York sirloin with green olive and herb chimichurri served with fried polenta and grilled asparagus for $26. Reservations recommended but not necessary; a downstairs bar that serves the full menu is first come, first

served. Wine-d Down Wednesdays offer featured wines and a special martini menu.

The Inn of Exeter's New Epoch Restaurant and Bar (603-772-5901; 800-782-8444; theexeterinn.com), 90 Front St., Exeter. Open year-round. Breakfast from 7 daily; lunch Mon.–Sat. 11–2; dinner 5:30–9 during the week, till 10 on Fri. and Sat.; Sun. brunch 11–2. The newly renovated restaurant has exposed brick, a wall of smoked-glass Palladian windows, and a menu that offers the same kind of classic but casual elegance. Lunches run from $3 for a cup of locally farmed gazpacho to $13 for a steak salad enhanced with field greens, feta cheese, and seasonal vegetables. Dinner selections range from fresh seafood to Continental favorites; prices from $17 for vegetable lasagna to $34 for a grilled filet mignon accompanied by Maine lobster, broccolini, and bacon truffle mashed Yukon gold potatoes. Half portions are available for some entrées. The award-winning Sunday brunch is a local favorite. There's also a lounge with a "nosh" menu, including either Spinney Creek oyster shooters with vodka-infused Brandywine tomatoes or a trio of Kobe beef sliders with various cheeses for $10.

Pimento's (603-583-4801), 69 Water St., Exeter. Open Mon.–Sat. 4:30 PM–midnight. Painted the color of an olive rather than its center, this new addition to Exeter's Water Street dining spots opened in early summer 2008. The fare is casual gourmet fare, primarily American but with a French touch reflective of chef-owner Rob Miller's culinary training. He and co-owner Ken Linn have credentials from working several seacoast restaurants. Downstairs offers a lounge with a view of the river. In the more formal upstairs dining room, the menu ranges from baby arugula and grilled squid with basil parsley pesto for $11 to pan-seared native scallops with raisin caper sauce atop an herb ragout with French beans, red and yellow peppers, and roasted sunchokes for $2.

The 401 Tavern (603-926-8800; the401tavern.com), 401 Lafayette Rd., Rt. 1, Hampton. Open daily 11 AM–1 AM. A local favorite, boasting three different areas and atmospheres: old-style tavern/pub, modern sports bar/lounge, and well-stocked wine bar. Haddock, schnitzel, prime rib, chicken, and shrimp or lobster scampi priced $14–20; sandwiches and burgers $8–9. International wine tastings ($15, with complimentary cheese platter) are held weekly.

Ron's Landing at Rocky Bend (603-929-2122; ronslanding.com), 379 Ocean Blvd., Hampton 03843. Open daily for dinner in summer 4–10, also Sun. brunch 11–3. Winter hours are 4–9, Sun. 11–7. Locals say this is the best place in town for casually elegant dining. Great ocean views, white linens, fresh flowers, and candles. While the menu makes a nod to the inveterate carnivore, this seaside dining room takes advantage of its nearby largesse. Fish lovers can count on lobster, tuna, scallops, sole, and more, prepared with appropriate flair. Entrées between $17.95 and $25.95.

The Old Salt Eating & Drinking Place at Lamie's Inn (603-926-8322; oldsaltnh.com), 490 Lafayette Rd., Hampton. Open all year. Breakfast, lunch, then dinner served Mon.–Thu. until 9 PM, Fri.–Sat. until 10; noon–8 on Sun. Founded in 1931, this is one of the oldest restaurants in the area, and when Rt. 1 was the main road between Boston and Portland, the place was open 24 hours a day on major weekends. With huge beams, pine paneling, tavern tables, and a large fireplace, Lamie's has a Colonial atmosphere, but its menu adds a Continental accent to the mostly New England fare. Lunch, complete dinner, or à la carte are all inexpensive to moderate. A 32-room motor inn with Colonial decor is attached. Entrées $12.99 for fish-and-chips; $18.99 for surf and turf. Early-bird specials (3–5 PM, Mon.–Fri.) are $12.99 for soup or salad, entrée, and dessert.

Wings Your Way (603-964-3333; wingsyourway.com), 215 Lafayette Rd., North Hampton. Open daily 11 AM–10 PM, extended hours weekends and summer season. Way more than wings! Casual family dining with wraps, salads, burgers, burritos, well-priced kids' meals, and awesome desserts.

The Beach Plum (603-964-7451; thebeachplum.net), 17 Ocean Blvd., North Hampton. Open daily Apr. 1–mid-Nov., 10 AM–9 PM; till 11 PM in July and Aug. Considered to have the area's best chowder and and biggest lobster roll; also 78 flavors of ice cream and yogurt.

Joe's Meat Shoppe (603-964-9911; joesmeatshoppe.com), 229 Atlantic Ave. (Rt. 111 at intersection of Lafayette Rd.), North Hampton. This is where the locals send you for a great Angus beef burger washed down by a beer. Joe and Nancy Kutt turned the 1907-era Dow General Store into a meat market and lunch place back in 1984 and have attracted a local following ever since.

Ship to Shore Food and Spirits (603-778-7898; ship-to-shore.com), Rt. 108, Newfields. Open Tue.–Sat. for dinner from 5 PM. Constructed by a local shipbuilder in 1792, this half barn (built shorter than it is wide) has been restored and turned into an intriguing, antiques-filled restaurant. The menu ranges from baked shrimp and haddock to roast duckling, barbecued baby back ribs, and broiled seafood. Daily chicken, veal, seafood, and pasta specials. Entrées $17–27. Occasional special wine and game dinners.

The Tavern at River's Edge (603-772-7393), 163 Water St., Exeter. Open Mon.–Sat. 3–10 PM, for light fare; dinner 5:30–9, Sat. from 5 on. This cozy restaurant in the heart of town has reaped various awards and an admiring review from the *Boston Globe*. Its menu is interesting and comprehensive, ranging from vegetarian lasagna to rack of lamb. Some of the appetizer selections (wild mushroom and pear salad, for example) can double as a light meal. Moderate to expensive.

Zampa (603-679-8772; zampa.com), 8 Exeter Rd., Epping. Open Mon.–Sat., 5–9 PM. Young ideas in an old setting. The great-grandson of one of the original owners and his fiancée bring their Italian-influenced culinary proclivities to this early estate. *Zampa* is Italian for the paw prints embedded in the fireplace bricks. Appetizers include Italian rice dumplings with herbed beef, pecorino cheese, spinach, and tomato sauce. The homemade pasta is fresh daily. Occasional wine dinners and other events. Moderate to expensive.

EATING OUT Abercrombie & Finch (603-964-9774), 219 Lafayette Rd., North Hampton. Open daily 11:30–9, Sunday brunch 9–1. Locally popular restaurant and lounge with a large menu ranging from salads, soups, and sandwiches to full dinners. Vegetarian entrées, plus steaks, quiche of the day, lobster pie, baked scrod, stir-fries, and fried seafoods. Most entrées $8.95–13.95; a 16-ounce prime rib is $20.95; New England Sunday brunch buffet (eggs and omelets cooked to order).

The Baker's Peel (603-778-0910), 231 Water St., Exeter. Open Mon.–Fri.

7 AM–5:30 PM, Sat. until 3 PM. The Old World bakery atmosphere is authentic. Co-owner Suzanne Lovering hails from Switzerland, where husband Judson spent several years learning the trade. In addition to scrumptious pastries, stop by for great iced coffee with coffee ice cubes, plus a great selection of reasonably priced sandwiches, wraps, salads, and soups. The baker's peel (a wooden baking paddle) hangs on the wall.

✔ **Blue Moon Natural Foods & Green Earth Café** (603-778-6850), 8 Clifford St., Exeter. Mon.–Fri. 9–7, Sat. 9–5, Sun. noon–5. Café open for lunch only Mon.–Sat. 11–2:30. Vegetarians and others rejoice at this healthy place offering sandwiches and salads featuring tofu, tuna and egg salads, free-range chicken, and salad specials such as white bean, couscous, and hummus. There are also daily soup specials. On weekday afternoons the store offers heat-your-own meals from Mexican fare to quiche-to-go. Inexpensive.

Divine Café & Grille (603-773-2233; divinecafe.org), 50 Lincoln St., Exeter. Mon.–Fri. 6:30–2:30; Sat. 7:30–6:30. Near the railroad depot and the Handkerchief Company, one of Exeter's newest cafés draws plenty of folks seeking such all-day breakfast specialties as a "Gooey Pile" of roasted home fries, cheese, onions, zucchini, and cilantro for $5.95, or creative takes on burgers, sandwiches, salads, and soups. Eat outside on the deck and try a side of hand-cut sweet potato fries for $2.95 or the asparagus fries for $3.50.

♿ **Galley Hatch Restaurant & Pelican Pub** (603-926-6152; galleyhatch .com), 325 Lafayette Rd., Rt. 1, Hampton. Open daily 11 AM–10 PM, Fri.–Sat. until 11. A large and popular seacoast restaurant with a diverse and reasonably priced menu. Fish, chicken, steaks, pastas, and vegetarian entrées plus pizza, salads, and sandwiches. Breads and pastries are made in the Galley's own bakery, which is open to the public. Two lounges; light meals, special coffees, and desserts served in the lounge until closing. Weekend entertainment. Handicapped accessible. Dinner and movie specials with Hampton Cinema complex next door. Prices are moderate.

Loaf and Ladle, Inc. (603-778-8955), 9 Water St., Exeter. Open Mon.–Sat. 8:30 AM–9 PM, Sun. 9–9. A landmark since 1973, this restaurant has a long-time following. Folks come for the bread (60 different kinds, though not all at one time), which you can also buy by the loaf. Also sandwiches, soups, chowders, salads, and desserts; everything is fresh and homemade, served cafeteria-style by cheerful staff. Seating inside and out overlooking the river.

Margarita's (603-772-2274), 93 Portsmouth Ave., Exeter. A new locale, just off Exit 11 on Rt. 101, for this popular Mexican chain. Serves lunch from 11:30 AM and dinner 4–10 PM, Fri.–Sat. until 11. The bar stays open until 1 AM, Thu.–Sat.

Me & Ollie's Bakery & Café (603-772-4600), 64 Water St., Exeter and 61 High St., Hampton. Open Mon.–Sat. 8–6:30, Sun. 9–5:30. *Honest Food* is this restaurant's mantra. Hearty soups, healthy salads and sandwiches, or grilled panini. Make up your mind over a latte. There are two more sister cafés, including the original, in downtown Portsmouth.

✍ **Penang and Tokyo Restaurant** (603-778-8388), 97 Water St., Exeter. Open Sun.–Thu. 11:30–10, Fri.–Sat. until 11. Following the odd trend of seacoast-area combination restaurants featuring Malaysian, Chinese, and Japanese (there may even be some

Thai in there), this bustling eatery in the heart of Exeter plays host to Phillips Exeter Academy parents, students, families with children, and local business types who don't feel it's a day unless they consume sushi. Don't expect super-friendly service, but do come for the unique Malaysian food, like coconut scallops encrusted with sesame seeds or spicy apple chicken. Everything's well flavored, portions are huge, and the sushi laid out at the sushi bar is nothing if not artful. Prices top out at $25 and usually run $9–15. Look for luncheon specials.

Petey's Summertime Seafood and Bar (603-433-1937), 1323 Ocean Blvd., Rye. Open in-season, 11:30–10. "As good as it gets on paper plates" is what the locals say of this popular seaside spot. Fresh fish, fried and otherwise, is the draw for families, couples, seniors—seemingly the entire East Coast. The chowder, said to be the best on earth, is chocked with seafood, then souped up with real cream and fish stock. Take out, eat in, or compromise by dining on one of the outdoor picnic tables.

Purple Urchin Seaside Café (603-929-0800), 167 Ocean Blvd., Hampton Beach. Seasonal. Patio pub open 11 AM–10 PM; dining room opens at 5 for dinner. Afternoon entertainment Fri.–Sun. 2–6. Laid-back seaside fare with salads, sandwiches, appetizers, handcrafted pizza, and clam chowder served all day. Dinners range from pasta of the day for $13.95 to chargrilled filet mignon for $23.95. Lots of frozen drinks. A dessert alternative is the tiramisu martini rimmed with chocolate syrup.

LOBSTER AND SEAFOOD Fried seafood, chowder, steamed clams, and lobster in the rough are seacoast specialties. Local favorites include the following places:

Brown's Seabrook Lobster Pound
(603-474-3331), Rt. 286, Seabrook
Beach. Open year-round (weekends
mid-Nov.–mid-Apr). Boiled lobster,
steamed clams, fried and baked seafood. Its screened dining room is on the
marsh beside the Blackwater River—or
call ahead for take-out service.

Little Jack's Seafood (603-926-0444),
539 Ocean Blvd., Hampton Beach.
Open late spring–Labor Day.

Lobsters are a seacoast trademark. For
live or cooked lobsters, try the **New
Hampshire Lobster Company** (603-
926-3424), located at the Smith and
Gilmore Pier at Hampton Harbor,
open daily 9–5, summer until 6; or **Al's
Seafood** (603-946-9591), Rt. 1,
Lafayette Rd., North Hampton, open
daily. Al's is a lobster pound and fish
market with a small seafood restaurant
offering mainly fried seafood, but in
warm weather they serve lobster in the
rough on a porch.

✳ Selective Shopping

Christine & Co. (603-964-2380;
christinescrossing.com), 1000 Washington Rd., Rye. Open daily 10–6, Sun.
11–5. A three-story New England barn
featuring new and old, serious and
shabby treasures—all *très* chic. There's
furniture, textiles, lighting, china, art,
even buttons, along with a terrific
selection of women's clothing. The outlet store on Rt. 1 (60 Lafayette Rd.)
offers used clothing and more, though
not necessarily cheaper, furniture and
accessories.

Exeter's Water Street is a mother lode
of interesting shops, offering everything from antiques, art, and apparel to
books, chocolates, cheeses, crafts, garden furnishings and supplies, gifts,
jewelry, toys, and wine. Two old-time
favorites are:

Exeter Fine Crafts (603-778-8282),
61 Water St., Exeter. Open Mon.–Sat.
10–5. More than 200 craft workers,
many of them members of the **League
of New Hampshire Craftsmen**, supply a wide variety of distinctive handmade items.

**Exeter Handkerchief Fabrics and
Custom Draperies Co.** (603-778-
8564), 48 Lincoln St., Exeter. Open
Mon.–Sat. 9–5, Thu. until 8. Long a
destination for home sewers, this shop
features a huge selection of yard
goods, specializing in drapery and
upholstery fabric.

ORCHARDS, PICK-YOUR-OWN,
FARMER'S MARKETS ✿ **Apple-
crest Farm Orchards** (603-926-
3721), Rt. 88, Hampton Falls. Open
year-round, but the best times to visit
are in May when apple blossoms cover
the hillsides and in late summer–fall
when apples are harvested. Pick your
own apples and enjoy weekend festivals in-season. Also pick your own
strawberries, raspberries, and blueberries. Cross-country ski in winter. The
Apple Mart and gift shop are open
year-round.

Jewell Towne Vineyards (603-394-
0600; jewelltownevineyards.com), 65
Jewell St., South Hampton. Free tours
and complimentary tastings offered
May–Dec., weekends 1–5. Now in
operation for more than a decade, this
is New Hampshire's oldest winery.

Farmer's markets are open Tue.
afternoons June–Oct. at Sacred Heart
School, Rt. 1, in Hampton, and Thu.
afternoons at Swasey Pkwy. in Exeter.
Local homegrown vegetables, herbs,
flowers, fruits, and plants plus baked
goods and crafts.

✳ Special Events

Summer on the seacoast offers a nearly unlimited number of special events and activities for people of all ages. Check with local chambers of commerce for varied activities.

Mid-May: **Alewife Festival** (603-778-0885), Exeter. Activities and demonstrations focused on the river and its importance to the community. **New Hampshire Towing Association Wrecker Rodeo** (603-926-8717), Hampton Beach State Park. Scores of wreckers parade and compete for prizes. Parade 9 AM on Sun.

Mid-June: **Hobie Cat Regatta** (603-926-8717), Hampton Beach. A weekend of racing just off Hampton Beach makes a colorful spectacle.

Mid- to late June: **Master Sand Sculpting Competition** (603-926-8717). Seven thousand dollars in prize money goes to one of the 12 master sand sculptors who spend a week working and are judged. Past winning sculptures have included a depiction of carpenters building a house and frogs playing at the beach. Each year 250 tons of sand is dumped on the beach for contestants' use.

Late June–early August: **Concerts in the Park** (603-778-0595), Swasey Park, Exeter, every Thu.

July and August: **Hampton Beach fireworks**, every Wed. at 9:30 PM. **Hampton Beach concerts**, every night at 7 and 9:30.

Fourth of July: **Kingston Fair**, Rt. 125, Kingston. A weekend country fair.

Third Saturday of July: **Exeter Revolutionary War Festival**, Exeter. Historic demonstrations, militia encampments, battle reenactments, road race, canoe rally, and lots of family fun.

Late July: **Miss Hampton Beach Pageant**. A serious beauty pageant with evening gown and swimsuit competitions; 2 PM. **Stratham Fair**, Rt. 101, Stratham. A weekend, agricultural country fair with horse and cattle pulling, midway, children's events, fireworks.

✎ *Mid-August:* **Annual Children's Festival** (603-926-8717), Hampton Beach. **Hampton Idol competition** (603-926-8718), Hampton Beach.

September: **Seacoast Seafood Festival** (603-926-8717), Hampton Beach. Held the weekend after Labor Day, this annual gathering offers the chance to sample a variety of seafood prepared by area restaurants. **Reach the Beach Relay** (rtbrelay.com), 200-mile relay from Franconia Notch to Hampton Beach.

October: **Fall Festival** (603-772-2411), Exeter. Street vendors, crafts, hay rides, and family fun. **Annual Hamptons Marathon & Half** (info@hamptonsmarathon.com), Hampton.

Columbus Day weekend: **Harvest Day Festival and Craft Fair** (603-926-8718; hamptonbeach.org), Hampton.

December: **Holiday Open House and Festival of Trees** (603-772-2411), Exeter. Tree lighting, dozens of decorated trees, hayrides, special late hours for downtown stores. **New Year's Eve Fireworks Display** (hamptonbeach.org). Family fireworks at 8 PM so children can enjoy and still get home in time for bed.

DOVER, DURHAM, AND VICINITY

Durham is the home of the University of New Hampshire, whose beautiful campus dominates the center of the town. The Paul Creative Arts Center with its galleries, music, dance, theater, and intercollegiate athletics has the most to offer visitors, though these activities tend to happen during the school year, Sept.–May. First settled in 1623, Dover is the oldest continuous settlement in the state and the seventh oldest in the nation. During the past decade, the city has become a model of revitalization, attracting visitors from near and far. Today its historic mills house shops, restaurants, apartments, and offices. The Cochecho River, with its river walk, covered bridge, picnic areas, historic markers, and public boat launch, winds through the heart of Dover's downtown.

GUIDANCE **Greater Dover Chamber of Commerce** (603-742-2218; dovernh .org), 550 Central Ave., Dover 03820. The chamber offers a brochure with several self-guided heritage trails to explore the city's long history. See *To Do*.

University of New Hampshire main switchboard (603-862-1234) can provide details of various events or direct your questions to the proper office.

GETTING THERE *By car:* From Portsmouth, follow the Spaulding Tpk. (Rts. 4/16) north, then Rt. 4 West for Durham (Exit 6W), or remain on the turnpike and take one of the three Dover exits (Exits 6E–9).

By bus: **C&J Trailways** (603-430-1100; cjtrailways.com) provides many trips daily connecting Logan Airport and downtown Boston with Dover, Durham, and Portsmouth, New Hampshire; Newburyport, Massachusetts; and Portland, Maine.

By train: **Amtrak** (800-872-7245; amtrak.com). Slide down the Maine and New Hampshire coasts with ease on this short train that shuttles between Boston and Portland, Maine. The train runs year-round; one-way fares run about $12–21. On the seacoast the train stops at Dover, Durham, and Exeter. The Dover station, a short two-minute walk from downtown shops and restaurants, offers free parking.

GETTING AROUND *By bus:* **COAST** (Cooperative Alliance for Seacoast Transportation) (603-743-5777; coastbus.org), a local bus transportation network, connects Portsmouth and major outlying shopping centers with Durham, Dover, Newmarket, Rochester, and Somersworth, New Hampshire; and Berwick, Maine.

Wildcat Transit (603-862-2328) makes frequent trips among Dover, Portsmouth, and the University of New Hampshire in Durham.

By boat: **George's Marina** (603-742-9089), 33 Cochecho St., Dover. Reminiscent of the days when Dover's textile mills shipped their goods far and wide, boats still travel the Cochecho all the way to Portsmouth, Great Bay, and the Atlantic Ocean.

MEDICAL EMERGENCY Wentworth-Douglas Hospital (603-742-5252; wdhospital.com), 789 Central Ave., Dover, has 24-hour emergency walk-in service. **Dover ambulance:** 911. **Durham ambulance:** 603-862-1212.

✳ To See

GAME FARM Little Bay Buffalo Company (603-868-3300), 50 Langley Rd., Durham. Open daily except major holidays 10–5 or dusk. This family-owned and -operated wildlife estate offers an amazing view—a grand stretch of pastureland swooping down to a saltwater bay. Add a few dozen buffalo and call it unique. Sometimes guests can ride across the rolling landscape in a covered wagon pulled by a vintage Farmall tractor to view the bison as they breed and calve. Bison meat, bison jerky, and various other bison by-products are available for sale at the trading post gift shop.

HISTORICAL SOCIETIES AND MUSEUMS ∂ **The Children's Museum of New Hampshire** (603-742-2002; childrens-museum.org), 6 Washington St., Dover. Open Tue.–Sat. 10–5, Sun. noon–5, Mon. during summer and school vacation weeks; closed early Sept. Admission for children and adults is $8; ages 65 and over, $7; free admission under age 1. Formerly located in Portsmouth, the museum reopened in 2008 on the banks of the Cochecho River next to Henry Law Park in the heart of downtown Dover. Many of the museum's exhibits reflect the area's maritime heritage. Kids can explore the yellow submarine, ride in the lobster fishing boat, or climb inside a human-sized kaleidoscope to see unending reflections of themselves. There are many other hands-on exhibits, changing displays, organized activities, and interactive fun for kids of all ages.

A HANDS-ON EXHIBIT ABOUT THE GUNDALOW, ONCE THE SIGNATURE SAILING CRAFT ON THE PISCATAQUA RIVER, AT THE CHILDREN'S MUSEUM OF NEW HAMPSHIRE.

Children's Museum of New Hampshire

Durham Historical Museum (603-868-5436), corner of Main St. and Newmarket Rd., Durham. Open Sept.–May, Tue. and Thu. 1–3; June–Aug., by appointment only.

Mill Museum (603-231-2600), 100 Main St., Dover. Located in the Cocheco Mill-works in the heart of downtown Dover. Impressive photographic collection and artifacts documenting Dover's brickyards, and shoe and textile industries. This city was visited by Abraham Lincoln, Franklin Roosevelt, and other historic figures. It was also the site of the first women's labor strike in the United States.

Lee Historical Society (603-659-5925), Mast Rd., Lee. Open on Lee Fair Day (the Sat. after Labor Day) and June–Aug., Sat. 9–2. Local artifacts, including farm tools, household items, and antique photographs, are housed in an old railroad freight station, moved to this site between the town library and the police station.

Newmarket Historical Society (603-659-7420), Granite St., Newmarket. Open by appointment and June–Aug., Thu. 2–4. The old Granite School Museum has old tools and local artifacts plus photographs of Newmarket mills and shoe shops.

Woodman Institute Museum (603-742-1038), 182 Central Ave., Dover. Open Apr.–Nov., Wed.–Sun. 12:30–4:30. $6 adults, $5 students and seniors, $3 ages 6–15, ages 5 and under free. This three-building complex is Dover's historical museum. The Woodman House (1818) is a research library that has galleries and natural history and war-related museum rooms. The 1813 Hale House is a historical museum with period furniture. The Damm Garrison, built in 1675, is a unique building that was used as a home and fortress by early settlers.

✳ To Do

❧ **Jenny Thompson Pool and Guppey Park** (603-516-6085), Portland Ave., Dover. Dover native Jenny Thompson holds the prize, a dozen Olympic medals, more than any other American in history. Maybe it's the water.

❧ **Dover Bowl** (603-742-9632), 887 Central Ave., Dover. Candlepin and 10-pin bowling center with fun house and arcade, pro shop, food, full bar, and frequent live entertainment. "Rock and Bowl" on Friday nights.

❧ **Twice the Fun** (603-740-9099), 881 Central Ave., Dover. Indoor play area for children from 3 months to 12 years. Climbing structure, 20-foot trampoline track, mini indoor soccer and basketball courts, playhouses. Friday Family Fun Nights.

❧ **Paint for Fun** (603-617-3595), 157 Portland Ave., Dover. Open daily. Children and adults can paint plaster figurines, piggybanks, wall hangings, and gifts. No firing required, so you can take home pieces the same day. Art classes also available.

❧ **Dover Ice Arena** (603-516-6060), 110 Portland Ave., Dover. Year-round hockey, figure skating, and youth programs. Skate rentals available.

❧ **Hilltop Fun Center** (603-742-8068), 145 Rt. 108, Somersworth. You name it, this place has it. Mini golf, driving range, baseball and softball batting cages, go-carts, arcade, laser tag, snack bar.

❧ **Coppal House Farm** (603-659-3572; nhcornmaze.com), 118 N. River Rd., Lee. Scenic 78-acre family farm with seasonal activities including horse-drawn wagon and sleigh rides, a corn maze, and a farm stand.

GOLF Nippo Lake Golf Course (603-664-7616), Province Rd. (off Rt. 126), Barrington. Open Apr.–Nov. Nine holes, cart rentals, full bar and food service year-round; call for starting times on weekends.

The Oaks Golf Links (603-692-6257), Rt. 108, Somersworth. Open mid-Apr.–mid-Nov. Eighteen holes, cart rentals, practice facility and pro shop, full bar and year-round food service. Call for starting times on weekends.

Rochester Country Club (603-332-9892), Rt. 125, Gonic. Open mid-Apr.–mid-Nov. Eighteen holes, cart rentals, full bar and food service, and pro shop; call for starting times on weekends.

Rockingham Country Club (603-659-9956), Rt. 108, Newmarket. Open mid-Apr.–mid-Nov. Nine holes, cart rentals, pro shop, full bar and food service; call for starting times on weekends and holidays.

✄ **Wadleigh Falls Golf Driving Range** (603-659-4444; wadleighfallsgolf.com), Rt. 152, Newmarket. Open May 1–fall. Fully lighted family driving range with ice cream stand and gardens in a country setting.

Sunningdale Golf Course (603-742-8056), 301 Green St., Somersworth. Open mid-Apr.–mid-Nov. Nine holes, cart rentals, full bar, and light food.

Granite Fields Golf Club (603-642-9977; granitefields.com), Rt. 125, Kingston. Eighteen-hole golf course and driving range.

WALKING TOURS **Dover's Heritage Trails** (603-742-2218), 299 Central Ave., Dover. The chamber of commerce offers a brochure with a series of walking tours exploring Dover's long history. Guided Points of Interest tours are offered May–Oct. on Sat. at 10:30 AM for $5 per person.

✳ Green Space

Great Bay National Estuarine Research Reserve (603-868-1095; greatbay .org), 37 Concord Rd., Durham. Great Bay, with some 4,500 acres of tidal waters and tidal wetlands and 800 surrounding upland acres, has been designated part of the national estuarine research system. Famous for winter smelt fishing, oystering, and waterfowl, the bay is a unique resource in the midst of the rapidly growing towns of the seacoast. Some 23 rare or endangered species, including bald eagles in winter, depend on the shallow bay as a refuge. It is an important stop for migrating birds of all species. Its status as a research reserve will help continue the scientific studies conducted since 1970 by the University of New Hampshire's Jackson Estuarine Lab on **Adams Point**. From Rt. 108 in Durham, follow Bay Rd. to Adams Point, where there is a launch ramp and a self-guiding nature trail. Return to Bay Rd. and follow it south to Newmarket, an especially scenic drive with views across the bay. Just across the bay from Adams Point is the **Great Bay National Wildlife Refuge** (603-431-7511), part of the Pease International Tradeport. The public is welcome at the **Sandy Point Discovery Center** on Depot Rd., just off Rt. 101 in Stratham (603-778-0015). It's free and open to the public May–Sept. (plus weekends in Oct.), Wed.–Sun. 10–4. Nearby on Rt. 108 in Stratham is **Chapmans Landing**, a launching site with restroom facilities. There is another launch ramp in the middle of **Newmarket** on Rt. 108. Although the bay has a large surface area, its average depth is only 8 feet, making navigation in larger boats a challenge. Some of the Portsmouth tour boats offer fall foliage cruises on the bay and its tributaries. The bay drains through the Piscataqua River, the boundary between Maine and New Hampshire.

⚓ **Hilton Park** is located on Dover Point, bisected by the Spaulding Tpk. It has a boat-launching ramp, picnic tables, outdoor grills, and play area. It is named for Edward Hilton, who acquired a land grant in 1623 from King James of England.

Cochecho River Trail (603-749-4445), Strafford County Farm at County Farm Rd. and County Farm Cross Rd., Dover. An easy 1-mile loop trail that crosses an old floodplain with scenic river vistas and through forests rich with tall pines and ancient oaks. Trail maps and interpretive materials are available at the trailhead.

UNH's Department of Campus Recreation publishes an excellent little booklet of self-guiding hikes on and around the university's sprawling, wooded campus. Call UNH's main switchboard (603-862-1234) or drop by the New England Conference Center (see *Lodging*, below) to pick up a copy of *Running and Walking Routes*.

✳ Lodging

HOTELS 🐾 ♿ ⁕ᴵ⁕ **The Hotel New Hampshire** (603-868-1234; hotelnewhampshire.net), 2 Main St., Durham 03824. Located just a short walk from the University of New Hampshire, this hotel with the literary reference to Exeter native John Irving's novel of the same name has become Durham's go-to property for lodging. It offers 68 guest rooms plus two luxury suites. Rates include continental breakfast, flat-screen televisions with 70 cable channels, high-speed Internet access both wired and wireless, complimentary beer and wine in the evenings, and other extras. The hotel also offers a guest computer station, guest laundry, and two meeting rooms. Nonsmoking; the public spaces and some guest rooms are handicapped accessible. Rates vary seasonally and include continental breakfast. May–Oct., $119, Nov.–Apr., $99. Pet-friendly.

BED & BREAKFASTS Durham Point B&B (603-868-1162), 1 Sunnyside Dr., Durham 03824. A well-kept new Colonial-style home set back from the road on the way to Durham Point. Philip and Elena Rainville offer two air-conditioned rooms with shared bath at $80 each; a third with private bath goes for $90. Breakfast included.

⁕ᴵ⁕ **The Governor's Inn** (603-332-0107; governorsinn.com), 78 Wakefield St., Rochester 03867. The Georgian Colonial Revival home of former New Hampshire governor Hunter Spaulding plus a neighboring family estate have been combined and turned into a popular restaurant and inn with 20 guest rooms. Accommodations are cozy and comfortable with an expansive continental breakfast. More than 20 guest rooms offer private bath, cable TV, A/C, WiFi, and lush grounds with a gazebo, gardens, bocce ball, horseshoes, and swing.

Highland Farm (603-743-3399; highlandfarmbandb.com), 148 County Farm Rd., Dover 03820. Open year-round. This interesting brick Victorian country house is on the outskirts of the city in a unique pastoral setting. There are nature trails for walking or cross-country skiing along the nearby Cochecho River. Four guest rooms, two with private bath; the other rooms share two baths. Beds include a queen-sized with a canopy. Most rooms have a queen bed or two twins. Common rooms include a living room, wood-paneled library, sunroom, and dining room. Furnishings are antiques, enhanced by the unusual woodwork and architectural design of this house. Full breakfast. Rates are $90–145 for two.

🐾 ⚓ **The Inn at Packers Falls** (603-659-5500; 866-995-6500), 191 Packers Falls Rd., Durham 03824. There are five rooms, each with private bath and double or king bed, in this comfortable home owned and operated by retired social science professor Richard Dewey and his daughter Marilyn. The front lawn dips down to the Lamprey River, and you can too if you're in the mood for a swim. Children and pets accepted; breakfast included; and rates, at $70–100 ($20 per extra person), are a bargain for the area.

⟨†⟩ Silver Fountain Inn (603-750-4200; silverfountain.com), 103 Silver St., Dover 03820. A three-story, late-1800s Victorian with a mansard roof, in the midst of a residential neighborhood but an easy walk to downtown shopping, restaurants, and Amtrak service. Nine romantic guest rooms, all with private bath, TV/DVD, phone, WiFi, A/C, hair dryers, and robes, range $89–129, depending on season and day of the week. A sumptuous breakfast, plus afternoon tea and cookies, is included.

Three Chimneys Inn (603-868-7800; 888-399-9777; threechimneysinn.com), 17 Newmarket Rd., Durham 03824. Open all year. Seemingly no expense was spared when Sagamore Hill, Inc., purchased Durham's oldest home in 1997 and transformed it into the area's poshest public lodgings. During three and a half centuries the original 1649 house on a hill has gone through several expansions and incarnations, each time reflecting the owners' rising fortunes. The inn, overlooking its own formal gardens, the Oyster River, and Old Mill Falls, is an easy walk to the University of New Hampshire campus and 10 miles from Portsmouth. The 23 guest rooms—all with private bath, many with gas fireplace—are luxuriously furnished with four-poster beds, Edwardian bed draperies, tapestries, and Oriental rugs. Added comforts include desk, sitting area, and Internet service. Wedding and conference facilities are available for up to 150. Rates ($249 for two in high season, $109 the rest of the year) include a full breakfast served in the Maples dining room (see *Dining Out*). Children over 6 welcome; $25 charge for third person in a room.

& The Williams House Inn (603-750-4200; 800-871-4177; thewilliams houseinn.com), 103 Silver St., Dover 03820. Open year-round. Located on a residential street, this gray, mansard-roofed B&B was built in the 1880s by a wealthy leather machine belt manufacturer who spared nothing in the way of Gilded Age elegance. Many of the architectural details, including mahogany, crystal, slate, and Caen stone, were imported from Western Europe, and the craftsmanship of the molded plaster ceilings and hand-painted dining room walls reflects the sumptuousness of the age. Eight rooms (all with private bath) have air-conditioning, telephone, hair dryer and robes, plus cable TV with DVD and a video library to choose from. One downstairs room is handicapped accessible. Its king-sized bed, surrounded by rose silk wall panels and custom crown molding, makes the room truly fit for royalty. The dining and living rooms and the ornate library are comfortable and have fireplaces. Full breakfast. Rates are $109–149 July–Columbus Day weekend; $99–129 the rest of the year.

✳ Where to Eat

DINING OUT Blue Latitudes Bar & Grill (603-750-4222; bluelatitudes .net), 100 Main St., Suite 102, Dover. Open Tue.–Thu., 11–9 (bar till 10); Fri.–Sat., 11:30–10 (bar till 11); Sun., 10–8. The high wooden ceilings and brick walls recall this restaurant's mill origins, but the stylish decor and sophisticated menu are evidence of a new day dawning. The menu breaks tradition with such lunch offerings as

South American empanada, and gravlax pumpernickel crostini. For dinner there's three-pepper lamb chops at $22.95, veal Milanese with apple cinnamon compote at $19.95, and a Malaysian stir-fry with tuna strips, wild mushrooms, pineapple, and coconut milk for a dollar less. Sunday brunch, 10–2, features jazz along with everything from two eggs, bacon or sausage, toast, and rosti potatoes for $7 to a lobster scramble with shrimp sauce and vegetable for $15.

Foxfire Grille (603-679-3700; thefox firegrille.com), 96 Calef Hwy., Rt. 125, Epping. Open Sun.–Thu. 11–2 for lunch, 5–9 for dinner, Fri. and Sat. until 10. Breakfast served from 7 on weekends. Opened in 2002 in what was once the local hardware store, this restaurant has been winning acclaim for its casual feel and gourmet food. Chef Andrew Robinson once aspired to be a musician; now he says his art is cooking. For the full menu, choose the dining room. Otherwise, you can loll on the deck or play billiards in the lounge.

Orchard Street Chop Shop (603-749-0006; orchardstreetchopshop .com), 1 Orchard St. (adjacent to the municipal parking off the lower square), Dover. Open daily for lunch from 11:30, dinner from 5. Reservations recommended for dinner. Housed in a remodeled 1830s firehouse, this may be the most elegant example of Dover's dining renaissance. The walls are red, the atmosphere mellow, the menu memorable. Appetizers range from wild boar sausage with creamy cabbage slaw and mustard seed emulsion, to beef carpaccio with saffron aioli (both $9). Entrées include free-range chicken, center-cut veal chop, ahi tuna, and a wide selection of USDA prime-grade beef. Continue the indulgence with fine Napa wines and a Cuban-style cigar lounge. Upstairs, the "Top of the Chop" offers a lower-priced lunch menu.

Three Chimneys Inn (603-868-7800; 888-399-9777; threechimneysinn.com), 17 Newmarket Rd., Durham. Open year-round with dinner served nightly from 5. Whether dining in the formal Georgian-style room, the granite-walled tavern, or alfresco on a terrace under an old English grape arbor, you can count on style here, both in surroundings and food. Oysters, chowder, mussels, smoked salmon crêpes, hazelnut-crusted chicken livers, and chilled jumbo shrimp crown the appetizer menu. The entrées range from pork shank osso buco with red beans and rice ($18.95), to stuffed calamari with sausage and eggplant ($18.95), to beef tenderloin with lump blue crab meat and classic béarnaise ($26.95).

EATING OUT Alexander's Italian Restaurant (603-742-2650), 489 Portland Ave. (Rt. 4), Rollinsford. Tue.–Thu. 11:30–9, Fri. until 10, Sat. 4–10, Sun. noon–8. This popular restaurant is located just west of downtown Dover. For antipasti select red peppers and anchovies or eggplant parmigiana, then try calamari with linguine in red sauce, octopus with linguine, or shrimp with garlic and butter on linguine. Meat entrées range from veal parmigiana and roast veal to chicken cacciatore, pork chops, and New York strip steak. Also pizza (white with Fontina cheese), lasagna, and fettuccine carbonara. Inexpensive.

The Barn Tavern (603-742-1231), 17 Portland Ave., Dover. Open daily 11–9 (to 10 on weekends; closed Sun. in winter). This historic waterfront barn overlooking the Cochecho River offers a casual pub atmosphere with reasonably priced sandwiches, salads, pasta dishes, and entrées for lunch and dinner. Full-service bar. Located directly behind the Schooner House Inn, once a sea captain's home, which now offers short-term rental suites.

Café on the Corner (603-742-0314), 478 Central Ave., Dover. Open for breakfast, lunch, and coffee until midnight. A cozy spot that draws most of its clientele from nearby UNH, Café on the Corner features great coffee, sandwiches, soups, and salads as well as Internet access (there's a minimum charge even if you're just quickly checking your e-mail), board games, books, and comfortable seating. It's very friendly, and even if the crowd is younger than you might like, it's open for a bite or a coffee far later than almost anything else in the seacoast area. Try the bananas Foster smoothie.

Cartelli's Bar & Grille (603-750-4002; cartellis.com), 446 Central Ave., Dover. Open from 4 PM daily. Traditional Italian dishes plus fresh sushi and a raw seafood bar. Full bar and frequent live entertainment.

Christopher's Third Street Grille (603-740-0044; christophersthirdstreet grille.com), 16 3rd St., Dover. Open Mon.–Thu. 11:30–9, Fri. till 10, Sat. noon–10. This popular restaurant features a full menu with fresh ingredients and a creative twist. Flatbread pizzas at $10; grilled ribs, steak, and seafood $13–21; also sandwiches, salads, pasta, and special house entrées.

Kelley's Row Restaurant (603-750-7081), 421 Central Ave., Dover. Open 11–1 AM daily, Sun. until 9. Last call at 12:30. Another of Dover's downtown mill conversions, this one with a patio overlooking the old Cochecho Mill Pond, great for a midsummer meal or drink. The menu features soups, salads, big sandwiches served on a bulkie roll with choice of french fries or pasta salad, and low-carb, low-priced options such as a 6-ounce haddock fillet, or grilled salmon with salad or vegetable for $9.50.

Khaophums Taste of Thailand (603-749-9300), 555 Central Ave., Dover.

Open Mon.–Thu. 11:30–9:30, Fri.–Sat. until 10:30, Sun. until 9. Authentic Thai with fresh ingredients. Chef's specials run $14.95–17.95 but most entrées are $7.95 for lunch, $10.95 for dinner. Also soups, salads, curries, noodles, and appetizers.

Margaritas Restaurant (603-743-6363; margs.com), 23 Members Way, Dover. Open 11:30–1 AM. Mucho gusto with Mexican food, furnishings, and fiesta-like atmosphere.

Newick's Lobster House and Restaurant (603-742-3205; newicks .com), 431 Dover Point Rd., Dover. Open daily 11–9, Memorial–Columbus Day; Sun.–Thu. 11–8:30, Fri.–Sat. 11–9 the rest of the year. Fresh fish and lobster right off the boat are the specialties at this large, very popular restaurant overlooking Great Bay. Not fancy dining, but you can have deep-fried (in cholesterol-free vegetable oil) fish of all kinds with combinations of scallops, oysters, haddock, clams, and shrimp. Portions are huge. For those with lighter tastes, try boiled lobsters, steamers, or broiled, baked, or stuffed fish dinners. Also chicken, sandwiches, chowders, and lobster stew. Expect a wait at weekend dinnertimes. $4.50–20 and above.

Oriental Delight (603-742-5611; orientaldelightdover.com), 436 Central Ave., Dover. Open Sun.–Thu. 11:30–9:30; Fri.–Sat. until 10:30. Attractive restaurant with Chinese Szechuan, Mandarin and Japanese cuisine, including a sushi bar. Dine in or take out.

Strafford Farms Restaurant (603-743-3045), 58 New Rochester Rd., Rt. 108, Dover. Open Sun.–Thu. 6 AM–9 PM, Fri. and Sat. till 10. Sixty years ago Leo Allen and the Rollins families opened a milk-processing plant, which soon expanded to sell ice cream, and eventually became a full-fledged restaurant serving breakfast, lunch, and dinner. Today, despite its location on a busy strip of fast-food restaurants and chain stores, Strafford Farms continues to offer such homemade, back-on-the-farm specialties as Yankee pot roast, meat loaf, and turkey croquettes. The full menu also includes hot and cold sandwiches, seafood entrées, Black Angus beef, homemade soups, salads, and several Italian dishes. Most are priced under $10. Turkey potpie in a bread bowl with vegetable and roll is $7.25; a 20-ounce prime rib with all the trimmings is $16.95.

Weathervane Seafood Restaurant (603-749-2341; weathervaneseafoods .com), 2 Dover Point Rd., Dover. Open 11–9 Sun.–Thu., 9:30 on weekends. A regional restaurant chain with well-priced fresh seafood and other dishes prepared from old family recipes. Full bar, booth and table seating, dine in or take out.

Weeks Restaurant (603-749-4673), 1 Locust St., Dover. Open daily 6 AM–2 PM, Sun. 7–1. A treasured local hangout that serves breakfast till closing, along with soup, salads, and sandwiches for lunch.

✳ Entertainment

✄ **Cochecho Arts Festival** (603-742-2218; cochechoartsfestival.org), Rotary Arts Pavilion, Dover. Open July–late Aug. In the center of Dover beside the Cochecho River is a huge textile mill complex, recently remodeled into a business center. The pavilion is the location for Friday-night Headliners' Series performances. There is also a Children's Series on Tuesday morning and a Thursday Luncheon Series with performances beginning at noon. In summer there's also a Wednesday-afternoon Market Series to correspond with the nearby farmer's market. All feature a wide variety of regional music groups—acoustic, blues, folk, funk, rock and swing artists—plus puppeteers,

magicians, storytellers, acrobats, and musical entertainment for kids.

✄ **Garrison Players Performances** (603-740-0069; 603-450-4ART; garrison players.org), Garrison Players Arts Center, Rt. 4 (corner of Roberts Rd.), Rollinsford. Year-round community theater group that performs plays, musicals, and revues geared for family audiences. Also youth theater productions.

Mill Pond Center for the Arts (603-868-2068; millpondcenter.org), 50 Newmarket Rd., Durham. You'll be amazed at the bounty of performing arts housed in this historic former inn set in the woods. Year-round chamber music, dance, and theater performances. Call for schedules and pricing information.

Whittemore Center Arena (603-862-4000; whittemorecenter.com), 128 Main St., Durham. A 6,100-seat multi-purpose sports and entertainment facility (everything from the nationally ranked UNH Wildcats ice hockey games to Ludacris) on the University of New Hampshire campus.

✳ Selective Shopping

Calef's Country Store (603-664-2231; 800-462-2118; calefs.com), Rts. 9 and 125, Barrington. Open daily 8–6, Sun. till 5. Since 1869, five generations of Calefs have operated this old-fashioned country store. Penny candy, cheddar cheese, maple syrup, Barbados molasses, jams and jellies, pickles and crackers in the barrel, dried beans for baking, hand-dipped candles, pumpkins in fall, gifts, and more.

The Christmas Dove (800-550-3683; christmasdove.com), junction of Rts. 125 and 9, Barrington. Open daily 10–5; Nov.–Christmas Eve, 10–8. This Dover establishment, which has sister stores in New York, Boston, and Ogunquit, Maine, has been around for more than a quarter century. Trimmings, lights, nutcrackers, candles, and nativities turn the complex into a southerly North Pole, allowing organized shoppers to ho-ho-ho all year. Also stocks seasonal decor, including Halloween.

Farmer's market, Henry Law Park, Dover. Wed. afternoons, June–Oct. Locally grown veggies and fruits, home-baked goods, and crafts.

Flag Hill Winery (603-659-2949; flaghillenterprises.com), 0.25 mile off Rt. 155 in Lee. Rolling hills and French hybrid grape vineyards surround this 200-year-old, family-run farm. Wine-tasting bar, vineyard tours, and gift shop, Wed.–Sun., 11–5.

Habitat for Humanity ReStore (603-750-3200; senhhabitat.org), 15 4th St., Dover. Open Wed.–Fri. 10–6, Sat. 9–5. Everything including the kitchen sink can be found here, depending on what's recently been donated by local builders, businesses, and individuals. If you're renovating or just looking for a bargain, this is the place to find a cache of reusable, even some new and vintage materials.

Lucy's Art Emporium (603-740-9195), 303 Central Ave., Dover. Changing array of local artisans' works, including wall hangings, jewelry, clothing, accessories, sculpture, and household gadgets with an original flair.

⌀ **Noggin Factory** (603-742-0012), 330 Central Ave., Dover. Independent toy store just steps away from the Children's Museum with free activities and plenty of quality games, puzzles, teaching aids, costumes, puppets, and pretty much anything else to engage a child's imagination.

Now and Then Home Décor Shoppe (603-692-3237), 60 High St., Somersworth. Open Mon.–Sat. 9:30–4:30. Vintage furnishings, some hand-painted, along with homespun accessories.

Salmon Falls Stoneware (603-749-1467; salmonfallsstoneware.com), the Oak Street Engine House, Dover. Open Mon.–Sat. 8–5, Sun. from 9. Salmon Falls Stoneware has gained a following for its line of cobalt-blue country designs on salt-glazed pottery. The casserole dishes, crocks, dinnerware, mugs, and pie plates are ovenproof, and microwave and dishwasher safe. There's a shop that sells both first-quality items and selected seconds, as well as a studio where you can watch potters at work.

Red's Famous Shoe Barn (603-742-1893), 35 Broadway Rd., Dover. New Hampshire's largest shoe store, featuring more than 100 famous brands at discount prices for the entire family. Open seven days and five nights.

The Sugar Shack (603-868-6636; 800-57-MAPLE; maplesugarshack .net), 0.5 mile from the Lee traffic circle on Rt. 4W in Barrington. Open Feb.–Dec., Wed.–Sat. 10:30–5:30. All-you-can-eat spring breakfasts begin the last weekend in Feb. and run through Mother's Day. The shop is open for sampling and buying a variety of maple products, many produced on the premises. The maple syrup is finger-lickin' good—naturally!

Tuttle's Red Barn (603-742-4313), Dover Point Rd., Dover. Open daily 10–6. Tuttles have lived on this site since 1632, making this the oldest continuously operating family farm in America. Once just a seasonal farm stand operating from the large, old red barn, it has been expanded as a market and garden center. While the surroundings can no longer be called quiet or country, much of the produce, especially sweet corn, comes from the surrounding fields in-season. There's also good bread and a wide variety of fruits, vegetables, and cheeses.

Wiswall House Antiques (603-659-5106; jmcarter5@comcast.net), 28 Wiswall Rd., Durham. Open Mar.–Dec., Wed.–Sat. 10–5, Sun. afternoon by chance or appointment. Interesting selection of American furnishings, unusual lighting, linens, and more.

✳ Special Events

April: **Seacoast Flower, Home & Garden Show** (603-862-1199), Whittemore Center Arena, 128 Main St., Durham. This popular annual event features landscapers, Realtors, and remodelers offering valuable home tips, demonstrations, and displays.

May: ✿ **Children's Museum of New Hampshire Annual 5K Road Race and Fun Run** (603-742-2002), 6 Washington St., Dover. Runs through downtown Dover, the first leg in the popular Seacoast Road Race Series. Face painting, food, entertainment, and children's activities follow. **Antiques Appraisal Day** (603-742-1038), Woodman Institute, 182 Central Ave., Dover. Bring the family heirlooms. **Lilac Family Fun Festival** (603-332-2577), downtown Rochester. Features games, rides, eating and baking contests, live entertainment.

June: ✿ **Seacoast Irish Festival** (603-742-2218), Rotary Arts Pavilion, Henry Law Park, Washington St., Dover. Irish bands, food, beer, crafts, and fun for all ages. ✿ **Somersworth International Children's Day**, an all-day event with four entertainment stages including one for children, a craft fair, food booths, a hands-on craft tent for children, and an activities section for children. **Great Cochecho Boat Race** (603-868-1494). Sponsored by the Strafford Rivers Conservancy, this canoe race proves a challenge to all participants and is great fun to watch. ✿ **Children's Fishing Derby**, Willow Pond, Dover. ✿ **New Hampshire**

Soap Box Derby (603-743-4547), Central Ave., Dover. Coasting race for small, gravity-powered cars built by their drivers and assembled within guidelines on size, weight, and cost.

July–August: ✿ **Cochecho Arts Festival** (603-742-2218), Rotary Arts Pavilion, Dover. Music and children's programs, several times weekly.

August: **Seacoast Irish Festival** (603-516-6100), Dover Lodge of Elks, Rt. 108, Dover. Features live performances by a variety of Irish bands with food, beer, and fun for all ages.

Early September: **Lee Fair Day**, Mast Rd., Lee. A community fair with exhibits, games, and food.

Mid-September: **Rochester Fair** (603-332-6585), 72 Lafayette St., Rochester. A 10-day fair with a midway, agricultural exhibits, and pari-mutuel harness racing. **Antique and Classic Car Show**, (603-742-1038), Woodman Institute Museum, Dover. View and vote for your favorite antique autos.

First Saturday in October: ✿ **Apple Harvest Day** (603-742-2218), Dover. An all-day craft fair with entertainment, food, petting zoo, children's activities, and more.

November: **Holiday Parade** (603-742-2218), Central Ave., Dover. Santa Claus always shows for this traditional holiday parade held on the Sunday following Thanksgiving.

December: **Holiday Home Tour** (603-740-2818), Dover. Self-guided tour of elegant homes decorated for the holidays. ✿ **Santa Claus House** (603-740-6435), Cocheco Courtyard, Dover. Thu. and Fri. 5–7 PM, Sun. 1–4. Santa stops by on weekends to listen to kids' Christmas wish lists. **Winter Solstice** (603-740-9700), downtown Dover. Organized by Dover Yoga Studio to celebrate holiday customs around the world.

The Merrimack Valley

THE MANCHESTER/NASHUA AREA

THE CONCORD AREA

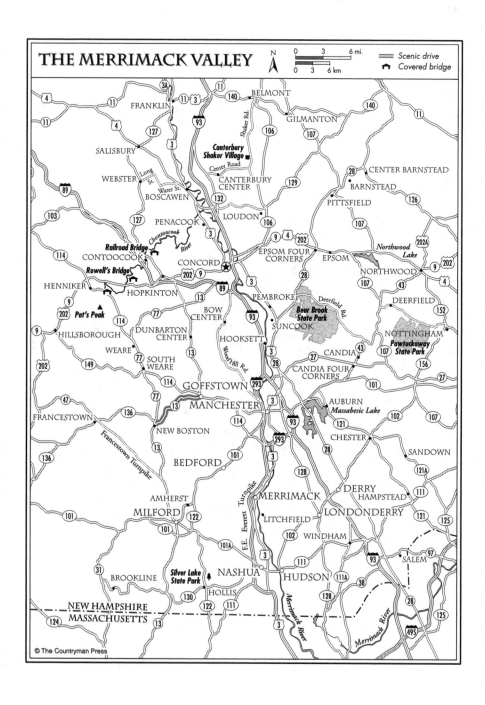

THE MERRIMACK VALLEY

N

0   3   6 mi.
0   3   6 km

Scenic drive
Covered bridge

© The Countryman Press

INTRODUCTION

The Merrimack, New England's second longest river, was an early New Hampshire highway, and today it's paralleled by I-93, New Hampshire's north–south transportation spine. One of the state's first settled corridors, the Merrimack Valley has enjoyed another migrational rush from hundreds of companies and thousands of families moving north from Massachusetts to take advantage of New Hampshire's tax breaks (no sales or income tax).

Relatively few visitors, however, venture farther into this area than the fast-food chains just off I-93. The very way the highways slice through and around both Manchester and Concord does little to encourage exploration. Over recent decades, the southern tier of New Hampshire has become a mecca for Massachusetts émigrés and other expatriates looking for the simple life once exemplified by rural New Hampshire. While tourists see mainly crowded highways and strip malls, those who make this area home know better. Most towns have retained large tracts of conservation land with nature trails and continue to take pride in their old meetinghouses and town halls. Alongside the more recent Rockingham Park Mall is its namesake, Rockingham Park, one of America's most historic racetracks. Nearby is one of the country's oldest amusement parks (Canobie Lake Park), while Nashua, with a bevy of fine restaurants, is frequently named one of the nation's most livable cities.

Manchester's proud old brick shopping streets, its Currier Museum of Art, and its Amoskeag Mills—once the world's largest textile "manufactory"—are rewarding stops. So are Concord's state capitol building, the Museum of New Hampshire History, and the McAuliffe-Shepard Discovery Center. The headquarters for the New Hampshire Audubon Society (just off I-89) and the Society for the Protection of New Hampshire Forests (just off I-93) are also well worth the small detours they require.

Other genuine finds are salted around this little-touristed central New Hampshire corridor. Canterbury Shaker Village, just 15 miles north of Concord, remains a working Shaker community in addition to being one of New England's most interesting museums. "America's Stonehenge" is at Mystery Hill in North Salem. The town of Henniker offers skiing and some fine lodging, dining, and shopping, while Hopkinton village's Main Street, a simple loop between two exits off I-89, presents a picture-perfect slice of early American architecture. There are also numerous state parks with sandy beaches.

THE MANCHESTER/NASHUA AREA

Manchester is by far New Hampshire's largest city (just over 100,000 people). It's also arguably New England's most interesting "mill city," an image the city has begun to re-embrace.

When white men first traveled up the Merrimack, they found a large Native American village at Amoskeag Falls. In 1650 the English missionary John Eliot set up one of his "Praying Indian" communities and called it Derryfield. The Native Americans were later displaced by a white settlement early in the 18th century. By 1810 local judge Samuel Blodgett foretold the community's future, suggesting that its name be changed from Derryfield to Manchester, then the world's biggest manufacturing city (in England).

This early American Manchester population was just 615, but Judge Blodgett raised money to build a canal around Amoskeag Falls enabling flat-bottomed boats to glide downstream and onward, via the Middlesex Canal, into Boston. Both the canal and the town's first cotton mill opened in 1809.

It was a group of Boston entrepreneurs, however, who put Manchester on the map. By the 1830s these "Boston Associates" had purchased waterpower rights for the entire length of the Merrimack River and had begun developing a city full of mills in Lowell, Massachusetts, 32 miles downriver from Manchester. Incorporating themselves as the Amoskeag Manufacturing Company, they then bought 15,000 acres around Amoskeag Falls and drew up a master plan for the city of Manchester, complete with tree-lined streets, housing, churches, and parks.

Like Lowell, Manchester enjoyed an early utopian period during which "mill girls" lived in well-regulated boardinghouses. It was followed by successive periods of expansion, fueled by waves of foreign immigration. With direct rail connections to Quebec, Manchester attracted predominantly French Canadian workers, but Polish, Greek, and Irish communities were (and are) also substantial.

At its height in the early 20th century, the Amoskeag Manufacturing Company employed 17,000 workers, encompassed 64 mill buildings lining both sides of the Merrimack River for a mile and a half, and contained the world's largest single mill yard. Imagine this space filled with the noise and movement of nearly 700,000 spindles and 23,000 looms! Today visitors can get a sense of this history at Manchester's Mill Yard Museum, and even view the former mill yard replicated in LEGOs at Manchester's SEE Science Center.

Life for workers was unquestionably hard. The tower bells rang each morning

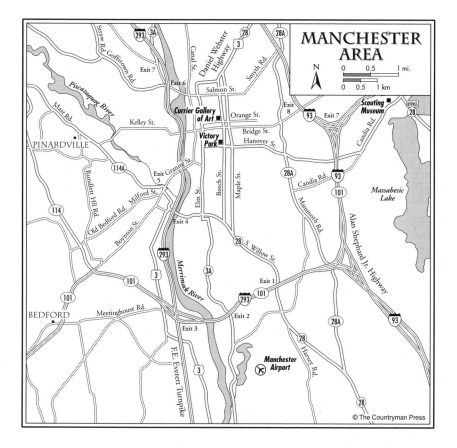

MANCHESTER AREA

© The Countryman Press

at 4:30, and the first call for breakfast was 5:30; the workday began at 6:30, lasting until 7:30 in the evening. But it's a way of life that many workers remember fondly in the oral histories recorded in *Amoskeag: Life and Work in an American Factory-City* by anthropologist Tamara Hareven and photographer Randolph Langenbach. Based on interviews with thousands of former Amoskeag employees, this interesting book, published in 1978, vividly conveys what it was like to live within Manchester's tightly knit ethnic circles, reinforced by a sense of belonging to a full city of workers united like one family by a single boss.

The Amoskeag Manufacturing Company went bankrupt in 1935, and the following year the mills were shut down. In desperation a group of local businessmen formed Amoskeag Industries, Inc., purchased all the mills for $5 million, and managed to lease and sell mill space to diversified businesses.

"Diversify" has been the city's slogan ever since. Having once experienced complete dependency on one economic source, Manchester now prides itself on the number and variety of its industries and service businesses as well as on its current status as a financial and insurance center. New business and residential buildings rise high above the old mill towers.

Loosely circled by hills and with buildings that rise in tiers above the mills on the eastern bank of the Merrimack, Manchester is an attractive city with a Gothic

Revival town hall, handsome 19th-century commercial blocks, the gemlike Palace Theater, and the new 10,000-seat Verizon Wireless Arena featuring such top acts as Bob Dylan and Elton John, as well as the city's own American Ice Hockey League team, the Manchester Monarchs. The recently expanded Currier Museum of Art, one of the country's outstanding small art museums, is also located here.

GUIDANCE Greater Manchester Chamber of Commerce (603-666-6600; manchester-chamber.com), 54 Hanover St., Manchester 03101. Open Mon.–Thu. 8:30–5, Fri until 4. The chamber office stocks a first-rate *Visitors Guide to Greater Manchester.*

Greater Nashua Chamber of Commerce (603-881-8333; nashuachamber.com), 151 Main St., Nashua 03060. Open until 4:30 PM.

Salem, New Hampshire Chamber of Commerce (603-893-3177; salemnh chamber.org), 224 N. Broadway, Salem 03079.

GETTING THERE *By bus:* From the **Manchester Transportation Center** (603-668-6133), 119 Canal St., you can get anywhere in the region; Concord Trailways and Boston Express stop regularly.

By air: The **Manchester-Boston Regional Airport** (603-624-6539) is not only the largest in the state, it's also one of the fastest growing in the country. Carriers include Air Canada (888-247-2262), Continental (800-525-0280, Delta (800-221-1212), Southwest (800-435-9792), United (800-241-6522), and US Airways (800-428-4322). There are nonstop flights to Atlanta, Baltimore, Charlotte, Chicago, Cleveland, Detroit, Fort Lauderdale, Las Vegas, Newark, New York, Orlando, Philadelphia, Phoenix, Tampa, and Washington. Alamo, Avis, Budget, Dollar, Enterprise, Hertz, National, and Thrifty Car Rental are all here and offer free airport transfers. For parking information call 603-641-5444.

By car: The biggest problem with Manchester is finding your way in. It's moated by interstate highways 93 and 293 more effectively than it ever was by canals and mill walls. The simplest access points to downtown are marked from I-293. A handy map, available from the chamber of commerce (see *Guidance*), pinpoints parking garages, and there are reasonably priced (warning: and well-monitored) meters.

GETTING AROUND Hudson Bus Lines (603-424-2446), 22 Pond St., Nashua, offers limousine service among pickup points in Concord, Manchester, Nashua, downtown Boston, and Logan International Airport. City dispatch services are offered by **Flightline, Inc.** (800-245-2525; info@flightlineinc.com, **Town and Country** (603-668-3434), **Yellow Cab** (603-622-0008), and **Executive Airport Service** (603-625-2999).

MEDICAL EMERGENCY Catholic Medical Center (603-668-3545), 100 MacGregor St., Manchester.

Dartmouth-Hitchcock Medical Center (603-577-4000; dartmouth-hitchcock .org), 591 Hollis St., Nashua. Additional branches in Hudson, Merrimack, and Milford.

Elliot Hospital (603-669-5300), 1 Elliot Way, Manchester.

St. Joseph Hospital (603-882-3000; stjosephhospital.com), 172 Kinsley St., Nashua.

Southern New Hampshire Medical Center (603-577-2000; snhmc.org), 8 Prospect St., Nashua.

✻ To See

MUSEUMS ♿ **Currier Museum of Art** (603-669-6144; currier.org), 150 Ash St., Manchester. Open Mon., Wed., Fri., Sun. 11–5, the first Thu. of the month until 8, Sat. 10–5. $10 per adult, $9 per senior, $8 per student; under 18, free. Free admission Sat. until noon. See the Zimmerman

Currier Museum of Art, Manchester

CURRIER MUSEUM OF ART, MANCHESTER

House (below) for rates with museum admission. This excellent regional museum, already one of New England's finest, underwent a major 33,000-square-foot expansion in 2007 that added the dramatic Winter Garden Café, an expanded museum shop, 50 percent more gallery space, and a 180-seat auditorium. It offers unexpected treasures: a lovely landscape by Claude Monet; a spooky 1935 Edward Hopper Maine coastal scene titled *The Bootleggers*; a 1940s painting by Sheeler of the Amoskeag mills; and a recently acquired abstract by Mark Rothko. Paintings range from a 13th-century Tuscan *Madonna and Child* to 20th-century works by Rouault, Picasso, Wyeth, Matisse, and Maxfield Parrish. Silver, pewter, art, glass, textiles, and an extensive collection of early furniture are also displayed. Special exhibits are frequently outstanding. Inquire about frequent lectures and concerts. The Currier is in a residential neighborhood on the site of the Victorian home of Moody and Hannah Currier, the couple who donated the property and who specified in their will that their house be torn down to make way for the museum. The trick to finding it is to begin at either highway exit from which it's marked (the Amoskeag Bridge exit on Rt. 293 and the Wellington St. exit on I-93), then follow the trail of signs.

The Zimmerman House (603-669-6144; currier.org), 201 Myrtle Way. Open year-round except Jan.–Mar. Tours Mon. at 2, Thu. at 11:30 and 2, Fri. at 2, Sat. at 1, and Sun. at 11:30 and 1:30. Tour prices for the Zimmerman House include general admission to the Currier Museum of Art and are $20 adults, $19 seniors, $16 students, and $8 ages 7–17. Please note that children under 7 are not permitted to tour the Zimmerman House. This

AMOSKEAG CANAL, 1948, BY CHARLES SHEELER

Currier Museum of Art, Manchester. Museum purchase: Currier Funds, 1948

Usonian home designed in 1950 by Frank Lloyd Wright—his only house open to the public in New England—is also maintained by the Currier. The hour-and-a-half tour of the house offers details about the Zimmermans, life in the 1950s and '60s, and the architecture of Frank Lloyd Wright. Additional in-depth tours focus on the Zimmermans' love of photography, music, and architectural detail.

Franco-American Centre (603-669-4045; francoamericancentrenh.com), 52 Concord St. Open Mon.–Fri., 10–4. Handy to Elm St. and other downtown museums, this is a leading source of information about French culture, heritage, and history in North America. The Beliveau Gallery mounts changing exhibits, primarily by Franco-American artists.

New Hampshire Institute of Art (603-623-0313; 866-241-491; nhia.edu), 148 Concord St., Manchester. Open Mon.–Fri. 9–5, Sat. until noon. Just across Victory Park from the Historical Association, New Hampshire's only independent college of art now occupies a dozen buildings in the Victory Park neighborhood. In addition to changing exhibits of regional and national importance, it features frequent lectures and theatrical performances. A gift and art supply shop offers handcrafted items.

Alva deMars Megan Chapel Art Center, Saint Anselm College (603-641-7470; anselm.edu), 100 Saint Anselm Dr., Manchester. Exhibits open 10–4 Tue.–Sat., till 8 on Thu. Changing exhibits by regional and nationally known artists often coincide with lectures, tours, and concerts. Admission is free and open to the public.

HISTORICAL MUSEUMS AND SITES ✏ ♿ **Millyard Museum** (603-622-7531; manchesterhistoric.org), 225 Commercial St., Mill #3 (corner of Commercial and Pleasant), Manchester. Open Tue.–Sat. 10–4 PM, Sun. noon–4. $6 adults, $5 students and seniors, $2 ages 6–18, under 6 free; family maximum $18. A branch of the Manchester Historic Association, this new museum in former Mill 3 offers a glimpse into what was once the world's largest textile enterprise. Originally conceived as a planned industrial center, the buildings of the former Amoskeag Manufacturing Company still represent one of the country's leading examples of 19th- and early-20th-century industrial architecture. The four- and five-story-high mills stand in two rows along the eastern bank of the river. Built variously from the 1830s to 1910, they look fairly uniform because, as the older mills were expanded, their early distinctive features were blurred. The adjoining blocks lined with tidy, brick mill housing, however, reflect a progression of

DINING ROOM OF THE FRANK LLOYD WRIGHT–DESIGNED ZIMMERMAN HOUSE
Currier Museum of Art, Manchester

styles from the 1830s to 1920. The two large mills on the western side of the river were once connected to these by tunnels and bridges. The museum documents the area's history, beginning with a permanent exhibit about the Native Americans who used to catch salmon at Amoskeag Falls. Multimedia exhibits, programs, and guided walking tours of the mill yard and beyond offer more insights into the social and architectural history of the area. Many of the Amoskeag Manufacturing Company records, along with city records and family papers, are available in the Henry Fuller Gallery at the museum.

American Credit Union Museum (603-629-1553; acumuseum.org), 418–420 Notre Dame Ave., Manchester (main entrance on Armory St.). Open Mon., Wed., and Fri. 10–noon and 1–4. Home of the nation's first credit union, which opened its doors in 1908 to mill workers seeking the American dream. Exhibits, artifacts, and a video present the story of the credit union movement.

Manchester City Hall (603-624-6500; ci.manchester.nh.us), 1 City Hall Plaza (west side of Elm St.), Manchester. This Gothic-style structure, built in 1845, houses rotating exhibits by local artists, permanent public exhibits of city paintings and photographs, and the Primary Room with exhibits celebrating New Hampshire's first-in-the-nation primary.

Diocesan Museum (603-624-1729), 140 Laurel St., Manchester. Built in 1896, this historic chapel, once part of the Sisters of Mercy convent, is of interest for its stained-glass windows and marble altars as well as for changing exhibits of religious art and memorabilia.

Sargent Museum of Archaeology (603-627-4802), 1045 Elm St., Suite 303, Manchester. Usually open Tue.–Thu. 9:30–5:30 and other times by appointment, but best to call in advance to be sure. The late Howard R. Sargent, a revered anthropology professor, spent a lifetime collecting Native American and other artifacts from across the continent. His influence ranged far and wide; at the museum's opening in 2001, Steven Tyler, lead singer of Aerosmith, reminisced about finding an arrowhead when he was a kid digging in one of Sargent's excavations. In addition to housing Sargent's collection of artifacts and his 7,000-volume library, the museum serves as a center for field studies, workshops, and lectures focusing on the archaeology, anthropology, and history of New Hampshire and New England.

Nashua, New Hampshire's second largest city, has its share of monumental mill buildings along Water and Factory Sts., built by the Nashua Manufacturing Company, which was chartered in 1823 to produce cotton fabric.

Robert Frost Farm (603-432-3091; nhstateparks.org), 2 miles south of Derry on Rt. 28. Open end of June–Labor Day, daily 10–4; Sun. only in May, June, and throughout Sept. until Columbus Day. New Hampshire residents: adults $4, children under 17 and seniors over 65 free. Nonresident adults $5 and ages 6–17, $3. Grounds open free at all times. This 1880s clapboard house in which the poet lived between 1901 and 1909 is filled with original furnishings. An interpretive nature trail runs through surrounding fields and woods, past the "mending wall." Frost did the bulk of his writing here. Programs—including special tours, displays, and poetry readings—are offered to the public at no charge and run May–Oct.

Nashua Historical Society (603-883-0015; nashuahistoricalsociety.org), 5 Abbott St., just off Rt. 101A., Nashua. Call for hours. The Florence Speare Memorial

Museum offers changing exhibits plus a wealth of information regarding Nashua's origins, its evolution into a mill town in the 1800s, and its continued growth as a leading manufacturing and technological center. The neighboring Abbot-Spalding House, a fully furnished Federal-era mansion built by Daniel Abbot, "Father of Nashua" and founder of the city's first cotton mills, is an extension of the museum. It also contains a library of Nashua history and materials.

Taylor Up and Down Saw Mill (603-271-2214; nh.gov/dred/divisions/forest andlands/bureaus/communityforestry/taylormill.htm), Island Pond Rd., Derry. A 200-year-old, water-powered up-and-down sawmill located in a 71-acre state forest. The mill operates at about 60 strokes per minute to process logs into boards. Open usually in spring when the water level is high enough to power it and approximately every other Sat., June–Sept. For precise operating times call the Department of Resources and Economic Development or consult the website.

Old Sandown Railroad Museum (603-887-6100), Rt. 121A, 1 Depot Rd., Sandown. Open May–Oct., Sat. and Sun. 1–5. Railroad memorabilia, telegraph equipment, old magazines, posters, photographs, and Civil War letters are among the exhibits.

Valley Cemetery (603-624-6514; valley-cemetery.com), corner of Pine and Valley Sts., Manchester. Walking tours and programs highlight this Victorian garden cemetery, established in 1841, the burial place for many of Manchester's founding families.

FOR FAMILIES *ℰ* **Amoskeag Fishways** (603-626-3474; amoskeagfishways.org), Amoskeag Dam, 6 Fletcher St. (Exit 6 off I-293), Manchester. Open Mon.–Sat. 9–5 throughout the year; daily during fish migration season. There's a fish ladder where you can watch fish returning to spawn in the Merrimack River during May and June. Year-round educational exhibits highlighting the natural history of the Merrimack River watershed include a historic diorama and waterpower displays.

ℰ **Canobie Lake Park** (603-893-3506; canobie.com), I-93 Exit 2, Salem. Open Memorial Day–Labor Day, daily noon–10; mid-Apr.–Memorial Day and Labor Day–late Sept., weekends noon–6. In operation since 1902, this remains one of the country's finest traditional amusement parks and one of New England's largest. Situated on Canobie Lake and dotted with large old trees, this well-kept, well-landscaped complex offers more than 40 rides, including a big roller coaster, extensive Kiddieland, water park, swimming pool, wild log flume ride, antique carousel, and excursion boat and mini train ride around the park. Lots of treats, traditional and otherwise, in more than a dozen food stands.

ℰ **Charmingfare Farm** (603-483-5623; visitthefarm.com), Rt. 27, Candia. Open daily May–Oct., 10–4; Nov.–Apr., weekends only, 11–3. $17 admission includes pony, tractor-train, and horse-drawn rides around the grounds; $11 without rides (kids under 1 are free). The farm includes a petting zoo with farm animals, Community Supported Gardens and livestock, summer camp, guided horseback trail rides, weddings, seasonal events, and more.

ℰ **The Lawrence L. Lee Scouting Museum** (603-669-8919; scoutingmuseum .org), Blondin Rd. off Bodwell Rd., Manchester. Open Mon.–Sat. in July and Aug., 10–4; Sept.–June, Sat. only, 10–4. Considered the finest collection of Scouting memorabilia and books in the world; exhibits include original drawings and letters

of Scouting founder Lord Robert Baden-Powell. The library of 3,000 books and
bound periodicals also relates to Scouting.

✎ **Mystery Hill** (603-893-8300; stonehengeusa.com), 105 Haverhill Rd. (off Rt. 111), Salem. Open daily 9–5 except Thanksgiving and Christmas. $10 adults, $9 over 65, $7 ages 6–12; ages 5 and under free. Billed as "America's Stonehenge, one of the largest and possibly the oldest megalithic . . . sites in North America." How and why these intriguing stone formations originated is a mystery, whether built by Native Americans or migrant Europeans, but what's known for sure is that they remain an amazing example of prehistoric astronomical and architectural prowess. There's snowshoeing in-season and a celebration of astrological events throughout the year.

✎ ♿ **SEE Science Center** (603-669-0400; see-sciencecenter.org), 200 Bedford St., Manchester. Open Mon.–Fri. 10–4, Sat. and Sun. 10–5 Housed on two floors of a former textile mill building, this science discovery center allows children of all ages hands-on experience of the principles of electricity, momentum, sound, light, and other technology. You can walk on the moon, play with giant bubbles and gyroscopes, and see a two-million-piece LEGO replica of the circa-1905 mill yard, complete with running water; it's the world's largest LEGO exhibit outside LEGOLAND Park. $6 per person.

SCENIC DRIVES Goffstown to New Boston. With its bandstand and country stores, New Boston is an unusually handsome town, and the ride between it and Goffstown is one of the most pleasant around. The road follows the winding Piscataquog River, a good stream for fishing and canoeing. Take Rt. 114 west from Manchester and Rt. 13 to New Boston.

Londonderry. For a glimpse of southern New Hampshire's agricultural past, call the Londonderry town offices at 268B Mammoth Rd., Londonderry, 603-432-1100, ext. 134, to obtain a map for a tour of country roads through blossoms in spring and apples in fall.

✳ To Do

BALLOONING High 5 Ballooning (603-893-9643), 4 Joseph St., Derry. Gift certificates available.

Splash & Dash Hot Air Ballooning (603-483-5503), 107 Hook Rd., Candia. Balloon rides offered over Lake Massabesic.

BASEBALL Fisher Cats Ballpark/MerchantsAuto.com Stadium (603-641-2005; nhfishercats.com), S. Commercial St., Manchester. This 6,500-seat stadium along the Merrimack River is an occasional venue for such big-time acts as Bob Dylan, but more regularly it hosts the area's hotshot members of the AA Eastern Baseball League, the New Hampshire Fisher Cats. Fans are avid about this very competitive team.

Holman Stadium (603-883-2255), 67 Amherst St., Nashua. The Nashua Pride may be a minor-league team (it's part of the Atlantic League of Professional Baseball), but around here it's major summertime fun. Built in 1937, the stadium hosted what is considered the first integrated baseball team in the modern era, when Roy Campanella and Don Newcombe played for the then Nashua Dodgers in 1946.

BOATING There's public access to the Merrimack River's kayak course from Arms Park in downtown Manchester. Lake Massabesic offers two public launches for sailing, powerboating, and canoeing. The **Merrimack River Watershed Council** (603-626-8828; merrimack.org) offers detailed boating maps of the Merrimack River and a series of free trips down southern New Hampshire rivers Apr.–early Oct.

FACTORY TOURS Anheuser-Busch Brewery (603-595-1202; budweisertours .com/toursMER.htm), 221 Daniel Webster Hwy., Merrimack (between Manchester and Nashua). Tours of the brewery (the brew hall, cold cellars, high-speed packaging operations, and the Budweiser Clydesdales in their Old World–style hamlet), complete with complimentary tastings, are offered daily 10–5 June–Aug., 10–4 during May and Sept.–Dec., and Thu.–Mon. 10–4 the rest of the year. The shop where you can buy Budweiser logo merchandise stays open an hour later.

Stonyfield Farm Yogurt Visitor Center (603-437-4040, ext. 3270; stonyfield .com), 10 Burton Dr., Londonderry. Open Mon.–Fri. 8–5, Sat. 9:30–5; closed Sun. and holiday weekends. Stonyfield Farm is known for good yogurt and good sense with its environmentally friendly operation. The visitors center offers samples and discount prices, plus information about the organization's origins and earth-friendly business practices. There's a shop for Stonyfield wearables, kids' stuff, eco-goodies, and kitchen helpers.

GOLF Bedford Golfland (603-624-0503), 549 Donald St., Bedford. Year-round driving range and 18-hole miniature golf course. **Apple Hill Golf Course** (603-642-4414), East Kingston. **Atkinson Country Club** (603-362-5681), Atkinson. **Buckmeadow Golf Club** (603-673-7077), Amherst. **Campbell's Scottish Highlands** (603-894-4653), Salem. **Candia Woods Golf Links** (603-483-2307; 800-564-4344; candiawoods.com), Exit 3, Rt. 101, High St., Candia. Eighteen holes, open to the public, tee times taken five days in advance. **Countryside Golf Club** (603-774-5031), Dunbarton. Nine holes. **Derryfield Country Club** (603-669-0235), 625 Mammoth Rd., Manchester. **Granite Fields Golf Club** (603-642-9977; granitefields.com), Kingston. **Green Meadow Golf Club** (603-889-1555), Hudson. **Legends Golf & Family Recreation** (603-627-0099), 18 Legends Dr. (behind Walmart), Hooksett. Miniature golf and lighted driving range, along with lessons by a PGA professional and free tips on Wed. night. Also batting cages for baseball and softball. **Londonderry Country Club** (603-432-9789), Londonderry. **Stonebridge Country Club** (603-497-8633), 161 Gorham Pond Rd., Goffstown. Eighteen holes, open to the public.

✍ ⬥ **Victorian Park Mini-Golf & Family Entertainment Center** (603-898-1803; victorianpark.com), 350 N. Broadway, Salem. Open end of Apr.–Halloween, daily 10–10. Victorian-motif ice cream parlor, video arcade, and challenging 18-hole mini golf course.

HOCKEY Verizon Wireless Arena (603-644-5000; 603-626-PUCK; 603-626-7825), 555 Elm St., Manchester. The Manchester Monarchs, an affiliate of the Los Angeles Kings, field this American Hockey League team at New Hampshire's largest sports and entertainment facility. The season lasts mid-Nov.–the first week in Apr.

MOTORCYCLING EagleRider (603-626-6300; 877-736-8431; eaglerider.com),
336 Lincoln St., Manchester. As unlikely as it may seem, one of the state's busiest weekends is in June when Harleys crowd most roads heading north toward Weirs Beach and Laconia. If you're a Hog or a wannabe, call the EagleRider motorcycle tourism company to join them.

✳ Green Space

Bear Brook State Park (603-485-9874; campground 603-485-9869), off Rt. 28 in Allenstown. Open daily mid-May–Labor Day; call for other times. Take the Hooksett exit off I-93. Fee. The park has 9,600 heavily forested acres with six lakes, swimming, rental boats, picnicking for up to 1,500 visitors under tall pines, a physical fitness course, nature trails, fishing (Archery Pond is reserved for fly-fishing), and camping with 97 tent sites on Beaver Pond (where the swimming beach is reserved for campers). The Bear Brook Nature Center also has programs, two nature trails, and more than 30 miles of hiking trails in the park with separate routes for ski tourers and snowmobilers in winter. Very crowded on summer weekends but not too bad midweek.

Massabesic Audubon Center (603-668-2045; nhaudubon.org/sanctuaries/massabesic.htm), Auburn. Open Tue.–Sat. 9–5, Sun. noon–5. Free. Miles of scenic trails for hiking, snowshoeing, and skiing. Live animals, osprey viewing, and large nature store with snowshoe and binocular rentals.

Northwood Meadows State Park (603-485-2034), off Rt. 4, Northwood, offers 675 acres of wilderness open year-round. Hiking, picnicking, fishing, nonmotorized boating, snowmobiling, and cross-country skiing, depending on season. Free.

Pawtuckaway State Park (603-895-3031), off Rt. 156, Nottingham. Open weekends only Memorial Day weekend–mid-June, then daily through Columbus Day; call for winter hours. At Raymond, 3.5 miles north of the junction of Rts. 101 and 156. The attraction is a small beach on 803-acre Lake Pawtuckaway, with good swimming, a bathhouse, a 25-acre picnic area, and hiking trails. Rental boats are available, outboard motors are permitted, and the lake is stocked for fishing. Horse Island and Big Island, both accessible to cars, have a total of 170 tent sites, many right on the water; campers have their own boat launch. Trails lead up into the Pawtuckaway Mountains. Both cross-country skiing and snowmobiling are popular here in winter.

Silver Lake State Park (603-465-2342), Rt. 122, Hollis. Open weekends only Memorial Day–mid-June, then daily through Labor Day. Fee. A great beach with a bathhouse, a concession stand, picnic tables, and a diving raft. More than 100 picnic sites are scattered through the pine groves. Summer weekend crowds come from Nashua, but midweek is pleasant.

Clough State Park (603-529-7112), between Rts. 114 and 13, about 5 miles east of Weare. Open weekends only Memorial Day–late June, then daily through Labor Day. Fee. The focus here is 150-acre Everett Lake, created by the US Army Corps of Engineers as a flood-control project. The 50-acre park includes a sandy beach and bathhouses, a picnic grove, and a playground. Motorized boats are not permitted, but there is a boat launch and rental boats are available.

Ponemah Bog (603-224-9909), Amherst. A 100-acre open bog and botanical preserve with boardwalk and trails open year-round.

Mines Fells Park (603-589-3370), Nashua. Part of Nashua's Heritage Trail, the 325-acre park offers wetlands, forests, open fields, and the Nashua River canal for walking, jogging, biking, and cross-country skiing.

✳ Lodging

HOTELS ✍ ⅊ "❢" **Radisson Hotel Manchester** (603-625-1000; 800-333-3333; radisson.com/manchesternh), 700 Elm St., Manchester 03101. Originally named The Center of New Hampshire, this hotel, located in the center of downtown near the Verizon Wireless Arena, is the state's major convention venue. Two restaurants, 250 guest rooms (with computer dataport and WiFi Internet access), and garage parking all under one roof. $139–179; group rates and package plans available.

✍ ⅊ **The Highlander Inn** (603-625-6426; 800-548-9248), 2 Highlander Way, Manchester 03103. A very nice 88-room hotel in a well-landscaped, 33-acre setting with outdoor pool, hot tub, and exercise center, just 2 minutes from the airport. $115–170 for Jacuzzi suites with 24-hour shuttle and discounted airport parking.

INN ✍ ⅊ "❢" **Bedford Village Inn** (603-472-2001; 800-852-1166; bedfordvillageinn.com), 2 Olde Bedford Way, Bedford 03110. This is the inn the big-name media folks prefer when they're in town to cover New Hampshire's first-in-the-nation presidential primary. Once a working farm, the circa-1810 dairy barn now offers a dozen elegant guest suites plus Woodbury Cottage. All the rooms are spacious, equipped with large HDTV, WiFi, four-poster king-sized beds, and whirlpool tubs, and are handsomely decorated with period antiques, custom fabrics, paintings, and Oriental rugs. The complex also includes a patrician-looking Federal home that houses a restaurant with eight intimate dining rooms and a taproom tavern (see *Dining Out*). Expensive.

BED & BREAKFASTS Ash Street Inn (603-668-9908; ashstreetinn.com), 118 Ash St., Manchester 03104-4345. One of Manchester's rambling old Queen Anne houses, this one (circa 1885) is the setting for the Queen City's poshest B&B. In addition to plush queen-sized beds, private bath, and cable TV, the five rooms offer air-conditioning, wireless access, and voice-mail phones. There's a full breakfast in the dining room and a fireplace in the parlor. $169–265 with breakfast and complimentary shuttle. Packages include dining and museum admission. Nonsmoking; no children or pets.

"❢" **Stephen Clay Homestead B&B** (603-483-4096; stephenclaybedandbreakfast.com), 193 High St., Candia. Ed and Therese Sterling operate a three-bedroom B&B in this classic twin-chimney, white village colonial surrounded by stonewalls and well-kept herb, vegetable, and perennial gardens. Three queen-bedded rooms with shared bath rent for $98. A two-room suite with private bath features a queen-sized, double, and twin bed, and ranges from $135 for two to $195 for four occupants. Full breakfast by the fireplace in the dining room. Central air-conditioning and WiFi.

Stillmeadow B&B (603-329-8381; still-meadow.com), 545 Main St., Hampstead. Open all year. After a couple of decades as members of the British Institute of Innkeeping, the Mitchells moved from Scotland to southern New Hampshire to take over this Italianate home built in 1850 by one of the area's leading families. Centrally air-conditioned, the inn offers three guest rooms, one with an adjoining sitting area, fireplace, and mini kitchen. There's a full breakfast (maybe venison sausage or Margaret's porridge made the Scottish way) served in the formal dining room. The leftovers can be packed for a brown-bag lunch at the nearby Robert Frost Farm. $135–165.

Tiffany Gardens B&B (603-432-0418; tiffanygardens.com), 15 King John Dr., Londonderry 03053. The accent here is on garden, as in ¾ acre of flowering trees, shrubs, and perennials with five water features, including a swimming pool, and plenty of information about area garden centers. Each of the two guest rooms offers a queen bed, private bath, and balcony overlooking the gardens. $145 includes a full breakfast served outdoors, weather permitting.

For **camping sites**, see Bear Brook State Park and Pawtuckaway State Park under *Green Space*.

❋ Where to Eat

DINING OUT **Bedford Village Inn** (603-472-2001; 800-852-2001; bedfordvillageinn.com), 2 Olde Bedford Way, Bedford. Open for breakfast, lunch, and dinner daily; Sun. brunch. This beautifully restored 18th-century house is now a Four Diamond restaurant with a variety of elegant dining rooms. The glassed-in porch has off-white furniture and mint-green carpeting with floral design; another room boasts mahogany paneling. There's also a cheery tavern with its own less expensive menu. Breakfast is a production—specialty omelets and crêpes, plus treats like deep-fried fruit fritters. The seasonally changing dinner menu might include pan-seared jumbo sea scallops served with chive risotto and butternut-apple salad ($27), or veal porterhouse with red wine demiglaze, shallot mashed potatoes, and wilted greens ($29).

Baldwin's on Elm (603-622-5975; baldwinsonelm.com), 1105 Elm St., Manchester. Open weekdays for lunch 11:30–2, nightly for dinner 5–9:30, Fri. and Sat. until 10. Closed Sun. The talk of the town since the Verizon Wireless Arena brought new buzz to Elm Street, this restaurant opened in October 2001 with Nathan Baldwin, the former executive chef at the Bedford Village Inn, at the helm. There's a three-course wine-tasting dinner on Mon. for $35. The cosmopolitan menu matches the sleek, contemporary atmosphere with small plates and bowls from $10 for semolina fried calamari on baby greens to larger entrées such as grilled venison chop with roasted corn polenta, chanterelle mushrooms, and red wine sauce for $29.

The Colosseum (603-898-1190), Breckenridge Mall, 264 N. Broadway, Rt. 28, Salem. Open daily except Mon. for dinner from 4 PM (Sat. and Sun. from noon), and Tue.–Fri. for lunch 11:30–3. Popes, politicians, and celebrities have given their blessing to this multi-award-winning restaurant. The extensive menu boasts daily trips to Boston for fresh ingredients and includes a variety of antipasti, pastas, and beef, veal, chicken, and fish dishes at reasonable prices. Among the specialties are pork loin stuffed with provolone, mint, fresh basil, bread crumbs, and garlic, sautéed in a tomato sauce with onions and oregano, for $13.95. A scaloppine of veal sautéed with mushrooms in a sherry sauce with cheese and served with ziti is $18.95.

Commercial Street Fishery (603-296-0676; csfishery.com), 33 S. Commercial St., Manchester. Open Sun.

4–8, Mon.–Thu. until 8:30, Fri. and Sat. to 9:30. Whether you like your seafood raw, fried, wood grilled, or pan blackened, this is the place to get it fresh and innovatively prepared. Cotton's chef Jeffrey Paige is one of the owners of this moderately priced, attractively restored mill-house restaurant. Children's menu; tropical thirst quenchers for adults.

✦ & **Cotton** (603-622-5488; cotton food.com), 75 Arms Park Dr., Manchester. Open Mon.–Thu. 5–9 PM, Fri. and Sat. until 10, Sun. 4–8. Lunch is served Mon.–Fri. 11:30–2:30, with a bar menu 2:30–5. Located below Canal St., the bold font and tilted martini glass on the marquee herald the casually sophisticated, slightly 1950s retro look of this trendy bistro in Manchester's historic old mill complex. Jeffrey Paige, once the chef at Canterbury's Shaker Village, is well known for his innovative dishes and cookbooks using fresh seasonal ingredients. Now he's earning a name for his presentations from the likes of *Bon Appétit* magazine, which named this eatery one of the best neighborhood restaurants in the East. Asian-style tuna stacked on a sesame rice cake and topped with warm crab salad is typical of his style. Moderate.

C. R. Sparks (603-647-7275; crsparks .com), 18 Kilton Rd., Bedford. Open Mon.–Thu. 11:30–3 and 4:30–9:30; Fri. and Sat. until 10:30, Sun. 4–8. Warm woods, comfortable booths, an open concept, and an exhibition-style kitchen form the centerpiece of this restaurant dedicated to casual gourmet dining. Locals regard it as the best stop in town for roast beef and steak. Also has function facilities.

Fratello's (603-624-2022; fratellos .com), 155 Dow St., Manchester. Open for lunch weekdays 11:30–2; for dinner Mon.–Sat. from 4:30, and Sun. from noon. Located in an old mill building, Fratello's is one more entry on the city's Italian dining scene. The restaurant offers a good, moderately priced menu with steaks, seafood, Italian specialties, and major desserts.

Gauchos Churrascaria (603-669-9460), 62 Lowell St., Manchester. Open Tue.–Sat. 4–10 PM, Sun. noon–9. This fun, Brazilian-style eatery offers the best high-protein diet around, starting with a salad bar and followed by round after round of pork, beef, lamb, and chicken served at your table and dexterously sliced from skewers by waiters who know what they're doing. Side dishes include black beans, fried plantains, and rice. The restaurant's new location in an old brick-walled livery stable is both handsome and appropriate. Fixed price $19.95. The front room offers a pastry bar with Starbucks coffee.

Loafers American Restaurant (603-890-6363; loafersnh.com), 43 Pelham Rd., Salem. Open daily for lunch and dinner. Interesting menu with moderately prices in an attractive, "doggy-themed" setting.

Michael Timothy's (603-595-9334; michaeltimothys.com), 212 Main St., Nashua. Afternoon menu served daily 3–5, dinner till closing. White tablecloths, Tuscan colors, and fresh flowers set the tone for this long-standing Nashua favorite (opened in 1995). The wood-grilled pizza is high-style and delicious—for instance, caramelized onion and crispy bacon with duck confit ($21)—as are such other dinner entrées as the sautéed veal scaloppine with half-dried tomatoes, leeks, white wine, and prosciutto-wrapped baked asparagus ($22).

Richard's Bistro (603-644-1180; richardsbistro.com), 36 Lowell St.,

Manchester. Open daily with lunch starting at 11:30, dinner at 4:30, Sun. brunch at 10 AM. Just off Elm Street in downtown Manchester, this attractively mellow, French-style restaurant is good for unusual soups and salads at lunch and for Sunday brunch dishes like salmon hash and poached eggs topped with horseradish dill cream, or a frittata of fresh vegetables baked with feta. Dinner entrées might include pecan-dusted chicken breast with kiwi, mango, and sweet potato garnished with raspberries, and char-broiled filet mignon with shiitake mushrooms and focaccia potatoes. For dessert try the raspberry trifle or one of Richard's famous pastries. A number of wines are available by the glass, and the wine list is respectable.

Saffron Bistro (603-883-2100; the saffronbistro.com), 80 Main St., Nashua. Open Tue.–Sat. for dinner 5–9:30, bar and lounge 4–closing. The refined atmosphere—gilt mirrors, glittering chandeliers, artwork, and a baby grand in the corner—echoes the highly regarded American classic cuisine. Entrées range from pecan-crusted chicken at $19 to New Zealand rack of lamb for $32. Lighter fare also available.

Surf (603-595-9293; surfseafood.com), 207 Main St., Nashua. Open Tue.–Sat. from 4:30. Super-fresh seafood imaginatively prepared by chef-owner Michael Buckley has earned repeated accolades for this upscale eatery, the place for seafood and atmosphere in the Gateway City. Green and blue hues and gossamer fabrics introduce an ocean theme, which the menu continues. A good raw bar plus plenty of entrées ranging $17–36. We liked the **Portuguese seafood stew with** cod, mussels, clams, scallops, and shrimp with chorizo sausage, simmered in white wine, tomatoes, red pepper, stock, garlic, herbs, and butter ($28).

Unum's (603-821-6500; unums.com), 47 E. Pearl St., Nashua. Open Tue.– Sat. 5–closing. Colorful and eclectic with an open kitchen design, the restaurant features entrées ranging $14–32 as well as gorgeous build-your-own pastas and flatbreads, the latter served at the bar or at white-linen-draped tables.

Thousand Crane (603-634-0000), 1000 Elm St., Manchester. Open Mon.–Thu. 11–10, Fri. and Sat. until 11, Sun. noon–9:30. An extensive menu ranging from Japanese sushi to popular Chinese dishes. Moderate.

Tiya's Restaurant (603-669-4365), 8 Hanover St., Manchester. Open for lunch Mon.–Fri. 11–3, for dinner on Fri. and Sat. 5–10. An attractive Thai eatery right downtown at the corner of Elm and Hanover. You can get a tuna salad or Reuben, but stir-fried dishes like shrimp, scallops, sea legs, broccoli, pepper, and mushrooms are the same price. The house specialty is pad Thai: stir-fried egg, chicken, bean sprouts, and spicy sauces garnished with crushed peanuts. Moderate.

Villa Banca (603-598-0500; villabanca .com), 194 Main St., Nashua. Open Mon.–Thu. 11:30–9, Fri. to 9:30, Sat. 4–10, Sun. 4–8. Classic and contemporary Italian dishes served in a former bank building. The lunch menu includes soups, salads, pastas, panini, and reasonably priced entrées; dinner the same. The pesto chicken and lobster sautéed with sun-dried tomatoes and spinach in a pesto Alfredo sauce and served over fettuccine is $19. Seasonal dining outside. A piano player or strolling violinist adds to the weekend ambience.

XO's (603-296-0292), 827 Elm St., Manchester. Open Tue.–Thu. 4–11, Fri. and Sat. until 1 AM. Tapas bar and variety of European entrées. Moderate.

EATING OUT **The Athens** (603-623-9317), 31 Central St., Manchester. Open daily for lunch and dinner. Standard Greek dishes, generous portions, moderately priced.

Black Brimmer Bar & Grill (603-669-5523; blackbrimmer.com), 1087 Elm St., Manchester. Open daily except Sun. and Mon., weekdays from 11:30 AM, Sat. from 5 PM, most nights until 1 AM. Wood paneling, high ceilings, and crystal chandeliers give this an old-fashioned tavern atmosphere. Good food and drinks with frequent live music. Moderate.

Chez Vachon (603-625-9660), 136 Kelly St., West Manchester (minutes from I-293). Open daily 6 AM–2 PM. A small Franco-American eatery with a big following for its salmon pie, pork pie, French crêpes, and the like.

Down 'n Dirty Bar BQ (603-624-2224), 168 Amory St., Manchester. Open Thu.–Sat. 11:30–9, Sun. 1–6. Real southern pit barbecue, eat in or take out. Pulled pork, ribs, chicken, beef, catfish, and shrimp, all cooked lovingly over hickory wood. Hush puppies and pecan-topped sweet potato pie, with a little blues music for background, will have you whistling "Dixie."

The Element Lounge (603-627-1855), 1055 Elm St., Manchester. Open daily except Tue. with live jazz on Thu. from 8 PM. Outside, this popular lounge features sidewalk drinks and light dining in season. Inside, there are two rooms, one with private circular booths, the other with wall-to-wall velour couches and high-definition projection TV. The only nonsmoking bar in town.

Lala's Hungarian Pastry Shop (603-647-7100), 836 Elm St., Manchester. Open daily except Sun. 7–5, Wed.–Sat. until 8. Home-style restaurant with authentic Hungarian food and pastries.

Martha's Exchange and Brew Pub (603-883-8781), 185 Main St., Nashua. Open daily for lunch and dinner from 11 AM, weekend brunch 8:30–3. Large selection of beer and ale plus expected accompaniments. Well priced and popular.

The Peddler's Daughter, 48 Main St., Nashua. Irish restaurant and pub with indoor and outdoor seating overlooking the Nashua River. Serves traditional Irish fare and a selection of draft beers, along with various homemade items. Live music venue featuring traditional Irish music and Celtic rock.

Pine Street Eatery (603-886-3501), 136 Pine St. (between Lake and Kinsley), Nashua. Open Mon.–Tue. 6 AM–7:30 PM, Wed.–Sat. 8 AM–9 PM, Sun. 6 AM–3 PM. Homey atmosphere with diner-style food and breakfast served until 3 PM. Seniors over 60 get a 15 percent discount.

Puritan BackRoom (603-669-6890; puritanbackroom.com), 245 Hooksett Rd., Manchester. This longtime Manchester meeting place offers a good, moderately priced menu served in a comfortable setting. Ice cream takeout in season.

Red Arrow Diner (603-626-1118), 61 Lowell St., Manchester. Open 24/7 just a block off the main drag of Elm St. A city landmark since 1922, this small, friendly diner was voted one of the top 10 diners in the country by *USA Today*. It's the kind of place with a brass hanger for your coat and a mug of coffee that's brought the moment you sit down. Specialties like meat loaf, chicken potpie, and hot sandwiches.

Shorty's Mexican Roadhouse (603-472-3656; shortysmex.com), 230 Rt. 101 West, Bedford; Manchester (603-625-1730), 1050 Bicentennial Dr.; and Nashua (603-882-4070), Nashua Mall, Rt. 3 to Exit 6. Open daily. This is a local favorite: a 1940s roadhouse atmosphere with southwestern and Mexican reliables like tacos, fajitas, and enchiladas; also dinner specials like chicken mole and grilled fish with salsa. Same menu, including 20 vegetarian dishes, all day.

Strange Brew Tavern (603-666-4292; strangebrewtavern.net), 88 Market St., Manchester. Open daily 4 PM–1 AM. The food's good but people go for the beer—the largest draft selection in town—and live nightly jazz and blues performances. Dancing.

Venetian Canal Espresso Caffé (603-627-9200), 805 Canal St., Manchester. Open Tue.–Thu. 7–4, Mon. and Fri. until 3; Sat. 8–1. Soups, salads, sandwiches, pastry, and enough yummy coffee, tea, and chai drinks to float a gondola.

Ya Mamma's (603-578-9201), 75 Daniel Webster Hwy., Merrimack. Open weekdays 11:30–9, Sat. 4–10, Sun. 1–8. Extensive, moderately priced Italian menu and casual atmosphere have made this restaurant a longtime local favorite.

✳ Entertainment

Adams Memorial Opera House (603-437-0505; derryarts.org), 29 W. Broadway, Derry. Built in 1904 and renovated in 2000, this theater, now on the National Historic Register, continues its tradition of hosting concerts, plays, and other arts and civic performances.

The Dana Center, St. Anselm College (603-641-7710; anselm.edu), 100 St. Anselm Dr., Manchester. A state-of-the-art regional performing arts center presenting a full program of nationally acclaimed theater, dance, and music.

Majestic Theatre (603-669-7469; majestictheatre.net), 281 Cartier St., Manchester. A full-time community theater that produces more than a dozen plays, musicals, and dinner theaters each year.

✧ ⟳ **The Palace Theatre** (603-668-5588; palacetheatre.org), 80 Hanover St., Manchester 03101. Opened in 1915, reopened and restored in 1974, this 883-seat theater is a beauty—with small, glittering chandeliers, bright local art, and an intimate feel. In addition to a calendar of nationally known artists, the theater has its own resident company, which mounts several productions a year. During the summer there is children's programming and a July summer camp. Phone for the current program.

Stage One Productions (603-669-5511; stageoneproductions.net), 124 Bridge St., Manchester. Buffet dinner theater at the **Chateau Restaurant** (603-627-2677), 201 Hanover St., Manchester, Nov.–Apr.

Tupelo Music Hall (603-437-5100; tupelohalllondonderry.com), 2 Young Rd. (0.1 mile west of the intersection of Rt. 102 and Mammoth Rd./Rt. 128), Londonderry. Bo Diddley, Christine Lavin, and Ronnie Earl are among the nationally recognized musicians who have performed in this intimate venue named for Elvis's Mississippi birthplace. Check online or call for upcoming schedule. Light snacks, nonalcoholic drinks, and desserts available for purchase. BYOB wine and beer only. Nonsmoking.

⟳ **Verizon Wireless Arena** (603-644-5000), 832 Elm St., Manchester. The state's major (10,000-seat) venue for big-time concerts, wrestling, dirt shows, figure skating, hockey, basketball, arena football, and political forums. Tickets to most events are available through Ticketmaster at 603-868-7300 or ticketmaster.com.

✳ Selective Shopping

ART GALLERIES Art 3 Gallery
(603-668-9983; art3gallery.com), 44 W.
Brook St. (off Canal), Manchester.
Open Mon.–Fri. 9–3 and by appointment. Contemporary and traditional
work by a range of artists.

East Colony Fine Art Gallery (603-
621-7400; eastcolony.com), Langer
Place, 55 S. Commercial St., Manchester.

E. W. Poore Gallery (603-622-3802),
531 Front St., Manchester. This well-
established, well-stocked art supply
store includes a gallery featuring local
artists' work.

**SPECIAL SHOPS Absolutely New
Hampshire** (603-880-3039), 113 Main
St., Nashua. New Hampshire–themed
marketplace featuring items made in
and about the Granite State. Offers
personalized service, shipping, and
extended holiday hours.

With Heart & Hand Unique Gifts
(603-625-8100; withheartandhand
.com), 823 Elm St., Manchester. Open
daily except Sun. Country and primitive Americana linens, lighting, furniture, and tableware.

MALLS Reluctantly we include directions to malls along Salem's and Manchester's "strip," because that's what
many out-of-staters are here for; New
Hampshire's lack of sales tax has its
appeal.

Just across the Massachusetts border
on Rt. 28 (Exit 1 off I-93) in Salem,
Rockingham Park Mall, with the
usual suspects including JCPenney,
Filene's, and Macy's, holds sway over a
host of smaller strip mall entries. In
Manchester the **Mall of New Hamp-**

shire, 1500 S. Willow St., claims the
distinction of being the state's largest.
Willow Tree Mall, 575 Willow St.,
and **TJ Maxx Plaza**, 933 S. Willow St.,
are also large.

✳ Special Events

May: **Hillsborough County Annual
Sheep and Wool Festival**, New
Boston.

June–mid-October: **Manchester
Farmer's Market**, on Concord St.
between Chestnut and Pine, next to
Victory Park.

June: **Talarico Downtown Jazz &
Blues Festival** (603-668-5588): music,
crafts, food. **Strawberry Shortcake
Festival** (603-647-7309), Valley Cemetery, Manchester. Free shortcake and
guided tours with characters dressed in
1800s-era costumes.

July: **Family Outdoor Discovery
Day**, Bear Brook State Park Campground.

August: **Annual Antique Dealers
Show**, Manchester. **Latino Festival**
(603-644-7023), Manchester. Parade,
live music, dancing, ethnic foods, and
crafts.

September: **A Taste of Downtown**
(603-645-6285) offers food from the
city's best restaurants all for one ticket.
Glendi (603-622-9113) is the largest
Greek festival north of Boston, featuring Greek bands, dancing, and delicacies. **Hillsborough County
Agricultural Fair** (603-674-2510),
New Boston. **Deerfield Fair** (603-
463-7421), Deerfield.

October: **Annual Weare Craft
Bazaar**, Weare. **Head of the Merri-
mack Regatta** (603-888-2875),
Nashua.

THE CONCORD AREA

The golden dome of the state capitol building still towers above downtown Concord. Since 1819, when it was built out of local granite by convict labor, this building has been the forum for the state's legislature—now numbering 400 members—said to be the third largest deliberative body in the English-speaking world.

The Native Americans called this site Penacook, or "crooked place," for the snakelike turns the Merrimack makes here. Concord's compact downtown clusters along the western bank of the river, and it's encircled by the concrete wall of I-93 along the opposite bank.

Concord owes its prominence to two forgotten phenomena: the Middlesex Canal—opened in 1815 to connect it with Boston—and the steam railroad from Boston, completed in 1842. Today Concord remains an important transportation hub—the point at which I-89 forks off from I-93 to head northwest across New Hampshire and Vermont, ultimately linking Boston with Montreal.

Concord is really just a medium-sized town of a bit over 40,000 residents, and you are quickly out of it and into the countryside of East Concord at the Society for the Protection of New Hampshire Forests headquarters, or into the western countryside at Silk Farm, New Hampshire's Audubon Society.

While still very much in the Merrimack Valley, Concord, in contrast with Manchester, is just beyond southern New Hampshire's old industrial belt with its ethnic mix. Some of Concord's surrounding towns are as Yankee, and as picturesque, as any in New England.

Canterbury Shaker Village, a striking old hilltop community, is a gathering of white wooden buildings surrounded by spreading fields. Hopkinton, a proud, early-19th-century town, boasts one of New England's most classic Main Streets, and Henniker is a mill-town-turned-college-town with more to offer visitors than many resorts.

GUIDANCE **The Greater Concord Chamber of Commerce** (603-224-2508), 40 Commercial St. (just off I-93 Exit 15W), Concord 03301. Open year-round, Mon.–Fri. 8–5. Although not in the center of town, this office is well located for many tourists and visitors, and not far off the beaten path for anyone with a car. Plenty of parking by the new Concord Courtyard Marriott & Grappone Conference Center. Staff are exceptionally friendly and helpful. The chamber also maintains an information kiosk downtown on State House Plaza, open weekends June–Columbus Day, depending on the availability of volunteers.

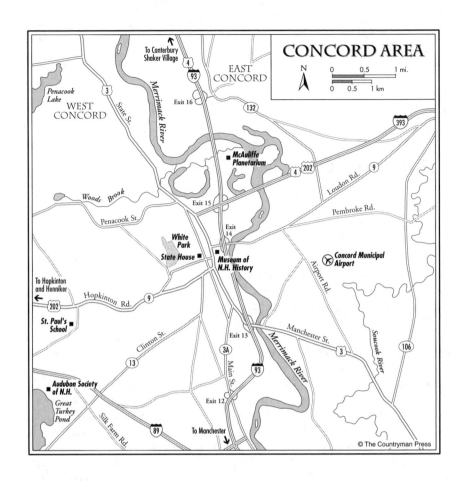

GETTING THERE *By bus:* **The Concord Bus Terminal** (603-228-3300), Stickney Ave., is served by Concord Trailways, Peter Pan Bus Lines, and Vermont Transit. Free parking.

GETTING AROUND *By taxi:* **A&P Taxi** (603-224-6573), **Central Taxi** (603-224-4077), **Concord Cab Company** (603-225-4222), **Main Street Taxi** (603-226-8888). **Celebrity Express Limousine** (603-776-5775), and **Grace Limousine** (603-226-0002) offer limousine service among pickup points in Concord, Manchester, downtown Boston, and Logan International Airport.

MEDICAL EMERGENCY Concord Hospital (603-225-2711), 250 Pleasant St., Concord.

✳ Villages

Henniker. West of Concord at the junction of Rts. 9/202 and 114 (take Exit 5 off I-89), "the only Henniker on earth" is a delightful college town with an outstanding small ski area, a cross-country ski center, and a number of interesting shops and restaurants. Well into the 20th century Henniker was a bustling crossroads town with a thriving inn, a number of farms, and three mills on the Contoocook River—one mill making bicycle rims; another, handles; and the third, leatherboard for shoes. Several mills, however, were destroyed by a 1936 flood, and in the 1940s **New England College** was established. With a combined student and faculty population of 1,000, the college now forms the heart of the town. The former Henniker Inn is the administration office, the art gallery next door showcases New England art, and shops and restaurants line a green strip along the Contoocook River across the street. Just across the bridge, the Simon Student Center provides a handsome venue for frequent lectures by nationally known visiting scholars and political insiders.

Hopkinton. Just west of Concord off I-89, Hopkinton village boasts a Main Street lined with picturesque churches, early white-clapboard mansions, a traditional town hall that once served as the state capitol, and the Hopkinton Historical Society, an excellent local museum and gallery with changing exhibitions. Beyond the village center are lovely back-road drives. Be sure to stop at Beech Hill Farm, still owned by the Kimball family nine generations after the king's grant, for Donna's home-baked coffee cake and make-your-own sundaes. Another old family property, Gould Hill Orchards, is located high enough to see Mount Washington on a clear day. It offers "pick-your-own" and a barn filled with seasonal gifts, homemade goodies, fruit, and ice cream. Three miles west on Rt. 103, Contoocook village (one of three villages that form the town of Hopkinton) is host to the large annual Hopkinton Fair. The Hopkinton Town Library, just off Fountain Square on Pine Street, is a handsome shingle-style building set on a former 68-acre farm. Its screened reading porches overlook soccer and baseball fields, and the Local History Room features a dozen outstanding murals with area scenes painted by talented local artists.

✳ To See

MUSEUMS ✐ **McAuliffe-Shepard Discovery Center** (603-271-STAR [7827]; starhop.com), 2 Institute Dr., Concord. Take I-93 Exit 15E, drive east on I-393 to Exit 1, and follow signs. Exhibit area and Science Store are open 7 days a week 10–5. The Count-down Cafe is open Sat.–Thu. 9:30–4:30 and Fri 9:30–8. Honoring New Hampshire's very own space pioneers, Christa McAuliffe (the first teacher in space, who died in the *Challenger* tragedy of 1986) and Alan Shepard (the second person and first American in space), the Discovery Center is a place to explore, discover, and be inspired. Using state-of-the-art technology, the Discovery Center offers a world-renowned planetarium, simulation experiences, observatory, NASA Educator Resource Center, truly awesome

MCAULIFFE-SHEPARD DISCOVERY CENTER
Chris Tree

CANTERBURY SHAKER VILLAGE

🐌 (603-783-9511; shakers.org), 288 Shaker Rd., Canterbury 03224. Open May 15–Oct. 31,, daily 10–5 and Fri.–Sun. in Nov. 10–4. $17 adults, $8 ages 6–17; under 6 free. Family and group discounts.

Designated a National Historic Landmark and arguably the single most rewarding sight to see in central New Hampshire, this complex of 24 buildings set in 694 acres conjures up a unique, almost vanished way of life that produced many inventions and distinctive art, food, and music. Between the 1780s and 1990 some 2,300 Shaker men, women, and children lived in this rural community, putting their "hands to work and hearts to God." In the 1850s, when this Shaker village owned 4,000 acres with 100 buildings, it was one of 18 such American communes extending from Kentucky to Maine to Ohio. Today just six communities survive to tell their story, and Canterbury is one of only two settlements that have never been out of Shaker hands. In 1969 Eldress Bertha Lindsay (who died in 1990) had the foresight to incorporate the present buildings and property as a nonprofit museum.

The last village to assume the "Lead Ministry," Canterbury absorbed a number of brethren from other communities as they closed and so conveys a vivid sense of Shaker life from the 1880s to about the turn of the 20th century. Visitors are guided through a dozen buildings and encouraged to try the Shaker-inspired food served at the village restaurant (see *Dining Out*). You can also follow the nature trail around Turning Mill Pond, one of the eight that once powered a variety of mills on a 4,000-acre spread. The vintage-1792 Meeting House now doubles as exhibit and performance space. The Laundry is immense and fascinating; the brightly lit sewing room is furnished with exquisitely crafted tables and hung with the "Dorothy Cloaks" invented here, popularized by Mrs. Grover Cleveland, who wore one to her husband's inauguration in 1885. The infirmary is equally fascinating, restored to trace the evolution of medical care here. Herbs in the built-in drawers are

permanent and traveling exhibits, conference areas, a science store, and a café. There are several shows daily, but reservations are strongly recommended. Call for pricing and reservations.

🐌 **Museum of New Hampshire History** (603-228-6688; nhhistory.org), 6 Eagle Square, off Main St., Concord. Follow directions to parking from I-93 Exit 14. Open Tue.–Sat. 9:30–5, Sun. noon–5. Also open Mon. 9:30–5 in Dec. and July–Oct. 15. $5.50 adults ($4.50 if over age 55), $3 ages 6–18, under 6 free; $17 family maximum; free on Thu. evenings. Opened in 1995 by the New Hampshire Historical Society. Exhibits fill two floors of a 19th-century stone warehouse with one floor devoted to the densely packed permanent exhibit, New Hampshire Through Many Eyes. Chronological displays draw you through the state's history, left from the last time they were used, and the tools on the dentist chair are just as Elder Henry Blinn left them. (Also known as a cartographer and geologist, Blinn began practicing dentistry here in 1860.) In the School House it's easy to assume that the pupils are just out for recess and will be rushing back in, up the graceful staircase and into the bright, wood-paneled room that is filled with books, hung with maps. The blackboard bears a reminder written there by Sister Bertha: NO ONE WILL FIND A SPIRIT-REAL HEAVEN, UNTIL THEY FIRST CREATE EARTHLY HEAVEN.

Note the many special happenings listed at the end of this chapter under Special Events.

Southbound on I-93, the village is marked from Exit 18. Northbound, use Exit 15E and follow I-393 east for 5 miles; then take Rt. 106 north for 7 miles and turn at the sign for Shaker Rd.

THE MEETING HOUSE AND DWELLING HOUSE AT CANTERBURY SHAKER VILLAGE

from the Native Americans (in addition to an ancient dugout canoe and Indian artifacts, there is a wigwam in which youngsters can sit and hear an old Abenaki tale) to 20th-century industry. The exhibit captions tell some fascinating stories, like that of an exquisite porcupine quill belt (woven in 1763 by a young girl who had been captured by Native Americans) and of a piece of linen made by Henniker's "Oceanborn Mary" (who was such a captivating baby that she charmed pirates out of capturing a ship). The collection includes the predictable Portsmouth-made highboy, Revolutionary War muskets, and, of course, a Concord Coach (3,000 were made in this town), but what's most interesting about the exhibit is its chronicle of past New Hampshire residents. You can hear Eldress Bertha Lindsay of Canterbury Shaker Village (thanks to the sound tape from

Walpole resident Ken Burns's Shaker documentary) and ponder the fact that Christian Science founder Mary Baker Eddy (born in Bow, New Hampshire), poet Robert Frost, President Franklin Pierce, and *Peyton Place* author Grace Metalious are all in the same corner. The top floor, accessed through a staircase that suggests the look and view (through murals) of a White Mountains fire tower, is devoted to changing exhibits. There's no need to pay admission to access the extensive gift shop, featuring New Hampshire books and other interesting gift items related to the history of the state and beyond. The historical society's headquarters, in its original neoclassical building enhanced by Daniel Chester French's frontispiece, is nearby at 30 Park St., and contains changing exhibits and the excellent Tuck Library.

The Hopkinton Historical Society (603-746-3825), Main St., Hopkinton 03229. Open year-round, Thu. and Fri. 9–4, Sat. 9–1. On a street full of white-clapboard Colonials, this redbrick Palladian-windowed building is notable for its 1890s architecture, as well as for its genealogical materials, research library, local memorabilia, and paintings. There is an appealing shop and changing exhibits, including a popular autumn art show of exceptional regional talent. Ask for a brochure that includes a driving tour of local attractions.

HISTORIC HOMES AND SITES A leaflet describing a self-guided walking tour of Concord, *Concord on Foot*, is available from the chamber of commerce's Capital Region Visitor Center (see *Guidance*). It includes some of the following:

Benjamin Kimball House and Capitol Center for the Arts (603-225-1111), 44 S. Main St., Concord. This Romanesque Revival house was built around 1885 by Benjamin Kimball, but later became the state headquarters of the Masonic Order. Now the house and adjoining 1920s-era theater are the core of the Capitol Center for the Arts, a regional cultural art center that hosts internationally known theater troupes, dance companies, and musical acts.

The Eagle Hotel, N. Main St., Concord. For more than 135 years the Eagle Hotel was the center of Concord's social and political happenings. Andrew Jackson, Benjamin Harrison, Jefferson Davis, Charles Lindbergh, and Eleanor Roosevelt were all guests. The hotel, now handsomely renovated as the Eagle Square Marketplace, houses mostly offices with a few shops and a restaurant.

First Church of Christ, Scientist, N. State and School Sts., Concord. Mary Baker Eddy, born in nearby Bow in 1821, formulated the spiritual framework of the Christian Science faith. She contributed $100,000 toward the construction of this Concord granite building, whose steeple makes it the tallest in the city.

Kimball-Jenkins Estate (603-225-3932), 276 N. Main St., Concord. Built in 1882, this high-Victorian brick-and-granite mansion has hand-carved oak woodwork, frescoed ceilings, Oriental rugs, and many original furnishings. Inspired by a directive in the late Carolyn Jenkins's will, the estate now houses two galleries and a thriving community art school.

Mary Baker Eddy Historic House (603-225-3444; longyear.org), 62 N. State St., Concord. Open May 1–Oct. 31, Mon. and Sat. 11–2 (and by appointment all year). Mary Baker Eddy was born on a small farm in Bow (just outside Concord) and later moved to Rumney, New Hampshire, where she battled family disappointment and bad health, then went on to inspire millions by founding the Christian Science religion in 1866. At the age of 68, Eddy moved from Boston to this mid-19th-century Greek Revival house, where she revised her original treatise and wrote her biography. The house has been recently restored. Inside is a large scale model of Pleasant View, the house and grounds (no longer standing) she later built on the western edge of town. In all, Eddy spent 18 years in Concord. Admission is free.

New Hampshire State House and the State House Plaza (603-271-2154), 107 N. Main St., Concord. Open year-round, weekdays for guided and self-guided tours 8–4:30. A handsome 1819 building, this is the oldest state capitol in which a legislature still meets in its original chambers. A visitors center contains dioramas and changing exhibits. More than 150 portraits of past political figures are displayed, and the plaza boasts statues of several New Hampshire notables. The gift shop, located just off the lobby, offers posters, scarves, ties, books, and other items related to the state's natural resources and political history. The House is typically in session on Wed., Jan.–June. Visitors interested in viewing democracy in action are welcome to take a seat in the balcony of Representatives Hall.

The Pierce Manse (603-224-5954; 603-225-2068), 14 Penacook St. (at end of N. Main St.), Concord. Open mid-June–mid-October, Mon.–Fri. 11–3, or by appointment. Closed holidays. $7 adults, $6 seniors, $3 children. $15 family. Built in 1838 and moved to its present site in 1971, this Greek Revival structure was home for Franklin and Jane Pierce from 1842 to 1848, between the time Franklin served in the US Senate and was elected 14th president of the United States. Exhibits include many items owned by the Pierce family prior to 1869.

St. Paul's School (603-225-3341), 325 Pleasant St., Concord. Founded in 1855 by Dr. George Shattuck, St. Paul's is one of the country's premier preparatory schools, a four-year boarding school with more than 500 students and 100 faculty members. Although the 2,000-acre campus is private, many of the lectures and theater and dance performances are open to the public. Exhibitions in the Tudor-style Hargate Art Center are scheduled throughout the school year, and feature a variety of works by well-known and up-and-coming professional and student artists, as well as occasional highlights from the school's collection of works. Past exhibitions have featured works by artists such as Robert Motherwell, Jacob Lawrence, Andrew Wyeth, Milton Avery, Arthur Dove, Eugene Atget, Thomas Buechner, Joyce Tenneson, and others. The school's Ohrstrom Library is also of particular interest. Designed by postmodern architect Robert Stern and opened in 1991, the building references a variety of features from other buildings on campus and offers an outstanding view of Turkey Pond from the reading room.

Upham-Walker House (603-271-2017), 18 Park St., Concord. One of the best examples of late Federal architecture in the area, this building is open to the public by appointment and offers a glimpse into the lifestyle of successive generations of a prominent Concord family.

Covered Bridges Henniker–New England College bridge. A single-span, 150-foot bridge across the Contoocook River on the New England College campus.

Hopkinton–Rowell bridge, West Hopkinton. Built in 1853 across the Contoocook River; rebuilt in 1997.

Hopkinton bridge, Contoocook village. No longer operating, the bridge spans the Contoocook River at Fountain Square and is said to be the oldest railroad covered bridge in the United States. The nearby depot has been recently restored.

FOR FAMILIES ✑ **New Hampshire Fish & Game Department Discovery Room** (603-271-3211), 2 Hazen Dr., Concord. Open year-round, Mon.–Fri. 8:30–4. Visit the Wild New Hampshire nature center and discover the state's wide variety of landscapes, among them a beaver pond, meadow, vernal pool, and boreal (spruce/fir) forest. Kids will enjoy the chance to get up close and personal with the life-sized replica of a moose cow and calf.

✳ To Do

BALLOONING What's Up Ballooning (603 428-3128), 39 Flanders Rd., Henniker. Traditional champagne balloon flights year-round.

CANOEING See *Boating* in "The Manchester/Nashua Area" for the Merrimack River Watershed Council.

In addition to the Merrimack, stretches of the Contoocook River between Henniker, Hopkinton, and Concord provide popular canoeing and kayaking. Originating in Rindge, the Contoocook flows approximately 66 miles northeast to join the Merrimack River in Penacook. The Nubanusit, Warner, and Blackwater Rivers are the main tributaries. Quickwater can be found in early spring when the river is high, but by late April the river becomes flat for the summer months. Take a swim; stop for a picnic; fish for bass, pickerel, and trout; or simply enjoy the scenery and occasional wildlife.

Contoocook River Canoe Company (603-753-9804; contoocookcanoe.com), 9 Horse Hill Rd., Concord. Canoe and kayak rentals, instructions, guided tours, and shuttle service.

CAR RACING New Hampshire International Speedway (603-783-4931; nhis.com, Rt. 106, Loudon. New England's largest sports facility and home of the region's professional motor sports, this 101,000-seat complex annually attracts an estimated 400,000-plus motor-sport enthusiasts. "The Magic Mile" offers a wide range of activities, including professional and amateur motor sports, bicycle racing, driving and racing schools, special performance-related activities, and even soap-box derby trials. Races include the world-class NASCAR Winston Cup series, the NASCAR Busch series, and many more. Call for current schedule.

NEW HAMPSHIRE INTERNATIONAL SPEEDWAY

Courtesy NHIS

FISHING The New Hampshire Fish and Game Department (603-271-3211), 2 Hazen Dr., Concord. A source of information about where to fish as well as how to obtain licenses. Trout fishing is particularly good in this area.

GOLF Beaver Meadow Golf Course (603-228-8954), Concord, 18 holes on the oldest course (1896) in the state. **Duston Country Club** (603-746-4234), Hopkinton, nine holes. **Loudon Country Club** (603-783-3372),

Loudon, 18 holes. **Plausawa Valley Country Club** (603-224-6267), Pembroke, 18 holes. **Canterbury Woods Country Club** (603-783-9400; canterburywood-scc.com), 15 West Rd., Canterbury, is an 18-hole championship course.

DOWNHILL SKIING ✄ **Pats Peak** (603-428-3245; 888-PATS-PEAK; patspeak .com), Rt. 114, Henniker. The mountain rises steeply right behind the base lodge. It's an isolated, 1,400-foot-high mountain, its face streaked with expert trails and a choice of intermediate and beginner runs meandering down one shoulder, half a dozen beginner runs—served by their own lifts—down the other. Big old fir trees are salted around the summit, and some of the intermediate trails—certainly Zephyr, the 0.25-mile-long beginner's trail off the top—convey the sense of skimming through the woods. When it comes to expert runs, Tornado and Hurricane are wide and straight, but Twister is an old-timer—narrow, twisty, and wooded. The Turbulence Terrain Park offers a changing menu of jumps, rails, and hips for snowboarders and freestyle skiers. This is a family-geared ski and snowboard area that provides a great place to learn, along with some of the most accessible yet challenging skiing in southern New England. The Patenaude family, which has owned and operated the area since 1963, has spent millions of dollars on expanding and updating lifts, snowmaking equipment, and après-ski facilities.

Lifts: 10, including 3 double chairs and 2 triple chairs to the summit.

Trails: 22.

Snowmaking: 100 percent.

Night skiing: 22 trails, 10 lifts.

Facilities: Ski and snowboard school, rentals, ski shop, lounge, cafeteria, child care.

Rates: Check out patspeak.com for the latest rate information. Midweek packages include WOW (Women's Only Wednesday, a seven-week program that includes breakfast and lunch plus weekly clinics and lessons) and Adult Clinics (seven half-days of professional lesson clinics including lunch with your instructor). On Saturday night Pay One Price (POP) includes skiing, snowboarding, tubing, rentals, lesson tips, and entertainment for one low price 3–10 PM.

✳ Green Space

Elm Brook Park and Wildlife Management Area, off Rt. 127, West Hopkinton. Swimming and picnic areas; built and managed by the US Army Corps of Engineers.

Hannah Duston Memorial, west of I-93 Exit 17 (4 miles north of Concord), Boscawen. The monument is on an island at the confluence of the Contoocook and Merrimack Rivers. It commemorates the courage of Hannah Duston, a woman taken prisoner from Haverhill, Massachusetts, during a 1696 Indian raid. She later made her escape, killing and scalping 10 of her captors (including women and children) at this spot on the river. The 35-foot-high monument, erected in 1874, depicts a busty lady with a tomahawk in one hand and what look like scalps in the other. Open all year, but the trail from the parking lot is not plowed in winter.

Silk Farm Wildlife Sanctuary (603-224-9909; nhaudubon.org), 3 Silk Farm Rd. (follow Audubon signs from I-89 Exit 2), Concord. Open year-round, Mon.–Fri. 9–5, Sat. from 10, and from noon on Sun. The McLane Center, named for longtime New Hampshire legislator and environmental activist Susan McLane, is the headquarters of the Audubon Society of New Hampshire, offering an overview of Audubon centers and programs in the state. The environmentally friendly "green" building with wood pellet heating, composting toilets, and optimum solar siting has a Discovery Room with a "touch table," a research wildlife library, an aerie for spotting birds, a newly expanded hummingbird and butterfly garden, a raptor enclosure, and a gift shop with bird feeders, optics, birdseed, books, clothing, jewelry, and much more. Trails thread forests and wetlands around Great Turkey Pond and traverse orchards and fields with a variety of flora and fauna.

Society for the Protection of New Hampshire Forests Conservation Center (603-224-9945), Portsmouth St., Concord. Bring a picnic and hike along the Merrimack River on 90 acres of nature trails, or enjoy exhibits in the recently expanded and award-winning passive-solar "green" building.

✍ **White's Park**, Liberty and School Sts., Concord. In summer feed the ducks or swing on the playground; in winter sled or ice skate, just as Concord residents have done for generations. This well-kept park is located in a residential area a few blocks west of downtown.

✳ Lodging

INNS & ❝❞ **Centennial Inn** (603-227-9000; 800-360-4839; thecentennial hotel.com), 96 Pleasant St., Concord 03301. Built in 1896 as a home for the aged, this impressively turreted brick building now boasts the city's most luxurious accommodations. Recent renovations have introduced a modern, urban-contemporary flair to the beautiful Queen Anne landmark. Each of the 32 spacious, earth-toned guest rooms is uniquely fitted into the building's architectural elements; some even have their own private porch. All have every modern convenience, including WiFi, LCD TVs with VCR, independent climate control, and spa-like baths. Your choice of queen, king, or two queen beds. There are exercise and meeting facilities on the premises, as well as a popular restaurant. $139–249. Packages available.

Colby Hill Inn (603-428-3281; 800-531-0330; colbyhillinn.com), just west of the village center off Western Ave., The Oaks, P.O. Box 779, Henniker 03242. Cindi and Mason Cobb's rambling 1795 farmhouse offers yesteryear charm and comfort on 6 acres just 0.5 mile from downtown Henniker. Despite the popular public dining room (see *Dining Out*), there's privacy for inn guests: a comfortable living room with hearth off by itself, and a game room. There are 10 rooms in the inn itself, 4 more in the neighboring Carriage House, 6 with working fireplace, all with phone, air-conditioning, and private bath (2 have two-person Jacuzzi). Rooms are wallpapered in flowers and furnished with antiques, with beds ranging from twins to king sized. Facilities include a pool that's sequestered behind the barn, as well as croquet and badminton; tennis is across the street. A full breakfast is served in the glass-walled dining room, overlooking birds feeding in the barnyard. It's included in the rates: $139–265.

BED & BREAKFASTS
❝❞ **Henniker House Bed and Breakfast** (603-428-3198; 866-428-3198; hennikerhouse.com), 2 Ramsdell Rd., P.O. Box 191, Henniker 03242. Built in 1859 on the banks of the Contoocook River,

this Victorian house is comfortable and convenient, just steps away from the campus of New England College and surrounding restaurants and stores. Five bedrooms, each with private bath, cable television, WiFi access, and window air conditioners, are decorated in vintage style, three with king-sized beds. The $95–145 double rate includes a full breakfast served in the dining room solarium overlooking the river. Packages are available featuring regional crafts and other attractions.

🐾 ✄ **Lovejoy Farm** (603-545-2016; lovejoy-inn.com), 268 Lovejoy Rd., Loudon 03301. Sequestered up a back road (10 minutes' drive from I-93 and 5 miles from the Canterbury Shaker Village, 6 from the New Hampshire International Speedway), this classic Federal mansion looks truly grand with its attached carriage barn set against landscaped grounds and acres of surrounding woods and fields. Both the formal dining room and parlor retain their original, richly colored woodwork and the parlor, its extensive 1810 stenciling. There's also an informal sitting room/library and a large country kitchen in which the only stove is a vintage wood-and-gas Kalamazoo. Our favorite guest room, the Lovejoy Suite, is upstairs, with a working fireplace, four-poster bed, cottage furniture, and wing chairs, but there are two other smaller rooms in the main house and five more open-beamed rooms created from scratch upstairs in the carriage barn. All have private bath. The hosts are world travelers and gourmet cooks, and pride themselves on the quality of the full breakfasts included in the $115–135 double rate (can be higher during NASCAR events, Motorcycle Week, and other special occasions). Call ahead to arrange for pets or children ages 8 and above. No smoking.

🐾 **Meadow Farm Bed and Breakfast** (603-942-8619; bbonline.com/ nh/meadowfarm), 454 Jenness Pond Rd., Northwood 03261. This authentic, beautifully restored 1770 New England colonial is located a few miles off Rt. 4's "Antique Alley," about halfway between Concord and Portsmouth. Surrounded by 55 acres of fields, woods, and extensive gardens (including many historic varieties of roses), the property is a short walk down a country lane to a private waterfront where guests may swim, canoe, and view the loons. In addition to three guest rooms furnished in period antiques (one with fireplace and private bath; the other two share a bath), this home for all seasons offers several charming sitting areas, including a library with television and fireplace, a rustic screened porch furnished in twig furniture, an outdoor stone wall patio, and a large country kitchen with woodstove. Room rates, $80 for single to $105 double occupancy, include a full breakfast served in front of the fireplace in the paneled keeping room. There's also a cottage on the lake, available for rent by the week for $1,100 during the summer, or for a three-night minimum stay during Sept. and Oct. for $175 a night. Arrange ahead to bring pets (including horses) or children over 3.

🐾 **Wyman Farm** (603-783-4467), Wyman Rd., Loudon 03301. Open year-round. Despite its location just a few minutes east of Concord and a five-minute drive from Canterbury Shaker Village, the remote, storybook setting of this hilltop farm makes it feel like one of those places you could search for forever and never find. The 200-year-old "extended" Cape rambles along the very top of a hill, with lawns and fields that seem to roll away indefinitely. With small-paned windows and original woodwork, the living room exudes age and comfort, and each of the three air-conditioned guest rooms has its own bath and sitting room, all furnished with carefully selected antiques. (In some cases innkeeper Judith Merrow has equipped even the bathrooms with vintage furnishings; in addition to a shower stall, one has a wooden, copper-lined tub she picked up years ago at an antiques show.) The farm has been in the family for many generations, and accommodating guests has been a tradition since 1902 when this was "Sunset Lodge" and the going rate for room and board was $5 a week. Today, with room rates ranging $65–95 (including tax), Wyman Farm remains a bargain for the genuine luxury it offers. Merrow provides a tea tray in the afternoon, and breakfast, which includes homemade breads, is cooked to order from the menu guests receive when they check in.

✷ Where to Eat

DINING OUT & **Angelina's Ristorante Italiano** (603-228-3313; angelinasrestaurant.com), 11 Depot St., Concord. Open Mon.–Fri. for lunch 11:30–2, dinner Mon.–Thu. 5–9, Fri. and Sat. until 10. Exposed brick, soft pink walls, black chairs, and white tablecloths make this one of the handsomest restaurants in town. Well-prepared regional Italian cuisine and decadent desserts complete the experience. Moderate.

& **The Barley House** (603-224-6363; thebarleyhouse.com), 128 N. Main St., Concord. Open Mon.–Sat. 11–1 AM. Directly across Main Street from the capitol building, this watering hole for press and politicians offers billiards, darts, frequent live music performances, and a dozen micro beers on tap, plus a full menu of hearty cuisine in both the pub and the more sedate dining room.

& **Chen Yang Li Restaurant** (603-228-8508), 520 South St., Exit 2 just off I-89 in Bow. Open Sun.–Thu. 11:30–10, Fri. and Sat. until 11. Extended hours in the bar. New owners have brought new style to this handy way stop built on an old mill site next to the Hampton Inn. The extensive menu features American classics and Asian specialties, including sushi, in a fine-dining atmosphere.

& **Colby Hill Inn** (603-428-3281), off Western Ave., Henniker. Open daily 5:30–8:30 PM. Candlelight makes the paneling and furniture glow, and the view of fields and gardens adds to the romantically elegant feel of this dining room. The chef's signature dish is chicken breast stuffed with lobster, leeks, and Boursin cheese, served with a supreme sauce. Leave room for dessert. Expensive.

& **The Common Man** (603-228-3463; thecman.com), 25 Water St. (Exit 13 just off I-93), Concord. Open daily for lunch from 11:30, for dinner from 5; Sun. brunch 10–2:30, dinner 2:30–close. What looks like a large green Colonial home that somehow survived the surrounding commercialization of Concord's South Main Street is actually a recently built restaurant. Post-and-beam construction provides two spacious, high-ceilinged dining rooms plus four function areas. Fireplaces and a mix of Yankee artifacts lend a cozy atmosphere. Lobster corn chowder and a deli board to make your own sandwich are among the lunch specialties; dinner entrées, including thick-cut roast prime rib, are the usual moderately priced quality fare expected from this chain of highly successful eateries.

& **Country Spirit** (603-428-7007), junction of Rts. 202/9 and 114, Henniker. Open daily 11–9, Fri. and Sat. until 10; closed Christmas and Thanksgiving. Walls are festooned with memorabilia from "the only Henniker on earth": old tools, signs, and photos. Specialties include the restaurant's own smoked meats, aged Angus sirloin, fresh seafood, and vegetarian dishes.

Crystal Quail Restaurant (603-269-4151; crystalquail.com), 202 Pitman Rd., Center Barnstead. Open Wed.–Sun. 5–9 PM. Reservations only. Dining in this old 18th-century post house is an experience. Service is limited to a dozen patrons per night, who are offered a "verbal menu," the better to provide what's fresh and good at the moment. Three entrées are offered, usually including chefs Harold and Cynthia Huckaby's specialty quail or pheasant. Vegetables are picked from the extensive organic garden, and vegetarian dishes can be prepared with advance notice. Needless to say, everything is made from scratch, and the desserts (Belgian gâteau au chocolat or crème caramel, for example) are exquisite. Be sure to ask for directions—there is no sign outside, and Barnstead is one of those towns webbed with back roads; even the owners admit to not knowing them all. The five-course dinner is $70 prix fixe. BYOB. Reservations required. No credit cards.

Daniel's (603-428-7621; danielsof henniker.com), Main St., Henniker. Open daily at 11:30 AM. Friendly and attractive with a great view of the Contoocook River from the dining room and deck; there's also a brick-walled lounge. Lunch can be a Mediterranean salad (fresh greens, roast turkey, smoked ham, and imported cheeses garnished with marinated vegetables) or simply a Cajun burger. For dinner you might try chicken Contoocook—a breast of chicken baked with an apple, walnut, and sausage stuffing and glazed with maple cider sauce. Moderate.

&. **Granite Restaurant & Bar at the Centennial** (603-225-7102; 800-360-4839; graniterestaurant.com), 96 Pleasant St., Concord. Open for breakfast daily 7–10:30; lunch Mon.–Fri. 10:30–2:30; Sun. brunch 10:30–2:30; dinner Mon.–Thu. 5–9, Fri. and Sat. until 10, Sun. to 8. This former old folks' home has undergone a major makeover with upscale contemporary furnishings, mellow jazz, and an up-to-date menu featuring New American cooking with Caribbean, Pacific Rim, and Latino influences. Most dinner selections are offered in two sizes. Maple-bourbon-glazed Niman Ranch pork tenderloin with sweet potato and plantain puree and micro baby bok choy runs $26 for a full serving, $16 for a smaller plate. The bar with an array of martinis and microbrews is the place to see and be seen locally.

Greenwood's at Canterbury Shaker Village (603-783-4238; shakers.org), 288 Shaker Rd., Canterbury. Open May 15–Oct. 31 for lunch only; other times for special events. Four family-style seatings on the half hour 11:30–2:30. This beautifully designed restaurant offers Shaker-inspired cuisine with fresh ingredients, many grown on the property.

&. **Hermanos Cocina Mexicana** (603-224-5669; hermanosmexican .com), 11 Hills Ave., Concord. Open daily for lunch Mon.–Sat. 11:30–2:30, dinner 5–9, Fri. and Sat. until 10. This Mexican restaurant has gotten high ratings for its authenticity and incredible margaritas since it first opened around the corner in 1984. Some successful years later it moved to new digs and expanded; now several dining rooms on two floors are nearly always full. Live jazz Sun.–Thu. evenings.

Ichiban Japanese Steak House & Sushi Bar (603-223-3301; ichiban concord.com), 118 Manchester St. Open daily for lunch and dinner. A family-owned restaurant in an attractive Asian *cum* art deco space, serving traditional Japanese cuisine. Sushi specials after 8:30 on Fri. and Sat. nights.

&. **Makris Lobster & Steak House** (603-225-7665; eatalobster.com), Rt. 106, Concord. Open daily 11–9, Fri. and Sat. until 10; closed Mon. in fall and winter. The Makris family has been in the food business for 90 years, operating half a dozen restaurants around the city. Dozens of entrées with lobster are perennial favorites. Summer dining on the back porch patio; weekend entertainment in the lounge.

Margarita's (603-224-2821; margs.com), 1 Bicentennial Square, Concord. Open nightly from 4. This former city jail is now a favorite (and very festive) gathering spot for locals and travelers alike. Ask for a table in one of 16 old cells for an intimate dining experience. The menu is typical Mexican fare—there are now Margarita's throughout New England, though they started here—with fajitas and margaritas as good as they get.

&. **Moritomo** (603-224-8363), Fort Eddy Plaza (Exit 14 off I-93), Concord. Open for lunch and dinner Mon.–Sat.; Sun. 2–9:30 PM. Yes, it's in a mall, but inside this Japanese restaurant there are several attractive sitting and dining choices: a Benihana-style grill, cushioned chambers for up to six, or regular tables in the main dining room; also a sushi bar and extensive menu with a variety of tempura, teriyaki, noodles, soups, and salads.

Siam Orchid (603-228-1529), 158 N. Main St., Concord. Open for lunch Mon.–Fri. 11:30–3, dinner Mon.–Fri. 5–10, Sat. to 10:30, Sun. 4–9:30. Concord's first Thai restaurant continues to draw a well-satisfied clientele. Excellent specialties and service in an attractive, well-located setting at the intersection of Main and Bridge (Centre) Sts.

Sunny's Table (603-225-8181; sunnystable.com), 11 Depot St., Concord. Open Tue.–Sat. 11:30–2:30 for lunch; Tue.–Thu. 5–9 for dinner, Fri. and Sat. until 10. Closed Sun. and Mon. A gray-and-pomegranate color scheme with copper-topped tables and bar make this a stylish setting for a local farm-to-table favorite. First courses range from soups and root vegetable with petite lettuce salads to pan-seared scallops with hot and spicy green curry sauces. Entrées are innovative. Miso-braised beef short ribs with roasted local carrots and caramelized ginger mash is $22; soy-braised tofu is $17. Desserts are expensive but delicious.

EATING OUT Bistro Rustica (603-224-2110; ninamjv@yahoo.com), 80 N. Main St., Concord. Open Mon.–Sat. 7 AM–2 PM, Sun. 11–4. Excellent, moderately priced panini, cold sandwiches, salads, desserts, and traditional Mediterranean and Middle Eastern specialties. Sidewalk dining in-season.

&. **Bread and Chocolate** (603-228-3330), 29 S. Main St., Concord. Open Mon.–Wed. 7:30 AM–6 PM, Thu. and Fri. until 8, Sat. 8–4. Concord's own *konditorei*, operated by Franz and Linda Andlinger. This European-style bakery offers the best selection of breads and pastries in town, as well as *gemütlich* atmosphere for lunch or tea. Great sandwiches and superlative pastries, plus browsing privileges and inside access to Gibson's Book Store.

Café Indigo (603-224-1770; cafeindigo.com), 128H Hall St., Concord. Open Mon.–Fri. 9–5; Sun. brunch 10–2 on the second and fourth Sundays of the month. If you're not put off by its industrial park setting and you don't mind driving a couple of minutes out of downtown, your search for a vegan alternative will be rewarded by a menu filled with natural organic goodness and a carrot cake that's universally described as a touch of heaven.

Caffenio's (603-229-0020), 84 N. Main St., Concord. Open every day but Sun. 7:30–5. Live music the first Friday evening of the month. An attractive coffee bar with homemade soups, sandwiches, salads, sweets, and some Greek-inspired lunch dishes. Outside dining in-season.

&. **In a Pinch Café** (603-226-2272), 146 Pleasant St., Concord. Open Mon.–Sat. 7–3. A cheerful, informal café locally known for its gourmet sandwiches, soups, salads, and an assortment of luscious pastries. Take out or picnic inside on a snazzy, wicker-filled sunporch. No table service.

✱ **Intervale Farms Pancake House** (603-428-7196), Rt. 114 and Flanders Rd. (bottom of Pat's Peak access road), Henniker. Open daily 5:30 AM–noon, on weekends until 1:30 PM. Shaped like a giant red sugar shack, this spacious, friendly, family-run restaurant is one of the very best places for breakfast in the state, featuring the farm's own homemade syrup.

The Sandwich Depot (603-228-3393), 49 Hall St., Concord. Open Mon.–Fri. 7–3:30, Sat. 8–12:30. What started as a neighborhood eatery in an abandoned train depot in 1989 now attracts those-in-the-know from Concord and towns around. Nancy Stewart is a fine but unlikely-looking poet who spends her days in ball cap and apron dishing out corned beef hash, burritos, and homemade muffins. She and her husband, Gary, are always good company, even first thing in the morning.

The Shaker Box Lunch & Farm Stand (603-783-9511; shakers,org), 288 Shaker Rd., Canterbury. Open

daily 10–4, May 15–Oct. 31. Sandwiches, salads, soups, baked goods, and other light lunch options in a bucolic setting.

Susty's Café (603-942-8425), 159 1st New Hampshire Tpk. (Rt. 4), Northwood. Open Mon.–Wed. 11–3, Thu.–Sat. until 9, Sun. 8. The name *Susty's* is a fusion of *sustainable sustenance* and the *Simpsons* TV show's Krusty the Clown. Such mile-a-minute witticisms and one-of-a-kind victuals from owner-chef Norma Koski have earned this novel eatery a gold plate from a Boston food critic and a full-page spread in the *New York Times Magazine*. Lavender walls adorned with stars and swirls provide the celestial atmosphere; vegetarians and beyond find the ever-changing menu equally heavenly. Check out the attached gift shop for everything from natural-fiber clothing to juggling clubs.

The Works Café/Bagelworks (603-226-1827), 42 N. Main St., Concord. Open Mon.–Sat. 6–6, the first Fri. of the month until 8 PM. A bagel bar that also offers soups, salads, sandwiches, sweets, and more—all served with a smile.

&. **Washington Street Cafe** (603-228-2000; 603-226-2699), 88 Washington St., Concord. Open Mon.–Fri. 7–5, Sat. until 2 PM. Deli sandwich shop that also offers take-out, catering, and outstanding Middle Eastern fare.

✳ Entertainment

✱ &. **The Capitol Center for the Arts** (603-225-1111; ccanh.com), 44 S. Main St., Concord. Once a candidate for demolition, this onetime vaudeville venue and movie house is now the largest, and arguably best, performing arts center in the state. Since the mid-1990s the 1,307-seat facility has been twice expanded, modernized, and

restored. Its 1927 Egyptian-motif art-work is an outstanding example of the King Tut era of theater decoration. The center hosts a wide mix of nationally known entertainers and events, including Broadway shows; dance, music, and opera performances; pop and country stars; family entertainment; school programs; and business conferences. Governor's Hall provides a full-service function room for up to 350 guests; the adjacent Kimball House is a Victorian mansion featuring a stately dining room and boardroom.

♪ ♿ **Concord City Auditorium** (603-228-2793; concordcityauditorium.org), Prince St. (between city hall and the city library), Concord. Affectionately known as "The Audi," this 850-seat theater has been a mainstay of the capital city's community and entertainment life since 1904. In recent years an impressive group of community angels and volunteers has partnered with the city to enable the renaissance of this gilded, classically lovely venue, now host to more than 75,000 patrons and 100 musical and theatrical events per year. The reception lobby, although a 21st-century addition, features century-old stained-glass windows and period furnishings.

Red River Theatres (603-224-4600; redrivertheatres.org), 11 S. Main St., Concord. A nonprofit theater showing a lineup of independent and foreign films, classics, documentaries, and cult favorites, often accompanied by guest discussion leaders. The three-screen theater is located in the lower two levels of the Capital Commons office building. Two of the areas feature stadium seating; the third is a smaller screening room and multi-function hall. Beer, wine, sandwiches, desserts, and traditional movie snacks are available.

✳ Selective Shopping

ANTIQUES Rt. 4 between the Epsom Circle and the Lee Rotary is widely known as **Antique Alley** (nhantique alley.com). More than two dozen shops in the four towns of Chichester, Epsom, Lee, and Northwood represent more than 500 dealers; the primary customers are antiques store owners and other dealers from throughout the country. This area is just far enough off the beaten tourist path to make for exceptional pickings. Along Rt. 4 in Northwood, **Hart's Desire Antiques** (603-942-5153) has a large group shop with 150 dealers on three floors, and the **Parker-French Antique Center** (603-942-8852) represents 135 dealers. Some shops, such as **The Betty House** in Epsom (603-736-9087), specialize, this one in tools and household gadgets, while **On the Hill Collectables** (603-942-8169) in Northwood has over 200,000 vintage postcards. Other shops represent a full range of antiques, from country furniture to quilts, folk art, china, and jewelry.

Antiques & Findings (603-746-5788) and **The Covered Bridge Frame Shop & Gallery** (603-746-4996) offer sometimes rare and always interesting items within walking distance of each other on Main Street in Contoocook village.

The Brick House (877-563-2421; brickhouseshop.com), intersection of Rts. 107 and 140 in the historic district of Gilmanton. Open daily 10–5. What appear to be museum-quality furnishings and an ever-changing inventory of Americana are actually antique reproductions, all for sale, from the rooms of Doug Towle's imposing home.

Concord Antique Gallery, Inc. (603-225-2070), 97 Storrs St., Concord. Open Mon.–Sat. 10–6, Sun.

11–5. Just below Main Street, this popular shop offers good browsing right downtown. Two floors of merchandise from more than 125 dealers.

Henniker Kennel Company Antiques (603-428-7136), 2 Old Ireland Rd., Henniker. Deals only with antique and collectible canines.

ART GALLERIES The Art Center in Hargate, St. Paul's School (603-229-4644), 325 Pleasant St., Concord. Exhibits vary throughout the school year, from student work to private collections to traveling shows by well-known contemporary artists and photographers. Gallery hours are Tue.–Sat. 10–4.

Kimball-Jenkins Estate (603-225-3932; kimballjenkins.com), 266 N. Main St., Concord. Open Tue. and Fri. 11–5, Wed. until 6. The longtime residence of a prominent Concord family, this estate is now home to an art school and two exhibition galleries: the Jill Coldren Wilson Gallery, which hosts historic artwork in the Victorian mansion, and another space for currently practicing artists in the nearby Carriage House Gallery.

McGowan Fine Art Inc. (603-225-2515; mcgowanfineart.com), 10 Hills Ave., Concord. Open Mon.–Wed. 9–5, Thu. and Fri. 9–7, Sat. 10–2. Perhaps the state's premier outlet for contemporary art, this gallery features changing exhibits by the region's best-known artists.

Mill Brook Gallery & Sculpture Garden (603-226-2046; themillbrookgallery.com), 236 Hopkinton Rd., Rt. 202/9, Concord. Open Apr.–Dec. 23, Tue.–Sat. 11–5; winter hours and other times by appointment. Juried outdoor sculpture exhibit with large and small sculpture, fountains, and birdbaths displayed in seasonal gardens; rotating

gallery exhibitions in a distinctive contemporary gallery on a country estate.

New England College Gallery (603-428-2329), Preston Barn, Main St., Henniker. An interesting, eclectic schedule of shows throughout the year, all of which look first-rate in this high-ceilinged exhibit space. The gallery is open Mon.–Thu. 9:30–6, Fri. and Sun. 11:30–3.

BOOKSTORES The Book Emporium (603-225-0555), 202 S. Main St., Concord. Open Tue.–Fri. 10–6, weekends 11–4:30. A small shop with a big, helpful attitude; 8,000 used and collectible books on site, another 8,000 in stock.

& **Borders Books, Music & Café** (603-224-1255; bordersstores.com), 76 Fort Eddy Rd., Exit 14 off I-93, Concord. Open Mon.–Thu. 9 AM–10 PM, Fri. and Sat. until 11, and Sun. 10–8. Always busy and nearly always open, this is a great place to browse and buy. Their calendar includes frequent author visits, concerts, and special events.

✔ **Gibson's Book Store** (603-224-0562; gibsonsbookstore.com), 27 S. Main St., Concord. Open Mon.–Wed. 9–6, Thu. and Fri. 9–8, Sat. 9–5:30, plus expanded holiday hours. Nourish both body and soul in Michael Hermann's friendly, well-stocked bookstore linked to a European-style bakery and café. There's a cosmopolitan selection of poetry, literary fiction, memoirs, travel, gardening, and cookbooks, plus children's story hours, book discussion groups, and frequent author signings.

Henniker Book Farm (603-428-3429), 2 Old West Hopkinton Rd. (just off Rt. 202/9), Henniker. This longtime "bookies" destination continues with its old woodstove. More than 30,000 titles of general interest, plus the owner's personal interests of history, literary criticism, and biography, continue to make this shop a magnet for browsing.

Old Number Six Book Depot (603-428-3334), 26 Depot Hill Rd., Henniker (up the hill from the town hall). Open daily 10–5. Boasts nearly 150,000 volumes with general and scholarly stock in all fields.

CRAFTS Canterbury Shaker Village (603-783-9511), Shaker Rd., Canterbury. The museum shop features Shaker crafts.

The Capitol Craftsman (603-224-6166), 16 N. Main St., Concord. Fine jewelry and handcrafts.

The Elegant Ewe (603-226-0066), 71 S. Main St., Concord. Designer yarns, rug-hooking and spinning supplies, Tuesday-night knitting clinics, quality handcrafted gifts, and the area's best selection of recorded Celtic music.

The Fiber Studio (603-428-7830; fiberstudio.com), 9 Foster Hill Rd. (off Rt. 202/9), Henniker. Open year-round, Tue.–Sat. 10–4, Sun. by chance. Wide selection of natural knitting and weaving yarns and spinning fibers; looms, spinning wheels, knitting machines, handwoven and knit items, workshops.

Heritage Herbs and Baskets (603-753-9005), 1 Hannah Dustin Rd., Canterbury. Open May–mid-Dec., daily 10–5:30. Herb gardens plus a charming country barn stocked with herbs, plants, handcrafted baskets, wreaths, books, and related New Hampshire crafts.

The League of New Hampshire Craftsmen (603-228-8171), 36 N. Main St., Concord. Open Mon.–Fri. 9:30–5:30, Sat. 9–5. The league's downtown shop is located in the old Phoenix Hall and has works by juried craftspeople in a range of media,

including glass, pottery, jewelry, metalwork, woodwork, and fiber arts.

Mark Knipe Goldsmiths (603-224-2920), 2 Capital Plaza, Main St., Concord. Open Mon.–Thu. 10–5:30, Fri. 10–6, and Sat. 10–2. Studio and gallery with beautifully designed, custom-made jewelry.

SPECIAL SHOPS ✿ Beech Hill Farm (603-223-0828; beechhillfarm .com), 107 Beech Hill Rd., Hopkinton. Open May–Aug., daily 11–9; until 8 in Sept.; till 7 through Oct. 31. A direct descendant of the first white child born in Hopkinton, Bob Kimball and his wife, Donna, have converted their ninth-generation dairy farm into a showplace for New Hampshire products and agricultural history. There are 50-plus flavors of New Hampshire–made ice cream with make-your-own sundaes, plenty of friendly animals to pet, a garden of cut-your-own flowers, and a barn filled with Donna's home-made goodies, as well as Kimball farm artifacts and regionally produced soaps, cheese, maple products, and decorative accessories. Kids and adults alike will enjoy navigating the 2-acre "amaizing" corn maze. With luck, you'll happen onto one of the frequent concerts, dances, or other festive gatherings in the big red barn. On a hot summer night, this place is filled with locals and visitors alike. It's not only the ice cream that gives this a real sense of New Hampshire's old-time community flavor.

Butter's (603-225-5995; 815-642-4662; buttersfinefood.com), 70 N. Main St., Concord. Open Mon., Tue., Wed., Sat. 9 –6 PM, Thu.–Fri. until 7. A handsome store and excellent source of special breads, cheeses, pâtés, spreads, and other tempting edibles.

Caring Gifts (603-228-8496), 18 N. Main St., Concord. Specializes in personalized baskets filled with everything from toys to gourmet foods.

Company C (603-226-4460), 102 Old Turnpike Rd., Concord. This brick-and-concrete warehouse hides a colorful cluster of casual contemporary furnishings, all at knockoff prices. Owner Walter Chapin is the son of a Pottery Barn founder, and his wife, Chris, has a background in fabrics. The two design the merchandise, which is manufactured offshore, then distributed to such upscale marketers as L.L. Bean and Neiman Marcus, as well as Company C's offshoot, Kate's Paperie on Prince Street in SoHo.

Gondwana and Divine Clothing Company (603-228-1101), 13 N. Main St., Concord. Open Mon.–Wed. and Sat. 10–6, Thu.–Fri. until 7. This store recently moved down the street and doubled its size, a reflection of growing customer satisfaction with its selection of expressive clothing and decorative accessories from around the world.

✂ **Gould Hill Orchards** (603-746-3811; gouldhillfarm.com), 656 Gould Hill Rd., Contoocook. Open daily Aug.–Nov. 1, 10–5; Nov. 2–30, 10–4; Dec., weekends only, 10–4. A 200-year-old family farm located high on Gould Hill with spectacular 75-mile views to the White Mountains. A nature trail winds through the orchard, and the inviting store is filled with fruit (including peaches, nectarines, plums, and 80 varieties of apples), baked pies, ice cream, cider doughnuts, maple syrup, honey, dips, jams, cider, and gifts of the season. The barn also houses The Little Nature Museum featuring displays of seashells, birds' nests, fossils, and stuffed animals.

✂ **Granite State Candy Shoppe** (603-225-2591; 888-225-2531), 13 Warren St., Concord. A great old-fashioned candy shop that's been in business since 1927, and a great spot for you and the kids to watch master candy craftsmen make a wide assortment of chocolates and other confections using the original copper pots and family recipes. Along with the hand-pulled crunchy nut brittle, truffles, fudge, and taffy, this newly expanded shop now offers homemade ice cream.

Little River Oriental Rugs (603-225-5512), 10 N. Main St., Concord. A unique selection of rugs, plus tea, sympathy, and knowledgeable service.

✧ **L.L. Bean Factory Store** (603-225-6575), Fort Eddy Rd., Concord. Discounted clothing and outdoor gear from the well-known Maine purveyor.

Fox Country Smoke House LLC (603-783-4405; foxcountrysmokehouse .com), 164 Briarbush Rd., Canterbury. Open daily Sept.–Christmas Eve, 10–4, Sun. noon–4; closed Mon. the rest of the year. Gift baskets of home-cured and smoked cheeses and meats in an interesting old building near Canterbury's bucolic town green.

Things Are Cooking (603-225-8377; 866-225-7300; thingsarecooking.com), 74 N. Main St., Concord. Open Mon.–Sat. 9–6, Thu. until 7, Sun. 11–4. Everything for the kitchen.

GOULD HILL ORCHARDS, HOPKINTON/CONTOOCOOK

Viking House (603-228-1198), 19 N. Main St., Concord. Open Mon.–Wed. 9–6, Thu.–Fri. 9–8, Sat. 9–5:30, and Sun. 12:30–4:30. A large selection of Norwegian sweaters, Vera Bradley products, and Scandinavian and other crystal, china, textiles, food, and gifts temptingly displayed.

✳ Special Events

June: **Garden Day**, Shaker Village, Canterbury. Herbal demonstrations, land management lectures, beekeeping. **New Hampshire Concord Coach & Carriage Festival**, New Hampshire Technical Institute, Concord. Horse-drawn parade, rides, competitions. **Wood Day**, with folk musicians and furniture makers demonstrating traditional techniques.

July: **Fourth Fireworks**, Memorial Field, Concord. **Strawberry Festival**, Contoocook. A 5K road race, 5-mile canoe race, parade, strawberries. **Fireman's Muster**, Pembroke. **Downtown Market Days**, Concord. Main Street closes to traffic for three days of entertainment, street food, and special sales. **Canterbury Fair**, Canterbury. Chicken barbecue, auction, antiques, juried crafts, Morris dancers. **Annual Bean Hole Bash weekend**, Northwood. Food, games, raffle, auction, flea market.

August: **Annual Hot Air Balloon Rally**, Drake Field, Pittsfield. Twenty balloons usually come; arts, crafts, entertainment. **Annual Northwood Community Craftsmen's Fair**, Northwood. Country fair, more than 60 craftspeople, music, food, folk dancers, flower show. **Annual New Hampshire Antiques Show**, Manchester.

Labor Day weekend: **Annual Hopkinton State Fair** (603-746-4191). **Annual Kiwanis Antique & Classic Car Show**, New Hampshire Technical Institute, Concord. **Annual Wool Day at Shaker Village**, Canterbury. Natural dyeing, rag-rug weaving, fleece-to-shawl. **NASCAR Craftsman Truck Series**, New Hampshire International Speedway, Loudon.

October: **Annual Harvest Days at Shaker Village**, Canterbury. Farm stands, produce, applesauce making, music. **Classic Car Show**, Canterbury Shaker Village. **Northern New England Sled Dog Trade Fair & Seminar**, Hopkinton Fair Grounds.

November: **Annual Holiday Craft Sale** at Shaker Village, Canterbury. Demonstrations and sales by a variety of artists and craftspeople from around the state. **Annual Gingerbread Showcase** features a landscape of edible edifices.

December: **Annual Contoocook Artisans Craft Show and Sale**, Hopkinton Town Hall.

The Monadnock Region

3

PETERBOROUGH, KEENE, AND
SURROUNDING VILLAGES

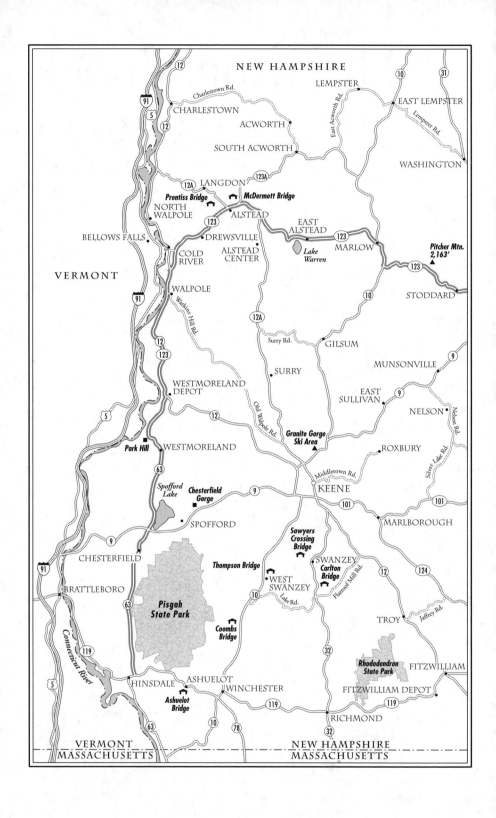

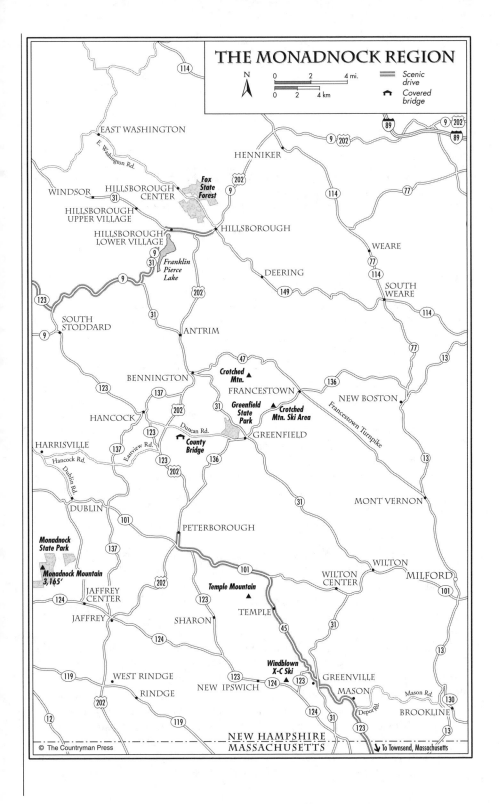

THE MONADNOCK REGION

N

0   2   4 mi.

0   2   4 km

Scenic drive

Covered bridge

114

EAST WASHINGTON

E. Washington Rd.

89
9 202

9 202

89
9 202

HENNIKER

202

9

Fox State Forest

114

77

WINDSOR

HILLSBOROUGH CENTER
31

HILLSBOROUGH UPPER VILLAGE

HILLSBOROUGH

WEARE
77

HILLSBOROUGH LOWER VILLAGE
9
31

Franklin Pierce Lake

DEERING

149

SOUTH WEARE

DEERING
149

114

123

9

SOUTH STODDARD

9
31

202

ANTRIM

77

114

47

Crotched Mtn.

13

BENNINGTON
123

137

FRANCESTOWN

136

NEW BOSTON

202

31

Greenfield State Park

Crotched Mtn. Ski Area

Francestown Turnpike

HANCOCK

Duncan Rd.

GREENFIELD

123

HARRISVILLE
137

Fairview Rd.

County Bridge

136

13

Hancock Rd.

123

202

Dublin Rd.

31

MONT VERNON

DUBLIN
101

PETERBOROUGH

137

WILTON

Monadnock State Park

101

WILTON CENTER

MILFORD

Monadnock Mountain 3,165'

202

Temple Mountain

101

JAFFREY CENTER
124

123

TEMPLE

31

JAFFREY

SHARON

45

13

124

Windblown X-C Ski

119

WEST RINDGE

123

NEW IPSWICH
124

GREENVILLE

123

MASON

Mason Rd.

130

202

RINDGE

124

31

Depot Rd.

BROOKLINE

12

119

NEW HAMPSHIRE
MASSACHUSETTS

123

13

© The Countryman Press

To Townsend, Massachusetts

PETERBOROUGH, KEENE, AND SURROUNDING VILLAGES

Mount Monadnock's 3,165-foot-high bulk towers above the surrounding roll of southwestern New Hampshire. Not only is the mountain visible from up to 50 miles in every direction, but it's also as much a part of the dozens of surrounding towns as the steeples on their meetinghouses. Uplands around the mountain, in turn, rise like an island 2,000 feet above the rest of southern New Hampshire. Hardy spruce, fir, and birch are the dominant trees, and the rugged terrain—with the help of many grassroots efforts—has deflected both developers and interstate highways.

Depending on where you draw the line, the Monadnock Region as a whole encompasses some 40 towns, most characterized by narrow roads, quintessential New England villages, and mountain vistas. A region of rushing streams, this entire area was once spotted with small 19th-century mills, and many of these buildings survive. Harrisville, with its two cupola-topped mills graceful as churches, is said to be the country's most perfectly preserved early-19th-century mill village. Larger brick mill buildings in West and South Peterborough and in Keene now house shops and restaurants, and half a dozen old mills are still producing a wide variety of useful products.

Mount Monadnock itself spawned the region's tourism industry early in the 19th century. Around 1800 and then in 1820 major fires exposed the mountain's bald pate. Once this bare spot was created, alpine flora (usually found only on mountains twice as high) took root, and hikers could enjoy not only the high-altitude landscape but also the spectacular view, which can extend more than 100 miles.

"Grand Monadnock" quickly became a famous freak. By 1823 a shed, the Grand Monadnock Hotel, was selling refreshments just below the summit, and a rival, Dinsmore's Comfortable Shantee, opened high on the mountain a few years later. By the 1850s local farmers and innkeepers had blazed trails up every side of Monadnock, and from 100 to 400 people could be found hiking them on any good day.

In the 1850s the mountain inspired works by Henry David Thoreau and Ralph Waldo Emerson, and around the turn of the century Dublin became known as a literary and art colony. Writers included Samuel Clemens and Willa Cather, who is buried in Jaffrey Center. Artists included Abbot Thayer, Frank Benson, and Rockwell Kent. In 1908 the MacDowell Colony in Peterborough became one of the country's first formal retreats for musicians, artists, and writers. The region's cultural climate remains rich, expressed through the unusual number of art galleries and musical and theatrical productions.

Most of the 19th-century summer hotels around Mount Monadnock are long gone, but half a dozen of the region's earlier stagecoach taverns survive, and over the past decades attractive bed & breakfasts have opened. The Monadnock Region is a destination area once more—but a low-key one. Residents take pride in the fact that Mount Monadnock is the world's second most heavily hiked mountain (after Mount Fuji in Japan), but everyone wants to keep the region's roads as delightfully traffic-free as they are.

While Mount Monadnock is the region's spiritual and physical hub, mountains do divide. In addition to Monadnock, there are other mountains—Pack Monadnock and Crotched and Temple for starters. Countless hills further divide the region into a patchwork of small areas that are surprisingly self-contained, especially in winter.

Broadly speaking, Mount Monadnock divides the region in two; all roads west of the mountain seem to converge in Keene, while in the hillier area to the east they run to Peterborough.

Keene is the shire town of Cheshire County, home of Keene State College and the place most residents of southwestern New Hampshire come to go to the movies or the hospital or to seriously shop. Far smaller Peterborough prides itself on having "the first tax-supported Free Public Library in the world," on having inspired Thornton Wilder to write *Our Town*, and on serving as home for one of New England's oldest summer theaters. Together with neighboring Jaffrey, this small area offers a large concentration of visitor-geared shops, dining and lodging, and easy access to Mount Monadock.

Hillsborough, 16 miles north of Peterborough, also counts itself part of this upland region. In truth, however, it's the hub of another little-touristed area along the Contocook River, one that's pocked with ponds and laced with hiking trails.

In the northwestern corner of this region Walpole, 18 miles northwest of Keene, is another destination in its own right, a part of the Connecticut River Valley as well as the Monadnock Region. A 19th-century resort town, it has recently been rediscovered, primarily as a dining destination—but it offers much more.

The Monadnock Region remains pristine in part because of its location: too near Boston to be generally viewed as a place to spend the night, too far from Manhattan to draw New Yorkers. So it happens that, despite the region's beauty, its ski and hiking trails, its biking routes, its wealth of antiques shops, and the quality of its inns, B&Bs, and restaurant, prices are relatively and refreshingly low. The only way to truly experience and explore the region, moreover, is to stay at least overnight.

GUIDANCE The website **monadnocktravel.com**, sponsored by the Monadnock Travel Council, is the best online info source for this area.

Greater Peterborough Chamber of Commerce (603-924-7234; peterborough chamber.com), P.O. Box 401, Peterborough 03458. Open weekdays 9–5; in summer and fall, Sat. 10–3. The chamber publishes a thick, useful guide to the 20 central and eastern towns in the region, and the walk-in information center at the junction of Rts. 101 and 202 is unusually friendly and helpful.

Greater Keene Chamber of Commerce (603-352-1303; keenechamber.com), 48 Central Square, Keene 03431. Open weekdays 9–5. The Keene chamber's easy-to-find walk-in office is a source of brochures about the western side of the region

Jaffrey Chamber of Commerce (603-532-4549; jaffreychamber.com) maintains a useful website and walk-in information center at 7 Main St.

Hillsborough Chamber of Commerce (603-464-5858; hillsboroughnhchamber .com) publishes a brochure and maintains a helpful website as well as an office at 25 School St., open Tue.–Thu. 9–3.

GETTING THERE *By air:* **Manchester Airport** (603-624-6539; flymanchester .com) offers connecting service to the world; see *Air Service* under "What's Where."

By bus: **Greyhound/Vermont Transit** (800-229-9424) stops in Keene with slow service to Boston via Springfield, Massachusetts.

GETTING AROUND *By car:* Although the beauty of this region is its winding country roads, it's also worth noting the straightest, quickest routes: **Rt. 101**, which connects with Rt. 9 in Keene, bisects the region from east to west, linking with Boston via Rts. 101A and 3 or Rts. 12 and 140 to Rt. 2; **Rt. 202** serves as a north–south spine linking I-89 north of Hillsborough with Rt. 2 (via Rt. 140) in Massachusetts. These two high roads cross at the lights in Peterborough, site of the region's prime information center.

Note: Free town maps are readily and suspiciously available. Snap them up! Given the web of roads with changing names, it's easy to get turned around. GPS and usually dependable atlases can lead you astray. Our map is just an overview.

WHEN TO GO This high and hilly region frequently gets old-fashioned winters. Two small ski areas survive, but this is primarily a summer and fall destination.

MEDICAL EMERGENCY 911 covers the entire region. **Cheshire Medical Center and Dartmouth-Hitchcock** (603-354-5400; cheshire-med.com), 580 and 590 Court St., Keene. **Monadnock Community Hospital** (603-924-7191; monadnockhospital.org), 452 Old Street Rd., Peterborough, has a 24-hour emergency department.

✳ Villages

No other area in New England is as thickly studded with picture-perfect villages—clusters of clapboard and brick buildings around commons that have changed hardly at all since the mid-19th century. Each has a town clerk, listed with directory assistance, who can furnish further information. See *Getting Around* and *Scenic Drives* for suggestions on ways to thread these villages together.

Alstead (pop. 2,013). There are actually three Alsteads (pronounced like the name *Al*), a grouping of quiet hill towns in the northwestern corner of the region not far from the Connecticut River. From the handsome old white houses and the Congregational church in **East Alstead**, Rt. 123 dips down by Lake Warren and into Mill Hollow, by 18th-century water-powered **Chase's Mill**, and by **Vilas Pool**—an unusual dammed swimming area with an elaborate island picnic spot, complete with carillon. The center of **Alstead** includes a general store and the **Shedd-Porter Memorial Library**, a domed, Neoclassical Revival building given by native son John Shedd, an associate of Marshall Field, who gave an almost identical library to his hometown of Conway. Turn left at the library and follow Hill Rd. up into **Alstead Center**, a hilltop cluster of old homes. The town also boasts two covered bridges.

Dublin (pop. 1,586). The flagpole on Rt. 101 sits 1,493 feet above sea level, marking New Hampshire's highest village center. But the best views (a mile or so west on Rt. 101) are of Mount Monadnock rising above **Dublin Lake**. Artist Abbott H. Thayer and the cigar-smoking poet Amy Lowell were among the artists and writers who summered here in the late 19th and early 20th centuries, an era in which some 50 large, elaborately rustic summer homes were built in town, many still sequestered in the greenery around the lake and on wooded heights that enjoy this view. The offices of *Yankee Magazine* and *The Old Farmer's Almanac* are in the middle of the village, along with "oldest public library in the United States supported by private funds." The post office and general store have moved downhill.

Fitzwilliam (pop. 2,292). Rt. 119 crosses Rt. 12 and snakes through this famously handsome village, by the green with its vintage-1816 steepled town hall, its four-tiered spire, a bell cast by Paul Revere, and Ionic pillars set in granite quarried right in town. The green is circled by a number of pillared and Federal-style homes. One is now a library, and another is a friendly historical society, the **Amos J. Blake House** (fitzhistoricalsociety.org), open Memorial Day weekend–Labor Day weekend, Sat. 1–4 and Thu. 9–11. Exhibits include a law office, old-time schoolroom, military room, and vintage-1779 fire engine. On a mid-July Saturday it's also a focal point for the annual mid-July **Fitzwilliam Historical Society Antiques Show & Sale**, usually featuring more than 50 dealers and drawing shoppers from as far as Boston. Rt. 119 continues on by the turnoff for **Rhododendron State Park** and angles north by **Laurel Lake**. In-season the **farmer's market** is every Saturday on the common, 9–noon.

Francestown (pop. 1,579). Named for Governor Wentworth's wife, Francestown has an almost feminine grace. The white-pillared, 1801 meetinghouse stands across from the old meetinghouse at the head of a street lined on both sides by graceful Federal-era houses. One of these is now the **George Holmes Bixby Memorial Library** (603-547-2730), 52 Main St., with wing chairs, Oriental rugs, and a children's story corner that many a passing adult would like an excuse to curl up in; inquire about the historical collection upstairs. Pick up a guide to local antiques shops in the **Francestown General Store**. Contra dances are held the second Saturday of every month in the town hall. **Crotched Mountain**, the area's prime ski area, is just up the road.

Greenfield (pop. 1,770) is best known for **Greenfield State Park** with camping and swimming on **Otter Lake**, and for the **Crotched Mountain Rehabilitation Center**, which sits high on the shoulder of the mountain, with spectacular views. In the village the vintage-1795 **Congregational church** is the oldest meetinghouse in New Hampshire, serving as both a church and a town hall. It stands tall with maples in front and a graveyard curving up the hill behind.

Hancock (pop. 1,805). **The Hancock Inn**, one of the oldest continuously operating inns in New England, forms the centerpiece of this village, and **Norway Pond** shimmers on the edge. There's also a green with a bandstand. A number of the

HARRISVILLE

aristocratic old homes have been occupied by "summer people" since the mid-19th century. The **Harris Center for Conservation Education** offers hiking, kayaking, and year-round programs.

Harrisville (pop. 1,098). What excites historians about this mill village is the uncanny way in which it echoes New England's earliest communities. Here life revolved around the mills instead of the meetinghouse: The mill owner's mansion supplanted the parsonage, and the millpond was the common. What strikes other people about Harrisville is its beauty. This little community of brick and granite and white-trimmed buildings clusters around a millpond and along the steep **Goose Creek Ravine** below. The two mills have cupolas, and the string of wooden workers' houses, "Peanut Row," is tidy. Decades ago when the looms ceased weaving, townspeople worried that the village would become an industrial version of Old Sturbridge Village. Instead, new commercial uses have been found for the old buildings, a few of them appropriately filled by **Harrisville Designs**, founded by John Colony III the year after his family's mill closed. "Wool has been spun here every year since 1790," he notes. The **Harrisville General Store**, now owned by Historic Harrisville, is an appealing gathering spot.

The Hillsboroughs (pop. 5,522). This is one town for which a map is a must, and luckily it's readily available from local businesses and the chamber of commerce. Downtown Hillborough is technically **Bridge Village**, a funky mill town with wooden mills still to be found along the Contoocook River. Note the "Dutton Twins," two Greek Revival 1850s mansions on Main St. The oldest part of town, **Hillsborough Center**, is well worth finding, a photogenic grouping of more than a dozen late-18th- and early-19th-century houses with a church, graveyard, pond,

HILLSBOROUGH CENTER

and several open art and craft studios. It's up School St. beyond the **Fox State Forest**. The **Franklin Pierce Homestead** is in **Lower Village**, out W. Main St. (Rt. 9) and north on Rt. 31. North of the homestead a right onto Shedd Rd. brings you to one of the town's four famous **stone arched bridges** dating from the 1850s. A left turn here onto Beard Rd. brings you to two more stone bridges and to **Gleason Falls**, a local picnicking spot. Swimming, kayaking, and hiking are to be found in town.

Jaffrey (pop. 5,500) is a lively, multifaceted town with it own chamber of com-

Hillsborough Chamber of Commerce

STONE ARCH BRIDGE, HILLLSBOROUGH

merce (jaffreychamber.com) maintaining a walk-in information center at 7 Main St. (603-532-4549). **Jaffrey Center**, west on Rt. 124, on the way to **Mount Monadnock**, is a gem. Its centerpiece is a white, steepled meetinghouse built in 1773, the site of the summer lecture series known as the **Amos Fortune Forum Series**. Willa Cather (1873–1947), who spent many summers in attic rooms at the former Shattuck Inn writing two of her best-known books—*My Antonia* and *Death Comes for the Archbishop*—is buried in the cemetery here. So are Amos Fortune (1710–1801), an African-born slave who bought his freedom, established a tannery, and left funds for the Jaffrey church and schools, and "Aunt" Hannah Davis (1784–1863), a beloved spinster who made, trademarked, and sold this country's first wooden bandboxes. On Thorndike Pond Rd. in Jaffrey Center, a Greek Revival schoolhouse built in 1833 houses an eclectic collection of Jaffrey artifacts (open July and Aug., weekends 2–4). The **Monadnock Inn** marks the middle of the village. Downtown Jaffrey itself is a mix of shops, restaurants, and former mills at the junction of major Rts. 202 and 124. The **Jaffrey Civic Center** (jaffreyciviccenter.com; 603-532-6527), 40 Main St., includes historical society exhibits and is the scene of frequent lectures and performances. Note *Buddies*, the World War I monument outside, carved from a single block of granite.

BUDDIES, WORLD WAR I MONUMENT, JAFFREY

WALPOLE HISTORICAL SOCIETY MUSEUM

Chris Tree

Walpole (pop. 3,594) is a handsome and visitor-friendly town in the northwest corner of the Monandock Region, set high above the Connecticut River. A number of its mansion-sized houses date from the 1790s, but more from the early and mid-19th century when Walpole was a popular summer haven. At one time three large inns served passengers who arrived on six trains a day from Boston; five daily trains from New York stopped across the river in Westminster, Vermont. Louisa May Alcott summered here, and Emily Dickinson visited. In the 20th century James Michener came here to research the opening chapter of *Hawaii*—the one about the New England–born missionaries and their families.

The old hotels went the way of Boston trains around the time that residents voted to reroute the state highway (Rt. 12) away from the village, down to the river's edge. That highway was then backroaded by I-91, running up the Vermont side of river. For half a century Walpole dozed.

In 1993 chocolate maker Lawrence Burdick drove up I-91 from Brooklyn, looking for a place to raise his family and grow his business. He turned a small Walpole shop into a chocolate factory/café but soon outgrew it and collaborated with filmmaker Ken Burns, a longtime Walpole resident, to purchase the vacant former IGA in the heart of the village. Together they transformed it into a destination chocolate shop and Parisian-style brasserie. Patrons now drive from as far as Boston for brunch at Burdick's.

Walpole is still just far enough off the beaten path to offer a sense of discovery. Burdick's original café now houses **Walpole Artisans Cooperative**. **Ruggles & Hunt** is another treasure trove, hidden behind the gas station. From the village, quiet roads climb into surrounding hills, up the past **Hooper Golf Club**, a holdover from the town's previous resort era. These roads and their views are their own reward, but bonuses include wine at **Walpole Mountain View Winery**, cheese at **Boggy Meadow Farm**, and a variety of farm stand and PYO fruit at **Alyson's Orchards**, which also offers lodging. So does **Valley View Farm**, a colonial-era gentleman's farm set on 150 acres with a sense of expanse and peace, inside and out.

The **Walpole Historical Society** (603-756-3349; open June–Oct., Wed.–Sat. 2–4) fills three floors of the tower-topped Academy Building in the middle of the village with displays chronicling the town's unusual history.

Note: In previous editions of this book we have positioned Walpole in the Connecticut River chapter because it is closely linked to Bellows Falls, Vermont. Walpole's founder, Colonel Benjamin Bellows, was the original owner of the land on both sides of the 56-foot drop in the river here. Unfortunately, at this writing the main bridge linking the Walpole with Bellows Falls is closed for a lengthy reconstruction. However, the **Great Falls Regional Chamber of Commerce** (802-463-4190; gfcc.com) in Bellows Falls remains its prime source of information for this area, and from points south I-91 Exit 5 remains the primary access.

VALLEY FARMS

Chris Tree

VIEW OF MONADNOCK BY RICHARD MERYMAN   Courtesy, Thorne-Sagendorph Gallery at Keene State College

MONADNOCK

Monadnock is reportedly an Algonquian word loosely translated as "mountain that stands alone." In the early 19th century the name spread from this mountain to designate every solitary prominence in the world that rises above its surroundings. To distinguish it from all others, purists now call this mountain "Grand" Monadnock. It acquired its bald summit in the 1820s (see the introduction to this chapter). In 1885 the town of Jaffrey acquired 200 summit acres with the help of the Society for the Protection of New Hampshire Forests (SPNHF). **Monadnock State Park** (603-532-8862; nhstateparks.org) now encompasses most of the mountain, some 5,000 acres. There are 40 miles of trails and five primary routes up to the 3,165-foot summit. First-timers, however, are advised to follow either the White Dot or the White Cross Trail from the state park headquarters on the eastern side of the mountain, marked from Rt. 124 northwest of Jaffrey Center. Experienced hikers tend to prefer the less trafficked trails. A favorite is the Dublin Trail, accessible from the northwestern side of the mountain. Check the map online at nhstateparks.org, but pick up a detailed trail map locally. The store at the park entrance is open year-round.

Detailed information about the mountain is available at the visitors center, open weekends and holidays in winter, otherwise daily. There are also restrooms, a snack bar, and picnic grounds. The park offers both group and family tent sites, open year-round but with flush toilets and showers, water in general, unavailable in winter. Reservations are available Memorial Day–Columbus Day but it's first come, first served in winter; the central reservation number is 603-271-3618. Eight miles of cross-country trails are marked but not groomed in snow season. Admission is $4 for ages 12 and older, $2 for those 6–11. *Dogs are strictly prohibited by law from all areas and trails on Mount Monadnock.*

Hikers were few on a bright February afternoon, and park manager Patrick Hummel had time to share observations and advice about visiting the country's most heavily hiked mountain:

- *Allow enough time.* Set aside four to five hours (in good conditions) for the roundtrip trek on the White Dot and White Cross Trails, the shortest and most heavily hiked trails. Be aware of the time the sun sets and allow an hour for

HIKERS ON MT. MONADNOCK

each hiking mile. Also be sure to stay on your original trail, because not every trail brings you back to the same place.

- *Avoid peak weekends.* September and October are the busiest months. Weekdays in June, September, and October are also popular with school groups. In May and June be sure to bring insect repellent.

- *Dress appropriately.* Bring a windbreaker and hat and wear sturdy hiking shoes (sneakers are discouraged) on even the hottest day. The higher the elevation, the colder, windier, and wetter the weather. Warmer gear is needed in fall, winter, and spring. Also, bring at least 2 quarts of water per person (it's just as important in winter as in summer), along with food and snacks. Check the website (nhstateparks.org) for weather before starting out. Calls are welcome (603-532-8862), so you might want to check ahead on trail conditions.

- *Stay on the trail!* Hiking on the edges of trails or parallel to them to avoid puddles, mud, or ice causes serious erosion problems. Plants are trampled, soil is compacted, and a route is created for the uncontrolled flow of water down the trails. These problems are sometimes impossible to repair.

MOUNT MONADNOCK SUMMIT

Mason (pop. 1,352). Another picture-perfect cluster of Georgian- and Federal-style homes around a classic Congregational church, complete with horse sheds and linked by stone walls. A historic marker outside one modest old house explains that this was the boyhood home of Samuel Wilson (1766–1844), generally known as "Uncle Sam" because the beef he supplied to the army during the War of 1812 was branded U.S. We were lucky enough to first visit Mason with Elizabeth Orton Jones, illustrator of the Golden Book *Little Red Riding Hood.* Today the house that served as a basis for "Grandmother's House" is **Pickity Place**, a popular herb farm and restaurant.

Nelson (pop. 656). This quiet gathering of buildings includes 1841 Greek Revival and Gothic Revival churches and an early, plain-faced but acoustically fine town hall.

Stoddard (pop. circa 1,000). Sited on a height-of-land that's said to divide the Connecticut and Merrimack River watersheds, Stoddard is known for the fine glass produced in three (long-gone) 19th-century factories. **Pitcher Mountain**, with a picnic area and trailhead on Rt. 123, is a short hike yielding a spectacular view.

Temple (pop. 1,560). The common is framed by handsome old homes and a classic tavern, now the **Birchwood Inn**. Known for its glasswork in the 18th century, Temple is now known chiefly for its band, founded in 1799.

Wilton. Downtown Wilton is just off Rt. 101, worth finding for the movie theater housed upstairs in the massive town hall and for the **Melting Pot** restaurant across the street. The other gem here is **Wilton Center**, also off Rt. 101 a few miles west. Look for the sign (across from the Mobil Station) for **Frye's Measure Mill**. This road, Isaac Frye Hwy., brings you to a ridgeline of grand old houses ranging from 18th-century to late-19th-century summer homes. The old Grange Hall houses **Andy's Summer Playhouse** (andyssummerplayhouse.org) with presentations by young performers. Continue through the village center, following signs to a shingled water-powered mill that's been in business more than 150 years, with a gift shop selling its Shaker-style boxes, woodenware, and more.

✴ To See

MUST-SEE The beauty of the villages, the roads that connect them, and the surprises that you'll find along the way—swimming holes, antiques shops, art galleries, summer music, and small-town celebrations—are what this area is about. Peterborough is the most visitor-friendly town, good for dining and shopping. The significant "sight to see" is **Mount Monadnock** itself.

In Keene

A small city (pop. 22,893), Keene serves as shopping hub for a tristate area that includes southeastern Vermont and much of upcountry Massachusetts. Keene's long **Main Street**, the widest in New England, is well worth exploring. It includes the historic houses described below as well as **Keene State College** (keene.edu) buildings like Elliot Hall, worth stepping inside to see the Barry Faulkner mural depicting Keene's **Central Square**. Some first-rate restaurants are clustered around the square itself, site of the high-steepled **United Church of Christ** (built in 1786), the town hall, and the chamber of commerce.

Thorne-Sagendorph Gallery at Keene State College (603-358-2720; keene .edu/tsag), Wyman Way off Main St. on the campus. Drive in and look for patron parking in front of the building. Open during the academic year, daily noon–4,

Thu. and Fri. until 7; in summer, open Wed.–Sun. noon–4. A handsome, modern gallery. The permanent collection includes many 19th-century landscapes from the Dublin Art Colony, but these may not be on view; check the exhibit calendar. Parking is available right at the building.

Historical Society of Cheshire County (603-352-1895; hsccnh.org), 246 Main St., Keene. Open Tue.–Fri. 9–4, Wed. evening until 9, Sat. 9–noon. An archival center for much of New England that features products once made in the area, including Keene and Stoddard glass. Changing exhibits are often worth checking, as is the museum store. The society maintains the **Wyman Tavern** (603-357-3855), 339 Main St., Keene. Open June–Labor Day, Thu.–Sat. 11–4, or by appointment. Maintained to represent the period between 1770 and 1820, this was the scene of the first meeting of the trustees of Dartmouth College under President Eleazar Wheelock in 1770. It was also from this site that 29 of Keene's Minutemen set out for Lexington in April 1775. Tours are offered by costumed guides.

Horatio Colony House Museum (603-352-0460; horatiocolonymuseum.org), 199 Main St., Keene. Guided tours are offered May–mid-Oct., Wed.–Sun. 11–4; winter hours by appointment; free. A Federal-era home filled with elegant family furnishings and souvenirs collected by Horatio and Mary Colony from their extensive travels throughout the world. Special collections include cribbage boards, walking sticks, Buddhas, beer steins, paperweights, and thousands of books.

In Peterborough

Far smaller than Keene, Peterborough (pop. 6,140) offers more than its share of dining, shopping, and entertainment. Its walkable core is **Depot Square**, a gathering of galleries, shops, and restaurants that also offers parking and riverside picnicking. The former depot itself is now a popular restaurant; the old A&P is a bookstore and café, and the **Sharon Arts Center**'s craft and art gallery is a destination in itself. On Sunday mornings in-season, an outdoor antiques mart is popular.

The **Peterborough Historical Society, Museum and Archives** (603-924-3235; peterboroughhistory.org), 19 Grove St. Open year-round Tue.–Sat. 10–4; $3; free under age 12. A large and handsome facility with an extensive research library. The downstairs museum room showcases a 1785 kitchen, vintage furnishings, and decorative arts; the upstairs space is family-friendly. Check for special exhibits and programs. It's worth at least stepping into the front hall to view a photo montage on the town's history. A circa-1800 mill house has been preserved behind the museum, as well as an 1824 one-room schoolhouse are open by appointment to groups.

DOWNTOWN PETERBOROUGH

Chris Treew

&. **Mariposa Museum & World Culture Center** (603-924-4555; mariposa museum.org), 26 Main St., open in summer daily 11–5, off-season Wed.–Sun. $5 per adult, $3 per child. Call or check online for First Friday and frequent special programs and weekly performances. Housed in a former Baptist meetinghouse, three floors of exhibits and performance space feature folk art, local and world-wide. Visitors are invited to try on costumes, play instruments. There's also a gift shop.

FOR FAMILIES ✿ **Friendly Farm** (603-563-8444; friendlyfarm.com), Rt. 101, Dublin. Open daily 10–5 (weather permitting), late May–Labor Day, and then weekends through mid-Sept. $6.75 adults, $6 children. Operated since 1965 by Allan and Bruce Fox, this 7-acre preserve is filled with barnyard animals: cows, horses, pigs, goats, sheep, donkeys, chickens, geese, turkeys, rabbits, and a working beehive. Feeding and cuddling welcome. Don't forget your camera. We treasure photos of our presently 6-foot, 3-inch son feeding a Friendly Farm goat when he was still small enough to heft.

✿ **Stonewall Farm** (603-357-7278; stonewallfarm.org), 242 Chesterfield Rd. (a turn to the north off Rt. 9), Keene. This not-for-profit education center and working organic farm welcomes visitors on weekdays, 8:30–4:30; call for weekend hours and special programs. Cows are milked at 4:30 daily, and there are hiking trails, a wetlands boardwalk, and a learning center. No admission fee. A gift shop sells local products.

Elsewhere

HISTORIC HOUSES Barrett House (603-878-2517; historicnewengland.org), 79 Main St. (Rt. 123), New Ipswich. Open June–mid-Oct., second and fourth Sat. for tours hourly 11–4. $5 adults. One of New England's finest Federal-style, rural mansions, built in 1800 as a wedding gift. The bride's father is said to have boasted that he would furnish as large a house as the groom's father could build. Both fathers outdid themselves, and it remained in the family until 1948. The rich furnishings are mainly Empire and Victorian, and they offer a sense of the surprisingly early sophistication of this area. Inquire about teas and other frequent special events. Operated by Historic New England.

Franklin Pierce Homestead (603-478-3165), 3 miles west of town near the junction of Rts. 9 and 31, Hillsborough. Open daily in July and Aug., 10–4, Sun. 1–4; otherwise weekends only in June and Sept.; July 4 and Labor Day 10–4. Nominal admission for adults; under 18 free. This is the restored, vintage-1804 home of the 14th president of the United States (1853–1857), the only one from New Hampshire. The hip-roofed, twin-chimney house was built in 1804 by Benjamin Pierce, Franklin's father, two-time New Hampshire governor. It is beautifully restored to illustrate the gracious home Franklin knew as a boy, operated by the Hillsborough Historical Society.

SCENIC DRIVES From the Boston area to Peterborough. Take Rt. 119 to West Townsend and turn right over the bridge up Rt. 123, but at the first fork bear right on the unnumbered road to Mason. Then take Rt. 123 into Greenville, a classic mill village; Rt. 45 to Temple; and Rt. 101 into Peterborough.

Hinsdale to Walpole. Take Rt. 63, a high, rural road, past the entrance to **Pisgah State Park** and on up to the hilltop village of **Chesterfield**. Drive across Rt. 9

COVERED BRIDGES

The Swanzey area, just south of Keene, boasts one of the densest concentrations of covered bridges east of Madison County. Our favorite is the white, red-roofed **Winchester–Ashuelot**, built in 1864 across the Ashuelot River just off Rt. 119 in Ashuelot. The 1830s **Winchester–Coombs bridge** across the Ashuelot is west of Rt. 10, 0.5 mile southwest of Westport. The 1860s **Swanzey–Slate bridge** across the Ashuelot is east of Rt. 10 at Westport. The 1830s, 155-foot **Swanzey–West Swanzey bridge** across the Ashuelot is east of Rt. 10 at West Swanzey. **Swanzey–Sawyer's Crossing**, rebuilt in 1859, bridges the Ashuelot 1 mile north of Rt. 32 at Swanzey village. The **Swanzey–Carlton bridge** across the South Branch of the Ashuelot River is east of Rt. 32, 0.5 mile south of Swanzey village. Pick up a detailed map, locating the bridges, at the **Swanzey Historical Museum**, 720 W. Swanzey Rd. (Rt. 10). It's open mid-May–foliage season, weekdays 1–4, weekends and holidays 10–4, and displays a Concord Coach, an Amoskeag steam fire pumper, and much more. Off by itself 1 mile east of Rt. 202 or 3.5 miles west of Greenfield is the **Hancock–Greenfield bridge**, built in 1937, which spans the Contoocook.

WINCHESTER-ASHUELOT COVERED BRIDGE

Robert J. Kozlow

(careful: It's a major east–west highway) on up Rt. 63 past **Spofford Lake** and through Westmoreland, another vintage village, then on to **Park Hill**, a showstopper even by Monadnock village standards. Its meetinghouse was built in 1762, and a Paul Revere bell was installed in 1827; handsome early homes frame the hilltop common. At Westmoreland Depot continue north on Rt. 12 until you reach the yellow blinking lights, then go left up the hill into Walpole village.

Walpole to Hillsborough. Take Rt. 12 to Rt. 123 and drive through **Drewsville** (another village you can fit in a photograph) to Alstead, then on through East Alstead (unless you want to check out the two covered bridges on the way to Acworth) to Marlow, a pretty village by a lake. Be sure to stop at the trailhead for **Pitcher Mountain**, because it's a quick hike to the fire tower for a panoramic view. From here the road plunges down to Stoddard and on to its Mill Village, where two adjacent general stores divide the town. Continue on along Rt. 23 to Rt. 9.

✳ To Do

BIRDING **New Hampshire Audubon** (nhaudubon.org) maintains the Pack Monadnock Raptor Observatory in Miller State Park (Temple), a prime hawk-viewing site during migration season (Sept.–Oct.), also some exceptional sanctuaries. See *Green Space*.

BICYCLING The Monadnock Region's many miles of back roads and widely scattered lodging places endear it to bicyclists of all abilities. It was once also webbed with rail lines, now abandoned and transformed into recreational trails. See **nhtrails.org** (603-271-3254). Check out the **Rindge Rail Trails**, some 6 miles, from Winchendon to the Jaffrey line, and the **Cheshire Recreational Trail** with parking on Rt. 119 near the old train depot and on Rt. 12 across from the State Line Store.

Peterborough's **Common Pathway** provides a relatively easy walking/bicycling experience from just south of downtown north to the Hancock border. Get a map at the chamber of commerce.

Asheulot Rail-Trail. This 21.2-mile former rail route begins on Emerald St., near Keene State College, and heads south along the Ashuelot River through West Swanzey and Winchester to Hinsdale (the trailhead is 2.1 miles south of the village on Rt. 63). You pass several covered bridges en route. The surface is hard-packed cinder.

BOATING **Boat rentals** are available at **Greenfield State Park** (603-547-3497)—which also offers a boat launch on Otter Lake; at **Eastern Mountain Sports** (603-924-7231) north of Peterborough on Rt. 202; and at **Pelletier's Sport Shop** (603-532-7180) in Jaffrey.

Public boat landings are available (ask locally to find them) in Antrim on **Franklin Pierce Lake**, **Gregg Lake**, and **Willard Pond**. The latter, a 2-mile gem hidden away in the Audubon Society of New Hampshire's dePierrefeu–Willard Pond Wildlife Sanctuary, is rich in water wildlife (motors prohibited; access on Rt. 123, 3.7 miles west of Hancock village). In Bennington there is a launch area on **Whittemore Lake**; in Dublin on **Dublin Lake**; in Francestown on **Pleasant Pond** and **Scobie Lake**; in Hancock on **Norway Pond**; in Jaffrey on **Frost Pond**; and in Rindge on the **Contoocook River**, **Emerson Pond**, **Grassy**

Pond, and **Pool Pond**. A popular canoe route begins in Peterborough, where the Contoocook River crosses under Rt. 202, with a take-out at Powder Mill Pond in Bennington. There is also a canoe launch at Edward MacDowell Lake in West Peterborough.

CARRIAGE RIDES, SLEIGH RIDES, HAYRIDES, AND HORSEBACK RIDING **Inn at East Hill Farm** (603-242-6495), Jaffrey Rd., Troy, offers year-round trail rides open to the public, weather permitting. Children (ages 5 and up) can go out on the trail after they take a lesson and are deemed qualified; there are pony rides for younger kids. Sleigh rides along with cross-country skiing are also offered.

Silver Ranch (603-532-7363; silverranch-stables.com), 183 Turnpike Rd (Rt. 124), Jaffrey. The third generation to operate this property offers carriage rides, hayrides, sleigh rides, and both riding and driving lessons. We can vouch for the sleigh rides through the woods.

Sleeper Hill Farm (603-478-1100), 20 Severance Rd., Hillsborough. Horseback riding and lessons.

Stonewall Farm (603-357-7278), 243 Chesterfield Rd., Keene. Specializes in groups of 15 or more; hayrides, sleigh rides.

FISHING Anglers have discovered the **Contoocook River** as a source of cold-water species, especially above Hillsborough and the stretch along Rt. 202 north of Peterborough. The North Branch is stocked with trout. The New Hampshire Fish and Game Department (fishnh.com) publishes a glossy guide to the fish and fishing holes of southwestern New Hampshire. Suggestions include **Edward Mac-Dowell Lake** (603-924-3431), marked from Union St. in West Peterborough, and **Powder Mill Pond** in Greenfield (also known as Bennington Bog); from Rt. 202 turn east on Forest Rd. Access is just after the covered bridge.

GOLF & **Bretwood Golf Course** (603-352-7626; bretwoodgolf.com), E. Surry Rd., Keene. Two full-length 36-hole layouts, par 72; driving range, pro shop, golf carts, snack bar, function room.

Crotched Mountain Golf Club and Resort (603-588-2000; crotchedmountain golf.com), Rt. 47, Francestown. Donald Ross design, 18 holes, par 72. Full pro shop, packages including dining, lodging, and golf school.

The Shattuck (603-532-4300; sterlinggolf.com), 53 Dublin Rd., Jaffrey. An 18-hole championship course at the foot of Mount Monadnock with a pro shop, restaurant, and reception space.

Monadnock Country Club (603-588-2000; monadnockcc.com), 49 High St., Peterborough. Dating back to 1901 on land donated by summer resident Edward MacDowell specifically to play golf; two Plexipave tennis courts are also available, along with grill service and a lounge.

Woodbound Inn and Resort (603-532-8341; woodbound.com), Woodbound Rd., Jaffrey. Nine holes, rental clubs, par-3 course.

Pine Grove Springs Country Club (603-363-4433; pgscc.com), 292 Rt. 9A, Spofford. Not far from Spofford Lake, nine challenging holes, open to the public with a restaurant and rentals.

Hooper Golf Club (603-756-4080; hoopergolfclub.com), 166 Prospect Hill Rd. Overlooking hills on both sides of the Connecticut River, it's highly rated. Check the website for current lunch and dinner options in the handsome clubhouse, the colonial-era Hooper Tavern.

HIKING Also see the Mount Monadnock sidebar and *Green Space*.

Crotched Mountain. Three trails lead to this 2,055-foot summit. The start of the Bennington Trail is marked 3 miles north of Greenfield on Rt. 31. The Greenfield Trail starts just beyond the entrance to Crotched Mountain Rehabilitation Center (also on Rt. 31). The Francestown Trail starts beyond the entrance to the former Crotched Mountain Ski Area on Rt. 47.

Willard Pond (see *Boating*) is an Audubon wildlife sanctuary in Antrim, accessible from Rt. 123 in Hancock, with Bald Mountain on the north, surrounded by large glacial boulders. You can walk around the northern side of the pond and hike to the top of Bald Mountain, from which there is a spectacular view.

Pinnacle Hiking Trails, Fitzwilliam. Maintained by the Fitzwilliam Conservation Commission, this is a series of trails on a former alpine ski area, also used for cross-country skiing in winter. Access is from Richmond Rd. (off the common), just beyond the Fitzwilliam Inn.

Long-distance trails. Hikers are advised to pick up trail maps to the following trails from the Monadnock State Park Visitors Center (see the "Monadnock" sidebar).

The **Metacomet Trail** is the northernmost 14 miles of a trail that theoretically leads to Meriden, Connecticut. The two most popular sections are Little Monadnock, accessible from the parking lot at Rhododendron State Park in Fitzwilliam, and Gap Mountain, accessible from trailheads on Rt. 124 west of Jaffrey Center from a spot just east of the Troy town dump. The trail is marked with white rectangles and is famed for its abundance of wild blueberries in July.

Monadnock–Sunapee Trail. The 47-mile, northern continuation of the Metacomet Trail, originally blazed in the 1920s by the SPNHF, was reblazed in the early 1970s by Appalachian Mountain Club volunteers. It descends Mount Monadnock on the Dublin Trail, then cuts across Harrisville, through Nelson village, up and down Dakin and Hodgeman Hills in Stoddard, up Pitcher Mountain (a rewarding stretch to hike from Rt. 123 in Stoddard), and up Hubbard Hill (prime blueberry picking). It then goes up 2,061-foot Jackson Hill, through Washington, and up through successive high ridges in Pillsbury State Park to Sunapee. Sounds great to us, but since we've never done it, be sure to pick up a detailed trail map from the Ecocenter, which displays a topographic relief map of the entire trail.

Wapack Trail. A 21-mile ridgeline trail with many spectacular views from North Pack Monadnock in Greenfield to Mount Watatic in Massachusetts. The trail crosses roads about every 4 miles. Just west of Miller State Park on Rt. 101, turn right onto Mountain Rd., continue until the road makes a T, and then turn right. After the road turns to gravel, look for a trail to your right. You will see a parking area. A 45-minute climb here yields great views.

RACING Winchester SpeedPark (603-239-6040; winchesterspeedpark.com), 517 Keene Rd., Winchester. Motorcycle and NASCAR races.

SPA The Grand View Inn & Resort (603-532-9880; thegrandviewinn.com), Rt.
124, 4.5 miles west of Jaffrey, open by reservation. Housed in a converted stable, this attractive day spa offers a full menu of services: a variety of massages, herbal, mud, and parafango wraps, as well as a steam room and sauna, great for the day after hiking.

The Green Spa (603-924-7444), 174 Concord St., Peterborough. Facials, foot and body treatments; Reiki also offered.

SPECIAL PROGRAMS Harrisville Designs (603-827-3996; harrisville.com), Harrisville 03450. Open Tue.–Sat., 10–5. The weaving tradition that once shaped the life of this village continues in the Weaving Center, an old brick textile factory overlooking the original millpond. Weekend and multiday weaving workshops, as well as sessions featuring knitting, felting, and other skills, are held throughout the year; some are simply introductions to weaving, while others are specialized and advanced courses. Lodging is available in nearby B&Bs as well as the Cheshire Mills Boardinghouse, built in 1850 for transient weavers. Daylong workshops are also offered; request a schedule.

Sharon Arts Center (603-924-7256; sharonarts.org), Rt. 123, Sharon. This rebuilt facility is a venue for year-round day, weekend, and multiday courses in drawing and painting, glass, basketmaking, photography, weaving, jewelry, ceramics, and more. See *Selective Shopping* for its extensive gallery and store in Peterborough's Depot Square.

SWIMMING Although the region is spotted with clear lakes and ponds, public beaches are jealously held by towns—understandably, given their proximity to Boston. Guests at local inns and B&Bs have access to local sand and water.

In Alstead: **Vilas Pool**, just off Rt. 123. Open in summer Wed.–Sun. A dammed pool in the Cold River with bathhouse and picnic area. **Lake Warren** has swimming from the public landing.

In Gilsum: **Otter Brook Lake Park**, Rt. 9. Maintained by the US Army Corps of Engineers, a sandy beach with picnic tables and grills. $1 fee.

In Greenfield: **Greenfield State Park** (603-547-3497), off Rt. 136, offers a beach that's mobbed on summer Sundays but not midweek. Modest fee.

In West Peterborough: **Edward MacDowell Lake** (603-924-3431). Marked from Union St. west of town. Maintained by the Army Corps of Engineers, a swim beach as well as boating, fishing, and picnicking.

In Hillsborough: Options include **Franklin Pierce Lake** (Manhattan Park is just off Rt. 9) and **Beard Brook** (along Beard Rd.), both at the shaded public beach and at the Gleason Falls bridge.

In Jaffrey: **Contoocook Lake Beach**—a small but lovely strip of soft sand along Quantum Rd. east of the junction of Rts. 124 and 202—and **Park Beach** on Thorndike Pond near the main entrance to Monadnock State Park are both open to nonresidents; weekend fee.

In Rindge: **Pearly Pond** adjacent to the Franklin Pierce College campus is good for swimming and picnicking.

In Roxbury: **Otter Brook Recreation Area**, Rt. 9, northwest of Keene. A human-made lake with lawns and sandy beach that can fill the bill on a hot day. Fee.

In Spofford: **Spofford Lake**, Rt. 9A. Town-run beaches: On North Shore Rd. off Rt. 9A there is a sandy beach with lifeguards, grills, and bathhouse. Farther along Rt. 9A is Wares Grove Beach, with lifeguards, a concession stand, and shallow water for a long way out, great for toddlers.

In Stoddard: **Center Pond**. Off Rt. 9 follow Center Pond Rd. The spring-fed pond has a small beach.

In Surry: **Surry Mountain Lake Recreation Area**, Rt. 12A not far north of Keene, offers a sand beach, as well as picnicking. Small charge for swimming.

In Swanzey: **Swanzey Lake** and **Wilson Pond**.

✳ Winter Sports

DOWNHILL SKIING Crotched Mountain (603-588-3668; crotchedmountain .com), 615 Francestown Rd., Bennington. A popular family-geared mountain.

Vertical drop: 875 feet.

Lifts: Five, including two quad chairs.

Skiable terrain: 75 acres with 23 trails and glades (28 percent novice, 50 percent intermediate, 22 percent expert).

Snowmaking: 100 percent coverage.

Night skiing and snowboarding on all trails, six nights. Midnight Madness on Fri., Sat. in Jan.–Feb. until 3 AM.

Facilities: Lodge with food court and well-equipped, self-serve rental center.

Granite Gorge (602-358-5000; granitegorge.com), 341 State Rd. 9, Roxbury. Five miles east of Keene.

Vertical drop: 525 feet.

Lifts: Four, including a double chair to the summit.

Skiable terrain: 55 acres, 18 glades and trails (30 percent novice, 40 percent intermediate, 30 percent expert).

Snowmaking: 69 percent.

Night skiing and snowboarding on 10 trails.

Facilties: Base lodge, tubing and terrain parks.

CROSS-COUNTRY SKIING Also see *Green Space.*

Windblown (603-878-2869; windblownxc.com), Rt. 124 west of the village, New Ipswich. Open daily 9–5 when snow conditions permit. In 1972 Al Jenks began transforming this alpine area into a 24-mile network that frequently has snow when the ground is bare just 10 miles away. A massive ice storm in 2008 tragically felled hundreds of trees on the 308-acre property, resculpting its landscape. Heart-breaking as this was, the volunteer cleanup effort and level of support for Al and Irene Jenks was equally overwhelming. The best developed, high-altitude cross-country center within easy striking distance of Boston, Windblown's future at present is the focus of an ambitious fund-raising effort by the nonprofit Central New England Nordic Council, with plans that include world-class racing trails and

Chris Tree

WINDBLOWN IN NEW IPSWICH IS KNOWN FOR ITS WELL-GROOMED TRAILS

snowmaking. Hopefully, readers will find this magical place with its varied trails, homemade soups, spiced cider, and home-baked munchies before Al and Irene retire. Rentals, instruction. Trail fee (no credit cards). Check conditions before you come.

The Inn at East Hill Farm (603-242-6495), Jaffrey Rd., Troy. Trails meander gently around this property with its great view of Mount Monadnock. Rentals and instruction are offered, and informal meals are available at the inn. A warming hut on the trail, with fireplace and woodstove, serves hot drinks on weekends. Trail fee.

Woodbound Inn (603-532-8341), Jaffrey. Fourteen kilometers of wooded trails; rental equipment. Trail fee.

Granite Gorge (603-358-5000; granitegorge.com), Rt. 9, 5 miles east of Keene. Lessons, rentals and a 12-mile trail system at the base of the alpine ski area. Open Wed.–Sun. Check for hours.

Mount Monadnock State Park (603-532-8862), Dublin Rd. from Rt. 124, Jaffrey Center. A 12-mile, well-marked but ungroomed system of trails webs the base of the mountain; loops run from 1 mile to more than 7 miles. Winter camping is also available. Entrance fee. No dogs allowed. See the sidebar on the 40-mile trail system radiating from the mountain summit.

✳ Green Space

Also see *Hiking* and *Swimming* under *To Do*.

In the Keene area

Annette State Park, Cathedral Rd., 2 miles off Rt. 119, Rindge. Shaded picnic sites and walking trails on 1,336 acres near Cathedral in the Pines.

Bear Den Geological Park, Rt. 10, Gilsum. Look for a large pull-off area on your right (heading north). This is a geologically fascinating area, with glacial pot-holes, caves, and ledges, believed to have once been a denning area for bears.

⊙ **Cathedral of the Pines** (603-899-3300; cathedralofthepines.org), marked from Rt. 119, a few miles east of Rt. 202, Rindge. Open for an Easter sunrise service, then May–Oct., 9–5. The 1938 hurricane exposed the magnificent view from this ridgetop property, and the infamous December ice storm of 2008 destroyed most of the tall, century-old pine trees for which it is named. With fresh landscaping and an enhanced view, the 400-acre site continues to be a popular venue for weddings as well as services. Mount Monadnock is the backdrop for the altar. Created as a memorial by Douglas and Sibyl Sloane for their son, killed in World War II, it was recognized by the 1956 Congress as a national memorial to all American war dead. There's a stone Memorial Bell Tower with four bas-reliefs designed by Norman Rockwell, honoring American women. A museum in the basement of the Hilltop House is a mix of religious and military pictures and artifacts, thousands of items donated by visitors from throughout the country. Visitors are welcome to stroll the extensive grounds. Please: No dogs, no smoking, no picnicking (the Annett Wayside Area is a mile up the road).

Charles L. Pierce Wildlife and Forest Reservation, Stoddard. From Rt. 9 in Stoddard, follow Rt. 123 north approximately 2 miles; turn right at the fire station; cross the bridge. At the junction go straight on a dirt road approximately 1 mile; park in the lot 300 feet beyond the woods road, on the left. The 5-mile Trout-n-Bacon Trail, beginning at a small brook to the left of the road, offers outstanding views from Bacon Ledge and leads to Trout Pond. This is a 3,461-acre preserve with more than 10 miles of hiking trails and woods roads that wind over ridges, through deep forest, and around beaver dams. The Society for the Protection of New Hampshire Forests (SPNHF) also owns the 379-acre Thurston V. Williams Forest and the 157-acre Daniel Upton Forest in Stoddard.

Chesterfield Gorge (603-239-8153), Rt. 9, Chesterfield. Open weekends. Footpaths along the gorge were carved by a stream that cut deep into ledges. The 0.75-mile trail crosses the stream several times, and there are plenty of picnic tables within sound and sight of the rushing water. Volunteers staff the park visitors center, which houses a logging tool collection and displays of local mammals.

Horatio Colony Trust, off Daniels Rd. (take a left 0.5 mile west of the blinking light on Rt. 9), Keene. A 450-acre bird and animal preserve with marked trails through the woods.

Piper Memorial Forest, off Rt. 9, East Sullivan. A 199-acre wooded SPNHF property traversed by a loop trail to the top of Boynton Hill.

Pisgah State Park (603-239-8153), Chesterfield, Hinsdale, Winchester, with entrances off Rts. 9, 10, 63, and 119. A largely undeveloped 13,500-acre area with pit toilets and old logging trails (good for hiking, hunting, and cross-country skiing), plus ponds to satisfy the adventurous angler. Parking and maps at all six major trailheads. No camping or fires allowed.

Rhododendron State Park (603-239-8153), Rt. 119 west of the village, Fitzwilliam. $3 day-use fee; children 11 and under are free. The wild rhododendrons grow up to 30 feet high and are salted along paths above wildflowers and ferns and under pine trees. It is one of those deeply still and beautiful places.

These rhododendrons reach maximum bloom in mid-July. A great place for a picnic.

In the Peterborough and eastern Monadnock area

Note: See the Monadnock sidebar under *To See* for Monadnock State Park.

☙ **Pack Monadnock Mountain in Miller State Park** (603-924-7672), Rt. 101, 3 miles east of Peterborough. $4 adults, $2 children. Open weekdays in May, then full-time late June–early Nov. Pets are permitted. For those who don't feel up to climbing Mount Monadnock, this 2,300-foot-high summit is a must. A 1.5-mile winding, steep, but paved road leads to the top, where there are walking trails, picnic sites, and views of Vermont to the west and (on a good day) Boston skyscrapers to the south. Opened in 1891, this was New Hampshire's first state park. A hotel was opened in 1892 but burned down in 1896, replaced by a smaller lodge that burned in 1924. This is the terminus of the 21-mile-long **Wapack Trail** (see *Hiking*) and a popular site for viewing migrating hawks in Sept.–Oct. (see *Birding*).

Greenfield State Park (603-547-3497), Rt. 136, 1 mile west of Greenfield Village. $4 adults, $2 ages 6–11. A 401-acre preserve with 0.5-mile frontage on Otter Lake, this is the region's prime public camping spot, with 252 tent sites (no hookups) that access their own beach. There's also a popular public beach. Snowmobiling and cross-country skiing in winter.

The **Harris Center for Conservation Education** (603-525-3394; harriscenter .org), 83 Kings Hwy., is a 12,000-acre super-sanctuary offering 7 miles of hiking trails, kayaking, and some 100 year-round programs, including guided hikes and snowshoeing treks. Follow signs from Hancock village.

Fox State Forest (603-464-3453; nhdfl.org), 309 Center Rd., Hillsborough. Twenty miles of trails within 1,445 acres of woodland. An extensive trail system geared to hikers, bikers, and cross-country skiers is marked. Pick up a map in the mailbox at the main entrance parking lot.

Gap Mountain Reservation, Jaffrey. From Troy, follow Rt. 12 south 0.4 mile; turn left onto Quarry Rd.; continue past transmission lines. At a sharp left in the road, a woods road continues straight uphill. Park and hike up the hill. Near the top, trail markers bear left through the woods. Gap Mountain is a favorite with berriers and picnickers. The 1,107-acre preserve includes three peaks, two bays, and a rich variety of plants and wildlife.

The Heald Tract, off Rt. 31 in Wilton. A Society for the Protection of New Hampshire Forests (SPNHF) preserve with fairly flat trails, pond views.

MacDowell Reservoir (603-924-3431), Wilder St., West Peterborough. Good for picnicking, boating, fishing, swimming, and hiking. Maintained by the US Army Corps of Engineers.

McCabe Forest, Antrim. Take Rt. 202 north from Antrim for 0.2 mile; turn right onto Elm St. Extension; turn right to the parking area. This former 192-acre farm has 2 miles of trails, including a fine self-guided interpretive trail, and a variety of wildlife.

Otter Brook Dam and Lake, Roxbury, Keene. There's picnicking and swimming with a sandy beach and lawns at this human-made lake. Free admission.

Pierce Island State Park (Spofford Lake). This 5-acre island, densely wooded with hemlocks, lies less than a mile from the state boat landing. No facilities.

☙ **Shieling Forest**, off Old Street Rd., Peterborough (marked from Rt. 202 north of town). This is one place you can walk your dog. There are 45 acres of tree-covered ridges and valleys, and a forestry learning center.

✳ Lodging

Note: The Monadnock Lodging Association maintains an excellent website: **nhlodging.org**. Also check lodging listings at **monadnocktravel.com**.

INNS

In and around Keene

✪ ෴ ☙ ✎ ⅙ ⁗**T**⁗ **Chesterfield Inn** (603-256-3211; 800-365-5515; chesterfieldinn.com), P.O. Box 155, West Chesterfield 03466. Innkeepers Phil and Judy Hueber have created a comfortable, romantic getaway that's well positioned for exploring much of southern Vermont as well as the Monadnock Region and Connecticut River Valley. The inn is set well back from busy Rt. 9, 2 miles east of Brattleboro, Vermont. The original house, which served as a tavern from 1798 to 1811, has been skillfully expanded to include a spacious dining room, attractive parlor, and 15 guest rooms divided between the main house and newer Guest House. All rooms have a sitting area, phone, controlled heat or air-conditioning, and optional TV and wet bar; some have a working fireplace and/or double whirlpool. $175–345 double includes breakfast; $25 higher during foliage season and holiday weekends. Inquire about MAP rates. Pets are accepted with advance permission. Also see *Dining Out*.

✎ ⅙ ⁗**T**⁗ **E. F. Lane Hotel** (603-357-7070; 888-300-5056; eflane.com), 30 Main St., Keene 03431. Shop till you drop in downtown Keene, then check into what was once Goodnow's, known for a century as the area's finest department store. This stately 1890 brick-and-granite structure is now the city's "inn" spot. The 31 elevator-accessed rooms and nine suites vary in size from large to two-story Chairman Suites suitable for a small household. Although no two are alike, each is furnished in period style. Many suites offer whirlpool tub and separate sitting room. The Salmon Chase Bistro (see *Dining Out*) offers a light breakfast buffet, included in the $139–194 room rate. Check for packages.

✪ ☙ ✎ **Inn at East Hill Farm** (603-242-6495; 800-242-6495), 460 Monadnock St., Troy 03465. This isn't a fancy place, but over the years (since 1973) three generations of the Adams family have created a lively, friendly family resort. The core of the complex is an 1830s inn with a fireplace in its living room and a large dining room in which meals are served at individual small tables; it's frequently cleared for square dances and other events. In all there are now 70 guest rooms and family units, all with private bath. Facilities include an indoor and two outdoor pools, Perkins Pond for boating and fishing, tennis, shuffleboard, and boats. Water-skiing, horseback riding, and a children's program are also available, and the barn is filled with animals. $104–126 per adult plus 15 percent gratuity; children's rates are geared to age; all three meals are included, and weekly rates are available. Credit cards are accepted but not for gratuities. Pets are $10 per day.

✎ ⁗**T**⁗ **The Fitzwilliam Inn** (603-585-9000; historicfitzwilliaminn.com), 62

Rt. 119 West, Fitzwilliam 04447. This three-story, double-porched, Greek Revival landmark serves as a centerpiece for one of the region's most handsome villages. It's looking good again, freshly painted and with chimneys repaired by Scott Nickerson and Lucia Crocker from Leverett, Massachusetts, who reopened it in September 2009. There are currently just six attractive, second-floor guest rooms, each with private bath ($125–150 including breakfast). On the frosty winter evening we stopped by, a fire was blazing in the tavern hearth and tempting smells emanated from the kitchen. At this writing the tavern (see *Eating Out*) is open just Thu.–Sun., but the energetic trio of female managers promise that this will increase.

In and around Peterborough

☯ 🐾 ✧ "1" **Woodbound Inn** (603-532-8341; 800-688-7770; woodbound .com), 62 Woodbound Rd., Rindge 03461. This is once more the region's premier resort, a rambling old complex set in 200 wooded acres on Contoocook Lake. It had fallen on hard times in 2008 when well-known local restaurateurs Aylmer and Cindy Given bought the property and, with the help of other local investors, gave the core inn—with its 16 guest rooms and their baths—a total and tasteful makeover. There are gracious spaces to relax downstairs, but the focal point here is now **Aylmer's Grille**, a sleek and informally inviting dining area (open to the public for lunch and dinner), named for the couple's former downtown restaurant (see *Dining Out*). There are 14 motel-style rooms, each with two double beds, in the neighboring Edgewood building, which also includes a ballroom, a venue for weddings and other functions, and 11 lakeside cabins with fireplaces (2 are pet-friendly). Facilities include a nine-hole par-3 USGA-sanctioned golf course, cross-country ski trails and rentals, and a private beach. B&B rates are $159–279 for rooms in the inn, $139–149 in Edgewood, $149–299 in cabins.

& **The Hancock Inn** (603-525-3318; 800-525-1789; hancockinn.com), 33 Main St., Hancock 03449. Built in 1789 and the state's oldest, this inn has a late-19th-century look, thanks to two-story pillars and a mansard roof. We arrived on a midsummer evening and, after a rum punch in the tavern, attended a free concert of classic blues just outside on the village green before returning to the inn's elegant deep-cranberry-colored dining room for dinner. Innkeeper Robert Short offers 15 guest rooms (all with private bath, some with Jacuzzi), with elegantly classic country inn decor: canopy and four-poster beds, handmade quilts, braided and hooked rugs, rockers, wingback chairs, and several fireplaces. One room is decorated with genuine Rufus Porter murals, and authentic 1830s stencil patterns decorate many of the other rooms as well. Both the tavern room, which serves light meals in the

WOODBOUND INN, JAFFREY

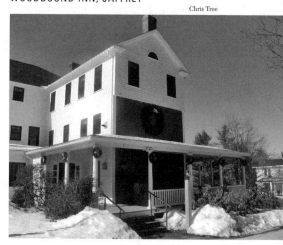
Chris Tree

HANCOCK INN

evening, and the dining room (see *Dining Out*), are open to the public. $125–240 double, less in winter; no smoking, no children under 12.

⊙ **The Monadnock Inn** (603-532-7800; 877-510-7019; theinnatjaffrey center.com), 379 Main St., Jaffrey 03452. Known for several years as The Inn at Jaffrey Center, this gracious old landmark has recently reacquired its original name. Under ownership by Noel and Stephen Pierce and his brother Max Mitchell, it's become known for dining. We lament the loss of the parlor, now another dining room, but we understand that the food is superb. The 11 rooms on the second and third floors are nicely decorated in soft, pleasing colors, each different and varying widely in size but all with private bath. The old plumbing has been retained: Claw-foot tubs have been glazed and sinks refitted. Furnishings are a mix of antiques and reproductions. While families are welcome and some guest rooms are quite large (there's also a two-room suite), shared space is limited to the tavern and dining areas. Room rates range $110–160, depending on season, including breakfast.

♨ ⁿ¹⁾ **The Birchwood Inn and London Tavern** (603-878-3285; the-birchwoodinn.com), 340 Rt. 45, P.O. Box 23, Temple 03084. Henry Thoreau is counted among past guests at this small brick inn, now on the National Register of Historic Places. Built around 1800 in the center of a tiny back-road village, today the inn is owned by two Brits, Andrew and Nick, and their American partner, Trish. The trio have renovated the three rooms ($89–109) and two suites ($139), furnishing each with authentic items from the English communities for which each is named. Downstairs the food and atmosphere are of a cheerful, authentic English pub. Inquire about frequent special-occasion meals served in the fine little dining room with 1820s murals by Rufus Porter (see *Dining Out*).

BED & BREAKFASTS

In and around Keene

✪ ♨ ✿ ⁿ¹⁾ **Ashburn House** (603-585-7198; ashburnhouse.net), 20 Upper Troy Rd., Fitzwilliam 03447. This town is so exceptionally rewarding (see *Villages*) that until recently it drew enough visitors to fill a full-service inn and several B&Bs. We are grateful to Carole and Ken Beckworth for preserving the town's long tradition of hospitality and offering a gracious entrée for visitors to this special corner of the region. Their Federal-era house is just off the common, with wide 1790s floorboards, books, and fresh flowers; there are also formal and informal parlors, both with Rumford hearth, one with board games and a piano, the other with TV, VCR, and DVD. Of the three upstairs guest rooms, two are rather grand, and a third can be part of a family suite. We agonized between the Rose and Blue Rooms (both with fireplace) and settled in the smaller Blue, with its elegant settee and lacy canopy bed. Breakfast, served in the wainscoted, flower-papered dining room with a boar's head above the fireplace, is full and included in $85–120 rates, depending on season. Children welcome.

✓ **The Carriage Barn Guest House** (603-357-3812; carriagebarn.com), 358 Main St., Keene 03431. Dave Rouillard, a retired fifth-grade teacher, is the enthusiastic host of this B&B attached to the back of a large home just past the college on the southern end of Keene's Main St. His librarian wife, Marilee, knows the area well and can direct you to downtown shops, movies, restaurants, and a host of nearby activities. Behind their large home, a converted Civil War–era barn now holds four guest rooms, each with private bath, a large sitting room with TV and phone, and a sunny breakfast room. $70–110 double includes tax as well as a continental "plus" breakfast. Children over 5 are welcome.

Colony House (603-352-0215), 104 West St., Keene 03431. This is a classic vintage 1819 brick mansion built by the founders and longtime owners of the nearby Colony Mill that's presently a major shopping/dining complex. The wonder is that it's still in the Colony family. Proprietor Joslin Kimball Frank has named each of the four second floor bedrooms for a forebear who either lived in or frequented the house. Unfortunately West St. is now a major, heavily trafficked main drag, but the upside is that the establishment is easy to find and within walking distance of downtown. The house is elegantly comfortable throughout. An expanded continental breakfast is served in the cheerful, expansive kitchen; the guest pantry is fitted with fridge, microwave, and electric teapot.

$135 for one night, $120 for two or more, with discounts for longer stays. Checks or cash only.

In Walpole

✪ ✓ "♦" **The Inn at Valley Farms B&B Cottages and Vacation Farmhouse** (603-756-2855; 877-327-2855; innatvalleyfarms.com), 633 Wentworth Rd., Walpole 03608. This 1770s rural mansion is set in 105 rolling acres bordering an apple orchard, not far from Walpole village. It offers exceptionally handsome, antiques-filled guest rooms along with a series of lovely common rooms, including a formal parlor, a library, a dining room, and a glass-walled sunroom with a guest fridge and pantry, overlooking a lovely perennial garden. Upstairs is a two-bedroom suite with bath, along with two other bedrooms, each with four-poster bed, private bath, phone, and WiFi. Niceties include fresh flowers, plush robes, and Burdick chocolate goodnight treats. Family travelers can choose one of two cottages, each with three bedrooms, kitchen, and living area. Innkeeper Jacqueline Caserta is a serious organic farmer/gardener and raises pastured organic chickens and turkeys and grass-fed beef. Jacki grew up down the road and bought the property when it was threatened by

ASHBURN HOUSE, FITZWILLIAM

Chris Tree

development. Guests are invited to walk the hill, past the four-story red barn to a hilltop meadow with a long view down the valley. On a late-spring morning breakfast began with a fresh rubarb compote laced with mint and followed by hot popovers and the farm's eggs with flowering fresh chives. Rates for the inn are $175–215 double occupancy, including breakfast. Cottages, which sleep six, are $220 for two, plus $20 per person under 12; $35 per person over 12. A basket of homemade breads and muffins is delivered each morning to your door. Inquire about the three-bedroom farmhouse with a full kitchen for longer stays.

∞ ☃ ⁰ᵀ⁰ **The Caleb Foster Farmhouse & Rochambeau Lodge at Alyson's Orchard** (603-756-9800; 800-756-0549; alysonsorchard.com), P.O. Box 562, Wentworth Rd., Walpole 03608. Alyson's Orchard (see *Selective Shopping—Farms*) is a popular wedding venue, and these three distinct lodging options across the road are frequently all used by the wedding party. Rochambeau Lodge is a rustic, renovated barn with a fully equipped kitchen, dining area, and two and a half baths; it sleeps 16 to 18 in eight

INN AT VALLEY FARMS, WALPOLE

Chris Tree

bedrooms. The neighboring Caleb Foster Farmhouse has been divided into two recently renovated upscale units with WiFi. Both have modern kitchens and spacious common areas; Foster West has three bedrooms and a two-bedroom suite, and Foster East, three bedrooms. The 500-acre orchard is known for its heirloom apples and invites visitors to use its miles of trails for cross-country skiing or hiking. It includes several spring-fed ponds, friendly fenced llamas, and a children's play area. The Orchard Room is available for wedding receptions and conferences.

The Walpole Inn B&B (603-756-3320; walpoleinn.com), RR 1, Box 762, 297 Main St., Walpole 03608. Originally this distinguished Colonial was home to Colonel Benjamin Bellows, commander of Fort No. 3, a strategic garrison along the Connecticut River during the French and Indian Wars. Now, in another life, it offers eight guest rooms, each furnished with a pencil-post queen-sized bed and simple tailored linens. Four have walk-in shower; the others feature a luxurious soaking tub with shower. You can choose among chess in the paneled parlor, tennis on the grounds, or golf at the nearby Hooper Golf Course. A full breakfast comes with an artist's view of meadows and hills, and is included in the $145–175 rate.

⁰ᵀ⁰ **The Bridges Inn at Whitcomb House** (603-357-6624; bridgesinn .com), 27 Main St., Swanzey 03446. Dating in part from 1790, this is a rambling, welcoming inn with largely Victorian detailing and decor. Each of the five guest rooms is named for one of the town's covered bridges, and all have private bath (check if you need it to be en suite). Five miles south of Keene, the inn is in the handsome village of West Swanzey. Innkeeper

Susan Schuster and her family welcome you. Son David, a local chef, prepares a multicourse breakfast, included in $100–130.

&. "Ψ" **Inn of the Tartan Fox** (603-357-9308; 877-836-4319; tartanfox .com), 350 Old Homestead Hwy., Swanzey 03446. This Arts & Crafts–style stone-and-shingle cottage, with mahogany woodwork and cobblestone fireplace, is banked behind pines, across the road from Keene's airport (no commercial service). Meg Kupiec and Wayne Miller offer four guest rooms, each appointed with Eastlake-era antiques and a different tartan plaid. Several of the private bathrooms have heated marble tile floors. A ground-floor guest room, which opens onto a terrace, has a shower wide enough for a wheelchair. The second-floor Manor Room is our favorite. The couple make and sell their own jams and woodwork and raise Rhode Island Reds, which contribute their eggs to the four-course breakfast, included in the $90–150 rate (for two).

In and around Peterborough

"Ψ" **Little River Bed & Breakfast** (603-924-3280; littleriverbb.com), 184 Union St., Peterborough 03458. A mile west of downtown Peterborough, this renovated farmhouse overlooks the Nubanusit River. In the early 20th century it served as a dorm for the Mac-Dowell Colony, housing the likes of Thornton Wilder. Rob and Paula Fox have thoroughly renovated the house, keeping the wood-burning fireplace in the living room but installing electric hearths in three of the four guest rooms. All are nicely furnished, and Paul has installed cork floors in the bathrooms (what a good idea!). Our favorite is the second-floor Beech Tree Room with its iron queen-sized bed, writing desk, and river view. There's a flat-screen TV in the large living room

and a cozy upstairs sunporch with river views—a great spot to read within earshot of the river, as is the back deck. Breakfast is a serious affair here, served in the sunny dining area off the open kitchen, included in $95–125.

"Ψ" **Three Maples B&B** (603-924-3503; threemaples.com), Rt. 123, Sharon 03458. Directly across from the Sharon Arts Center, a fine old country home dating in part to 1795, set behind three, century-old sugar maples. Linda Claff has created an appealing haven with three guest rooms. One downstairs, furnished in white cottage furniture and a brightly quilted bed, has a two-person sauna as well as a bath. Upstairs are two more nicely furnished rooms, one with a four-poster canopy queen and an extra-deep jet tub. The living room and two of the guest rooms feature gas fireplace. A full breakfast is included in the $95–125 rates. Children are welcome if the family rents all three rooms.

"Ψ" **The Benjamin Prescott Inn** (603-532-6637; benjaminprescottinn .com), Rt. 124, East Jaffrey 03452. This stately, 1850s Greek Revival farmhouse has been meticulously restored. Each of the 10 guest rooms has a private bath and charm of its own, and several work as suites. Our favorite is the upstairs suite (sleeping four) with views out across the fields; another suite, off by itself, is ideal for honeymooners. A full breakfast is served in the large, attractive combination dining room/sitting room. $95–190 double. Two-day weekend minimum in Oct. No children under 10.

The Harrisville Inn (603-827-3163), 797 Chesham Rd., Harrisville 03450. Scottt and Deirdre Oliver own this rambling white-clapboard roadside farmhouse just west of the center of Harrisville (see *Villages*), one of New

England's earliest and most photogenic mill villages. There are five guest rooms, all with private bath. $95–115 includes breakfast.

❦ ☀ ♪ **Auk's Nest** (603-878-3443; auksnest@cs.com), 204 East Rd., Temple 03084. Anne Lunt's 1770s Cape sits at the edge of an apple orchard and is filled with books and antiques. There's a low-beamed living room with a Rumford fireplace; upstairs are three guest rooms, two baths. A newly renovated garden-level efficiency suite can accommodate families. A country breakfast is served in a stenciled dining room or on the screened-in porch overlooking a meadow. From $70 single to $135 double for rooms, $175 for the suite, $25 per extra person, full breakfast included.

In Hillsborough

∞ ☀ "ⵏ" **Stonewall Farm** (603-478-1947; stonewallfarmbandb.com), 235 Windsor Rd., Hillsborough 03244. This imposing farmhouse is a few minutes off Rt. 9 and centuries off the beaten track. Built in 1785, the home crowns a quiet ridge, looking much the same as it probably did when neighbors Franklin Pierce (the only New Hampshire native to serve as president) and his father, Benjamin, used to come calling. Skip and Meg Curtis have researched the home's history, and nearly every room has a framed photo or document evoking its past. There are five guest rooms. A first-floor suite has a gas fireplace and a bath with claw-foot tub, while four attractive upstairs rooms have king or queen beds. The most romantic is the Stowewall Room with a queen-sized, pencil-post canopy bed. On a snowy day we gravitated to the big country kitchen with its blazing, wood-fed Glenwood stove. Breakfast is served in the formal dining room or outside. This is a favored wedding spot in spring when,

Meg tells us, more than 100 lilac trees bloom on the grounds. These add up to 6 acres and include walking paths, good for cross-country skiing in winter. Meg is a serious cook who throws her all into breakfast, included in $120–185 double. She is also a font of suggestions about ways to enjoy the local area. Crated, trained dogs are welcome.

Stone Bridge Farm B&B (603-478-0809), 44 Jones Rd., Hillsborough 03244. This classic Federal brick 1820s mansion was built by a counterfeiter. Abby and Jeff Rand have converted its wooden wing into a two-bedroom apartment, one with its own tasteful sitting room/cooking and dining area. Each of the two guest rooms has a private bath and can be rented either individually or as a unit (but never to two different parties). $175 for either bedroom June–Oct., $150 off-season (except school vacations), includes a full breakfast served in the formal dining room. The house is on a quiet back road, just up from one of the town's famous arched bridges. The property comprises some 300 acres.

In the eastern Monadnock Region

❦ ☀ ♿ **The Inn at Crotched Mountain** (603-588-6840; innatcrotchedmt .com), Mountain Rd., off Rt. 47, Francestown 03043. The 1822 brick farmhouse is now a centerpiece for wooden wings, but it still contains a gracious parlor and two dining rooms. The Pine Room also serves as a small gathering space for guests. The real beauty of this place is its setting at 1,300 feet, high on a ridge with sweeping views. Three of the 13 rooms have working fireplace, and 8 have private bath. Amenities include a pool, sited to take advantage of the view, tennis courts, and cross-country skiing. $85–110 double, including full breakfast served 8–9; holidays and foliage season, $20 more. Closed Apr. and first three weeks of Nov.

✪ 🐾 🐱 ✎ ⁘⸰ **Stepping Stones Bed & Breakfast** (603-654-9048; 888-654-9048; steppingstonesbb.com), Bennington Battle Trail, Wilton Center 03086. This remarkable house—flower and sun filled, at once unusually cozy and airy—is hidden away in a bend off a back road that leads to a picture-perfect old village. Guests enter through a skylit kitchen/sitting room that is one of the most pleasant we know. There are two more sitting rooms. The three upstairs guest rooms are small but cheerful, one with a queen, one with a double, and one with twin beds, all with handwoven rugs and throws and down comforters; all have private bath. A full breakfast is served in the solar garden room, with its many books and plants. The gardens are inviting and extensive, reflecting Ann Carlsmith's training and skill in landscape design. The house is accessed up stone steps and walkways winding through mature plantings, hence the name. The back is terraced, graced with several unusual trees, and usually filled with birds. Breakfast is served on the porch or terrace, weather permitting. Chuckles the coon cat is a permanent resident, and other pets are welcome. $75–85 double occupancy includes a full, imaginative breakfast and tea. Inquire about the nearby waterfall.

OTHER LODGING 🐱 ✎ ⁘⸰ **The Jack Daniels Motor Inn** (603-924-7548; jackdanielsmotorinn.com), 80 Concord St. (Rt. 202 North), Peterborough 03458. An attractive 17-room motel, nicely furnished in cherry with all the comforts: climate control, remote-control cable, and WiFi access. It's just north of town on busy Rt. 202 but positioned with its side to the road to minimize noise. $89–134, depending on season, number of people, and day

of week. Pets are allowed in some rooms for $25 per stay.

∞ **The Grand View Inn & Resort** (603-532-9880; thegrandviewinn.com), 580 Mountain Rd., Jaffrey 03452. Weddings are the specialty at this white brick mansion set off in its own 330 acres at the base of Mount Monadnock. The former stables, just below the inn, house a spa with a full menu of treatments, and **Churchill's**, a restaurant geared to special functions. There are formal living and dining rooms, a large screened porch, and a breakfast room. Guest rooms, divided between the mansion and the neighboring Tom Thumb Cottage, run $100–125 for the three smallest (two with shared bath), $170–175 for the remaining five. Facilities include a pool, outdoor hot tub, and game room. Horses can be boarded in the stables across the road.

Riverside Hotel (603-256-4200; nhriversidehotel.com), 20 Riverside Dr., West Chesterfield 03466. Right on the Connecticut River beside the classic iron bridge connecting Rt. 9 with Brattleboro, Vermont. Built from scratch on the site of the old Riverside Motel, this gleaming new facility has 34 rooms with river views and many balconies. Posted rates are higher, but on a July 4 weekend they were $150–199. Continental breakfast included.

The Little House (603-585-3023; cmfarm.com), 325 Richmond Rd., Fitzwilliam 03447. The Little House is a separate two-story cottage on a road through the woods between Richmond and Fitzwilliam. Andrew and Sherri Walters have renovated the country Victorian building, adding a slate roof and dormers, Rumford fireplace, wraparound porch overlooking the flower garden, and new 1920s-style kitchen complete with icebox and Glenwood stove. The house, rented by the night, weekend, or week, is a romantic get-away. Rates are $175 per night, $310 per weekend, $780 per week. The house is stocked with breakfast fixings, or a full breakfast is prepared.

✳ Where to Eat

DINING OUT

In and around Keene

& **Nicola's Trattoria** (603-355-5242), 39 Central Square, Keene. Open for dinner Tue.–Sun. 5–9; Fri. and Sat. until 10. Reservations recommended. With its open kitchen, chef Nicola Bencivenga's handsome trattoria is elegant. The dinner menu is studded with pasta dishes like ziti della casa (chicken sautéed in olive oil with broccoli rabe, arugula, and portobello mushrooms) or osso buco (thick veal shank simmered with onions, tomato, carrots, celery, and fresh Italian herbs). Everything is made to order with fresh ingredients, and you can taste it. Dinner entrées $20–25.

& **Luca's Mediterranean Café** (603-358-3335; lucascafe.com), 10 Central Square, Keene. Open for lunch (11:30–2) and dinner (5–9) Mon.–Thu.; Fri. and Sat. 5–10. Also Sun. Apr.–Dec. 5–8 PM. Reservations advisable for dinner, and come early to snag a table for lunch. Be prepared for a culinary journey with a menu that translates the flavors of the Mediterranean from simple Italian to elegant French to hearty Moroccan fare. Owner-chefs Luca Parks, a native of Turin, Italy, and his wife Cindy (Swanzey-born) have brought their culinary degrees and New York City experience to this delightful, deep storefront with its creamy mocha walls, white napery (even at lunch), and sidewalk café tables. Dinner entrées might include Moroccan-inspired chicken in phyllo with lemon tahini yogurt sauce, bouillabaisse, and Greek-marinated lamb kebabs; $15–26. Lunch is reasonably priced.

& **Tony Clamato's** (603-357-4345), 15 Court Square, Keene. Closed Mon., otherwise open for dinner and beyond, 4:30 PM–1 AM. Italian trattoria decor and menu with pasta specialties like fettuccine alla Siciliana (egg noodles with prosciutto, mushrooms, and peas) and pollo Gamberi Francese (chicken and shrimp in egg batter, sautéed with lemon, butter, and wine sauce). Entrées $13.95–19.95.

Chesterfield Inn (603-256-3211), Rt. 9, West Chesterfield. Open for dinner every night except Christmas Eve and Christmas Day. Chef Bob Nabstedt has an enviable reputation for imaginative dishes, and the setting is an 18th-century tavern expanded to create one of the most attractive dining areas in the region, with views of Vermont hills. Entrées on a summer menu might range from black bean and baby vegetable ratatouille on wild mushroom risotto ($19) to five-spice-marinated duck breast with tomato and ginger chutney on toasted pistachio wild rice ($29); or, for those with an eye to eating light, an appetizer smoked salmon on a Grafton cheddar and ale cheesecake with fresh chives ($9).

In and around Peterborough

Acqua Bistro (603-924-9905), 18 Depot Square, Peterborough. Open for dinner Tue.–Sat. from 4 PM; Sunday 11–10. Reservations advised. With its chic decor and menu, this restaurant gets rave reviews. In summer dine on the expanded patio overlooking the brook. There are also a variety of sophisticated stone-baked, thin-crust pizzas. In addition to beer and wine, the fully licensed bar offers specialty drinks and marvelous martinis. Expect to spend $80 for dinner for two.

✪ & **Burdick's Bistro and Café** (603-756-2882; burdickchocolate.com), 47 Main St. (next to the post office), Walpole. Open Tue.–Sat. 11:30–9, Sun. brunch 10–2. Closed Mon. off-season. Reservations suggested for brunch or dinner. Chocolatier extraordinaire Larry Burdick and his friend, filmmaker Ken Burns, have transformed the town's former IGA into a destination dining spot. With its warm yellow walls, soft lighting, and artfully placed mirrors, this is as close to a Paris brasserie as you get in New Hampshire. Like the decor, the menu, much of which changes daily, is understated but close to perfect. The "Brasserie Menu," available all day, features soups, artisanal cheeses and pâtés, gravlax, salads, and charcuterie. On a summer day we discovered how good a salad of goat cheese with red and orange beets, walnuts, and greens can be. It came with French bread and oil and a pot of tea with lemon. On winter afternoons the signature hot chocolate is a draw, with or without a scrumptious pastry. Around 5 PM the ambience shifts. White tablecloths appear, and the café morphs into a more formal restaurant. Dinner might be oven-roasted chicken with Calvados and cream, caramelized apple, scallion, whipped and straw potatoes; or maybe a pork chop stuffed with chèvre. The bread is crusty; the wine list, top-notch; the chocolate desserts, to die for. Entrées are $14–22.

BURDICK'S BISTRO AND CAFE

Courtesy, Burdick Chocolate

Aylmer's Grille at the Woodbound Inn (603-532-4949; woodbound.com), 247 Woodbound Rd., Rindge. Open Tue.–Sat for lunch (11–2) and dinner (5–9); Sun. brunch 10:30–2. Reservations recommended. A Culinary Institue of America graduate, chef Aylmer Given grew up around here but worked in many parts of the country before opening Aylmer's, first in 2003 on Main St. in Jaffrey and now at the region's premier resort, which had fallen on hard times until he bought it (with help from friends and family). The stylish restaurant with its open kitchen is now the heart of the renovated inn (see *Lodging*). Given has transformed the place, putting his heart into the design and quality of the inn's stylish restaurant. On a late-winter day dinner entrées included butternut squash ravioli served with toasted almond and caramelized onion cream ($17.95), and grilled beef tenderloin medallions in a wild mushroom sauce flamed with brandy ($25.95). "Small Plates"—such as a ragout of wild mushrooms served with a puff pastry shell, and a corn cake topped with grilled jumbo shrimp—were also available ($7.95–12.95). The Sunday brunch buffet is $19.95, while lunch choices begin at a $9.95 for a cup of soup and half sandwich.

✪ **Sunflowers Café** (603-593-3303; sunflowerscatering.com), 21B Main St., Jaffrey. Closed Tue.; otherwise open for lunch (11–2) and dinner (5–9); brunch Sun. 9–3, and breakfast Sat. 6–9. Carolyn Edwards relocated her popular café from Fitzwilliam to the middle of Jaffrey in spring 2009. It's a real winner with an open kitchen and a bright, spacious dining area. Dinner entrées range from spinach-portobello ravioli ($14.99) to pan-seared duck breast ($22.99), and we hear nothing but raves. At lunch we feasted on the chicken salad of the day

and coveted the sweet potato home fries that came with workman-sized sandwiches ordered by companions at the bar.

Pearl Restaurant and Oyster Bar (603-924-5225), Jaffrey Rd. (Rt. 202), Peterborough. Open for dinner daily. Sequestered in the corner of the small shopping mall just south of the Rt. 101 junction, this upscale Asian fusion restaurant offers elegant decor and rave reviews for its seafood—oysters and otherwise. Make a meal of oysters ($2.15 each) and fish tacos with citrus slaw and chipotle cream ($14.95) or shrimp and tofu noodles ($13.95). Entrées such as soy-marinated grilled pork chops and lemongrass chicken run $17.95–18.95.

The Monadnock Inn (603-532-7800; 877-510-7019; theinnatjaffreycenter.com), 379 Main St., Jaffrey Center. Open for dinner and Sunday brunch except Tue.; also closed Wed. off-season. Known recently as The Inn at Jaffrey Center but recently reverting to the name by which it was known for more than a century. Under any name this classic country inn is sited at the center of one of the Monadnock Region's prettiest villages, not far from the entrance to Monadnock State Park. Under current ownership the focus is on fine dining, with tables filling both the old dining room and the parlor. Menu choices range from vegetarian pastas and seafood dishes to bacon-wrapped beef tournedos and rack of lamb. Entrées $16–24. Sunday brunch $7–12 with similarly priced lunch options. There's also an informal tavern with a pub menu.

🦞 **The Hancock Inn** (603-525-3318), Main St., Hancock village. Open for dinner Tue.–Sat. An 18th-century inn with an award-winning, candlelit, cranberry-colored dining room and a far-ranging menu that usually features grilled rack of lamb and filet mignon and might also include Asian five-spice pomegranate-glazed salmon, or grilled chicken and portobellos stacked with Boursin and served on a twist of angel-hair pasta tossed with fresh basil and tomatoes. Entrées are $19–28. A tavern menu that includes brick-oven-baked thin-crust pizza as well as sandwiches and burgers is available, along with the regular menu, in the genuine old tavern.

○ ☙ **The Birchwood Inn/London Tavern** (603-878-3285; thebirchwood inn.com), Rt. 45, Temple. Main restaurant open for dinner Fri. and Sat. year-round by reservation. Tavern open Wed.–Sun. 5–10:30 and after noon on Sat. and Sun. British-born innkeeper-chefs Andrew and Nick, and their American counterpart Trish, have infused this cozy restaurant and pub with Anglo cheer and cuisine. They dub their menu, which includes steak-and-ale pie and bangers and mash as well as more geographically diverse weekly specials, "a taste of Old England in New England." The charming candlelit dining room is especially noteworthy for its Rufus Porter mural dating to the early 19th century. Entrées are $14.50—but inquire about special dinners, offered regularly.

Del Rossi's Trattoria (603-563-7195), Rt. 137, Dublin. Open for dinner Tue.–Sat. 5–9. This is an Italian trattoria in a pleasant old house just north of Rt. 101. Inquire about scheduled music and poetry readings. Honestly we haven't eaten here, but local patrons we ask give mixed reviews. Homemade pastas are a specialty, as are Italian classics like bisteca and scaloppine with penne pasta Alfredo. Entrées from $19.95 for shrimp and tomato tart.

J. P. Stephens and Tavern on the Pond (603-899-3322), Rt. 202, Rindge. Open for lunch through dinner except Mon. Under new ownership this justly popular landmark, formerly Lilly's on the Pond, has been refurbished but retains the same chef and wait staff. Floors have been sanded and walls painted but the woodstove is still crackling on wintry days and a wall of windows still overlooks the pond. The core of this restaurant was built in 1790 as a sawmill. It's been a restaurant under various names since 1952.

In the eastern Monadnock Region
☙ **Pickity Place** (603-878-1151; pickity place.com), Nutting Hill Rd., Mason. Open year-round daily for three lunch sittings: 11:30, 12:45, and 2. Reserve ahead because there are just 15 tables in this 200-year-old house. Home-grown herbs are the draw here, and you come for "herbal lunches." The set menu changes each month. When we stopped by, it included roasted garlic herb soup; wild mushroom strudel with grilled trout over julienned vegetables with cranberry vin blanc; or Mediterranean spinach fettuccine, along with home-baked breads and dessert. Children can have a Little Red Riding Hood basket of sandwiches and

BIRCHWOOD INN/LONDON TAVERN IN TEMPLE

Chris Tree

fruit; they come to see "Grandmother's bed" in the Red Riding Hood Museum. The five-course luncheon for adults varies each month ($16.95). The gift shop specializing in everything herbal is an attraction in its own right.

In Hillsborough

Nonni's Italian Eatery (603-464-6766; nonnisitalianeatery.com), 17 Main St., Hillsborough. Open for dinner Mon.–Thu. 5–9, Fri.–Sat. until 10; Sun. 5–10. Brooklyn-born owner-chef Matthew Mitnitsky began his career working at Balducci's, then graduated from the Culinary Institute of America before earning additional stripes at such upscale eateries as New York's 21 Club and River Café. Now he and his wife have brought a little bit of Italy to downtown Hillsborough with white-washed walls, a brick pizza oven, a handsome wine bar, and authentic Mediterranean cuisine. Entrées include veal scaloppine in a lemon cream reduction and a wide choice of pastas: $18.99–27.99. Pizza (from $13.99) and gluten-free entrées are also options.

Tooky Mills Pub (603-464-6700; tookymillspub.com), 9 Depot St., Hillsborough. Sun.–Thu. 11:30–9, Fri. and Sat. until 10. Housed in a 150-year-old downtown mill building on the Contoocook River, with seasonal tables on the patio. A local favorite for both lunch and dinner with burgers, sandwiches, and salads at lunch, pastas and pub food such as stuffed chops, bacon-wrapped sirloin, and garlic balsamic steak tips at dinner. Dinner entrées all under $15. Wine, beer, and spirits.

EATING OUT

In and around Keene

✪ ✐ **Pappagallo's** (603-352-9400), 9 Monadnock Hwy., Swanzey (southeast on Keene Rt. 12). Open except Mon. 11–10. An immensely popular family-priced restaurant with varying atmosphere in its several dining rooms and a large Italian-flavored menu. All entrées $15.50 or less, and there are reasonably priced house wines.

The Stage Restaurant (603-357-8339), 30 Central Square, across from the County Courthouse, Keene. Open Tue.–Fri. 11:30 AM–11 PM, Sat. from 8:30 AM; Sun. 8–4. A trendy, family-owned café with a playbill decor and a large menu: burgers, sandwiches, pasta, steaks, and salads. Full bar. Entrées $9.95–15.95. Live jazz on Thursday.

Sakura (603-358-9902), 601 S. Main St., Keene. Open Tue.–Sat. for lunch (11:30–3) and dinner (4:30–9:30; 10:30 on weekends); Sun. noon–9:30. First-rate Japanese fare: sushi, tempura, donburi, and udon (Japanese noodles). Entrées $9.95–14.95, less at lunch.

&. **Thai Garden** (603-357-4567), 118 Main St., Keene. Open daily 11:30–3 and 5–10 for lunch and dinner. An attractive restaurant featuring traditional Thai soups and noodle dishes. Moderately priced luncheon specials.

Keene Fresh Salad Co. (603-357-6677), 44 Main St., Keene. Open Mon.–Sat. Hours vary seasonally. Soups and salads are the specialties with everything made from scratch, from baked goods to soup stocks.

❝❞ **The Market at Luca's** (603-358-3337), 11 Central Square, Keene. Open Mon.–Fri. 9–7, Sat. 10–4. Great grilled panini, salads, and specialty wraps, great value for a quick lunch or take-out.

✐ **Pedraza's Mexican Restaurant** (603-352-3199), 43 Central Square, Keene. Open 11–10, later on weekends. A popular new restaurant with a large south-of-the-border menu with plenty to please, including desserts like "Xango" (fried tortilla filled with cheesecake) and deep-fried vanilla ice cream.

Timoleon's Restaurant (603-357-4230), 27 Main St., Keene. Open daily 6 AM–9 PM. This is the kind of place every town once had: a long counter and booths with better-than-average service, deli and club sandwiches, hot sandwiches, salads, fried haddock, and ham steak with a pineapple ring, served with salad, a roll, and potato. Like all Keene restaurants, it's now smoke-free, and we're told business has picked up as a result.

Elm City Brewing Co. (603-355-3335), 222 West St., Keene. Open daily for lunch and until 11 PM Mon.–Thu., until midnight on Fri. and Sat.; Sun. 11:30–8:30. In the Colony Mill, a large, attractive brewpub with its own ales, draft, and a large, varied, and reasonably priced menu.

Audrey's (603-3316), Rt. 101, Marlborough. Open Tue.–Fri. 7–2, Sat., Sun. 8–3, closed Mon. Destination breakfasting on the weekend for folks from miles around (try the New England French toast, stuffed with apples and cheese) and a good bet any day for lunch. Built in the 1920s as "Esquimo Lodge," it has the feel of a longtime local favorite. Come early to snag a booth. Specials the day we lunched included a terrific asparagus omelet.

Lindy's Diner (603-352-4273), 19 Gilbo Ave., just off Main St. across from the bus station, Keene. Open daily 6 AM–8 PM, Fri. until 9. The same quick and hearty fare that's been a staple of this location for decades. Good pies and take-out ice cream.

Eva's Bakery & Café (603-242-3044), on the common, Rt. 12, Troy. Open Thu.–Sun. 6–6, otherwise 7–4. Eva Duz is a true pastry chef and offers elaborate cakes as well as breads, morning croissants as well as muffins, soups, and sandwiches. There are tables, and coffees are on tap.

Thistle & Crown Tavern at the Fitzwilliam Inn (603-585-9000; historicfitzwilliaminn.com), on the common, Rt. 119, Fitzwilliam. Open Thu.–Sat. for dinner. As we go to press, the inn has been open just six, mostly winter months and plans call for more hours. The handwritten menu includes pizza, grilled pork chop with sauerkraut and applesauce, and grilled T-bone veal steak with salad. There's a wood fire in the brick hearth by the bar, and tables are scattered through adjoining parlors. Inquire about live music on Saturday; Thursday is open mike.

Mt. Pisgah Diner (603-239-4101), 18 Main St., Winchester. Open Mon.–Fri. for early breakfast through lunch; Sat., breakfast only. An authentic 1930 Worcester diner (#769) that's sparkling clean and pridefully maintained by Joni Otto. The food's not bad, either! We went for the kielbasa omelet but might have sampled sausage gravy over biscuits with two eggs and home fries.

Murray's, Walpole village. Open daily 6 AM–3 PM. Walpole's longtime local hangout, this is the kind of place where everyone looks up when a stranger walks in. But that's okay; the

MT. PISGAH DINER, WINCHESTER

Chris Tree

food is great. On a summer day the pepper pot soup and fresh fruit cocktail were splendid.

& **Walpole Village Tavern Restaurant & Bar** (603-756-3703), 10 Westminster St., Walpole village. Open Mon.–Sat. 11:30–9. Closed Sun. The menu offers the usual suspects—soups, salads, sandwiches, burgers, wraps, and panini. At dinner you can go anywhere from a quesadilla or pulled-pork basket to Delmonico steak ($8.99–21.99). There's also a kids' menu and full bar.

Casey J's (603-585-9577), junction of Rts. 12 and 119, Fitzwilliam. Open for all three meals except on Mon. Good road food.

In and around Peterborough
Note: Also see **Sunflowers Café** in Jaffrey under *Dining Out*, a great lunch spot that can be very reasonably priced for dinner as well.

Harlow's Pub (603-924-6365), 3 School St., Peterborough. Open daily noon–9, bar open until 1 AM. A funky, lively middle-of-town gathering space with good pub food and frequent, live entertainment, some outdoor tables.

Nature's Green Grocer (603-924-2233), 374 Union St. in the Union Mill, West Peterborough. Open Mon.–Fri. 9–7, Sat. 9–6. A health food store with an organic café in back, good for freshly made soups and "handcrafted" sandwiches plus salads like "farmhouse apple," maybe strawberry spinach. There are tables inside, but the payoff is the back riverside patio.

Lee & Mt. Fuji at the Boiler House (603-924-7770), 50 Jaffrey Rd. (Rt. 202), Peterborough. Open except Tue., 11–9:30. Mount Fuji is, of course, the Japanese mountain that's the world's most frequently climbed, after which Mount Monadnock ranks second. The moderately priced menu offers a mix of Indian as well as Chinese and Japan-

ese dishes. The restaurant, which offers a view of a waterfall, fills an attractive space in a former mill building that has been home to a series of restaurants in recent years.

✍ **Aesops Tables at the Toadstool Bookshop** (603-924-1612), 12 Depot Square, Peterborough. Open except Sun. 9–4. An inviting corner of this outsized bookstore. The blackboard menu lists sandwiches and café fare like bagels, raspberry squares, and Brazilian chocolate cake. There's a play corner for small fry and a choice of gourmet coffees on tap.

Nonies (603-924-3451), 28 Grove St., Peterborough. Open Mon.–Sat. 6 AM–2 PM, Sun. 7 AM–1 PM. Doughnuts made daily, full breakfasts, soups, sandwiches, local gossip.

The Peterborough Diner (603-924-6202), Depot St., Peterborough. Open daily 7AM–8 PM. A 1950s green-and-yellow diner featuring dependable diner food including homemade soups, pies, daily and nightly specials, beer. Choose the counter or wooden booth.

✍ **Cantine Mexican Kitchen** (603-924-3883; cantinemex.com), Monadnock Community Plaza, Rt. 202 just south of its junction with 101. Open for lunch, dinner, and Sunday brunch. Closed Mon. Family-friendly and priced, a cheerful venue for a variety of tacos, burritos, and quesadillas as well as soups and salads. Dinner entrées include Mexican pot roast and roast chicken with pecan-dried plum mole. New in 2009, this is under the same ownership as the neighboring Pearl Restaurant and Oyster Bar (see *Dining Out*).

Twelve Pine (603-924-6140; twelve pine.com), Depot Square, Peterborough. Open Mon.–Fri. 8–7, Sat. 9–6, Sun. 9–4. The aroma is a mix of coffee, spices, and baking, which—combined with the array of salads, quiches, cal-zones, and soups—is something to savor before deciding on any one thing. This former train depot is now filled with delectable deli and baked items, cheeses, and Italian ices; also specialty foods, flowers, fruit, and wine to take home. Small tables are scattered throughout; or dine outside on one of the two porches or the patio—a great place to people-watch.

Grand Finale Bakery & Café (603-532-5678), junction of Rts. 202 and 124, Jaffrey. Open 6:30–5 weekdays, 8–2 weekends, longer in summer. Just the spot for bagels and muffins with a wide choice of brews, also build-your-own panini and deli sandwiches.

Fiddleheads Café (603-525-4432), 28 Main St., Hancock. Open Mon.–Sat. 8 AM–8 PM, Sun. 8–3. This café in the middle of Hancock village offers gourmet-to-go plus an attractive sitting room designed for patrons to simply read and relax. Sherry Williams serves several daily soups as well as scones and muffins, pizzas and calzones, and coffees and teas. Local art on the walls is for sale.

✪ **Harrisville General Store** (603-827-3138), 29 Church St., Harrisville. Open Mon.–Sat. 8–6, Sun. 8–2. Owned by Historic Harrisville, this old brick store is more a place to eat than to shop, a great option in this historic mill village. There's an open kitchen and blackboard menu with soups, salads, sandwiches, and apple cider doughnuts, made fresh each morning. The Monday daily special is polenta casserole with Italian sausage or wild mushrooms, Tuesdays it's chicken pot-pie or shepherd's pie, and so on. In warm weather customers tend to spill over to tables and picnic sites by the neighboring millpond.

Brady's American Grill (603-924-9322), Rt. 202 North, Peterborough.

Open daily for lunch and dinner with a sports bar and good food: burgers, sandwiches, salads, pasta, and a surprising choice of dinner entrées. Beer and wine served.

Dublin General Store (603-563-8410), 1257 Main St. (off Rt. 101 by the post office). Open Mon.–Sat. 6–8, Sun. 6–5. Good, reasonably sandwiches, pizza on Thursday.

In the eastern Monadnock Region
✪ **The Melting Pot** (603-654-5150), 47 Main St., Wilton, off Rt. 101. Open Wed.–Fri. for lunch 11–2, dinner Wed.–Sat. 5–8. Worth finding even for lunch, this family-owned freestanding restaurant at the center of the village is a real find, with an attractive ambience and a menu that brings in a full house most days—but especially for dinner before first-run vintage and art films shown across the street in the town hall. For lunch, there's a variety of pizzas, salads, burgers, and other sandwiches. Moderately priced dinner entrées change weekly. Chef Mark Worcester works in the open kitchen and his wife, Cynthia, greets patrons. Lunch specials might include cauliflower cheddar and scallion potato

PETERBOROUGH DINER

Chris Tree

pancake, or mushroom and Swiss quiche, both with salad. Our sautéed pork tenderloin ($12.95) was topped with a creamy green peppercorn sauce and was delicious. Specials might also include wolf fish Veronique and mushroom ravioli. Beer, wine, and cordials.

𝒮 Gary's Harvest Restaurant (603-654-9969), Rt. 101, West Wilton. Open 6:30–3, until 8:30 PM Fri.–Sat., from 7 AM Sun. A classic road-food source with welcoming booths by the windows and a counter with TV, friendly service. Specials included beef stew over biscuits on the day we lunched on the chicken salad sandwich and a cup of soup. In business over 35 years with a loyal following. Ice cream and take-out in-season.

Alberto's (603-588-6512). Rt. 31, Bennington. Open daily at 5 PM. A red-sauce Italian place with a big menu that includes 11 kinds of pizza, garlic bread, and 19 Italian dishes like manicotti, lasagna, and chicken cacciatore.

Union Street Grill (603-672-4180), 4 Union St., Milford. Open Mon.–Fri., 6–2, Sat. until 1, Sun. until 12:30. After honing his culinary skills at area restaurants, Milford native Kevin Stephens headed home a few years back and opened this cheery restaurant just beyond the center of town. The yellow-and-blue color scheme features a chicken motif, in keeping with the restaurant's specialty omelets. Folks from around the area consider it a good stop for lunch as well.

SNACKS Ava Marie's Handmade Chocolates and Ice Cream (603-924-5993; avamariechocolates.com), 43 Grove St. in the Grove Village Shoppes, Peterborough. No ordinary chocolates these, and we've heard their turtles are "to die for."

German John's Bakery (603-464-5079), 5 West Main St., Hillsborough.

Open year-round Wed.–Sat. 9:30–5; also on Sun. and Tue., July–Christmas. Closed Mon. Best known for their authentic German soft pretzels, but the soft sweet almond and raisin are also worth trying. Or sample a slice of kuchen or streusel, then bring home a loaf of bread.

Kimball Farm Ice Cream, Rt. 124 at Silver Ranch, Jaffrey. Open Apr.–Oct., 10 AM–9 PM. A Massachusetts import, delicious in every conceivable flavor.

&. Burdick's Bistro and Café (603-756-2882; burdickchocolate.com), 47 Main St. (next to the post office), Walpole. See *Dining Out*. The café is great for midafternoon teas, coffees, rich hot chocolate, and sinful pastries—like "the Burdick," layers of almond wafers and rum ganache, topped with white chocolate and pistachio.

Walpole Grocery (603-756-9098), 47 Main St. Open Mon.–Sat. 8–8, Sun. 10–5. A few doors down from Burdick's, this upscale little market offers fabulous breads, local cheeses, and a deli—a good picnic source.

Walpole Creamery (603-445-5700), 532 Main St. (Rt. 12), Walpole. Fresh, creamy ice cream made from scratch, one batch at a time, from local cows. Open daily noon–8.

✳ Entertainment

LECTURE AND PERFORMANCE SERIES 🕭 Amos Fortune Forum Series (amosfortune.com), Jaffrey Center Meeting House. Ongoing since 1947, the Forum continues the legacy of this fine old venue by providing free speakers from around the area on topics of interest, Friday evenings at 8 in July and Aug.

Monadnock Summer Lyceum (603-924-6245; monadnocklyceum.org), Unitarian Church, Main St., Peterborough. Originally established in 1828, the Lyceum offers free programs by well-known speakers, often people who live or vacation in the region, every Sunday in July and Aug. at 11 AM.

MUSIC 🐾 ♿ Apple Hill Chamber Players (603-847-3371; 800-472-6677; applehill.org), Apple Hill Center for Chamber Music, Apple Hill Rd., East Sullivan. The Apple Hill Summer Chamber Music School attracts 275 participants of all ages; inquire about free weekly concerts by faculty (Tue. at 7:30 PM) and students (check current calendar) in June, July, and Aug.; all concerts are in the hilltop Apple Hill Concert Barn. This noted group also performs throughout the country and the world.

Monadnock Music (603-924-7610; 800-868-9613; monadnockmusic.org), Peterborough. This is a prestigious summer series of concerts and orchestra performances, many of them free, staged by highly professional artists in churches and meetinghouses throughout the region, from the Walpole Unitarian Church to Marlow's Jones Hall, the Unitarian Church in Wilton Center, and the Jaffrey Center Meeting House. A subscription series is available for those performed at the Town House in Peterborough.

The Peterborough Folk Music Society (603-827-2905), P.O. Box 41, Peterborough 03458, features performances by talented new as well as legendary folk musicians. Performances are at the Union Congregational Church, 33 Concord St. (Rt. 202). Call ahead to join in a potluck dinner. Tickets are available by mail or by credit card at ticketstage.com/PFMS. Cash and checks only at the door.

🐾 Temple Band (603-878-2829), said to be the oldest town band in the country, performs at the Sharon Arts Center, the Jaffrey Bandstand, and a

number of scheduled festivities throughout the summer. Past masters of oompah-pah.

🐾 Jaffrey Bandstand. Performances Wed. evenings in summer.

Walpole Common. Free Sun. concerts 7–8:30 PM during July and Aug.

LIVE THEATER Peterborough Players (603-924-7585; peterborough players.org), 55 Hadley Rd., Peterborough. Since 1933 this professional group has performed everything from Will Shakespeare to Tom Stoppard. One of New England's better-known summer theaters, presenting five to seven plays, often with well-known Broadway and Hollywood talent, each summer in a renovated, air-conditioned 19th-century barn. In winter the Metropolitan Opera live in HD is a popular draw on a 10-by-16-foot screen.

The Colonial Theatre (603-352-2033; thecolonial.org), 95 Main St., Keene. A majestic, magical old theater featuring big-name performers and Broadway road companies plus a schedule of current and classic films.

The Arts Center on Brickyard Pond at Keene State College in Keene and Franklin Pierce College in Rindge.

MONADNOCK MUSIC STAGES DOZENS OF PERFORMANCES THROUGHOUT THE REGION.

MacDowell Colony (603-924-3886; macdowellcolony.org), 100 High St., Peterborough. This is the country's oldest and arguably most prestigious artists' retreat. Since its founding in 1907 by the noted American composer Edward MacDowell and his wife, Marian, it has offered some 6,000 artists in a range of disciplines the freedom to create in supportive and inspiring surroundings.

Colony fellows have won more than 60 Pulitzer Prizes as well as many other major awards. Famous residents have included Thornton Wilder, Leonard Bernstein, Edward Arlington Robinson, James Baldwin, Willa Cather, Aaron Copland, Alice Walker, Jonathan Franzen, Michael Chabon, and many more. Some artists—like Robinson, who was in residence 24 times—bonded for life with the colony, while others also embraced the Monadnock Region. Wilder used Peterborough as the model for the typical New England community in his enduringly popular play *Our Town*, and Cather, who grew up in Nebraska, chose to be buried in the old graveyard in Jaffrey Center.

The colony had its beginnings in 1896 when the MacDowells bought Hillcrest Farm in Peterborough where they spent summers and he felt he did his best work. A few years later, to give her husband more seclusion, Marian built a rustic log cabin on a wooded hillside. Still standing, it became the inspiration for the 32 studio cabins now scattered around the 450-acre property. A year before his death in 1908 the couple had the then-novel idea of creating an interdisciplinary community where artists could enjoy the company of their peers while working in the beautiful, peaceful surroundings that had so inspired Edward. To

HEINZ STUDIO INTERIOR

Courtesy, MacDowell Colony

that end they deeded Hillcrest to the newly created Edward MacDowell Association, which still runs the colony. Marian MacDowell, who died in 1956 at the age of 98, resumed her musical career as a pianist—specializing in interpretations of her late husband's work—to raise funds for the new colony, which became nationally known as "The Peterborough Idea." She spent the rest of her life working on the colony's behalf and is buried on the grounds with Edward.

Although well-known philanthropists such as Andrew Carnegie were supporters, the most consistent support in the early years came from women's clubs and musical organizations. From the beginning women have been an important part of the colony. Indeed, the first so-called Colonists, who arrived in 1907, were two sisters: sculptor Helen Farnsworth Mears and writer Mary Mears. Originally a summer community, the colony is now open year-round. Typically, there are 20 to 30 artists in residence.

EDWARD MACDOWELL   Courtesy, MacDowell Colony

To protect the privacy of the artists, the MacDowell Colony is closed to the public. An exception is the annual Medal Day, usually the second or third Sunday in August, when the Edward MacDowell Medal is presented to a creative artist who has made an outstanding contribution to American culture. The award is rotated among writers, visual artists, and composers. A presentation address is given by a noted authority in the medalist's discipline. Medal Day usually attracts hundreds of spectators, most of whom picnic on the grounds before the ceremony. After the presentation address, artists open their studios to the public for a few hours to display and discuss their work.

The colony also has an outreach program called MacDowell Downtown, a series of presentations in downtown Peterborough on the first Friday of the month from March to November. Programming includes film screenings, readings, concerts, talks, and more. All presentations are free to the public and listed in the "At MacDowell" column in the *Monadnock Ledger-Transcript*.

Both stage musical, theatrical, and dance performances. Check local listings.

✍ **Andy's Summer Playhouse** (603-654-2613; andyssummerplayhouse .org), Wilton. An innovative theater program begun 35 years ago to foster creative collaborations between children and professional artists working in a variety of media: performance art, theater, dance, music, puppetry, video, set and lighting design, and playwriting. Frequent performances in July and Aug. in the old Grange Hall in Wilton Center.

FILM ✪ **Wilton Town Hall Theatre** (603-654-3456), 40 Main St., Wilton. This genuine gem is hidden away upstairs in Wilton's ornate 1886 town hall, a vaudeville stage before 1912, when it began showing silent films. Since 1973 it has been operated by its dedicated film-buff owner, Dennis Markaverich. A small sign on the street lists current movies, usually a mix of first-runs and art films. Well-worn steps lead to the second floor, where the large theater seats 250 in well-spaced rows facing a curtained stage. Across the hall, beyond the counter with its fragrant popcorn, a smaller screening room seats 60. Inquire about Saturday-afternoon classic and silent films (shown with an accompanying keyboardist). Tickets are $6 adults, $4 children and seniors, free if you can answer the film-buff question of the day. There's usually plenty of parking on the street.

The Colonial, Keene. See *Live Theater*.

Peterborough Community Theater (603-924-2255; movies.com), Depot Square, Peterborough.

Milford Drive-in (603-673-4040; milforddrivein.com), 531 Elm St.

(marked from Rt. 101/101A), Milford. One of New England's few surviving drive-ins, open seasonally.

✳ Selective Shopping

The area is studded with shopping finds, ranging from unusual crafted items and antiques to exceptional chocolates.

ANTIQUARIAN BOOKSHOPS
Bequaert Old Books (603-585-3448; beqbooks.com), 37 Rt. 119 West, Fitzwilliam. Open Apr.–Nov., weekdays 9–5, weekends 11–5. Closed on Wed. In the vintage barn beside their house near the Fitzwilliam village green, the Bequaerts stock some 45,000 titles, including technical books as well as volumes on mountaineering, fiber arts, and cookbooks.

MindFull Books & Ephemera (603-532-8300), 29 Main St., Jaffrey. A mix of antiques and antiquarian books with the coffeepot always on and an invitation to browse and gab.

Eagle Books (603-357-8721), 19 West St., just off Central Square, Keene. Open Wed.–Sat. 11–5; 12,000 volumes specializing in WPA writers' project books and New Hampshire town histories.

Homestead Bookshop (603-876-4213), Rt. 101 just east of Marlborough village next to the Marlborough Country Store. Open weekdays 9–5, weekends until 4:30 every day but Christmas and Thanksgiving. They stock some 45,000 volumes specializing in Americana, children's art, New England local history.

Hurley Books (603-399-4342; hurley books.com), east side of Rt. 12 (just north of Rt. 63), Westmoreland. Open by appointment or chance; 35,000 volumes specializing in religion, farming, and gardening.

ANTIQUES Listing the more than 50 antiques stores in the Monadnock Region would simply be confusing. Be it said that antiquing is big but composed of many small shops, thickest in the Jaffrey and Fitzwilliam areas. Free, frequently updated flyers describing these shops and their whereabouts are available locally. Pick up the pamphlet guide *In Peterborough*. **The Red Chair** (603-924-5953) in Depot Square offers distinctive antiques, accessories, and jewelry featured in national publications and TV shows.

Bloomin' Antiques (603-585-6688), open Thu.–Sun., has been in business more than 30 years and remains the anchor for several other dealers on and around the village green in *Fitzwilliam*, which remains the venue for the region's largest, most colorful **Antiques Show** in mid-July; details at fitzhistoricalsociety.org. *In Jaffrey:* **Seaver & McLellan Antiques** (603-532-8500; smantiques.net), 2 Main St., a large and eclectic collection that ranges from classic furnishings to a table that perches atop a life-sized carved hippo. *In Keene:* **Antiques at Colony Mill** (603-358-6343; colonymill.com), 222 West St., open daily 10–9, 11–6 Sun. A major destination for antiques buffs with some 75 dealers. **Antiques & Collectibles Mall of New England** (603-878-0606; antiquesandcollectiblesmall.com), 8 Dunster Ave. (Rt. 45), Greenville, provides good hunting grounds for table linens, china, glassware, and silver. **New Hampshire Antique Coop** (603-673-8499; nhantiquecoop), 323 Elm St. (Rt. 101A), Milford, is another major complex, with 200 dealers. **Knotty Pine, Inc.** (603-352-5252), Rt. 10, West Swanzey, generally holds auctions every Thursday. *In Peterborough:* The Depot Square Outdoors Antiques Mart is held Sunday in-season.

The Directory of New Hampshire Antiques Dealers, available from most chambers of commerce and antiques shops, lists dozens of dealers in this area.

ART GALLERIES Sharon Arts Center Gallery (603-924-7878), 30 Grove St., Peterborough. Open Mon.–Sat. 10–5, Sun. noon–5. A showcase for the best current art and craft work in this creative corner of the state. The gallery, running a block through from Grove St. to Depot Square, displays a wide variety of original art in many media. This is also a great place to shop for quality gifts ranging from toys to jewelry. Workshops and studio space are at the center's original locale in Sharon.

New England Art Exchange (603-355-9906; neartexchange.com), 29 Central Square, Keene. Open Mon.–Sat. 11–4:30, or by appointment. Ken Spector and Jane Larmon have been buying and selling fine prints and period paintings from this location since 1989. They specialize in the Cornish Colony and other artists, primarily from the mid-19th to the mid-20th centuries.

BLOOMIN' ANTIQUES, FITZWILLIAM

Chris Tree

Peterborough Fine Art (603-924-7558), Depot Square, Peterborough. Open year-round, Tue.–Sat. noon–5. A serious gallery specializing in 19th- and early-20th-century landscape paintings, especially those of the Dublin Art Colony, also some contemporary work.

Peterborough Art Academy and Gallery (603-924-4488), Depot Square, Peterborough. Regional artists' gallery, children's and adult classes, summer art camp and art supplies.

BOOKSTORES The Toadstool Bookshop (603-924-3543), 12 Depot Square, Peterborough; the Colony Mill (603-352-8815), Keene; and Lorden Plaza (603-673-1734) in Milford. Outstanding bookstores with a wide range of general titles, including many regional and art books. Under *Eating Out* note Aesops Tables, a café in the immense Peterborough store (a former A&P).

Yankee Publishing, Rt. 101, Dublin Village. Open 8:30–5. The home of *Yankee Magazine* and *The Old Farmer's Almanac* offers a friendly front office selling books, magazines, and calendars. Browsers welcome.

Also see *Antiquarian Bookshops.*

CRAFTS Frye's Measure Mill (603-654-6581), 12 Frye Mill Rd., Wilton.

HARRISVILLE DESIGNS IS HIDDEN INSIDE ONE OF HARRISVILLE'S MILLS

Chris Tree

Open Tue.–Sat. 10–5, Sun. noon–5 most of the year. Closed Tue. in winter but open seven days a week from the day after Thanksgiving to Dec. 22. The seven-room shop is housed in part of a 19th-century mill that retains its original machinery, some still water powered to make Shaker boxes and woodenware. Quilts and coverlets, salt-glaze pottery, and other country folk art items are also sold. Inquire about tours.

Harrisville Designs (603-827-3996; harrisville.com), Harrisville. Open Tue.–Fri. 10–5:30, Sat. till 5. Handweaving looms are designed and made here, priced from $700 to $5,000. Check out the new children's weaving looms and kits. A variety of yarns and weaving accessories are also sold in the Weaving Center, housed in an 1850 brick storehouse by the millpond. Inquire about used looms.

Gibson Pewter Shop (603-464-3410; gibsonpewter.com), 18 E. Washington Rd., Hillsborough Center. Open Mon.–Sat. 9–5; Sun. by chance. The shop is a 200-year-old barn in the picturesque village of Hillsborough Center, and Jon Gibson is the second generation of his family to craft the family's highly rated pewter in traditional and contemporary designs.

Sharon Arts Center Gallery(603-924-7256), Depot Square, Peterborough. This is the region's leading craft shop, *the* place to pick up a distinctive, hand-crafted gift or accessories for your wardrobe and home. See *Art Galleries.*

Hannah Grimes Marketplace (603-352-6862), 46 Main St., Keene. Open daily. A major outlet for 250 artisans, craftspeople, cooks, and farmers, all in New Hampshire.

Walpole Artisans Cooperative (603-756-3020; walpoleartisans.org), 52 Main St., Walpole. Open Wed.–Sat. 11–6, Sun. 11–3. Painting, woodworking, pottery, wearables, and much more. This shop showcases work by artists and artisans on both sides of the river within easy commute. An annual open studio tour is held the weekend after Thanksgiving.

Chrysalis Farm (603-352-7878; chrysalisfarmstudiogallery.com), 129 Westport Village Rd., Swanzey. Check for hours. Some 40 artists and craftspeople, also special shows and events.

Granite Lake Pottery (603-847-9908), Rt. 9, Munsonville. Open year-round, Tue.–Sat. 10–4. Hand-thrown dinnerware and accessories from mugs to lamps and bathroom sinks (the sinks are a specialty).

Country Artisans (603-352-6980), 53 Main St., Keene. Offers a wide selection of crafts produced in New England and beyond.

SPECIAL STORES

In the Peterborough Area

✿ **Eastern Mountain Sports** (603-924-7231; ems.com), 1 Vose Farm Rd., off Rt. 202 North, Peterborough. Open Mon.–Thu. and Sat. 9–6, Fri. 9–8, Sun. 11–5. Founded in 1967 and specializing in quality and hard-to-find equipment and clothing for backpacking and climbing enthusiasts, EMS now has 50 stores across the country. This is the corporate headquarters and one of the largest stores, one with a discount corner. Pick up a pamphlet guide to hiking and other outdoor sports possibilities in the Monadnock Region.

Peterborough Basket Co. (603-371-9020), 130 Grove St. (south of Rt. 101). Open daily 9–5, Sun. 1–5. The showroom is impressive and prices are reasonable, but the real fun of this outlet is the seconds room with its bins of baskets and major markdowns on large items like woven hampers. Basketmaking has been an important industry in

Peterborough since the 1850s, and this company traces its origins to 1875.

Joseph's Coat Peace Crafts (603-924-6683), 15 Depot Square, Peterborough. Colorful clothing, jewelry, shawls, alpaca yarn, quilts, puppets, and gifts from around the world. Fair Trade goods.

The Renaissance Room (603-924-7934), Depot Square, Peterborough. Jacqueline Perry owns this boutique featuring high-style clothing and wearable art. It's the place to find that special outfit or accessory for women who don't mind standing out in a crowd.

Steele's, 40 Main St., Peterborough. In business since 1860, the nicest kind of stationery, card, and generally useful supply store.

In Walpole

Burdick's Chocolate (603-756-2882; burdickchocolate.com), 47 Main St. (next to the post office), Walpole. Exquisite, hand-cut chocolates are crafted from French Valrhona chocolate without extracts or flavorings in the small shop, then shipped to the best Manhattan restaurants and customers throughout the country. We can attest to the quality of the mocha square and white pepper truffle. Burdick's signature is a chocolate mouse, handmade with toasted almond ears. Combined with the excellent bistro and bakery (see *Dining Out*), this is a must-stop.

Ruggles & Hunt (603-756-9607; rugglesandhunt.com), 8 Westminster St., Walpole. Open Mon.–Sat. 11–6. Tucked in behind the gas station, this is an urbane country store bursting with colorful and unusual gifts, household furnishings, and men's, women's, and children's clothing and accessories from around the world—things you never realized you needed and suddenly do.

SHOPPING COMPLEX Colony Mill Marketplace (603-357-1240; colonymill.com), 222 West St., Keene. Open daily 10–9, Sun. 11–6. This 19th-century brick woolen mill now offers the region's most interesting, weather-proofed shopping, featuring specialty shops. There's a food court and an attractive brewpub, Elm City Brewing Co.; a Toadstool Bookshop and the vast, multidealer Antiques at Colony Mill are the anchors.

FARMS, PICK-YOUR-OWN, CUT-YOUR-OWN Cut your own Christmas tree at **Farmstead Acres** (603-352-8730) in Westmoreland, **Wright's Tree Farm** (603-352-4033) in Keene, and **Zahn's Berry and Christmas Tree Farm** (603-673-1908), 211 Jennison Rd. in Milford.

Barrett Hill Farm (878-2351), Barrett Hill Rd., Mason. Strawberry fields forever, daily 8–6, from mid-June into July.

Alyson's Orchard (603-756-9800; 800-856-0549; alysonsorchard.com), Wentworth Rd., Walpole. Some 500 acres of fruit trees cover this beautiful hilltop overlooking the Connecticut River Valley. Heritage-variety apples,

RUGGLES & HUNT, AN URBANE COUNTRY STORE IN WALPOLE

Chris Tree

peaches, pears, blueberries, raspberries, hops, and firewood are available at the farm stand in-season. This is also a site for weddings, corporate retreats, and more (see *Lodging*).

High Hopes Orchard (603-399-4305), 582 Glebe Rd., Westmoreland. Raspberries in July, blueberries in July and Aug., apples in Sept. and Oct., and pumpkins (wagon rides) in Sept. and Oct.; gift shop, cider, homemade pies, apples, doughnuts, and apple gift packs Aug.–Dec.

Maple Lane Farm (603-352-2329), 220 Gunn Rd., Keene. PYO apples—dwarf trees make it easy. Also cider, pumpkins, and seasonal specialties. Call for times.

Rosaly's Farmstand (603-924-7774; rosalysgarden.com), Rt. 123 just south of Rt. 101, Peterborough. Open mid-May–mid-Oct., daily 9–6. Thanks to reader Alexandra Kelly for her recommendation of Rosaly Bass's you-pick flower and herb gardens and farm stand featuring organic vegetables, most grown on the property. Rosaly also sells hand-painted T-shirts, maple syrup, and muffins, cakes, and bean salads on which you can picnic with a view of the fields and Mount Monadnock.

Monadnock Berries (603-242-6417; monadnockberries.com), 545 West Hill Rd., Troy. Open mid-July–mid-Sept., daily 8–7. With 9,000 PYO bushes, they offer "berry big" pickin's of blueberries, raspberries, black and red currants, and gooseberries, with a spectacular mountain view.

FARM STANDS Barrett's Greenhouse and Farm Stand (603-352-8665), Rt. 32, Swanzey. Bedding plants, perennials, vegetables, pumpkins, produce, and floral bouquets throughout summer and fall.

Butternut Farm (603-673-2963), 483 Federal Hill Rd., Milford. Open

July–Sept., daily 8–6. Named for the tree, not the squash, this farm offers a lovely setting to cut your own floral bouquets, with annuals ranging from asters to zinnias. There are also veggies for sale in the barn.

Chauncey Farm (588-2857), 3 Old Concord Rd., Rt. 202, Antrim. Open mid-July–Halloween, 10–6. Cut your own flowers in summer; in fall, come for straw bales, gourds, Indian corn, mums, and sunflowers plus a variety of fall vegetables. A host for the annual Columbus Day weekend Wool Arts Tour.

Tenney Farm (603-588-2020; tenney farm.com), 1 Main St. (Rt. 202), Antrim. A locally popular source of seasonal fruits and vegetables, plus chicken and duck eggs year-round.

HERBS Harvest Thyme Herbs (603-563-7032; harvestthyme.com), 91 Dooe Rd., Dublin. The handsome post-and-beam barn showroom is open mid-Oct.–Dec., 10–5. Herbal baskets, dips, and related gift items.

Pickity Place (603-878-1151), Nutting Hill Rd., Mason. A large herb garden and gift shop, catalog. (Also see *Dining Out* and *Villages.*)

Red Oak Farm (603-585-9052), 487 Royalston Rd., Fitzwilliam. Herb and perennial plants, dried herbs and flowers, wreaths.

Sage Knoll (603-478-5461), 955 E. Washington Rd., Hillsborough. Open Memorial Day–Labor Day, Tue.–Sat. 10–4. Herbs and perennials, specializing in hardy, farm-grown plants, old-fashioned and colonial varieties.

WINE AND CHEESE Walpole Mountain View Winery (603-756-3948; bhvineyard.com), 114 Barnett Hill Rd., Walpole. Susan Carter has planted more than 1,000 hardy grapevines on the hillside beside her home, one with a glorious view west to Vermont. The tasting room/shop is open seasonally. Call before coming.

Boggy Meadow Farm (877-541-3953; boggymeadowfarm.com), 13 Boggy Meadow Lane, Walpole; marked from Rt. 12. The dairy farm has been in the Cabot family since 1820, and Powell Cabot was one of the first local farmers to begin producing artisanal cheeses. These are made by hand twice a week in the barn across from the dairy parlor, using raw milk and vegetable rennet that pasteurizes naturally during the 60-day curing process. Call ahead to make sure the retail shop is open. The drive along the river to the shop is a treat in itself. Otherwise you can buy the cheese at Walpole Grocery (see *Snacks*).

SUGARING Maple sugaring season in the Monadnock Region is Mar.–mid-Apr., but farmers may not be "boiling" (40 gallons of sap boil down to 1 gallon of syrup) every day, so phone ahead to make sure there's something to see— and something to eat. Most maple producers offer "sugar parties": sugar-on-snow (usually crushed ice these days) and maybe the traditional accompaniment (a pickle). Most sell a variety of maple products year-round. Call the New Hampshire Maple Phone (603-225-3757) or visit nhmaple producers.com for an updated report on the season.

Parker's Maple Barn (603-878-2308; parkersmaplebarn.com), 1316 Brook-line Rd., Mason. Open Valentine's Day–Christmas, Mon.–Fri. 8–2, Sat. and Sun. 7–4. The specialty here is obvious—pancakes, waffles, French toast—whatever conduit you prefer to heap on the maple syrup, which is made on the premises. For lunch, you can continue the theme with maple baked beans or maple BBQ ribs, or break out and order from a selection of soups, salads, sandwiches, and moderately priced entrées. There's a covered bridge, nature walk, and sugarhouse to add to the barnboard-rustic ambience.

Bascom's Sugar House (603-835-6361), Sugar House Rd. between Alstead and Acworth off Rt. 123A. One of the largest maple producers in New England, a huge sugarhouse and warehouse set high on Mount Kingsbury. Visitors are welcome to tour the plant, which uses unusual reverse-osmosis evaporators. Open year-round weekdays and Sat. mornings.

Ben's Sugar Shack (603-924-3177), 83 Webster Hwy., Temple. Ben Fisk gives tours of his sugarhouse and sells syrup, cream, and candy.

Clark's Sugar House (603-835-6863), 14 Currier Rd., Alstead. Award-winning syrup boiled over a wood fire. Maple treats and free tours. Will ship.

Stonewall Farm (603-357-7278; stonewallfarm.org), 242 Chesterfield Rd., Keene. Gift shop open year-round. A sap-gathering contest in-season features up to 20 teamsters and their draft horse teams; call for dates.

Stuart & John's Sugar House and Pancake Restaurant (603-399-4486), 19 Rt. 63 at the junction of Rt. 12, Westmoreland Depot. Open weekends (7–3) in spring (Feb.–Apr.) and fall (Sep.–Nov.). A family business for more than 40 years. Plenty of people drive up from Boston to sample their four different kinds of pancakes and several grades of syrup. The family farm spreads across a rise above the Connecticut River. Syrup is sold year-round from the house beside the sugar house.

✳ Special Events

February: Keene's annual **Ice and Snow Fest** features ice sculptures and a carving contest.

April: **"Greenerborough" Green Living Expo & Festival**, Sat. before Earth Day (April 22), Peterborough.

May: **Spring concert**, Monadnock Chorus and Orchestra.

✐ *Mid-May:* **Children and the Arts Festival**, Peterborough.

June–September: **Peterborough Players Summer Theater**.

Late June: The annual **Rock Swap** in Gilsum (behind the elementary school on Rt. 10) attracts 8,000 to 10,000 mineral buffs.

July–August: **TGIF Summer Music Series** in Depot Park, Peterborough. Also see *Entertainment* for more music, theater, and lecture series.

July–September: **Monadnock Music Concert Series** (see *Entertainment*).

Fourth of July: The most unusual July 4 celebration around is perhaps held July 3 in **Greenville**: At midnight all the bells and sirens in town ring and residents march down Main Street banging pots and pans, leading a parade that includes fire engines, floats, and baby carriages. In **Peterborough** the Fourth is also a gala celebration. Stoddard's annual **Olde Home Days** includes a tour of some of the town's early homes.

Third week of July: **Fitzwilliam Antiques Fair**, more than 40 dealers.

Third weekend of July: The Old Homestead, a pageant/play, is performed in the Potash Bowl, a natural amphitheater in Swanzey. **Balloon Fest and Fair**, Hillsborough. **Monadnock Festival of the Arts**, Peterborough.

August: **Oak Park Festival**, Greenfield. **Medal Day**, MacDowell Colony, Peterborough (a public picnic and open house). **Old Home Days**, Hancock.

September: **Labor Day Festival**, Francestown. Annual **Balloon**

NHDTTD/photographer

KEENE'S ANNUAL PUMPKIN FESTIVAL FEATURES MORE THAN 1,000 LIGHTED, HAND-CARVED JACK-O'-LANTERNS.

Festival, Monadnock Travel Council. Annual **Music Festival** in Keene.

October: Keene's **Pumpkin Festival** has made national news in recent years: Two 40-foot-high scaffold pyramids are erected on Main Street to display more than 1,000 lighted, hand-carved jack-o'-lanterns. **Foliage Festivals** are also held in Francestown and Greenfield. **Antique Auto Show** and **Octoberfest** at Crotched Mountain Foundation. German music, food, and classic cars. Annual **Book Fair**, Mac-Dowell Colony, Peterborough. Also **Into Peterborough**, an annual shopping festival during the "peek" of this Currier and Ives community's foliage season on the Saturday after Columbus Day. Biannual **Monadnock Festival of Quilts**, Monadnock Quilters Guild. **Wool Arts Tour** of farms and crafts studios in the Francestown-Antrim-Hillsborough area.

November: **Monadnock Music Christmas Fair**, South Meadow School, Peterborough.

December: **Christmas teas** at the Sharon Arts Center. **Messiah Festival** at Franklin Pierce College. **Monadnock Chorus Christmas Concert** at Peterborough Town House.

The Connecticut River Valley

4

UPPER VALLEY TOWNS

LOWER COHASE

Ct. River Joint Commissions

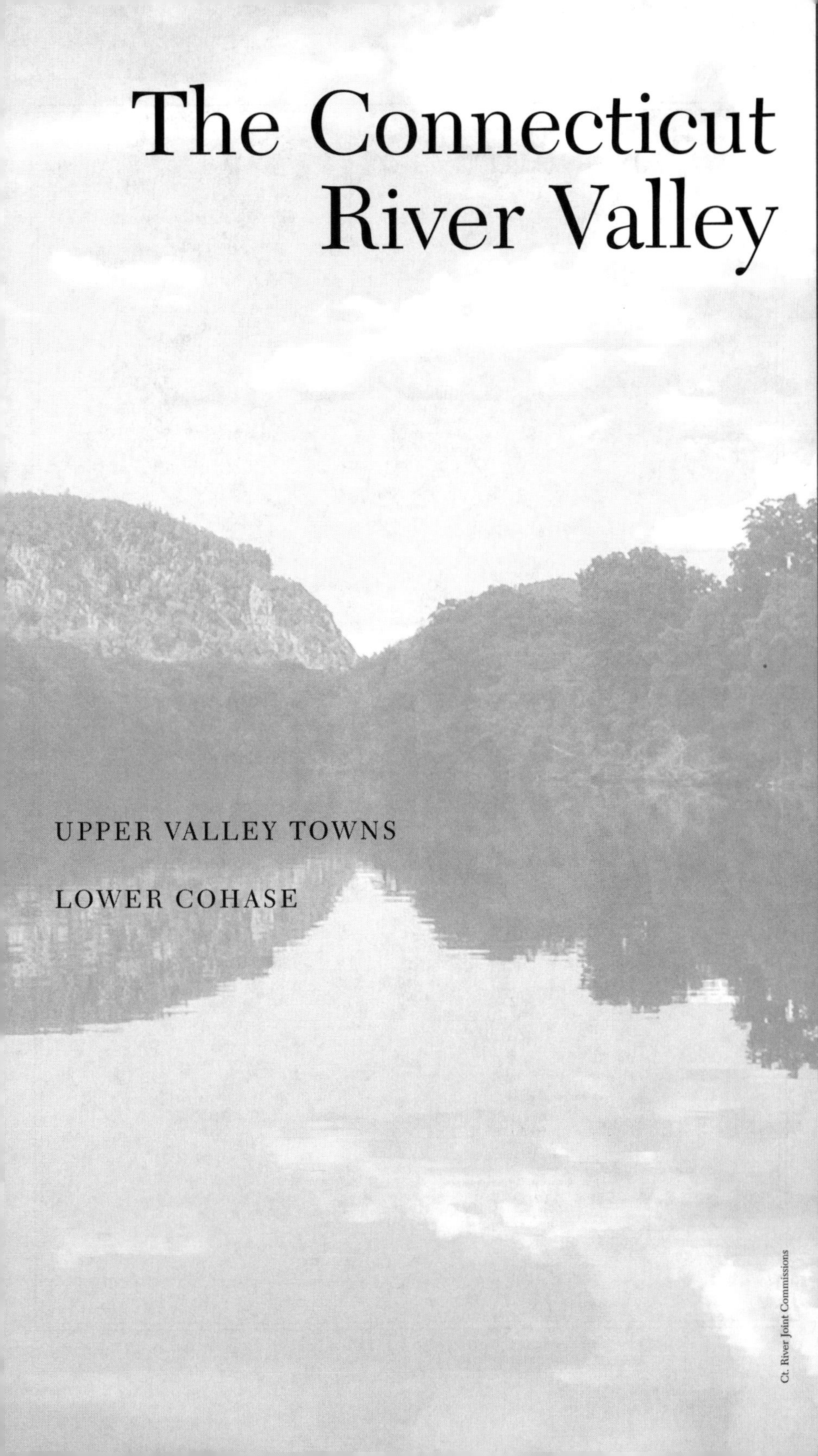

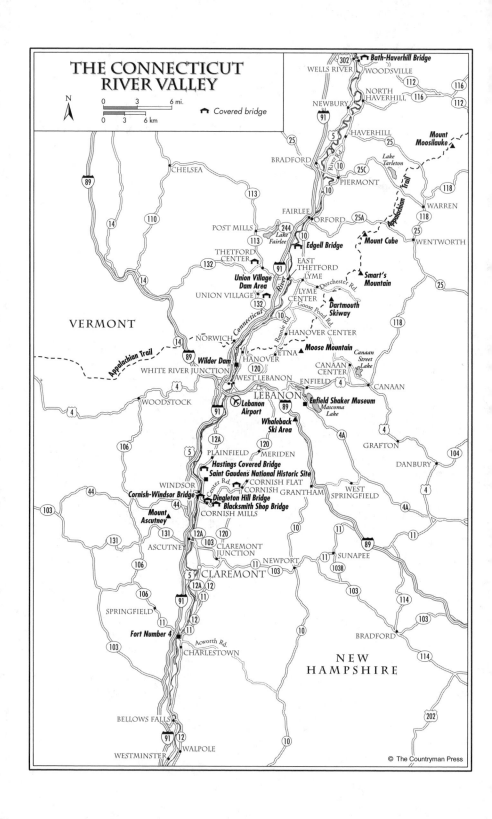

THE CONNECTICUT RIVER VALLEY

N

0   3   6 mi.
0   3   6 km

🏠 *Covered bridge*

VERMONT

NEW HAMPSHIRE

Bath-Haverhill Bridge

302
WELLS RIVER   WOODSVILLE
112
NORTH
HAVERHILL   116   116
116   112
NEWBURY
91
5   HAVERHILL   25   *Mount Moosilauke*
25
BRADFORD   River Rd.   25C
Lake Tarleton
PIERMONT   118
10

CHELSEA
113   WARREN
89
FAIRLEE   25A   118
14   110   POST MILLS   244   ORFORD   118
113   Lake Fairlee   10   *Mount Cube*   25
THETFORD   Edgell Bridge   WENTWORTH
CENTER   132   EAST
14   91   THETFORD   *Smart's Mountain*
Union Village   LYME   Dorchester Rd.   25
Dam Area
UNION VILLAGE   132   LYME   *Dartmouth Skiway*
CENTER   Goose Pond Rd.   118
10
HANOVER CENTER
NORWICH   Rennie Rd.   *Moose Mountain*
89   Wilder Dam   ETNA   Canaan Street Lake
WHITE RIVER JUNCTION   HANOVER   CANAAN
120   CENTER
WEST LEBANON   ENFIELD   4
4   LEBANON   CANAAN
WOODSTOCK   91   Lebanon   Enfield Shaker Museum
Airport   89   Mascoma Lake   4
4   Whaleback
106   Ski Area   GRAFTON
12A
PLAINFIELD   120   104
5   MERIDEN
Hastings Covered Bridge   DANBURY
Saint Gaudens National Historic Site   WEST   4
WINDSOR   Center Rd.   CORNISH FLAT   SPRINGFIELD
Cornish-Windsor Bridge   CORNISH   GRANTHAM   4A
44   Dingleton Hill Bridge
103   *Mount   44   Blacksmith Shop Bridge
Ascutney*   CORNISH MILLS   10   11
131   12A   120   11   89
ASCUTNEY   103   CLAREMONT   11   SUNAPEE
106   JUNCTION   NEWPORT   103B
5   CLAREMONT   103   103
SPRINGFIELD   12A   12   114
106   11   103
91   11
12   10   BRADFORD
Fort Number 4   11
103   Acworth Rd.   114
CHARLESTOWN
NEW
HAMPSHIRE
202

BELLOWS FALLS
91   12
WESTMINSTER   WALPOLE   10

© The Countryman Press

INTRODUCTION

The Connecticut River flows 410 miles from its high source on the New Hampshire–Quebec border to Long Island Sound in the state of Connecticut. What concerns us here are its 270 miles as a boundary—and bond—between the states of New Hampshire and Vermont. Defying state lines, it forms one of New England's most beautiful and distinctive regions, shaped by a shared history.

Judging from 138 archaeological sites along this stretch of the river, its banks have been peopled for many thousands of years. Evidence of sizable Western Abenaki villages have been found at Newbury, Vermont; at Claremont, New Hampshire; and at the Great Falls at present-day Bellows Falls. Unfortunately, these tribes, along with those throughout the "New World," were decimated by disease contracted from English traders.

By the late 17th century English settlements had spread from the mouth of the Connecticut up to Deerfield, Massachusetts, just below the present New Hampshire–Vermont border. In 1704 Deerfield was attacked by French and Indians, who killed 40 villagers and carried off more than 100 as captives to St. Francis, a full 300 miles to the northwest. This was one in a series of bloody incidents drily dismissed in elementary schools as "the French and Indian Wars."

Recent and ongoing scholarship is deepening our sense of relationships among Frenchmen, Western Abenaki tribespeople, and Englishmen during the first half of the 18th century. By 1700 many settlers had adopted the canoe as a standard mode of travel and, according to Dartmouth professor Colin G. Calloway in *Dawnland Encounters*, in 1704 New Hampshire passed a law requiring all householders to keep "one good pair of snow shoes and moqueshens [moccasins]." Settlers and Abenaki traded with each other. Beaver remained the prime source of revenue for the settlers, and the Indians were becoming increasingly dependent on manufactured goods and alcohol. Both at Fort Dummer—built in 1724 in what, at the time, was Massachusetts (now Vernon, Vermont)—and at the Fort at No. 4, built 50 miles upriver in 1743 in present Charlestown, New Hampshire, settlers and Indians lived side by side. Unfortunately, during this period former friends and neighbors also frequently faced each other in battles to the death. In 1759 Major Robert Rodgers and his Rangers retaliated for the many raids from the Indian village of St. Francis (near Montreal) by killing many more than 100 residents there, including many women and children. The suffering of "Rodgers' Rangers" on their winter return home is legendary. A historic marker on Rt. 10 in Haverhill, New Hampshire, offers a sobering description.

Ct. River Joint Commissions

KAYAKING, BRUNSWICK, VT

After the 1763 Peace of Paris, France withdrew its claims to New France and English settlers surged up the Connecticut River, naming their new communities for their old towns in Connecticut and Massachusetts: Walpole, Plainfield, Lebanon, Haverhill, Windsor, Norwich, and more.

This was, however, no-man's-land.

In 1749 New Hampshire governor Benning Wentworth had begun granting land on both sides of the river (present-day Vermont was known as "The New Hampshire Grants"), a policy that New York governor George Clinton refused to recognize. In 1777, when Vermont declared itself a republic, 16 towns on the New Hampshire side opted to join it. In December 1778, at a meeting in Cornish, New Hampshire, towns from both sides of the river voted to form their own state of "New Connecticut," but neither burgeoning state was about to lose so rich a region. In 1779 New Hampshire claimed all Vermont.

In 1781 delegates from both sides of the river met in Charlestown, New Hampshire, and agreed to stick together. Vermont governor Chittendon wrote to General Washington asking to be admitted to the Union, incorporating towns contested both by New Hampshire and New York. Washington replied: Yes, but without the contested baggage.

In 1782 New Hampshire sent 1,000 soldiers to enforce their jurisdiction. Not long thereafter Washington asked Vermont to give in—and it did. Needless to say, the river towns were unhappy about this verdict.

The Valley itself prospered in the late 18th and early 19th centuries, as evidenced by the exquisite Federal-era (1790s–1830s) meetinghouses and mansions still to be seen in river towns. With New Hampshire's Dartmouth College (established 1769) at its heart and rich floodplain farmland stretching its length, this valley differed far more dramatically than today from the unsettled mountainous regions walling it in on either side.

The river remained the Valley's highway in the early 19th century. A transportation canal was built to circumvent the Great Falls at present-day Bellows Falls, and

Samuel Morey of Orford, New Hampshire, built a steamboat in 1793. Unfortunately Robert Fulton scooped his invention, but the upshot was increased river transport—at least until the 1840s, when railroads changed everything.

"It is an extraordinary era in which we live," Daniel Webster remarked in 1847, watching the first train roll into Lebanon, New Hampshire, the first rail link between the Connecticut River and the Atlantic. "It is altogether new," he continued. "The world has seen nothing like it before."

In places the railroad totally transformed the landscape, creating towns where there had been none, shifting populations from high old town centers like Rockingham, Vermont, and Walpole, New Hampshire, to the riverside. This shift was most dramatic in the town of Hartford, where White River Junction became the hub of north–south and east–west rail traffic.

The river itself was put to new uses. It became a sluiceway down which logs were floated from the northern forest to paper mills in Bellows Falls and farther downriver. Its falls had long powered small mills, but now a series of hydro dams were constructed, including the massive dam between Barnet, Vermont, and Monroe, New Hampshire, in 1930. This flooded several communities to create both Comerford Reservoir—and the visual illusion that the Connecticut River stops there. At present 16 dams stagger the river's flow between the Second Connecticut Lake above Pittsburg, New Hampshire, and Enfield, Connecticut, harnessing the river to provide power for much of the Northeast. By the 1950s the river was compared to an open sewer and towns turned their backs to it, depositing refuse along its banks.

Still, beyond towns, the river slid by fields of corn and meadows filled with cows. In 1952 the nonprofit Connecticut River Watershed Council was founded to "promote and protect wise use of the Connecticut Valley's resources." Thanks to the 1970s Clean Water Act and to acquisitions, green-ups, and cleanups by numerous conservation groups, the river itself began to enjoy a genuine renewal. Visitors and residents alike discovered its beauty; campsites for canoeists were spaced along the shore. At present kayaks as well as canoes can be rented along several stretches.

The cultural fabric of towns on either side of the river has remained close knit and, although many bridges were destroyed by the hurricane of 1927, the 21 that survive include one of the longest covered bridges in the United States (connecting Windsor, Vermont, and Cornish, New Hampshire). It's only because tourism promotional budgets are financed by individual state taxes that this stretch of the river valley itself has not, until recently, been recognized as a destination by either New Hampshire or Vermont.

Happily, a respected nonprofit, bistate group, the Connecticut River Joint Commissions—founded in 1989 to foster bistate cooperation and protect the Valley's resources—has stepped into this breach, with dramatic results. It has now spawned the Connecticut River Scenic Byway Council dedicated to, among other things, creating an infrastructure to identify appropriate places in which to promote tourism and the cultural heritage.

At this writing nine "waypoint" information centers are salted along the river. Those in Brattleboro, Bellows Falls, Claremont, Windsor, White River Junction, Wells River, Haverhill, St. Johnsbury, and Colebrook are serving visitors and in the process restoring the Connecticut to its rightful place as the centerpiece of a genuine region. Their work has been enhanced by the federally funded Silvio O.

Conte National Fish and Wildlife Refuge, which seeks to preserve the quality of the natural environment within the entire Connecticut River watershed. For a sense of wildlife and habitat in this area, stop by the Montshire Museum (the name melds both state names) in Norwich, Vermont.

The Connecticut River corridor is now officially "the Connecticut River National Scenic Byway." We are proud to note that for the past 20 years both our *New Hampshire* and *Vermont Explorer's Guides* have included an Upper Valley section describing both sides of the river. Visually visitors see a river, not state lines. While Interstate 91 on the Vermont side is conduit for through traffic, Rt. 5 in Vermont and Rts. 10 and 12A along the New Hampshire bank are genuinely scenic byways, threading historic towns, farm stands, local scenic spots, and the river, close at hand. Access to the river via canoe and kayak has increased in recent years, thanks to both outfitters and conservation groups that maintain launch areas and campsites.

Within this chapter prime sights to see shift from one side of the river to the other; the same holds true for places to eat, stay, hike, and generally explore this very distinctive region. Of course in this book we focus primarily on New Hampshire while in *Vermont: An Explorer's Guide* the focus is more detailed on that state.

As the River Flows, an excellent film on view in the Waypoint Visitors Center at the Amtrak station in Bellows Falls, Vermont, is a great introduction to the lower 40-mile stretch of the river between the two states.

Please note: In this edition we have repositioned Walpole (see page 144), across the river from Bellows Falls, in "The Monadnock Region." This very special village, a destination in its own right, is a part of both regions, and travelers approaching the Upper Valley up I-91 should allow time to explore it. (Take Exit 5 off I-91 to Rt. 12 and follow signs.)

GUIDANCE **ctrivertravel.net**, an excellent, noncommercial website covering the entire stretch of the Connecticut shared by Vermont and New Hampshire, is main-

COMERFORD DAM, BARNET, VT.

Ct. River Joint Commissions

tained by the **Connecticut River Scenic Byway Council**. Also look for "way-

point" information centers serving both sides of the river, described under *Guidance* in ensuing chapters.

Helpful pamphlet guides available from the **Connecticut River Joint Commissions** (603-826-4800; crjc.org) include:

Explorations Along the Connecticut River Byway of New Hampshire and Vermont (a map/guide).

Connecticut River Heritage Trail (a 77-mile driving/biking tour for the historically and architecturally minded).

RECOMMENDED READING *Proud to Live Here in the Connecticut River Valley of Vermont and New Hampshire* by Richard J. Ewald with Adair D. Mulligan, published by the Connecticut River Joint Commissions (crjc.org).

Confluence: A River, Politics, and the Fate of All Humanity by Nathaniel Tripp (Steerforth Press, Hanover, NH).

This American River: Five Centuries of Writing About the Connecticut by Walter Wetherell (University Press of New England, Hanover, NH).

Where the Great River Rises: an Atlas of the Connecticut River in Vermont and New Hampshire by the Connecticut River Joint Commissions (University Press of New England, Hanover, NH).

UPPER VALLEY TOWNS

The Upper Valley ignores state lines to form one of New England's most rewarding and distinctive regions.

Upper Valley is a name coined in the 1950s by a local daily, *The Valley News*, to define its two-state circulation area. The label has stuck, interestingly enough, to the group of towns that back in the 1770s tried to form the state of "New Connecticut." The Dartmouth-based, pro–New Connecticut party was, however, thwarted (see the introduction to "Connecticut River Valley").

In 1769 Eleazar Wheelock had moved his Indian school—which had been funded through appeals made by Mohegan preacher Samson Occum in England and Scotland to "spread Christian knowledge among the Savages"—from Lebanon, Connecticut, to Hanover, New Hampshire. Initially Dartmouth College recruited Indian students, but the school also served whites and the percentage of Native Americans quickly dwindled.

The Valley itself prospered in the late 18th and early 19th centuries, as evidenced by the exquisite Federal-era meetinghouses and mansions still salted away along the Connecticut. The river was the area's only highway in the 18th and early 19th centuries and was still a popular steamboat route in the years before the Civil War.

The Upper Valley phone book includes towns on both sides of the river, and Hanover's Dresden School District reaches into Vermont. This was the first bistate school district in the United States. Several Independence Day parades start in one state and finish across the bridge in the other. The Montshire Museum, founded in Hanover but now in Norwich, Vermont, combines both states in its very name.

Dartmouth College in Hanover remains the cultural center of the Upper Valley. With the nearby Dartmouth-Hitchcock medical complex and West Lebanon shopping strip, this area forms the region's hub, handy to the highways radiating, the way rail lines once did, from White River Junction, Vermont. North and south of the Hanover area, old river towns drowse and the river roads are well worth finding.

GUIDANCE

Listed from south to north

Greater Claremont Chamber of Commerce (603-543-1296; claremontnh chamber.org), Moody Building, 24 Opera House Square, Claremont, N.H., is open weekdays 8:30–4:30. It's housed in the city's central, most distinctive building. Pick

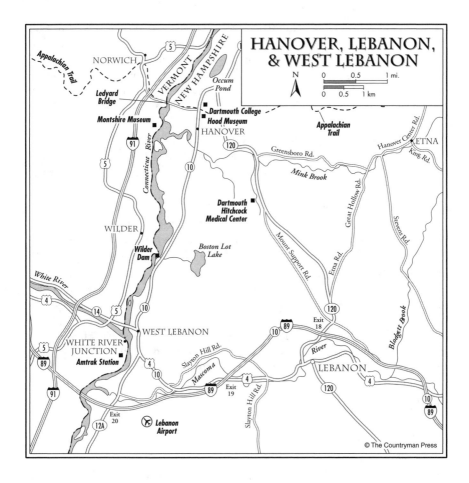

up a walking guide. No public restrooms. A new Waypoint Visitors Center on North St. (Rt. 11/103) offers restrooms but minimal visitors info and no visitors staffing.

Windsor Welcome Center (802-674-5910), 3 Railroad Ave., Windsor, Vt. Hidden down by the Windsor Station Restaurant, off Main St. Open weekdays 10–2.

The Greater Lebanon Chamber of Commerce (603-448-1203; lebanon chamber.com), 1 School St. (next to the post office), Lebanon, N.H., is open weekdays 9–5 and maintains a seasonal information center across the street in Colburn Park (8:30–4:40).

White River Junction Welcome Center (802-281-5050; hartfordchamber.com) 100 Railroad Row in the Amtrak station, White River Junction, Vt. Open 10–4 except Sun.

Hanover Chamber of Commerce (603-643-3115; hanoverchamber.org), 216 Nugget Arcade Building, Main St., Hanover, N.H., welcomes visitors weekdays 9–5 and maintains a seasonal (early June–Sept.) information booth on the Dartmouth green.

GETTING THERE *By car:* Interstates 91 and 89 intersect in the White River Junction Vt.–Lebanon N.H. area, where they also meet Rt. 5 North and South on the Vermont side; Rt. 4, the main east–west highway through central Vermont; and Rt. 10, the river road on the New Hampshire side. From New York and points south the way to Claremont, Cornish, and Plainfield is I-91 to Vt. Exit 8 in Ascutney, then Rt. 103 west to Claremont or Rt. 5 north to Windsor and across the covered bridge to Rt. 12A in Cornish.

By bus: "1" **Dartmouth Coach** (603-448-2800; 800-637-0123; dartmouthcoach .com) stops at the Hanover Inn and at the Dartmouth Region Transportation Center, 90 Etna Rd., Lebanon, with service to Boston and Logan Airport and to Stanford, Connecticut, and NYC.

By air: The **Lebanon Regional Airport** (603-298-8878; flyleb.com), West Lebanon (marked from the junction of I-89 and Rt. 10), has frequent service to Boston and New York/White Plains via Cape Air (flycapeair.com). Rental cars are available from Avis, Hertz, and Alamo; the airport is also served by **Big Yellow Taxi** (603-643-8294).

By train: **Amtrak** (800-872-7245) serves Claremont, N.H., Windsor, Vt., and White River Junction, Vt., en route to and from New York/Washington and Essex Junction, Vt. Connecting bus service to Montreal.

MEDICAL EMERGENCY Dartmouth-Hitchcock Medical Center (603-650-5000), off Rt. 120 between Hanover and Lebanon, is generally considered the best hospital in northern New England. **The Valley Regional Hospital** (603-542-1822), 243 Elm St., Claremont, also offers 24-hour emergency service.

Call **911**.

✳ Communities

Listed from south to north

Charlestown (pop. 4,929) was a stockaded outpost during the French and Indian Wars. Its Main St. was laid out in 1763, 200 feet wide and a mile long, with more than five dozen structures that now make up a national historic district; 10 buildings predate 1800. Note the 1840s Congregational church; the former Charlestown Inn (1817), now a commercial building; the vintage-1800 Stephen Hassam House, built by the great-grandfather of impressionist painter Childe Hassam; and the Foundation for Biblical Research, housed in a 1770s mansion. At this writing the reconstructed stockade and museum, The Fort at No. 4, is closed.

Claremont (pop. 13,344). Massive textile mills and machine shops line the Sugar River as it drops 300 feet from the city's compact core around Opera Square. At this writing the mills are being rehabbed. Opera Square retains some magnificent 1890s buildings, notably the massive Italian Renaissance Revival–style city hall with its magnificent and well-used second-floor **Opera House**, and the Moody Building, built originally as a hotel in 1892. Adjoining Pleasant St. is lined with shops. The mammoth brick **Monadnock Mills** on Water St. (off Broad and Main) on the Sugar River are among the best-preserved small 19th-century urban mills in New Hampshire; note the 1840s gambrel-roofed brick Sunapee Mill across the river and the small brick overseers' cottages (also 1840s) on Crescent St. The railroad was an essential contributor to Claremont's industrial and cultural heyday. It remains an Amtrak stop. The **Claremont Historical Society** (603-543-1400), 26

Mulberry St., is open June–Sept., Sun. 2–. A walking tour pamphlet is available from the chamber of commerce. **West Claremont** (3 miles west on Rt. 103) is a vanished village graced by New Hampshire's oldest Episcopal and Catholic churches. It seems that the Catholic priest who founded St. Mary's parish in 1824 was the son of the Episcopal rector who built St. John's across the street. Both buildings are interesting architecturally. The only sign of the congregations that both men taught and served is the West Part Burying Ground adjoining the church

Cornish. In the 1880s these riverside hills were far more open, mowed by thousands of sheep, but the wool bubble had already burst and farms were selling cheap. Many were bought by artists and writers, friends of sculptor **Augustus Saint-Gaudens** whose home is now a National Historic Site. By the turn of the 20th century 40 families had bought old farms or built homes in Cornish and neighboring Plainfield. This "Cornish Colony" included artists, writers, and other creative and wealthy bohemians, prominent in their own right. It also included artist Ellen Wilson, whose husband, President Woodrow Wilson, spent a portion of the summers of 1914 and 1915 here at the home of writer Winston Churchill (note the historic marker near the Plainfield–Cornish line). Best remembered of the artists is Maxfield Parrish (1870–1966), in whose honor an 11-mile stretch of Rt. 12A in Cornish and Plainfield has recently been named the Maxfield Parrish Highway.

Plainfield. A one-street village, Plainfield still clings to the memory of onetime resident Maxfield Parrish. In the 1920s Parrish painted a stage set in the **Plainfield Town Hall** picturing Mount Ascutney and the river in the deep blues for which he is famous. Stop by the vintage-1798 building, open Sunday. You might also want to follow **River Rd.,** where you'll find produce at local farms.

Enfield (pop. 4,618). On the eastern edge of the Upper Valley, wedged between I-89 and Rt. 4, Enfield is best known for Mascoma Lake and as the home of a former Shaker community, one that's commemorated in the impressive five-story Great Stone Dwelling built in 1837 and now the **Enfield Shaker Museum**. The Shakers arrived in 1793 and established their "Chosen Vale" on the southwestern shore of the lake; it grew to include several "families." They packaged seeds and made brooms and brushes, spinning wheels and furniture. To ship these products they constructed the 1849 bridge across the lake, linking their communities with the railroad in Enfield, where the commercial center evolved. The **La Salette Brothers** (603-632-4301) maintain a shrine and center adjacent to the Shaker Museum. Also see **Shaker Bridge Theatre** in *Entertainment*.

CLAREMONT MILLS

Chris Tree

Lebanon (pop. 14,000). As near to the junction of I-91 and I-89 as it can be while still on the New Hampshire (no-sales-tax) side of the Connecticut River, "West Leb" is the shopping center of the Upper Valley. The strip of

malls is a good bet for most basics, and the **Powerhouse Mall** (north of I-89) offers some pleasant surprises. Positioned between the Connecticut River and Mascoma Lake, with old mills lining the Mascoma River, Lebanon itself—once you find it (east on Rt. 4)—is a city with a small-town feel. The common is circled by handsome buildings—a vintage-1828 church, substantial homes, and public buildings, including an opera house—and is the site of summer band concerts. Shops and restaurants are found along adjoining traffic-free streets.

White River Junction (pop. 2,569; whiteriverjunction.org) is one of five villages within the town of Hartford, Vt. As noted in this chapter's introduction, downtown White River—which at its peak saw 100 steam locomotives chug into the station daily—is now a bit of cul-de-sac. Still, it's well worth finding. **Northern Stage**, a professional theater company, performs year-round in the old Briggs Opera House. The Tip Top building, a former commercial bakery, is honeycombed with artists' studios, and there is natural food co-op, some interesting shops, a choice of restaurants, and the groundbreaking **Center for Cartoon Studies** (a two-year program with a library endowed by Charles M. Schulz, creator of *Peanuts*). The station itself is a seasonal departure point for the **White River Flyer** (see *To Do*). Follow the walkway along the tracks to the free **Main Street Museum** (802-356-2776; mainstreetmuseum.org), open Thu.–Sat. 1–6. Housed in a former firehouse, this "cabinet of curiosities" seems a parody of the museum genre. Owner David Fairbanks (as in St. Johnsbury's Fairbanks Museum) Ford's exhibits include Elvis Presley's gallstones and an eclectic range of stuffed and "found" objects. Check the website for ongoing events. At the center of the village is the **Hotel Coolidge** (see *Lodging*), one of the last of New England's railroad hotels. In its former incarnation as the Junction House, the hotel's clientele included Lillian Gish and President Calvin Coolidge, for whose father it is named. Ask to see the hand-painted murals in the Vermont Room, depicting the state's history from wilderness to the 1940s. Lovingly preserved by its present owners, the Coolidge is rich in character, something conspicuously absent from the interstate-geared, brand-name motels and fast-food stops along the village periphery.

Hanover is synonymous with Ivy League **Dartmouth College** (dartmouth.edu), chartered in 1769 and one of the most prestigious colleges in the country. Dartmouth's student population averages 4,300 undergraduate men and women and 600 graduate students. Its handsome buildings frame three sides of an elm- and maple-lined green, and the fourth side includes a large inn, an arts center, and an outstanding art museum. The information booth on the green is the starting point for historical and architectural tours of the campus. **Baker Memorial Library**, a 1920s version of Philadelphia's Independence Hall, dominates the northern side of the green. Visitors are welcome to see a set of murals, *The Epic of American Civilization*, by José Clemente Orozco, painted between 1932 and 1934 while

DARTMOUTH COLLEGE

Hanover Chamber of Commerce

he was teaching at Dartmouth. (Some alumni once demanded these be removed or covered because of the Mexican artist's left-wing politics.) In the Treasure Room (near the western stair hall on the main floor), Daniel Webster's copies of the double elephant folio first edition of John Audubon's *Birds of America* are permanently displayed. The **Hopkins Center for the Arts** was designed by Wallace Harrison a few years before he designed New York's Lincoln Center (which it resembles). It contains three theaters, a recital hall, and art galleries for permanent and year-round programs of plays, concerts, and films. It's also home base for the Dartmouth Symphony Orchestra. **Dartmouth Row**, a file of four striking white Colonial buildings on the rise along the eastern side of the green, represents all there was to Dartmouth College until 1845. You might also want to find **Webster Cottage** (603-646-3371), N. Main St., Memorial Day–Columbus Day, Wed., Sat., and Sun. 2:30–4:30, maintained as a museum by the Hanover Historical Society. Built in 1780 as the home of Abigail Wheelock (daughter of Dartmouth founder Eleazar Wheelock), it was also the senior-year (1801) residence of Daniel Webster and birthplace in 1822 of Henry Fowle Durant, founder of Wellesley College. The vintage-1843 **Shattuck Observatory** (603-646-2034) is open weekdays 8:30–4:40, also Tue. and Thu. evening by reservation. Don't miss the **Hood Museum**, and allow time to explore downtown Hanover, which compresses an ever-expanding wealth of places to eat and to shop within a few walkable streets.

Lyme is known for its splendid **Congregational church**, completed in 1812, a Federal-style meetinghouse complete with Palladian window, an unusual tower (three cubical stages and an octagonal dome), and no fewer than 27 numbered horse stalls. The gathering of buildings, including the inn, fine old houses, and general stores, is one of New Hampshire's most stately. There's good shopping, dining, and lodging. Take **River Rd.** north by old farms and cemeteries, through an 1880s covered bridge.

Orford is known for its **Ridge Houses**, a center-of-town lineup of seven houses so strikingly handsome that Charles Bulfinch has been (erroneously) credited as their architect. They were built instead by skilled local craftsmen using designs from Connecticut Valley architect Asher Benjamin's do-it-yourself guide to Federal styles, *The Country Builder's Apprentice.* These houses testify to the prosperity of this valley in the post–Revolutionary War era. Each was built by an Orford resident—with money earned in Orford—between 1773 and 1839. The best remembered of the residents is Samuel Morey. While all his neighbors were in church one Sunday morning in 1793, Morey gave the country's first little steam-powered paddle-wheeler a successful test run on the river. Sam kept tinkering with the boat and in 1797 came up with a side-wheeler, but at this point Robert Fulton, who had encouraged Morey to talk freely with him and demonstrate the invention, went into the steamboating business, using a boat clearly patterned after Morey's. It's said that an embittered Morey sank his boat across the river in the Vermont lake that now bears his name. He also heated and lighted his house with gas, and in 1826 he patented a gas-powered internal combustion engine. The **Samuel Morey House** is the oldest of the seven, a centerpiece for the others.

✳ **Must-See**

The Saint-Gaudens National Historic Site (603-675-2175; nps.gov/saga; also check sgnhs.org), 139 Saint Gaudens Rd., off Rt. 12A, Cornish. Grounds open daily, dawn–dusk. Buildings open 9–4:30 daily late May through Oct. $5 adults (good for a week); free under age 17. This glorious property with a view of Mount Ascutney includes the sculptor's summer home and studio, sculpture court, and formal gardens, which he developed and occupied between 1885 and his death in 1907. Augustus Saint-Gaudens (1848–1907) is remembered primarily for public pieces: the Shaw memorial on Boston Common, the statue of Admiral Farragut in New York's Madison Square, the equestrian statue of General William T. Sherman at the Fifth Avenue entrance to Central Park, and the *Standing Lincoln* in Chicago's Lincoln Park. He was also the first sculptor to design an American coin (the $10 and $20 gold pieces of 1907). His home, Aspet, is furnished

U.S. Dept. of the Interior, National Park Service,
Saint-Gaudens National Historic Site, Cornish.N.H.

ADAMS MEMORIAL AT THE SAINT-GAUDENS NATIONAL HISTORIC SITE. COMMISSIONED BY HISTORIAN HENRY ADAMS FOR THE GRAVESITE OF HIS WIFE, MARION HOOPER ADAMS.

HOUSE AND GARDENS OF THE SAINT-GAUDENS NATIONAL HISTORIC SITE

U.S. Dept. of the Interior, National Park Service, Saint-Gaudens National Historic Site, Cornish.N.H.

much as it was when he lived there. A visitors center features a 28-minute film about the artist and his work. Augustus Saint-Gaudens loved the Ravine Trail, a 0.25-mile cart path to Blow-Me-Up Brook, now marked for visitors, and other walks laid out through the woodlands and wetlands of the Blow-Me-Down Natural Area. Saint-Gaudens was the center of the "Cornish Colony," a group of poets, artists, landscape artists, actors, architects, and writers who included Ethel Barrymore, Charles Dana Gibson, Finley Peter Dunne, and Maxfield Parrish; President Woodrow Wilson's wife was drawn into this circle, and the president summered at a nearby home from 1913 to 1915. *Note:* Bring a picnic lunch for Sunday-afternoon chamber music concerts, at 2 PM in July and August.

∞ **Enfield Shaker Museum** (603-632-4346; shakermuseum.org), Rt. 4A, Lower Shaker Village, Enfield, marked from I-89 Exit 17. Open year-round, Mon.–Sat. 10–4, Sun. noon–4. Last tour at 3. $7.50 adults, $6.50 seniors, $5 students, $3 ages 10–18. It's less ($5/$4/$3) if you just want to walk around the first floor and visit the outbuildings, but really the tour's the thing. *Note:* It's also possible to stay in one of the 20 guest rooms (see *Other Lodging*) and to both stay and dine as part of frequent special events. The entire Great Stone Dwelling can also be rented. The Shaker community, founded in 1793 in this "Chosen Vale" between Mount Assurance and Mascoma Lake, prospered through the 19th century, with some 300 men, women, and children living in three separate families in the 1840s; 13 buildings survive. The six-story (eight floors if you count the basement and belfry) Great Stone Dwelling, completed in 1841, was said to be the tallest building north of Boston at the time and is the largest Shaker building anywhere. It remains the centerpiece of the museum, which also includes seven other structures. Visitors begin with a video about the Shaker community and tour the second-floor Meeting Room, hung with portraits of past elders and rooms displaying the community's work and lifestyle. The third and fourth floors are restored "dwelling rooms." Unfortunately the Great Stone Dwelling no longer stands alone. Next door is the basilica-like Mary Keene Chapel, built by the Catholic Order of La Salette, which bought the Shaker property in 1927. That property is now further cluttered by lakeside cottages built by developers who bought a portion of the property in the 1980s. Still, this is a magical place, and now the chapel, stone mill building, West and East Brethren's Shops, Ministry House, chapel, and laundry/dairy are part of the museum. Note the single stone commemorating the resting place of 330 Shakers. You might want to climb the dirt road that begins next to the stone shop; it's a steep 0.5-mile walk to the holy Feast Ground of the Shakers of Chosen Vale. Check the website for school vacation children's programs as well as lectures, weekend workshops, garden tours, and more.

Hood Museum of Art, Dartmouth College (603-646-2808; hoodmuseum .dartmouth.edu), on the Dartmouth Green, Hanover. Closed Mon.; open Tue.–Sat. 10–5, Wed. until 9, Sun. noon–5. Free. An outstanding collection of world-class art

THE ENFIELD SHAKER MUSEUM IS OPEN YEAR-ROUND

Chris Tree

Chris Tree

DARTMOUTH ROW BY ANN FRANCES RAY, CA. 1840, COURTESY OF THE HOOD MUSEUM OF ART

from almost every area of the world and historical period. Featuring ninth-century Assyrian reliefs from the Palace of Ashurnarsipal II at Nimrod (present-day Iraq), European Old Master prints and painting, two centuries of American paintings, portraits, drawings, and watercolors; American decorative arts; ancient and Asian objects; traditional and contemporary African, Oceanic, and Native American collections; cutting-edge contemporary art; and a stunning set of murals by Jose Clemente Orozco. Two floors of galleries, permanent collections, traveling exhibitions. Explore on your own or arrange for a tour by calling 603-646-1469. Hood Museum of Art Shop has something for all ages and budgets.

✐ **Montshire Museum of Science** (802-649-2200; montshire.org), 1 Montshire Rd., Norwich. Open daily 10–5 except Thanksgiving and Christmas; $10 adults, $8 ages 2–17, free for members and children under 2. Use of the trails is included with admission. Few cities have a science museum of this quality. This hands-on

MONTSHIRE MUSEUM INTERIOR

Courtesy, Montshire Museum

science center with more than 100 exhibits is sited on 110 trail-webbed acres beside the Connecticut River. The name derives from Ver*mont* and New Hamp*shire*, and the focus is on demystifying natural phenomena in the world in general and the Upper Valley in particular. The Montshire exhibits include an elaborate 2.5-acre Science Park outdoors: Water bubbles from a 7-foot Barre granite boulder, and from this "headwater" a 250-foot "rill" flows downhill, snaking over a series of terraces, inviting you to manipulate dams and sluices to change its flow and direction (visitors are advised to bring towels). You can also shape fountains, cast shadows to tell time, and push a button to identify the call of birds and insects within actual hearing. Note Ed Kahn's *Wind Wall*, a billboard-sized sheet attached to the museum's tower, composed of thousands of silver flutter disks that shimmer in the breeze, resembling patterns on a pond riffled by wind.

The Montshire is also a visitors center for the Silvio O. Conte National Fish and Wildlife Refuge. Inside the museum exhibits include a giant moose and tanks of gleaming local fish. The museum theater features ViewSpace, a program showing the latest images, movies, and animations from the Hubble Telescope and other NASA observatories. Some of our favorite exhibits include the fog machine up in the tower, the see-through beehive, the gravity well, a heat camera, and the physics of bubbles. There are also astounding displays on birds, moths, and insects. Most exhibits are hands-on. While there's a corner for toddlers (Andy's Place) and some demonstrations geared to youngsters, this is as stimulating a place for adults as for their offspring. The gift shop alone is worth stopping for. Inquire about special events, programs, and visiting exhibitions. In summer and fall the excursion train **White River Flyer** (800-707-3530) offers roundtrip excursions from Union Depot in White River Junction up along the Connecticut River to the museum.

MONTSHIRE MUSEUM, NORWICH, VT.

Courtesy, Montshire Museum

Listed from south to north

Rockingham Meeting House. Vermont's oldest unchanged public building is off Rt. 103 between Chester and Bellows Falls, and open Memorial Day–Columbus Day, 10–4. Built as a combination church and town hall in 1787, this Federal-style structure stands quietly above its graveyard. It's striking inside and out. Inside, "pigpen"-style pews each accommodate 10 to 15 people, some with their backs to the minister. The old burying ground is filled with thin old markers bearing readable epitaphs.

The American Precision Museum (802-674-5781; americanprecision.org), 1961 S. Main St., Windsor, Vt. Open Memorial Day–Oct, 10–5 daily; $6. Billed as the largest collection of historically significant machine tools in the country, housed in the 1846 Robbins, Kendall & Lawrence Armory, itself a national historic landmark, said to be the "birthplace of this country's modern system of industrial design and production." At the 1851 Great Exposition in London the firm demonstrated machine tools and rifles with interchangeable parts. The British army ordered 25,000 rifles and 141 metal-working machines on the spot and coined the name "the American System" for this revolutionary approach to gun making. Excellent special exhibits feature machine tools from the collection, tracing their impact on today's world.

Old Constitution House (802-674-6628; historicvermont.org), N. Main St., Windsor, Vt. Open mid-May–mid-Oct., weekends 11–5. Nominal admission. This is Elijah West's tavern (but not in its original location), where delegates gathered on July 2, 1777, to adopt Vermont's constitution, America's first to prohibit slavery, establish universal voting rights for all males, and authorize a public school system. Excellent first-floor displays trace the history of the formation of the Republic of Vermont; upstairs is the town's collection of antiques, prints, documents, tools and cooking utensils, tableware, toys, and early fabrics. Special exhibits vary each year. A path out the back door leads to Lake Runnemede.

CORNISH-WINDSOR COVERED BRIDGE WITH MT. ASCUTNEY IN THE BACKGROUND

Chris Tree

COVERED BRIDGES At 460 feet the **Cornish–Windsor covered bridge**, Rt. 12A, one of the country's longest covered bridges, is certainly the most photographed in New England. A lattice truss design, built in 1866, it was rebuilt in 1989. There are also three more covered bridges in Cornish, all dating from the early 1880s: Two span Mill Brook—one in Cornish City and the other in Cornish Mills between Rts. 12A and 120—and the third spans Blow-Me-Down Brook (off Rt. 12A). On the Meriden road in Plainfield another 1880s, 85-foot bridge spans Bloods Brook. Near the Lyme–Orford line the **Lyme–Edgell bridge** (154 feet long) spans Clay Brook (off Rt. 10).

BALLOONING **Balloon Vermont** (802-333-9254), Post Mills Airport, West Fairlee, Vt. Brian Boland offers morning and sunset balloon rides. On the summer evening we tried it, the balloon hovered above hidden pockets in the hills, and we saw a herd of what looked like brown and white goats that, on closer inspection, proved to be deer (yes, some were white!). After an hour or so we settled down gently in a farmyard and broke out the champagne. Boland builds as well as flies hot-air balloons and maintains a private museum of more than 100 balloons and antique airships. He also maintains rustic cabins on the premises for patrons ($70 per night) and offers packages in conjunction with nearby **Silver Maple Lodge** (800-666-1946; ballooninnvermont.com), which includes the balloon rides on its website.

BICYCLING Given its unusually flat and scenic roads and well-spaced inns, this area is beloved by bicyclists. Search out the river roads (for some reason they're not marked on the official New Hampshire highway map): from Rt. 12A (just north of the Saint-Gaudens site) on through Plainfield until it rejoins Rt. 12A; from Rt. 10 north of Hanover (just north of the Chieftain Motel) through Lyme, rejoining Rt. 10 in Orford. A classic, 36-mile loop is Hanover to Orford on Rt. 10 and back on the river road. The loop to Lyme and back is 22 miles. For inn-to-inn guided tours in this area, contact **Bike Vermont** (802-457-3553; 800-257-2226; bikevermont.com). The Sugar River Trail, a multiuse recreational path, follows the Sugar River east from Charlestown to Newport.

Northern Rail Trail (fnrt.org) runs 25 miles from Lebanon east along the Mascoma River to Mascoma Lake, through Enfield and up through Canaan (climbing 600 feet in altitude), then down through Grafton to Danbury (see "Sunapee/Newfound Lakes Region"). In Lebanon the trailhead is on Rt. 120 south of I-89 Exit 18, at the intersection of Taylor and Spencer Sts.

BOATING With its usually placid water and scenery, the Connecticut River through much of the Upper Valley is ideal for easygoing canoeists. The Connecticut River Joint Commissions (603-826-4800; ctrivertravel.net) has published a useful *Boating on the Connecticut River* guide. Information on primitive campsites along this stretch of the river can be found on the website maintained by the Upper Valley Land Trust (uvlt.org).

The most frequently photographed reach of the Upper Connecticut is the 3 miles above the Cornish–Windsor covered bridge, set against the dramatic lone peak of Mount Ascutney. This is part of a popular 12-mile paddle that begins just below Sumner Falls, 0.5 mile of rolling water and jagged rock worth mentioning because it's so deceptive and so deadly.

♪ **North Star Livery** (603-542-6929; kayak-canoe.com), 58 Bridge St., White River Junction, Vt. With over 90 boats, including 30 kayaks, this is the largest and oldest commercial rental service on the Connecticut River. For more, see the description of its home base in Cornish ("Lower Connecticut").

The Ledyard Canoe Club (603-643-6709), Hanover, is billed as the oldest canoe club in America. It's named for a 1773 Dartmouth dropout who felled a pine tree, hollowed it out, and took off downriver (with a copy of Ovid), ending up at Hartford, 100 miles and several major waterfalls downstream. Hidden on the riverbank

Chris Tree

NORTH STAR CANOE LIVERY

north of the Ledyard Bridge, down beyond Dartmouth's slick new rowing center, Ledyard is a mellow, friendly, student-run place, usually open mid-May to mid-Oct. The canoeing and kayaking center for the 40 river miles above Wilder Dam, it offers kayaking clinics as well as cruising canoe and sea kayak rentals. No shuttle service.

Fairlee Marine (802-333-9745), Rt. 5 in Fairlee, Vt., rents pontoons, kayaks, canoes, rowboats, and small motors for use on the Connecticut and two local lakes.

FISHING You can eat the fish you catch in the Connecticut River—it yields brown and rainbow trout above Orford. There's a boat launch on the Vermont side at the Wilder Dam, another just north of Hanover, and another across the river in North Thetford, Vt. Lake Mascoma (look for boat launches along Rt. 4A in Enfield) and Post Pond in Lyme are other popular angling spots.

GOLF Hanover Country Club (603-646-2000), Rope Ferry Rd., off Rt. 10, Hanover. Open May–Oct. Founded in 1899, an 18-hole facility with 4 practice holes, pro shop, PGA instructors. **Carter Golf Club** (603-448-4483), Rt. 4, Lebanon. Nine holes, par 36. **Lake Morey Country Club** (802-333-4800; 800-423-1211), Fairlee. Eighteen holes.

HEALTH CLUBS CCBA (Carter-Witherell Center) (603-448-6477; joinccba .org), 1 Taylor St., Lebanon. Nonmembers can purchase day passes to use the facilities of this community health center. Includes use of pool, whirlpool, and saunas; exercise and weight room; tennis and basketball courts; and child care.

River Valley Club (603-643-7720; rivervalleyclub.com), Centerra Market-place, Rt. 120, Lebanon. Open Mon.–Thu. 4:45 AM–10 PM, Fri. 4:45–9, Sat.–Sun. 7–7. Offers day spa services to nonmembers in its luxurious facility: massages, herbal wraps, facials, hydrotherapy, and more. Call for rates. Included: indoor and outdoor pools, whirlpool and sauna, exercise and weight room, fitness classes, and child care. A climbing wall, hair salon, and café lounge are also part of the complex.

Upper Valley Aquatic Center (802-296-2850; uvac-swim.org), 100 Arboretum Lane, junction of Rts. 89 and 91, White River Junction, Vt. Featuring a 25-meter competition training pool, three-lane lap pool, splash park with children's area, fitness center, and café. Open to the public.

HIKING The **Appalachian Trail** (AT) crosses the Connecticut River over the Ledyard Bridge and runs right through Hanover on its way to Mount Katahdin in Maine; note the marker embedded in the sidewalk in front of the Hanover Inn. Follow the white blazes down S. Main St. to find where the trail reenters the woods just past the Hanover Food Co-op.

Short hikes in the Hanover area itself abound; a map of area trails is available from the Hanover Chamber of Commerce. Inquire locally or pick up the *Dartmouth Outing Guide*, published by the Dartmouth Outing Club. Suggested hikes include **Balch Hill Summit** north of town, the **Mink Brook Trail** off S. Main St., **Smarts Mountain** in Lyme, **Mount Cube** in Orford, and **Moose Mountain** (another section of the AT) in Etna. The westernmost peak in the White Mountain range, 4,802-foot-high Mount Moosilauke, is 50 miles north of Hanover, visible from much of the Upper Valley.

RAILROAD EXCURSION ♦ **Trains Around Vermont** (802-463-3069; 800-707-3530; rails-vt.com), Union Depot, 102 Railroad Row, White River Junction, Vt. Take a roundtrip along the Connecticut River to the Montshire Museum and Thetford on the White River Flyer. Frequent roundtrips mid-June–Labor Day and weekends in foliage season (mid-June–mid-Oct.) plus the Polar Express in Dec. $15–21 adults, $12–17 children. $16 group.

SWIMMING Ask locally about swimming holes in the Connecticut River and public swimming in Lake Mascoma in Enfield.

Canaan Street Lake offers a small town beach on Canaan St.

♦ **Storrs Pond Recreation Area** (603-643-2134), off Rt. 10 north of Hanover (Reservoir Rd., then left). Open June–Labor Day, 10–8. Bathhouse with showers and lockers, lifeguards at both the (unheated) Olympic-sized pool and 15-acre pond. Fee for nonmembers.

🐾 ♦ **Treasure Island** (802-333-9615), on Lake Fairlee, Thetford, Vt. This fabulous town swimming area is on Rt. 244 (follow Rt. 113 north of town). Open late June–Labor Day, 10–8 weekends, noon–8 weekdays. Sand beach, picnic tables, playground, tennis. Nominal admission.

Union Village Dam Recreation Area (802-649-1606), Thetford, Vt. Open Memorial Day–mid-Sept.; five swimming areas along the Ompompanoosuc River. Also has walking and cross-country skiing trails, picnic tables, and grills.

✳ Winter Sports

CROSS-COUNTRY SKIING **Dartmouth Cross Country Ski Center** (603-643-6534), Rope Ferry Rd. (off Rt. 10 just before the country club), Hanover. Open in-season, Mon.–Fri. 9–7, weekends 9–5. Twenty-five kilometers of trails through the Storrs Pond and Oak Hill areas; rentals, lessons, waxing clinics. "The country's oldest collegiate outing club" rents a full line of skis, snowshoes, rock climbing equipment, and camping gear to the public from the basement of Robinson Hall.

Lake Morey Inn Resort (802-333-4800; 800-423-1211), Fairlee, Vt. The golf course turns into a touring center in winter; rentals, instruction.

DOWNHILL SKIING

Listed from south to north
Arrowhead Recreation Area (603-542-7016; arrowheadnh.com), Claremont, is a family ski and tubing hill open weekends, also Sat. nights and holiday weeks. There's a free ice-skating rink and 2km of cross-country trails. A pony lift gets you halfway up the hill, and a snowcat pulls you the whole way. Check the website for extended hours and snow conditions. Equipment rentals and lessons. Very reasonable rates.

✔ **Ascutney Mountain Resort** (802-484-7771; 800-243-0011; ascutney.com), Rt. 44, Brownsville (I-91 Exit 8 or 9), Vt. A family-geared, self-contained resort. Facilities include a 215-unit condo hotel (time share), a sports center with indoor and outdoor pools, weight and racquetball rooms, a full restaurant, and a base lodge. Expert trails on North Peak are served by a mile-long quad chair.

Vertical drop: 1,800 feet.

Lifts: Six.

Trails: 56.

Snowmaking: 95 percent.

Features: Nine double-diamond advanced trails, expert tree skiing, a terrain park, a tubing slope, and a separate lift-served Learning Park.

For children: Nursery/child care from six weeks.

Rates: $60 adults weekend, $45 seniors/juniors; $60/$44 midweek. Half-day and multiday tickets are offered.

Whaleback Mountain (603-448-1489; whaleback.com), I-89 Exit 16. Zero Gravity Skate Park open year-round, winter hours with skiing/snowboarding: weekdays noon–9, Sat. 9–9, Sun. 9–4:30. This beloved family mountain, just off I-89, is now an "action sports center." Reopened under new, local ownership in 2006, it offers 35 trails served by a double chair and four surface lifts (with 80 percent snowmaking), plus night skiing. What's new: a renovated base lodge, indoor and outdoor skate parks, and seasonal mountain biking. Planned: a water ramp, BMX track, and paintball. The staff are headed by two-time Olympian Evan Dybvig and all about teaching action sports. Weekday ski/snowboard rates: $25 adult, $20 at night skating, $12.

✔ **Dartmouth Skiway** (603-795-2143; skiway.dartmouth.edu), Lyme Center, an amenity for families as well as the college, with a snazzy 16,000-square-foot timber base lodge. Open 9–4 daily; rentals and ski school.

Vertical drop: 968 feet.

Lifts: One quad chair, one double chair, a beginners' J-bar.

Trails: 32.

Snowmaking: 65 percent.

Rates: $38 adults, $25 juniors on weekends; $26 and $18 weekdays; also half-day, senior, military, and more rates.

ICE SKATING Occom Pond, next to the country club, Hanover. Kept plowed and planed, lighted evenings until 10 unless unsafe for skating; warming hut. The Dartmouth Outing Club (603-646-2429) rents skates.

✳ Green Space

Pine Park, just north of the Dartmouth campus between the Hanover Country Club and the Connecticut River, Hanover. Take N. Main St. to Rope Ferry Rd. Park at the trail sign above the clubhouse. These tall pines along the river are one of the beauty spots of the valley. The 125-year-old trees were saved from the Diamond Match Company in 1900 by a group of local citizens. The walk is 1.5 miles.

Rinker Tract, Rt. 10, 2.5 miles north of Hanover. This is an 18-acre knoll with a pond at the bottom of the hill below the Chieftain Motel. The loop trail is marked by blue blazes.

The city of Lebanon maintains several wooded parks for which trail maps are available from the recreation department, just inside the door of city hall (on the common). These include **Farnum Hill**, an 820-acre property with a ridge trail commanding some magnificent views. On the Connecticut River, **Chambers Park** (just off Rt. 10) offers trails through riverbank terrace, upland forest, and open field. The 286-acre **Boston Lot** lies between the river and the city reservoir, with trails good for hiking, biking, and cross-country skiing, and with picnic tables on the northern edge of the reservoir. **Goodwin Park**, adjoining Storrs Hill Ski Area, offers a 1.5-mile exercise trail.

⟁ **Montshire Museum of Science Trails**, Norwich, Vt. The museum's 110 acres include a 12-acre promontory between the Connecticut River and the marshy bay at the mouth of Bloody Brook. The 0.25-mile trail leading down through tall white pines to the bay is quite magical. The 1.5-mile Hazen Trail runs all the way to Wilder Village. These trails are hard packed, accessible to strollers and wheelchairs.

Thetford Hill State Park (802-785-2266; vtstateparks.com), 622 Academy Rd., Thetford Center, Vt. Open Memorial Day–Labor Day. Developed by the Civilian Conservation Corps in the 1930s, 177 acres with a **campground** (14 tent/trailer sites, two lean-tos, hot showers), hiking and cross-country trails (maintained by Thetford Academy).

✳ Lodging

Listed from south to north
INNS AND HOTELS

⁗ᵀ⁗ **The Common Man Inn** (603-542-0546; thecman.com), 21 Water St., Claremont 03743. This recent addition to "the Common Man family" is a welcome one in downtown Claremont. Housed in former brick mill building, it offers 35 tastefully decorated, brick-walled rooms with large, shuttered windows and gas fireplaces as well as a restaurant (see *Dining Out*). $89–289 per night includes continental breakfast.

✪ "ıʼ **Juniper Hill Inn** (802-674-5273; 800-359-2541; juniperhillinn .com), 153 Pembroke Rd., Windsor, VT 05069. "There's a warmth and glow to a real fire," innkeeper Robert Dean will tell you. "It's like candlelight," he adds. "Everyone looks better." Dean wouldn't think of replacing wood with far more common and less romantic gas logs.

Guests are usually met at the door either by Dean or partner Ari Nikki and get a quick tour of the inn's several common rooms, which include an informal "living parlor" with a bar and plasma TV as well as hearth. The innkeepers tell about Max Evarts, the man who built this 28-room Colonial Revival mansion in 1902. A hugely wealthy 19th-century industrialist, he helped save the Morgan horse breed and fund the nearby Cornish Art Colony. "Juniper Hill reflects the stories of people who have lived and visited here," Robert Dean will tell you. It's a theme that Dean, a professional interior designer, evokes in the guest rooms, each named for a former guest. There's the richly colored Teddy Roosevelt Room with its queen canopy and wing chairs as well as the Calvin Coolidge, the Woodrow Wilson, the Maxfield Parrish, and the Isadora Duncan Rooms, most walled in period paper and all furnished with a mix of antiques and designer furniture. Like the firelight itself, these rooms are subtly, genuinely luxurious. Roosevelt's bathroom features a European air-jetted tub with chroma light therapy (changing to fit your mood); most rooms feature deep, claw-foot soaking tubs. No fewer than 11 guest rooms have fireplace, and all but 4 of those burn wood. Each is fitted with a customized mattress, a decanter of sherry, bedside chocolates, fine linens, fluffy robes, and Egyptian cotton towels. Our

favorite is the Evarts Room, the original master bedroom with its fireplace in an alcove and views south across the lawn and valley to Mount Ascutney. Usually obscured by the winter dark when guests arrive, this is also the view at breakfast in the Cabernet-colored dining room, warmed—of course—by a glowing hearth (see *Dining Out*). $135–295 per room, full breakfast included.

INNS ✪ ⚭ ♿ **Home Hill Country Inn** (603-675-6165; homehillinn.com), River Rd., Plainfield 03781. Built in 1818, this is one of those magnificent, four-square mansions spaced along the Connecticut River (see the introduction to this chapter); it sits at the end of a 3.5-mile road, surrounded by 25 acres. It was a private home until 1981 and has been owned since 1996 by Cornish resident Robert Gordon, furnished throughout with fine antiques and paintings. Chef-innkeeper Paula Snow offers three elegant guest rooms and a two-room suite with a fireplace in the main house; there are also six guest rooms in the Carriage House and a small cottage with a bedroom and sitting room beside the pool. Amenities include an outdoor pool, putting green, croquet, and tennis court as well as a fitness room. Lovely as it is otherwise, this inn is all about outstanding food; check *Dining Out*. $160–250 per couple includes breakfast and afternoon refreshments.

♿ **The Hanover Inn** (603-643-4300; 800-443-7024; hanoverinn.com), corner of Main and S. Wheelock Sts., Hanover 03755. This is the Ritz of the North Country. It overlooks the Dartmouth Green and exudes a distinctly tweedy elegance. Guest rooms are each individually and deftly decorated, and the junior suites—with canopy beds, eiderdown quilts, armchairs, a silent valet, couch, and vanity—are pamperingly luxurious. A four-story, 93-room, neo-Georgian building owned and operated by Dartmouth College, the "inn" traces itself back to 1780 when the college's steward, General Ebenezer Brewster, turned his home into a tavern. Brewster's son parlayed this enterprise into the Dartmouth Hotel, which continued to thrive until 1887, when it burned to the ground. The present building dates in part from this era but has lost its Victorian lines through successive renovations and expansions. It remains, however, the heart of Hanover. In summer the front terrace is crowded with faculty, visitors, and residents enjoying a light lunch or beer. Year-round the lobby, the porch rocking chairs, and the Hayward Lounge (a comfortable sitting room with clawfoot sofas and flowery armchairs, dignified portraits, and a frequently lit hearth) are popular spots for friends to meet. Roughly half the inn's guests are Dartmouth related. Both Zins Winebistro and the more formal Daniel Webster Room (see *Dining*

Out) are popular places to dine before attending performances at neighboring Hopkins Center. Rates range from $265 for a standard room to $315 for a junior suite, no charge for children under age 12; senior citizens' discount; honeymoon, ski, golf, and seasonal packages. Handicapped accessible.

 The Hotel Coolidge (802-295-3118; 800-622-1124; hotelcoolidge .com), White River Junction, VT 05001, is one of the last of the old railroad hotels. It's located in a railroad town that's undergoing a small renaissance with some good shopping and dining. All 30 elevator-served guest rooms have private bath, phone, and TV. Some back rooms are dark, but others are quite roomy and attractive, and the family suites (two rooms connected by a bath) are a real bargain. We'd request Room 100, or a similar suite. The hotel sits across from the Amtrak station and next to the Briggs Opera House. Local buses to Hanover and Lebanon stop at the door, and rental cars can be arranged. Search out the splendid Peter Michael Gish murals in the Vermont Room, painted

HOME HILL COUNTRY INN

Home Hill Country Inn

in 1950 in exchange for room and board while the artist was studying with Paul Sample at Dartmouth. Owner-manager David Briggs, a seventh-generation Vermonter, takes his role as innkeeper seriously and will arrange for special needs. $89–109 per room double, $169 for a suite.

∞ ⅙ ☻ ⁙ **Norwich Inn** (802-649-1143; norwichinn.com), 325 Main St., Norwich, VT 05055. Just across the river from Hanover and also very much a gathering place for Dartmouth parents, faculty, and students. The present three-story, tower-topped inn dates from 1889 (when its predecessor burned). Innkeepers Joe and Jill Lavin have made major additions, recently replacing two small annexes with two brand-new buildings: Ivy Lodge has four king-bedded rooms with gas fireplace, two of them pet-friendly, and Walker House has 18 rooms of varied sizes, shapes, and decors, all with gas fireplace. The 16 rooms in the main inn also have private bath, telephone, and cable TV. The brewpub, Jasper Murdock's Alehouse, features a wide variety of inn-made brews (see *Eating Out*). There is also a formal dining room; the inn is open except Mon. for breakfast, lunch, and dinner. $149–169 in the main inn, to $199 in the annexes.

⅙ ⁙ **The Lyme Inn**, on the Common, Lyme 03768. Dating back to 1809, this substantial inn stands at the head of a classic common. Most recently it was called the Alden Country Inn but had been closed for several years before it was totally renovated, reopening in 2010. The 14 rooms with private bath are on the second and third floors (there's an elevator). The dining room and tavern are open to the public.

∞ ✐ ⅙ **Lake Morey Resort** (802-333-4311; 800-423-1211; lakemorey

resort.com), Club House Rd., Fairlee, VT 05045. On the shore of Lake Morey, this sprawling, lakeside landmark best known for its golf course is also a winter getaway for cross-country skiers, snowshoers, and ice skaters. In summer supervised children's programs are included with MAP. Given the landscaped grounds and reception areas, this is a wedding venue as well. The resort dates from the early 1900s and was owned by the Avery family for some 20 years beginning in the 1970s, then sold and reclaimed several years ago. It has since been completely renovated. There are 130 rooms and suites. The splendid lake view remains key, along with a player-friendly 18-hole golf course. Facilities include an indoor swimming pool, Jacuzzi, sauna, fitness center, and the Waters Spa, with a full menu of treatments. There are also tennis courts, cross-country ski and snowmobile trails. All three meals are served. Winter EP rates are per room and include up to two children sharing a room with parent: $105–149 per room, $172–217 for suites. MAP per-person summer and fall rates are $123–279 with a $35–54 charge for children, depending on age. Inquire about golf and other packages, and about cottage rentals.

BED & BREAKFASTS

Listed from south to north
Note: Also see Inn at Valley Farm and other Walpole listings.

Dutch Treat (603-826-5565; the dutchtreat.com), P.O. Box 1004, Charlestown 03603. Open year-round. Formerly Maple Hedge, this handsome, 1820s Main St. house has been completely refurbished by Dob and Eric Lutze, natives of Holland who have also lived in Canada, England, and Austria and speak French and German. There's a Dutch theme to guest rooms with names like the Tulip Suite (our favorite) and the Delft Room, both big sunny guest rooms in the front of the house. Smaller rooms—the Lace Maker (honoring the Dutch painter Vermeer), the twin-bedded Tasman Room (named for the Dutch explorer who discovered New Zealand and Tasmania), and the Generals Room (with a picture of a forefather who fought under both Napoleon and Wellington)—are also inviting. The sunny, square dining room is elegant. There's a big comfortable parlor, wicker on the porch, and an outdoor hot tub. Dob and Eric are delighted to help guests explore the best of the area. $119–159 includes breakfast.

⊙ **Chase House** (603-675-5391; chasehouse.com), 1001 Rt. 12A, Cornish. This classic Federal mansion, begun around 1775, was moved back from the banks of the Connecticut River in the mid-1940s to make way for the Sullivan County Railroad. Salmon Portland Chase, born here in 1808, is remembered as Lincoln's secretary of the treasury, the namesake of the Chase Manhattan Bank, and the man on the $10,000 bill. Previous owners restored the house and added another vintage-1810 building (from Vermont) onto the back, creating a large "rafter room" designed to accommodate weddings and functions, now the specialty of the house. There are nine guest rooms. Amenities include a hot tub, sauna, and exercise room. Current owners Paul and Terry Toms have created extensive hiking, snowshoeing, and cross-country trails on the 160-acre property, which includes frontage (across the road and railroad tracks) on the river. $165–265 per couple B&B, two-night minimum.

✪ ¶ **Shaker Hill B&B** (603-632-4519; shakerhill.com), 259 Shaker Hill, Enfield 03748. This is a gem, a big, airy white house with a wraparound porch, much expanded from the Jewett Farmhouse that forms its core. It was here in the 1790s that the first group of Shakers lived before building their village (presently preserved in part as a museum). The four guest rooms are decorated with taste; all have private bath, wide floorboards, and air-conditioning as well as computer access. A sitting room has a TV and is well stocked with games and books. Our corner bedroom had wide pumpkin pine floorboards and furnishings that included a graceful bird's-eye dresser, an antique Shaker-style rocker, a country-style armoire, and a desk with a pottery lamp. We pulled down the shades and snuggled under a warm colored and patterned coverlet and a patchwork quilt, and slept soundly. Mascoma Lake is minutes away, and the 23-acre grounds include gardens and ski/walking trails. $90–110 with a full breakfast and afternoon tea. Innkeepers Nancy and Allen Smith are knowledgeable and helpful about the surrounding area.

¶ **The Trumbull House** (603-643-2370; 800-651-5141; trumbullhouse .com), 40 Etna Rd., Hanover 03755. Four miles east of Dartmouth College, Hillary Pridgen offers four bright and spacious, tastefully decorated guest rooms in her gracious house. There's also a suite and a guest cottage. Amenities include private baths, down comforters, cable TV, and WiFi. The suite has a king-sized bed, a sitting area with TV/VCR, a trundle bed, and two baths, one with a Jacuzzi tub. $145–240 for rooms, $260–310 for the suite and guest cottage, from $125 for singles, midweek. Rates includes a full breakfast—guests choose from a menu that includes scrambled eggs with smoked salmon and a portobello mushroom and Brie omelet. The 16 country acres include a swimming pond, hiking trails, and cross-country ski trails. Guests enjoy access to the River Valley Club.

Breakfast on the Connecticut (603-353-4444; 888-353-4440; breakfaston thect.com), 651 River Rd., Lyme 03768. This 1990s B&B is off on its own 23 acres, right on the Connecticut River, with a private dock. The 15 guest rooms are divided between the main house and a 12-sided "barn," connected by an enclosed passageway, which also connects with a whirlpool tub in a gazebo. Rooms vary. Some have gas fireplace and skylights; many have river views and in-room whirlpool tub; all have TV/VCR and individual climate control. Innkeepers Donna and John Anderson offer a warm welcome. $115–185 per night double occupancy for rooms, $199–250 for suites, including breakfast, served in the large, sunny living/dining/sunroom. Two-night minimum on most weekends. Inquire about the guest house, sleeping four.

∞ ▝▌▘ **Dowd's Country Inn** (603-795-4712; dowdscountryinn.com), Lyme 03768. On Lyme's classic common, geared to groups and weddings. You'll find a large living room, a meeting space, a small dining room, a cheery breakfast room, and 20 guest rooms. The presidential suite can accommodate a family of five. Rooms $125–175 in-season, double occupancy, including breakfast and afternoon tea.

White Goose Inn (603-353-4812; 800-358-4267; whitegooseinn.com), Rt. 10, P.O. Box 17, Orford 03777. This is an 1830s brick house—four-chimneyed and green-shuttered, with the original 1766 clapboard home now an el at the back. Marshall and Renee Ivey offer eight antiques-furnished guest rooms with private bath and two that share. $89–149 includes a full breakfast. Inquire about floorcloth workshops.

Guests can take advantage of Peyton Place (see *Dining Out*) next door.

✪ ▝ ▝ ✎ ⟆ **Silver Maple Lodge & Cottages** (802-333-4326; 800-666-1946; silvermaplelodge.com), 520 Rt. 5 South, Fairlee, VT 05045. Situated just south of the village on Rt. 5, Silver Maple was built as a farmhouse in 1855 and has been welcoming travelers for more than 80 years. Now run by Scott and Sharon Wright, it has seven nicely appointed guest rooms in the lodge and eight separate, pine-paneled, shaded cottages. The farmhouse has cheerful sitting rooms with exposed 200-year-old hand-hewn beams in the living room and dining room, where fresh breads appear with other continental breakfast goodies. The newest cottages with kitchenette and working fireplace are real beauties. Play horseshoes, croquet, badminton, or shuffleboard on the lawn, or rent a bike or canoe. Scott will also arrange a ride in a hot-air balloon for you at neighboring Post Mills Airport. Scott grew up on a Tunbridge farm and takes pride in introducing visitors to Vermont. $79–109 per couple. Pets are accepted in the cottages, one of which has wheelchair access.

OTHER LODGING ∞ **The Great Stone Dwelling at the Enfield Shaker Museum** (603-632-4346; shakermuseum.org), Rt. 4A, Lower Shaker Village, Enfield 03748, marked from I-89 Exit 17. This striking six-story centerpiece of the museum (see *Must See*), completed in 1841 and said to be the largest Shaker building anywhere, offers 20 spacious, nicely furnished guest rooms with the original Shaker built-ins on its third and fourth floors. These are available to individuals on a nightly basis ($95–135 per night) or as part of frequent special events and workshops that also include meals. The entire Great Stone Dwelling can also be rented.

⊗ ✔ **Pierce's Inn** (603-643-2997; piercesinn.com), 261 Dogford Rd., Etna 03750. Set high in the hills above Hanover but just 6 miles from the college, this homey lodge is a bit of a Dartmouth secret. Specializing in family and college reunions, weddings and gatherings, the 1940s lodge originally opened with a ski tow for the hill behind the inn. Since 1971 it has been run by the Pierce family. Innkeeper Cindy Pierce, the youngest of seven children, ably carries on the tradition of warm, capable hospitality, informal atmosphere, and plenty of good food. Reasonably priced.

🐾 ✔ "𝐓" **Chieftain Motor Inn** (603-643-2550; chieftaininn.com), 84 Lyme Rd. (Rt. 10), Hanover 03755. Set high above the river, this attractive motel has 22 rooms with river views, some with king or two full-sized beds. Amenities include phones, an outdoor pool, barbecue, and access to canoes. Continental breakfast is also included in $119–140. Many special discounts, including for AT hikers, for whom there is free shuttle service.

Note: The **Hotel Coolidge** in White River Junction (hotelcoolidge.com/hostel) is affiliated with Hosteling International USA and offers both bunk rooms and double rooms in its hostel wing from $32 (HI members) and $55 (for a double room) nonmembers. It also sells HI memberships. Credit cards only (no cash). For more about the Coolidge see *Inns*.

✷ Where to Eat
DINING OUT

In Hanover/Norwich

Canoe Club Bistro and Music (603-643-9660; canoeclub.us), 27 S. Main St., Hanover. Open daily for lunch and dinner with light fare between meals (2–5) and late-night menus Thu.–Sat. Reservations suggested for dinner. Acoustic music nightly, also Sunday jazz brunch. "Sensational" is the way local residents describe this attractive addition to Hanover's dining options. The lunch may include wild mushroom stroganoff, pulled pork quesadilla, and warm smoked sausage with port-braised cabbage, a grilled baguette, and ale mustard. A winter dinner might be a shared platter of charcuterie followed by seared salmon with local butternut squash and goat cheese ravioli, apple cider and maple syrup glaze, with sautéed chard, leeks, and bacon. Dinner entrées $12–27.

Salubre Tratttoria (603-643-2007; salubrehanover.com), Hanover Park Building, 3 Lebanon St. Open Tue.–Sun. 5–9. Reservations suggested. Lee and John Hester's welcoming new restaurant, just off the beaten path, is a winner with Hanover's sophisticated locals. The low-lit ambience is informal with the focus on well-sourced and -prepared food, well presented. Begin with beef carpaccio or beet salad with warm goat cheese, then dine on pastas or pan-seared

GUEST ROOM AT THE GREAT STONE DWELLING, ENFIELD SHAKER VILLAGE

scallops over saffron rice with frisole tomatoes, roasted garlic, and saffron cream, leaving room for amaretto flourless cake. Entrées $15–25.

Hanover Inn (603-643-4300; 800-443-7024), Dartmouth Green, Hanover. The **Daniel Webster Room** is a large, formal dining room (open daily for breakfast, lunch, Sunday brunch, and evening events) with a seasonal terrace dining overlooking the Dartmouth Green. **Zins Winebistro** is open for lunch and dinner nightly, featuring wines by the glass, local brews, and locally sourced ingredients. The dinner menu ranges from burgers to shrimp and scallop scampi with greens, linguica, and white beans. The long dining bar is a welcome option for single travelers. Dinner entrées $9–28.

Carpenter and Main (802-649-2922; carpenterandmain.com), 326 Main St., Norwich, Vt. Open for dinner except Tue. and Wed.; tavern 5:30–10, dining room 6–9; reservations suggested. Chef-owner Bruce MacLeod is known for locally sourced, seasonal food with a French accent. On a winter night you might begin with a house pâté with cornichons or a warm trout soufflé with dill crème fraîche; then dine on pan-roasted pork loin with garlic sausage and toasted spaetzle. Entrées $24–34 in the dining room, $10–19 in the Tavern.

Norwich Inn (802-649-1143; norwich inn.com), 325 Main St., Norwich, Vt. Open for breakfast, lunch, and dinner, also Sun. brunch, but closed Mon. Across the river from Hanover, the dining room in this classic inn is popular with Dartmouth faculty. The same menu is available all day in both the dining room and Jasper Murdock's Alehouse (see *Eating Out*); the latter, also on the premises, is beloved for its handcrafted brews, sold only here. Dinner entrées $13–22. Grilled twin

quail with tomato wine broth, risotto cake, and Swiss chard is available in both large ($20) and small ($14) plates. The wine list is a point of pride in the dining room.

Elsewhere, listed from south to north

Home Hill Country Inn (603-675-6165; homehillinn.com), River Rd., Plainfield. Open for dinner Wed.–Sun. 5–9, Sun. brunch 9–2. Reservations suggested. The dining room in this four-square 1820s mansion by the river is bathed in light from floor-to-ceiling French doors, with warmly colored walls, white-draped tables, specially designed chandeliers and furnishings, and a working (not gas) hearth. Chef-innkeeper Paula Snow is a passionate believer in locally sourced produce. The inn also creates its own breads, sausages, cured salmon, mozzarella cheese, pasta, and ice cream. On an autumn evening half a dozen appetizers might include handmade crayfish ravioli with smoky local sweet corn and Andouille sausage; for an entrée you might choose veal with slow-roasted tomato, Fontina cheese, grilled polenta, and broccolini. Entrées $16–24, with less pricey daily specials such as (local) chicken potpie. Reasonably priced Sunday brunch is a great excuse to drive to this lovely spot. (Also see *Lodging*.)

Elixir (802-281-7009; elixirrestaurant .com), 188 S. Main St., White River Junction, Vt. Open Tue.–Sat. 5–11. Housed in a former freight house in downtown WRJ (keep going past the Hotel Coolidge), this is a casually upscale place with French-born and -trained chef Jean Pierre Debeuf in the kitchen. As in his former location (the Tunbridge Country Store), JP makes his own ice cream, focaccia, and desserts as well as entrées. You might dine on baked stuffed shrimp with spinach roasted garlic stuffing and risotto; a rosemary braised lamb shank with pumpkin tortellini; or a pulled-pork sandwich. Entrées $10–22. Cocktails are a specialty.

Simon Pearce (802-295-1470; simonpearce.com), The Mill, 1760 Main St., Quechee, Vt. Open daily for lunch and dinner (reserve). Let's face it—this is the one place no visitor to the Upper Valley wants to miss. It's frequently crowded and touristy, but a special place with delicious food. Housed in a mill that once formed the centerpiece for a village, with views of the waterfall. The tableware features hand-blown, hand-finished glass designed and blown in the mill and sold in the adjoining gift shop. At lunch try the shepherd's pie or coho salmon smoked here at the mill. Dinner entrées $23–30.

Stella's Kitchen & Market (603-795-4302; stellaslyme.com), 5 Main St., Lyme. Tue.–Sun. for lunch, closed Sun. for dinner and all day Mon. You enter through an unpromising door (beside the bank) into a smallish market (good for deli, wines, and prepared foods) and don't expect the restaurant itself to be as sleek and spacious as it is, hung with local art. The menu

BOB COYLE OF STELLA'S KITCHEN & MARKET, LYME

Chris Tree

includes a wide choice of pizza and pastas as well as staples like (free-range) chicken portobello with mushrooms, a Marsala and shallot demiglaze, and crumbled blue cheese; and Tuscan steak (pan-seared filet mignon topped with mushrooms, Gorgonzola, garlic, sun-dried tomatoes, and a Marsala demiglaze). Dinner entrées $14.50–21.50.

♿ **Peyton Place** (603-353-9100; peytonplacerestaurant.com), Rt. 10, Orford. Open for dinner Wed.–Sun. 5:30–10:30; in the off-season, Wed.–Sat. Reservations a must. Destination dining, this restaurant (named for Chef Jim and Heidi Peyton) is housed in the 1773 Mann Tavern. There's a genuine old taproom with a Rumford fireplace as well as a more formal dining room and seasonal terrace. Since 1993 Jim has offered highly seasonal, locally sourced menus. Dinner entrées might include house-made vegetarian or lamb ravioli and (organic) veal scaloppine from nearby Robie Farm, sliced thin, served with mushroom sauce and saffron risotto. Ice creams and sorbets are handmade. Wine and spirits are served. Dinner entrées $12–24. Inquire about cooking classes.

⨁ **Bunten Farmhouse Kitchen** (603-353-9252; thebuntenfarm.com), 1322 Rt. 10, Orford. Dinner by reservation Thu.–Sun., Sun. brunch 10–2. Chris Bunten grew up in this handsome brick farmstead before working in restaurants nationwide and marrying classically trained chef Bruce Balch. Today the couple turn super-rich milk from their Devon cattle into butter, cheese, yogurt, and ice cream, served up along with other local ingredients in multiple courses with entrées like roasted eggplant with sun-dried pesto and Devon mozzarella cheese. Brunch options might include a fiddlehead, asparagus, onion, tomato, and moz-

Chris Tree

CHRIS BUNTEN TURNS HER ORFORD
FARM'S RICH MILK INTO BUTTER, CHEESE,
YOGURT, AND ICE CREAM.

zarella frittata with home fries and toast ($10), or French toast with strawberry rhubarb sauce and whipped cream ($9). Four-course meals $32–36. BYOB.

EATING OUT

In Lebanon/Hanover

Three Tomatoes Trattoria (603-448-1711; threetomatoestratorria.com), 1 Court St., Lebanon. Open for lunch Mon.–Fri. 11:30–3, and nightly from 5 for dinner. A trendy trattoria with a sleek decor, a wood-fired oven and grill, and a reasonably priced menu: plenty of pasta creations like penne con carciofi—sautéed mushrooms, spinach, roasted garlic, and olive oil tossed with penne ziti regate. There are also grilled dishes like pollo cacciatora alla gorgolia—boneless chicken topped with tomato basil sauce, mozzarella, and Romano cheese, and served with linguine—and no less than 16 very different pizzas from the wood-fired oven. Wine and beer are served. Dinner entrées $14.95–17.75; less for pasta.

Gusanoz (603-448-1408; gusanoz .com), 410 Miracle Mile, Lebanon. Open Mon.–Sat. 11–10, until 11 Fri., Sat.–Sun. 11–9. The Upper Valley's hottest Mexican restaurant is squirreled away in a Lebanon mini mall (off I-89 Exit 19; look for a movie theater and the DMV). Maria Limon and Nick Yager have already tripled their seating in answer to demand since their 2005 opening. Specialties include chicken mole, carnitas, tamales, and pork asado, all staples of Limon's girlhood in Durango, Mexico.

Koto (603-298-2925), 288 N. Plainfield Rd. (Rt. 12A), West Lebanon. A well-regarded Japanese steak house, where servers fling knives into the air while grilling your steaks or fish; also sushi and standard Japanese fare.

✐ **Lui, Lui** (603-298-7070), Powerhouse Mall, West Lebanon. Open daily for lunch straight through dinner until 9:30. The former boiler house for the brick mill complex makes a multitiered, attractive setting for this popular, informal Italian restaurant. Pastas, salads, calzones, and specialty pizzas fill the bill of fare.

Four Aces Diner (603-276-3120), 23 Bridge St., West Lebanon. Open for breakfast and lunch except Wed. 6 AM–2 PM. A classic Worcester diner is hidden beneath the unremarkable red-sided exterior. Good, reliable food, fountain drinks, and homemade pie served at booths with jukeboxes.

Yama Restaurant (603-298-5477), 96 S. Main St., West Lebanon. Open Tue.–Sat. (until 10 PM) for lunch and dinner; Sun. from 3 PM. The fare is essentially Korean and terrific, if you like a large choice of udon noodle, miso, seaweed, and spicy soups, as well as house specials like "Yukyejang," which turned out to be shredded beef and vegetables in a spicy broth with side dishes of pickled cucumber and sweet but firm baked beans. There are also donburi, tempura, and teriyaki dishes, and a reasonably priced sushi bar (served with miso soup). Wine and beer.

Salt Hill Pub (603-448-4532), 2 West Park, on the mall, Lebanon. Weekdays 8:30 AM "till late," Sat. from 11 AM, Sun. noon–9. Soups, salads, sandwiches, and burgers plus hand-battered onion rings. At dinner, bangers and mash, fish-and-chips, Irish country pie. A cross between café and Irish pub atmosphere with music Tue. and Thu.–Sat. evenings. *Note:* The latest Salt Hill Pub can be found at 7 Lebanon St., Hanover (603-676-7855).

Baited Hook (603-448-1135), Rt. 4A, Lebanon. This seasonal eatery is a real summer find for lunch and dinner, overlooking Mascoma Lake, also good for take-out and ice cream.

Riverside Grill Restaurant (603-448-2571; riversidegrillnh.com), Riverside Dr., Lebanon. Just off I-89 Exit 17, near Mascoma Lake; the sign is visible from the interstate. This is a good road-food stop. Owned by the Laware family for 60 years, it hasn't changed much in the past 30. We stop for the freshly squeezed lemonade and usually order a BLT. The dinner menu features fries seafood and classics like ham steak and liver, bacon and onions. Beer and wine are served.

In Hanover
Lou's Restaurant and Bakery (603-643-3321; lousrestaurant.net), 30 S. Main St., Hanover. Open for breakfast and lunch weekdays 6–3, weekends from 7. Since 1947 this has been a student and local hangout—and it's great: a long Formica counter, tables and booths, fast, friendly service, all-day breakfast, homemade corned beef hash, good soups, sandwiches, and daily specials, and irresistible peanut butter cookies at the register.

Murphy's on the Green (603-643-4075), 11 S. Main St., Hanover. A traditional college rathskeller with a dark, pubby atmosphere and a wide-ranging beer list; burgers, soups, sandwiches,

and more. It can be crowded and noisy, but the food and service are reliable.

Molly's (603-643-2570), 43 Main St., Hanover. Open daily for lunch and dinner. The greenhouse up front shelters a big, inviting bar that encourages single dining. The menu is immense and reasonably priced: big salads, enchiladas, elaborate burgers at lunch, pasta to steak at dinner.

Yama Restaurant II (603-643-4000), 72 N. Main St., Hanover, is reputedly as good (although Asian aficionados don't agree) as the original and so popular that, with no reservations allowed, a seat can be hard to come by on Saturday night.

Jewel of India (603-643-2217), 27 Lebanon St., Hanover. This restaurant-in-a-house is just hard enough to find to deter tourists but well known to students and locals. A good, reasonably priced bet for quick service and well-spiced dishes.

Jesse's (603-643-4111), Rt. 120, Hanover. Open for lunch and dinner daily, this steak and seafood tavern has long been a mainstay for Upper Valley diners. Daily fish and shellfish specials, three salad bars, burgers, and prime rib. The atmosphere varies from Victorian to Adirondack to Greenhouse but is comfortable for all ages throughout. Entrées $14.50–21.95.

Elsewhere, listed from south to north
Note: Also see **Burdick's Bistro and Café** (burdickchocolate.com) in Walpole, worth a detour off I-91 Exit 5, en route to the Upper Valley.

The Common Man (603-542-6171; thecman.com), 21 Water St., Claremont. Dinner nightly 5–9, Sun. brunch/ dinner 11–9; lounge open 4–11 with light grill menu 9–11. Housed in the Woven Label Building attached to a former mill and to the newest Common Man Inn, this is an attractive brick-walled space with a deck overlooking the Sugar River, the latest addition to the "Common Man Family" of New Hampshire restaurants known for dependably good food and service. The menu varies seasonally but might include sole stuffed with spinach and lobster cream sauce, chicken potpie, and rib-eye steak. Entrées $15–20.

Daddypops Tumble-Inn Diner (603-542-0074), Tremont Square next to the Moody Building, Claremont. Open 6 AM–2 PM. A genuine classic 1941 Worcester diner (#778), with blue tile, a counter, and booths, that has received a new lease on life from owner Debbie Kirb. It's a local hangout: The menu includes corned beef hash and homemade fries. The turkey soup we had here on our last visit hit the spot, and the coffee was good.

China Delight (603-542-0021), 38 Opera House Square, Claremont. Closed Sun., Mon.; otherwise open 11–9, till 9:30 Fri. and Sat. The restaurant space is spacious and bright, and the food is good. No MSG.

✍ "ᵀ" **Mickey's Roadside Café** (603-632-9400; mickeyscafe.net), 330 Rt. 4, Enfield. Open daily 7 AM–9 PM, closing 8 PM Sun. A great roadside eatery, good for pizza, a char-grilled veggie sandwich, or a fried fish platter. Fully licensed. Children's menu.

The Tip Top Café (803-295-3312; tiptopcafe.com), 85 N. Main St., White River Junction, Vt. Chef-owner Eric Harting presides in this glass-fronted bistro on the ground floor of a former commercial bakery. The decor is spare and arty with changing art and brown paper instead of tablecloths. Lunches include soups, salads, and unusual sandwiches such as balsamic figs with spinach and Gorgonzola on rosemary focaccia. Dinner might begin with artichoke fritters with lemon jalapeño preserve. Entrées might include sesame-crusted tilapia with mango salsa and mixed greens. Lunch $6–10, dinner entrées $10–18. This spot is also excellent for lunch.

Jasper Murdock's Alehouse (802-649-1143) in the Norwich Inn, Main St., Norwich, Vt. Open 5:30–9 PM daily. The house brew comes in more than a dozen varieties; we favor the Whistling Pig Red Ale. A comfortable, green-walled room popular with locals, the Alehouse serves the full inn menu, which includes tavern food.

✍ **Gilman's Fairlee Diner** (802-333-3569), Rt. 5, Fairlee, Vt. Closed Tue., otherwise 5:30 AM–2 PM; Thu. until 7 PM and Fri., 8 PM. Turn left (north) on Rt. 5 if you are coming off I-91. This is a classic wooden diner built in the 1930s (across the road from where it stands), with wooden booths, worn-shiny wooden stool tops, and good food. The mashed potato doughnuts are special, and both the soup and the pie are dependably good. Daily specials.

ICE CREAM Wade's Ice Cream, 488 Main St., Claremont. Many flavors

FAIRLEE DINER, FAIRLEE, VT.

Chris Tree

and generous, reasonably priced servings in a riverside setting.

Ben & Jerry's (603-643-2663), 11 Lebanon St., Hanover. For those who need their B&J fix.

Whippi Dip (802-333-3730), 158 Rt. 5, Fairlee. Open 6 AM–9 PM. Known for BBQ and generally good food as well as hard and soft ice cream. Try the World's Fair Sundae: fried dough topped with vanilla ice cream, maple syrup, mixed nuts, and whipped cream.

Mountain Scoops, Rt. 10, North Haverhill. Open Memorial Day–Columbus Day, 11–9. This colorful stand in the middle of town is the source for Rhonda Abrams's homemade ice cream.

SPECIAL BREWS, BAKERIES, AND MORE ✪ Umpleby's Bakery

(603-643-3030; umplebys.com), 3 South St., Hanover. Open Mon.–Sat. 7:30–6, Sun. 7:30–3. We have followed baker Charles Umpleby and his wife, Carolyn, from their original space in the Bridgewater (Vt.) Mill and are delighted to see them ensconced in the heart of Hanover. Everything here is from scratch with no chemical infusions. Breakfast croissants and the like can't be beat. For lunch try a chicken, mushroom, and leek pie, a chicken curry pie, or a pork sausage roll. Sandwiches are on house-made bread; check out "The Mungo Park," grilled vegetables with portobello mushroom, roasted red peppers, and zucchini, plus curry mayonnaise.

"ʏ" Rosey's Coffee and Tea (603-643-5282), 15 Lebanon St., Hanover. Open weekdays 7:30 AM–6:30 PM, from 8:30 Sat.; Sun. 10–5. This stylish European-style café with painted floors and marble-top tables offers great coffee, baked goods, gourmet sandwiches, desserts, and a pleasant place to linger. A bit pricey, but good.

Dirt Cowboy Café (603-643-1323), 7 S. Main St., Hanover. Open 7–6. This is a busy place, thanks to dedication to that perfect cup of Jamaican Blue or Ethiopian Yirgacheffe brew. Also limited sandwiches, bagels, and pastry. Great student-watching inside and (seasonally) out.

"ʏ" Tuckerbox (802-359-4041), 1 S. Main St., White River Junction, Vt. Open Mon.–Sat. Same ownership as the Tip Top but a great coffee shop just where it's needed, right on the corner, the obvious hub of White River Junction. Coffees, teas, and "Eats": soups, sandwiches, and pastries.

Alléchante Patisserie and Cafe (802-649-2846), Main and Elm Sts. Open Mon.–Fri. 7:30–6; until 5 Sat. Nicky Barraclough's shop is in a small shopping complex, easy to miss but well known to local residents who drop by for a morning brioche and latte and to check the daily sandwich board. This might include freshly roasted beef with homemade horseradish cream on white sourdough, and imported fresh goat cheese with sliced tomatoes and green olive spread on a baguette. There are daily baked artisan breads and pastries, plus a full deli with a weekly changing take-out dinner menu. This is also a place to pick up farmstead cheeses. The name is French for "mouthwatering."

✱ Entertainment

MUSIC AND THEATER Hopkins Center (box office 603-646-2422; hop.dartmouth.edu), on the Dartmouth green, Hanover. Sponsors some 150 musical and 20 theater productions per year, plus 200 films, all open to the public.

Lebanon Opera House (603-448-2498), in town hall, Coburn Park. This 800-seat, turn-of-the-20th-century theater hosts frequent concerts, lectures, and summer performances by the North Country Community Players.

&. **Claremont Opera House** (603-542-4433; claremontoperahouse.com), Opera House Square, Claremont. A restored vintage-1897 second-floor theater with a frescoed ceiling and seating for 787, the scene of frequent concerts, plays, and live performances. It's home to the Connecticut River Valley Orchestra. Inquire about children's shows.

⚘ **Northern Stage** (802-296-7000; northernstage.org), Briggs Opera House, White River Junction, Vt. Semiprofessional community theater offers high-quality productions year-round. Special children's theater classes and summer arts education classes.

Opera North (603-448-0400; opera north.org), Lebanon Opera House, 20 Park Square. Excellent, semiprofessional summer performances feature visiting soloists from major opera companies.

Shaker Bridge Theatre (603-632-4013; shakerbridgetheatre.org) stages off-Broadway-style productions year-round in Whitney Hall, 23 Main St., Enfield. Check the website for per-

formances, Fri.–Sat. at 8 PM, Sun. matinees at 3 PM.

The Parish Players (802-785-4344), based in the Eclipse Grange Hall on Thetford Hill, Vt., is the oldest community theater company in the Upper Valley. Its Sept.–May repertoire includes classic pieces and original works; summer presentations vary.

For music, also see **Canoe Club** under *Dining Out* and **Salt Hill Pub** under *Eating Out*.

FILM ⚘ **Fairlee Drive-In** (802-333-9192), Rt. 5, Fairlee, Vt. Summer only; check local papers for listings. This is a beloved icon, the last of the valley's seasonal drive-ins. It's attached to the Fairlee Motel and has a famously good snack bar featuring "Thunderburgers," made from beef on the family's farm across the river in Piermont. The gates open at 7; films begin at dusk.

Dartmouth Film Society at the Hopkins Center (603-646-2576). Frequent showings of classic, contemporary, and experimental films in two theaters.

Nugget Theaters (603-643-2769), S. Main St., Hanover. Four current films nightly, surround sound.

Sony Theatres (603-448-6660), Miracle Mile Shopping Center, Lebanon. Six first-run films nightly.

✴ Selective Shopping

Listed from south to north
ANTIQUES **William Smith** (603-675-2549) holds antiques auctions at the Plainfield Auction Gallery, Rt. 12A in Plainfield, year-round.

Colonial Antique Markets (603-298-8132), Colonial Plaza, Rt. 12A, West Lebanon. Open year-round Mon.–Thu. 10–5, Fri.–Sun. 9–5:30. This looks like nothing from the outside because it's all basement level: dozens of dealers

HOPKINS CENTER

Chris Tree

with art, antiques, collectibles, jewelry, clothing, books, tools, and fun old stuff. It's easy to find once you know it's there: Take Exit 20 off I-89 and follow signs for the airport (it's next to the highway); as soon as you turn onto Airport Rd., take a quick left into Colonial Plaza. The unpromising entrance is around the corner of the brick building on your left, across from the Seven Barrel Brewery.

Quechee Gorge Antiques Mall (802-295-1550), Rt. 4 in Quechee, Vt., with 450 dealers, offers the largest selection on the Vermont side of the river.

ART GALLERIES AND CRAFTS CENTERS

Aidron Duckworth Art Museum (603-469-3444; aidronduck worthmuseum.org), 21 Bean Rd. in the center of Meriden, just off Rt. 120, across from the library. Open May–late Oct., Fri.–Sun. 10–5. A former schoolhouse that served as home and studio for artist Aidron Duckworth until 2001. It now displays his work and changing exhibits by guest artists. Check the website.

AVA Gallery (603-448-3117; ava gallery.org), 11 Bank St. (Rt. 4 just west of Coburn Park), Lebanon. Open Tue.–Sat. 11–5. From its Hanover beginnings, the Alliance for the Visual Arts has grown to fill a sunny former mill building. The Soho-style (and -quality) gallery mounts frequent exhibits of arts and crafts. Classes and workshops are also offered.

Gemstar GemStone Co. in Enfield (603-632-7115), 427 Shaker Blvd., Enfield. Off the beaten path, wholesale importers of gems and beads, knowledgeable and known for high quality, low prices.

Tip Top Media & Arts Building, 85 North St., White River Junction, Vt. A warren of 40 studios and changing galleries, worth a look.

League of New Hampshire Craftsmen (603-643-5050), 13 Lebanon St., Hanover. Closed Sun. Next to Ben & Jerry's; a wide selection of local and regional crafts pieces. Craft classes offered.

Spheris (603-640-6155; spherisgallery .com), 59 South St., Hanover. This is a high-quality contemporary art gallery that we have followed from Walpole to Bellows Falls to this present space.

Long River Studios (603-795-4909), 1 Main St., Lyme. Open Mon.–Sat. 10–5. A regional cooperative with a wide selection of art in many media, also cards, books, pottery, clothing, jewelry, and more.

Simon Pearce Glass (802-674-6280), Rt. 5 north of Windsor, Vt. Open daily 9–5. Pearce operated his own glassworks in Ireland before moving to Ver-

LONG RIVER STUDIOS, LYME, IS AN EXCEPTIONAL REGIONAL COOPERATIVE.

Long River Studios

mont in 1981. Here he acquired the venerable Downer's Mill in Quechee and harnessed the dam's hydropower for the glass furnace (see *Dining Out*). In 1993 he opened this new, visitor-friendly glass factory featuring a catwalk that overlooks the gallery where glass is blown and shaped. Of course, there's a big showroom/shop featuring seconds as well as first-quality glass and pottery.

BOOKSTORES Dartmouth Bookstore (603-643-2348; dartmouth books.bncollege.com), 33 S. Main St., Hanover. Open Mon.–Thu. 8 AM–9 PM, until 10 Fri., Sat. and Sun. 11–5. Now operated by Barnes & Noble College Books, this is a gathering space and source of Dartmouth paraphernalia, clothing, and gifts as well as textbooks; also children's and general-interest titles. Author readings and events.

The Norwich Bookstore (802-649-1114), Main St., Norwich, Vt., next to the post office. This is a light, airy store with well-selected titles and comfortable places to sit. The staff are very knowledgeable. Frequent readings, and a good children's section.

Left Bank Books (603-643-4479), 9 South St., Hanover. Closed Tue. Otherwise 9:30–5:30; Sun.11:30–4. Nancy Cressman has created an inviting upstairs aerie filled with used books and comfortable places to read. Inquire about the many programs, including a Tue.-evening series of readings, slide shows, and discussions.

Violet's Book Exchange (603-542-4222; violetsbookexchange.com), 28 Opera House Square, Claremont. Open daily. Two floors of new and used books, a great place to browse.

Borders Books Music & Café (603-298-9963), Walmart Plaza, West Lebanon. Open Mon.–Thu. 9–9, Fri.–Sat. 9–10, Sun. 9–8.

SPECIAL SHOPPING CENTERS Centerra Marketplace, Rt. 120, Lebanon. Anchored by the co-op grocery store, this complex also features a trendy restaurant.

Powerhouse Mall, Rt. 10, West Lebanon. Open Mon.–Fri. 10–9, Sat. 10–6, Sun. noon–5. A total of 40 stores are in this unusual complex, which combines an old brick electric powerhouse, a large, new but mill-style, two-story arcade, and several older buildings moved from other places, all offering a genuine variety of small specialty stores. Anchored by **Eastern Mountain Sports** (603-298-7716) and **L.L. Bean** (603-298-6975) featuring sporting gear, other noteworthy shops include the **Anichini Outlet Store** (603-298-8656; anichini.com); open 10–8 except Sun., when it's noon–5, featuring the Tunbridge, Vt.–based company's nationally lauded line of antique and fine linens at substantial savings; and a surprising choice of women's clothing stores.

SPECIAL SHOPS King Arthur Flour Baker's Store (802-649-3361; kingarthurflour.com), Rt. 5, Norwich, Vt. Open Mon.–Sat. 8:30–6, Sun. until 4. Home as well as prime outlet for the country's oldest family-owned flour company (since 1790), this store draws serious bakers and would-be bakers from several time zones. The vast post-and-beam building itself is a marvel, its shelves stocked with every conceivable kind of flour, baking ingredient, and a selection of equipment and cookbooks, not to mention bread and pastries made in the adjacent bakery (with a glass connector allowing visitors to watch the hands and skills of the bakers). Next door too is the Baking Education Center, offering baking classes ranging from beginner to expert, from making piecrust to braided breads and elegant pastries.

Dan & Whit's General Store (802-649-1602), Main St., Norwich, Vt. This quintessential Vermont country store justifies a trip across the river. Hardware, groceries, housewares, boots and clothing, farm and garden supplies, and a great community bulletin board: If they don't have it, you don't need it.

Shackleton Thomas (603-676-7214), 15 South Main St., Hanover. This handsome store showcases work by Charles Shackleton, one of Vermont's foremost furniture makers and his wife, Miranda Thomas, a distinguished potter.

Dartmouth Co-op (603-643-3100), 25 S. Main St., Hanover. Incorporated in 1919 and now owned by Dartmouth alumni, a source of sports clothes and of course an extensive line of Dartmouthiana: T-shirts, sweats, boxers, mugs, cushions.

Pompanoosuc Mills (802-785-4851; pompy.com), Rt. 5, East Thetford, Vt. Dartmouth graduate Dwight Sargeant began building furniture in this riverside house, a cottage industry that has evolved into a riverside factory with showrooms throughout New England. Some seconds. Open daily until 6 PM, Sun. noon–5. Note the branch on Lebanon St. in Hanover. The Memorial Day weekend tent sale draws shoppers from afar.

Chapman's (802-333-9709), Fairlee, Vt. Open daily 8–6, 7–5 on Sun. Since 1924 members of the Chapman family have expanded the stock of this old pharmacy to include 10,000 hand-tied flies, wines, Mexican silver and Indonesian jewelry, used books, maple syrup, and an unusual selection of toys.

FOOD AND FARMS North Country Smokehouse (603-542-8323; ncsmokehouse.com), 471 Sullivan St. (formerly Airport Rd.), Claremont. Open Mon.–Fri. 8–5. The meats made here—ham, turkey, bacon, sausages, and kielbasa, some applewood smoked, some maple cured—have been deli staples since Mike Satzow's grandfather established the business in 1912.

Thyme & Ewe Farm (603-542-1746), 688 Chestnut St., Claremont. This family farm rescues farm animals and offers free tours. Seasonal events such as haunted trailer rides and tree lighting. There's a greenhouse and a small retail store that sells jams, pickles, baked goods, and seasonal produce.

Claremont Farmer's Market (603-542-8687), Broad Street Park, downtown Claremont. Mid-June–Oct., Thu. 4–7. Locally grown vegetables, homemade baked goods and crafts, live music in the evening.

Edgewater Farm (603-298-5764) in Plainfield offers pick-your-own strawberries and raspberries; there are also greenhouses with bedding plants, and a farm stand on Rt. 12A. Also on River Rd., **Riverview Farms** (603-298-8519) offers apples, pumpkins, cider pressing, and hayrides in fall. **McNamara Dairy** (603-298-MOOO) sells its own glass-bottled milk and eggnog.

CLAREMONT FARMER'S MARKET

Chris Tree

Poverty Lane Orchards and Farnum Hill Ciders (603-448-1511; farnumhillciders.com), 98 Poverty Lane, Lebanon. The orchard's retail store is open Labor Day–Halloween, weekdays 8–6, weekends 10–5. Minutes from I-89; follow signs for the airport. Also inquire about PYO. There are more than 100 varieties of heirloom apples. Visitors can sample the hard sparkling and still ciders, which are crafted in small batches from heirloom apples in this hilltop orchard overlooking the Connecticut River. There's nothing not to like about these throwbacks to the favored drink at New England's earliest taverns. The cider is available throughout New England. Check the website for special tastings.

Hanover Farmers Market. June–Sept., Thu. on the green.

MAPLE SUGARING Mid-Feb.–early April, the following local sugarhouses welcome visitors to watch them "boil off" and sample the new syrup. Most also sell their own syrup year-round.

Putnam Bros. Sugarhouse (603-826-3196), 39 Old Cheshire Turnpike, off Rt. 12 about 3 miles south of Charlestown. This is a beautiful old family dairy farm, with the sugarhouse open during sugaring season when they are boiling and on weekends, 10–5, for sugar-on-snow with homemade doughnuts and coffee. Guests are also welcome to come up to the barn.

Brokenridge Farm (603-542-8781), Rt. 120, Cornish. Sap is gathered with horses on weekends; sugar-on-snow, tours.

Orford has the biggest local concentration of maple-syruping operations, including: **Gerald and Toni Pease** (603-353-9070), Pease's Scenic Hwy., off Rt. 25A. Draft horse with wagon or sleigh. Gale and Peter Thompson (son

of a former governor) operate a traditional sugarhouse and serve pancake breakfasts at **Mount Cube Farm** (603-353-4709), Rt. 25A. There's also **Sunday Mountain Maple Products** (603-353-4883), Rt. 25A.

✳ Special Events

For details about any of these events, phone the town clerk, listed with information.

Mid-February: **Dartmouth Winter Carnival**, Hanover. Thu.–Sun. Ice sculptures, sports events, ski jumping.

March: **Meriden Wild Game Dinner**, Kimball Union Academy's Miller Student Center. Usually a Saturday. At this benefit for the Meriden Volunteer Fire Department, bear, raccoon, and boar are usually on the menu.

Mid-May: **Dartmouth Pow-Wow**, Hanover. A gathering of Native American craftspeople and dancers on the second Saturday of May; sponsored by Native Americans at Dartmouth (603-646-2110) and the Native American Studies Program (603-646-3530).

Third weekend in June: **Quechee Balloon Festival and Crafts Fair** (802-295-7900), Quechee, Vt. Some 20 hot-air balloons gather, offering rides at dawn and dusk; barbecue, skydiving, crafts, food booths. **Summer Strawberry Festival**, Plainfield Historical Society Clubhouse, Rt. 12A, Plainfield. **Lyme Summer Suppers and Horse Sheds Crafts Festivals**, Lyme Congregational Church horse sheds, Lyme. Beginning the last Wednesday in June, then every other week for four Wednesdays. The crafts festivals begin at 1 PM and the suppers, also at the church, begin at 6 PM.

Fourth of July: **Independence Day Open Fields Circus**, Thetford, Vt. A takeoff on a real circus, by the Parish

HANOVER STREET FEST DRAWS SHOPPERS FROM THROUGHOUT THE UPPER VALLEY.

Players. **Fourth of July celebration**, Plainfield. Community breakfast, footraces, parade, firemen's roast beef dinner. Lebanon stages the largest fireworks display in the area.

Mid-July: **Hanover Street Fest** (603-643-3115; visithanover.com). All day for one July Saturday, downtown Hanover is a pedestrian mall. Street bazaar, hay-wagon rides, fireworks, entertainment. **Norwich (Vt.) Fair**. Mix of old-time country fair and honky-tonk carnival. Lobster dinner, parade, ox pulling.

Late July: **Hanover Center Fair**, Hanover. Friday-night games, dancing, food; Saturday starts with a children's costume parade, ox pulling, food, games. **La Salette Fair** (603-632-4301), at the La Salette Shrine, Rt. 4A, Enfield. Usually a midway with rides, flea market, craft booths. **Thetford Hill Fair**, Thetford Hill, Vt. Small but special: a rummage sale, food and plant booths, barbecue.

Mid-August: **Cornish Fair**. Horse and ox pulling, agricultural exhibits, ham and bean suppers, a Saturday woodsmen's field day.

Late August: **Quechee Scottish Festival**, Quechee, Vt. Sheepdog trials, Highland dancing, piping, Highland "games," ladies' rolling-pin toss, more.

Mid-October: **Horse Sheds Crafts Fair**, at the Lyme Congregational Church, Lyme. Saturday of Columbus Day weekend 10 AM–4 PM; also a **Fall Festival** lunch at the church.

Mid-December–Christmas: **Christmas Pageants** in Norwich and Lyme. **Revels North**, in the Hopkins Center. Song and dance. **Christmas Illuminations**, at the La Salette Shrine, Rt. 4A, Enfield.

LOWER COHASE

*C*ohase (pronounced *co-hâs*) is an Abenaki word meaning "wide valley." That's according to the chamber of commerce by that name that now embraces this gloriously little-touristed 15-mile stretch of the Connecticut north of the Upper Valley.

Its southernmost towns are sleepy Piermont, New Hampshire, and (relatively) bustling Bradford, Vermont, built on terraced land at the confluence of the Waits River and the Connecticut. Bradford is a 19th-century mill village that produced plows, paper, and James Wilson, an ingenious farmer who made America's first geographic globes. Handsome Low's Grist Mill survives across from the falls, now housing a popular restaurant, and a golf course spreads below the business block across the floodplain. From Bradford the view across the river encompasses Mount Moosilauke, easternmost of the White Mountains.

Moving upriver, Haverhill and Newbury, Vermont, two of northern New England's most handsome and historic towns, face each other across the river.

Haverhill is immense, comprising seven very distinct villages, including classic examples of both Federal-era and railroad villages. Thanks to a fertile floodplain, this is an old and prosperous farming community, even now. Haverhill Corner was founded in 1763 at the western terminus of the Coos Turnpike that wound its way up the Baker Valley and over the mountains from Plymouth. It became the Grafton County seat in 1773; a graceful 19th-century courthouse has recently been restored as a performance and information center. The village itself is a gem a grouping of Federal-era and Greek Revival homes and public buildings around a double, white-fenced common.

Just north of Haverhill Corner (but south of the junction of Rts. 10 and 25) a sign points the way down through a cornfield and along the river to the site of the Bedell Bridge. Built in 1866, this was one of the largest surviving examples of a two-span covered bridge, until it was destroyed by a violent September windstorm in 1979. The site is still worth finding because it's a peaceful riverside spot, ideal for a picnic.

In North Haverhill you come unexpectedly to a lineup of modern county buildings—the courthouse, a county home, and a jail—and then you are in downtown Woodsville, a 19th-century rail hub with an ornate 1890s brick Opera Block and three-story, mustard-colored railroad station. The Haverhill–Bath covered bridge, built in 1829 and billed as the oldest covered bridge in New England, is just beyond the railroad underpass (Rt. 135 North).

Newbury is one of Vermont's oldest towns, founded in 1761 by Jacob Bailey, a Revolutionary War general still remembered as the force behind the Bayley-Hazen Road, conceived as an invasion route to northwest to Canada. It was abandoned two-thirds of the way along, but after the Revolution it served as a prime settlement route. A plaque at the northern end of the business block in Wells River (a village in Newbury) notes the beginning of the trail, while another in Hazen's Notch marks its terminus. Newbury was the site of a Native American village for many thousands of years, and its mineral springs drew travelers as early as 1800. Wells River marked the head of navigation on the Connecticut through the 1830s. In the 1840s river traffic was upstaged by the railroad, which transformed Woodsville.

GUIDANCE Lower Cohase Regional Chamber of Commerce (802-222-5631; 866-526-4273; cohase.org), P.O. Box 209, Bradford, VT 05033, publishes a helpful map/guide and maintains a seasonal welcome center in Wells River, Vt., just west of the bridge on Rt. 302.

Alumni Hall (603-989-5500), Court St., Haverhill Corner. Open mid-June–mid-Oct., 10–4. Built gracefully in brick in 1846 as the Grafton County courthouse, later part of Haverhill Academy and recently restored as a venue for performances, art shows, and the like and as a Connecticut River Scenic Byway interpretive center. Cultural map/guides and books published by the Joint River Commissions are featured, along with local info.

✳ To Do

BALLOONING See **Balloon Vermont** in the "Upper Valley River Towns."

BICYCLING Given the beauty of the landscape and the little-trafficked, level nature of Rt. 10 and of this stretch of Rt. 5, the appeal to bicyclists is obvious. Less obvious are the long-distance routes that draw serious cyclists up over the White Mountains on Rts. 116 and 25.

BOATING Hemlock Pete's Canoes & Kayaks (603-667-5112; hpcanoes.com), off Rt. 10, North Haverhill. Scott Edwards teaches at the local high school and actually makes as well as rents canoes and kayaks and offers shuttle service; guided War Canoe tours, too. His seasonal shop is the barn across from the fairgrounds. Call or check the website for directions off-season.

GOLF Bradford Golf Club (802-222-5207), Bradford, Vt. Nine holes down by the river. **Blackmount Country Club** (603-787-6564; blackmountcountryclub .com), 400 Clark Rd., North Haverhill. Cart rentals, driving range, practice green, A par-36, nine-hole golf course.

SWIMMING Lake Tarleton State Park, Rt. 25C in Piermont, Warren, and Benton. More than 5,000 acres surrounding Lake Tarleton, smaller Lakes Katherine and Constance, and much of Lake Armington are now public land divided between White Mountain National Forest conservation trusts and a state park featuring the sand beach on Lake Tarleton (part of a onetime resort). The property was slated for major development in 1994 when preservation forces, spearheaded by the Trust for Public Land, raised more than $7 million to preserve this magnificent woodland with its views of Mount Moosilauke. The lake is stocked with trout and also beautiful for canoeing and kayaking (public boat launch). Hiking trails are taking shape, including a connector to the Appalachian Trail, which passes through the property 0.5 mile from the lake.

✳ Lodging

🐾 ✄ ♿ **Piermont Inn** (603-272-4820; piermontinn.com), 1 Old Church St., Piermont 03779. A 1790s stagecoach stop with six rooms, four in the adjacent carriage house (only the two in the inn are available year-round), all with private bath. The two in the main house are outstanding rooms, both carved from the tavern's original ballroom, high ceilinged and spacious, with writing desks and appropriate antiques. The carriage house rooms are simple but cheery; one is handicapped accessible, and pets are accepted ($20 per night). Common space includes a living room with a fireplace, TV, wing chairs, and a nifty grandfather clock. Charlie and Karen Brown are longtime Piermont residents who enjoy tuning guests in to the many ways of exploring this upper (less touristed) part of the Valley, especially canoeing the river. Rooms in the main house are $139, and in the carriage house $99. Full breakfast available for $9.

🐾 **The Gibson House** (603-989-3125; gibsonhousebb.com), RR 1, Box 193, Haverhill 03765. Open June–Oct. New innkeepers Susie Klein and Marty Cohen have kept this amazing place exactly as Artist Keita Colton restored it. One of the valley's finest Greek Revival homes, it was built in 1850 on the green in Haverhill Corners and at one point was a stagecoach inn. The eight guest rooms, especially the four big second-floor rooms, are artistic creations, each very different from the next. Taj North is the most opulent and exotic with its faux balcony, rich colors, and glowing stained-glass moon. We enjoyed the golden, Asian-themed Bamboo Room, but our favorite is the Seashore Room, with its quilts and colors (twin beds), overlooking the garden. While the house fronts on Rt. 10, the 50-foot-long sunny back porch with wicker seats and swing takes full advantage of the splendid view west across the terraced garden and the Connecticut River. A full breakfast is served, weather permitting, in the fanciful dining room or on the first-floor screened porch. $135 weekdays, $150–175 weekends includes a full breakfast.

🍑 **Peach Brook Inn** (802-866-3389), Doe Hill, off Rt. 5, South Newbury, VT 05051. Joyce Emery has opened her spacious 1837 home with its splendid view of the Connecticut River. What a special place! Common space includes two nicely furnished parlors with exposed beams and a fireplace, an open kitchen, and a screened porch with a view of Mount Moosilauke across the river. The house is on a

PIERMONT INN, PIERMONT

Piermont Inn

country lane in the almost vanished village of South Newbury, once connected to Haverhill, New Hampshire, across the river by a long-gone covered bridge. Plenty of farm animals are within walking distance. There are three comfortable guest rooms; $75 with shared bath, $85 with private, including full breakfast. No smoking. No children under 10, please; under 18 are $10.

The Hayloft Inn at Blackmount (603-787-2367; hayloftinn.com), 440 Clark Pond Rd., North Haverhill 03774. The plain exterior of this house belies its airy, open post-and-beam interior. Innkeeper Joyce Read is a native of Plainfield, where her mother modeled a couple of times as a young girl for painter Maxfield Parrish. Read has been collecting the artist's distinctive prints all her life and displays them in a special gallery room. There's a large room with king-sized bed and bath downstairs ($100); upstairs there are two bright, tastefully furnished guest rooms with private bath ($85). A hearty breakfast is served at 8 AM. The Blackmount Country Club is next door.

✃ ✆ 🍴 **The Whipple Tree Bed & Breakfast** (802-429-2076; 800-466-4097), 487 Stevens Place, Wells River, VT 05081. High on a wooded slope with views across the Valley to the White Mountains, William Bailey has built a splendid home designed as a bed & breakfast with six spacious guest rooms, all with private bath. Carol Bailey's decor throughout is casual, country elegant. Amenities include air-conditioning, TVs, a guest fridge, a game room, and a big outdoor hot tub. Bill Bailey is, incidentally, the great-great-great-great-grandson of General Jacob Bailey, the Revolutionary War hero responsible for the Bayley-Hazen Road (see the chapter introduction). While the feel is remote, the house is

just over 2 miles up country roads from Rt. 302 and little more than that from I-91 Exit 17. A full country breakfast is included in $140–190, $15 per extra person.

🐾 ✆ ✆ 🍴 **Nootka Lodge** (603-747-2418; 800-626-9105), 4982 Dartmouth College Hwy. (junction of Rts. 10 and 302), Woodsville 03785. This attractive 34-unit log motor inn offers efficiencies, connecting rooms for families, and two-bedroom suites with Jacuzzi and fireplace. Amenities include TV, air-conditioning, a pool, and indoor whirlpool and game room. $70–175 for rooms.

✳ Where to Eat

DINING OUT The Perfect Pear Café (802-222-5912; theperfectpear cafe.com), the Bradford Mill, Main St., Bradford, Vt. Open Tue.–Sat. 11:30–3 for lunch, Tue.–Sun. 5–8:45 for dinner. Dinner reservations recommended. Adam Coulter, formerly at the Norwich Inn, is now chef-owner. This remains a charming bistro, housed in a historic brick mill by a falls, especially appealing in summer when there's dining on the flower-decked patio overlooking the Waits River, churning along because the big falls are just across the road. Lunch is reasonably priced with choices like Gorgonzola and candied walnut salad with maple balsamic vinaigrette, and a lamb and rosemary sausage sandwich on whole grain with honey mustard. Dinner might begin with crispy pork dumplings and feature crabmeat-stuffed rainbow trout with a pesto cream, or pork tenderloin served with polenta, as well as vegetarian choices like truffled cannellini bean ravioli with a shiitake Marsala sauce and braised greens. Dinner entrées $12–18.

🍷 ✆ **Warners Gallery Restaurant** (802-429-2120), just off I-91 Exit 17, 2284 Rt. 302, Wells River. Open

Tue.–Sat. 5–9 PM, Sun. 11–8 with brunch 11–2. This is a find, a dependable all-American family restaurant with an eating-out, candlelit atmosphere. Entrées usually include twin stuffed lobster tails, a fisherman's platter, and roast prime beef au jus. Dinner entrées $13–23, including the generous salad bar. On Tuesday the sirloin, haddock, and BBQ chicken are all $10 (we took advantage of this!), Wednesday is "bring a friend" night (half price on the second dinner), and on Friday kids eat free. The Sunday buffet draws folks from throughout the North Country. Full liquor license.

EATING OUT *Note:* For lunch in Bradford/Piermont, check **Perfect Pear** under *Dining Out.*

✍ **Colatina Exit** (802-222-9008), Main St., Bradford, Vt. Open daily 5–9 PM; weekends until 10:30. Carol Meagher's Vermont trattoria has been here more than 30 years but recently doubled in size, added a wood-fired pizza oven, and expanded its to-go menu. We still like the original dining room best: candles in Chianti bottles, Italian scenes on the walls, checked (green in summer, red in winter) tablecloths, and a few tables in back with a view of the river. The big menu offers plenty of antipasto and insalata choices and traditional Italian dishes like "lasagna classico" and veal parmigiano; also some nice surprises like grilled chicken portofino (with sautéed portobello mushrooms and fresh spinach in a red Marsala marinara sauce) and wood-roasted scallops carbonara (with spinach and smoked bacon). Plenty of pizza choices and calzones. There's also an upstairs pub with river views.

Bliss Village Store and Deli (802-222-4617), Main St., Bradford, Vt. Housed in a former 19th-century hotel, this is a classic general store but with Crock-Pots full of soup, chili, or stew-fried chicken and a deli with daily specials; tables are in the back—including a booth with the best river view in town.

Newbury Village Store (802-866-5681), 4991 Rt. 5, Newbury, Vt. Open 6 AM–8 PM weekdays, Sat. 7–8, Sun. 8–6. This is the new breed of nouvelle general store. Gary and Maggie Hatch have added comfortable seating near the periodicals and expanded the deli to feature sandwiches named for local landmarks like "The Oxbow" ("basil herb roasted turkey breast with Vermont cheddar, ripe tomatoes, leaf lettuce and the house garlic cream cheese spread on multi grain bread"). There's also a hummus wrap and "The Flatlander" ("shaved black pastrami warmed and piled high on rye and pumpernickel swirl bread, topped with swiss cheese and deli mustard"). There are staple groceries, also a selection of wine and Vermont products. Locals tells us these are the best sandwiches around. There are tables in the back, overlooking the river.

Happy Hours Restaurant (802-757-3466), Rt. 5, Wells River, Vt. Open daily 11:30–8, later in summer. This large, pine-paneled family restaurant in the middle of town has been lightened and brightened in recent years and hums with a sense of friendly service and satisfied patrons. Most entrées include the salad bar—and servings are generous. We couldn't finish a tender sirloin topped with red wine mushroom sauce, with baked potato and good coleslaw (a $12.99 special). Dinner entrées $11.99–22.99.

✍ **P&H Truck Stop** (802-429-2141), just off I-91 Exit 17 on Rt. 302, Wells River, Vt. Now open just 6 AM–10 PM for hot meals but still 24 hours for to-go premade sandwiches, pies, and the like. Dozens of rigs are usually parked outside on one side, with a broad range of license plates on cars in the other lot. This is a classic truck stop with speedy service, friendly waitresses, and heaping portions at amazing prices. Plus which the bread is homemade; ATM and phone are available (cell phones don't tend to work around here, and pay phones are scarce).

Shiloh's Cabin Cooking (603-747-2525), 202 Central St., Woodsville. Open 7 AM–9 PM, closing Sun. at 8 PM. Nicole and Miranda Fenoff fill the need for good road food in Woodsville. The beef and as many other ingredients as possible are local.

ICE CREAM Mountain Scoops, Rt. 10, North Haverhill. Open Memorial Day–Columbus Day, 11–9. This colorful stand in the middle of town is the source of Rhonda Abrams's homemade ice cream.

✳ Entertainment

Old Church Community Theater (802-222-3322), 137 Main St., Bradford, Vt. (call Paul Hunt: 802-222-4254).

Alumni Hall (603-989-5500), Court St., Haverhill Corner. Open mid-June–mid-Oct., 10–4. Built gracefully in brick in 1846 as the Grafton County courthouse, later part of Haverhill Academy and recently restored as a venue for concerts and other performances, art shows, and the like. Call for current schedule.

Summer band concerts can be found in Bradford, Woodsville, and Haverhill; for details see cohase.org.

✳ Selective Shopping

Copeland Furniture (802-222-5300; copelandfurniture.com), 64 Main St., Bradford, Vt. Open Mon.–Fri. 10–6, Sat. 9–5. Contemporary, cleanly lined, locally made furniture in native hardwoods displayed in the handsome showroom in the converted 19th-century brick mill across from Bradford Falls. Seconds.

Farm-Way, Inc. (800-222-9316), Rt. 25, Bradford, Vt. One mile east of I-91 Exit 16. Open Mon.–Sat. until 8 PM. Billed as "complete outfitters for man and beast," this is a phenomenon: a family-run source of work boots and rugged clothing that now includes a stock of more than two million products spread over 5 acres: tack, furniture, pet supplies, syrup, whatever. Recently expanded: Shoes and boots remain a specialty, from size 4E to 16; 25,000 shoes, boots, clogs, sandals, and sneakers in stock; also kayaks, sporting equipment, furnishings, and gifts.

South Road Pottery (802-222-5798; brucemurraypotter.com), 3458 South Rd., Bradford. Open May–Oct., 10–5. Bruce Murray is a long-established, nationally known potter whose studio-showroom is in a timber-frame 18th-century barn surrounded by farm fields. It's well worth the scenic drive to this exceptional studio with its wide variety of handmade and hand-decorated stoneware, both functional (lamps, vases, unusual butter dishes—really mini crocks that keep butter soft) and decorative (wall tiles and plaques). Inquire about workshops and about the **Barn Bridge Guest Room**, an attractive guest unit with a private deck, bath, and galley kitchen ($150 per night).

Robie Farm & Store (603-272-4872), 25 Rt. 10, Piermont. Six generations of Robies have farmed this property. The farm store sells dairy beef free from antibiotics and hormones, also low-fat and skim raw milk as well as pints of cream; eggs from free-range chickens; a variety of cheeses, including our favorite, Toma—a traditional Italian Alpine-style cheese made from their own raw milk; and ice cream made in small batches (flavors vary seasonally and may include rhubarb, brownie, and pumpkin). Also baked goods and local products.

Round Barn Shoppe (603-272-9026), 430 Rt. 10, Piermont. Open May 2–Christmas, Thu.–Mon. 9–5; Jan.–May 1, Fri.–Sun. This 1990s post-and-beam round barn replicates the authentic 1906 barn across the road. It houses a shop selling New England products ranging from baskets and dolls to local dairy milk and fresh pies. Some 300 New England craftsmen and 100 small manufacturers are represented.

4 Corners Farm (802-866-3342), just off Rt. 5, South Newbury, Vt. Bob and Kim Gray sell their own produce and flowers. An exceptionally pretty farm, just off but up above the highway, known for strawberries, PYO vegetables.

Windy Ridge Orchard (787-6377), Rt. 116, North Haverhill. Open daily Labor Day–Thanksgiving, 9–6; weekends Thanksgiving–Christmas, 9–4. Pick-your-own apples and pumpkins, farm animals, kids' corral playground, nature trails, picnic tables, Cider House Café, gift shop. Apple picking begins in mid-August and lasts through mid-October depending on the variety. There are 3,500 apple trees on 20 acres, overlooking the valley and Green Mountains. There's also a Christmas tree plantation—and you can cut your own trees.

Woodsville Bookstore (603-747-3811), 91 Central St., Woodsville. Open weekdays 9–6, Sat. 9–4. Dave Major's friendly, well-stocked bookstore is an unexpected find here, the best for many miles around. One room of new, one of used books.

✳ Special Events

Note: Farmer's markets are held in Woodsville on Wednesdays.

Late November: **Bradford United Church of Christ Wild Game Supper**, Bradford, Vt. The Saturday before Thanksgiving this town nearly doubles its population as hungry visitors pour into the church to feast on 2,800 pounds of buffalo, venison, moose, pheasant, coon, rabbit, wild boar, and bear. $25 adults, $12 for children under 10. The problem is that you can't simply show up. Checks to the BUCC, along with a SASE and the seating you would like (on the hour: 2:30–6:30), must be sent on or after Oct. 19 (don't wait too long) to UCC Wild Game Supper, P.O. Box 861, Bradford, VT 05033.

July: **4th of July Parade and celebration in Woodsville and Wells River**—marching bands, floats, horses, chicken barbecue, dancing, fireworks. **Connecticut Valley Fair** (*midmonth*), Bradford. **Cracker Barrel Bazaar** (*third or final weekend*), Newbury, Vt., includes plenty of fiddling (802-866-5521). **Connecticut Valley Fair** (connecticutvalleyfair.com), Bradford, Vt. Ox and horse pulling, sheep show, midway, demolition derby. The **North Haverhill Fair** (*last weekend*) is an old-style fair with ox and tractor pulls, pig races, and more.

Last weekend of September: **Whole Hog Blues & BBQ Festival** (*last weekend*). Blues music by leading bands, roast pig cook-off, arts and crafts.

Weekend before Columbus Day: **Vermont North by Hand**—crafts and art studios hold open house (cohase.org).

The Lakes Region

5

THE SUNAPEE/NEWFOUND LAKES
REGION

THE LAKE WINNIPESAUKEE REGION

OSSIPEE VALLEY

Chris Tree

THE SUNAPEE/NEWFOUND LAKES REGION

From Lake Sunapee to Newfound Lake, this region is spotted with lakes big and small, all set in open, rolling countryside, each with a view of one of the area's three mighty mountains: Sunapee, Kearsarge, and Cardigan.

All three summits make rewarding hikes, and the lakes offer attractive shoreline lodging as well as swimming, fishing, and boating. But this entire area is far less well known than the Winnipesaukee region, because most of the old lakeside hotels have long since been replaced with second homes. Still, these "summer people" continued to patronize summer theater, shops, ski areas, and restaurants. When lodging places began proliferating again, as they have over the past few decades, these amenities were all in place.

The year-round hub of the area is the handsome old college town of New London, with a rambling, 18th-century inn and Colby-Sawyer College at its center and two small lakes—Little Sunapee and Pleasant Lake—on its arms.

The region's most famous lake is Sunapee. Unusually clear (it is still a source of drinking water) and unusually high (1,100 feet), Lake Sunapee sits midway between the Connecticut River Valley and the Merrimack River Valley. Ten miles long and 3 miles wide, with a shoreline that's still almost entirely green, it's a special place.

Lake Sunapee, however, is also a tease. Stand on the summit of Mount Sunapee (accessible by chairlift) and its 10-mile-long expanse shimmers below, seemingly inviting you to jump in. Back on level ground, though, reaching the water is elusive. You can swim at the beach in Lake Sunapee State Park, choose from two excursion boats, or rent almost any kind of boat; but no road circles the lake because, from the 1850s until the 1920s, everyone came and went by train and got around the lake itself by steamboat. The largest cluster of hotels and busiest steamboat landing was Sunapee Harbor, still the summer focal point of the lake.

Pristine Newfound Lake to the northeast (8 miles west of I-93) has 22 miles of shoreline and views to the west of Mount Cardigan. It offers a sandy state beach, as does smaller Kezar Lake in North Sutton (I-89 Exit 10). Other lakes accessible to guests at local inns include Little Sunapee Lake, Pleasant Lake, Lake Todd, and Lake Massasecum in Bradford; Highland Lake in East Andover; and Webster Lake in Franklin.

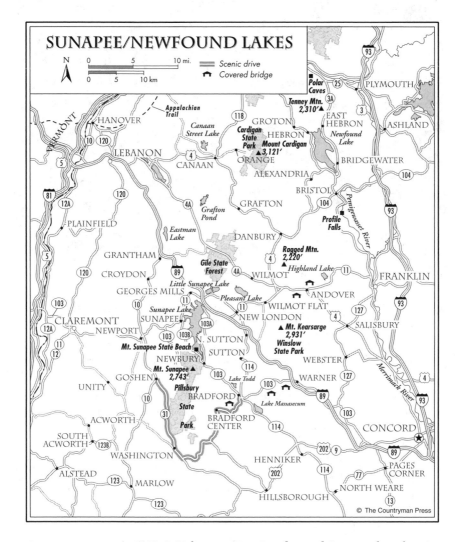

Since its opening in 1968, I-89 has put New London and Sunapee less than 2 hours from Boston, but the increase in tourist traffic has not been dramatic. In winter, skiers tend to day-trip from Boston as well as Concord to Mount Sunapee and to Ragged Mountain in Danbury. Lodging prices are relatively low—and even lower in the northern part of this region, which has been backroaded since I-89 replaced Rt. 4 as the region's major east–west route.

In New Hampshire state promotional literature you'll find much of this area described under "Dartmouth/Lake Sunapee Region." We don't want to confuse the issue, but it does seem that Sunapee is a big lake in a lakes region and that Dartmouth is the historic hub of the Connecticut River Valley, which we describe in another chapter.

GUIDANCE "*ℹ*" **Lake Sunapee Region Chamber of Commerce** (603-526-6575; sunapeevacations.com) maintains a helpful walk-in information center with a restroom in the middle of New London at 328 Main St. Open year-round,

VIEW OF LAKE SUNAPEE FROM MOUNT SUNAPEE

Mon.–Fri. 9–5, Sat. 9–noon, Sun. 11–2; another seasonal information booth for Sunapee in Sunapee Lower Village is open May–Oct., Wed.–Sun. 10–4.

The Newfound Region Chamber of Commerce (603-744-2150; newfound chamber.com) maintains a seasonal information booth on Rt. 3A, Bristol, at the foot of the lake.

The Newport Chamber of Commerce (603-863-1510; newportnhchamber.org), 2 N. Main St., maintains a seasonal information booth in the center of town.

GETTING THERE ʰⁱ⁰ *By bus:* **Dartmouth Coach** (800-637-0123; dartmouth coach.com) stops regularly en route from Boston's Logan Airport and South Station to Hanover. The stop is just off I-89 Exit 12, 3 miles from downtown New London; there's parking but no station. Buy tickets online or with cash from the driver.

By car: I-89 cuts diagonally across the heart of this region, putting it within an hour and a half of Boston; via I-91 it's also two and a half hours from Hartford.

By air: See *Getting There* in "Upper Valley Towns" and "The Manchester/Nashua Area."

MEDICAL EMERGENCY Dial **911**.

New London Hospital (603-526-2911), 270 County Rd., New London, has a 24-hour walk-in clinic.

✳ Villages

Andover (pop. 2,010). This is an unusually proud town, with Proctor Academy, established in 1848 (it actually moved to Wolfeboro in 1865, then back in 1875), at its core—hence the B&Bs and unusually good dining. The **Andover Historical Society Museum** (603-735-5694), housed in a vintage-1874, Victorian-style railroad station at 105 Dept St. (Rt. 4/11) in the tiny village of Potter Place, is open weekends Memorial Day–Columbus Day, Sat. and Sun. 1–3. The restored station complex now includes a caboose and freight car as well as the general store and post office, preserved as a museum. There is also the grave of Richard Potter, a 19th-century black magician who performed throughout America. This is also an entry point to the **Northern Rail Trail**, with a popular stretch running from here to **Highland Lake** in East Andover.

Bradford Center. Just off the main drag (Rt. 103), but it feels like a million miles away. Coming north, the turn for River Rd. is a left just beyond the junction of Rts. 103 and 114. You go through the Bement covered bridge, built in 1854. Continue up the hill, up and up until you come to the

Courtesy, Andover Historical Museum

POTTER PLACE RR STATION MUSEUM

old hill-town crossroads. Turn left, and you will find the old schoolhouse and vintage-1838 meetinghouse with its two doors and Gothic-style tower topped with decorative wooden spikes, resembling upside-down icicles. The old graveyard is here, too. The present town hall was moved from this village down to what is now the business center of Bradford when the train arrived in the 1860s.

Canaan Center is a classic hill town: a proud, old agricultural community left high and dry when the railroad came through in the 1860s and the town's business shifted to the area (now the village of Canaan) 3 miles down the road, around the depot. Like Old Deerfield Village in Massachusetts, the houses here—a few 18th-century homes and the rest built before 1850—line a single street, and over the years the community itself has become known as **Canaan Street**. Its unusual beauty—and that of its lake—was recognized early on; the train to Canaan soon began bringing summer tourists, hotels opened to accommodate them, and an elaborate pier was built. The **Canaan Historic Museum** (open July–Oct., Sat. 1–4 PM) displays souvenir dishes with CANAAN STREET and color pictures printed on them.

Hebron (pop. 499) is a classic gathering of white-clapboard houses around a common—with bandstand, general store, post office, and handsome, two-story 1803 meetinghouse—at the northwestern corner of Newfound Lake. It's home to the **Paradise Point Nature Center**.

New London (pop. 4,463). Sited on a ridge, good for summer views and winter skiing, New London is the home of **Colby-Sawyer College** (colby-sawyer.edu), a four-year, coed college founded as a Baptist academy in 1837. The 80-acre campus includes the **Marion G. Mugar Art Gallery**, with changing exhibits by recognized artists and by college faculty and students. The **New London Historical Society Museum and Library** on Little Sunapee Rd. is an ambitious gathering of restored buildings. New London is also home to the **Barn Playhouse**, one of New England's oldest and best summer theaters. The town's hidden gems are **Cricenti's Bog** and **Little Sunapee Lake**, site of **Twin Lake Village**, one of New England's most authentic and low-profile 19th-century family resorts.

Chris Tree

SUNAPEE HARBOR

Newport is an old mill town and commercial center with some elaborate 19th-century buildings including the circa-1886 **Newport Opera House** on Main St., scene of frequent concerts, plays, and dances. It's also the scene of the annual presentation of the Sarah Josepha Hale Medal to the likes of Arthur Miller and Arthur Schlesinger. (Hale, the town's best-known citizen, was the author of the famous children's poem "Mary Had a Little Lamb" and was instrumental in promoting Thanksgiving as a national holiday.) **The Richards Library Arts Center** (603-863-3040), 58 N. Main St., hosts continuous exhibits by local artists. Also note the vintage 1823 brick **South Congregational Church** on Main St. No longer an outlet for the woolen mill across the street, the **Dorr Mill Store** has become a destination for rug hookers and quilters looking for supplies.

Sunapee Harbor. In the **Sunapee Historical Society Museum** (see *To See*) you browse through scrapbooks filled with pictures of the village's half a dozen vanished hotels, most notably the four-story, 100-room Ben-Mere, which sat until the 1960s on a knoll in the middle of "the Harbor." You also learn that village mills once included a tannery, a pulp mill, and clothespin and wooden harness parts factories. This is now a busy seasonal gathering spot and departure point for boat excursions.

Sutton, off I-89 Exit 10, and south on Rt. 114. **South Sutton** is a 19th-century mill-village center with a 1790s meetinghouse and a former general store that's now the **Old Store Museum** (603-938-5843). **North Sutton** is also an appealing village with a meetinghouse, general store, and historic marker noting the several large summer hotels that used to stand here by **Kezar Lake**. Only the annex of one (now the Follansbee Inn) survives, but **Wadleigh State Beach** offers access to the lake. **Muster Field Farm** conveys a sense of both the beauty and the history of the area.

Warner (pop. 2,946). This is the region's first town that travelers up I-89 from points south tend to hit. Gas and fast-food services are an easy off/on at Exit 10 just north of the village, but it's worth taking the previous exit and exploring Main St. Warner offers the easiest approach to 2,937-foot **Mount Kearsarge** through **Rollins State Park**; it's home to the Mount **Kearsarge Indian Museum** as well as the **New Hampshire Telephone Museum**. There's also the **Warner Historical Society** (603-456-2437), 15 Main St., open Tue. 1–4 with frequent presentations at Main Street Bookends—which with The Foothills Restaurant serve as the kind of gathering spots every town should have. There are two covered bridges and several farms worth finding. From the 1930s through World War II this was a popular ski destination, but the big event now is the **Warner Fall Foliage Festival** (wfff.org), one of the most colorful in New England.

Washington (pop. 895). A gem of a village with a cluster of imposing buildings, a meetinghouse completed in 1789 (the Asher Benjamin–style steeple was added later), an 1840s Gothic-style Congregational church, and a two-story, 1830s schoolhouse—all huddled together on the northern side of the common. According to a historical marker, this is the birthplace of the Seventh-Day Adventist Church (April 1842) and also the first town in the country incorporated (December 13, 1776) as "Washington." It's home to **Pillsbury State Park**.

✳ To See

MUSEUMS Muster Field Farm Museum (603-927-4276; musterfield-farm.com), Harvey Rd., off Keyser St., which runs along Kezar Lake from North Sutton village. Grounds and farm buildings open daily year-round; hiking, cross-country skiing, snowshoeing. These 250 hilltop acres have been farmed since the 18th century. The original Matthew Harvey Homestead remains remarkably intact; it changed ownership only once—in the 1940s—before acquiring its current status as a nonprofit trust. On any given day visitors are welcome to stroll around, inspect

SUTTON

Chris Tree

MUSEUMS IN WARNER

&. **Mt. Kearsarge Indian Museum** (603-456-2600; indianmuseum.org), 18 Highland Rd. off Kearsarge Mountain Rd., near the entrance to Rollins State Park. Open May–Oct., Mon.–Sat. 10–5, Sun. noon–5. Open Sat. and Sun. from Nov. to the weekend before Christmas, also for special programs and by appointment Jan.–Apr. Guided tours at 2 PM, otherwise self-guided. $8.50 adults, $6.50 ages 6–12, $7.50 seniors. This is one of the most impressive displays of Native American artifacts in the Northeast. Frankly, we weren't prepared for the quantity or quality of this collection, amassed by former curator Bud Thompson, over more than 50 years. Thompson transformed a former riding arena into a showcase for hundreds of priceless and evocative pieces: dozens of intricate sweetgrass baskets from the Penobscot, carved ash

MT. KEARSARGE INDIAN MUSEUM, WARNER

a dozen and a half outbuildings like the 1881 springhouse from a long-vanished hotel in Bradford, and buy vegetables and fruit in-season. The main house, an excellent example of rural Georgian architecture, is open Sun. 1–4 during June, July, and Aug. During the course of the year, the farm hosts several special events—Ice Day, Harvest Day, and Farm Days, among others—designed to highlight New Hampshire's agricultural traditions. The **Annual Muster Field Farm Days**, the weekend before Labor Day weekend, involves more than 100 exhibitors demonstrating crafts and traditional farming methods. $5 admission ($2 seniors) on event days, otherwise a nominal parking fee. Farmstead open in summer, noon–6.

The New London Historical Society (603-526-6564; 603-526-6201; newlondon historicalsociety.org), Little Sunapee Rd (Rt. 114), New London. Guided tours are available on Sun. 12:30–3:30 Memorial Day–Columbus Day weekend as well as on Tue. 12:30–3:30 during July and Aug.—but call to see if the schedule has changed. Special events are listed on the website. The society owns and maintains a village of 19th-century buildings, including a farmhouse, two barns, a schoolhouse, meetinghouse, hearse house, violin shop, and blacksmith shop. In addition, the recently constructed Transportation Building houses the group's outstanding collection of wagons, carriages, and sleighs, including an original Concord Coach. Most of the buildings have been moved to the property.

baskets from the Passamaquoddy, intricate quillwork from the Micmac, Anasazi pottery from Chaco Canyon in New Mexico (dating from somewhere between AD 800 and 1200), Navajo Yei rugs, elaborate saddlebags beaded by the Plains Indians, cradleboards from Idaho, and much, much more. Note the statue carved from a single tree cut from the slopes of Mount Kearsarge. The archaeology exhibit in the lobby features the collection of Howard Sargent, the first professionally trained archaeologist to focus on New Hampshire. The self-guided Medicine Woods Trail highlights more than 100 plants Native Americans used for food, medicine, dye, shelter, and tools. Proceeds from the gift shop (dreamcatcher.org) help support programming.

New Hampshire Telephone Museum (603-456-2234; nhtelephonemuseum.com), 22 E. Main St. Open May–Oct., Tue. Thu., Sat. 10–4; Nov.–Apr., Wed.–Sat. 10–4. $5 adults, $4 seniors, $3 students. Father and son Dick and Paul Violette, both veterans of a local independent telephone company, have amassed a collection covering 130 years of telephone history beginning with Alexander Graham Bell. Displays include manual switchboards, party lines, and rotary phones. Did you know that phone lines were once strung on trees as well as poles? That the first cell phones were the size and weight of small bricks? Do you really understand what makes this familiar phenomenon work? This is a genuine museum, built for the purpose just off Main St. There's a video to start with, and before you know it you've spent an hour.

Sunapee Historical Society Museum (603-763-9872; newlondonhistorical society.org), 74 Main St., Sunapee Harbor. In summer, open Tue. and Thu.–Sun. 1–4, Wed. 7–9 PM; closed Mon. In fall, open weekends until Columbus Day 1–4. A former livery stable filled with photos of Sunapee's grand old hotels and steamboats. You discover that visitors began summering on Lake Sunapee as soon as the railroad reached Newbury in 1849. The lake's resort development was sparked by the three Woodsum brothers from Harrison, Maine (another lake resort), who began running steamboats to meet the trains. Soon there were two competing ferry lines (one boat carried 650 passengers) serving dozens of small landings on the shore and islands. Check for special lectures and events.

Daniel Webster Homestead (603-934-5057; 603-271-3556), 131 North Rd., marked (badly) from Rts. 11 and 127 in Franklin. Open weekends and holidays Memorial Day–Labor Day, 10:30–5:30. $7 adults, $3 ages 6–17; 5 and under and New Hampshire residents 65 and over are admitted free. This is a small, clapboard, 18th-century cabin filled with replicated furnishings. Webster (1782–1852), Dartmouth class of 1801, represented New Hampshire in Congress from 1813 to 1817 and Massachusetts in the Senate from 1827 to 1841. He was a champion of states' rights and involved in many of the major issues of his day. His legendary oratorical skills were memorialized in Stephen Vincent Benet's play *The Devil and Daniel Webster.*

⊙ **The Fells State Historic Site at the John Hay National Wildlife Refuge** (603-763-4789; thefells.org), Rt. 103A between Newbury and Blodgett's Landing. The vintage-1891 lakeside estate is open year-round dawn–dusk. The house and shop are open seasonally 10–4: weekends and holidays beginning Memorial Day, then Wed.–Sun. late June–Labor Day and again weekends through Columbus Day; $8 adults, $7 seniors and students, $3 ages 7–15; under 5 free. Call for a schedule of programs and workshops. The former summer home of John Hay, a poet as well as Teddy Roosevelt's secretary of state, The Fells sits high above the eastern shore of Lake Sunapee. Although the 22-room mansion is partially unfurnished, there is a gallery and gift shop. The 164.5-acre trail-laced property (it was originally 1,000 acres) provides an example of one of New England's finest early-20th-century gardens—a delightful mix of rugged landscape, cultivated perennials, and formal terraces. Walk from the exquisite Alpine Garden 0.5 mile down along meadowlike lawn to the water. In spring the 0.5-mile walk from the parking area is magnificent with century-old stands of rhododendron and mountain laurel. In all, there are more than 5 miles of hiking paths. This is a popular setting for weddings.

A SCULPTURE AMONG THE GARDENS AT THE FELLS HISTORIC SITE, NEWBURY

Note: Also see **Enfield Shaker Museum** (shakermuseum.org), described in the Upper Valley chapter.

COVERED BRIDGES **The Keniston bridge**, built in 1882, spans the Blackwater River, south of Rt. 4, 1 mile west of Andover village.

The Cilleyville bridge, now open to foot traffic only, was built across Pleasant Stream in 1887; it's now at the junction of Rts. 11 and 4A in Andover.

The Bement bridge, built in 1854, is on River Rd. in Bradford Center.

The Corbin covered bridge, rebuilt by a group of Newport citizens after being destroyed by arson in 1993, crosses the Sugar River west of Rt. 10 in North Newport.

The Warner–Dalton bridge, originally built in 1800 and rebuilt in 1963, crosses over the Warner River, south of Rt. 103 in Warner village (multiple kingpost truss).

The Warner–Waterloo bridge, rebuilt in 1972, is 2 miles west of Warner village, south of Rt. 103 (Town lattice truss).

FOR FAMILIES *𝄞* **Ruggles Mine** (603-523-4275; rugglesmine.com), off Rt. 4, Grafton. Open weekends mid-May–early June; daily mid-June–mid-Oct. Hours 9–5, until 6 in July and August. $23 adults, $13 ages 4–11. Children of all ages will love this place; you don't have to be a mineral buff. The eerie shape of the caves high up on Isinglass Mountain is worth the drive up the access road, and the view includes Cardigan, Kearsarge, and Ragged Mountains. Commercial production of mica in this country began here in 1803. The story goes that Sam Ruggles set his large family to work mining and hauling the mica (it was used for lamp chimneys and stove windows) to Portsmouth; from there it was shipped to relatives in England to be sold. When the demand for his product grew, these trips were made in the dead of night to protect the secrecy of the mine's location. The mine has yielded some $30 million over the years. It was last actively mined by the Bon Ami Company for feldspar, mica, and beryl from 1932 to 1959. An estimated 150 different minerals can still be found. There's a snack bar, picnic area, and a gift shop with minerals so visitors can take home a piece of the rock. Collecting is permitted.

SCENIC DRIVES **Bradford Center to Washington to Sunapee.** The most difficult part of this tour is finding the starting point, just west of the stoplight at the junction of Rts. 104 and 114 in Bradford. The road immediately threads a covered bridge, then climbs 2.4 miles to Bradford Center. Stop to see the original town buildings (just out of view on your left), but turn right and follow that road 1.8 miles until a sign on a tree points the way to East Washington. The route passes the Eccardt Farm barnyard; visitors are welcome to stroll through the operating dairy farm, and to see the collection of live birds along with horses, cows, goats, and antique farm equipment. You might also want to park your car at Island Pond and walk up the hill to the Baptist church grounds and cemetery. The old schoolhouse here, with its desks, foot organ, and vintage textbooks, is open on summer Sundays 1–3 PM. Turn north (right) on Rt. 31 into Washington, a photographer's delight with its 1787 meetinghouse, school, and Congregational church all conveniently arranged to fit into one picture. Continue north on Rt. 31 to Pillsbury State Park. Just north of Goshen village, a right brings you back to Rt. 103 and Mount Sunapee.

Around Newfound Lake. This crystal-clear gem of a lake is circled by roads that hug most of its 22-mile shoreline and offer access for both walkers and paddlers. Plan to spend the day. The approach is Rt. 104, and whether you're coming from Danbury to the west or I-93 to the east, the gateway town is Bristol, a mill town that's mellowed. Follow Rt. 3A north for 9 miles (pick up a map at the information center just south of the lake) with views of the lake and Mount Cardigan. Turn left onto North Shore Rd., following signs to **Paradise Point Nature Center**, a New Hampshire Audubon property that's a great place to hike, bird, or rent a kayak. From here you may want to continue on through the classic village of Center Hebron and follow signs to **Sculpted Rocks Natural Area**. Retrace your route

(3.2 miles) as far as Hebron and turn down the West Shore Rd., which runs south along the lake, by a string of summer cottages and past **Sugarloaf Ledges** to **Wellington State Park**. Continue on back to Bristol or west into the Shem Valley to the base of Mount Cardigan.

✳ To Do

BICYCLING The region's many back roads through vintage villages appeal to bicycle tourers. Two rail-trails can also be found in this area. The first is a popular 10-mile piece of the **Northern Rail Trail** (fnrt.org), which runs from Potter Place through Andover (along Highland Lake) to Webster Lake in West Franklin; another 25-mile section of the trail presently runs from Danbury to Lebanon. In addition, the **Sugar River Trail** links Newport and Claremont.

Granite State Vacations (603-735-6426; granitestatevacations.com). Four local lodging places work together to offer guided or self-guided inn-to-inn bike tours. These include Highland Lake Inn, The Rosewood Country Inn, and the Blue Acorn (see *Lodging*).

Bob Skinner's Ski & Sports (603-763-2303), Rt. 103, Newbury, rents mountain bikes. Inquire about the many mapped local routes.

Outspokin Bicycle & Sport Shop (603-763-9500), junction of Rts. 103 and 103A, Newbury. Another good spot for biking gear, rentals, and information.

Village Sports (603-526-4948), 140 Main St., New London. All-season rental for bikes.

BOAT EXCURSIONS ⋖ **M/V *Mount Sunapee II*** (603-938-6465; sunapee cruises.com), Sunapee Harbor. Weekends mid-May–foliage season; daily at 2 PM late June–Labor Day. $18 adults, $8 ages 3–12; 5 and under free. Hour-and-a-half narrated cruises of the lake. This is unquestionably the best way to see Lake Sunapee, complete with the captain's retelling of its history and major sights. New

LAKE SUNAPEE EXCURSION BOATS

Chris Tree

London's long swath of eastern shore is entirely green, with rustic cottages hidden in woods above occasional docks. In Newbury on the south, you see Blodgett's Landing, a tight cluster of gingerbread cottages descended from the tents of the 1890s Sunapee Lake Spiritualist Camp Meeting Association. All children aboard are invited to take a turn at the helm. Private and group tours also available.

M/V *Kearsarge* (603-938-6465), Sunapee Harbor. Summer months. A re-creation of a 19th-century steamer offers hour-and-a-quarter narrated cruises twice daily, as well as a single dinner cruise (see *Dining Out*).

BOATING **Sargents Marina** (603-763-5036), Cooper St., Sunapee, rents canoes, boats, and motors. A great source of advice on where to fish.

Sunapee Harbor Boat Rentals (603-763-4521) rents pontoon boats.

Kayak Country (603-381-8685; kayakcountry.com), 27 Kearsarge Valley Rd. (off Rt. 11), Wilmot Flat. This seasonal shop offers a selection of used kayaks as well as rentals and guided trips on nearby lakes and ponds.

Paradise Point Nature Center (603-744-3516), on Newfound Lake in Hebron, rents canoes, kayaks mid-May– Sept., except on Sun. Call ahead to reserve.

Canoe/kayak put-ins can be found on Lake Sunapee; Pleasant Lake; Otter Pond in Georges Mills; Rand Pond in Goshen; Lake Todd, Blaisdell Lake, and Lake Massasecum in the Bradford area; Little Sunapee in New London; Kezar Lake in North Sutton; and Kolelemook Lake in Springfield.

Public boat launches are found in Sunapee Harbor, at Blodgett's Landing (shallow), at Sargents in Georges Mills, and at Sunapee State Park Beach.

FISHING **Sargents Marine** in Georges Mills (see *Boating*).

Lake Sunapee is good for salmon, lake trout, brook trout, smallmouth bass, pickerel, perch, sunfish, hornpout, and cusk. Otter Pond, Perkins Pond, and Baptist Pond yield bass, pickerel, and perch. Rand Pond, Croydon Pond, Long and Lempster Ponds, and the Sugar River are good for trout. Pleasant Lake has salmon, trout, and bass. Inquire locally about what other lakes offer.

FISHING IN LITTLE LAKE SUNAPEE
Thea Dodds, courtesy Twin Lake Village

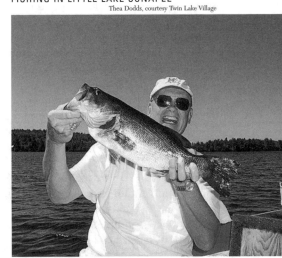

GOLF **Country Club of New Hampshire** (603-927-4246; playgolfne.com), Kearsarge Valley Rd., North Sutton 03260. Twice rated one of the top 75 public courses in the United States by *Golf Digest*. Dining, cart rentals; reservations required.

Eastman (603-863-4500; 603-863-4500; Eastman@golflinks.com), Grantham. Public. Reservations required.

Newport Golf Club (603-863-7787), 112 Unity Rd., Newport. Eighteen holes. Reservations required on weekends.

Ragged Mountain Golf Club (603-768-3600; 800-400-3911; raggedmountain resort.com), 620 Ragged Mountain Rd., Danbury. A Jeff Julian par-72, 18-hole course with PGA pros.

Twin Lake Village Golf Course (603-526-2034), Twin Lake Village Rd., New London. Nine-hole, par-3 course by the lake.

HIKING Mount Cardigan. From **Mount Cardigan State Park** in Orange (east of Canaan) on the western side of the mountain, the **West Ridge Trail** takes you to the summit in just 1.3 miles. From **Old Baldy**, the principal peak, the view is of Mount Sunapee and Mount Ascutney in Vermont. A ridge trail runs north to **Firescrew Peak** and south to South Peak. In all, a network of 50 miles of trails accesses the summit from various directions. Although this western ascent is the shortest and easiest, many hikers prefer the eastern climbs. You might ascend by the **Cathedral Spruce** and **Clark Trails** (2.5 miles to the summit; average time two hours 10 minutes, not including stops) or by the more difficult **Holt Trail** (1.9 miles to the summit, not to be attempted in wet or icy weather), and return on the **Mowglis Trail** (3 miles from the summit). The **Appalachian Mountain Club Cardigan Lodge** (see *Lodging*), nestled at the mountain's eastern base, is the departure point for these and other year-round ascents; the AMC also maintains a year-round rustic cabin near the summit.

Mount Kearsarge. Despite controversy about the cell phone tower on top of this peak, the view remains one of the most spectacular in New England, especially for people familiar enough with the landscape to know what they're looking at. The sweep is from Mount Sunapee on the southwest to Moosilauke (the westernmost of the White Mountain peaks), to the Sandwich and Ossipee ranges and Mount Washington. Serious hikers prefer the 2-mile ascent from **Winslow State Park** on the northern side of the mountain to the mere 0.5-mile saunter up from **Rollins State Park**. The **Northside Trail** to the summit begins in the southeastern corner of the picnic area, climbs through birch and spruce into fir, and emerges onto smooth ledges, then barren rocks. Roundtrip time on the Northside Trail averages an hour and a half each way—or you can do it in 20 minutes from the other side. Either way, it's a lot of bang for the buck and a favorite hang-gliding spot.

Mount Sunapee. In winter you can opt for the chairlift, but the most popular hiking trail up is the **Andrew Brook Trail** (1.8 miles to Lake Solitude) from a marked trailhead 1.2 miles up Mountain Rd., which is off Rt. 103 roughly 1 mile south of Newbury. The most ambitious approach to Mount Sunapee is along the 47-mile **Monadnock–Sunapee Trail**, which begins atop Mount Monadnock. The last and perhaps the most rewarding stretch of this trail is from **Pillsbury State Park**, which offers primitive camping and its own 20-mile system of trails. In all there are six campsites along this stretch. From Sunapee it's possible to follow a 75-mile loop north to 2,937 foot-high **Mount Kearsarge** and the **Ragged Mountain** massif.

SKIN DIVING LaPorte's Skindiving Shop (603-763-5353), 1053 Rt. 103, Newbury. Equipment for sale, plus lessons and rentals.

SWIMMING Sunapee State Park Beach (603-263-4642), Rt. 103, 3 miles west of Newbury. Open weekends mid-May–mid-June and Labor Day–mid-Oct., daily in between. Fee. A 900-foot stretch of smooth sand backed by shaded grass, picnic tables, a snack bar, and a bathhouse.

Wellington State Park (603-744-2197), Rt. 3A, 4 miles north of Bristol. Open weekends from Memorial Day, daily mid-June–Labor Day. Fee. This is a beauty: a sandy, 0.5-mile-long beach on a peninsula jutting into Newfound Lake. Picnic tables are scattered along the shore, away from the bathhouse and snack bar, under pine trees.

Wadleigh State Beach (603-927-4724), on Kezar Lake, Sutton. Marked from Rt. 114. Open weekends from Memorial Day, daily mid-June–Labor

Thea Dodds, courtesy, Twin Lake Village

SWIMMING IN LITTLE LAKE SUNAPEE

Day. Fee. Smaller, less well known, and less crowded than nearby Sunapee; a pleasant beach sloping gradually to the water. Facilities include a shaded picnic area, a bathhouse, and a large playing field.

Town beaches. Many more local beaches can be accessed by guests at local inns.

TENNIS Mountainside Racquet and Fitness Center (603-526-9293), 23 Summit Rd., New London. Open 6:30 AM–9 PM weekdays, 8 AM–5 PM weekends (until 1 PM in summer). Tennis, exercise machines, sauna, and yoga classes open to the public.

Colby-Sawyer College (603-526-2010), New London. The Hogan Sports Center with indoor swimming and fitness machines is open to the public.

✳ Winter Sports

CROSS-COUNTRY SKIING ♻ 🐾 **Pine Hill XC Ski Club** (603-381-8685; 603-526-6772; pinehillskiclub.com), 220 Mountain Rd. off Shaker St., marked from Rt. 11 (just east of the country club), New London. John Schlosser discovered the sport while attending the University of Oslo in 1972 and with his wife, Nancy, opened Norsk at the Lake Sunapee Country Club in 1976, drawing fans regularly from as far as Boston. In 2005 the Schlossers established the Pine Hill Ski Club to maintain local ski and snowshoe trails. Schlosser grooms 10 trails—for a total of 22km—including 1 snowshoe and 2 pet-friendly trails, 4km for skating, and the remainder for touring. Most trails follow wooded, rolling terrain, suitable for beginner and intermediate skiers; one trail is for advanced skiers. With an elevation of 1,300 feet and superb grooming, the trails are usually the best around. Rentals are available at **Village Sports** (603-526-4948), 394 Main St., New London. $10 trail fee; free under age 12. Rob's Hut (hot drinks, snacks) is open Saturdays. Check the website for conditions and special events.

Dexter's Inn Trails by Norsk Outdoors (800-232-5571; dextersnh.com), 258 Stagecoach Rd., Sunapee. A 30km trail system, 20km groomed and tracked. From the inn, trails wind through the 20-acre property and into surrounding conservation land. Equipment rentals and small ski shop. $10 fee ages 6 and over. The inn offers a lunch menu noon–2 on winter weekends.

Eastman Cross Country Ski Center (603-863-4500; eastmannh.org/ski), turn right off I-89 (you can't miss the sign), Grantham. Open in-season with 36km of groomed trails.

DOWNHILL SKIING ✪ **Mount Sunapee** (603-763-3500; snow phone 603-763-4020; mountsunapee.com), Rt. 103, Newbury. This is a major, family-geared ski area, one of the most convenient to Boston. The Sunapee Express quad accesses half a dozen swooping, intermediate-to-expert runs from the summit, each at least a mile long. Off the North Peak Triple Chair, our favorite is Flying Goose, a quick, steep, and addictive run. There are also challenging glades and wide mogul trails. The two base lodges—at the opposite ends of the parking lot—and the summit lodge help disperse the crowds at lunchtime. When all trails are open, skiers can choose from trails and slopes on five separate mountain areas.

Until 1998 Mount Sunapee was operated by the state. In the decade that followed, Tim and Diane Mueller—the owners of Mount Okemo in Vermont—leased the ski area and spent more than $15 million upgrading lifts, snowmaking, and amenities.

Vertical drop: 1,510 feet.

Lifts: 10: a high-speed detachable quad, plus 2 other quads, as well as 2 triple lifts, 1 double, and 4 surface lifts.

Skiable terrain: 232 acres.

Trails: 65 (20 percent novice, 58 percent intermediate, 22 percent expert).

Snowmaking: 97 percent.

Terrain parks: Three including the Six O' Three Terrain Park with a 4,000-watt sound system.

Facilities: PSIA ski and snowboard school, and day care available. The South Peak Learning Area offers 14 beginner-friendly trails serviced by five lifts. The area is home to the New England Handicapped Sports Association (NEHSA) and offers

SKIER AT MOUNT SUNAPEE

Mount Sunapee

lessons, racing programs, and other services to disabled skiers. Guest services throughout are exceptionally friendly and helpful.

Rates: $68 weekends, $64 midweek for adults; $56 and $48 ages 13–18 and 65–69; $42 and $38 ages 6–12 and 70-plus. Free skiing for those 5 and under. Various specials, including a midweek Super Pass to Mount Sunapee, Okemo, and Stratton.

In addition to the Annual League of New Hampshire Craftsmen's Fair, Mount Sunapee hosts weddings and other events including a Car Show, Bike Race, and concerts. The Sunapee Express chair operates during the Craftsmen's Fair and several other weekends including fall foliage.

🍴 ♂ **Ragged Mountain Ski Area** (603-768-3600; raggedmountainresort.com), 620 Ragged Mountain Rd., off Rt. 4, Danbury. A pleasant, intermediate, genuinely family-friendly mountain that offers snowmaking and a red barn look-alike base lodge with a soaring, three-sided fireplace. Still just enough off the beaten track and little known enough to be relatively uncrowded. In 2007 the 2,000-acre property was purchased by RMR Pacific, LLC, which plans to develop a four-season resort community.

Vertical drop: 1,250 feet.

Lifts: One six-pack, two triple chairs, one double, and one surface tow.

Trails: 45 (30 percent novice, 40 percent intermediate, 30 percent expert).

Snowmaking: 84 percent.

Facilities: Ski school, ski shop, rentals, restaurant, lounge, child care, and lodging.

Rates: $62 adults weekends, $52 weekdays; $49/39 teens; $39/29 juniors and seniors.

✳ Green Space

STATE PARKS Mount Cardigan State Park, off Rts. 4 and 118, 4.5 miles east of Canaan. Open mid-May–mid-Oct. This western approach to the mountain includes a picnic area sited among pines and rocks. For more about the West Ridge Trail, the shortest and easiest route to the 3,155-foot-high summit of Mount Cardigan itself, see *Hiking.*

♿ **Pillsbury State Park** (603-863-2860), Rt. 31, 3.5 miles north of Washington. Open weekends from Memorial Day, daily from mid-June. Day-use and camping fees. What a gem! This 9,000-acre near wilderness was once a thriving settlement with its share of mills. Today the dams are all that survive of "Cherry Valley." Camping is restricted to 41 superb primitive sites on May Pond, and there's both stream and pond fishing. A 51-mile hiking trail from Mount Monadnock to Mount Sunapee passes through the park. Inquire about trails to nearby mountains.

Rollins State Park (603-456-3808), off Rt. 103, 4 miles north of Warner. Open weekends from Memorial Day, daily early June–Oct. A 360-degree view of villages, lakes, and a patchwork of pastures is an easy half-hour amble from the parking lot/picnic area here. A 3.5-mile road, built originally as a scenic toll road in 1874, ascends 300 vertical feet to wooded picnic sites roughly 0.5 mile below the summit, with views south to Monadnock. A walking trail (good for the elderly, young, or lazy) accesses the bald summit of Mount Kearsarge. There's a fire tower for those who want an even higher view.

Winslow State Park (603-526-6168), off Rt. 11, 3 miles south of Wilmot. Open weekends from Memorial Day, daily from early June; fee. An auto road climbs to the 1,820-foot level of 2,937-foot Mount Kearsarge. There are picnic tables and comfort facilities, and you can inspect the cellar hole of a big 19th-century resort hotel, the Winslow House. A steep, mile-long trail leads to the summit for a 360-degree panoramic view. The park is named for Admiral John A. Winslow, commander of the sloop *Kearsarge* when she sank the Confederate gunboat *Alabama* in 1864.

OTHER AREAS Newfound Audubon Center (603-744-3516; nhaudubon.org), North Shore Rd., East Hebron. This 43-acre preserve includes an extensive, rocky, and unspoiled stretch of shore on Newfound Lake. The property is webbed with trails and includes the **Paradise Point Nature Center** (open July–Sept. 1, 10–4 daily) with hands-on and wildlife exhibits, a library, and the **Ash Cottage and Nature Store**. During summer a natural history day camp and a variety of work-shops and special events are also staged. **Hebron Marsh Wildlife Sanctuary** is another 1.4 miles down the road toward Hebron Center (drive past the red Ash Cottage and take the next left down the dirt road; park off the road on your left by the sign). The 36-acre property includes the field directly across the road from Ash Cottage down to the Cockermouth River and the field to the southwest of the cot-tage. The marshes are teeming with bird life; follow signs to the observation tower. Kayak and canoe rentals are available except Sundays (call ahead and reserve). Inquire about directions to the West Shore Rd. trailhead for **Bear Mountain**.

Sculptured Rocks State Park, west of Groton village on Sculptured Rocks Rd. From Paradise Point (above), continue west and follow the signs. The parking area is across the road from the river. With grottoes formed by waterfalls, this is mer-maid/merman territory. The Cockermouth River has carved a deep chasm through which it tumbles from pool to pool, forming a popular local swimming spot. There's a bridge; a path, with plenty of large rocks for picnicking, follows the water down.

Bradford Pines, Rt. 103, Bradford. Twelve giant white pines stand on 5 acres of preserved land.

Cricenti's Bog, Rt. 11, New London. A genuine bog with a nature trail. Wooden walkways thread a pond that's been filled with sphagnum moss and rare bog flora.

Gardner Memorial Wayside Area, Rt. 4A, Wilmot. Picnic site along a scenic brook and stone foundation.

Grafton Pond, off Rt. 4A. A 935-acre Society for the Protection of New Hamp-shire Forests preserve. North from Wilmot take a sharp left at the Grafton–Sullivan County line; take the first left, then an immediate right, and park at the dam site. The only amenity is a public boat ramp. The pond has a 7-mile shoreline. Good boating and fishing.

Knights Hill Nature Park, County Rd., New London. Sixty acres of fields and forest, fern gardens and a pond, a marsh, and a stream, all linked by easy trails. No dogs. Inquire at the town information booth about guided hikes.

Profile Falls, Rt. 3A, 2.5 miles south of Bristol. A popular (and dangerous) local swimming hole. This is a 40-foot falls with the profile of a man silhouetted against the water at its base.

Also see **The Fells State Historic Site** under *To See*.

✳ Lodging

Note: The website **nhcountryinns .com**—representing Country Inns of the Dartmouth–Lake Sunapee Region—is well worth checking.

RESORT ✪ ☜ ⚬ ☙ Twin Lake Village (603-526-6460; twinlakevillage .com), 164 Twin Lake Villa Rd., New London 03257. Open late June–Labor Day. Nothing fancy unless you count its idyllic lakeside setting, but this 1890s resort is much beloved by those who stay here. Many families have been coming for generations. Opened by Henry Kidder in 1897, it is presently owned and managed by three generations of Kidders and accommodates 160 guests among the rambling Villa and a number of Victorian houses scattered throughout surrounding trees. Sited on Little Lake Sunapee, it has a private beach and a boathouse with canoes, rowboats, and kayaks. A nine-hole golf course stretches from the rocker-lined veranda (note the untraditional rocker colors) down to the lake. All three daily meals, supervised children's mornings in the Playbarn, and old-fashioned evening entertainment— maybe a suppertime picnic on Mount Kearsarge, or bingo—are included in weekly rates that start at $430 per person. Shorter stays are possible as the season gets under way.

INNS

In the Lake Sunapee area
✪ ∞ ☙ The Inn at Pleasant Lake (603-526-6271; 800-626-4907; innat pleasantlake.com), 853 Pleasant St., P.O. Box 1030, New London 03257. Open except for parts of Apr. and Nov. This is a gem, a many-gabled inn that's evolved from one of many farms in this area that began taking in boarders in the 1880s. Guests came from New York and Boston, and strangers were expected to bring letters of introduction. These days innkeepers Linda and Brian MacKenzie (Brian is a graduate of the Culinary Institute of America) welcome guests with such amenities as afternoon tea, elegant dining, and towels for use at their beach on Pleasant Lake across the way. The 12 second- and third-floor rooms include several with sitting rooms; most overlook the lake and Mount Kearsarge beyond. All have private bath and are furnished in antiques with comfort and flair. Two canoes and a kayak are available to guests. Full breakfast and tea are included in rates of $155–215; also see *Dining Out.*

∞ ☙ ⚬ New London Inn (603-526-2791; 800-526-2791; newlondoninn.us), P.O. Box 8, 353 Main St., New London 03257. Built originally in 1792, this substantial inn marks the middle of New London, next door to Colby-Sawyer College. It's always busy, but guests can usually find quiet space in a corner of the large, graciously furnished living room. The New London Barn Playhouse is just down Main St., which is lined with attractive shops and eateries. Stroll around town or simply rock an hour away, watching the activity from the second-story gallery porch. The inn has been lucky down through the decades, with most owners—like

TWIN LAKE VILLAGE

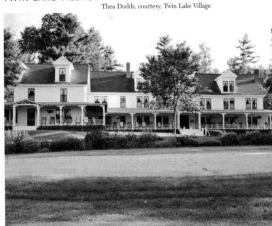
Thea Dodds, courtesy, Twin Lake Village

NEW LONDON INN

Chris Tree

current innkeepers Bridget LeRoy and Eric Johnson—updating but preserving its essential character. The 23 rooms range over three floors, and to say that each is individually decorated is an understatement (you might want to check out the choices pictured on the inn's website). It's worth noting that a number feature a sleeping arrangement for prospective college students with parents. All have private bath. $99–225 per couple includes breakfast. For details about Rockwell's at the Inn, see *Dining Out*.

♥ ᵬ **Colonial Farm Inn** (603-526-6121; 800-805-8504; colonialfarminn .com), 499 Andover Rd. (Rt. 11), New London 03257. John and Heidi Greene are the innkeepers of this informally gracious inn with six guest rooms, all individually climate controlled with private bath and comfortably furnished in antiques, all $149 including a full breakfast. The 1836 house features three fireplaces, restored wooden floors, and a century-old pool table. The dining room is open to the public except Tue.; see *Dining Out*.

∞ **Back Side Inn** (603-863-5161; backsideinn.net), 1171 Brook Rd., Goshen 03752. Open year-round. Still off the beaten track on the backside of Sunapee, this onetime family farm first

opened its doors to overnight guests as a hunting lodge in the 1920s. Ninety years later the inn retains its getaway feeling, set in 120 acres with frontage on Rand Pond. There are 10 guest rooms, 6 with private bath plus 2 double suites with shared bath. The grounds include gardens, croquet, badminton, bocce, and—in winter—access to a state snowmobile route (snowmobilers are welcome). Afterward, relax in the TV room or in the living room by the wood-burning fieldstone fireplace and walk no farther than the dining room for dinner. Chef-owner Anne Bernroth maintains the inn's tradition of Sunday brunch and dinner Fri.–Sat. (other nights depending on the season), open to the public by reservation ($12.95–26.95 BYOB). Room rates are $99 double weekdays, $119 weekends, including a full breakfast.

∞ ♥ ᵔ ᵬ **Dexter's Inn** (603-763-5571; 800-232-5571; dextersnh.com), Stagecoach Rd., Sunapee 03782. Open year-round. This hilltop house dates in part from 1801, but its present look is 1930s, when it became a summer home for an adviser to Herbert Hoover. In 1948 Dexter and Janelle Richards purchased the home and transformed it into Dexter's Inn, an après-ski getaway for guests coming to the newly opened Mount Sunapee Ski Resort. Current innkeepers Emily and John Augustine offer 17 guest rooms, each individually decorated, all with private bath. The best views are from the annex (with two handicapped-accessible rooms) across the road. A pool is set in the landscaped backyard, which also offers croquet, lawn games, and three all-weather tennis courts. Fields across the road, in front of the house, slope toward Lake Sunapee in the distance. Common spaces include a formal living room; a pubby, pine-paneled library/lounge; and a kids' playroom with videos, games, toys, and stuffed animals. Altogether, this has the look and feel of a casual, unpretentious country club. Also see *Cross-Country Skiing*. Rates per double are $110–180 with breakfast. Pets are permitted in the annex. Inquire about The Holly House Cottage, with a living room with fireplace, a kitchen, and two bedrooms; also about a two-bedroom, one-bath efficiency condo, sleeping up to six.

⟨↑⟩ The Follansbee Inn on Kezar Lake (603-927-4221; 800-626-4221; follansbeeinn.com), Kezar St., off Rt. 114, P.O. Box 92, North Sutton 03260. Open year-round. Located in a small-town center that time seems to have forgotten. You'll find comfortable low-beamed living and dining rooms. On the upper floors the 17 guest rooms, all with private bath, are divided by wide halls. The white, green-trimmed structure was built originally as an annex for the huge but long-gone Follansbee Inn that once stood across the street. The property abuts Kezar Lake, and guests can swim or boat from the inn dock; for those more comfortable with a lifeguard on duty, Wadleigh State Beach is just down the road. Guests have access to bikes, kayaks, and snowshoes; many discover the joys of the 3-mile walk, bike, or jog around the lake. In winter there's snowshoeing out the back door and at Muster Field Farm, which is also a summer attraction with its museum and farm stand. The $137–198 per-couple rate includes breakfast. No children under age 10 please.

⟨∞⟩ & ⟨↑⟩ The Rosewood Country Inn (603-938-5273; rosewoodcountry inn.com), 67 Pleasant View Rd., Bradford 03221. Whatever it is that makes a place romantic, this rose-shuttered inn has it. Off the beaten path, set in gardens, surrounded by woods and meadows, the 11 spacious rooms and suites are furnished with a tasteful mix of old

and new. Nine are fitted with gas fireplace, four with Jacuzzi. Common spaces include a cozy tavern and ample corners for snuggling. Three-course breakfasts are served with candlelight and crystal. From $129 in low season to $299 in high (for a two-room suite with all the bells and whistles).

In Danbury

♪ ⟨↑⟩ The Inn at Danbury (603-768-3318; 866-DANBURY), 67 Rt. 104, Danbury 03230. With Ragged Mountain just 5 miles away, this Bavarian-flavored getaway is geared to skiers and great for groups and families, children age 8 and over. Fourteen individually decorated guest rooms vary widely, from couples geared to family rooms and suites, all with private bath. Rates range $120–155 on weekends (double occupancy), 15 percent less midweek, with full breakfast in the Alphorn Bistro (see *Dining Out*), access to the inn's heated, indoor pool, and use of the hot tub (adults only); ski and golf packages available.

On Newfound Lake

∞ ⟨↑⟩ The Inn on Newfound Lake (603-744-9111; newfoundlake.com), 1030 Mayhew Turnpike, Rt. 3A, Bridgewater 03222. Open year-round. Although thoroughly rehabbed, this 1840s inn still looks its age with a full veranda overlooking sunsets on the state's fourth largest lake. Across the road, there's a 300-foot sandy beach and a dock. Inside, the main inn has 16 guest rooms, 11 with private bath, and the adjoining Elmwood Cottage offers 12 more rooms, each with bath. There are comfortable parlors in each facility. For more about the Pasquaney Restaurant, the inn's dining room, see *Dining Out*. Summer is high season here, and there's a two-night minimums on weekends. Mid-May–Oct. 25, rates are $135–165 double occupancy $295–355 for a two-room suite, continental breakfast included. With its newly completed reception barn, this is a popular venue for weddings.

BED & BREAKFASTS

In the Lake Sunapee area

✪ ✍ ¹⁰ **Maple Hill Farm** (603-526-2248; 800-231-8637; maplehillfarm .com), 200 Newport Rd., New London 03257. Just off I-89 but seemingly light-years away, this capacious old farmhouse offers the same genial hospitality that it did in the 19th century. A path leads through its back acreage to Little Sunapee Lake, where a canoe and rowboat await. There are also barnyard animals, including chickens that yield those fresh eggs for breakfast. Other amenities include a spa tub on the deck and, in the barn, a seasonal indoor basketball court in the barn that doubles as a dance floor. Dennis Aufranc is a consummate host and cook who offers a choice of full breakfasts and will happily cook dinner for groups. There are 10 guest rooms, 6 with private bath, in the main house where, depending on season, rates run $90–135 and include a choice of full breakfasts. Or you can book a three-bedroom, four-and-a-half-bath lakefront home of your own for $3,000 a week or $500 a night. It's fully furnished with fireplace, spa, steam shower, and wet bar and comes with kayaks. Ski-and-stay packages are a great deal here.

✍ **Blue Goose Inn** (603-763-5519; bluegooseinn.com), 24 Rt. 103B, P.O. Box 2117, Mount Sunapee 03255-2117. A 19th-century roadside farmhouse in the shadow of Mount Sunapee, this country B&B has a wraparound porch overlooking 3.5 acres of lawn and woods, adjacent to the former Newport-to-Claremont railroad bed, now a trail for hiking, biking, cross-country skiing, snowshoeing, and snowmobiling. There are four attractive guest rooms, each with private bath, including a two-room family suite. $110–130 double with full country breakfast; extra adult, $25.

Twin Doors (603-763-2236; twindoors .com), 49 High St., Sunapee 03782. Rose and Hess Gates have transformed this vintage Sunapee Harbor duplex into one of the area's most charming B&Bs. Each of the four tastefully decorated guest rooms has a king or queen bed, a Jacuzzi in the bathroom, and individually controlled heating/cooling as well as ceiling fans. We particularly like the bright, book-lined dining room, the venue for full breakfasts— maybe a smoked salmon and asparagus frittata. $129–165 per night also includes tea.

The 1806 Inn at Mount Sunapee (603-763-2040; 1806inn.com), 1424 Rt. 103, Newbury 03255. Sited almost at the entrance to Mount Sunapee, this classic old Cape is surrounded by extensive gardens. There are five guest rooms, all with private bath, and ample common space. Innkeepers Karen and Bill Carruth are helpful hosts. $95–150 double includes a buffet breakfast plus a hot dish.

The Blue Acorn Inn (603-863-1144; blueacorninn.com), 21 Sleeper Rd., Sunapee 03782. This 1847 farmhouse offers six individually decorated rooms (two with private baths) minutes from Mount Sunapee. $100–140 includes breakfast. Given the shared baths and ample, comfortable common spaces, this is a good choice for groups.

In the Kezar Lake area

✪ **Dragonflies** (603-927-4053; dragon fliesbnb.com), 9 Keyser St., P.O. Box 3, North Sutton 03260. Just off I-89 Exit 10. The street side of this charming home faces the town's old-time general store; the back of the house has a wide view of Lake Kezar. Inside, Christine and Iain Gilmour offer the warm hospitality they became known for when they operated a prestigious Massachusetts inn. Here there are just two guest rooms, both with queen-sized bed, private bath, and views of the lake, but the comfortable furnished living room with hearth and lake views is as spacious as any to be found in the area's major inns. Weeknight room rates begin at $105, weekends at $125 with a two-night minimum or $140 if booking just one night. This includes a full breakfast served outside on the lakeside patio or glorious screened porch, or in the cozy, book-lined dining room with its woodstove. A large selection of mostly classical music helps soothe you into the day, while a trip in the Gilmours' two kayaks helps keep the stress at bay.

🐚 **The Village House at Sutton Mills Bed & Breakfast** (603-927-4765; villagehousebnb.com), 14 Grist Mill Rd., Sutton Mills 03221. Outside, Marilyn and Jack Paige's 1857 Victorian house sits neat as a bandbox atop a granite-stepped slope; inside, her stenciled floor cloths and his hand-wrought iron beds add a unique touch to the three stylishly furnished guest rooms. Each has its own bath, one a claw-foot tub. Downtown Sutton Mills is both a minute and a century away, with a quaint and quiet Main Street that boasts a town hall and library. In winter guests can cross-country ski from the door. Jack has his shop open early evenings and on weekends all year. $120 double includes a full country breakfast. Children 3 years and older welcome.

Candlelite Inn (603-938-5571; 888-812-5571; candleliteinn.com), 5 Greenhouse Lane, Bradford 03221. Built in 1897 as a guest house, this inn had different names and owners for nearly a century before Les and Marilyn Gor-

don took over in 1993. The Gordons have added much pampering to the late-Victorian structure, which is set in 3 acres that include a pond. The inn offers six pretty pastel guest rooms, each with queen bed and private bath (some with claw-foot tubs), where you can rest up for a multicourse breakfast that includes dessert. Rates range $129–199, the high end for a first-floor mini suite with a soaking tub and access to the gazebo-like porch. Contact the Gordons for a calendar of special weekend activities. No children under 12 please. The place lends itself to a groups and can accommodate 25.

In the Newfound Lake area

🎵 ⑪ **Meadow Wind Bed and Breakfast** (603-744-9532; meadowwindbedandbreakfast.com), 41 North Shore Rd., Hebron. Across the road from the Audubon Society Marsh Wildlife Sanctuary and on the edge of the Hebron historic district, this 1820s farmhouse is the perfect setting for bird-watching or a Sunday-afternoon band concert. In summer you can hike from the back door, or kayak and swim in the Cockermouth River. In winter there are groomed trails for snowshoeing, cross-country skiing, and snowmobiling, plus a hot tub in the barn. Tenney Mountain Ski Area is 10 minutes away by car; Ragged Mountain, 20 minutes. The six guest rooms include a two-bedroom suite as well as a loft apartment with kitchen that sleeps up to six. Karen Corey has furnished all of them attractively with top-of-the-line mattresses and a mix of antiques. The common room has a woodstove and satellite TV. Rates run from $75 for a small room in the old servants' quarters to $150. Breakfast is served in the dining room or on one of three porches overlooking extensive vegetable and flower gardens.

⁰ᵀ⁰ **Pleasant View Bed & Breakfast** (603-744-5547; pleasantviewbandb .net), 22 Hemp Hill Rd., Bristol 03222. A big old white farmhouse with a wide-open view of Mount Cardigan. The home has been in the business of putting up guests since around the turn of the last century, when two men came over the hill from Dartmouth and asked if they could stay overnight. New owner Heidi Milbrand offers six recently renovated guest rooms, all with private bath. Rates are $105–135 all year, including a full country breakfast. Newfound Lake is just a mile off. No children under age 18 please.

⁰ᵀ⁰ **Bridgewater Mountain Bed and Breakfast** (603-968-3966; bridgewater mountain.com), 984 Bridgewater Hill Rd., Bridgewater 03264-5809. Once a working farm, this was Tom and Virginia Slayton's family vacation home for 60 years before they redesigned it to accommodate guests in summer and fall. Each of the three guest rooms has a private bath, queen- or king-sized bed, air-conditioning, wireless Internet connection, and views of flowers, fields, mountains, and woods. The Loft also includes a kitchen, living room with futon, and separate entrance. The downstairs common area features a fireplaced living room and reading space, as well as a wicker-filled back porch and breakfast area. Rates, $110–160, include a full breakfast with organic produce in-season.

⁰ᵀ⁰ **A Newfound Bed & Breakfast** (603-744-3442; 877-444-3442; anew foundbnb.com), 94 Mandi Lane, Bristol 03222. Sondra Keene has transformed her hillside home into an exceptional B&B. The atrium-style, double-tiered living room is walled in windows overlooking Newfound Lake and Cardigan Mountain in the distance. On the spring day we stopped by Cardigan was still snowcapped, the lake was blue, and we didn't want to leave. The four guest rooms all enjoy this view. The largest has a working fireplace dividing it from a bath with hot tub. There are gas stoves, flat-screen TVs, clock radios, and quality linens throughout. Guests have access to kitchen facilities and a guest panty, also a seasonal barbecue and fire ring as well as lawn games. $199–250 includes a full breakfast.

Sculptured Rocks Farm (603-744-6159; sculpturedrocks.com), 363 Sculptured Rocks Rd., Groton 03241. Restoring this vintage-1865 Gothic Revival farmhouse was a work of love for carpenter Michael Lemieux. Architecturally striking, it was built by the owner mill owner and showcases the variety of fine woods produced in his mill. Walls have been further enhanced by Dawn Lemieux's colorful murals. Accessed by a spiral staircase, two of the rooms share a bath; the third has both bath and king-sized bed. At the opposite end of the house, a two-room suite can sleep six. This is a casual, homey place with a soapstone wood-stove in the kitchen and the only TV in the parlor. Part of the appeal is a lovely off-the-beaten-path location, within walking distance of Sculptured Rocks State Park and enjoying easy access to both Newfound Lake and hiking trails up Cardigan Mountain. You can also snowshoe and cross-country ski out the back door. $85–140, $5 less per day for multiday stays, includes a full breakfast.

⊗ ✿ ✎ ⁰ᵀ⁰ **CopperToppe Lodge and Retreat Center** (603-744-3636; coppertoppe.com), 8 Range Rd., Hebron 03241. The view from this highly unusual, circa-1999 home is a cascade of forested mountains descending to the blue waters of Newfound Lake. Bill Powers and Sheila Oranch offer three guest rooms, each with private bath, cable TV, phone, and balcony. The Garnet Room also boasts a four-poster bed, fireplace, large whirlpool bath, and separate shower. The casual, comfortable common spaces appeal to small groups. Rooms run $175–275, less in winter; $30 charge per person for more than two in a room. Expect Sheila to ask your breakfast preferences when you make your reservation.

&. **Henry Whipple House Bed and Breakfast** (603-744-6157), 75 Summer St. (5.6 miles from I-93 Exit 23), Bristol 03222. Solidly built and elaborately embellished, this turreted Queen Anne–style inn was built in 1902 for the town's mill owner. It offers six spacious guest rooms, two with working fireplace, all with private bath and cable television. A first-floor room is designed for handicapped guests. There are also two carriage house suites, one with a self-catering kitchen. This is right downtown on a busy route, handy to I-93, but Newfound Lake is nearby as well. $100–155 per night for rooms and suites includes a full breakfast (with the exception of the self-catering suite, which is $140 double); additional charge for children over 12.

In the Highland Lake area

∞ ❦ ✐ **Highland Lake Inn** (603-735-6426; highlandlakeinn.com), P.O. Box 164, 32 Maple St., East Andover 03231. The lovely old property, which dates from 1767, retains 7 of its original acres, overlooks Highland Lake, and abuts a nature preserve. Peco and Gail Beufays speak French and German and have decorated each of the 10 spacious guest rooms with taste and an eye to comfort. Beds are fitted with high-quality Italian linens; there are flat-screen TVs, baths with European-style showers (no bathtubs) and luxurious amenities. Several rooms are designed to accommodate parents and

prospective students visiting nearby Proctor Academy. Breakfast in the sun-filled dining room with its lake view is an event, perhaps Belgian waffles or crêpes and a bread basket with croissants, included in $170–190 double occupancy. Wedding are a specialty; this is also home to Granite State Vacations (see *Biking*) and a stop on the Northern Rail Trail. A former international hotel executive, Peco enjoys tuning guests in to the natural and historic beauty of this off-the-beaten-path area. Highland Lake offers swimming, paddling, and a lovely 4.5-mile walk or run around its circumference.

Elsewhere

❦ ✐ **The Maria Atwood Inn** (603-934-3666; atwoodinn.com), 71 Hill Rd., Rt. 3A, Franklin 03235. The first time we visited this inn, three women from Florida had just checked into a trio of rooms, each of which drew more oohs and aahs than the last. Innkeepers Sandi and Fred Hoffmeister bought this well-preserved, elegant 1830 brick Federal home in 1997, then turned it into a charming B&B with seven romantic, antiques-filled guest rooms, each with private bath, four with working fireplace. Two years later, lightning struck, literally, topped off with hurricane floods while the roof was being repaired. But the Hoffmeisters made lemonade from their troubles, transforming their third floor into two post-and-beam family guest rooms. A full breakfast is served in the library; snacks and beverages are always available. Rates are $97–127 double. Well-behaved children are encouraged to bring their parents; those under 12 stay free.

Also see **Shaker Hill B&B** (shakerhill.com) in Enfield, one of our favorite places to stay on the western edge of this region. We've described it in detail in the Upper Valley chapter.

OTHER LODGING ✪ ✄ "♦" **Sunapee Harbor Cottages** (603-763-5052; sunapeeharborcottages.com), 4 Lake Ave., Sunapee Harbor 03782. Times change, as these charming cottages, rebuilt in 2002 on the site of the old Whispering Pines Cabins Resort, testify. Location! Location! Sited smack in the center of Sunapee Harbor with lake views, the six clustered cottages represent a fabulous find for families. Each is nicely designed and delightfully decorated in true cottage style with work by local artisans. Each offers kitchen facilities, phone, and an attractive gathering space with a gas fireplace. Most sleep five; Loon's Nest sleeps seven. Owner Sheila Thomas Whitcomb lives and works in the house next door and is happy to help orient guests and to arrange for amenities ranging from babysitting and catered meals to pontoon boat rental and massage therapy. Rates are $200–250 for two, $250 for three to five, and $325 for Loon's Nest. Check the website for special rates and packages.

"♦" **Best Western Sunapee Lake Lodge** (603-763-2010; sunapeelakelodge.com), 1403 Rt. 103, Mount Sunapee 03255. Sited at the entrance to Mount Sunapee Ski Resort and the state park beach, this is a 55-room motor lodge with phones and free HBO. Deluxe units have fold-out couches, fridge and microwave. Food and drink are next door at Digby's Burger Bar and Saloon. $119–209.

Mountain Edge Resort (603-763-4600; mountainedgeresort.com), 1380 Rt. 103, Mount Sunapee 03255. This is a condo resort with a great location right below the entrance to the ski area and overlooking the lake. Time-share but regular guests welcome. Amenities include an indoor pool, a full-service spa and restaurant. From $289 per night with a two- to three-night minimum.

✴ Where to Eat

DINING OUT

In the Lake Sunapee area
Rockwell's at the Inn (603-526-2791; rockwellsattheinn.com), 353 Main St. at the New London Inn. Open Tue.–Sat. for dinner. Reservations recommended. Chef-owner Jerod Rockwell's fare is more inventive than you might expect to find in this traditional inn dining room. Entrées might include Alaskan halibut with poppy seed spaetzle, bacon lardoons, caramelized onions, and artichoke and Brie broth; or rosemary roasted filet mignon with Yukon gold and blue cheese butter and sautéed spinach. Entrées $18–30. Tavern menu features comfort food like rosemary meat loaf with "really good gravy" ($9–25).

The Inn at Pleasant Lake (603-526-6271; 800-626-4907), 853 Pleasant St., New London. Reservations required. Fixed price ($55), five-course dinner Wed.–Sun. in summer; to Sat. in winter. Chef-owner Brian MacKenzie is a Culinary Institute of America graduate who has put this lovely old inn on the culinary map. Guests are asked to arrive around 6:15 for a drink, and Brian lovingly describes the menu while serving cocktails and canapés on the glassed-in porch. Dinner, too, is a ceremony, including an entremezzo course of, say, fresh citrus sections with a splash of sherry. Follow that with rack of lamb with roasted garlic rosemary demiglaze, or mahimahi served with an exotic mushroom salad and yellow pepper oil; then perhaps a rosette of white chocolate mousse in a lace cookie cup with a trio of sauces. Star billing is shared with a view of the lake. Half-portion, half-price children's servings.

⅃ **Millstone American Bistro and Wine Bar** (603-526-4201), Newport

AMC Cardigan Lodge (603-466-2727; outdoors.org), 774 Shem Valley Rd., Alexandria (mail: RFD 1, Bristol 03222). Open late June–late Oct. for full service (breakfast, dinner, and trail lunch with towel and linens supplied); otherwise self-service (kitchen use and BYO sleeping bag). Meals are also served on winter weekends and during the Presidents' Week school vacation. Check the website for precise dates. The Appalachian Mountain Club, founded in 1876 to blaze hiking trails through the White Mountains, maintains a number of no-frills, outdoors-oriented huts, lodges, and family camps in New Hampshire.

Cardigan Lodge opened as a truly pioneer ski lodge in 1934, nestled in the Shem Valley on the eastern side of 3,155-foot-high Mount Cardigan. Ski trails were blazed with the help of the CCC, and the lodge was built almost entirely by volunteers. A rope tow was installed and the lodge remained a hugely poplar winter destination through World War II. However, with the opening of new, more sophisticated ski areas after the war, Cardigan's popularity waned, and its focus shifted to summer and fall hiking programs. In 2005 it was totally renovated. There are now 13 shared bunk rooms of various sizes and two private rooms with bath. Walk out the door to access literally dozens of trails to the three peaks generally known as Cardigan (the other two are South Peak and Firescrew). Many of the lower trails are used by cross-country and back-country skiers and snowshoers in winter. This is one of the most pristine, off-the-beaten-path corners of the Lakes Region, with 6,000 surrounding acres of woodland and Newfound Lake down the road. Summer at Cardigan includes volunteer-led hikes and swimming. $50–76 per adult with three meals. Inquire about primitive campsites and a rustic (self-service) high cabin near the summit. Call or check the website for current programs.

CARDIGAN LODGE

Jerry & Marcy Monkman, courtesy of the AMC

Rd., New London. Open for lunch and dinner daily. A veteran of the area restaurant scene claims this is where he goes when he doesn't want to be disappointed. Entrées, ranging from Maine crab pie to Jaeger schnitzel, are creative and consistently good. Original art, warm colors, plants, and nice light shining through French doors and skylights lend a note of relaxed gentility to this bistro and wine bar. Dinner options might include pan-seared veal scaloppine with spinach, crispy potato gnocchi, and a sage prosciutto broth, or semi-boneless half ducking with orange, roasted beets, and truffle oil over lentils. Entrées $19–27. A lighter menu (from $8) is offered on the lounge side of the bar. More than 50 wines by the glass are featured.

Café Andre (603-863-1842), Rt. 103 just west of the Mount Sunapee traffic circle, Sunapee. Open daily, except Tue., 4 PM–1 AM. Reservations recommended. Chef Andre Woldkowski's long history in the restaurant business dates to working at his family's establishment while he was growing up in Poland. Before opening his own place with partner Mary Stillwell in December 2001, he worked for a decade— winters at restaurants in Vermont, summers on Block Island. He describes his menus as "intercontinental." One offers formal dining choices: escargots, tournedos of beef, duck, and other classics. The other is served at the more casual pub. The dining room has white tablecloths, soft lighting, and a display of local art. Entrées $12.95–23.50.

Colonial Farm Inn (603-526-6121; colonialfarminn.com), 499 Andover Rd. Open except Tue. for dinner. The charming fireplaced dining room in this early-19th-century inn is the setting for candlelight dining. The menu might include potato-crusted chicken breast, sautéed with fresh sage and crimini and shiitake mushrooms, and finished with Marsala cream sauce; or seared duck breast with cranberry ruby port sauce. Entrées $19–28.

& **Traditions Restaurant at Lake Sunapee Country Club** (603-526-6040), Rt. 11 and Country Club Lane, New London. Open year-round for lunch and dinner but selective days; check. The attractive dining room with views of the fairway is locally known for its fare. You might dine on pork schnitzel or seafood pie. From $16 for a roast turkey dinner to $22 for certified Angus beef, the specialty.

Alphorn Bistro (603-768-3318; innat danbury.com), 67 Rt. 104, Danbury. Open Wed.–Sat. 5–9 PM. The annual "Best of the Wurst" festival is a good description of this restaurant's exuberantly Bavarian atmosphere. The owners, Netherlands-born Alexandra and chef Robert Graf, have created a yearlong Oktoberfest, complete with dirndl-clad waitresses, blue-and-white-checked tablecloths, an extensive beer list, and a menu of German and other European specialties. Entrées range $14–22.

& **La Meridiana** (603-526-2033), Rt. 11, Wilmot. Open for dinner nightly. This is the favorite restaurant of local children's author Tomie dePaola, who based one of his books on an Italian legend he learned here. The menu, like chef-owner Piro Canuto, is northern Italian, and the specialties are tender scaloppine and bistecca. Pastas and pastries are outstanding, and the wine list is moderately priced. Patrons are welcome to order just the appetizers, pastas, or entrées off an à la carte menu that has remained the same for 24 years—but there are also nightly, seasonally based specials. Pastas $9–18.95, entrées $12.95–26.95.

Dexter's Inn (603-763-5571), 258 Stagecoach Rd., Sunapee. Reservations suggested. Dinner is served on weekends at the inn (see *Lodging*). The menu might range from Tuscan vegetable lasagna to Jaeger schnitzel; desserts like blueberry bread pudding are a specialty. Choose from the menu (entrées $18–24) or from a three-course prix fixe menu ($32, $39 for four courses).

☙ **M/V *Kearsarge* Dinner Cruise** (763-5477; mvkearsarge.com), Sunapee Harbor. May to October, there's no lovelier place to be on a warm evening than aboard the *Kearsarge* for the nightly roast beef buffet (full bar). It's $36 for adults, $26 for kids. Meals are catered by the Appleseed Restaurant (see *Eating Out*)

ち **The Old Courthouse** (603-863-8360), 30 Main St., Newport. An 1820s courthouse hidden behind the Victorian Opera House. Open Wed.–Sat. for lunch and dinner; Sun. brunch 9:30–1:30. Reservations suggested. Family owned and a special place, a dining room that preserved the elegant simplicity of the Federal era. Dinner options might range from wild mushroom risotto with wilted spinach to grilled New York strip sirloin with roasted shallot and tarragon butter. $16–22.

In the Newfound Lake area

ち **The Homestead** (603-744-2022; homesteadnh.com), Rt. 104, Bristol. Dinner daily from 4:30; Sun. brunch 11–2. Closed Mon. between Columbus Day and Memorial Day. This handsome old 1788 roadside Colonial, now painted pale yellow with dark green shutters and awnings, has been a restaurant since 1978. A series of dining rooms range from traditional to glass to stone walled. The menu offers a choice of more than 40 entrées,

priced from $15.95 for vegetarian ravioli to $27.95 for a lobster casserole.

ち **Pasquaney Restaurant in The Inn on Newfound Lake** (603-744-9111), 103 Mayhew Turnpike, Rt. 3A, Bridgewater. Serves dinner Wed.–Sun., plus Sun. brunch 10–2. The traditional old hotel dining room has been deftly updated with forest-green walls, white wainscoting, and flowery chintz window swags. There's also patio dining overlooking the lake. The seasonal menu might include pan-sautéed forktender veal cutlet topped with prosciutto and fresh sage, or baked Atlantic salmon glazed with pecans and maple syrup. Entrées $12–29. The **Wild Hare Tavern** serves a lighter menu along with drinks.

EATING OUT

In and around New London

☙ **MacKenna's Restaurant** (603-526-9511), New London Shopping Center. Open for breakfast, lunch, and dinner. Every town should have a place like this: clean, friendly, fast, and inexpensive. Homemade soups, great sandwiches on homemade bread (chicken salad is exceptional), steak dinners, and broiled or fried seafood and chicken; children's plates.

The Flying Goose Brew Pub & Grille (603-526-6899; flyinggoose .com), 40 Andover Rd. (Rts. 11 and 114). Open for lunch and dinner daily 11:30–9, Sun. until 8. Same ownership as the Millstone Restaurant but a more casual atmosphere. This 195-seat restaurant has become a widely prized, nonsmoking acoustic venue for musicians, offering seasonal Thursday-night concerts with locally and sometimes nationally known rock, folk, blues, country, jazz, and swing stylists (call for current schedule). It features 14 handcrafted ales and homemade root beer on tap, as well as a large menu that includes daily specials and burgers, sandwiches, ribs, superb soups, pastas, deep fries, and a variety of entrées, $9.95–19.95.

Ellie's Cafe/Deli (603-526-2488; elliescafeanddeli.com), 207 Main St. In summer open 7–5, Sun. 8–2. With cloth napkins and a hearth, the sense is of a special place. Breakfast choices might include crème brûlée French toast or whole-grain banana and walnut pancakes. Lunch on flatbread pizza or jumbo lump crabcakes.

Screwie Lewiez Ristorante (603-526-6600), 420 Main St. Open except Sun. 11–8. Ms. Wally and Mr. Bud serve up super hand-tossed pizzas and a wide choice of sandwiches on homemade bread, salads, and more.

On and around Lake Sunapee

The Anchorage at Sunapee Harbor (603-763-3334), 71 Main St. Open mid-May–mid-Oct. for lunch and dinner 11:30–9. A Lake Sunapee waterside tradition that's simply a great spot. Lunch on a grilled fish salad if you don't want a burger. Reasonably priced dinner options include Redneck Yacht

THE ANCHORAGE AT SUNAPEE HARBOR
Chris Tree

Club meat loaf with a mushroom sauce, fish-and-chips, and grilled tuna steak. Live entertainment in the lounge Thu.–Fri.

Double Diamond Café (603-863-9837; doublediamondcafe.com), 53 Rt. 103, Sunapee. Open 7–2, a great breakfast and lunch spot, from omelets to a steak sizzler.

Bubba's (603-763-3290), Rt. 103, Newbury Harbor. Open 11:30–9. Just where you might want to want to stop—at the southern toe of Lake Sunapee—this cheerful eatery offers a truly tasty burger, beer-battered onion rings, BBQ, pizza, pasta, steak, and more. Good for lunch, dinner, and anything in between.

Elsewhere

✿ **Appleseed Restaurant** (603-938-2100; appleseedrestaurant.com), 63 High St. Open year round, Tue.–Sun. 5–9, Sun. brunch 9–noon. This delightful family-run and -geared restaurant describes itself as "in between everywhere," but it's easily accessible from Mount Sunapee. In summer you can dine on the deck overlooking Lake Todd; in the winter the woodstove blazes away in the dining room. Go for the roast beef dinner, but you can also dine on a BBQ beef sandwich—and don't pass up the hand-battered onion rings or the house "Bitin' Bloody Mary" at brunch.

○ **The Foothills Restaurant** (603-456-2140), 15 Main St., Warner. Open daily 6 AM–2 PM. For tourists, a pleasant pit stop in a picture-perfect small town just off I-89. For locals, this is the place to come to see everyone they know, even at 6 AM! Weekdays and weekends, folks from Warner and surrounding towns flock here for homemade breakfasts (huge pancake platters; great corned beef hash; toasted, buttered muffins) that are better than home since someone else does the cooking. Fast friendly service, daily baked specials, and a front porch with rocking chairs in case there's a wait. All sandwiches are $7.55, with a choice of sides. We usually settle for The Foothills: turkey, bacon, tomato, and Swiss on rye.

Blackwater Junction Restaurant (603-735-5099), 730 Main St., Andover. Open Wed.–Sun. 5–3. Ample portions of from-scratch diner food make this a huge local favorite.

Bradford Junction Restaurant and Bakery (603-938-2424), Rt. 114, Bradford. Open daily 6 AM–2:30 PM. A remnant of the area's railroad days, this dinerlike restaurant was once a depot, and is still the showcase for an elaborate model train that tracks the perimeter of the cheery dining room. Homemade bread, muffins, soups; maybe pot roast and baked haddock.

✋ **Salt Hill Pub** (603-863-7774), 58 Main St., Newport. Open Mon.–Sat. from 11, Sun. from noon, until 1 AM weekends. This handsome brick building dates from 1825, when it was built as a hotel to serve the new courthouse (now also a restaurant; see *Dining Out*). Rehabbed from top to bottom, it is presently an Irish pub with the focus on perfect pints and music.

Pat's Seafood and Pizzaria (603-744-0004), 34 Central Square, Bristol. Open daily for lunch through dinner. There are other seasonal spots in this gateway town to Newfound Lake, but this is a realizable bet with booths, a pleasant atmosphere, and blackboard specials. Specialties range from homemade onion rings to bouillabaise. Beer and wine.

✳ Entertainment

THEATER ✋ **New London Barn Playhouse** (603-526-6710; 603-526-4631; nlbarn.org), 84 Main St., New

London. June–Labor Day; performances are Tue.–Sat. 8 PM, Sun. at 5. One of New England's oldest and best summer-stock theaters, featuring dramatic, musical productions by professional and rising actors. In 2010 the half-dozen productions include *Hello Dolly*, *Hairspray*, *Carousel*, and *Harvey*. The season traditionally kicks off with a free Straw Hat Revue and includes Kids Theatre on Thursdays at 11 and 2.

Newport Opera House (603-863-1212; newportoperahouse.com), 26 Main St., Newport. Rebuilt in 1886 after a fire, this majestic building boasts "the finest acoustics and largest stage north of Boston." It hosts a variety of live productions.

MUSIC Summer band concerts. June–Aug., the Springfield band performs weekly at the grandstand in Sunapee Harbor, and at New London's Mary D. Haddard Memorial Bandstand on Sargent Common. **Wilmot Music on the Bandstand** is mid-July–Aug., Sat. 6–8 at Town Hall in case of rain. **Newport Concerts on the Common** are every Sun. 6–8, in the Opera House in case of rain.

Summer Music (603-526-8234), a nonprofit association, sponsors a series of concerts ranging from chamber music to symphony orchestras, late June–early Aug. at local venues.

✳ Selective Shopping

Antiques Prospect Hill Antiques (603-763-9676), Prospect Hill Rd., Georges Mills. The selection is immense, and the quality outstanding. If you are searching for an armoire or an end table, a desk or a stool, this barn, filled with more than 1,000 pieces of furniture and hundreds of collectibles, is worth checking.

Antiquing in the Lake Sunapee–New London Region. A map/guide to local antiques dealers is available at local information booths and from the New London Chamber of Commerce.

CRAFTS Artisans (603-526-4227; artisansnewlondon.com), 195 Main St. (corner of Pleasant), New London. A colorful selection of handcrafted jewelry, pottery, prints, paintings, woodenware, glass, cards, clothing, books by local authors, and much more.

Braided Rug Shop (603-863-1139; braidedrugshop.com), P.O. Box 2154, Mount Sunapee. Braiding woolen fabric and supplies, plus rugs and novelty items made to order. Instructions for groups and individuals.

Carroll Art Gallery (603-456-3947; carrollartgallery.com), 237 E. Main St. (Rt. 103), Warner. Open Sat. and Sun. 10–5, most other days by chance or appointment. A unique shop with original affordable art, mostly to do with nature, by all members of the Carroll family, including prizewinning author-illustrator-naturalist David Carroll.

Hodgepodge Handicrafts & Ransom's Furniture (603-863-1470), 59 Belknap Ave., Newport. Open Mon.–Fri. 9:30–5, Sat. until 4. Specializing in spinning and knitting supplies, including spinning wheels, homespun yarns, and even a selection of hand-knit wearables.

Earthly Treasures & Iron Horse Metal Works (603-744-5331), 150 Lake St. (Rt. 3A), Bristol. Worth a stop on the way to Newfound Lake: more than 450 artists and artisans, featuring iron wrought on the site.

SPECIAL SHOPS ☙ Main Street BookEnds of Warner (603-456-2700; mainstreetbookends.com), 16 E. Main St., Warner. Open Tue.–Sun. 9–6. This combination bookstore, art gallery, and community heartbeat has a wonderful selection of books, cards, and CDs of local interest, with a big, inviting children's section and toys. Also changing art exhibits, fun and savvy staff, and an amazing array of literary, historical, musical, political, and community programs including Friday-evening book-related films. At this writing the Jim Mitchell park and amphitheater is taking shape at the rear of the store, a play and performance space envisioned by the store's former co-owner.

☙ Morgan Hill Bookstore (603-526-5850; morganhillbookstore.com). Open weekdays 9–5:30, Sat. until 5, Sun. 11–3. A spacious full-service bookstore with a unique, inviting children's area set up like a barn. Specializes in fine fiction and travel; also cards and CDs. Special programs, including signings and talks by area authors, including children's book author-illustrator Tomie dePaola.

Vessels and Jewels, 207 Main St., New London (adjacent to Ellie's Café and Deli). Open daily except Tue. 10–6, Sat. until 8, Sun. until 3. Work by local artists and craftsmen, along with a make-your-own bead shop.

Wingdoodle (603-456-3515; wingdoodle.com), 19 E. Main St., Warner. Open Wed.–Fri. 10–5, Sat. 10–4, Sun. noon–3. A colorful and creative center

ARTISANS, NEW LONDON

Chris Tree

Lee. Booker

MAIN STREET BOOKENDS IN WARNER

offering classes and gifts for all ages. Original artwork, cards, stickers, rubber stamps, journals, toys, puppets, and more.

Rowe Mountain Fair Trade Shop (603-456-2404; rowemountain.com), 17 E. Main St., Warner. Open Wed.–Sat. 10–5, Sun. 10–2. Haitian wall art, wall hangings from Laos and Pakistan, hand-carved salad bowls from Kenya, hemp shoulder bags from Nepal, and much, much more.

The Dorr Mill Store (603-863-1197; dorrmillstore.com), Rt. 11/103, Guild (between Newport and Sunapee). Open Mon.–Sat. 9–5; also Sun. at holiday time. A longtime outlet for the former woolen mill across the street, still featuring 100 percent wool used for hooking and braiding, along with bolts of fabrics, wool blankets, and classic clothing, specializing in sweaters, woolens.

Sunapee Landing Trading Co. (603-863-2275), 356 Rt. 103. Sunapee. Open Mon.–Sat. 10–5. A major local source of furniture, lighting, rugs, art, and antiques.

Renaissance Shoppe (603-526-6711), 107 Newport Rd., New London. A sec-

ondhand trove benefiting the Lake Sunapee Visiting Nurse Association.

FARMER'S MARKETS Bradford Community Farmers' Market (603-938-6228), 134 E. Main St., June–Oct., Thu. 3–6.

Newbury Farmer's & Artisan's Market (603-763-0181), Newbury Library Playground, Rt. 103. July–Oct., Fri. 3–6. Music, local produce, and crafts.

Newport Farmer's Market (603-863-3837) on the common, N. Main St., Newport. Mid-June–Oct., Thu. 3–6.

Warner Area Farmers' Market (603-456-2319), Town Hall lawn. Mid-June–mid-Oct., Sat. 9–noon. Music, crafts, produce, concluding with Warner Fall Foliage Festival.

FARMS, PICK-YOUR-OWN Yankee Farmer's Market (603-456-2833), 360 Rt. 103, Warner. Open Thu.–Mon. A working farm with live buffalo and a retail store selling bison, venison, ostrich, poultry, and pork.

Bartletts Blueberry Farm (603-863-2583), 648 Bradford Rd., Newport. Blueberries mid-July–Sept.

Huntoon Farm (603-768-5579), Huntoon Rd., Danbury. Open Memorial Day–Oct., weekends 10–5. A variety of offerings including baked goods, maple syrup, pumpkins, naturally raised beef, and fall hayrides.

Meadowbrook Farm/Walker's (603-744-8459), 2760 Smith River Rd., Bristol. Fresh corn, tomatoes, and assorted vegetables plus maple syrup, ice cream, and cheese.

Spring Ledge Farm (603-526-6253; 603-526-8483), 220 Main St., New London. Open seasonally 9–6. A succulent selection of produce and plants plus pick-your-own strawberries and flowers.

✴ Special Events

Note: The following entries represent a fraction of summer happenings in this region; check local listings.

July: July 5 fireworks and Sunapee Harbor Parade. **New London Garden Club Annual Antiques Show**. **Hebron Fair**.

August: **New London Hospital Fair**. Annual **League of New Hampshire Craftsmen's Fair**, Mount Sunapee State Park. The biggest event of the year by far. The country's oldest and still one of its best craft fairs: a nine-day gathering of more than 500 juried artisans. Music, an art exhibit, a wide variety of craft demonstrations, and workshops are included in the admissions ticket, good for two days—the time you need to take in the full range of exhibits, try your own hand at crafting something, and see the featured demonstrations that vary with the theme of the day. **Old Home Day**, Sutton. **Annual Lake Sunapee Antique Boat Show and Parade**. **Alexandria Fair**. **Muster Field Farm Days**, North Sutton village, offers more than 100 demonstrations of colonial skills, a Grand Parade, and a roast beef dinner the last weekend of the month—the same weekend as the decades-young **Annual Apple Pie Craft Fair** in Newport.

September: **Mount Sunapee Triathlon**. **Danbury Grange Fair**.

Columbus Day weekend: **Warner Fall Foliage Festival** (wfff.org). Crafts, parade, food, entertainment, and traditional small-town hospitality, one of New England's oldest and biggest small-town fall foliage events.

December: **Magical Christmas**, first weekend in Sunapee Harbor.

A METALSMITH DEMONSTRATES HOW SPOONS ARE MADE AT THE ANNUAL LEAGUE OF NEW HAMPSHIRE CRAFTSMEN'S FAIR.

Courtesy, League of New Hampshrie Craftsmen

THE LAKE
WINNIPESAUKEE REGION

Winnipesaukee is one of the larger natural freshwater lakes in the country and by far the largest in New Hampshire. Twenty-four miles long and varying in width from 1 to 15 miles, it harbors no fewer than 274 habitable islands and 72 square miles of very deep, spring-fed water. Ringed by mountains, it is magnificent.

It's also convenient. Sited in the very center of New Hampshire, Lake Winnipesaukee is less than two hours from Boston. Not surprisingly, its shore is lined with cottages, year-round homes, condominiums, and mansions, and every property owner seems to have at least one boat. On major holiday weekends the lake is jammed with everything from sailboards and Jet Skis to high-speed runabouts, from canoes to luxury cabin cruisers.

The message is clear. The first thing to do here is to get out on the water, and it's easy. The M/S *Mount Washington*, New Hampshire's flagship excursion boat, offers frequent daily cruises, and many marinas and outfitters rent boats, from canoes and kayaks on up.

Where you stay along Winnipesaukee's 200 miles of shoreline makes a huge difference in what you experience. Wolfeboro and Weirs Beach are, for instance, not just at opposite corners of the lake but worlds apart.

Wolfeboro, tucked in an eastern corner of Winnipesaukee and backing on Lake Wentworth, is New Hampshire's tidiest, most compact and upscale resort town, with independently owned, year-round shops and restaurants as well as seasonal small museums. It offers easy access to beaches, bike trails, and cross-country skiing as well as to boats.

Weirs Beach centers on a Victorian-style boardwalk, evoking the late 1800s when it was known for religious "Grove Meetings" and the large wooden hotels and gingerbread cottages that flanked its Victorian depot and docks. Fire has destroyed many buildings here, including the elaborate Weirs Hotel and the original train station, but the present depot and docks are impressive, summer home of both the M/S *Mount Washington* and the Winnipesaukee (excursion) Railroad. This remains the amusement center for the lake, one with a public beach.

Along the north shore, lake views and access are limited unless you are a property owner or guest at a local property. Many public beaches are restricted to local

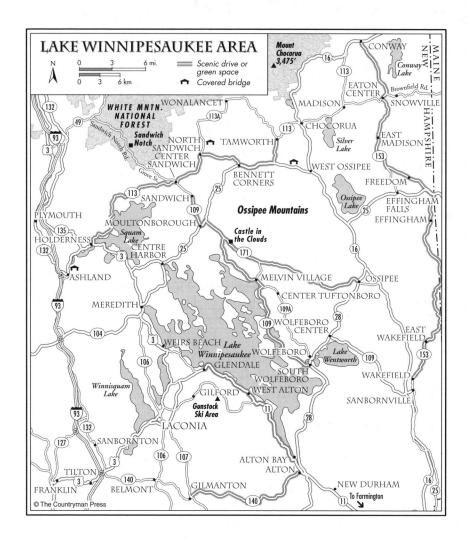

LAKE WINNIPESAUKEE AREA

N   0   3   6 mi.
     0   3   6 km

Scenic drive or green space
Covered bridge

Mount Chocorua 3,475'

residents and guests. For more than 20 miles northwest of Wolfeboro, the lake is obscured by numerous "necks," lined with private homes. Happily, one of the more opulent old estates here, the Castle in the Clouds in Moultenborough, set high in the Ossipee Range—with splendid lake views and more than 5,000 trail-laced acres—is open to the public.

The western and southern shores of the lake—from Meredith in the west, along through Weirs Beach to Gilford on the southern shore and Alton Bay in the very southeast—do offer dramatic views of the lake and its mountains. Ellacoya State Park in Gilford is the only big public beach, but there are many smaller strands.

In sharp contrast with Winnipesaukee's heavy summer traffic, both on and off the water, Squam Lakes are the quiet haven pictured in the movie *On Golden Pond*. Just northwest of Winnipesaukee, pristine Big Squam and Little Squam (which together add up to New Hampshire's second largest lake) have been carefully, sensibly preserved, but it's also surprisingly visitor-friendly—on its own terms.

Kayakers, canoeists, hikers, and naturalists of every ilk are welcome. The Squam Lakes Natural Science Center offers nature trails with views of wild animals in their (almost) natural habitats.

The villages of Meredith and Center Harbor, while on Winnipesaukee, double as shopping centers for nearby Holderness (Squam Lakes) and for Sandwich, an exceptional hill town best known for its annual agricultural fair and as birthplace of the League of New Hampshire Craftsmen. Center Sandwich still showcases fine craftsmanship; more can be found by following its numerous and heart-stoppingly beautiful byways. Several scenic drives lead to Tamworth, the home of the Barnstormers, oldest summer theater in the country, and an equally inviting destination described in "Ossipee Valley." East of Winnipesaukee, Rt. 153 through Wakefield and Effingham is also described in that chapter.

Some visitors to the Winnipesaukee area come for the entire summer, staying in their own cottages (or mansions) or renting housekeeping cottages. Many families have owned their summer places for generations, and many renters have returned to the same cottages for the same week year after year.

Winter brings skiing, snowmobiling, and ice fishing. Gunstock offers both alpine and Nordic skiing, and there are several cross-country facilities in the region. Members of the Winnipesaukee tribe who frequented this lake and named it either "smile of the Great Spirit" or "beautiful water in a high place" (no one seems sure which) wintered over on the site that's now Weirs Beach and fanned out around the lake itself only in warm weather.

The area's mill towns are year-round, workaday communities. Laconia, "the City on the Lakes," is by far the largest (still under 20,000 people) local community, connected to Winnipesaukee but also bordering Lake Winnisquam, and Paugus and Opechee Bays. At its core stands the tower-topped brick Belknap Mill, built in 1823 and said to be the oldest unaltered textile mill in the country. It now serves as a gallery and an entrée to the city's colorful industrial history.

Beginning in the 1840s rail lines on this western side of Winnipesaukee invited expansion of mills in Ashland and Tilton, two towns that also served as transfer points for summer visitors, a role they still play as I-93 exits. Ashland (Exit 24) remains an obvious dining and shopping stop en route to Squam Lake and Center Harbor; Tilton is now known for its outlet shopping and the commercial strip at Exit 20. The town itself is west of I-93, worth checking for its public monuments.

MUST SEE AND DO Cruise Lake Winnipesaukee aboard the M/S *Mount Washington* or rent your own boat. Visit Castle in the Clouds in Moultonborough and the Science Center of New Hampshire at Squam Lake in Holderness. Sunbathe. Swim. Hike.

GUIDANCE Lakes Region Association (800-60-LAKES; lakesregion.org), maintains a walk-in information center Rt. 140 in Tilton, just east of I-93 Exit 20. Open 8:30–5 daily, year-round.

Note: The following are the most active chambers. Others are included in the *Villages* descriptions. All are good for finding summer cottage rentals.

Wolfeboro Chamber of Commerce (603-569-2200; 800-516-5324; wolfeboro chamber.com). The walk-in office is at the old railroad station, 32 Central Ave.

Meredith Area Chamber of Commerce (603-279-6121; 877-279-6121;

Currier Museum of Art, Manchester. Gift of Barney Elsworth

UNTITLED (POSSIBLY A VIEW OF LAKE WINNIPESAUKEE) BY BENJAMIN NUTTING, 1853

meredithcc.org), maintains a walk-in information center center in a white cottage at 272 Daniel Webster Hwy. (corner of Rt. 3 and Mill St).

Lakes Region Chamber of Commerce (603-524-5531; laconia-weirs.org), 383 S. Main St. (Rt. 106 heading out of Laconia), open weekdays. A summer information booth is open weekends on Rt. 3, just south of Weirs Beach.

Squam Lakes Area Chamber of Commerce (603-968-4494; visitsquam.com) maintains a helpful website. **Squam Lakes Association** (603-968-7336) in Holderness is a nonprofit source of maps and information about hiking and boating.

GETTING THERE *By air:* There is regular service to airports in Manchester (see "The Manchester/Nashua Area") and Lebanon (see "Upper Valley Towns"), both of which are just a short drive via rental car from the Winnipesaukee region.

By bus: **Concord Coach Lines** (800-639-3317; concordcoachlines.com) provides scheduled service from Boston's Logan Airport to central and northern New Hampshire via Tilton, Laconia, New Hampton, Meredith, and Plymouth. Daily service varies.

MEDICAL EMERGENCY 911 covers this area.

Lakes Regional General Hospital (603-524-3211; 800-852-3311), 80 Highland St., Laconia. Walk-in care 9 AM–9 PM; 24-hour emergency service.

Huggins Memorial Hospital (603-569-2150), S. Main St., Wolfeboro.

✳ Villages

Alton Bay. One of the lake's early tourist centers, Alton Bay's waterfront area appears little changed from the turn of the 20th century, when train passengers transferred to steamboats. The **Alton–Lakes Region Chamber of Commerce** maintains a seasonal information booth in the old railroad station at the M/S

Mount Washington dock; concerts are held in the bandstand. Cottages around the bay shore evoke memories of the days when summer places were small houses, not condos. The nearby **Harold S. Gilman Museum**, corner of Main St. and Rt. 140, showcases an eclectic collection that include a stereopticon with 1890s views and a working toy steam engine. Open by appointment: 603-875-2161.

Ashland, the gateway town to the Squam Lakes area from I-93, is a delightfully visitor-friendly upcountry mill village. It's been this way since the 1850s, when the Boston & Montréal Railroad arrived, bringing lakes-bound visitors. The village offers good shopping and dining. The **Ashland Historical Society** (603-968-7716; oldashlandnh.org) maintains the **Ashland RR Station**, 69 Depot St. (Rt. 132), as a seasonal museum (inquire about special excursion rides) along with the **Whipple House Museum**, 4 Pleasant St., home of 1934 Nobel laureate Dr. George Hoyt Whipple; exhibits relate to his life. The nearby **Pauline Glidden Toy Museum**, housed in a circa-1810 Cape at 49 Main St., exhibits vintage games, toys, and books.

Center Sandwich (discoversandwich.com). This quintessential white-clapboard, green-shuttered New England village, complete with steepled churches, is exceptionally visitor-friendly, with the inviting tavern in **The Corner House** at its center. Next door is the **Sandwich Historical Society** (603-284-6269; sandwich historical.org), 4 Maple St. (open 10–4 for tours late June–late Aug., Tue.–Sat.; Sept.–early Oct., Wed.–Sat.), displaying portraits by native Albert Gallatin Hoit as well as special annual exhibits. Across the road is **Sandwich Home Industries**, founded in 1926 to promote traditional crafts, a project that evolved into the present League of New Hampshire Arts & Crafts. See *Selective Shopping* for several more shopping possibilities scattered along the back roads that web this mountainous, 100-square-mile town. Note Rt. 113A to Tamworth, described in "Ossipee Valley." Also see Sandwich Notch Rd. in *Hiking*. A century ago there were two hotels in the village itself, along with some 40 "guest farms" that took in summer boarders. The **Sandwich Fair**, held the three days of Columbus Day weekend, is

CENTER SANDWICH

Robert J. Kozlow

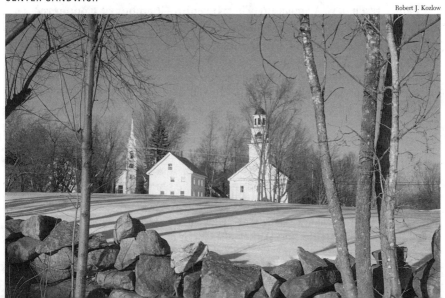

the last one of the year, famed for its old-fashioned feel and for the traffic it attracts to the fairgrounds (south of the village on Rt. 109).

Center Harbor. At the head (northwestern corner) of Lake Winnipesaukee, this is the winter home of the M/S *Mount Washington*. The village is bisected by Rt. 25, but it retains its 19th-century character. The town was named for the Senter family, but the *S* became a *C* somewhere along the way. Whether it's *Centre* or *Center* is still debated. The original name is preserved in its core shopping complex, Senter's Marketplace, best known for Keepsake Quilting, a mecca for quilters from the world over. Unfortunately, the village's big old 19th-century summer hotels, Senter House and the Colonial Hotel, are long gone, but the dock and a small beach survive. Note the bronze goose that's a fountain, sculpted by S. R. G. Cook, a student of Augustus Saint-Gaudens. The **Center Harbor Historical Society** (603-253-7892), Plymouth St. (Rt. 25B), maintains its collection in an 1886 schoolhouse, open Sat. 10–2 in July and Aug.

Melvin Village. The antiques center of the eastern Winnipesaukee region, the little town of Melvin Village still looks as it did in the 19th century, when many of the houses lining Main St. were built. The **Tuftonboro Historical Society** (603-544-8131), Main St. (Rt. 109), Melvin Village, open seasonally, displays photographs and literature relating to Lake Winnipesaukee.

Meredith. Rt. 3 now runs along Meredith's waterfront, meeting Rts. 104 East and 25 at a busy junction. The village, with its shops, restaurants, and B&Bs, is actually up above, bordering Lake Waukewan. In 1818 a canal was built from the site that is now John Bond Swase Park down to Lake Winnipesaukee, a 40-foot drop that eventually powered a number of mills. Despite disastrous fires, one four-story wooden 1820s textile mill survived, functioning off and on until the 1960s, but it was largely hidden by cinder-block industrial buildings. Thanks to local developer Rusty McLear, the mill and falls have been resurrected, making this town a major destination for its shops, restaurants, and four large inns, two with views of the lake and two directly on the water. The **Meredith Historical Society** (603-279-1190), 45 Main St., is open Memorial Day–Columbus Day weekend, Wed.–Sat. 11–4. Formerly the Oak Hill Church, the museum exhibits tools, costumes, photographs, "made-in-Meredith" items, and local historical information. Inquire about the Farm Museum, 61 Winona Rd. The **Meredith Chamber of Commerce** maintains a walk-in information center (see *Guidance*).

Tilton is now better known for its chain stores and discount malls than its village atmosphere, but the part of town west of I-93 does boast more statues than any other American town of its size. From the interstate, you first notice the 55-foot-high, granite Tilton (actually in Northfield) arch, an exact copy of a Roman memorial built in AD 79. Beneath it is a Numidian lion carved from Scottish granite, a tribute to Charles E. Tilton, the town's wealthiest mid-19th-century citizen and a descendant of the first settler. He persuaded the town of Sanbornton Bridge to change its name to Tilton in 1869, a decision no doubt made easier by his gift of statuary. Such allegorical figures as America, Asia, and Europe can still be found around town, along with Tilton's mansion, now the library of the private preparatory Tilton School, founded in 1845.

Wakefield. The sprawling town of Wakefield is composed of several villages: **Union**, **Brookfield**, **Sanbornville**, and **Wakefield Corners**, the latter now a historic district of more than two dozen mostly white-painted, 18th- and 19th-century houses and public buildings, well worth finding (it's just off Rt. 16). Sanbornville, several miles south, is the commercial center. **The Greater Wakefield Chamber of Commerce** (603-522-6106; wakefieldnh.org) furnishes maps and brochures. For lodging/dining in this area see "Ossipee Valley."

✔ **Weirs Beach**, at the junction of Rts. 3 and 11B, is the attractions center of the region—the place to go for many folks, and a place to avoid for others. It is difficult to be ambivalent about miniature golf, a go-cart track, the country's largest arcade, and a strip of pizza parlors, fast-food spots, gift shops, and penny arcades. No trip to the Lakes is actually complete without at least a stroll on the boardwalk. It's a great people-watching place. Right beside all this activity is a summer reli-

WEIRS BEACH BOARDWALK

Chris Tree

gious conference center dating back to the turn of the 20th century, the wharf for the M/S *Mount Washington*, and the home base of the **Winnipesaukee Railroad**. There is also a fine public beach beside the **Endicott Rock Historical Site**, a large boulder found in 1652, when a surveying party claimed this region for the Massachusetts Bay Colony, said to be the second oldest historic landmark in the country. The **Lake Winnipesaukee Historical Society** (603-366-5950) maintains a seasonal, free museum exhibiting vintage photos and memorabilia in a renovated farmhouse, 503 Endicott St. (Rt. 3), Weirs Beach.

Wolfeboro. Billed as "America's oldest summer resort," Wolfeboro remains a lively but low-key, old-fashioned resort village with some outstanding shops, restaurants, and museums as well as entrées to the lake and surrounding countryside. The campus of **Brewster Academy**, a private prep school, is the venue for summer music. **The Wolfeboro Historical Society** (603-569-4997), 337 S. Main St., maintains three buildings, open in July and Aug., Wed.–Fri. 10–4, Sat. 2–10. The complex includes the restored and furnished 1778 Clark House, an 1820 one-room schoolhouse, and the replica 1862 Monitor Engine Company, complete with a restored 1872 horse-drawn, Amoskeag steam-pumper fire engine and an 1842 Monitor hand

WOLFEBORO LAKEFRONT

Chris Tree

engine. The **New Hampshire Antique and Classic Boat Museum** (603-596-4554), a fine collection of antique boats and related artifacts, is at 397 Center St. (Rt. 28 North). Also note the **Governor Wentworth Historic Site**, Rt. 109, the site of Royal Governor John Wentworth's summer estate. Daily late June–Labor Day (seasonal weekends before and after), 45-minute narrated tours aboard **Molly the Trolley** (603-569-1080) depart regularly from the town docks. **Cate Park** on the waterfront by the town wharf is the site of occasional concerts and art exhibits in summer, a delightful place to relax anytime. The exceptionally helpful **Wolfeboro Chamber of Commerce** maintains an information center in the former depot at 32 Central Ave. Also see the museums described under *To See*.

> 🐾 **Squam Lakes Natural Science Center** (603-968-7194; nhnature.org), junction of Rts. 25 and 113, Holderness. Open May–Nov. 1, daily 9:30–4:30 (last admission at 3:30). $13 adults, $11 seniors, $9 ages 3–15; two-week family pass $50. Combined tickets with the popular lakes cruise (see *To Do*) are offered. Check for programs year-round. This nonprofit organization offers a hospitable welcome center and well-equipped gift shop and features a system of walking trails filled with scurrying chipmunks and lined at intervals with child-friendly educational displays and viewing stations (through glass) of live wildlife, including black bears, white-tailed deer, bobcats, foxes, owls, and raptors such as bald eagles, owls, and hawks. The animals are confined within generous areas resembling their natural habitat (the otters have a stream). In all there are 200 acres of meadow and forest, laced with streams and brooks. Daily live "up close" animal programs are offered on the hour 11–3 during July and Aug. The adjoining **Kirkwood Gardens** display perennials designed to attract birds and butterflies. One-day and weeklong activities are also offered for children ages 4–13.

ONE OF THE FEW ANIMALS THAT ISN'T FOR REAL AT THE SQUAM LAKES NATURE CENTER

✳ To See

◐ ♂ ♿ **Libby Museum** (603-569-1035), Rt. 109, 4 miles north of Wolfeboro village, is open Memorial Day–Labor Day, daily except Mon. 10–4. This wonderfully old-fashioned natural history museum has changed little since it was built in 1912 by Wolfeboro native Dr. Henry Forrest Libby, who believed "A museum of natural history should be a place for study, but if the specimens are not studied, it should, at any rate, be a place to flash before the eyes certain awakening influences; a spot where the mystery and drama of life up from the lost ages, may somehow make its appeal to the imagination and from imagination to curious investigation." Now operated by the town, the museum showcases mounted bird, fish, and animal specimens; Native American relics, including a dugout canoe; as well as antique maps and photographs. Programs—lectures, concerts, children's programs, and art exhibits—are well worth checking. Nominal fee.

Wright Museum (603-569-1212; wrightmuseum.org), 77 Center St., Wolfeboro. Open May–Oct., daily 10–4, Sun. noon–4; also Tue. 6:30–9 for lectures in July, Aug.; by appointment the rest of the year. This facility is devoted to the spirit of American enterprise as it was expressed during the war years of 1939–1945. The collection includes memorabilia, artifacts, vehicles (fully operating jeeps, tanks, command cars, and half-tracks), and films from the period. Gift shop and snack bar. A 200-yard walking path connects the museum with downtown Wolfeboro. $6 adults, $5 veterans and seniors, $3 children.

♂ **New Hampshire Farm Museum** (603-652-7840; farmmuseum.org), 1305 White Mountain Hwy. (Rt. 125) off the Spaulding Turnpike (Rt. 16) Exit 18, Milton. Open May–Oct., Wed.–Sun. 10–4. New Hampshire's rural agricultural heritage is maintained in this unusual collection of buildings, situated about midway between the Lakes Region and the seacoast. The three-story Great Barn is filled with wagons and a host of other farm artifacts. The Jones Farmhouse is furnished to reflect its ownership by the Jones family from 1780 to 1900; you'll also find the adjoining Plummer Homestead, blacksmith and cobbler shops, a well-stocked country store (good for historical books, reproduction toys, and much more), and 50 acres with picnic areas and a self-guiding trail. An annual Old-Time Farm Day, with many farmers, artists, and craftspeople gathered to demonstrate their skills, takes place in mid-Aug. $6 adults, $3 ages 3–17. See the website for a detailed program of year-round events. Also see *Villages* for more museums.

COVERED BRIDGES The **Graton covered bridge** just off Rt. 3 in Ashland was built for the town by resident Milton Graton, a renowned builder and restorer of covered bridges

LIBBY MUSEUM, WOLFEBORO

Chris Tree

✪ ⓓ ✐ **Castle in the Clouds** (603-476-5900; castleintheclouds.org), 455 Old Mountain Rd., Rt. 171 (2 miles east of the Rt. 171/Rt. 109 intersection), Moultonborough. Open weekends early May–mid-June, then daily until late Oct., 10–4:30. Plan to spend the better part of a day on the 5,500-acre estate set high in the Ossipee Mountain Range. At least come for lunch at the **Carriage House**, with its 270-degree view of the lake from the patio that's seemingly suspended 1,300 feet the panorama below. Locals know to tell the gatekeeper down on Rt. 117 that they are coming just for lunch so they don't have to pay the castle admission fee ($12 per adult, $5 per youth above age 6, $9 for seniors)—but really it would be a shame to drive all the way up and not to tour the state's standout showplace.

The 16-room Arts & Crafts–style stone mansion was built in 1912–1913 by 1,000 workers—primarily using wood and stone from the property—at a cost of $7 million for T. G. Plant (1859–1941). The eccentric 5-foot-1 multimillionaire had made his fortune in the Massachusetts shoe industry, retired at age 51, and remarried. He amassed 6,300 acres that stretched from the Ossipee Mountains all the way down to the lake. With his wife, Olive, Plant continued to live here until his death in 1941; the mansion has since survived remarkably intact. Under current ownership by the Lakes Region Conservation Trust and managed by its offshoot Castle Preservation Society, restoration continues. Visitors are welcomed in ways that we wish more historic properties would emulate.

A guide greets groups in the solarium, telling the mansion's story and explaining how thoroughly revolutionary many of its features—forced hot-air heating and air-conditioning using springwater, an intercom system, and central vacuum cleaning system—were for its era. Visitors are then free to wander the amazing rooms in which docents stand ready to answer questions and point out features like the secret room in the library with its low-cut door, the brine-cooled refrigerator, and the "needle showers" in the bathrooms.

throughout the Northeast. The **Whittier bridge** crosses the Bearcamp River, just off Rt. 16 and north of Rt. 25, in West Ossipee. The **Cold River bridge** is a little difficult to find but well worth the effort. It is located off Rt. 113A just north of North Sandwich.

SCENIC DRIVES To the east of Lake Winnipesaukee, **Rt. 153** from Sanbornville to Conway (see "Ossipee Valley") is a wandering alternative to busy Rt. 16. Another rewarding drive is **Rt. 113** east from Rt. 3 in Holderness, or **Rt. 109** north from Rt. 25 in Moultonborough. Either way you reach Center Sandwich and can opt—assuming you have a high, rugged car—for the **Sandwich Notch Rd.** or

Visitors buy tickets for the house tour and can generally relax in the Carriage House below the mansion (a shuttle van as well as a path links the two). In addition to the Café there's an upstairs function room, a popular venue for wedding receptions. Another building houses a gift shop and art gallery. The 127 acres immediately surrounding the castle include gardens, waterfalls, and Shannon Pond, complete with giant trout. Inquire about Monday "walks and talks" geared to kids. The grounds pass for the property is $5 (free for 6 and under). Check the website for many special events.

The 5,500-acre current property is webbed with more than 45 miles of trails, ranging in length from 20 minutes to three hours. For more about hiking on the property see *Green Space*.

FRONT LAWN AT THE CASTLE IN THE CLOUDS, MOULTENBOROUGH   Chris Tree

Rt. 113A to North Sandwich, Whiteface, and Wonalancet, then on to Tamworth. **Rt. 171** from Center Ossipee to Moultonborough, **Rt. 11** from Alton Bay to Glendale, and **Rt. 140** from Alton to Gilmanton are all great scenic drives.

✳ To Do

AMUSEMENT AREA ✈ **Weirs Beach**, at the junction of Rts. 3 and 11B, is the attractions center of the region, with two waterslides, miniature golf, a go-cart track, the country's largest arcade, and a strip of pizza parlors, fast-food spots, gift shops, and penny arcades. **Funspot** (603-366-4377; funspotnh.com), Rt. 3, 1 mile north of Weirs Beach is open daily year-round 10–closing: more than 550 games, billed as the largest complex of its type in the country. From pinball to video and driving games to simulcast golf, this has something for people of all ages, including both candlepin (a mostly New England game) and 10-pin bowling, a driving range, and miniature golf. Most seasonal attractions are open weekends Memorial Day–mid-June, then daily until Labor Day. They include **Daytona Fun Park** (603-366-5461), featuring Indy go-carts, mini golf, batting cages, an arcade, and a climbing wall.

BICYCLING **The Cotton Valley Trail** is an evolving 12-mile rec path that begins at the Wolfeboro Depot and follows the old rail line toward Wakefield. It's a great way to accesss the two beaches on Lake Wentworth, Albee Beach and Wentworth State Park. **Nordic Skier** (603-569-3151; nordicskiersports.com), 47 N. Main St., Wolfeboro, rents bikes and dispenses a free map to the trail, also directions for rides to Lake Wentworth and Brewster and Carry Beaches.

Mountain Sports (603-279-5540), Rts. 3 and 106, Meredith, rents mountain bikes and supplies area maps. Also see Gunstock under *Sports Park*.

BOAT EXCURSIONS **M/S *Mount Washington*** (603-366-5531; 888-843-6686; cruisenh.com), Lakeside Ave., Weirs Beach. Mid-May–Oct. 31. The queen of the lake and a New Hampshire landmark. Special theme cruises and dinner and moonlight dancing excursions are delightful. For first-time Lakes Region visitors, a ride on this famous vessel is a great introduction to Lake Winnipesaukee. Her namesake ship was a wooden side-wheeler in service 1872–1939. She was replaced by the present steel-hulled boat, but remained in port for most of World War II, when her engines were commandeered for the war effort. In 1946 she returned to service, and in 1983 she was lengthened and changed to M/S (motor ship). Day trips two to three hours, $25; evening dinner/dance cruise (reservations required) $25–49; Sunday champagne brunch cruises, $40 adults, $20 ages 4–12. Reduced fares and special family package fares available.

AT WEIRS BEACH BOARD THE M/S *MOUNT WASHINGTON* FOR A SAIL AROUND THE LAKE.

Chris Tree

M/V *Sophie C* (603-366-5531), Lakeside Ave., Weirs Beach. Mid-June–week after Labor Day, Mon.–Sat. 11 AM and 2 PM. This is the oldest floating post office in the country. Her cruises wind around the islands, into coves and channels, delivering mail to residents on five islands. Some of the two-hour cruises include mail stops. Light refreshments available. $16 adults $16, $5 ages 4–12; under 4 free.

Chris Tree

GETTING OUT ON THE LAKE IS A MUST.

M/V *Doris E* (603-366-5531), Lakeside Ave., Weirs Beach 03246. Departs Meredith and Weirs Beaches. June–Labor Day there are three daytime cruises and one sunset cruise. Discover Meredith Bay and many islands on these one- or two-hour trips. $10 adults for one-hour cruise, $16 for two-hour, $5 ages 4–12; under 4 free.

M/V *Winnipesaukee Belle* (603-569-3016; 800-451-2389), Wolfeboro. Call the Wolfeboro Inn to find out how to charter this 65-foot side paddle-wheeler based at the Wolfeboro Town Docks.

M/V *Millie B* (603-569-1080), Wolfeboro. Half-hour boat rides in a classic 1920s motor launch departing from the Wolfeboro Town Docks; operated by the Wolfeboro Trolley Company. Daily late June–Labor Day, 10–5, weather permitting; weekends only Memorial Day–late June from 11 AM and again from post–Labor Day through the Columbus Day weekend.

Golden Pond Tour (603-968-7194; nhnature.org) departs from the bridge at Walter's Basin, but passengers gather 15 minutes before departure at Squam Lakes Natural Science Center. Cruises are Memorial Day–foliage season. Ninety-minute cruises in an all-weather pontoon boat offer views of loons, the islands, and the movie-filming locations for *On Golden Pond*. Reservations suggested. Inquire about special naturalist-guided cruises and about the combined nature Science Center and Lakes Cruise pass.

BOAT RENTALS No driver's license is required to operate a boat, but you must be 16 years old to operate one with more than 25 horsepower. There are, of course, marine patrol officers, speed limits at certain congested areas, and a number of accidents each summer. For boating regulations and education contact the New Hampshire Department of Safety's **Bureau of Marine Patrol in Gilford** (603-293-2037; 877-642-9700). Also, keep an eye on the weather, because high winds, sudden squalls, and thunderstorms can quickly whip the lake surface into waves as rough as the ocean, an especially dangerous situation for those in small boats who have no experience in such conditions. Most towns provide public launching sites, and boat rentals are too numerous to list.

CANOEING AND KAYAKING Many powerboat rental outfits also rent canoes and kayaks, but the following companies specialize in nonmotorized rentals.

Wild Meadow Canoes & Kayaks (603-253-7536; 800-427-7536; wildmeadow canoes.com) in Center Harbor offers rentals and sales of canoes and kayaks.

Squam Lakes Association (603-968-7336), Rt. 3, Holderness, offers kayak and canoe rentals along with lakeside tenting.

FISHING Gadabout Golder Guide Service (603-569-6426; gadaboutgolder .com), 79 Middleton Rd., Wolfeboro, offers guided fly-fishing trips on Winnipesaukee and nearby lakes and rivers, late Apr.–mid-Oct.

Note: Contact the **New Hampshire Fish and Game Department** (603-271-3421; 603-271-3422; wildlife.state.nh.us) for local fishing license outlets and advice.

GOLF Most courses in this region operate mid-Apr.–Oct., weather permitting, and all offer cart rentals.

Highland Links Golf Club (603-536-3452; highlandlinks.net), Mount Prospect Rd., Holderness. Nine holes with executive par 3, pro shop, and snack bar.

Indian Mound Golf Course (603-539-7733; indianmoundgc.com), off Rt. 16, Center Ossipee. Nine holes, bar, and restaurant.

Kingswood Golf Club (603-569-3569; kingswoodgolfclub.com), Rt. 28, Wolfeboro. Eighteen holes, full bar, and food service. This is a busy summer place with fully stocked pro shop and driving range, so call for tee times.

Oak Hill Golf Course (603-279-4438; oakhillgc.com), 159 Pease Rd., off Rt. 104, Meredith. Nine holes, full bar, and food service. Reasonable greens fees. No tee times.

Pheasant Ridge Country Club (603-524-7808; playgolfne.com), 140 Country Club Rd., Gilford. Eighteen holes, lake views, light food, and bar service.

Province Lake Golf (800-325-4434; provincelakegolf.cam), Rt. 153, Parsonfield, Maine. Eighteen holes, full bar, and food service; tee-time reservations available seven days in advance. The Maine–New Hampshire state line cuts through the course, and several holes line picturesque Province Lake. Multiple tees at each hole appeal to families.

Ridgewood Country Club (603-476-5930; ridgewoodcc.net), 258 Governor Wentworth Hwy. (Rt. 109). An 18-hole course; carts, fully stocked golf shop, aqua driving range, full-service restaurant, lessons.

Waukewan Golf Course (603-279-6661; waukewan.com), Waukewan Rd. off Rt. 3/25, Center Harbor. Eighteen holes, full bar, and food service, located on a wildlife sanctuary. No tee times, so plan ahead for busy weekend play.

White Mountain Country Club (603-536-2227), 3 Country Club Dr. off Rt. 3, Ashland. Eighteen holes, designed by Geoffrey Cornish, a full bar and food service.

HIKING Most people head for the White Mountains to hike, but the Winnipesaukee region offers a variety of trails with fewer hikers and splendid mountaintop lake views (although the peaks are not as high as those farther north). The **Squam Lakes Association**, which maintains many trails in this region, has a guidebook (see *Guidance*). We have listed only a few of the many possible trails in the region. We recommend using a guidebook, because many of these trails are traveled less and marked less than the more famous trails farther north. All times shown are for the ascent only. Hikers should carry their own water. (Also see *Green Space*.)

Sandwich Notch, from Center Sandwich to Rt. 49 in Campton. This ancient Indian trail was an important 18th- and early-19th-century route from the western White Mountains down to the lakes, and it's lined with stone walls that once marked open meadows. Once more wooded and now part of the White Mountain National Forest, this haunting, 11-mile road has been preserved as is (to widen and pave it would inevitably turn it into a heavily traveled shortcut between Winnipesaukee and Waterville Valley). Closed in winter, it remains popular with cross-country skiers and snowmobilers; in summer it's steep, rough, and slow going but passable for all but low-slung cars. It's also a popular walk, at least the 3.5 miles from Center Sandwich to **Beede Falls** (a town park). The **Wentworth Trail** to the summit of **Mount Israel** (elevation 2,620 feet), which offers fine views of the Lakes Region, begins 2.6 miles from Center Sandwich. Watch for signs to Mead Base, a Boy Scout camp. The 1.6-mile-long trail usually takes two hours to hike. Park in the field below the camp buildings and enter the woods at a sign at the left rear of the main building. Farther along the Notch Rd. (about 3.7 miles south of the junction with Rt. 49), the 4.5-mile-long **Algonquin Trail** ascends **Sandwich Dome** (elevation 3,993 feet). It's rough but offers fine views from its rocky ledges. Hiking time is three and a half hours.

Rattlesnake is a popular short hike on Squam Lake. From Holderness go 5.7 miles north on Rt. 113, past the ROCKYWOLD–DEEPHAVEN ROAD sign. Park on the left at the base of the Mount Morgan Trail but follow the old **Bridle Trail** (across the road). It bears left at the end of a row of maples and up a wide, gradual path to the summit of **West Rattlesnake** (0.9 mile). There's an excellent view to the southwest just below the summit.

Red Hill. A fine view of Lake Winnipesaukee is the prize at the end of the **Red Hill Trail**. In Center Harbor, at the junction of Rts. 25 and 25A, take Bean Rd. for 1.4 miles, then follow Sibley Rd. (look for the FIRE TOWER sign) to a parking lot with a gate. Past the gate is a jeep road that becomes the trail. The hike is 1.7 miles and requires just over an hour. A famous Bartlett lithograph, often found in local antiques shops, shows a gathering of Native Americans on Red Hill.

Belknap Range. On the western side of the lake is a low ridge of mountains with many trails. A good starting point is the Gunstock Recreation Area on Rt. 11A in Gilford. Several trails ascend beside the ski slopes. Ask for a map at the camping area office.

Mount Major. Located just north of Alton on Rt. 11, this is everybody's favorite climb. The **Mount Major Trail** is only 1.5 miles long and requires about an hour and 20 minutes; views across the lake are impressive. Hike on the right day and watch the M/S *Mount Washington* as she cuts through the waters of Alton Bay.

Also look for Knight's Pond Conservation Area in Alton, Rines Rd. off Rt. 28 south. You'll find more than 300 acres good for fishing as well as hiking.

In the Wolfeboro area several short hiking trails are rewarding. ✔ **Abenaki Tower**, Rt. 109 in Tuftonboro. A 5-minute walk takes you from the parking area to an 80-foot tower overlooking Lake Winnipesaukee and the Ossipee Mountains; great for short legs. In Wolfeboro itself the **Russell C. Chase Bridge Falls Path** behind the railroad station leads 0.5 mile to Wolfeboro Falls, and the **Cotton Valley Trail** stretches from the station 12 miles along the old railbed to the railroad turntable in Sanbornville. It traverses trestles and three lakes as well as woods and fields.

HORSEBACK RIDING Gunstock Cobble Mountain Stables (603-293-4341; 800-GUNSTOCK; gunstock.com), Rt. 11A, Gilford. Ages 8 and up can take a one-hour trail ride through the scenic Cobble Mountain area.

RAILROAD EXCURSIONS ✔ **Winnipesaukee Scenic Railroad** (603-279-5253; 603-745-5253; hoborr.com), 154 Main St., Meredith, and 211 Lakeside Ave., Weirs Beach. Open weekends and holidays from Memorial Day, daily late June–Labor Day, then weekends only until mid-Oct. Board from Meredith or Weirs Beach. Ride beside the lake on historic coaches of the 1920s and 1930s, or connect with the M/S *Mount Washington* for a boat ride (see *Boat Excursions*). Inquire about dinner trains and special excursions. $14 per adult, $11 ages 3–11.

Molly the Trolley (603-569-1080), Wolfeboro, offers 45-minute narrated tours of Wolfeboro, daily from 10 AM late June–Labor Day; weekends only starting at 11 AM from Memorial Day into June and again after Labor Day until mid-Oct. $5 adult, $4 ages 4–12.

SAILING Winni Sailboarders' School & Outlet (603-528-4110; sailboarders @mathbox.com), 314 Laconia Rd., Tilton. Open daily in summer; weekends only off-season, though it's best to call ahead. Sales (and some rentals) of sailboards, sailboats, kayaks, pedal boats, wet suits, inflatables, and GPS receivers. Lessons in windsurfing, kayaking, and GPS.

SCUBA DIVING Dive Winnipesaukee (603-569-8080; divewinnipesaukee .com), 4 N. Main St., Wolfeboro. Open all year. Lake and ocean diving, scuba certification programs, rentals, guided dives, charter trips.

SPORTS PARK Gunstock (603-293-4341; 800-GUNSTOCK; gunstock.com), Rt. 11A, Gilford. This 2,000-acre ski area is a four-season sports park offering mountain boarding, skating, skiing, tubing, mountain biking, and horseback riding, plus a swim pond, hiking, and camping. (Also see *Green Space*.)

SWIMMING ♿ **Ellacoya State Beach**, Rt. 11, Gilford. Open weekends from Memorial Day, daily mid-June–Labor Day. Fee charged. The only state beach on Lake Winnipesaukee. A 600-foot strand with refreshment stand and changing rooms; handicapped accessible. The view across the lake to the Ossipee Mountains is one of the best in the region. There's also a boat launch and a campground with 38 RV sites ($45 per night).

Chris Tree

SWIMMING AT LEAVITT PARK IN CENTER HARBOR

Wentworth State Park and Clow Beach (603-569-3699), Rt. 109 East, Wolfeboro. Open daily mid-June–Labor Day. Fee charged. This small park on Lake Wentworth has a bathing beach, play field, changing rooms, and shaded picnic area. **Albee Beach**, Rt. 28 north on Lake Wentworth, is open mid-June–Labor Day, 9 AM–dusk. Also in Wolfeboro but on Lake Winnipesaukee, **Brewster Beach** on Clark Rd. and **Carry Beach** on Forest Rd. are both open mid-June–Labor Day, 9 AM–dusk.

Weirs Beach, Rt. 3. This is a beach in more than name, and it's public.

In Meredith look for **Waukewan Town Beach**, Waukewan St. (sandy town beach with mountain views), and **Leavitt Park**, Rt. 25 on the way to Center Harbor on Lake Winnipesaukee, sandy beach and picnic area.

✳ Winter Sports

CROSS-COUNTRY SKIING Nordic Skier Wolfeboro Cross Country (603-569-3151; wolfeboroxc.org), 47 N. Main St., Wolfeboro. Open daily 9–5:30. Sales, rentals, and instruction for cross-country skiing, also sales and rentals of toboggans, skis, skates, and snowshoes. They schedule moonlight tours and races and maintain a 30km trail network for both skating and doubletrack. Visit the shop for directions to **Abenaki Trails** (15 challenging kilometers) or the **Sewall Woods Trails** (15km of easy, family-geared trails); also maps or suggestions for backcountry skiing. Trail passes ages 13–74: $10.

Gunstock Ski Area (603-293-4341; gunstock.com), Rt. 11A, Gilford. Telemark, cross-country, and downhill skiing plus snowshoeing, with full-service retail, rental, and lesson facility on 50km of trails, 38km skate groomed, 14km tracked, 12km backcountry. $15 per adult, $12 ages 6–12 and 65–69, $10 for 70+.

DOWNHILL SKIING Gunstock Ski Area (603-293-4341; 800-GUNSTOCK; gunstock.com), Rt. 11A, Gilford. The original trails in this county-operated area were designed by President Franklin D. Roosevelt's WPA in the 1930s. From the beginning it included cross-country as well as alpine trails (since then it's been almost entirely redesigned). Since 1937 it has been drawing families with intermediate-level terrain and a magnificent lake and mountain view.

Vertical drop: 1,400 feet.

Lifts: Eight lifts including two quads and two triples.

Trail and glades: 53, 61 percent intermediate.

Snowmaking: 90 percent coverage of 224 acres.

Snowboarding: All trails, terrain park, half-pipe.

Night skiing: 21 trails, five lifts, Thrill Hill Tubing Park and lift, Tue.–Sat.

Facilities: Rentals, nursery, ski school, cross-country and snowshoeing facilities. Nonskiers can plunge down the state's longest snow-tubing hill.

Rates: $66 adults weekends, $56 midweek; $54/44 for teens; $41/31 per child; seniors $41/31. Special night and half-day rates.

SLEIGH RIDES Cobble Mountain Stables at Gunstock Ski Area (603-293-4341, ext. 153; cobblemountainstables.com) offers sleigh rides, conditions permitting, except Mon.

✳ Green Space

✐ **The Loon Center and Markus Wildlife Sanctuary** (603-476-5666), Lees Mills Rd. (Box 604), Moultonborough. The center is operated by the Loon Preservation Committee of the Audubon Society of New Hampshire. This 200-acre site has 2 miles of walking trails through the woods and down to the shore of Lake Winnipesaukee, where a loon nest can be observed. There is also a gift shop and exhibit space, but the main purpose of the facility is to research the American loon, the large waterbird whose eerie calls symbolize wilderness. Overdevelopment of New Hampshire's lakes once appeared to doom the bird, but this organization has been influential in protecting nesting sites and building public awareness of the loon's plight. The organization has accumulated some 20 years of data on loons, which currently number about 550 in New Hampshire. There are programs for adults and children, and self-contained loon education kits that can be sent to schools.

Castle in the Clouds (603-476-5900; castleintheclouds.org), Rt. 171, Moultonborough. Now owned by the Lakes Region Conservation Trust, this 5,500-acre property is part of the Ossipee Mountain ring dike, a circular formation of volcanic rock 9 miles in diameter that rises like a heavily wooded island from the more developed countryside around it. Seven of the Ossipee Mountains' most prominent peaks are in this property, including two popular hiking destinations. The summit of **Mount Shaw** (2,975 feet) has a panoramic view of the White Mountains to the north, while **Bald Knob** overlooks Lake Winnipesaukee to the southwest. In all 45 miles of trails traverse the property. Parking for hikers is available off Rt. 171 by the information kiosk, just east of the Castle entrance and Severance Rd.

New England Forestry Foundation Area (also known as the **Chamberlain-Reynolds Memorial Forest**), off College Rd. near the junction of Rts. 3 and 25B north of Meredith village, is a 200-acre conservation area on the lake with 2 miles of gentle trails and two sandy beaches with picnic tables on the shore of Squam Lake.

Prescott Farm Environmental Education Center, 928 White Oaks Rd., Laconia. A 160-acre former family farm with more than 3 miles of hiking trails plus a pond and woodland. Inquire about exhibits and programs.

Ragged Island on Lake Winnipesaukee. Docking is available at the southern end of the island. Shuttle service and programs on the island are offered by the Squam Lakes Natural Science Center (see *To See*).

🐾 🍃 **Stonedam Island Wildlife Preserve** (603-279-3246), operated by the Lakes Region Conservation Trust, Box 1097, Meredith 03253. Open dawn–dusk daily from mid-May to mid-Oct. Stonedam Island is an undeveloped, 112-acre preserve in Lake Winnipesaukee. Visitors are welcome to walk the trails, relax under a tree on the shoreline, or pursue their own nature study. Private boats may dock at the 60-foot pier on the northeastern side of the island. Bring water, as none is available on the island; no pets, audio equipment, smoking, fires, or glass containers. Inquire about public water-taxi transport to the island from Wolfeboro.

Leonard Boyd Chapman Wildbird Sanctuary, Mount Israel Rd., Sandwich. A very special 150 acres, open year-round—but you would be well advised to have four-wheel drive in winter, because it's up a steep road (off Grove St. out of Center Sandwich). There's a trail network groomed for cross-country skiing and snowshoeing, along with picnic tables. A trail leads to Eacup Lake, and in winter the ice that forms on this small pond is cleared for family skating (no hockey sticks, please).

Unsworth Wildlife Area at the Squam Lakes Conservation Society, Holderness. These 159 acres are webbed with trails, rich in wildlife. A canoe awaits, but you have to bring your own paddle.

Gunstock Recreation Area (603-293-4341; 800-GUNSTOCK; gunstock.com), Rt. 11A, Gilford. Operated by Belknap County, this 2,000-acre facility includes the Gunstock Ski Area and a large campground with related facilities. The 420-site campground has swimming, fishing, horseback riding, a store, and a playground. Extensive hiking trails lead to the summits of the Belknap Mountains, one of which is Gunstock. Trail maps are available. Warm-weather events include dances, craft and woodsmen's festivals, and Oktoberfest.

Also see **Sandwich Notch Rd.** under *Hiking*.

✳ Lodging

INNS ♿ ⓣ **The Wolfeboro Inn** (603-569-3016; 800-451-2389; wolfeboroinn.com), 90 N. Main St., Wolfeboro 03894. Open all year. This inn dates back to 1812 but now offers some the region's finest rooms. Nine guest rooms are in the original front portion of the inn, while the modern addition, built with a contemporary design to resemble an old barn, brings the room count to 44, including some suites with four-poster beds. The country-style rooms have private bath and king, queen, double, or twin beds, with phone, TV, and individually controlled heat and air-conditioning. The deluxe water-view rooms in the addition have decks where you can watch lake activities or catch cooling breezes. Two rooms are handicapped accessible. The center sections of the three-story addition have open areas with chairs and reading nooks. The inn has a private beach, conference facilities, and large, informal tavern. From $119 midweek in winter to $319 for a suite on holiday weekends in summer. Summer rates for a standard room are $159–175 and include continental breakfast. Children over the age of 2 years are $15 extra.

The Inns at Mill Falls are four separate well-designed inns, totaling 159 rooms, built over the past decade or so along the lake in Meredith. All share the same ownership, phone numbers (603-279-7006; 800-622-MILL), website (millfalls.com), and address: Rt. 3, Meredith 03253. Rates range $109–479, and package plans are available for all four inns. The original **Inn at Mill Falls** is built around a tumbling waterfall and adjoins the old linen mill that's now a shopping complex. Each of the 54 rooms has New Hampshire–made maple or Shaker pine furnishings with easy chairs and desks, air-conditioning, TV, and telephone. Beds are queens, doubles, or a king, and half the rooms have views out to Meredith Bay. There is an indoor pool, a spa, a sauna, and two restaurants. The neighboring **Chase House at Mill Falls** offers 23 rooms and 3 one-bedroom suites. Rooms feature fireplace, whirlpool spa, and private balcony overlooking the lake. There is also a function room with fireplace, patio, and panoramic view. Camp, the inn's restaurant, offers great grub and a woodsy decor (see *Dining Out*). The 24-room gleaming, white-clapboard **Inn at Bay Point**, across Rt. 3 from its sister inns, extends into Lake Winnipesaukee, resembling a ship that's just pulled into port. Amenities include a dock, sauna, and whirlpool spa area. Many rooms have

lakeside balcony, fireplace, and whirlpool. All feature New Hampshire–made furnishings, including king or queen beds (some with pullout sofas) and easy chairs, desks, air-conditioning, TV, and telephone. Dine directly on the water at Lago (see *Dining Out*), or opt for a dinner for two on your balcony. The newest, most luxurious addition to the Mill Falls complex is **Church Landing**, a neo-Adirondack structure situated on a landscaped promontory overlooking the lake. Each of its 58 rooms and multi-room suites offers a gas fireplace and view of the lake. Many also have balcony, and some a two-person whirlpool tub. The property also has docking, an indoor/outdoor pool, and full-service health club and spa. The upscale log cabin decor extends into the Lakehouse Grille (see *Dining Out*).

&. ⁕†⁕ **Squam Lake Inn** (603-968-4417; 800-839-6205; squamlakeinn.com), 28 Shepard Hill Rd, Box 695, Holderness 03245. Open all year. Innkeepers Rae Andrews and Cindy Foster have transformed a Victorian farmhouse into one of the area's most welcoming, unpretentious, and comfortable inns. While there is no lake view here, each of the eight guest rooms and baths is decorated stylishly in a vintage lake theme, and most overlook gardens. There are two suites with gas fireplacs and room for an extra person; a ground-level room has wheelchair access. While a portion of the ground floor is now a seasonal café featuring local produce (see *Eating Out*) and the barn is a popular gift store, guests still have plenty of private space to relax with a book. Rates, which include a full breakfast, are $160–185 mid-May–Oct.; $10 less off-season.

⁕†⁕ **The Manor on Golden Pond** (603-968-3348; 800-545-2141; manor ongoldenpond.com), Shepard Hill Rd. and Rt. 3 (Box T), Holderness 03245. This golden stucco mansion overlooking Squam Lake ("Golden Pond") was originally built in 1907 as a summer estate for a wealthy Englishman and his new bride, and current owners Brian and Mary Ellen Shields continue to promote this Lord of the Manse feel. Set in 13 hillside acres, the inn overlooks the water and surrounding mountains but does not offer direct access to the lake. Its private, 300-foot beach with a boat dock, paddleboats, and canoes is down the hill and across Rt. 3. Rooms with English place-names feature leaded-glass windows, ornate woodwork, fireplace, and antiques along with two-person whirlpool bath (most are in the bedrooms or adjoining alcoves) in some rooms. There are 24 guest rooms in all, including 2 suites and a cottage. Two large common rooms have wood-burning fireplace, and there is a second-floor library. You'll also find tennis courts, croquet, and a heated outdoor swimming pool. Bistro and formal dining is open to the public (see *Dining Out*). High-season rates with breakfast for two and afternoon tea range $255–470. Inquire about packages that include dinner and a Squam Lakes cruise or golf. Off-season packages featuring cooking classes are also offered.

RUSTIC RESORT Rockywold-Deephaven Camps (603-968-3313; rdcsquam.com), P.O. Box B, Holderness 03245. June–third week of Sept. Turn off Rt. 113 several miles east of Holderness and plunge down woods roads leading to Big Squam Lake. This is the only place to stay right on Big Squam Lake and it's a gem, a holdover from another era. At a final junction you have to head to either Rockywold or Deephaven, established as separate "camps" by two "New England gentle-

women" in the 1890s. The two properties have long since merged and are now owned by shareholders (most are families who have been coming here for generations), managed by a board of trustees. There are still separate lodge facilities, each with 20 guest rooms and a large common area with fireplace and porch overlooking the lake. The 60 cottages, each accommodating from 2 to 14 people, are tucked discreetly along 1.5 miles of shorefront pines and granite outcroppings. Built early in the 20th century, each has twin beds, a bath, fireplace, screened-in porch, private dock, and antique icebox cooled by ice harvested from the lake, delivered, as is firewood, daily. Organized activities include hiking, tennis (eight courts), softball, boat tours, games, talent shows, square dances, canoe and road races, a morning program for 3- to 5-year-olds, and activities for older kids as well as activities for teens, square dancing, and talent shows. The activities and amenities are there to participate in or not as you wish. Weekly rates are $2,825 for two people but include *all* three meals, served buffet-style, and activities. Overnight lodge rates are $84.50 per person with modest charges for meals; both June and Sept. rates are discounted, with special programs (check the website) offered. While many families return year after year, there are always vacancies, especially in June and early July.

BED & BREAKFASTS

In Wolfeboro and vicinity
°ı° **123 North Main B&B** (800-577-9506), 123 N. Main St., Wolfeboro 03894. Open all year. This classic green-shuttered white Colonial is a handsome oasis just up the street from the bustle of Wolfeboro's shopping area. Since opening in 1997, Bob and

Barbara Branscombe (the true B&B) have built their clientele via word of mouth by offering guests a refined yet relaxing atmosphere. The house is filled with antiques and period reproductions. The three air-conditioned guest rooms have king-sized beds, fine linens, and television; the upstairs suite can accommodate four guests. Common space includes a back deck overlooking the garden. Gourmet breakfast; pastries and coffee available all day; a gluten-free breakfast is also offered. $175–200.

Tuc' Me Inn (603-569-5702; tucme inn.com), 118 N. Main St., Wolfeboro 03894. Open all year. This 19th-century inn, with screened porches, a large common room with a fireplace, TV, and guest telephone, is just two blocks from village shops and restaurants. There are seven rooms, three with private bath (the others share two full baths), with a choice of queen, double, and twin beds. New innkeepers Wes and Linda Matchett also offer a choice of three full breakfasts. $165–209.

Afton Inn (603-569-4262; 800-569-0866; aftoninn.com), 31 Waumbeck Rd., Wolfeboro 03894. On a quiet country road a couple of miles west of Wolfeboro, Paul and Debby Schmidt have renovated a rambling old farmhouse. Two spacious downstairs guest rooms have in-room whirlpool tub, and all four rooms have queen beds and are furnished in antiques, fitted with TV/VCR and air-conditioning. Common space includes a partially screened, wicker-furnished wraparound porch, an uncluttered, comfortable living room, and a dining room with a fireplace—the venue for full breakfasts that are included in $134–189 per couple.

In Sandwich
Jonathan Beede House (603-284-7413; jonathanbeedehouse.com), 711 Mount Israel Rd., Center Sandwich 03227. High up on a back road, this 1787 farmhouse offers four comfortable guest rooms furnished with family antiques. Built by one of Sandwich's early settlers, it has been lovingly restored by owners Susan and John Davies. The four upstairs guest rooms share three down-the-hall baths and range from two big corner rooms to a cozy double. All have white-curtained, historic paned windows with plenty of natural light, heirloom quilts, and intriguing books. Downstairs, the formal parlor and less formal keeping room feature similar books and inviting places to read. There is also a big screened porch/sunroom overlooking the meadows; next door the **Chapman Wildbird Sanctuary** beckons you to walk, snowshoe, or cross-country ski. The house is filled with a sense of history (before the Civil War it served as a stop on the Underground Railroad) and with a warm sense of hospitality. $80–95 includes a full breakfast served in the dining room with its 18th-century fireplace and Indian shutters.

Strathaven (603-284-7785; strathaveninn.com), P.O. Box 42, 566 North Sandwich Rd. (Rt. 113), North Sandwich 03259. Open all year. Thirty or so years ago Betsy and Tony Leiper started taking in overflow guests from a local inn, and they've never stopped: Guests become friends who return annually. Picture windows overlook beautiful grounds with extensive gardens, a trout pond for swimming or skating, and an English croquet court. Betsy is an embroidery teacher and has a flair for color. Her favorite, blue, shows up in her extensive collection of blue-and-white Meissen china in the dining room cabinet. There are four lovely rooms; two large rooms each have two double beds and a private bath, and two rooms share a bath. Many feature antiques as well as

Betsy's embroidery. Tony Leiper grooms cross-country ski trails that connect the inn with Sandwich Notch. From $70–80 for two with full breakfast. These grandparents insist there be no extra charge for small children.

In the Squam Lakes area

❀ '¶' **The Glynn House Inn** (603-968-3775; 866-686-4362; glynnhouse .com), 59 Highland St., Ashland 03217. The Heidenreich family maintain this 1890s Queen Anne–style mill owner's mansion and neighboring carriage house as an impressive B&B. Set above the village on a quiet hillside street, the house retains its handsome original woodwork, and each of the 13 rooms (8 suites) is furnished to period. Most have fireplace, and all have private bath; nine with whirlpool. Amenities include iPod radios, robes, discreet flat-screen TVs, complimentary water, and more. Your innkeepers are Pamela (born in England and started her own culinary school in Singapore), Ingrid (also a chef), and Glenn, who has spent 30 years working outside the US. A multicourse breakfast, afternoon tea, and evening wine and munchies are included in $149–299 double, depending on the room and season. Breakfast is served in the formal dining room at separate tables. Inquire about dinner.

✪ '¶' **The Inn on Golden Pond** (603-968-7269; innongoldenpond .com), Rt. 3, Box 680, 1080 Rt. 3, Holderness 03245. Open all year. Bill and Bonnie Webb have been operating this large, cheerful, friendly B&B since 1984. While this 1870s house doesn't overlook the lake, huge picture windows in the breakfast room and living room do frame meadows and woodland, a sampling of the inn's 50 wooded acres. The village of Holderness, departure point for lake cruises and boat rentals, is just down the road. Most of the eight rooms (two suites)

have queen-sized maple beds, and all have private bath and air-conditioning. All the rooms are furnished tastefully and comfortably "country"-style, complete with two easy chairs and perhaps a desk. Amenities include table tennis or darts in the separate sports shed. The living room has a fireplace, and a second common room has cable TV; there's also a small guest study with a computer and phone with toll-free dialing anywhere in the county. The Webbs are knowledgeable about everything to see and do locally and are delighted to share their knowledge with guests. $175 per couple includes breakfast.

❀ ✎ '¶' **Cheney House** (603-968-4499; 877-968-4499; cheneyhouse .com), 82 Highland St., Ashland 03217. Just up the street from Glynn House, this turreted 1895 high-Victorian home is colorfully shingled and richly paneled. Anthony and Bobbi Hoerter offer a comfortable, informal B&B with four guest rooms with private bath, three with Jacuzzi tub. Guest rooms all have cable TV/VCR and AC. There's a guest fridge as well as inviting common space with some unusual hearths. A full breakfast is served at the dining room table. Anthony hails from Greenpoint in Brooklyn and Bobbi, from Denver. $115–150 includes breakfast.

In the Center Harbor/Meredith area

♿ **The Meredith Inn** (603-279-0000; meredithinn.com), corner of Main and Waukewan Sts., Meredith 03253. Open all year. Innkeeper Janet Carpenter clearly knows her business, one she grew up with in Rangeley, Maine, where her parents owned the Rangeley Inn. This rambling Victorian "painted lady," the home of Meredith's leading physician for several decades, has been transformed into a charming B&B. The eight spacious rooms offer a choice of twin, queen-, and king-sized beds. Each is different, but all combine real comfort and charm. They are furnished in antiques and feature luxurious linens and large, well-equipped private bath; six of the rooms have a whirlpool tub. The living room has a fireplace and is well stocked with local menus and information. It's just over 0.25 mile in one direction to downtown shopping and restaurants, 0.5 mile the other way to Lake Waukewan. Children are welcome, but rooms accommodate only two people. Full breakfast is included in $134–209.

Tuckernuck Inn (603-279-5521; 888-858-5521; thetuckernuckinn.com), 25 Red Gate Lane, Meredith 03253. Open all year. Up the hill from Main St., this five-room inn is within walking distance of shops, restaurants, and Lake Winnipesaukee. Owners Donna and Kim Weiland have added baths for all five guest rooms as well as stenciled walls, handcrafted quilts, and period furniture; one room has a gas fireplace. The living room has a fireplace and a huge shelf of books and games to play. A full breakfast is included in $129–159 per couple. Lower off-season.

On the south shore
The Inn at Smith Cove (603-293-1111; innatsmithcove.com), 19 Roberts Rd., Gilford 03249. This 1890s home with a third-floor tower suite and wraparound porch is right on one of Lake Winnipesaukee's many sheltered coves. Bob and Maria Ruggiero offer nine guest rooms in the inn itself, most with a water view, all with private bath (the tower suite has a Jacuzzi). Coffee and juice are served in the morning. The Light House in the garden is a two-level suite with a Jacuzzi; the Little House—a cabin on the cove—has a porch overlooking the water. Handy in winter to skiing at Gunstock. $90–180 (20 percent less during low seasons) per couple. Inquire about weekly rates for cottages.

On Winnisquam Lake
✪ "ቸ" **Ferry Point House** (603-524-0087; ferrypointhouse.com), 100 Lower Bay Rd., Sanbornton 03269. Just 0.25 mile off Rt. 3/11, handy to I-93 Exit 20. Open year-round. This is an airy Victorian, with wide parlor windows and a wicker-filled veranda overlooking Lake Winnisquam. While it's just off the main drag, the setting is

FERRY POINT HOUSE ON WINNISQUAM LAKE

Chris Tree

more peaceful than nearby Lake Winnipesaukee, and in summer you are quickly drawn to the gazebo on a grassy point across the road. Guests cans swim or paddle out on the lake. Andrea Damato and Eric are warm, energetic hosts, especially helpful with dining suggestions. The nine guest rooms vary in decor but all are unfussily comfortable and have private bath (one with a Jacuzzi). Most have lake views, antique high-backed beds, and antique dressers. Breathe deep and you can smell the lake air. Our breakfast was an event, an individual soufflé with fresh fruit and home fries. No children under 10, please. $120–250 for two, depending on season.

⚓ **Lighthouse Inn** (603-366-5432; 877-543-5432; lighthouseinnbb.com), 913 Scenic Rd., Laconia 03246. Just off the main drag (Rt. 3) in Weirs Beach but on a quiet street, this is a 1930s house, nicely built by shipbuilder Byron Hedblon, who brought the M/S *Mount Washington* to Lake Winnipesaukee. There are five smallish but comfortable guest rooms, all on the ground floor and all with private bath and gas or electric hearth, one with a whirlpool tub and private patio. The sense of space here is in the open-raftered Great Room with its fireplace and a view of the lawn that slopes away to trees and a glimpse of the lake. Mike Recht and Pat Cassidy are helpful hosts and serve a full breakfast; $90–200 for two people.

VACATION RENTALS Weekly rentals and rental websites are numerous; each of the sources listed under *Guidance* offers lists of local Realtors specializing in rentals. Also note this holdover from the era in which lakeside cottages clusters were the norm:

Ames Farm Inn (603-293-4321; 603-742-3962; amesfarminn.com), 2800 Lake Shore Rd. (Rt. 11), Gilford 03246. Open Apr. (for fishermen) through Oct. Tradition! This 300-acre inn and cottage community has been here since 1890, having been operated by five generations of the Ames family. Needless to say, book early for the short peak season of July and August. Nineteen fully equipped housekeeping cottages are spread out on the lakefront. Each has one or two bedrooms, kitchenette, living room, and screened porch. The view across Lake Winnipesaukee stretches across the Broads for miles to the Ossipee Mountains and Mount Washington. Away from the shore are buildings with housekeeping apartments and 12 modern guest rooms with private bath. No charge to guests to launch and dock a boat. Some rental boats are available. The inn restaurant is open mid-June–Labor Day, daily 7:30 AM–2 PM. Weekly rates: $1,325–1,485 peak season; less off-season. From $90 per day for the private rooms.

MOTELS AND CAMPING Check the AAA and Mobil guides' motel listings if it's a motel you're after; we frankly have a hard enough time personally checking all the inns and B&Bs. Ditto for campgrounds, of which the area offers plenty.

✳ Where to Eat

Note: Here some of the best dining experiences are family geared and moderately priced (entrées $15–20). Because there are so many—and because Winnipeaukee is circled by 50, frequently traffic-clogged miles of road—we have grouped *Dining Out* as well as *Eating Out* options geographically around the lake. There are, however, several restaurants and cafés that are destinations in their own right.

Worth the extra miles

The Woodshed (603-476-2311; wood shedrestaurant.com), 128 Lee Mill Rd., off Rt. 109, Moultonborough. Open all year, Tue.–Sun. at 5 and for Sun. brunch (10–2) but check off-season. Reserve. To operate a successful restaurant in the countryside, on a side road, off a less-than-major route, in a small, spread-out town, you must have atmosphere and good food. This place has both in abundance. What began as a small restaurant in an old farmhouse has grown into a phenomenon attracting the likes of Sean Penn and Michelle Pfeiffer. Dining extends into the year-round porch as well as an exquisite barn with massive hand-hewn beams and spacious loft, all decorated with antiques and collectibles. An evening could begin at the raw bar for clams and oysters or escargots. Prime rib is the specialty, but options might include vegetarian torta rustica and Alaskan king crab. Cheesecake or "Chocolate Decadence" can complete the feast. Entrées $19.95–32.89.

⌀ **Castle in the Clouds Carriage House Café & Patio** (603-476-5900; castleintheclouds.org), off Rt. 171, Moultonborough. Open daily for lunch late May–late Oct. Inquire about Thursday Jazz at Sunset concerts, 5:30–8. The café's patio is a flowery terrace that seems suspended somewhere between the sky and Lake Winnispesaukee. It's part of a spectacular, 5,500-acre mountaintop estate. The mansion here is justly popular as a tourist attraction (see *To See*) that's set 1,300 feet high in the Ossipee Mountains. Admission to the mansion is extra, but locals know it's unnecessary if you are just coming to the café. Lunch options range from sandwiches to steak tips; our salad was delicious. Most items are under $10. Obviously the view is weather dependent.

The Coe House (603-253-8617; coehousenh.com), Senter's Marketplace, Rt. 25B, Center Harbor. Open in-season daily 5–9:30 PM; off-season Thu.–Sun. Reserve. A magnificent early-19th-century mansion listed on the National Register of Historic Places, set on a rise overlooking the lake. Coe family guests included Presidents Franklin Pierce, Ulysses Grant, and Grover Cleveland as well as poets Lucy Lacrum, Celia Thaxter, Henry Longfellow, and John Greenleaf Whittier—who is said to have influenced John Coe to open his home to the Underground Railroad. The current owners, chef Jeff Day and Luke Dupuis, have restored original windows, chimneys, and hearths. The ambience is relaxed elegance in the dining rooms; for especially romantic occasions, a couple can reserve the third-floor cupola. You might begin with homemade mozzarella oven-roasted tomatoes, pesto, and ham, then dine on grilled swordfish with ginger scallion butter and citrus basmati, or beef tenderloin with cheddar grits— but the vegetable stack of fresh greens with roasted garlic, mushrooms, Tuscan beans, and much more is equally delectable. Entrées $20–28.

⌀ **Corner House Inn** (603-284-6219; cornerhouseinn.com), 22 Main St. (Rt. 109), Center Sandwich. Open daily for lunch and dinner; live music Fri. nights and for Sun. brunch. An inn for 150 years and owned by Don and Jane Brown for more than 20, this landmark has always enjoyed a reputation for good food. It's served with candlelit ambience in the traditional low-beamed dining room—or you can enjoy comfort food by the wood fire in a rustic pub with informal seating as well as regular tables and a semicircular bar. Inquire about Storyteller Dinners, "Wine Not?" nights, and other

Chris Tree

COE HOUSE IN CENTER HARBOR IS ONE OF THE REGION'S BEST RESTAURANTS AS WELL AS MOST HISTORIC HOUSES.

special events. Whatever you do, try the lobster and mushroom bisque. Locally sourced ingredients are the specialty here, as is "Jane's Salad" with buttermilk-dill dressing. Roast prime ribs are featured Fri. and Sat. Options include shellfish sauté with lobster, shrimp, and scallions in a light sherry sauce, and New Hampshire–raised venison with sweet potato polenta.

The Common Man (603-968-7030; thecman.com), 60 Main St., Ashland. Open daily for lunch (11:30–3) and dinner from 5. The upstairs Bar'n Grill is open 3–11 with seasonal après-ski specials 3–5 PM. The "Common Man Family" is one reason why folks don't have to travel far in the Lakes Region— or most parts of New Hampshire—to find attractive and dependable "American fare with flair." Each of the 18 (as of 2010) restaurants is so distinct that it's impossible to call them a "chain," but for many fans this the original Common Man is a pilgrimage point of sorts. It opened in 1971 with Alex Ray in the kitchen, the dining room seating 35, and the young family living upstairs. It was an immediate success.

A few years later the carriage house behind the restaurant was converted to more dining space and the family finally moved into their own house nearby; the upstairs became the popular Bar'n Grill Above Lounge with couches, woodstove, and parlor games. The restaurant's decor features old posters, books, tools, and art, a comfortable feeling for relaxed dining. There is also a brick patio and lounge deck. It's a big menu. You might begin with pan-fried crabcakes, then dine on country meat loaf or filet mignon. As at all "C-Mans," dinners include salad, crackers and dip, breads, sides, and white chocolate. Plan on desserts like crème brûlée and chocolate java pudding. Entrées $13.99–23.99. Lighter fare in the bar. Note the Common Man Company Store across the street and The C-Man Express at the I-93 Exit 24, down the road.

DINING OUT

In and around Wolfeboro

Wolfe's Tavern (603-569-3016; wolfe boroinn.com), 90 N. Main St., Wolfeboro. Open all year, 7 AM–10 PM.

Located in the old section of the inn, the tavern serves a wide variety of lighter fare, from hot and cold sandwiches and salads to soups, pasta, munchies, and dinners. The 1812 Dining Room features New England–style cuisine (prime rib and seafood) as well as daily specials and homemade desserts. Sunday brunch (10–1) is popular with guests and locals alike. The daily salad bar features more than 30 items, including a block of cheddar cheese and homemade soup and Italian bread. There are lovely views of Wolfeboro Bay and gardens. Dinner entrées $12–28.

✪ **Garwoods** (603-569-7788; garwoodsrestaurant.com), 6 N. Main St., Wolfeboro. Open daily for lunch and dinner in summer, closed Wed. in winter. This deep, lakeside storefront that began life as a lady's clothing store in 1899 is now an attractive restaurant overlooking Wolfeboro Bay. The best seats are of course way in the back, beyond the bar (an inverted racing scull hangs above), with water views; there's also a seasonal patio. Lunch runs from burgers to salads and pastas or the signature sandwich of grilled chicken marinated in teriyaki sauce; dinner options range from burgers to filet mignon with choices like baked sea scallops and vegetable risotto between. Dinner entrées $9.99–32.99 (for an 8-ounce grilled tenderloin).

✎ **The Cider Press** (603-569-2028; theciderpress.net), 30 Middleton Rd., Wolfeboro. Serving dinner at 5 PM. Since 1982, this has been a popular rustic spot with barnboard walls, fireplaces, antiques, candlelight dining, and a varied menu. Steak béarnaise is a specialty along with barbecued baby back ribs and char-grilled lamb chops. Nightly blackboard specials. Entrées $16–24.

East of Suez (603-569-1648; eastofsuez.com), 775 S. Main St. (Rt. 28), Wolfeboro. Open Memorial Day weekend–early Sept., for dinner daily except Mon. Asian food—Japanese, Chinese, Philippine, Thai, Indian, and Korean—is prepared with authentic ingredients and condiments by the Powell family. Housed for more than 40 years in a century-old lodge just south of town, this is still something of a secret. Huge portions and moderate prices make it a local favorite. Sushi, daily grilled seafood, and home-grown organic vegetables are featured. BYOB.

Mise en Place (603-569-5788), 96 Lehner St., Wolfeboro. Open daily for lunch and dinner except Sun. Also closed Mon. off-season. This small, chef-owned and -operated restaurant off the main drag gets great reviews for creative fine dining. Reservations advised evenings. Entrées $12–26.

Wolfetrap Grill & Raw Bar (603-569-9900; wolfetrap.com), 19 Bay St., Wolfeboro. Open daily 11–11. Come by car, boat, or call for shuttle service from the town docks. The sit-down component of the Wolfecatch Fish Market, this is *the* place to come for fresh lobster, shellfish, steamers, oysters, and fried clams; also hand-cut certified Angus beef. Specialties include coriander sesame tuna with wasabi/balsamic reduction and seaweed salad, and shrimp on the barbie. The menu rangers from burgers to shore dinners ($5.99–26).

In Center Harbor/Meredith/ Moultonborough

Canoe Restaurant and Tavern (603-253-4762; eatatcanoe.com), 232 Whittier Hwy. (Rt. 25), Center Harbor. Open daily for lunch and dinner. Whether you come by canoe, car, or take the valet shuttle from the Center Harbor town dock, you're likely to like this place; patrons have been praising it since its opening in 2004. Each of its five dining rooms has an outdoor theme with canoes suspended from the ceiling and hooked into rugs. One outdoor room, a screened porch overlooking woods and the lake, has space heaters to keep you toasty into fall. The extensive dinner menu ranges from meat loaf with house mac and cheese ($15) to butternut ravioli ($16), braised beef short rib ($22), and rack of domestic lamb ($26).

Lemon Grass Restaurant and Sake Bar (603-253-8100; lemongrass.net), Rt. 25, Moultonborough (tucked behind Anthony's Pizza). Open 11:30–9 except Tue., Wed. Organic and natural ingredients rule here, along with chemical-free meats and great sushi. You might begin with crispy calamari or a yellowfin tuna martini (tossed tuna and sea salad on crispy noodles in a martini glass). The choice of sushi rolls is extensive. Dinner entrées include slow-roasted spiced free-range duck with citrus black bean sauce, and shellfish coconut curry. Lunch options include a bean cake seafood hot pot and a choice of bento boxes. Dinner entrées $16–25; lunch around $10.

✒ **Hart's Turkey Farm Restaurant** (603-279-6212; hartsturkeyfarm.com), 233 Daniel Webster Hwy., junction of Rts. 3 and 104, Meredith. Open all year at 11:15 AM for lunch and dinner. This landmark is a big barn of a place with multiple dining rooms that swallow bus groups. The specialty is turkey in every conceivable form, from sandwiches and turkey pie through turkey meat loaf and croquettes to turkey tempura and Marsala. There are also plenty of steaks, seafood, salads, and other sandwiches in this large, popular restaurant, owned and operated by the Hart family since 1954. Gift shop. From $5.99 for a turkey salad sandwich to $28 for Alaskan king crab legs. The jumbo turkey plate ($21) is over a pound of turkey.

Mame's (603-279-4631), 8 Plymouth St., Meredith. Open daily for lunch and dinner; Sunday brunch 11–2. An 1825 brick village home with barn, now with six dining rooms, Mame's offers varied and reasonably priced dining. Honestly, however, we haven't eaten here and have to report that the online reviews for food and service are mixed. Dinner entrées range from seafood au gratin ($14) and grilled beef tips ($15.50) to lobster scallop divan ($24.50).

The following three atmospheric, dependable bets are all part of "the Common Man family" (thecman.com) housed in various Inns at Mill Falls (millfalls.com).

✒ "♪" **Camp** (603-279-3003), 300 Daniel Webster Hwy. (Rt. 3) in the Chase House at Mill Falls, Meredith. Dinner Tue.–Sat. The decor is summer camp with a fieldstone fireplace and tin ceiling, appropriate in this kids'-camp-studded corner of the world. The focus is on comfort food like meat loaf and shepherd's pie, but you'll also find broiled scallops, apple Brie chicken, slow-roasted back rib, and New York sirloin—not your standard camp fare, though the s'mores for dessert may bring back memories. Dinner entrées $13–23, with lighter options and children's menu.

"♪" **Lago at the Inn at Bay Point** (603-279-2253), the Inn at Bay Point, 1 Rt. 25, Meredith. Open nightly for dinner. The decor and menu are northern Italian. With dark beams, stucco walls, and a great deck, this is your villa on the lake. Antipasti might include toasted ciabatta with marinated tomatoes, or basil and fresh mozzarella; the pastas are available either as "primi" or main courses. Other choices include seafood simmered in a fennel tomato broth over fettuccine and pork osso buco, also eggplant Parmesan and lasagna. Entrées $12–21.

¹⁰¹˝ The Lakehouse Grille (603-279-5221), Church Landing, 281 Daniel Webster Hwy. (Rt. 3), Meredith. Open for lunch Mon.–Sat., dinner daily, Sunday brunch 9–2. Adirondack-style, elegantly casual decor with a view of the lake and mountains. In the evening there's candlelight and a menu with a large selection of entrées, including pan-seared crabcakes, trio of duck, a seafood stew, and char-grilled pork tenderloin ($14–25).

On Squam Lake
The Manor on Golden Pond (603-968-3348; 800-545-2141; manoron goldenpond.com), Shepard Hill Rd. and Rt. 3, Holderness. Open daily for dinner 6–9. Reservations required; request a table with a good view if you are an outside guest (don't get stuck overlooking the parking lot). Dining is in the Manor's truly elegant Edwardian Van Horne Dining Room. There's candlelight, a hearth, fine linen, and a menu that changes weekly. Starters might include crab bisque or foie gras with orange tart for starters; entrées may be wild mushroom risotto or grilled lamb with Yukon and sweet potato, grilled asparagus, and a burgundy shallot reduction. At $10–16 for appetizers and $26–40 for entrées, the prices reflect the restaurant's AAA Four Diamond status. There's also the **M Bistro**, with a menu of tapas and entrées from $20 for vegetarian paella.

♻ ✿ Squam Lake Inn Café (603-968-4417; squamlakeinn.com), Shepherd Hill, just off Rt. 3. Open for lunch daily July–Aug., Thu.–Sun. in June and Sept.–Oct., 11:30–2; also for dinner in-season, Thu.–Sat. 5–8. This casual, charming café is a winner, featuring local, seasonal ingredients and indoor/outdoor dining. Dine on pan-seared scallops with apricot and chipotle lime sauce over cilantro risotto. Entrées $16.25–26.95, with lighter fare

like honey mustard chicken skewers served over romaine greens, red onion, and tomato ($9.50). Lunch choices include create-your-own-salads, flatbread pizza, sandwiches on homemade bread, and lobster rolls. Beer and wine are served; there's also a kids' menu.

Walter's Basin (603-968-4412; 603-968-7728), 15 Main St. at the bridge, Holderness village. Open all year, daily in summer, most days off-season; check hours. This popular restaurant cantilevered over Little Squam Lake in the middle of Holderness is easy to find, whether you arrive by land or water. This is in fact the only restaurant right on these lakes (it's at the point that they connect), and it's named for the elusive trout in the 1981 film *On Golden Pond*. Casual but polished decor complements upscale family dining with a full-time lunch menu; dinner entrées range from $15.40 for pasta primavera to $27 for a seafood stew of scallops, mussels, whitefish, and king crab simmered in spiced broth. It's also possible to dine in the dining room off the pub menu.

On Lake Winnipesaukee's south shore
✪ Lyon's Den Restaurant & Tavern (603-293-8833), 25 Dock Rd., Gilford. Reservations requested. Open in summer daily for lunch and dinner; closed Mon. off-season. Roland Lyons is the chef and Lauren the hostess here. The food is excellent, and the view is one of the best on the lake. Try the veal Lauren, scaloppine lightly seasoned, sautéed with shrimp, tomato, and artichoke, finished with sherry and cream. Entrées range from $16 for pasta primavera to $28 for filet mignon.

The William Tell Inn (603-293-8803; thewilliamtellinn.com), 1602 Mount Major Hwy. (Rt. 11), West Alton. Open for dinner daily except Mon. during spring, summer, and fall; Sun.

brunch starting at noon; call for seasonal hours. With a name from Switzerland and housed in a chalet, expect Swiss cuisine. Owned since 1980 by the Bossart family, this is one of the region's better restaurants, with a variety of Continental favorites. Wiener schnitzel with spaetzle, sauerbraten, venison, and cheese fondue share the menu with more conventional favorites such as filet mignon, New York sirloin, salmon, lamb, and seafood grill. The desserts feature dark Tobler chocolate imported from Switzerland. Early-bird specials Tue.–Fri., 5–6:30 PM, $11; entrées from $15.

EATING OUT

In the Wolfeboro area and along the north shore

Morrissey's (603-569-3662), 298 S. Main St., Wolfeboro. Open mid-May–Columbus Day for all three meals. Formerly Bailey's, this is an old favorite known for its ice cream. A full menu, from breakfast omelets and blueberry muffins to homemade clam chowder, baked Virginia ham, and barbecued stuffed chicken, keeps families happy year after year.

Wolfeboro Dockside Grille & Dairy Bar (603-476-2311), 11 Dockside St. Open seasonally 11–8. We lucked into a water-view booth on a summer day and feasted on a chicken salad sandwich with walnuts, sun-dried tomato, and toasted wheat bread. No surprises here, just old-fashioned fun fare from hot dogs through seafood platters to banana splits.

Strawberry Patch (603-569-5523), 50 North St., Wolfeboro. Open Mon.–Sat. 7:30–2 for breakfast and lunch, Sun. breakfast only, 7:30–1. Strawberry pancakes, shortcake, and sundaes, not to mention fresh strawberries rolled in brown sugar and sour cream. Salads, tacos, and quiche, too.

✐ **Pine Cone Café** (603-544-3800), 427 Rt. 109, Melvin Village. Open year-round. This great neighborhood restaurant is attached to the Pine Cone Motel, a great family spot for soups, salads and sandwiches, specialty pizzas, and fried fish.

In the Squam Lakes area

Holderness General Store (603-968-3446), 863 Rt. 3 in Holderness village. A large and visitor-geared emporium featuring yummy made-to-order specialty sandwiches, wraps, and panini, perfect for picnics—but there is also a counter at the back of the store. There's a slatted wood ceiling and track lighting. Possible provisions include live lobster, Asian tenderloin tips, and an extensive wine selection.

❝ɪ❞ **Mocha Rizing** (603-284-9995), 25 Main St., Center Sandwich. Open year-round 7–5, Nancy Papp's coffee shop specializes in Fair Trade coffees and teas, also smoothies and light fare such as bagels and muffins. At this writing the space is shared with the Sandwich Artisans Guild.

Also see **Corner House Inn** in Center Sandwich (under *Worth the Extra Miles*) and the **Common Man** in Ashland as well as **Walter's Basin** and **Squam Lake Inn Café** under *Dining Out*. All are great, reasonably priced lunch bets.

In the Center Harbor/Meredith area

Sam & Rosie's Café and Bakery (603-253-6606), Rt. 25, Center Harbor. Open 6:30–2:45 except Sun. Sam and Rose Blake run a first-rate breakfast and lunch place, with fresh baked goods and NASCAR decor.

George's Diner (603-279-8723; georgesdiner.com), 10 Plymouth St., Meredith. Open 6 AM–8 PM daily. Breakfast daily until 2 PM. Nothing fancy, just dependably good food.

The Town Docks (603-279-3445), 289 Daniel Webster Hwy. (Rt. 3), Meredith. Open summer only 11–11 for ice cream. Free tie-up at the public boat docks. Ice cream all day; lobster rolls, fried clams, hot dogs, steamers, and fresh salads for most of it. Eat inside or at picnic tables or the "beach bar" overlooking the water (and just about everyone in town).

In the Laconia/Tilton area

❦ **Tilt'n Diner** (603-286-2204), Rt. 3 at I-93, left off Exit 20, Tilton. Another member of the Common Man family, this diner is a takeoff on the 1950s, with period menu, music, and memorabilia. Open until 9 PM for breakfast, lunch, and dinner. Nothing's expensive; everything's filling. For quick food and lots of fun, this place is just "swell!"

Our Family Tree (603-524-1988), 927 Laconia Rd., Tilton. Open daily 11–8. This rambling old waterside roadhouse is family run, with booths and plain good sandwiches and fried fish plates, reasonably priced and a nice change form nearby chains and fast-food options.

ICE CREAM Bailey's Bubble (603-569-3612), Wolfeboro town docks. A summertime tradition for ice cream and a definite must for a visit to Wolfeboro.

Kellerhaus (603-366-4466; 888-KLR-HAUS; kellerhaus.com), Rt. 3, just north of Weirs Beach. Known for the ice cream made here for 90 years with a view of the lake, sundaes with a dozen different toppings, an old-fashioned candy store, and waffle breakfasts weekends only May–Oct.

Jordan's Ice Creamery (603-267-1900), Rt. 106, Belmont, just past the Belmont Park and Ride and difficult to spot until after you have passed it. A must for ice cream connoisseurs. It's all homemade.

The Sandwich Creamery (603-284-6675), Hannah Rd. off Rt. 113A, North Sandwich. A source of ice cream (ginger is the standout flavor), also Brie and cheddar cheeses.

✳ Entertainment

MUSIC New Hampshire Music Festival (603-253-4331; nhmf.org). For almost 60 years, this regional music institution has brought big-time classical musicians to the small towns of the New Hampshire's Lakes Region. The six-week summer season begins in early July at the Silver Cultural Arts Center at Plymouth State College. In addition to featuring world-class performers, the festival includes a preconcert lecture series, chamber music concerts, and year-round education programs in New Hampshire schools.

Meadowbrook Musical Arts Center (603-293-4700; meadowbrook.net), 72 Meadowbrook Lane, Gilford. A popular summer venue for country music.

Great Waters Music Festival (603-569-7710; greatwaters.org), on the Brewster Academy campus, Wolfeboro. July–Sept., a series of performances held in an acoustically designed tent.

Wolfeboro Friends of Music (603-569-3657) sponsor a series of 10 concerts held in local churches and auditoriums Sept.–June.

SUMMER THEATER Summer Theatre in Meredith Village (888-245-6374; interlakestheatre.com), Rt. 25 Meredith. Late June–Aug., Tue.–Sun. with Sat. and Wed. matinees, professional summer-stock productions of upbeat Broadway plays like *Fiddler on the Roof* and *Camelot*, also a Saturday matinee Children's Series, all staged in a newly renovated, 420-seat theater at Inter-Lakes High School.

SOUND OF MUSIC AT THE SUMMER THEATER IN MEREDITH VILLAGE

Winnipesaukee Playhouse (366-7377; winniplayhouse.com), 36 Endicott St. (Rt. 3), Alpenrose Plaza, Weirs Beach. Founded just in 2004 and now nonprofit, this group garners rave reviews for professional black-box summer productions and off-season community theater. Plans call for a move to a larger theater, the former Annalee Dolls factory site in Meredith, eventually transforming the 14-acre property into a performing arts center.

The Little Church Theater (603-968-2250), 40 Rt. 113 (across from the Squam Lake Science Center), Holderness. A nonprofit arts center with a variety of offerings throughout summer, including art shows, sing-alongs, puppet shows, cabaret, plays, and workshops, at mostly modest prices.

Also see **Barnstormers Theatre** (barnstormerstheatre.org) in nearby Tamworth, detailed in "Osippee Valley." It's New Hampshire's oldest professional theater, staging outstanding plays with Equity casts.

FILM Weirs Drive-in (603-366-4723), 76 Endicott St. North (Rt. 3), Weirs Beach. Open seasonally, showing first-runs.

BarnZ's Meredith Cinema (603-279-4161), 35 Rt. 25 in the Meredith Shopping Center; three screens, first-runs.

OTHER ⚓ Belknap Mill Society (603-524-8813), Mill Plaza, Laconia 03246. Open all year. Built in 1823, this is the oldest unaltered textile mill in the country. It's now a year-round art center with art exhibits, music, lectures, and children's programs as well as many special events.

✳ Selective Shopping

ANTIQUES Antiques shops abound in this section of the state. Pick up the widely available, current *Antiquing* pamphlet.

ART AND CRAFTS Sandwich Home Industries (603-284-6831; nhcrafts.org), 132 Main St., Center

Sandwich. Open mid-May–mid-Oct. This cooperative was founded in 1926 to promote traditional crafts, eventually spawning the current **League of New Hampshire Craftsmen** with its stores throughout the state and its big annual August Craftsmen's Fair at Mount Sunapee. The present shop, picturesquely situated beside the town green, dates from 1934. For many years a signature item in this particular shop has been the locally made botanical lamp shades. As in other league shops, you will also find a fine selection of handmade pottery, glass, clothing, toys, ornaments, jewelry, prints, furniture, and weavings. In Meredith the league maintains a year-round gallery (603-279-7920) next to the Inn at Church Landing, 279 Daniel Webster Hwy. (Rt. 3), displaying superb New Hampshire–made, juried crafts of all types including lamps, furniture, prints, carvings, textiles, pottery, and much more.

Also in Meredith

The Old Print Barn (603-279-6479), 343 Winona Rd., off Rt. 104, Meredith. Open year-round except Thanksgiving and Christmas, 10–5. One of the largest displays of original prints in New England, some 2,000 original antique and contemporary works from 1600 to the present, housed in a Civil War–era barn. We especially like the old New Hampshire views of the lakes and White Mountains, but you can find etchings, lithographs, and engravings covering virtually any subject from any continent as well as work by locally prominent and world-famous artists. The huge restored barn, with its detailed, 19th-century craftsmanship, is impressive, too. Free, but it will be hard to resist buying a print!

Oglethorpe (603-279-9909), at Mill Falls Marketplace, Rt. 3 in Meredith, a gallery representing work by some 300 craftspeople, including hand-forged ironwork and handcrafted jewelry.

In Wolfeboro

Cornish Hill Pottery (603-569-5626; 800-497-2556), 39 N. Main St., is a combination studio and showcase for Gogi Millner's stunning functional and decorative pieces, all hand thrown and decorated.

Kalled Gallery (603-569-3994), 38 N. Main St., open daily 10–5:30. This strikingly colorful gallery features imaginative jewelry by Jennifer Kalled and showcases work by artists in a wide variety of media from throughout the country.

Hampshire Pewter (603-569-4944), 9 Mill St. (just off Main St.), open year-round daily except Sun., 9–5. A factory store showcasing pieces made here; factory tours are offered spring–fall.

The Art Place (603-569-6159), 9 N. Main St., exhibits regional, original art and limited-edition prints, as does the **Blue Shutter Gallery** (603-569-3372), 19 Lehner St. **Made on Earth** (603-569-9100), N. Main St., showcases artisans from around the earth.

Elsewhere

Village Artists & Gallery (603-968-4445), 51 Main St., Ashland, is a new nonprofit cooperative representing 40 local artists, well worth checking.

Stamping Memories (603-528-0498; stampingmemories.com), 45 Court St., Laconia. Open 10–5 Mon.–Sat., later on class nights. The largest outlet in the state for scrapbooking supplies. Downstairs, Mike Verhoek operates a pottery studio and showcase at the **Laconia Pottery Gallery** (603-528-4997).

Lambert Folk Art Gallery (603-286-4882; jimlambertfolkart.com), 271 Main St., Tilton. Not the kind of shop you might expect to find in the middle of Tilton, but Jim Lambert points out that his whimsical creations perpetuate the town's tradition of striking sculptures. His own folk sculptures are the real finds here, but many other outstanding craftspeople, most of them regional, are represented.

BOOKS ✑ **Bayswater Book Co.** (603-253-8858), Rt. 25 and Main St., Center Harbor. Open Mon.–Sat. 9:30–6, Sun. 11–4. A well-stocked bookstore offering volumes of extra service including kids' story hours, a young adults' discussion group, art and craft workshops, journal-writing courses, frequent author signings, and coffee by the pound or cup.

Innisfree Bookshop (603-279-3905), Mill Falls Marketplace, Meredith. A major, full-service independent bookstore also carrying music, toys, and cards.

The Country Bookseller (603-569-6030; 800-877-READ), 23A N. Main St., Wolfeboro. An inviting, well-stocked independent bookstore in the middle of the village.

SPECIAL STORES Keepsake Quilting (603-253-4026; 800-865-9458; keepsakequilting.com), Rt. 25, Senter's Marketplace, Center Harbor. Open daily 9–6. Mon.–Sat., Sun. until 5. Billed as America's largest quilt shop, this is a destination for quilters from throughout the country and even the world. Many are members, paying a nominal annual fee to display their own work here (on consignment); thousands also subscribe to the catalog, which features—as does the store—everything and anything a quilter could desire. There is nothing, however, like actually seeing and fingering more than 10,000 bolts of 100 percent cotton cloth in a heady range of colors and patterns.

The Old Country Store (603-476-5750; nhcountrystore.com), 1011

Whittier Hwy. (Rt. 25), Moultonborough. Open daily. Built as a stagecoach stop in 1781, this rambling old building offers a small museum along with enough rooms to get lost in searching for weird and wonderful gifts, books, New Hampshire–made products, and typical country store items.

chi-lin (603-527-1115; 603-279-8663), 17 Lake St. (corner of Main), Meredith. Terry and Suzanne Lee have filled their shop with a selection of imported and custom-made cabinets, furniture, and accessories with an Asian sensibility. They have also created an oasis off this busy shopping area. Their **Satori tea garden** is open for light lunches and sweets with tea in summer, Wed.–Sat. 11–4:30. You can consult with them to implement your own design ideas.

Pepi Herrmann Crystal (603-528-1020; handcut.com), 3 Waterford Pl., Gilford. Turn off Rt. 110 onto Lily Pond Rd. Tue.–Sat. 9:30–5. Showroom and museum. Fine-quality, hand-cut crystal and giftware. Watch crystal cutters at work.

KEEPSAKE QUILTING, CENTER HARBOR

Chris Tree

Country Braid House (603-286-4511; countrybraidhouse.com), 462 Main St., Tilton. Open Mon.–Fri. 9–5, Sat. 9–4. A workshop and showroom featuring new and antique braided and hand-hooked rugs. Custom designs and kits available.

Black's Paper Store and Gift Shop (603-569-4444), Main St., Wolfeboro. Village life eddies around this wonderfully old-fashioned store, a source of newpapers and magazines, stationery, toys, cards, and a wide variety of necessities and not-so-necessaries.

The Common Man Company Store (603-968-3559), 59 Main St., Ashland. Across the the original Common Man restaurant, this is a source of New Hampshire–made products and an imaginative variety of gift items. We did some unexpectedly good Christmas shopping here on a June day.

Topiary at Owl's Rest Farm (603-934-3221; thetopiary.com), 252 Brook Rd., Sanbornton. Call to check hours. Handcrafted, custom-designed silk topiaries, floral arrangements, wreaths, and swags. Twenty-seven acres with garden tours, cooking classes, and English tea by reservation.

SHOPPING COMPLEXES **Tanger Factory Outlet** (866-665-863; tangeroutlet.com), Rt. 3 at I-93, left off Exit 20, Tilton. Open daily 10 AM–9 PM, Sun. 10–6. More than 50 tax-free factory outlets include Brooks Brothers, J. Crew, Ralph Lauren, Eddie Bauer, Samsonite, Old Navy, Coach, Easy Spirit, and Nike.

Mill Falls Marketplace Shops (603-279-6797; millfalls.com), Rt. 3, Meredith. Open daily year-round. This remarkable restoration of an 1820s mill beside its 40-foot falls now houses 15 shops including the Innisfree Bookshop and Oglethorpe (see above). The complex includes a spa, four inns, and seven restaurants; also public restrooms and an ATM.

FARMSTANDS **Moulton Farm** (603-279-3915), 18 Quarry Rd., just off Rt. 25 east of Meredith. Open May–Christmas Eve. A simply outstanding farm stand in a great setting. Fall corn maze.

Longhaul Farm at Squam Lake (603-968-9333), Rt. 113, Holderness. Local farm products offered seasonally with a festive "Taste of the Farm" meal, including live music, presented annually in early July.

Booty Family Farm (603-284-7163), 610 Mount Israel Rd., Sandwich. Open year-round. The sugarhouse was billowing sweet steam when we passed. Syrup is sold year-round, along with organic produce.

Bly Farm (603-569-1411), 620 Center St., Wolfeboro. Flowers, herbs, veggies, pumpkins, homemade ice cream.

Beans & Greens Farmstead (603-293-7070), 300 Gunstock Rd., Gilford. Open May–Oct. 9–6. Plants, perennials, vegetable plants, veggies, flowers, honey, syrup, local eggs.

Farmers Choice (603-875-2556), 5 Homestead Place, at the junction of Rts. 111 ad 28 in Alton. Fresh corn, fruit, vegetables, maple syrup.

Smith Farm Stand (603-524-7673), 95 Sleeper Hill Rd., Gilford. Open mid-June–Sept. 10–6; closed Wed. Vegetables, cut flowers and herbs, maple syrup.

FARMER'S MARKETS **Alton Farmer's Market** (603-364-5279), Rt. 11, Alton Bay. Sat. 10–1, late June–mid-Sept.

Laconia Farmer's Market (603-267-6522), Beacon St. East. An outdoor farmer's market located in the parking lot between the mill and town hall. Open mid-June–mid-Sept., Sat. 8:30–noon.

Wolfeboro Area Farmer's Market
(603-323-3369), 35 Center St. Open
last week in June–end of Sept., Thu.
1–5. In addition to baked goods,
organically grown veggies, and cut
flowers, there are occasional educational events and demonstrations.

Heritage Farm Tours (603-524-8188;
heritagefarm.net), 16 Parker Hill Rd.,
Sanbornton. ATV rentals, hay- and
sleigh rides, petting farm, homemade
ice cream, gift shop and farm stand,
corn maze.

Smith Farm Stand (603-524-7673),
95 Sleeper Hill Rd., Gilford. This fifth-
generation maple syrup producer boils
in a 1947 sap house. Syrup available
year-round.

✳ Special Events

Dozens of events are held each summer in the Winnipesaukee region, too
many to list here in detail. Check with
such organizations as the **Lakes
Region Association** (603-744-8664),
New Hampshire Farm Museum
(603-652-7840), **Belknap Mill Society** (603-524-8813), and **Gunstock
Recreation Area** (603-293-4341).

Early February: **World Championship Sled Dog Derby**, Opechee
Park, Laconia. Three days of racing by
colorful teams of sled dogs. **Annual
Rotary Fishing Derby**, Meredith.

Mid-February: **Winter Carnival** (603-
569-2758), Wolfeboro Lion's Club. A
week of events.

Early June: **Laconia Race Week** is
huge, the biggest annual event in New
Hampshire and the oldest motorcycle
rally in the nation. In one recent year
it drew some 375,000 motorcyclists
over nine days, a tradition dating back
to 1916. The races are held at the New
Hampshire Speedway in Loudon 10
miles away, but parades and rallies are
held at Gunstock and in the Lake City

itself. Two-wheeled visitors from
throughout the country fill every bed
for miles around. For a full schedule of
events log onto laconiamcweek.com or
call 603-366-2000. **Annual Barn Sale
and Auction** (603-652-7840), New
Hampshire Farm Museum, Milton.
Call for a detailed schedule of many
summer events.

July and August: **Alton Bay band
concerts**. Several free concerts are
held weekly during July and August,
plus a week of events during Old
Home Week in mid-August. Write the
chamber of commerce for a full schedule of summer activities.

Fourth of July: Regionwide celebrations with parades and fireworks, some
special events, some events held the
night before. Alton, Ashland, Center
Harbor, Laconia, Meredith,
Wolfeboro.

Mid-July: **Arts and Crafts Street
Fair**, downtown Laconia.

Late July: **Annual Antiques Fair and
Show** (603-539-5126), Kingswood
High School, Wolfeboro. **Antique and
Classic Boat Show**, Meredith. **Annu-
al Flea Market and Chicken Bar-
becue**, East Alton.

Early August: **Huggins Hospital
Street Fair** (603-569-1043), Brewster
Field, Wolfeboro. **Sandwich Old
Home Days**, an entire week of very
special events.

Mid-August: **Old Home Week** (603-
539-6323), Freedom and Alton. **Miss
Winnipesaukee Pageant** (603-366-
4377), Funspot, Weirs Beach.

Late August: **Annual Lakes Region
Fine Arts and Crafts Festival** (603-
279-6121), Meredith. A major, juried
outdoor exhibit with music, entertainment, and food.

Labor Day weekend: **Fireworks at
Weirs Beach** (603-524-5531). **Lakes**

Region Craft Fair (603-528-4014).

Mid-September: **New England Slalom Championships**, Back Bay, Wolfeboro (603-569-3017). **Foliage trains** along Winnipesaukee, Meredith, and Weirs Beach stations (603-279-5253; foliagetrains.com). **Annual Mustang/All Ford Show** at the Laconia Funspot in Weirs Beach (603-753-8134). **Vintage Race Boat Regatta**, Wolfeboro Town Docks (603-569-4554). **Annual Winnipesaukee Relay Race** (603-524-5531). Teams of runners circle the lake, beginning in the Gunstock Recreation Area. **Annual Lees Mill Steamboat Meet**, Moultonborough.

Early October: **Annual Antique and Classic Boat and Car Rendezvous**, Wolfeboro Town Docks (603-569-0087). **Annual Quilter Show** (603-524-8813), Belknap Mill Society, Laconia.

Columbus Day weekend: **Sandwich Fair** (603-284-7062; sandwichfairnh .com), three days: an old-fashioned fair with tractor pulls, ox, mule, and draft horse pulls, clogging, an antique auto parade, 4-H exhibits, fleece-to-shawl spinning, stage shows, a grand street parade, and much more.

November: **Holly Fair**, Center Harbor Congregational Church (603-253-7698; chcc.org). **Lakes Region Holiday Arts & Crafts Fair**, Winnipesaukee Expo Center Laconia (603-528-4014).

First weekend in December: **Annual Christmas in the Village**, Center Sandwich. Craft, bake, and book sale with the historical society decorated for Christmas. **Festival of the Trees** in Meredith, open house in shops.

OSSIPEE VALLEY

INCLUDING TAMWORTH, CHOCORUA, THE OSSIPEES, MADISON, AND EATON CENTER

J ust off the beaten path, betwixt and between more high-profile destinations, this area offers an increasingly rare combination: beauty, hospitality, and peace. Flanking Rt. 16, just south of the Mount Washington Valley and north of Lake Winnipesaukee, this is a hilly, wooded region, spotted with small lakes—White Lake, Chocorua Lake, and Silver Lake, not to mention Ossipee, Silver, Purity, and Crystal. Its villages include picture-perfect Tamworth, Eaton Center, and Freedom.

GUIDANCE Greater Ossipee Area Chamber of Commerce (603-539-6201; 866-683-6295; ossipeevalley.org) publishes a helpful booklet. A seasonal, volunteer-run information booth (603-539-5424) at the junction of Rts. 16 and 25 West is open weekends.

GETTING THERE Rt. 16 is the high road from I-95 at Portsmouth to the Mount Washington Valley. Also see Rt. 153 (*Scenic Drives*). Rt. 25 runs east to Portland and west to Lake Winnipesaukee and I-93.

☀ To See

VILLAGES Tamworth (pop. 2,600; tamworth.org). Settled in 1771, the town of Tamworth encompasses the villages of Wonalancet, Chocorua, Whittier, Tamworth Village, South Tamworth, Pequawket, and Bennett Corners. **Tamworth Village** is a compact crossroads community with a steepled church backed by the Ossipee range and set in open fields. The draws here are the **Barnstormers Theatre**, the country's oldest professional summer theater and a venue for year-round live performances, and the **Remick Country Doctor and Farm Museum**. The village gathering places are the inviting **Cook Memorial Library** and **The Other Store**. Inquire at either place about ski and walking trails. Head west on Cleveland Rd. to see **Ordination Rock**, north on Rt. 113A to Wonalancet, east on 113 to **Chocorua** (and Rt. 16), and south on 113 to **Whittier** (named for the poet John Greenleaf Whittier, who frequented the area). The town's many distinguished

Chris Tree

TAMWORTH

second-home owners included two-term president Grover Cleveland, whose son Francis moved here to stay, founding the Barnstormers with his wife, Alice, in 1931. In the era when the train stopped at Depot St., this was also a winter resort with skiing (there was a rope tow) and dogsledding, based at the famous Chinook Kennels in Wonalancet. It's still as pleasant a place to come in winter (Wonalancet is a genuine snow pocket) as summer. The **Tamworth Historical Society** (603-323-2900) is open by appointment.

Chocorua sits astride busy Rt. 16. It's named for its Matterhorn-like mountain, visible from the highway, across Chocorua Lake. The view from Rt. 16 across the waterfall and its millpond is another photo op.

Eaton Center. While its population is a third what it was in the 1850s, this remains an idyllic village with a much-photographed classic 1870s white, steepled church beside **Crystal Lake**. The **Eaton Center Village Store** serves as the source of all local information; the Palmer House Pub at the Inn at Crystal Lake is the local gathering spot.

The Ossipees. The town of Ossipee encompasses the villages of Center Ossipee, Granite, Ossipee Corners, and Water Village. Then there's West Ossipee, the crossroads gathering of restaurants at the junction of Rt. 25 (a major route to Lake Winnipesaukee and on to I-93). The Carroll County Courthouse is in Center Ossipee.

Freedom (pop. 1,361). Another picture-perfect village with a flagpole and a fountain. Moulton Brook flows by and behind Main St., foxgloves bloom behind picket fences, and both the church and town hall are white with green trim. **The Allard House and Works Museum** (open in July and Aug., Sat. 10–noon, Sun. 2–4) is worth checking out, depicting life in this small mill town at its most prosperous.

MUSEUM

✐ **Remick Country Doctor Museum and Farm** (603-323-7591; 800-686-6117; remickmuseum.org), 58 Cleveland Hill Rd., Tamworth. Open year-round Mon.–Fri. 10–4; also summer Sat. 10–4. $5 adult, $4 per child. On the edge of the village, this exceptional museum depicts the life of a country doctor through the past century, also offers many special events: ice harvesting and sleigh rides, hearthside dinners, maple sugaring, day camps, family workshops in old-time rural skills, and more. For children the farm animals, which include cows and horses, pigs and goats, are a big attraction.

Remicks have been active in Tamworth since the 1790s; between 1894 and 1993 two members of the family (father and son) served the medical needs of the town and outlying farms. The Remicks themselves farmed (their Hillsdale Farm's barn and stable are part of the museum) and lived frugally, judging from the vintage 1930s–1950s furnishing in the house, which doubled as doctor's office. The **Capt. Enoch Remick House**, also in the village and slightly grander, is also open on special occasions. One of four surviving farms in Tamworth, it's in the middle of the village.

REMICK COUNTRY DOCTOR MUSEUM AND FARM IS A FIND FOR FAMILIES.

GLACIAL ERRATICS "It is a folk saying that God created the world in six days and spent the seventh throwing rocks at New Hampshire," Keith Henney wrote in *The Early Days of Eaton*. Two famous examples of these "rocks" are:

Ordination Rock, Cleveland Hill Rd., Tamworth (a few miles west of the village). A curiosity, this cenotaph perched atop a giant boulder commemorates the ordination of Tamworth's first minister in 1792. A plaque, recalling that HE CAME INTO THE WILDERNESS AND LEFT IT A FRUITFUL FIELD, gives details of his tenure.

Madison Boulder Natural Area, on a dirt side road off Rt. 113, Madison. Open all year, although access is limited to walking in winter. Just a big rock but amazing to see. During the Ice Age, this massive chunk was plucked off a mountaintop and carried along by a glacier until it reached this spot. Some three stories high and more than 80 feet long, it is one of the largest glacial erratics in the world and has been designated a national natural landmark. No facilities and no fees.

SCENIC DRIVES **The Chinook Trail**. On the late-fall morning we drove this stretch of Rt. 113A, it was magical! Turn north at the four corners in Tamworth Village, heading through woods for several miles. Note the turnoff for Hemenway State Forest and the firehouse; this is the only clue that you've entered Wonalancet. Look for the monument in front of **Chinook Kennels**, named for its most famous resident, born in 1917 and sire of the still-famous breed (now around 500 dogs). Chinook himself served as lead dog on Admiral Byrd's expeditions to Antarctica, but the monument is for all dogs who did so. For many years these kennels were a big attraction; dogsleds met the trains. Traveling this direction it's easy to miss the **Wonalancet Chapel**, at the bend in the road as the countryside opens up around you (look back for the best view; it's a classic chapel in the middle of nowhere, a favorite for weddings). It's a glorious 10 miles from here to Sandwich, through the tiny village of Whiteface (note the swimming hole by the bridge), and on down to North Sandwich.

Rt. 153 from Wakefield through the Effinghams and Freedom to Eaton Center. This route begins in the Lake Winnipesaukee area, but we think it belongs here because you tend to be heading north on it, into the Mount Washington Valley. Frequently we begin looking for road food at this point; see *Eating Out* for details about the **Poor People's Pub** (lunch/dinner) and **Lino's Café** (breakfast/lunch) in Sanbornville. It's less than a mile east of Rt. 16. You might also want to stop by **Lovell Lake**, just up Rt. 109, with a town beach.

Sanbornville is one of several villages in the town of Wakefield, which bills itself as the geographic center of New England. Heading north up Rt. 153 you soon come to the old town center with its impressive lineup of early-19th-century houses, including the **Wakefield Inn**. If it's Saturday don't miss the **Wakefield Marketplace**, a major farmer's and artisans' market (Memorial Day–Columbus Day weekends, 9–3), corner of Wakefield Rd. and Rt. 16.

Continue up Rt. 153 to **Province Lake** with its narrow ribbon of sand between the road and the lake (you won't be the first to wade in) and a view of mountains to the west. Here, too, is the entrance to the **Province Lake Golf Club** with 18 holes. Technically, you are in Parsonfield, Maine. In Taylor City, part of South Effingham (the next village), stop by the **Ye Olde Sale Shoppe** (yeoldesaleshoppe .com) in Taylor City. Owner Bill Taylor will tell you that the state line runs almost down the middle of his two-story, vintage-1815 country store, every inch of which

Chris Tree

EFFINGHAM

is crammed with antiques, cards, local art, and more—an eclectic mix of possible purchases. Next comes **Effingham Center** with surprisingly substantial buildings for its size. Continuing north, your head also swivels at the sight of **Squire Lord's Mansion**, a three-story unmistakable Federal mansion with a large cupola in the middle of nowhere (please drive on; it's a private home). In **Effingham Falls** you cross Rt. 25, the high road west to Portland (44 miles) and east to Ossipee Lake (6 miles).

Be sure to detour the mile or so into the village of **Freedom**, a real beauty. Continue on through **East Madison** to **Eaton Center**, or turn west on Rt. 113 to **Chocorua** and **Tamworth**.

✴ To Do

GOLF Province Lake Golf Club (800-325-4434; provincelakegolf.com) with 18 holes, Rt. 153, Parsonfield, Me. Technically two holes are in Effingham, New Hampshire, and the remainder in Maine, but most have views of Province Lake and this highly rated course attracts an enthusiastic following from both states. Multiple tees at each hole appeal to families. Inquire about lunch and dinner.

Indian Mound Golf Club (603-539-7733), Old Rt. 16, Center Ossipee. 18 holes, pro shop, carts, lounge/tavern.

HIKING Mount Chocorua is only 3,475 feet high, but its rugged, treeless summit makes it a popular destination, and there are many trails to the top. The **Piper Trail** begins on Rt. 16 at a restaurant-campground parking lot (fee charged for parking) a few miles north of **Chocorua Lake**. The well-trod trail is 4.5 miles long and requires about three and a half hours' hiking time. The Liberty Trail begins on Paugus Mill Rd., which is off Rt. 113A, southwest of the mountain. Some 3.9 miles long, requiring about three hours and 20 minutes, this oldest trail on the mountain passes the Jim Liberty cabin, a mountainside cabin with bunks (there for anyone willing to use it). The Champney Falls Trail ascends the mountain from the Kancamagus Hwy. West of Chocorua are Mounts Paugus, Passaconaway, and Whiteface,

MOUNT CHOCORUA

This distinctive peaked mountain gets its name from a prophet of the Pequawket Indians who refused to leave the graves of his ancestors in Tamworth when his tribe fled to Canada. He lived amicably among the settlers and left his son in the care of a local farm family while he journeyed to visit his tribesmen. When he returned, his child was dead. Chocorua refused to believe the farmer's story that the boy had mistakenly eaten poison meant for a fox. In retaliation he killed the farmer's wife and children. The husband tracked him to the summit of this mountain and shot him, but not before Chocorua laid a curse on the settlers who, according to legend, soon fell sick; then their crops died, and the settlement was abandoned. Cattle continued to die in this area, it seems, until a University of New Hampshire professor tested the local streams and discovered that they contained muriate of lime, palatable to humans but not livestock.

MOUNT CHOCORUA

all of which can be climbed from a parking lot off Ferncroft Rd., in Wonalancet on Rt. 113A.

Foss Mountain. From Eaton Center head west on Brownfield Rd. and right on Stuart Rd., then take the first right and look for trailhead parking. Not particularly high but with a bald summit offering a 360-degree view: the full march of the Presidentials to the northwest and nearer, the Moat Mountains, Chocorua, and, to the southwest, the Ossipee Range.

FOR FAMILIES ✒ **Monkey Trunks** (603-367-4427; monkeytrunks.com), Rt. 16, Chocorua. Open daily in July and Aug.; weekends in May, June, Sept., Oct. An adventure park featuring ziplines, climbing walls, rappels, and ropes courses. $40 adults, $35 teens, $30 kids, $35 for ages 60-plus.

SWIMMING This area is truly spotted with lakes, but few invite visitors. Pristine **Chocorua Lake**, Rt. 16, in Tamworth is a case in point, with cool waters set against rugged Mount Chocorua and a sandy beach beckoning beneath shady pines. There is, however, a large RESIDENTS ONLY sign, a much-repeated message in this area. Ask around locally. Under *Scenic Drives* we have noted **Lovell Lake** in Sanbornville.

White Lake State Park (603-323-7350; nhstateparks.org) Rt. 16, Tamworth. Open late May–mid-Oct. Here is a sandy beach and campground. Rental boats and good trout fishing. The 1.5-mile trail around the lake takes you through a large stand of tall pitch pines, a national natural landmark. $4 adults, $2 children.

✷ Winter Sports

CROSS-COUNTRY SKIING In Tamworth inquire about the local trail along the Swift River, and see **Hemenway State Forest** under *Green Space*.

King Pine (see *Downhill Skiing*) also offers a 20km groomed trail network throughout the Purity Spring property and **Hoyt Audubon Sanctuary**. Lessons, rentals.

DOWNHILL SKIING, SNOWBOARDING, AND SNOWTUBING ♂ **King Pine Ski Area** (603-367-8896; kingpine.com), Rt. 153, East Madison. Dating back to the 1930s as a ski area, operated since 1962 by the Hoyt family and part of the Purity Spring Resort complex, this is a fine family ski area.

Vertical Drop: 350 feet.

Lifts: Six.

Trails: 17 trails (44 percent novice, 31 percent intermediate, 25 percent expert).

Night skiing and snowboarding: Eight trails, three lifts.

Facilities and features: 100 percent snowmaking coverage, tubing, nursery, PSIA-certified ski and snowboard school and equipment rentals, a half-pipe, hits and rails, snowshoeing tours, resort amenities at Purity Spring.

Lift tickets: $44 adults, $30 juniors and seniors; less on certain days and with lodging packages.

ICE SKATING **King Pine Ski Area Tohko Dome Ice Skating Arena** (king pine.com) is open to the public. If you purchase an alpine ski pass at King Pine you can use it for skating and cross-country skiing that same day.

✷ Green Space

Hemenway State Forest, Rt. 113A, Tamworth. There are two trails here: a short, self-guided nature trail, and a longer trail with a spur to the Great Hill fire tower offering views of the southern White Mountains. Brochures for both trails can usually be found in the box a few yards up each trail. Note Duck Pond near the parking area, good for a dip. In winter this is a popular, dependably snowy bet for cross-country skiing.

✳ Lodging

RESORT ✎ "ℐ" **Purity Spring Resort**
(603-367-8896; 800-373-3754; purity
spring.com), Rt. 153, East Madison
03849. Open year-round. Off by itself
southwest of the Conways, this low-
key, affordable, 1,000-acre, family-
geared resort has been run by the
Hoyt family since 1870. In summer
most guests stay a week, taking advantage of activities and of sports facilities
that include canoes, rowboats, and
water-skiing on Purity Lake as well as
tennis, volleyball, and arts-and-crafts
programs. The inn van delivers guests
to trailheads for guided hikes, to rivers
for a canoe trips, and to North Conway
for a play. In winter the draw is King
Pine Ski Area, also part of the resort.
Seventy-two country-style rooms are
divided among 10 buildings, ranging
from remodeled farmhouses and barns
(several are suited to family groups) to
condominiums at King Pine and the
sleek Mill Building, which also houses
the indoor pool, hot tub, and fitness
center. Rates are $44–146 per person
depending on season and meal plan.
Winter ski packages include skiing at
King Pine Ski Area (see *Skiing*).

INNS 🐾 "ℐ" **The Inn at Crystal
Lake** (603-447-2120; 800-343-7336;
innatcrystallake.com), Rt. 153, Eaton
Center 03832. Open all year. This distinctive four-story, triple-porched (one
on top of another) Greek Revival
building overlooks Crystal Lake. Built
in 1884 as a private home, it became
an inn almost immediately, then a private school. Happily, it's now an inn
again. Bobby Barker and Tim Osten-
dorf are opera and classical music buffs
with a large collection of recordings
and videos. They offer 11 rooms, all
with private bath, phone, cable
TV/VCR, and most with air-conditioning. There is ample common space,

plus the cheery, funkily decorated
Palmer House Pub in the rear (see
Dining Out). Guests may use Crystal
Lake for swimming. Rates per couple
are $129–199 in winter, $149–219 in
summer, including full country breakfast. No smoking. Children over 8
please.

∞ ✎ **The Brass Heart Inn** (603-323-
7766; 800-833-9509; thebrassheart
inn.com), P.O. Box 370, off Rt. 113,
Tamworth. Dating in part from the
18th century and a summer inn since
the 1890s. (Fom the 1960s into the
1990s it was known as Staffords in the
Fields.) The setting is 35 acres of walkable woods and meadow with Mount
Chocorua as a backdrop. The inn
offers six suites with sitting areas and
private baths in the main house
($120–160) and four cottages with
microwave, fridge, and coffeemaker,
sleeping two to eight people
($180–240); add $20 to rates in foliage
season.

Snowvillage Inn (603-447-2818; 800-
447-4345; snowvillageinn.com),
Snowville 03832. Built as a summer
home on Foss Mountain in 1912, with
views of the Presidential Range. Guest
rooms, all with private bath, are divided among the main inn, the Carriage
House, and the Chimney House (with
fireplaces in the rooms). Each building
also has a guest living room with books
and games; the main inn has a large
brick fireplace and spacious porch.

BED & BREAKFASTS ✪ ∞ "ℐ"
Riverbend Inn Bed and Breakfast
(603-323-7440; 800-628-6944), Rt. 16,
Chocorua 03817. Open all year. Up a
long driveway and facing the Chocorua
River behind it, this 10-room inn is
Yankee plain on the outside—but
inside, it's wonderful to behold.
Innkeepers Craig Cox and Jerry Weiss
have traveled widely in Asia and deco-

rated the inn, which has won interior design awards, with artwork they acquired. A statue of the South Indian god of doorways graces a living room with a wood-burning fireplace and persimmon-colored walls; decks overlook the river. Six rooms have private bath, the others semiprivate facilities. Each has a different decor but all have mahogany beds and Oriental rugs, equipped with robes, hair dryer, air conditioner, cable TV, and WiFi. The $100–250 room rate includes a full breakfast, served on a riverside deck or in a sunny patio room with linen-covered tables and a massive antique candelabra. Our breakfast began with gingered melon and apple coffee cake, followed by blueberry pancakes with local maple syrup. Our hosts were full of helpful suggestions about local explorations. This is a great place for small weddings.

∞ **The Wakefield Inn** (603-522-8272; 800-245-0841; wakefieldinn .com), 2723 Wakefield Rd., Wakefield 03872. Open all year. Janel and James Martin have opened a new chapter in the long life of this handsome former stagecoach stop, dating from 1804. The graceful spiral staircase climbs three stories, accessing five country-gracious guest rooms and two family suites. Downstairs offers another guest room and comfortable sitting space by a three-sided fireplace with a beehive oven. Janel is an accomplished French chef, and the couple offer cooking lessons as well as Friday and Saturday three-course, prix fixe dinners by reservation in a dining area with view of the meadow (see *Dining Out*). $90–170 per couple for rooms includes a full breakfast. Small weddings are a specialty.

∞ **Highland House Bed & Breakfast** (603-323-7982; highlandhouse tamworth.com), 654 Cleveland Hill Rd., Tamworth 03886. We have to admit that after many years of visiting, even staying in and writing about Tamworth, we only just recently discovered this lovely B&B, a real gem. The three-story Federal-period country mansion offers a rare sense of quiet and grace with a fireplace in the parlor and five nicely restored guest rooms. Innkeeper Dale Bragdon is a locally known caterer, adept at staging weddings and other events in the 18th-cen-

WAKEFIELD INN

Chris Tree

tury Cooper's Shed out back; tents are added for larger events. In winter cross-country ski trails begin right outside the back door. Breakfast is included in $85–95 per couple; more for private bath.

Freedom House Bed and Breakfast (603-539-4815), 17 Old Portland Rd., Freedom 03836. Open Apr.–Dec. Located by a millpond in a quiet village, this 140-year-old house is decorated in country Victorian style. Four rooms sleep two to three each and share two full baths. Guests can relax on two porches or in the parlor or library. Innkeepers Patrick Miele and John Immediato also run an antiques shop in the adjoining barn. Full breakfast and four o'clock tea. $75–90 single or $85–105 double occupancy. A nonsmoking inn. There is a minimum two-night stay on weekends June–Oct.

🐾 **The Lazy Dog Inn** (603-323-8350; 888-323-8350; lazydoginn.com), 201 Rt. 16, Chocorua 03817. Innkeepers Steven and Lauren Sousa describe their inn as "A truly dog friendly bed and breakfast." You get the message as soon as you pull up in front of the mid-19th-century former farmhouse, which is decorated with banners bearing the images of happy dogs of different breeds. WIPE YOUR PAWS! a sign by the front door advises. "We wanted to make this the kind of B&B we were always looking for when we traveled with our dog but couldn't find," Lauren says. There are seven guest rooms, four with private bath and three sharing a full bath and a half-bath. All are cozily furnished and decorated with dog-themed pictures, quilts, knick-knacks, and framed sayings like LOVE IS A FOUR-LEGGED WORD. There is no restriction on the number of dogs accommodated or their size; all breeds are welcome. Dogs can sleep in the same room as their owners but can't be

left alone in a room. A former barn has been converted into a climate-controlled "Doggie Lodge," a canine day care center with fenced-in play areas, toys and agility equipment, and piped-in soothing music. (The building has a smaller exercise room for two-legged guests.) There is also a large outdoor fenced dog run. A full breakfast is served, and there is a "bottomless jar" of dog treats in the kitchen. Rates are $95–190 double occupancy with one dog, dog-sitting included. Additional people or dogs are $25 each.

CAMPING *Note:* There are also several private campgrounds in this area.

♿ **White Lake State Park** (603-323-7350; nhparks.state.nh.us), Rt. 16, West Ossipee. Open mid-May–Columbus Day. There are 203 campsites on 72 pine-wooded acres. The trick is to get one of the couple of dozen with a water view. No pets permitted. $25–30 per night; family sites $50–75. Facilities include a camp store, showers, ice, and firewood. No hookups. The lake offers swimming, canoeing, and a 2-mile walking trail.

✳ **Where to Eat**

DINING OUT ✪ **Inn at Crystal Lake and Palmer House Pub** (603-447-2120; innatcrystallake.com). Open Tue.–Sun. from 5 PM. Reservations a must for the dining room on weekends. The intimate, comfy dining room showcases creative entrées such as curried pork medallions and vegetable paella, also smaller plates lie bruschetta and dinner salads. Entrées $18–29. The **Palmer House Pub** is a popular local gathering spot, featuring a walnut bar from Boston's Ritz-Carlton and a light menu that includes every imaginable cocktail as well as comfort foods like a crispy fish wrap and shepherd's pie. Inquire about pre-performance dinners in connection with the **Stone House Arts Center** (see *Entertainment*) in nearby Brownfield, Maine.

The Brass Heart Inn (603-323-7766; 800-833-9509; thebrassheartinn.com), off Rt. 113, Chocorua. Open for dinner Tue.–Sat. by reservation. The dining room is decorated in attractive wine and ocher colors and has a wood-burning hearth in winter, AC in summer. Entrées change frequently but might include seafood pasta, and rack of lamb. Entrées, including a house salad, warm bread, and a seasonable vegetable, are $14–25. Full liquor license. The pub (Wed.–Fri.) offers more casual fare.

The Wakefield Inn (603-522-8272), 2723 Wakefield Rd. Dinner Memorial Day–Columbus Day weekends, Fri. and Sat. nights by reservation. The dining area overlooks meadows at the rear of this venerable inn. Chef-owner Janel Martin specializes in five-course, prix fixe dinners showcasing her French cuisine. Several choices for each course might include a local goat cheese and leek tart to begin, then flank steak stuffed with spinach, smoked Gouda, and roasted red pepper, ending with lavender crème brûlée. $40–50 includes everything but wine, which is also served.

Sleigh Mill Grille at Snowvillage Inn (603-447-2818; 800-447-4345; snowvillageinn.com), Snowvillage.

EATING OUT

Listed south to north

✪ ♪ **Poor People's Pub** (603-767-9700), junction of Rts. 109 and 153, Sanbornville. Open daily 11–9, until 10 on Fri. and Sat. Since 1974 the Keating family have served up the special food and atmosphere that make this a favorite local gathering spot, a good bet for a sandwich or full meal. Daily specials, pizzas, great sandwiches. Try the Hobo Special: corned beef, Swiss cheese, and sauerkraut on grilled rye.

✪ ♪ **Lino's Café**, Rt. 109 by the tracks in the middle of Sanbornville Village. Open 7–2. A cheery breakfast/lunch stop with booths, superb omelets with homemade bread and hash browns, good burgers, soups and salads.

Mt. View Station (603-539-3993), 79 Main St., Center Ossipee. Open 6–2 Mon.–Thu., until 8 Fri., 7–8 Sat., 7–2 Sun. Gina and Larry Ross operate this friendly restaurant in Center Ossipee's surprisingly large old rail station, a vestige of a once-thriving tourist industry in the village. Check out the photos of privately owned railcars whose owners tend to congregate here before heading for Wolfeboro on the stretch of track out back. Try the B&M special or the clam chowder.

Jake's (603-539-2805), Rt. 16, West Ossipee. Open daily 11–9. Fried fish and seafood platters, pasta; a family restaurant that can be packed in summer.

The Yankee Smokehouse (603-539-7427), junction of Rts. 16 and 25, West Ossipee. An authentic open-pit barbecue and plenty of it. Beef and pork barbecue and other sandwiches. Full dinners, including combination plates with barbecued chicken, beef, pork, and baby back ribs. Wine and pitchers of beer.

✪ **Whittier House** (603-539-4513), junction of Rts. 116 and 25, West Ossipee. Open daily 11:30–9, until 11 Fri.–Sat., open from 8 AM Sun. A Victorian house, the site of a tavern since 1784. An earlier 19th-century counterpart was frequented by poet John Greenleaf Whittier. Inside it's surprisingly spacious and informal, obviously a local favorite. The menu is large, ranging from fish through some tempting vegetarian dishes like Popeye Pie (fresh spinach with almonds, walnuts, and mushrooms topped with puff pastry) to roast prime rib. We can recommend the beef tips. Dinner entrées $15–20. The choice of beers is wide.

Rosie's Restaurant (603-323-8611), 1547 White Mountain Hwy. (Rt. 16), Tamworth. Near White Lake State Park, a local gathering spot year-round for breakfast, also open for lunch, take-out, and ice cream in warm-weather months.

The Chequers Villa (603-323-8686), Rt. 113, south of Tamworth Village. Lunch on weekends, dinners nightly. Reasonably priced pizza, soups, and salads with atmosphere.

✪ ❀ **Daley Café at The Other Store** (603-323-8872), 77 Main St, Tamworth Village. Open daily 8–5, serving breakfast and lunch, this is a

dependable oasis with a counter, a few tables, and a seasonal deck overlooking the Swift River. Owner Kate Thompson shares this space with Indian Mound Hardware and offers a corner full of stationery items, local crafts, and a good selection of books about Tamworth and the area. The soup of the day (the tomato is freshly made, studded with real tomatoes), good sandwiches, pie and ice cream. Inquire about dinners served selected nights, popular in summer before shows at the nearby Barnstormers Theatre. Dinner features locally grown ingredients, BYO wine and beer. Owner Kate Thompson explains that this became known as "the other store" during the many years that it served as an annex to Remick's, as the general store was long known. Tickets are also sold here for ACT performances (see *Entertainment*).

✪ **Eaton Village Store & Restaurant** (603-447-2403), Rt. 153, Eaton Center. Open daily 6–6 with breakfast until 11:30, lunch until 3. The heart of Eaton Center, a combination post office, grocery store, and a pine-paneled restaurant with a long counter and half a dozen tables. Owned by the Eaton Village Preservation Society and operated by Phil Kelly, a White Mountains enthusiast and well-known native of Jackson. A blackboard menu lists "sandwiches particular to the premises," and we can vouch for the turkey, bacon, and cranberry. We understand that this is also a destination drive for burger lovers.

Also see the Palmer House Pub at the Inn at Crystal Lake under *Dining Out*.

THE OTHER STORE, HOME OF DALEY CAFÉ, TAMWORTH

✳ Entertainment

Stone Mountain Arts Center (866-227-6523; stonemountainartscenter.com), 695 Dugway Rd., Brownfield, Me. During Friday variety shows year-round, big-name groups perform in this red barn; check the website for schedule and dining options before shows.

The Arts Council of Tamworth (603-323-8693; artstamworth.org) presents monthly (except summer) performances—from string quartets to vaudeville—in the Tamworth-Sandwich area, mainly at the Barnstormers Theatre. Inquire about Saturday-night contra dancing.

Dances in the Tamworth Town House on summer Sunday afternoons.

Concerts by the River at The Other Store (see *Eating Out*).

✳ Selective Shopping

Chocorua Village Pottery (603-323-7182), 118 Deer Hill Rd. (Rt. 113). Open daily but off-season only Thu.–Sun. 10–5. Myles Grinstead produces a variety of functional tableware and much more. Worth checking.

Stonehedge Farm (603-323-8335), 61 Chocorua Rd., Tamworth. Seasonal source of fresh vegetables, fruits, jams, jellies, eggs, honey, and homemade cotton quilts.

Wakefield Marketplace (603-473-8762), Rt. 16/Wakefield Rd. (across from Palmer's Motel). Weekends Memorial to Columbus Days.

✳ Special Events

January–March: **Dogsled races** are held periodically in this area. Check the New England Sled Dog Club schedule: nesdc.org/events.

February: **Ice Harvesting/Winter Carnival**; contact the Remick Country Doctor Museum and Farm (800-686-6117) for more information.

Fourth of July: The **parade** in Tamworth is big.

August: **Old Home Days** in Freedom; **Tamworth History Day**.

Also see *Entertainment* and special events sponsored by the **Remick Country Doctor Museum and Farm** (800-686-6117; remickmuseum.org) in Tamworth Village.

  ♿ **Barnstormers Theatre** (603-323-8500; barnstormerstheatre.org), 100 Main St., Tamworth Village. The country's oldest professional summer theater, founded in 1930 by Alice and Francis Cleveland, son of the president. Barnstormers stages eight outstanding plays in July and August in the renovated, 282-seat air-conditioned theater. Musicals, some popular plays, and other lesser-known offerings. Dinner theater packages are available with the Daley Café at The Other Store.

The White Mountains

6

WHITE MOUNTAIN
NATIONAL FOREST (WMNF)

MOUNT WASHINGTON AND
ITS VALLEYS

THE WESTERN WHITES

NH State Parks

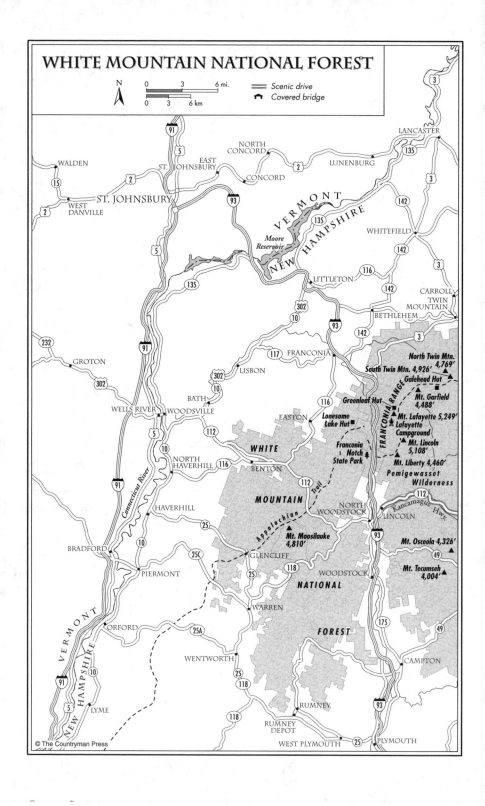

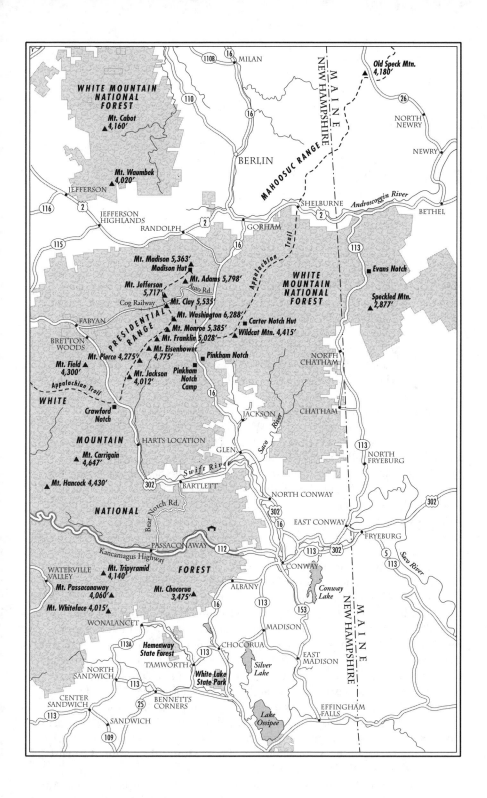

INTRODUCTION

Part of the Appalachian Mountain Range that runs from Maine to Georgia, New England's highest mountains march in a ragged line, heading diagonally northeast across New Hampshire, beginning near the Connecticut River with Mount Moosilauke and extending into Maine. They consist of several ranges among which the best known are the Presidentials, with each peak named for a different president and the highest of all for George Washington. As mountains go, these granite crags and domes are old, rounded by glaciers and "notched" with high passes. The most famous of these notches are Franconia, Crawford, and Pinkham.

In the 18th century several hardy innkeepers opened taverns in Franconia and Crawford Notches. Landscape artists W. H. Bartlett, Benjamin Champney, and Thomas Cole painted this landscape in the 1820s. Thoreau, Emerson, Hawthorne, and Whittier touted the White Mountains through prose and poetry in the 1830s. Starr King's *The Great White Hills*, first serialized in the *Boston Transcript*, brought them local city dwellers in droves, and after the Civil War steam trains linked the White Mountains with every major city in the East. Dozens of mammoth hotels dotted the entire region.

The hotels were patronized by the era's wealthy class, many of whom were also touring the Swiss Alps. It's worth noting that the **Cog Railroad**—"the Railway to the Moon"—was built up the western flank of Mount Washington in 1869, predating any Swiss cogs. The **Appalachian Mountain Club** (AMC) began opening "high huts," patterned on Alpine facilities, in 1888.

The AMC was founded in 1876 by Boston-based hotel patrons to blaze and map hiking trails through the White Mountains. Inevitably their interest in the beauty of the mountains put them on a collision course with the timber companies, which built extensive rail networks through the region to harvest the dense stands of mountain trees. Their clear-cutting technique left the steep mountain slopes denuded, leading to massive erosion and downstream flooding. The limbs and branches left behind in the woods quickly dried and fueled huge forest fires that threatened the uncut areas. The **Society for the Protection of New Hampshire Forests** was created as a spin-off from the AMC to energize support for the first national forest east of the Mississippi. The **White Mountain National Forest** was created by the Weeks Act in 1911.

Like the forests, tourism in the White Mountains proved resilient. World War I, income tax, and the invention of the reasonably priced Model T combined to doom the grand summer hotels, yet as these languished motor courts mushroomed in the 1920s and '30s, serving middle-class families out for a tour in their new cars. From Boston they traveled up Rt. 3 through Franconia Notch (designated as a state park to frame the Old Man of the Mountains in 1928), on up Rt. 3 to Twin Mountain and down along Rt. 302 through Crawford Notch on the other side of Mount Washington, down to North Conway and back down Rt. 16.

Some of the country's first roadside attractions—the Cog Railway and **Carriage Road** up Mount Washington, **Flume Gorge** in Franconia Notch, and **Lost River Gorge** in Kinsman Notch—already lined this route. Gradually these were augmented by many more attractions, ranging from **Clark's Trading Post** in the 1920s and the state-funded **Cannon Mountain Aerial Tramway** in 1938 (conceived as a summer as well as winter operation from the beginning), later by **Story Land, Six Gun City**, and **Santa's Village**. Over the years motels replaced motor courts; beginning in the mid-1980s, the few surviving grand hotels again came into vogue, along with inns and bed & breakfasts. Hiking, which had never ceased to attract enthusiasts, continues to thrive with an expanded AMC support system of shuttles and lodges. Both rock climbing and mountain biking in the WMNF draw athletes from throughout the country.

The White Mountains were also a proving ground for the American ski industry. In February 1905 Norman Libby of Bridgton, Maine, made the first recorded descent on skis of Mount Washington's western slopes, and a Forest Service trail from **Tuckerman's Ravine** (a high snow bowl on the eastern slopes of Mount Washington) drew pioneer skiers. In the 1930s the new sport exploded in popularity: Peckett's-on-Sugar-Hill claims "the country's first ski school," but several ski schools quickly followed in the town of Jackson. Acclaimed Austrian ski instructor Hannes Schneider established his famous ski school in North Conway, attracting hundreds of patrons who arrived every weekend on the "snow train" from Boston.

In the 1960s and '70s a new phenomenon was added to the region's half dozen "Ski areas": condo-based resorts such as **Loon** and **Waterville Valley**, evolving along with the transformation of Rt. 3 into I-93. In the 1970s the interstate brought this Western Whites region an hour closer to Boston, making it more accessible than the Mount Washington Valley, where similar condo clusters have since also turned several of the region's oldest ski areas into "ski resorts." Snowmobiling, tubing, and cross-country skiing have all contributed to their winter appeal for families.

School vacation periods aside, White Mountain ski areas tend to be relatively empty midweek. Summer and fall by contrast bring a steady stream of visitors. Tourists tend to follow the same route popularized in the 1930s, but now—since the opening of the east–west Kancamagus Highway through the heart of the White Mountain National Forest in 1959—it's a loop, "the White Mountain Trail," one of the country's national scenic byways. It continues to access a record number of attractions, both natural and human-made.

WHITE MOUNTAIN NATIONAL FOREST (WMNF)

The 800,000-acre White Mountain National Forest (WMNF) is the largest in the East. Its core 7,000 acres was established in 1918 after public outcry over uncontrolled logging and fires forced passage of the Weeks Act of 1911. Many forms of recreation—hiking, biking, fishing, camping, cross-country skiing, and snowmobiling—are popular within this vast, mountainous, and heavily wooded domain. It attracts more than six million visitors annually, but a national park it isn't. The mission of national forests is to conserve resources through a balance of activities and uses, including wildlife habitat, wilderness, recreation, clean water, timber, and forest products. Unlike national parks where land is set aside for preservation, national forests were set aside for conservation, or the wise use of resources through a balance of activities and uses. Timber harvesting occurs on roughly 0.05 percent of the entire forest at any given time, with approximately 29 million board feet of timber harvested annually. More than half of the forest is unavailable for harvesting, including 149,500 acres of congressionally designated wilderness.

GUIDANCE **The White Mountains Gateway Visitors Center** in Lincoln (603-745-8720; 800-346-3687; visitwhitemountains.com), just off I-93 Exit 32, includes an authentic post-and-beam barn housing a major WMNF information center. It features interactive displays about wildlife-watching and the history of the White Mountain National Forest. Rangers staff a desk (603-745-3816) stocked with hiking, biking, and cross-country maps, also information about biking trails, fishing, and camping. This is a source of the parking passes required within the forest (see *Parking*). The center is open daily year-round 8:30–5, July–Labor Day until 6. This is a great location, handy both to the east–west 34.5-mile-long Kancamagus National Scenic Byway through the heart of the national forest, and to Franconia Notch with its many trails just to the north.

The National Forest website is **fs.fed.us/r9/white**. Information is also available from:

WMNF headquarters (603-536-6100), 71 White Mountain Dr., Campton. Contact them, especially in the off-season, for details of campgrounds, fishing, hiking, or other activities. Visitors services and restrooms are open Mon.–Sat. 8–4:30 daily (weekends are seasonal). Office hours weekdays 8–4:30.

William Davis

LOWER FALLS SCENIC AREA

WMNF Saco Ranger Station (603-447-5448), 33 Kancamagus Hwy., just off Rt. 16, Conway. Open Mon.–Sat. 8–4:30 with restrooms. Rangers dispense timely information about camping, hiking, and biking. Maps, guides, and nature books are sold.

The following ranger stations are open varying hours, depending on the season:

WMNF Androscoggin Ranger Station (603-466-2713), 300 Glen Rd., Gorham. Visitors services and restrooms, weekdays 8–4:30.

WMNF Ammonoosuc Ranger Station (603-869-2626), 660 Trudeau Rd., off Rt. 302, Bethlehem.

AMC Pinkham Notch Camp (603-466-2725; outdoors.org), Rt. 16, Pinkham Notch, and the **AMC Highland Center Lodge at Crawford Notch** (603-466-2727; outdoors.org), Rt. 302, Crawford Notch. Center for hiking and camping information as well as lodging in Crawford Notch.

PARKING The **White Mountain National Forest Recreation Pass**. All unattended vehicles parked on national forest land are required—where signposted—to display a parking pass. In 2010 the fee is $3 a day, $5 per week, $20 for an annual pass; in 2011 fees are slated to rise to $5 per day, $10 per week, $30 for an annual pass, $40 for two cars in one family. Annual senior and access passes apply.

CAMPGROUNDS The WMNF operates 23 campgrounds ranging in size from 7 to 176 sites. No electrical, water, or sewer connections, no camp stores, no playgrounds. Toilets, water, tables, and fireplaces are provided. The sites were designed for tent camping, although trailers and RVs can be accommodated. Most of the campgrounds are open mid-May–mid-Oct., with a few opening earlier and closing later; several are open all winter, though the roads are not plowed. The daily fees range from $16 for a tent site to $20 per campsite on a first-come, first-served basis.

For some, where indicated below, reservations (877-444-6777; recreation.gov) are accepted. The reservation service operates Mar.–Sept. (Mon.–Fri. noon–9 PM, weekends noon–5 PM) and costs $9 in addition to the camping fee. Reservations may be made 120 days before arrival, but 10 days before arrival is the minimum time.

Not to confuse things, **Pro-Sport Inc.** (888-CAMPS-NH) also maintains a website listing campgrounds and offers to make reservations.

The six campgrounds along the **Kancamagus Highway** are among the most popular in the White Mountain National Forest (see *Scenic Drive*); of these, and only Covered Bridge Campground near Conway takes reservations.

Elsewhere in the Western Whites
Campton Family (Exit 28 off I-93; reservations accepted); **Russell Pond** (Tripoli Rd., Campton), **Waterville** (I-93 Exit 28; reservations accepted); **Wildwood** on Rt. 112, west of Lincoln, open mid-Apr.–early Dec., 26 sites, good fishing.

In or near Crawford Notch: Just south of Twin Mountain, off Rt. 302, reservations are accepted at **Sugarloaf I Campground** and **Sugarloaf II**; **Zealand Campground** is first come, first served.

In Pinkham Notch: **Dolly Copp Campground** has 176 sites.

Near Conway: **White Ledge**, Rt. 16, Albany; 28 sites; reservations accepted.

In Evans Notch on the Maine–New Hampshire border (Rt. 113 south of Rt. 2) there are five campgrounds: **Basin** (21 sites), **Cold River** (14 sites), **Crocker Pond** (7 sites), and **Hastings** (24 sites) all accept reservations; **Wild River** is first come, first served.

Backcountry camping is permitted in many areas of the WMNF but generally not within 200 feet of trails, lakes, or streams or within 0.25 mile of roads, most designated campsites or huts, at certain trailheads, or along certain trails. There are also many designated backcountry camping sites, some with shelters, others with tent platforms. The WMNF promotes a carry-in, carry-out, low-impact, leave-no-trace policy for backcountry hikers and campers; fires are prohibited in many areas, and the use of portable cooking stoves is encouraged, if not required. Restricted-use areas, which help protect the backcountry from overuse, are located in many parts of the forest. See fs.fed.us/r9/white for a copy of White Mountain National Forest Backcountry Camping Rules or check out one of the Forest Service's ranger stations listed above.

FISHING The WMNF publishes a comprehensive guide to trout fishing in the forest. More than 30 pond sites are listed, plus suggestions for stream fishing. A New Hampshire fishing license is required. A map showing "Fishing Opportunities on the White Mountain National Forest" can be downloaded from the WMNF website.

HIKING The WMNF is crisscrossed with 1,200 miles of hiking trails, some short and quite easy, others longer, and many challenging even for the most experienced backcountry traveler. A long, difficult section of the Appalachian Trail crosses the forest from the southwest to the northeast corner. The weather on the high mountains of the Presidential and Franconia Ranges can approach winter conditions in any month of the year, so hikers should be well prepared with extra food and proper clothing. Bring your own drinking water since *Giardia lamblia*, a waterborne intestinal bacterium, is found throughout the mountains. Although trails are well marked, a good map or guide is essential. We recommend the *AMC White Mountain Guide* (27th edition) and waterproof detailed maps published by the Appalachian Mountain Club, available locally and at outdoors.org.

Note the option of bunking down along hiking trails through the Presidentials, the highest of the White Mountains, in AMC huts. See *Appalachian Mountain Club* in "What's Where."

WINTER USE **Cross-country and snowshoe** trail maps are available at the nearest ranger stations. In the Western Whites: **Lincoln Woods Trails** at the western end of the Kanc. **Beaver Brook Loops**, a system of three loops in Twin Mountain–Franconia. **Greeley Ponds Trail**, accessible from the Kanc and from Waterville Valley. **Smarts Brook Trail** off Rt. 49 in Waterville Valley.

Elsewhere: **Connie's Way** in Pinkham Notch. **Hayes Copp**, parking at Dolly Copp Campground. **Spruce Goose**, from Zealand parking area.

Downhill skiing is available at Tuckerman's Ravine. For details see "Mount Washington and Its Valleys."

Snowmobiling. Large portions of the WMNF are off-limits to snowmobiling, trail bikes, and off-road vehicles. For details contact the Trails Bureau, New Hampshire Division of Parks and Recreation (603-271-3254; nhtrails.org).

SCENIC DRIVE **Kancamagus National Scenic Byway** (Rt. 112). The 34.5-mile paved highway is open all year, weather conditions permitting, but there are no motorists services on the road. Named for a local 17th-century American Indian chief, the highway was opened in 1959 but not fully paved until 1964. More than 750,000 vehicles travel this route, declared a National Scenic Byway in 1996, every year. On the western side of the mountains, the road begins on Rt. 112 just beyond Loon Mountain Resort (I-93 Exit 32). Stop at the White Mountains Gateway Visitors Center to pick up detailed hiking directions. Beginning at the eastern end on Rt. 16, just south of Conway village, look for the Saco Ranger Station. Both are comprehensive information centers, open daily year-round.

Note: The following descriptions are listed from west to east—Lincoln to Conway.

5 miles east of I-93 Exit 32 in Lincoln: **The Lincoln Woods Information Center** (603-745-3816), 200 Kancamagus Hwy., 5 miles east of Lincoln. This a log cabin ranger station staffed year-round. Stop and walk at least as far as the middle of the suspenion bridge across the Pemigewasset River, frequently a rushing torrent. From here the **Lincoln Woods Trail** follows an old logging railbed along the East Branch of the Pemi (a popular cross-country ski trail in winter), and the **Black Pond Trail** leads to a trout pond. The **Hancock Campground** (50 sites, 35 suitable for RVs) is also here. This marks the southern edge of the Pemigewasset Wilderness, one of the largest wilderness areas in the eastern United States.

7 miles east is the **Big Rock Campground** (28 sites).

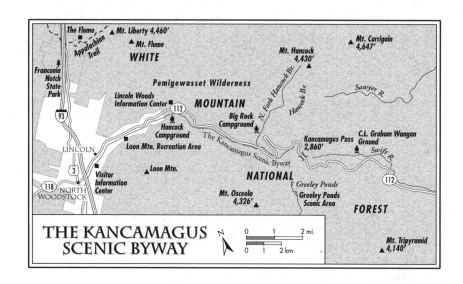

THE KANCAMAGUS SCENIC BYWAY

9 miles east you'll find the trailhead for the **Greeley Ponds Scenic Area**. Both ponds are good trout-fishing and picnicking spots. Hardy hikers and cross-country skiers continue into Waterville Valley.

Here the highway begins a long climb to **Kancamagus Pass** (2,860 feet), the highest point on this route, where there are several scenic lookouts. As you traverse the pass, you leave the valley of the Pemigewasset behind and cross over into the Swift River watershed.

SABBADAY FALLS

William Davis

C. L. Graham Wangan Ground is a picnic spot (a *wangan* was a logging company store) near picturesque **Lily Pond**.

Turn off for **Sabbaday Falls**. The falls are a very pleasant 10-minute hike from the highway. If you have time for only one stop along the Kanc, this is it. The trail is easy, and the falls flow through a gap between towering rock walls. Resist the temptation to swim in the pothole below; there is no swimming allowed here.

The **Russell Colbath House Historic Site** is another rewarding stop. The 1831 restored farmhouse (open daily mid-June–Labor Day, weekends Memorial Day–Columbus Day) is the only homestead remaining and, along with a small nearby cemetery, is all that's left of a once prosperous farming

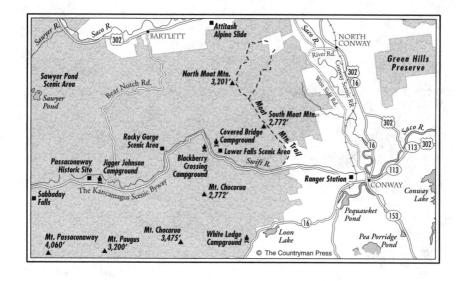

and logging community. The house, furnished with period antiques, is now a museum. A costumed National Forest Service volunteer tells visitors the story of the last resident, Passaconaway's postmistress Ruth Russell Colbath. In 1891 her husband, Thomas Colbath, left the house saying he would be back "in a little while." She never saw him again but kept a light burning in a window to guide him home every night until her death in 1930. Three years later, Thomas turned up and, after trying unsuccessfully to inherit her estate, disappeared again. A Colonial-style post-and-beam barn was recently constructed at the site. It has toilets and picnic tables and is used for ranger lectures and special events. **The Rail 'n' River Trail**, a 0.5-mile interpretive loop from this visitors center, is surprisingly varied. Just east is the Jigger Johnson Campground (74 sites).

12 miles from Rt. 16: **Bear Notch Rd.** (not maintained in winter) diverges right for Bartlett and Rt. 302. This 9.3-mile paved road has several impressive overlooks on its northern end.

About 1.5 miles east is the **Champney Falls Trail** (3.8 miles, three and a half hours) to Mount Chocorua. The falls are an easy 3-mile roundtrip on the lower section of the trail. They are named for Benjamin Champney, founder of the White Mountain School of Painting, who worked in this region of the mountains for more than 60 years.

About 9 miles from Rt. 16 is the **Rocky Gorge Scenic Area**, an interesting geological site where the rushing river has washed its way through the rocks. The footbridge leads to Falls Pond. Barrier-free restrooms, drinking water, and picnic tables are found at the scenic area.

Six miles from Rt. 16: Dugway Rd. diverges right, through the **Albany Covered Bridge** to the WMNF **Covered Bridge Campground** (49 sites, reservations accepted). The Albany covered bridge itself was built in 1858 and renovated in 1970; it is 136 feet long. Near the bridge the **Boulder Loop Nature Trail** (3.1 miles; allow two hours) leaves Dugway Rd. and ascends rocky ledges, offering views up and down the river valley. An informative leaflet, keyed to numbered

William Davis

ROCKY GORGE SCENIC AREA

stations, is available at the Saco Ranger Station. Across the valley is Mount Chocorua, and to its right are Paugus and Passaconaway, named, like the byway itself, for Native American chiefs who once lived in this region. Dugway Rd. can be followed east to a junction with the West Side Rd., just north of Conway village. Midway along this route, the road passes the trailhead for **South Moat Mountain** (2,772 feet), one of our favorite hikes. The 2.3-mile trail (two hours) offers magnificent views in all directions from its open, rocky summit. En route, in-season, can be seen lady's slippers and wild blueberries. This trail follows the long ridge to **North Moat Mountain**, then down to **Diana's Baths** and the River Rd., a total hike of 9.3 miles requiring about 6 hours to the WMNF Covered Bridge Campground. Opposite the junction of the Kancamagus Byway and Dugway Rd. is the **Blackberry Crossing Campground** (26 sites, open year-round; walk-in only in winter), and 0.5 mile west is the **Lower Falls Scenic Area**, which has restrooms, drinking water, and picnic tables. On a summer weekend afternoon you will be amazed at how many people can squeeze onto the rocks at this popular swimming hole. This is not a wilderness experience, but what a treat for people who spend most of their lives in the city!

Continuing east, the road closely parallels the winding, rocky Swift River, offering views across the rushing water to South Moat Mountain.

Also see scenic drives through **Crawford**, **Pinkham**, and **Evans Notches** in "Mount Washington and Its Valleys."

Note: Elsewhere in this chapter are descriptions of the following campgrounds:

White Mountain National Forest Campgrounds in Zealand Valley, 3 miles east of Twin Mountain off Rt. 302 on Zealand Rd. Open mid-May–mid-Oct. **Zealand Valley Campground** (first come, first served) has 11 grass pads, open sites , handicapped-access flush and vault toilets, fire ring, picnic tables and pump water ($16).Off the same access **Sugarloaf I** with 29 sites and flush toilets ($18) and **Sugarloaf II** with 32 sites and vault toilets ($16) can both be reserved (877-444-6777).

MOUNT WASHINGTON AND ITS VALLEYS

INCLUDING MOUNT WASHINGTON, NORTH CONWAY AREA, JACKSON AND PINKHAM NOTCH, CRAWFORD NOTCH, AND BRETTON WOODS

L iterally the high point of New England, Mount Washington has been New Hampshire's top tourist attraction for more than 150 years—despite its frequent cloud crown and temperatures more typical of a mountain three times its 6,288-foot height.

Improbably, its first recorded ascent was in June 1642 by Darby Field of Dover, assisted by Indian guides—only one of whom reluctantly accompanied him all the way to the summit. Local tribes revered the mountain as the seat of the Great Spirit.

Clearly visible from Portland, Maine (more than 60 miles to the east), Mount Washington is the central, pyramid-shaped summit in the White Mountains' Presidential Range, so called because each of its peaks is named for a different president. In 1819 legendary father-and-son innkeepers Abel and Ethan Crawford cut a bridle path (now named for the Crawford family, it's America's oldest continually used hiking trail) up the western side of the mountain, building a log cabin for patrons to rest up before venturing above tree line.

Artists and writers were among early patrons, and their work spread the mountains' fame. Dozens of mammoth hotels soon dotted the immediate area, some accommodating 500 or more guests. Hotel owners bought farms to raise their own produce, generated their own lights and power, built ponds, hiking trails, golf courses, and tennis courts, and maintained post offices. Atop Mount Washington itself a rude shelter was built soon after the bridle path opened and the first hotel, the Summit House, opened in 1852.

"We used to average 100 dinners a day . . . One noon there were representatives of 13 different nations as guests at dinner," its proprietor wrote. A rival, Tip-Top House, opened the next year. In 1861 stages began hauling tourists on the 8-mile-long Mount Washington Carriage Road up the mountain's eastern slopes; by 1869 the Mount Washington Cog Railway ("the world's first mountain-climbing cog railway") began transporting travelers from Bretton Woods at the mountain's

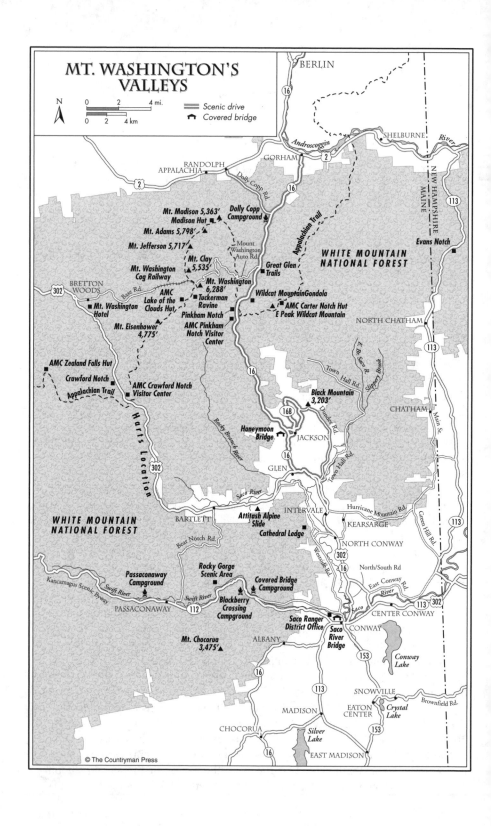

western base. Tradition has it that showman Phineas Taylor Barnum stood atop an observation tower on Mount Washington and, surveying the vista from the Canadian border to the Atlantic, observed the view to be "the second greatest show on earth."

By 1876 it was possible to buy a three-day $17 excursion that included a night at a hotel in Crawford Notch, a transfer to the Cog Railway to ride up Mount Washington, a night in a summit hotel, and then a carriage ride down the eastern side of the mountain to connect with a stage for a trip back to the railroad line.

The year 1876 saw the founding of the Appalachian Mountain Club (the AMC), which has cut, mapped, and maintained hundreds of miles of hiking trails through the White Mountains, erecting a series of eight "high huts," each a day's hike apart. While it's no longer possible to spend the night in a hotel atop Mount Washington, we recommend checking into the AMC's Mizpah Spring Hut off the Crawford Path or the Lake of the Clouds Hut above tree line on Mount Washington. The AMC also maintains appealing, hiker-geared lodging in Pinkham and Crawford Notches.

Unfortunately, most of the area's old hotels have gone the way of the railways. Still, the Omni Mount Washington Resort in Bretton Woods is as grand as ever and now open year-round, complemented by its own major ski area and cross-country trails. The smaller but still elegant Wentworth and the Eagle Mountain House in Jackson are also handy to both alpine and Nordic trails. Roughly the same number of visitors can be accommodated in the Mount Washington Valley today as in the 1890s.

So what and where exactly is the Mount Washington Valley? The promotional name was coined in the 1960s by a Boston publicist and the managers of its then three ski areas (Wildcat, Black Mountain, and Cranmore) specifically for the North Conway–Jackson area, which was known until then as the Eastern Slopes. It has since been expanded to apply to 28 towns surrounding Mount Washington, an area that now includes no less than seven alpine ski areas, six Nordic centers, 200 miles of snowmobiling trails, and, in summer, 12 "family attractions." There are also 10 golf courses, hundreds of miles of hiking and biking trails, 6,500 beds, more than 75 restaurants, and some 200 shops, boutiques, and outlet stores.

Virginia Moore, Mount Washington Observatory

Within this chapter we have divided the Mount Washington Valley into four distinct sections. We begin with "Mount Washington" itself, and an overview of how to explore it.

"North Conway" centers on the area's busiest and best-known village, which has been a summer haven for more than 150 years and in the 1930s became one of the country's first ski resorts, with lifts and trails on Mout Cranmore and a weekend ski train from Boston. It continues to offer the region's widest choice of accommodations, restaurants, and shopping, including the state's largest concentration of factory outlets.

"Jackson and Pinkham Notch" describes the distinctly 19th-century-style resort village with its many appealing lodging options and dramatic high pass that's become a year-round center for outdoor enthusiasts at the eastern base of Mount Washington. "Crawford Notch and Bretton Woods" details sights in this magnificent mountain corridor with its grand old hotel to the west of Mount Washington.

WHEN TO GO The Mount Washington Valley's winter season runs mid-December through February, with busy weekends and school vacations at Christmas and Presidents' Week. Genuine ski/stay bargains are available most weeks, when lodging can be combined with downhill skiing. March can be quite wonderful—off-season prices and plenty of snow—but check conditions before booking. Memorial Day–Labor Day it's consistently busy, but spring is mud season. Foliage peaks early in October. November offers plenty of special promotions and incentives to do your holiday shopping.

GETTING THERE Daily **"🚍" Concord Coach Lines** (800-639-3317; concord coachlines.com) stops daily in North Conway village and at the AMC Pinkham Notch Visitor Center en route from Logan Airport and Boston to Berlin, New Hampshire.

MOUNT WASHINGTON

HIKING GUIDANCE The Appalachian Mountain Club (outdoors.org) maintains two major visitors centers: **Pinkham Notch Visitor Center** at the eastern base of Mount Washington and **Highland Center at Crawford Notch** at the western base. Phone 603-466-2721 for weather, trail, or general information; 603-466-2727 for overnight or workshop reservations at either facility. Both serve as the information hubs for hiking throughout the Presidential Range. The AMC also operates hiker shuttles and maintains a system of eight huts, with the Lake of the Clouds on Mount Washington itself.

WMNF Androscoggin Ranger Station (603-466-2713), Rt. 16, Gorham. Open daily.

The Mount Washington Observatory website, **mountwashington.org**, offers current information about what's open and happening on the summit.

GETTING AROUND The **AMC Hiker Shuttle** operates daily, early June–early Sept., then weekends and holidays until mid-Oct. (no pets). The flat fare is $17 for AMC members, $19 for nonmembers; inquire about the $10-minute fare between specified points. The shuttle consists of two vans, one based at the Pinkham Notch Visitor Center, the second at the Highland Center. By changing at these transfer points, it's possible to reach all the area's major trailheads. It's suggested that you spot your car at the trailhead to which you intend to walk and take a van to the trailhead from which you begin to hike.

New Hampshire State Parks

VISITORS TO MOUNT WASHINGTON STATE PARK

✳ To See

✪ ♿ **Mount Washington State Park**, on the summit of the mountain, is open daily Memorial Day–Columbus Day (no pets). Although most of Mount Washington is part of the White Mountain National Forest, there are several other owners. The state of New Hampshire operates the Sherman Adams Summit Building, named for the former New Hampshire governor who was the chief of staff for President Eisenhower. This contemporary, two-story, curved building sits into the northeastern side of the mountain, offering sweeping views. Park facilities include a gift shop, snack bar, post office, restrooms (all handicapped accessible), and pack room for hikers. The old **Tip-Top House**, originally built as a summit hotel in 1853, has been restored and is open daily (free) as a reminder of the past. Other summit buildings include the transmitter and generator facilities of Channel 8, WMTW-TV, which provides transmitter service for radio stations and relays for state and federal government agencies.

Mount Washington Museum, on the summit. Open daily when the building is open. Located one flight below the main building, the museum is operated by the Mount Washington Observatory and offers historical exhibits and a wealth of scientific information on the meteorology, geology, botany, and biology of the mountain. A small gift shop helps support the activities of the observatory. Fee charged.

Mount Washington Observatory (603-356-2137; mountwashington.org), on the summit. Closed to the public, but members may tour the facility. There are, in fact, thousands of members around the world. With membership ($45 per adult, $70 for a family) comes the thick quarterly bulletin *Windswept* and the right to participate in workshops in subjects ranging from history and photography to geology. This private, nonprofit institution occupies a section of the Sherman Adams

A MOUNTAIN VIEW FROM ONE OF THE
AMC'S HIGH-MOUNTAIN HUTS

Summit Building and is staffed all year by crews of two to three people who rotate each week. Weather observations are taken every three hours, providing a lengthy record of data that extends back to the 1930s, when the institution was formed. In 2010 its long-held record for the highest winds ever recorded (231 mph) was proven to have been upstaged by 253 mph winds recorded during a 1996 typhoon on Barrow Island, Australia, but the observatory still styles itself "home of the world's worst weather." Various ongoing research projects study the effects of icing, aspects of atmospheric physics, and related subjects. The observatory has conducted research for a variety of commercial, institutional, and governmental organizations. Facilities include crew quarters, a weather-instrument room, a radio room, a photography darkroom, and a library. The staffers provide live morning weather reports on several area radio stations, including WMWV 93.5 FM in Conway. Inquire about **Edu-Trips**, permitting visitors to spend the night at the observatory.

✳ To Do

𝒮 **Mount Washington Cog Railway** (603-846-5404; thecog.com). See "Crawford Notch and Bretton Woods."

Mount Washington Auto (Carriage) Road (603-466-3988; mt-washington.com). See "Jackson and Pinkham Notch."

HIKING Mount Washington is crisscrossed with trails, but there are two popular routes. The **Tuckerman Ravine Trail** (4.1 miles, four and a half hours) begins at the AMC Pinkham Notch Camp on Rt. 16. It is nearly a graded path most of the first 2.5 miles as it approaches the ravine; then it climbs steeply up the ravine's headwall and reaches the summit cone for the final ascent to the top. The ravine area has open-sided shelters for up to 86 people, and each person has to carry up everything needed for an overnight stay. (Register at the AMC Pinkham Notch Camp; no reservations.) This is the trail used by spring skiers, and it can be walked as far as the ravine by anyone in reasonably good condition. The beginning of the trail is an easy 0.5-mile walk on a graded path to the pretty Crystal Cascade.

On the western side of Mount Washington is the **Ammonoosuc Ravine Trail** (in combination with Crawford Path, 3.86 miles, four and a half hours). It begins at the Cog Railway Base Station, located off Rt. 302 north of Crawford Notch. About 2.5 miles from the start is the AMC Lake of the Clouds Hut, one of the best areas to view the alpine flowers, near the junction with popular Crawford Path. This trail is 8.2 miles long and requires six hours to reach the summit of Mount Washington. It begins just above Crawford Notch and crosses a new, specially designed suspension bridge. After 2.7 miles comes the cutoff for the AMC Mizpah Spring Hut.

In the vicinity of the **AMC Pinkham Notch Visitor Center**, many short hiking trails are suitable for family groups. Ask for suggestions and directions at the camp. *A few words of caution about hiking on Mount Washington and the Presidential Range.* Most of these trails end up above tree line and should be attempted only by properly equipped hikers. Winter weather conditions can occur above tree line any month of the year. Annually some 50,000 hikers safely reach the summit, many in winter, but hiking is a self-reliant activity; even fair-weather, summer hikers are warned to climb well prepared, with extra clothing and food in addition to maps and a compass. Most of the trails to the summits are 4 to 5 miles in length and require four or five hours to reach the top. Although these trails are not exceptionally long, there is an elevation gain of some 4,000 feet, a distance that becomes painfully evident to those who are not in reasonably good physical condition. Western hikers, used to the higher Rockies, soon appreciate the ruggedness and the elevation change when climbing this mountain. About 100 people have died on these slopes, some from falls while hiking, rock or ice climbing, or skiing; but others have died in summer when they were caught unprepared by rapidly changing weather conditions. Since the weather can be most severe above tree line, cautious hikers will assess the weather conditions when reaching that point on a climb. The AMC provides daily weather information: 603-466-2721, ext. 4.

Since AMC staffers often volunteer for mountain rescues, they are careful to give considered advice to beginning and more experienced hikers. The *AMC White Mountain Guide* has the most comprehensive trail information available for hikers, but also see Daniel Doan and Ruth Doan MacDougall's *50 Hikes in the White Mountains* (Backcountry Guides).

SKIING Tuckerman Ravine (call the Appalachian Mountain Club, 603-466-2727), off Rt. 16, Pinkham Notch. Spring skiing has become an annual rite for many skiers, and there is nowhere better than the steep slopes of Tuckerman Ravine. There are no lifts, so you have to walk more than 3 miles to reach the

MOUNT WASHINGTON

Virginia Moore, Mount Washington Observatory

HIKERS' LODGING

✏ ♿ **Appalachian Mountain Club** (603-466-2727; outdoors.org) offers full-service year-round lodging and meals with discounts for its members in **Joe Dodge Lodge** in Pinkham Notch ($56–96 per adult, $35–52 per child with breakfast and dinner) and at the more luxurious new **Highland Center** in Crawford Notch ($59–174 per adult, $34–60 per child or $30–46 in the neighboring **Shapleigh Bunk House**). It's $70–116 per adult in the eight high huts in the Presidential Range, all accessible only by walking. Theoretically you can spend nine days hiking from one to the next, but in practice patrons usually just spend a night at one or two. June–mid-Sept. all but Carter Notch Hut are "full service," meaning you supply your sheets (or sleeping bag) and towels; they provide meals, bunks, blankets, and educational programs. Nonmember rates are $77–116 per adult, $46–69 per child for the night's stay with dinner and breakfast. Four huts continue to offer full service through mid-Oct. Three huts—Carter Notch, Zealand Falls, and Lonesome Lake—are also open in winter on a self-serve basis ($32–35 per person).

We know **Mizpah Spring Hut** better than the others, but all share the following essentials: Bunks are stacked (at Mizpah it's six to a room), equipped with three army blankets, a mattress, and a bare pillow. The two baths are dorm-style. Everything is immaculate, maintained by the youthful crew who also cook the gargantuan meals. Common space is attractive and well stocked with books, but the big draw here is your fellow hikers, who represent a span of ages

MEALTIME AT THE AMC'S GREENLEAF HUT

Courtesy, Appalachian Mountain Club

and, usually, several European countries. It's the kind of place that draws people together. Frequently a naturalist leads an after-dinner hike. Breakfasts tend to feature fresh-baked breads and crispy bacon. Also accessible from Crawford Notch, **Zealand Falls Hut** is popular with families because it's an easy hike in from Rt. 302 and sited by a waterfall. Serious hikers can continue on to **Galehead Hut** on Garfield Ridge and **Greenleaf Hut** on the western flank of Mount Lafayette. **Lonesome Lake Hut** is also popular with families because it's an easy hour's hike up from Franconia Notch. On Mount Washington itself **Lake of the Clouds** is frequently busy because it's above tree line en route to the summit and favored by Boy Scout troops. On the eastern flank of Mount Washington, **Madison Spring** is the most rugged of the huts, set above the sheer walls of Madison Gulf. **Carter Notch Hut** (open year-round on a self-service basis), the eastern-most hut, lies in a sheltered divide between Wildcat Mountain and Carter Dome. We cheated by taking the Wildcat Mountain Gondola up and walking in from there. For a detailed description of lodging at **Joe Dodge Lodge**, see "Jackson and Pinkham Notch," and for details about **Highland Lodge** see "Crawford Notch and Bretton Woods." *Note:* While all three meals are open to visitors at the Pinkham Notch Visitor Center and at the Highland Center, hikers are not invited to drop in for meals at the high huts.

Advice: If you are not a hardened hiker familiar with the huts, it's wise to check into one of the lodges for your initial night. This gives you a chance to not only recoup from a drive and tune in to the weather but also get valuable suggestions about trails. At Highland Lodge you can also take advantage of the L.L. Bean gear room, supplying guests with equipment from hiking boots to fleece.

THE AMC MAINTAINS EIGHT HUTS IN THE PRESIDENTIAL RANGE

Courtesy, Appalachian Mountain Club

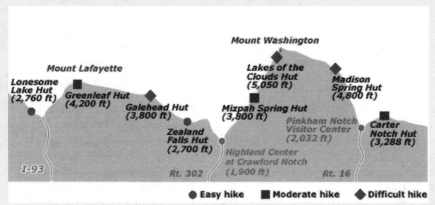

headwall of this cirque, a little valley carved out of the eastern side of Mount Washington by glaciers during the Ice Age. Winds blow snow from the mountain into the ravine, where it settles to a depth of 75 feet or more. When snow has melted from traditional ski slopes, it remains in the ravine; skiers by the thousands walk the 2.4-mile trail from the **AMC Pinkham Notch Visitor Center** to Hermit Lake, then on up to the floor of the bowl. The headwall is another 800 feet up. Skiing begins in early April, and we have seen some diehards skiing the small patches of snow remaining in the ravine in June.

Early in the season, when there is plenty of snow, the steep John Sherburne Ski Trail provides a brisk run from the ravine back to Pinkham Notch Camp. Spring sun warms the air, and many people ski in short-sleeved shirts and shorts, risking sunburn and bruises if they fall. Skiing here is for experts, since a fall on the 35- to 55-degree slopes means a long, dangerous slide to the bottom of the ravine. A volunteer ski patrol is on duty, and WMNF rangers patrol the ravine to watch for avalanches. The three-sided Hermit Lake shelters offer sleeping-bag accommodations for 86 hardy backpackers, who must carry everything up to the site for overnight stays. Winter-use-only (Nov.–Mar.) tent platforms are also available in the ravine. Register for shelters or tent platforms through the **AMC Pinkham Notch Visitor Center** (603-466-2727, no reservations; first-come, first-served only).

SCENIC DRIVE 100 Mile Loop. The 100-mile loop around the Presidentials, New Hampshire's highest mountain range (peaks are named for Presidents Pierce, Eisenhower, Franklin, Monroe, Clay, Jefferson, Adams, and Madison, as well as Washington), is said to be the region's most popular drive. Officially, the loop begins in Conway and heads west along the 34.5-mile **Kancamagus National Scenic Byway** (see p. 420) to Rt. 3 in Lincoln, up through **Franconia Notch State Park** (see p. 436) to Rt. 302 and south through Bretton Woods, passing the **Mount Washington Cog Railroad** and the **Omni Mount Washington Resort**, on down through **Crawford Notch** and back through Bartlett, by **Attitash** and through **North Conway** to Conway.

✳ Special Events

Third Saturday of June: The **Mount Washington Footrace** (603-863-2537; gsrs.com) was first held in 1936 and has been held consecutively since 1966; it's limited by lottery to 1,000 participants. Climb the 7.6-mile Mount Washington Auto Road from Rt. 16 in Pinkham Notch to the summit.

Mid-September: **Mount Washington Bike Race** (603-466-3988; mt-washington.com), Mount Washington Auto Road, Pinkham Notch. This event attracts some of the top US racers. *Note:* The year 2011 marks the 150th anniversary of the Auto Road, and many special events are planned throughout that summer.

NORTH CONWAY AREA

The town of Conway includes the villages of Conway, Kearsarge, and North, East, Center, and South Conway. It is North Conway, however, that dominates the region. A summer haven for more than 150 years and one of the country's first ski destinations, it is also now a major shopping mecca, with some 200 shops and factory outlets. It represents the state's largest concentration of inns, motels, and restaurants.

Early in the 19th century travelers began finding their way to the sleepy farming community in the broad Saco River Valley, the obvious staging ground for "adventure travel" into New England's highest mountains, visible a few miles to the north. By 1825 Conway had five inns, and by the 1850s hotels were sprouting on and around Mount Washington itself. Then in the 1870s rail service reached North Conway and was extended up through Crawford Notch. The town's status as the heart of the White Mountains was secured.

North Conway's most striking building remains its ornate, twin-towered rail station, built in 1874 to serve formally dressed ladies and gentlemen arriving to pass summer weeks and months at literally dozens of local hotels. The station is now the departure point for the seasonal Conway Scenic Railroad, with excursion trains running south along the Saco to Conway and north over Frankenstein's Trestle into Crawford Notch.

Regularly scheduled trains were still running in the 1930s when New Englanders discovered skiing. In 1938 Harvey Gibson, an enterprising North Conway businessman, designed and built the ground-hugging "Skimobile" to ferry skiers up the slopes of Mount Cranmore. A year later he brought famed Austrian instructor Hannes Schneider to town to teach folks how to ski down. Winter visitors came by ski train, found lodging in the village, and walked to the mountain.

The Skimobile is gone, but Mount Cranmore remains a popular family resort for boarding and tubing as well as skiing. The Valley's ski allure now includes extensive trails at Attitash a few minutes' drive (if you know the shortcut) northwest of the village, and there are some 40km of local cross-country trails.

This is one of the few resort areas in northern New England that you can still reach by bus, a service particularly popular with hikers from other countries, but virtually everyone now arrives by car, usually crammed on the way home with purchases.

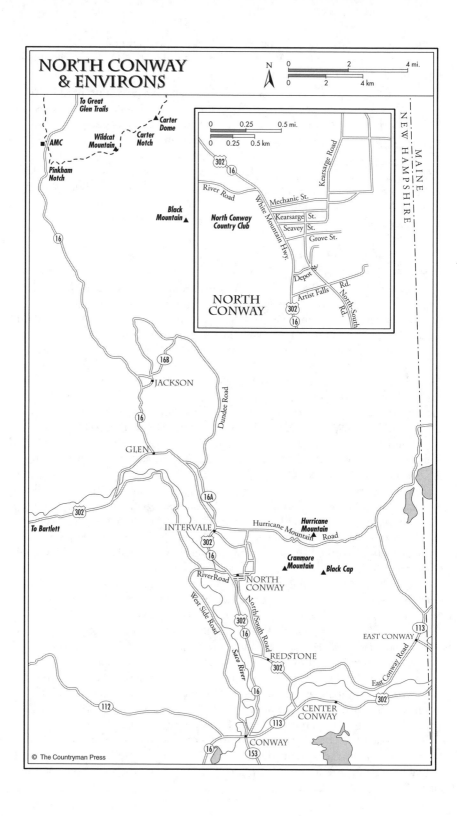

NORTH CONWAY & ENVIRONS

N

0   2   4 mi.

0   2   4 km

MAINE

NEW HAMPSHIRE

To Great
Glen Trails

▲ Carter
Dome

■ AMC

Wildcat
Mountain

Carter
Notch

Pinkham
Notch

Black
Mountain ▲

0   0.25   0.5 mi.

0   0.25   0.5 km

302
16

River Road

Kearsarge Road

White Mountain Hwy.

Mechanic St.

Kearsarge St.

Seavey St.

Grove St.

North Conway
Country Club

Depot St.

Artist Falls

North-South

Rd.

Rd.

NORTH
CONWAY

302
16

16

16B

JACKSON

16

Dundee Road

GLEN

16A

302

To Bartlett

INTERVALE

302

16

Hurricane
Mountain

Hurricane Mountain Road

RiverRoad

Cranmore
Mountain ▲

▲ Black Cap

NORTH
CONWAY

West Side Road

North South Road

Saco River

302
16

EAST CONWAY

113

REDSTONE

302

East Conway Road

112

16

113

CENTER
CONWAY

302

CONWAY

16

153

© The Countryman Press

As late as the 1930s, the strip along Rt. 16 south of North Conway village was a dirt road; but it was the only area left for development. With no zoning, commercial enterprises began appearing. In the 1980s this became one of the major factory outlet strips in New England.

On weekends in foliage season and the during the days just before Christmas, traffic can be stop-and-go on Rt. 16 for several miles north and south of the village. Both the West Side Rd. and a north–south bypass paralleling (to the east) the most traffic-clogged stretch of Rt. 16 are much appreciated by local residents.

Shopping aside, North Conway is a bustling village with an amazingly wide range of lodging and dining options, a hub for biking, climbing, canoeing, kayaking, and family forays. North Conway is what you make of it.

GUIDANCE **Mount Washington Valley Chamber of Commerce & Visitors Bureau** (603-356-5701; 800-367-3364; mtwashingtonvalley.org), Box 2300, North Conway 03860-2300. Free vacation guide, visitors information. The chamber also maintains a walk-in information center on Rt. 16 (Main St./White Mountain Hwy.) in North Conway village, open daily in summer and fall foliage season, weekends all year.

& **State of New Hampshire Information Center**, Rt. 16, at the "scenic vista" of Mount Washington in Intervale, 3 miles north of North Conway Village. This major new information center is open all year, daily until 6, weekends until 11. Restrooms, telephones, elevator, and well-stocked brochure racks and regional displays.

White Mountain National Forest Saco Ranger Station (603-447-5448), on the Kancamagus Hwy. just west of Rt. 16 in Conway. Open year-round from 8 AM, until 5 PM in summer, 4:30 in winter. Pick up maps and information on activities ranging from wildlife-watching to mineral collecting.

Conway Village Chamber of Commerce (603-447-2639; conwaychamber.com), junction of Rt. 16 and W. Main St. at the southern end of Conway village. Open daily in summer, weekends in winter.

See *Guidance* within each section of this chapter for other chambers of commerce.

GETTING THERE *By car:* Rt. 16 is the way from Boston and places south. In Conway it joins Rt. 302, the high road from Portland, Maine (just 62 miles to the east). Also see *Scenic Drives* in "Ossipee Valley" for details about **Rt. 153**, a variation on Rt. 16.

To access the **north–south bypass paralleling Rt. 16** to the east, take a right onto Rt. 302 (Eastman Rd.) at the traffic light at the intersection of Rts. 16 and 302. At the next light take a left onto the bypass, which is signposted to North Conway village. Settlers' Green and other shopping plazas can be accessed at the rear from the byway, and most of the side streets on the east side of Main St. (Mount Washington Hwy.) in the heart of the village connect to it. Coming from the north on Rt. 16, take a left onto Mechanic St. and then the first right onto North-South Rd. The **West Side Rd.**, the alternative and scenic route that also avoids the lights and traffic on Rt. 16, begins in Conway as Washington St., a left at the first light (junction of Rts. 16 and 153). Pass the two covered bridges, and at the fork bear right.

By bus: **⚊ Concord Coach Lines** (800-639-3317; concordcoachlines.com) stops at the Easter Slope Inn, North Conway, en route from Boston and Logan Airport via Manchester, Concord, and Meredith.

MEDICAL EMERGENCY 911 covers the area.

Memorial Hospital (603-356-5461), Rt. 16, north of North Conway village. As you might imagine, this facility has extensive experience in treating skiing injuries! North Conway ambulance: 603-356-6911. Conway ambulance: 603-447-5522.

✳ To See

⚲ **Mount Washington Weather Discovery Center** (603-356-2137; 800-706-0432; mountwashington.org), 2779 Main St. (Rt. 16). Open daily 10–5 through Oct.; closed weekends off-season. Free admission. Look for a brick building adjacent to the Citizens Bank, across from the Eastern Slope Inn on the northern edge of North Conway village. This is an extensive and fascinating museum in which you can experience what it sounded and felt like to be on top of Mount Washington in 231-mile-per-hour winds. A variety of hands-on exhibits illustrate the workings of weather. It's the public outreach center for the world-famous summit observatory.

⚲ **Tin Mountain Conservation Center** (603-447-6991; tinmountain.org), 1245 Bald Hill Rd., Albany. Posted on Rt. 16 just south of the junction with the Kancamagus Hwy., this handsome hilltop facility is a visitor-friendly "nature learning center" with an extensive library and meeting space, the venue for frequent lectures. Built as ecologically as you would expect, using local materials and craftspeople, it's also available for rent. Inquire about free, Wednesday-evening "walks and talks." The setting in a 138-acre trail-laced sanctuary with a pond and a beaver bog. Check the website for current programs.

Historical Society Conway Historical Society (603-447-5551; 800-447-5551; conwayhistory.org), the Eastman-Lord House, 100 Main St., Conway. Open Memorial Day–Labor Day, Wed. 2–4 PM, Thu. 6–8 PM. Donation. The **Eastman-Lord House** features a Victorian parlor and 1940s kitchen, plus local memorabilia and special exhibits, including paintings by 19th-century White Mountain artist Benjamin Champney.

Covered Bridges Saco River Bridge, on Washington St. (turn west at the Rt. 16 lights, junction of Rts. 16 and 153) in Conway village. Bear right at the fork to see this two-span bridge, originally built in 1890, rebuilt a century later. If you bear left (instead) at the fork, you come to the **Swift River bridge**. No longer used for traffic, this 144-foot, 1869 bridge has been restored (after being threatened with demolition) with picnic tables at its entrance, by the river. Covered-bridge buffs may also want to head out 9 miles east from Conway on the Kancamagus Hwy. and turn north at the sign to find the **Albany covered bridge** across the Swift River, dating from 1858. The **Bartlett covered bridge** on Rt. 302, 4.5 miles east of Bartlett village, is also the real thing despite its use as a gift shop. It has been closed to traffic since 1939.

SCENIC DRIVES West Side Rd., running north from the Conway village traffic lights to River Rd. in North Conway, is not only a scenic road that passes two covered bridges, working farms, and mountain views, but also a way to avoid much of the Rt. 16 traffic snarl between Conway and North Conway. In Conway it begins as Washington St., a left at the first light (junction of Rts. 16 and 153). Pass the two covered bridges, and at the fork bear right (a left would lead eventually to the Albany covered bridge on the Kancamagus Hwy.). At the intersection with River Rd., a right brings you quickly into North Conway village at the north end of Main St. Turn left for Echo Lake State Park, Cathedral Ledge, Diana's Baths, and Humphrey's Ledge, and then continue along the Saco River to join Rt. 302 just east of Attitash ski resort in Glen.

Hurricane Mountain Rd. and Evans Notch. For a satisfying day's loop turn east off Rt. 16 onto Hurricane Mountain Rd. It begins in Intervale, 3 miles north of North Conway (just north of the scenic vista turnout). Not for the fainthearted, the road climbs and twists across a ridge (not exactly a mountain ridge, although it is steep) to connect with north–south Green Hill Rd. Turn south (right) if you want the short loop back through East Conway and Redstone to North Conway. Turn north (left) to link up with Rt. 113, in tiny Stow, Maine, and equally rural Chatham, New Hampshire (pop. 274), surrounded by the national forest. Rt. 113 North is not maintained in winter, but it is a smoothly graded road through Evans Notch—one of the lesser known of the White Mountain passes but featuring four campgrounds, many hiking trails, and good fishing along the Wild River.

Cathedral Ledge. A winding, two-lane 1.7-mile-long road leads to the top of Cathedral Ledge with its fabulous view of the valley—an obvious place for a picnic. From the lights at the north end of North Conway village take River Rd. 1.4 miles to the marked turnoff.

Bear Notch Rd. Closed to vehicles in winter, this road through the White Mountain National Forest is a popular shortcut from the Kancamagus Hwy. to Crawford Notch (totally avoiding North Conway). It's also a beautiful woods road, however, and a good place to spot wildlife. From Conway head west on "the Kanc" (Rt. 110) to the turnoff near Jigger Johnson Campground. It meets up with Rt. 302 in Bartlett village.

✳ To Do

✎ **Conway Scenic Railroad** (603-356-5251; 800-232-5251; conwayscenic.com), North Conway village. Runs weekends mid-Apr.–Memorial Day, daily late June–fourth Sat. in Oct. The splendid Victorian North Conway depot, serving passengers 1874–1961, stood boarded and derelict for a dozen years until this excursion train company restored and reopened it as a base for its two trains and three different excursions: the Valley Train south to Conway (11 miles, one hour), and north to Bartlett (21 miles, one and a quarter hours), and the spectacular

CONWAY SCENIC RAILROAD

North Conway through Crawford Notch trip (50 miles, five hours). The latter trip traverses the most spectacular rail route in the Northeast (reservations a must). Lunch and dinner are served in a refurbished steel dining car (see *Dining Out*). The in-service rolling stock includes steam and diesel engines as well as vintage passenger cars and a parlor observation car. Historic buildings include the large turntable, roundhouse, freight house, and the old depot, which has a gift shop and exhibits. Rates begin at $14 per adult, $10 per child on the Conway run; $23 per adult, $16 per child for Bartlett; first-class parlor and dome tickets and meals (both lunch and dinner are offered) are considerably more.

BIKING **Bike the Whites** (800-448-3534; bikethewhites.com). This is a self-guided inn-to-inn biking package with your luggage transported; rentals are available. The distance is 20 miles per day over back roads. The three lodging places are the 1785 Inn in North Conway, Snowvillage Inn in Eaton Center , and the Brass Heart Inn in Tamworth.

Mountain bike rentals are easy to come by at North Conway sports stores, and bicycle routes abound. We can recommend the ride to and around **Echo Lake State Park** and on up or down the West Side Rd. At **Attitash** mountain bikers are welcome seasonally on ski trails. The **Conway Town Trail** (marked in yellow) is a designated recreation trail for mountain biking, running 4 miles along the river. Begin on East Conway Rd. off Rt. 302 in Redstone. Turn right immediately after the Conway Police Station onto Meeting House Hill Rd. for the parking lot. Also see **Whitaker Woods** under *Green Space*.

CANOEING AND KAYAKING The Saco is a popular canoeing river. Many people like to put in from River Rd. (turn west at the traffic lights at the northern edge of North Conway village), then paddle about 8 miles downstream to the Conway village covered bridge. In summer the river is wide and slow, except for light rapids between the Swift River covered bridge and the Conway (second) covered bridge. Take out after the second bridge at Davis Park.

Saco Bound (603-447-2177; sacobound.com), Rt. 302, Center Conway. Rentals, sales, instruction, canoe camping, shuttle service, and guided trips. They also maintain a seasonal information and sales and rental shop on Main St., North Conway.

Northern Extremes Canoe & Kayak (603-356-4718; 877-722-6748; northern extremes.com) in North Conway also offers rentals and Saco River kayak, canoe, and tubing excursions.

Saco Canoe Rental (603-447-2737) specializes in reasonably priced rentals (canoe, kayak, tubes) and shuttle service.

FISHING Brook and brown trout, lake trout, bass, and salmon are the target fish for anglers in this area. Try your luck in the Saco, Cold, or Swift Rivers; Conway Lake, the area's largest, is managed for landlocked salmon (the access is off Mill St. in Center Conway). **Mountain Pond** in Chatham (see *Scenic Drives*) is favored for brook trout. Fishing licenses are required.

North Country Angler (603-356-6000; northcountryangler.com), 2888 White Mountain Hwy. (Rt. 16), North Conway village. "The Biggest Little Fly Fishing

Shop in New Hampshire" offers gear and guiding on the Saco and Ellis Rivers.

Clear Water Fly Shop (603-447-1874), Rt. 16, Conway. New and used equipment, rentals, lessons, guiding.

FOR FAMILIES ✍ & **Story Land** (603-383-4293; storylandnh.com), Rt. 16, Box 1776, Glen 03838. Open daily 10–5 Memorial Day–Labor Day, weekends 9–6; Labor Day–Columbus Day, weekends 10–5. Created some 50 years ago and regularly expanded, Story Land is organized around well-known fairy tales and children's stories. Twenty-one family-friendly rides range from a pirate ship, railroad, and antique autos to an African safari, bamboo chutes, flume, and Dr. Geyser's Remarkable Raft Ride. Cinderella, the Old Woman Who Lived in a Shoe, the Three Little Pigs, and the Billy Goats Gruff are all here, along

White Mountains Visitors Center

with Heidi of the Alps, farm animals to pet and feed, and dozens of other favorites. There is a restaurant, gift shop, and free parking. Admission for those 3 and up is $26.99 per person, $24.99 for seniors, which covers all rides.

✍ **Mount Washington Valley Children's Museum** (603-356-2992; mwv childrensmuseum.org), 2936 White Mountain Hwy. (Rt.16/302), just north of North Conway village. Open Wed.–Sun. varying hours. Geared to children age 8 and under, $5 per person over age 1. An ever-expanding nonprofit resource with plenty to keep youngsters busy for hours: a camera obscura, a giant kaleidoscope, tree house, dress-up and stage, crafts, a reading corner, and more; frequent programs.

✍ **Attitash Alpine Slide, Waterslides, and Mountain Coaster** (603-374-2368; attitash.com), Rt. 302, Bartlett. Open late May–mid-June and Labor Day–early Oct., weekends 10–5; late June–Labor Day, open daily 10–6. A day pass (also good for the skate park, climbing wall, and mountain biking). Great fun for the kids and adults, too. The Alpine Slide includes a ride to the top of the mountain on the ski lift, then a slide down a curving, bowed, 0.75-mile chute on a self-controlled sled. Then cool off in the Aquaboggin Waterslide. New in 2010, the Mountain Coaster carries passengers 1,430 feet up the mountain on stainless-steel rails before dropping 316 vertical feet through a series of banked curves, dips, and straightaways at rider-controlled speeds of up to 25 mph.

✍ **Pirate's Cove Adventure Golf** (603-356-8807; piratescove.net/location16), Rt. 16, North Conway. Open May–mid-Oct. Eighteen-hole miniature golf with plenty of challenges for young and old.

✔ **Banana Village in North Conway** (bananavillage.com), Rt. 16, North Conway. Mini golf, waterslides, and an arcade.

Also see **The Red Jacket Mountain View Resort** (in *Lodging*) with its Kahuna Laguna—a 40,000-square-foot, state-of-the-art water park with four large slides (two you can take tubes in), a wave pool, kiddy area, dump tank, water basketball, and party-sized Jacuzzi. **Wildcat Mountain Gondola Ride** and zipline and the **Mount Washington Auto Road** are described in the "Jackson and Pinkham Notch" section; the **Mount Washington Cog Railway** is in "Crawford Notch and Bretton Woods."

GOLF North Conway Country Club (603-356-9391, pro shop), in the center of the village, North Conway. Eighteen holes.

Hales Location Golf Course 603-356-2140; whitemountainhotel.com), on the West Side Rd. A nine-hole course.

HIKING Black Cap Mountain Path (2.4 miles roundtrip). Highly recommended for young and/or lazy hikers. The trailhead is on Hurricane Mountain Rd., 3.7 miles east of Rt. 16. The trail is through the spruce and beech forest of The Nature Conservancy's Green Hills Preserve to the rocky summit of Black Cap for views north and west to the high peaks of the White Mountains.

Mount Kearsarge North Trail (3.1 miles one way, two and a quarter hours). Mount Kearsarge (elevation 3,268 feet) is just north of North Conway, and this hike has been popular since the turn of the 20th century. From Rt. 16 in Intervale follow Hurricane Mountain Rd. east for 1.5 miles to the trailhead. From the summit fire tower there are views across the Saco River Valley to the Moat Range, Mount Washington, and the Presidential Range.

Also see *Green Space*.

HORSEBACK AND HORSE-DRAWN RIDES Farm by the River Stables (603-356-6640; 888-414-8353), 2555 West Side Rd., North Conway. Year-round horseback rides offered daily, ponies for small children. Geared to novices. $40 per hour. Also wagon rides and sleigh rides ($15 per person).

The Darby Field Inn & Restaurant offers evening carriage rides Fri.–Sun. evening in summer. It's a classy small carriage on a wooded Bald Hill in Conway, with mountain views.

Attitash (603-374-2368; attitash.com) offers guided horseback tours along the Saco River in summer.

ROCK CLIMBING Cathedral Ledge is famous for its many challenging routes, and from the base you can observe climbers inching up its cracks and sheer faces. If you'd like to join the climbers, contact **Eastern Mountain Sports Climbing School** (603-356-5433; emsclimb.com) or **International Mountain Equipment Climbing School** (603-356-7064; ime-usa.com. **Cranmore Sports Center** (603-356-6301; cranmore.com) has an indoor climbing wall and offers instruction programs. If you are already an experienced climber, pick up Ed Webster's *Rock Climbs in the White Mountains of New Hampshire* (Mountain Imagery).

MOOSE-WATCHING MWV Moose Bus Tours (603-662-3159), operated by North Conway native Elwyn Wheaton, offer a safe and sure way to spot moose in and around the valley. Gorham-based **Dan's Scenic Tours** (603-723-2501) offers similar van tours, specializing in Jackson, Pinkham Notch, and points north.

SWIMMING Echo Lake State Park (603-356-2672; nhstateparks.org), West Side Rd., North Conway. Set against the backdrop of White Horse Ledge, this lovely lake offers a sandy beach, picnic area, and changing rooms. Nominal parking fee.

Diana's Baths. Lucy Brook cascades through a series of inviting (if chilly) granite basins below the waterfalls (swimming above is prohibited, because water there is piped into the public water supply). From North Conway follow River Rd. to the turnoff for Cathedral Ledge. A marked, 0.5-mile path leads from the parking lot.

Davis Park, Washington St., Conway. A great swimming beach with picnic tables next to the Saco River covered bridge, plus tennis and basketball courts.

Conway Lake, Center Conway. This is the area's largest lake, and the beach is public.

Saco River at Hussey Field, River Rd., North Conway. Turn onto Weston River Rd. at the light and park by the first bridge. This is a popular swimming hole, minutes from the middle of the village.

✳ Winter Sports

CROSS-COUNTRY SKIING Mount Washington Valley Ski Touring and Snowshoe Foundation (603-356-9920; crosscountryskinh.com). More than 50km of groomed trails through the valley, connecting inns. Rentals and information at **Ragged Mountain Equipment**, Rt. 16/302 in Intervale. Inquire about the chocolate festival in February.

🐾 **Bear Notch Ski Touring Center** (603-374-2277; bearnotchski.com), Rt. 302, Bartlett. With 65km of wooded, groomed trails, warming stations (snacks), and picnic tables, this is a visitor- and pet-friendly center; ski school, guided snowshoe and moonlight tours.

Also see the **Jackson Ski Touring Foundation** (jacksonxc.org), the region's most extensive network; **Great Glen Trails Outdoor Center** (greatglentrails.com) in "Jackson and Pinkham Notch"; and the **Bretton Woods Touring Center** in "Crawford Notch."

DOWNHILL SKIING AND SNOWBOARDING ⚓ **Attitash** (603-374-1960; snow phone 877-677-SNOW; lodging 800-223-SNOW; attitash.com), Rt. 302, Bartlett. This two-mountain ski area boasts New Hampshire's most powerful snow-making system.

Vertical drop: 1,750 feet at Attitash, 1,450 feet at Bear Peak.

Lifts: 11: 3 quads (2 high-speed), 3 triples, 3 doubles, 2 surface.

Trails: 78 trails and glades: 20 percent novice, 47 percent intermediate, 33 percent advanced.

Snowmaking: 98 percent coverage.

AERIAL VIEW OF ATTITASH

Snowboarding: Three terrain park with ramps with a variety of features including table tops, air hits, and jibs, plus a variety of rails.

Facilities: Base lodges with children's services. Three pubs and two cafeterias. Package plans include skiing, lessons, and lodging at the slope-side Grand Summit Resort Hotel and at Attitash Mountain Village with condos for 2 to 14 people, indoor pool, outdoor ice rink.

Lift tickets: Sat. and holidays: $69 adults, $54 juniors, $ 48 seniors. Weekdays: $62 adults, $48 juniors, $39 seniors.

✍ **Cranmore Mountain Resort** (603-356-5543; lodging 800-786-6754; cranmore .com), Skimobile Rd., North Conway. A granddaddy among New England ski areas and still a favorite for its in-town location, sunny and moderate slopes, and night skiing. This is a great family mountain with lift-serviced snow tubing, a relaxed place for anyone to learn to ski or snowboard. The sports center at the bottom is big, tubing is allotted its own space, and two lifts and a high-speed express quad chair have replaced the beloved old Skimobile. Inquire about the Mountain Meister racing series, billed as the largest citizens' racing program in the country, with as many as 800 racers in 15-person teams in two runs competing against one another and against the clock.

Vertical drop: 1,200 feet.

Lifts: Seven: one express quad, one triple, two doubles, one surface lift, two Magic Carpets.

Trails and glades: 50 (36 percent novice, 44 percent intermediate, 20 percent expert).

Snowmaking: 100 percent.

Snowboarding: All trails plus three customized terrain parks, including the highly ranked "Darkside."

Tubing: Seven lift-service lanes.

Night skiing and snowboarding: 12 trails, three lifts, two terrain parks.

Ski school: Cranmore's children's program is a special pride with programs designed to match developmental needs, along with creating a fun atmosphere that helps improve developmental skills.

Facilities: Base lodges with children's center and services; Meister Hut Summit Restaurant, Race Gate Grill, Legends Grill, The Beer & Bratt, Kaffeehous, Café Harvey's Deli, and Benno's Pizza & Pasta Bar; Cranmore Sports Center with indoor tennis courts, pool, exercise equipment, climbing wall; group fitness classes and the Indoor Family Fun Zone open weekends and vacation week; slope-side condos.

Events: Cranapalooza Saturday nights and holiday periods: live music, family activities.

Lift tickets: One price any day: $55 adults (19–64), $42 teens (13–28), $31 children (6–12) and seniors (65+). Ages 5 and under always ski free.

Also see **Wildcat Mountain** and **Black Mountain** in "Jackson and Pinkham Notch," and **Bretton Woods** in "Crawford Notch."

ICE CLIMBING North Conway is a world-class center for ice climbing, said to offer more businesses geared to technical climbing than anywhere else in the country. Foremost is the **International Mountain Equipment Climbing School** (603-356-7064; ime-usa.com), sponsor of the annual February Ice Fest, a series of shows, demonstrations, and clinics.

ICE SKATING The setting and price are hard to beat: **Schouler Park** in the center of North Conway in front of the train station is free. The **Ham Ice Arena**

CRANMORE MOUNTAIN RESORT IS A FAVORITE WITH FAMILIES

(603-447-5886), 87 W. Main St., Conway, is open year-round, featuring a 16-speaker sound system for music, rentals, and a café.

SLEIGH RIDES **The Darby Field Inn & Restaurant** (603-447-2181), off Bald Hill Rd. in Conway, offers sleigh rides in a classy small carriage through woods with mountain views.

Farm by the River B&B (see *Horseback Riding*) also offers sleigh rides.

SNOWMOBILING Corridor 19, one of the state's main snowmobile corridors, crosses Rt. 16 right in North Conway, also accessed from **Bear Notch Trails** (rentals). **Northern Extremes** (603-374-6000; northernextremessnowmobiling .com), 1328 Main St., Bartlett, offers rentals and guided tours. The local club is the Scrub Oak Scramblers (sossc.com).

SNOWSHOEING Snowshoe rentals are available from **Eastern Mountain Sports** (603-356-5433) and **Ragged Mountain Equipment** (603-356-9920).

✳ Green Space

Echo Lake State Park (603-356-2672; nhparks.org), off River Rd., 2 miles west of Rt. 16 in North Conway. Open weekends beginning Memorial Day, then daily late June–Labor Day. A swim beach with picnic tables and bathhouse plus dramatic views across the lake to White Horse (can you see the horse?) Ledge and a 1.7-mile road to the top of 1,150-foot Cathedral Ledge, good for broad views across the valley of the Saco. This is a favorite ascent for rock climbers and a nesting place for rare peregrine falcons, which can sometimes be seen soaring on the updrafts.

Whitaker Woods, Kearsarge Rd., North Conway. North of North Conway village on the east side of Rts. 16/302. A wooded, town-owned conservation area with trails for walking, mountain biking, or winter cross-country skiing.

Diana's Baths, River Rd., 2.2 miles west of North Conway. Watch for a dirt road on your left and park beside the road; it's a short walk to the stream. No swimming above the falls, since this is a public water supply. Lucy Brook has eroded and sculpted the rocks in this beautiful place. Moat Mountain Trail (4.2 miles, three and a half hours) leads to the summit of North Moat Mountain (3,201 feet).

Green Hills Preserve, North Conway. Access from Thompson Rd. with a designated parking area. This is a 2,822-acre preserve belonging to The Nature Conservancy, New Hampshire Chapter. It's home to several rare and endangered plants and a high-elevation stand of red pine. Half a dozen options include the Peaked Mountain Trail (2.1 miles, 1,739 feet) and Middle Mountain Trail (2 miles, 1,857 feet, with excellent views to the south, east, and west).

✳ Lodging

INNS ✪ "T" The Darby Field Inn and Restaurant (603-447-2181; outside New Hampshire 800-426-4147; darbyfield.com), 185 Chase Hill Rd., Albany 03818. Open all year. Operated by Marc and Maria Donaldson since 1979, this classic country inn is named for that intrepid first climber of Mount Washington, whose summit and other high peaks can be seen from the inn.

On a secluded hilltop south of Conway, the inn is set in landscaped grounds and woods that include 15km of cross-country trails. All 13 rooms have private bath; 6 suites now feature Jacuzzi, gas fireplace, TV/VCR, and a balcony with views north to the Presidentials. Rooms vary, and the key factor, to our thinking, is the views: Room 11 on the third floor is small and old-fashioned but has a fireplace and a great view, while Room 12 has all the bells and whistles plus view. The common room has a wood-burning fireplace; there's also an attractive pub with a wood-stove. Dinner (see *Dining Out*) is served by reservation. In summer there's a pool. Carriage and sleigh rides are a specialty, and there are ample hiking and snowshoeing possibilities. Tin Mountain Conservation Center is just down the road, and there's easy access to the Kancamagus. B&B $140–290, depending on the season and room. Add $170 per couple for dinner. Inquire about packages and midweek specials.

✸ **The 1785 Inn** (603-356-9025; 800-421-1785; the1785inn.com), Rt. 16 (mail: Box 1785, North Conway 03860), Intervale. Open all year. The vistas from many guest rooms in this genuine 1785 house are across the Saco River intervale to Mount Washington. Built by a Revolutionary War veteran when there was still plenty of space to choose from, it sits on a knoll with its dining room and guest living rooms, each with a large fireplace, facing the panorama. The inn's 17 rooms, 12 with private bath, have king-sized and double beds. Rooms are comfortably furnished, and some have two beds. Room 5 is a beauty; we also like 7 and 17. You'll definitely want a quiet room in the back of the inn as opposed to one on Rt. 16. The dining room is considered one of the best restaurants

in the valley (see *Dining Out*). There is a swimming pool, and many trails are handy for walking in summer or cross-country skiing. Longtime (since 1983) innkeepers Becky and Charlie Mallar charge $69–219 per couple, including a full breakfast.

✸ "🍴" **Eastern Slopes Inn Resort** (603-356-6321; 800-862-1600; easternslopeinn.com), 2760 White Mountain Hwy., North Conway 03860-0359. This big white Colonial Revival inn, first opened in 1926 in the middle of North Conway, is still the place that the Boston bus stops and a center of village life. Its history is that of this resort village, from its glory days under ownership by Harvey Gibson (see Cranmore Mountain Resort) and the initial home of the Eastern Slope Ski School and Carroll Reed Ski Shop to the bleak 1970s when it closed. The wonder is that it's now not only thriving once more but has been preserved as well as developed by local entrepreneur Joe Berry, who acquired the inn in 1980. He thoroughly renovated it and sold time-shares, doubled the number of units to 222. These vary from standard (lift-serviced) rooms on the upper floors with king or two twin beds in the rambling original inn to luxury suites with gas fireplaces and kitchen facilities in the Carriage House and Whitaker House, also several cottages to the rear of the inn and upstairs in the neighboring vintage buildings housing shops and restaurants. Everything seems efficiently run from the competent 24-hour front desk in the lobby. Amenities include a pool in a glass-sided wing off the lobby, the tiny but popular Frontside Grind (see *Breakfast*) and the Flatbread Company (see *Eating Out*). The Eastern Slope Playhouse (see *Entertainment*) is next door. Rack rates are $99–249 for rooms, $109–319 for cottages/town houses, $189–379 for suites. Packages and deals abound.

○○ 🏖 ∂ ⅊ "ı" **Red Jacket Mountain View Resort, Spa & Water Park** (800-RJACKET; redjacketresorts.com), 2251 White Mountain Hwy. (Rt. 16), North Conway 03860-2000. Set on 40 acres atop Sunset Hill, above the main drag, this 160-room facility has a lot going for it. The property began as a railroad baron's summer estate and has evolved into a sprawling full-service resort. The 148 rooms in the main building have all the basic amenities plus the view; 12 units are two-bedroom town houses. There is also a full-service spa. The lounge and **Champney's** (the restaurant named for the 19th-century artist whose painting hangs there) are at the core of the building, and the large, attractive lobby with its formal front desk is a source of information about frequent special happenings. The most recent addition is Kahuna Laguna, a 40,000-square-foot, state-of-the-art, indoor water park with four large slides (two you can take tubes down), a wave pool, kiddy area, dump tank, water basketball, and 25-person Jacuzzi. **Fox Ridge Resort**, a similar but seasonal 136-room property down the road, shares these facilities and has its own indoor and outdoor pools. Rates range $89–299.

○○ ∂ ⅊ **The White Mountain Hotel and Resort** (603-356-7100; 800-533-6301), West Side Rd. at Hale's Location, Box 1828, North Conway 03860. This is a 1990s motor inn with expansive grounds that include a nine-hole golf course and large condo development, near the base of Cathedral and White Horse Ledges. Geared to groups, tours, and weddings, there are 80 attractive rooms (they include 13 suites and 2 handicapped-accessible rooms), furnished in reproduction antiques, all with AC, TV, and phone. Facilites include an Irish pub, restaurant and lounge, all-season outdoor pool and Jacuzzi, sauna, fitness center, and tennis court. $99–269 per room depending on season and accommodations; many packages.

WATER PARK AT THE RED JACKET MOUNTAIN VIEW RESORT

⚘ **Grand Summit Resort Hotel and Conference Center** (603-374-1900; 888-554-1900; attitash.com), Rt. 302 at Attitash, Bartlett 03812. Located at the base of Attitash, a contemporary condominium resort now under the same ownership as the Eastern Slope Inn. The 143 guest rooms range from units with two queen-sized beds to three-bedroom suites. Most have a full kitchen and dining area. Facilities include a health club, year-round outdoor pool, whirlpool spa, arcade, a full-service restaurant, lounge, and on-site day care. $99–359.

The New England Inn and Resort (603-356-5541; outside New Hampshire 800-826-3466; newenglandinn .com), Rt. 16A, Box 100, Intervale 03845. Open all year. This is a valley landmark, dating back in part to 1809. We found rooms in the old main inn looking a bit tired, but the classic clapboard cabins with fireplaces are still attractive. The most recent addition is the Lodge, a two-story North Woods–style log structure across the road from the inn; rooms are named for woodland animals and feature Jacuzzi. Facilities include **Tuckerman's Tavern** and a swimming pool and fitness center housed in its own building, handy to the cottages.$139–199 for the cottages; $150–250 for the lodge and other adult-only units with Jacuzzi.

BED & BREAKFASTS ✪ ❦ ⚘
Spruce Moose Lodge and Cottages (603-356-6239; 800-600-6239; spruce mooselodge.com), 207 Seavey St., North Conway 03860. Open all year. This sunny, welcoming gabled house on a quiet street near Cranmore Mountain Resort is an easy walk to Main St. Nellie and Leon Filip are your outgoing, helpful hosts. In the lodge itself there are 10 cheery guest rooms, all with private bath and air-conditioning; the grounds also hold two studio "bungalows" with fireplace and Jacuzzi. There's a fireplace in the "great" room where a full breakfast is served and included in the rates ($99 and up). Off it is a well-equipped guest pantry. For families and groups the big appeal here are the three pet-friendly cottages (from $150), each with a full kitchen and living room with gas fireplace and, sleeping four to six people. Inquire about the neighboring Spruce Moose House and Little House, with two- to three-day minimums (but usually rented by the week), dog-friendly and good for up 10. Overall weekend rates are $109–275. Dogs are $10 per night; 20 percent goes to the Conway Area Humane Society.

❦ ⚘ **The Kearsarge Inn** (800-637-0087; kearsargeinn.com), 42 Seavey St. (mail: P.O. Box 9, North Conway 03860). Stuart Dunlap has totally renovated (from the studs up) this 19th-century inn on a quiet side street in the heart of the village. The 15 luxurious rooms and suites fall into four distinct categories, but all are furnished with antiques and reproductions of period furnishings; some have gas fireplace and Jacuzzi. Children of any age are welcome in family-geared suites but must be 12 or older to stay in the main inn. Winter rates: $99–349 (the high end is for the penthouse during Christmas week); summer: $99–259. Ask about golf and other packages. There's a onetime charge for dogs.

♿ **Cabernet Inn** (603-356-4704; 800-866-4704; cabernetinn.com), Rt. 16 (mail: Box 38, Intervale 03845). Begin with an 1840 house, raise it 13 feet, totally renovate and update it, and you have this striking inn just south of the intervale. Innkeepers Bruce and Jessica Zarenko offer 11 guest rooms, all with queen beds, air-conditioning, private phone, and bath. Two rooms have fireplace and Jacuzzi; three with gas fireplace open onto a back deck. One, with a private entrance, is totally handicapped accessible right down to the roll-in shower. There's a formal living room on the entry level as well as a comfortable downstairs den with a 10-foot-high hearth, TV/VCR, fridge, and board games. As with all properties on Rt. 16, we suggest you request a quiet back room with a view. The inn is on the valley's cross-country trail system. No children under 12, please. $90–235 includes a full breakfast.

✒ **Nereledge Inn** (603-356-2831; nereledgeinn.com), River Rd., North Conway 03860. Open all year. Nicely old-fashioned, in a quiet setting by a swimming hole in the Saco River and with a view of Cathedral Ledge, but steps from the summer playhouse and a short walk to the village. There are 11 cheerful but unfussy guest rooms (5 with private bath, 1 with a half-bath). Two adjoining rooms can be converted to a family suite. Guests have use of two comfortable sitting rooms, one with a woodstove, the other with dartboard, TV, and fireplace. This inn appeals to active people: Many of the guests are hikers, rock climbers, and cross-country skiers. Innkeepers Laura Glassover and Steve Hartmann include a full breakfast (served 7:30–9 from a blackboard menu) in the rates: from $75 weekdays, $95 on weekends, $150 for a family of four; children $1 per year to age 16. No smoking. Residents include cats and children.

✒ & **The Buttonwood Inn** (603-356-2625; 800-258-2625; buttonwoodinn.com), Mount Surprise Rd., Box 1817, North Conway 03860. This 1820s farmhouse sits snugly at the end of a road. There are two common rooms, a living room, and a downstairs game room that invites you to kick back in front of the fireplace and large-screen TV (BYOB). An outdoor swimming pool is set in gardens. Bill and Paula Petrone offer 10 guest rooms including 8 suites, 1 with a two-person Jacuzzi and 2 with gas fireplace; all have private bath. Just minutes from Mount Cranmore and Rt. 16, but with an away-from-it-all feel, handy in winter to cross-country trails. $99–299 includes a full breakfast.

The Red Elephant (603-356-3548; 800-642-0749; redelephantinn.com), 28 Locust Lane, Box 1763, North Conway 03860. This attractive gabled house is just of Rt. 16/302 in North Conway but on a quiet street. Nelson and Tana Hall have filled it with antiques and artwork collected in their travels. There are views across the valley from most of its eight well-furnished, air-conditioned rooms, the largest with a gas fireplace and two-person Jacuzzi tub. All rooms have private bath, four have king bed, three have queen, and one has a double bed. There's a swimming pool, a library with bay window, and a den with a big-screen TV and film. Full breakfast. No children under 13 please. $110–225 includes a full breafast.

∞ ✒ **The Farm by the River B&B with Stables** (603-356-2694; 888-414-8353; farmbytheriver.com), 2555 West Side Rd., North Conway 03860. Open all year. Built in 1785 on a land grant from King George III, this picturesque, three-story farmhouse and barn is part of a still-active farm. Surrounded by 70 acres with mountain views and Saco River frontage, the onetime boardinghouse is now a homey inn to which guests return year after year. Each of the 10 rooms, all named for former guests, is decorated with antiques and quilts. Some have a king-sized bed and two-person Jacuzzi bath and fireplace, and there are a couple of two-room suites, good for families. Innkeepers Rick and Charlene Browne-Davis provide horseback riding all year, as well as fall foliage wagon rides, Victorian carriage rides, and sleigh rides in winter. Snowshoes are provided for guest use on the property. Walk to the Saco for swimming and fly-fishing. Rick is a justice of the peace, and weddings are possible. $90–190 double includes a full patio or fireside breakfast.

☀ ✒ ⁗⒈⁗ **Cranmore Mountain Lodge** (603-356-2044; 800-356-3596; cranmoremountainlodge.com), 859 Kearsarge Rd., North Conway 03860. Open all year. This ramblng old inn up the road from Cranmore once belonged to Babe Ruth's daughter, and if it's not taken you can ask for the Babe's old room (number 2). Innkeepers Frederique and Thierry Procyk are French (Frederique is from the Alps) .They offer 20 rooms divided between the lodge and neighboring annex, all with private bath, microwave, and fridge. Several family suites have cooking facilities and sleep up to seven. Rates begin at $89 (the average is $113) and include a full breakfast, cooked to order (there are gluten-free choices), served in the big old-fashioned dining room. Facilities include a seasonal heated pool, year-round hot tub, regulation tennis court, basketball court, and stocked trout pond. Inquire about group rates.

⁗⒈⁗ **Wyatt House Country Inn** (603-356-7977; 800-527-7978; wyatthouse inn.com), P.O. Box 777, 3046 White Mountain Hwy., North Conway 03860. Set back from Rt. 16 north of the village, this expansive house enjoys a beautiful rear view across the valley to the Moat Mountains and north to Mount Washington. Elaine DiRusso and Trish Mansur have the right decor

touch (not too frilly). There are eight guest rooms, all with private bath, and five with two-person Jacuzzi and gas fireplace. No children under age 12, please. $84–190 includes a full breakfast.

⁗⒈⁗ **Glen Oaks Inn** (603-356-9772; 877-854-6535; glenoaksinn.com), 322 Rt. 16A, Intervale 03854. Open all year. Formerly the Forest Inn, this mansard-roofed hostelry has been welcoming guests for 120 years in a quiet byway between North Conway and Jackson. The eight rooms are decorated in country Victorian style with queen bed, private bath, TV, phone, and air-conditioning, some with fireplace. There are also three cottages with similar amenities plus fridge. Innkeepers Linda Trask and Mitch Scher serve a full breakfast and afternoon refreshments. There's an outdoor pool; hiking and cross-country ski trails are out the door. Inn rooms $99–219 depending on room and season, breakfast included.

Note: We have listed a small fraction of the large contemporary motor inns and motels that account for about two-thirds of the lodging options in the Conway area. Check for last-minute deals.

✴ Where to Eat

DINING OUT **Maestro's Café & Deli** (603-356-8790; maestrosnorth conway.com), 3358 White Mountain Hwy. (Rt. 16/302 north of North Conway). No reservations. Open for lunch 11–2:30; dinner 5–9. The local choice for fine dining and good value, this "Country Italian Cuisine" restaurant combines fresh ingredients with delicate flavoring. It's the antithesis of the usual "red sauce." Despite his name, chef Bill Bennett is the genuine article and claims to use recipes handed down through his family and practiced in the

New York restaurants he worked in for many years before opening a small restaurant on a side alley in North Conway village; he moved in 2009 to this expanded space across from Stonehurst Manor. Now there's a patio and windows overlook the Moat Mountains, but the combined lounge and restaurant are still not large. Dinner options include more than a dozen pastas and another dozen meat and seafood entrées. You might begin with Crostone (mushrooms, garlic, and spinach sautéed in olive oil and served on grilled country bread with Romano cheese; $5.75) and dine on vitello Marsala (veal scaloppine sautéed with mushrooms and shallots in a Marsala wine sauce). There are also a wide choice of salads. Dinner entrées $15.25–21.75 with pastas from $11.75 and dinner salads from $11.75. At lunch there are more than 30 sandwich choices on a variety of breads and lunch-sized pastas.The wine selection features Italian labels. Note that the restaurant closes 2:30–5.

White Mountain Cider (603-383-9061; whitemountaincider.com), 207 White Mountain Hwy. (Rt. 302), Glen. Reservations recommended. Open from 5 nightly. Housed in an 1890s farmhouse but with a a contemporary decor, this is a local favorite. Culinary Institute of America grad Teresa Stearns uses local ingredients, varying the menu seasonally. On a winter's evening starters included shaved brussels sprout and celery root salad with shaved Parmesan ($8); entrées, Gorgonzola crusted pork chop with crispy polenta and apple cider sauce ($26). Cider is pressed in the mill here mid-Sept.–early Dec.

The Darby Field Inn and Restaurant (603-447-2181; outside New Hampshire 800-426-4147; darbyfield .com), Bald Hill Rd., Conway. Dinner served weekends 6–9 PM, midweek depending on season; reservations required. Candlelight dining with a superlative view of the Presidentials in the distance (a diagram at the bottom of the menu locates the dozen peaks visible). You might begin with spanakopita or duck spring rolls, then dine on a boneless chicken breast with apple cheddar stuffing, finished with apple cider and maple glaze. Many patrons book a carriage or sleigh ride before, depending on the season (see *To Do*). The half dozen entrées run $21–33.

The 1785 Inn (603-356-9025; 800-421-1785; the1785inn.com), Rt. 16 at the Intervale. Breakfast weekdays 8–9:30; weekends and holidays 7–10. Open nightly for dinner at 5; also lunch during the cross-country season. Dependably outstanding. A wide choice of appetizers might include elk sausage, and among the entrées are such memorable dishes as veal and shrimp in a rum cream sauce with artichoke hearts, sherried rabbit, raspberry duckling, and rack of lamb. The wine list includes some 200 labels. There's a fireplace and, if you request the right table, a view of the intervale and Mount Washington. Entrées $17.85–29.85.

✒ **Bellini's Ristorante** (603-356-7000; bellinis.com), 1857 White Mountain Hwy. (Rt. 16/302), North Conway. Open from 4 PM except Tue. The Marcello family has more than 50 years' experience in the Italian food business, and they use all of their talents in this large and colorful restaurant in the Willow Place shopping plaza. The pasta is imported, but everything else is freshly prepared. All the well-known southern and northern Italian specialties are offered here, including 20 different kinds of pasta and braciola (sirloin rolled and filled with prosciutto, stuffing, garlic, and mozzarella), along with baked minestrone soup. Save room for gelato, canneloni, and tiramisu. Portions are large, but there's a children's menu. Entrées average $16–24.

Stonehurst Manor (603-356-3113; 800-525-9100; stonehurstmanor.com), Rt. 16, North Conway. Dining nightly 5:30–10; reservations suggested. Eat indoors surrounded by elaborate woodwork and stained-glass windows, or outside on the screened patio. In addition to a full menu of classic Continental favorites, offerings include gourmet pizza baked in a wood-fired stone oven. Entrées average $16.75–28.75. Bargain-priced midweek specials are advertised locally.

Decades Steakhouse (603-356-7080; 800-637-0087; decadessteakhouse .com), 32 Seavey St. Known primarily as a steak house, although seafood is also a specialty. The grilled filet mignon is topped by crispy fried onions and served with vegetables and veal demiglaze. Deep-fried jumbo shrimp and fresh haddock come with apple cabbage coleslaw. For some mysterious reason an antique motorcycle is the centerpiece of the dining room. Entrées $17.95–25.95. Martini club and great selection of martinis.

North Conway Scenic Railway (603-256-9009; conwayscenic.com). Weekends beginning late June, daily except Mon. from July 4 to Sept., then a reduced schedule again until foliage season (Sept. 10–Oct. 20). Lunch is served daily on the 11:30 AM run to Bartlett (an hour and 45 minutes) and the 1:30 PM to Conway (55 minutes); dinner on the 6 PM to Bartlett Thu.–Sat. It's a good idea to check the schedule. The venue is the refurbished, steel-exterior, oak-interior, 47-seat dining car *Chocorua*, built in 1922. The luncheon menu features soup or salad and a choice of entrées.

"Sunset" dinner trips to Bartlett, where the dining car is transformed into a deluxe restaurant with white linens and china, include an elegant four-course meal. Reservations strongly recommended for dinner. Full liquor license.

EATING OUT

In Conway village

🍴 🎷 **Horsefeathers** (603-356-2687; horsefeathers.com), Main St. Open daily 11:30 AM–11:30 PM. The best-known hangout and an all-around good bet for a reasonably priced meal in an attractive setting in the middle of the village. The menu is large and varied; the day's from-scratch soup may be curried crab and asparagus. Designer sandwiches like black pastrami with roasted peppers. Salads, pastas, fish-and-chips, plenty of desserts, fully licensed. Great specials. Kids' menu.

🎷 **Hooligan's** (603-356-6110), 21 Kearsage St. Open daily 11 AM–11 PM. "We don't do small," our waitress commented, about the size of our portions: two grilled center-cut chops of boneless pork browned in maple sugar and served with applesauce, mashed potatoes, and crisp green beans ($13.95). On a cold night it was complemented by Guinness on tap (superbly served up with a "clerical collar"). Other options range from burgers to Alaskan king crabs; there's a children's menu. Choose from the paneled dining room or lounge, a popular gathering space since 1984.

✪ 🎷 **Chef's Market of North Conway** (603-356-4747; chefsmarketnorth conway.com), 2723 Main St. Open 11–7, 6 in winter. Chef Bryant Alden presides over the open kitchen in the rear of this old store, creating delicacies like wild mushroom pie, balsamic bistro tenders, and risotto cakes that fill the deli case and are favorite take-homes in the valley. A 13th-generation descendant of *Mayflower* pilgrim John Alden, Bryant has also served as executive chef at some of the Valley's most prestigious hotels. There are also well-spaced tables here, great for a quick and delicious avocado focaccia, or a turkey sandwich with prosciutto and sun-dried mozzarella with pesto mayonnaise on homemade bread. Plenty of choices and a kids' menu.

Bangkok Café (603-356-5566), 2729 White Mountain Hwy. (Main St.). Open for lunch and dinner. Closed Tue. in off-seasons. This pleasant small restaurant has an extensive menu that's mostly Thai but includes some classic Chinese dishes. It gets consistent raves from Asian-food aficionados. Entrées $10.85–17.95. Lunch specials. Beer and wine.

Flatbread Company (603-356-4470; flatbread.net), Eastern Slope Inn, 2760 Main St. Open lunch through dinner. A pleasant space in the back of the hotel, featuring the distinctive pizza developed by the Vermont-based American Flatbread Company, made from 100 percent organically grown wheat and springwater, baked in a special wood-fired clay oven. Sun-dried tomatoes, fresh herbs, goat cheese, and olive oil figure in most of the toppings.

✔ **Rafferty's Restaurant & Pub** (603-356-6460; raffspub.com), 36 Kearsarge St. Open at 11:30 for lunch and dinner; closed Tue. Bright and casual with gluten-free options. Family owned and geared, serving pizza and sandwiches, reasonably priced dinners ranging from pastas to bistro filet.

North of Conway Village
Moat Mountain Smokehouse and Brewing Co. (603-356-6381; moatmountain.com), 3378 White Mountain Hwy. (Rt. 16), North Conway. Open daily for lunch and dinner. A restaurant specializing in its own microbrew

and southern fare like cornmeal-crusted catfish, St. Louis ribs, and a family-style barbecue dinner with generous platters of ribs, brisket, chicken, skillet corn bread, bowls of slaw, garlic mashed potatoes, and, naturally, black beans and rice. Of course you can also get by with a wood-grilled pizza, smokehouse sandwich, or burger, but don't pass up the brew. We lunched sumptuously in a mural-walled room with a view of "the Moats" across the valley.

✔ **The Red Parka Steakhouse & Pub** (603-383-4344; redparkapub.com), Rt. 302, Glen. Open daily 4–10 PM. A favorite with the locals and for après-ski, this is a traditional ski tavern, with skis dating back to the 1930s adorning the walls and ceilings. The motto is: "Good food and good times!" Outdoor dining on the patio. Famous for hand-cut steak and prime rib, the Red Parka Pub also features baked seafood, barbecued spareribs, and varied chicken dishes. An extensive salad bar rounds out the meal; special kids' menu. Open mike night in the pub every Monday plus seasonal events and live entertainment

✔ **Delaney's Hole in the Wall** (603-356-7776), Rt. 16, just 1 mile north of North Conway village. Open 11:30 AM–11 PM. A friendly, informal place, good for panhandle chicken, a portobello wrap, or baby back ribs. Fully licensed. Kids' menu. Sushi (only sushi in the Valley) and live entertainment on Wednesday nights.

South of Conway village
✔ **Shalimar** (603-356-0123), 2197 White Mountain Hwy. (Rt. 16/302). Open for lunch and dinner. Closed Mon. A popular Indian restaurant featuring a wide selection of vegetarian dishes as well as chicken, lamb, beef, and shrimp dishes. There's also a chil-

dren's menu that includes chicken fingers and cheese ravioli. Wine and beer served.

☙ **Muddy Moose Restaurant & Pub** (603-356-7696), 2344 White Mountain Hwy. (Rt. 16/302), North Conway. Open for lunch and dinner. This is a zany, fun place, both in decor and in menu options like buffalo burgers (the real thing), a wide choice of "trail stomping sandwiches," and "potato canoes." You can also have a plain old burger, spareribs, or baked haddock. In summer there's a nice deck.

In Conway

✪ **Chinook Café** (603-447-6300), 80 Main St. (Rt. 16). One of the valley's semi-hidden gems, well known to locals. Open daily 7–3; closing 2 in winter. Owner Laurel Tessier is a well-known chef who also caters and offers cooking classes. Breakfast on a freshly made bagel with caper and dill cream cheese, red onions, and tomatoes, served with sweet tomato home fries— or try polenta and goat cheese, served piping hot with a red bell pepper marmalade. Lunch on a curried chicken salad sandwich on sesame whole wheat, on chickpea latkes, or on white bean and portobello bruschette. The atmosphere is that of a colorful coffeehouse. There's also a bakery.

☙ **Café Noche** (603-447-5050), 147 Main St. (Rt. 16). Open daily 11:30 AM–9 PM. Many rate this the best Mexican restaurant in the North Country, plenty of atmosphere and all the classics, as hot as you like. Mexican beer and mean margaritas. Children's menu.

BREAKFAST ✪ ☙ **Peaches** (603-356-5860; peachesnorthconway.com), S. Main St., North Conway. Open 7–2. If ever there was destination breakfasting, this is it! We can't say enough for this cheery eatery that's larger than it

looks (regulars head for the rooms in the rear with a view). Daily specials are the way to go, judging from our superdelicious veggies-stuffed breakfast crêpe and banana French toast (bananas are cooked into the toast). Coffee flows, service is quick, and the menu is large with many additional lunch options, including BBQ pulled pork and open-faced panini.

☙ **Glen Junction** (603-383-9660; glenjunction.com), Rt. 302, Glen. Open daily 7–3; breakfast served all day. Kids (and adults) are fascinated with the two large-scale model trains that circle the dining rooms on tracks near the ceiling. Designer omelets, specialty sandwiches, apple pie and ice cream.The breakfast specialty is a thin and crispy pancake that fills the plate. Yum!

Priscilla's (603-356-0401; 2541 White Mountain Hwy. (Rt. 16/302), on the south edge of the village, behind the TD Bank. Open 6–2. Longtime Valley residents Carol and Ken Donabedian opened this bright, homey eatery in 2009; they already have an enthusiastic following and get rave reviews. Lunch (starting at 11:30) includes homemade tabouli and large salads served with pita bread.

Staircase Café (603-356-5200), 2649 White Mountain Hwy. (middle of the village). Breakfast and lunch. This place looks good but our breakfast was surprisingly expensive and skimpy, service slow.

COFFEEHOUSES ⁞ **The Met** (603-356-2332; metropolitancoffeehouse .com) is housed in a former bank building in the middle of the village, 2680 White Mountain Hwy. Open 8 AM–10 PM. Walls are hung with local art (for sale); WiFi.

⁞ **Frontside Grind Coffee & Espresso** (603-356-3603; frontside coffee.com), Eastern Slope Inn, North Conway village. Beans roasted on premises; we recommend the "fog lifter" dark roast coffee with a shot of espresso.

OTHER White Mountain Cider Co. (603-383-9061), Rt. 302, Glen. Open 7–5. Sited behind the restaurant (see *Dining Out*) and beside the cider mill, this is a deli take-out with plenty of great sandwiches, panini, and take-home specials (ask about nearby picnicking spots). Still, the reason we never fail to stop here on our way up or down the Valley is the cider doughnuts, simply the best! Wash them down with hot cider in winter.

Wine Thyme (603-356-VINE), 2697 White Mountain Hwy., corner of Kearsarge St. This is a wine bar and shop with 50 botttles by the glass plus tapas, appetizers, lunch, dinner, and weekend breakfast/brunch. It's an especially pleasant place in summer when the patio is used. Portions are small but tasty. Inquire about wine tastings.

✳ Entertainment

✐ **Arts Jubilee** (603-356-9393) offers summer musical performances, weekly afternoon children's programs, and a fall art show. Now at Cranmore Mountain Resort outside by the quad.

THEATER ✐ **Mount Washington Valley Theatre Company** (603-356-5776), Eastern Slope Playhouse, Main St., North Conway. Season: late June–Labor Day. Curtain at 8 PM, $24 tickets, good old chestnuts like *The Music Man* and *A Chorus Line*. Children's theater Friday mornings at 10 and 11:30.

M&D Theatre Productions (603-356-64449), 1857 White Mountain Hwy. (Rt. 16/302), North Conway, a lively community theater that offers plays, youth presentations, and other live entertainment with proceeds benefiting local nonprofits.

FILM Majestic Theater (603-447-5030), 32 Main St. (Rt. 16), Conway village, is a classic 1930s art deco movie hall with first-run movies on two screens.

First-run films can also be viewed at **North Conway Twin Theatre** (603-356-2921), Main St., and at **Mountain Valley Mall Theatre** (603-356-6410), intersection of Rts. 16 and 302.

MUSIC Stone Mountain Arts Center (866-227-6523; stonemountainarts center.com), 695 Dugway Rd., Brownfield, Me. A 200-seat open-timbered music hall is the area's major year-round venue for both name and local performers. Dinner is served but that's not what this place is about. Check the website for current acts and directions from North Conway.

Consult the area's two free newspapers, *The Conway Daily Sun* and *The Mountain Ear*, for current après-ski and other live entertainment. Likely venues include the **Red Parka Steakhouse & Pub**, **Delaney's Hole in the Wall** (see *Eating Out*), and **Tuckerman's Restuarant & Tavern** (603-356-5541) at the New England Inn. Also see "Jackson."

✳ Selective Shopping

OUTLETS From the junction of Rts. 16 and 302 north through North Conway may sometimes be motorist's hell—but it's shopper's heaven, with more than 200 specialty shops and outlets offering substantial savings, further sweetened by New Hampshire's zero sales tax. The outlet boom hit in the 1980s, and most of the leading manufacturers have opened stores here. The largest concentration, with more than

70 stores, is the **Settlers' Green Outlet Village** (settlersgreen.com), open 9–6 weekdays, until 9 Fri. and Sat.; longer hours in summer. The vast complex includes Brooks Brothers, J. Crew, Old Navy, Tommy Hilfiger, Van Heusen, Stonewall Kitchen, and Yankee Candle. The **Red Barn Outlet Center** factory outlet is another smaller complex. **L.L.Bean** (603-356-2100) is at 1390 White Mountain Hwy. (open 10–7, until 8 on Fri. and Sat.). Also see Eastern Mountain Sports under *Sports Equipment*.

ANTIQUES SHOPS **Richard M. Plusch Antiques & Appraisals** (603-356-3333; 603-383-9222), 2584 Main St., North Conway. Period furniture and accessories, glass, sterling, Oriental porcelains, rugs, jewelry, paintings, and prints. Open daily 10–5 in summer, rest of the year Sat. 10–5, Sun. noon–5 or by appointment.

ARTS AND CRAFTS **League of New Hampshire Craftsmen** (603-356-2441), 2526 White Mountain Hwy., North Conway village. Quality handmade crafts including pottery, jewelry, clothing, and furnishings. An added draw is the probability of watching Philip Jacobs at work here, forging glass in his adjoining **Earth & Fire Studio Gallery**. Jacobs specializes in special-order glass sconces but displays a variety of art glass.

Handcrafters Barn (603-356-8996), Rt. 16, North Conway. Open all year. Works by some 250 artisans as well as specialty foods, furniture, garden, and bath items.

White Mountain Artisans Gallery (603-356-6546 or whitemountain artisansgallery.com), 3358 White Mountain Hwy., north of North Conway, showcases art and crafts in a wide variety of media.

SPORTS EQUIPMENT This is New England's prime center for mountaineering equipment. The following is a partial listing.

International Mountain Equipment (603-356-6316; ime-usa.com), S. Main St., North Conway village. One step inside the door and it's obvious that this is no ordinary sports store. The long wall behind the counter is hung with climbing ropes, and the place is filled with specialized gear. We tend to come by in winter when the place is all about ice climbing with programs offered by the IMS Climbing School (603-356-6492), from an intro through steep, as well as guided ascents of Mount Washington. In summer it's all about rock climbing with programs on local ledges. Gear can be sold as well as rented. The school also offers climbing treks to Kilimanjaro and similar peaks.

Eastern Mountain Sports (603-356-5433; ems.com), 1498 White Mountain Hwy. Open daily, hours vary with seasons. This is a vast new store with a climbing wall and full line of skis plus hiking and climbing equipment. The climbing school (emsclimb.com) is here, too. Inquire about local day hikes, winter snowshoeing, hiking with ax and crampons, geocaching, winter camping, and more. Also see emsski.com and emstrek.com.

Joe Jones Ski & Sport (603-356-6474; joejonessports.com), Rt. 16 at the northern end of North Conway village, good for rentals as well as sales.

Ragged Mountain Equipment, Inc. (603-356-3042; 877-772-4433; ragged mountain.com), Rts. 16/302, Intervale. Here you'll find cross-country and snowshoe rentals in winter, plus a full line of equipment that varies with the season. Inquire about ski and snowshoe tours in winter, naturalist-led walks and hikes in summer.

Wild Things (603-356-9453; wild thingsgear.com), 1618 White Mountain Hwy. (Rt. 16), North Conway. Open Sun.–Thu. 10–5, Fri.–Sat. 10–7. Mountaineering equipment, climbing gear, backpacks, cold-weather clothing.

SPECIAL STORES Zeb's General Store (603-356-9294; 800-676-9294; zebs.com), Main St., North Conway village. Ye olde tyme tourist-geared general store with a 67-foot-long candy counter specializing in New England products, some 5,000 of them. Specialty foods top the list, and gift baskets—you assemble your own—are a draw. Upstairs there's plenty more stuff, a great place to browse.

5&10 Cents Store, Main St., North Conway village. This is the real thing: the local five-and-dime under the same family ownership since 1931. Children's books, toys, cards, stationery, and friendly old-timers at the checkout counter.

White Birch Books (603-356-3200; whitebirchbooks.com), 2568 Main St. (just south of Schouler Park). Be sure to stop by this tower-topped house, set back from the street. This attractive full-service independent bookstore is well stocked with everything from children's to travel books with plenty in between. Either Laura or Lucy has read whatever book you ask about, and there are handwritten commentaries attached to many covers. Specialties include New Hampshire, local writers, and all forms of outdoor adventure. The store has the Valley's largest selection of cards; there are also used and bargain books.

Fields of Ambrosia (603-356-3532; fieldsofambrosia.com), 26 Norcross Place (on Schouler Park), North Conway. Soaps, creams, and more body care products are made from plant and vegetable sources by the owner locally.

The shop also carries "**simple sacks**" (simplesacks.com), distinctive small purses made in the village.

Peter Limmer and Sons (603-356-5378), Rt. 16A, Intervale. Open 8–5 except Sun. If anything is a craft item, it is a pair of handmade mountain boots created by the third generation of the Limmer family. The boots are expensive, and you may wait a while for a pair custom-made to fit your feet. "Limmers" have gone from Mount Washington to Mount Everest, and many hikers wouldn't enter the woods without a pair. You'll also find stock shoes.

✳ Special Events

We have primarily listed annual events but not specific dates, which change each year. Contact the Mount Washington Valley Chamber of Commerce (mtwashingtonvalley.org) for details. Cranmore is often the host for professional tennis tournaments, and world-class skiing races are often held at valley ski areas.

March: **March Maple Madness** by the Country Inns of the White Mountains (603-374-2353).

July–Labor Day: **Arts Jubilee**. Free outdoor concerts in At Cranmore Mountain Resort.

Fourth of July: Fireworks and parade in North Conway.

Early September: **World Mud Bowl**, North Conway. Some people enjoy this annual football game, played in knee-deep mud. At least local charities benefit from the proceeds.

Mid-September: **Bark in the Park Expo**, billed as New England's largest pet expo, benefits the Conway Area Humane Society.

Late September: **Sherman Farm Corn Maize**, East Conway (603-939-2412 or shermanfarmnh.com).

First week in October: **Fryeburg Fair**, Fryeburg, Maine. This is a large agricultural fair, with horse and cattle pulling, livestock exhibits and judging, midway, and pari-mutuel harness racing. Just across the border from the Mount Washington Valley, this annual fair attracts a huge crowd in the middle of foliage season.

November: The **Harvest to Holidays Annual Promotion** is a big deal because this is such an obvious place to shop at what otherwise is low season for local shops and restaurants. Lodging and dining bargains, shopping coupons, and special events.

JACKSON AND PINKHAM NOTCH

Pinkham Notch is a high, steep-walled pass between the eastern slopes of the Presidential Range and neighboring mountains. Here Rt. 16 climbs steadily north, threading a 5,600-acre section of the White Mountain National Forest that includes Tuckerman Ravine, famous for spring skiing, adjacent Huntington Ravine, known for winter ice climbing, and the Great Gulf Wilderness, a larger glacial valley surrounded by the state's highest peaks.

Of course you see little of all this if you stick to Rt. 16. Nobody should. More than any other place in New England, Pinkham Notch has become the place ordinary folk come—year-round—to tune in to and engage with New England's highest mountains in all their splendor.

Back in 1861 the 8-mile "Carriage" (now "Auto") Road, billed as "America's first man-made attraction," opened the way for anyone to ride to the summit of Mount Washington, and it remains the route that most visitors take to the top. The hiking hub of the White Mountains, the Appalachian Mountain Club (AMC)'s Pinkham Notch Visitor Center, is just down the road, a place to learn about hiking trails and outdoor skills, to hear a free lecture, or to catch the "hiker's shuttle" that circles the base of Mount Washington, stopping at trailheads. At Wildcat Mountain a four-person gondola hoists passengers to the 4,062-foot summit, from which you can walk a ridge portion of the Appalachian Trail. Great Glen Trails Outdoor Center at the base of the Auto Road offers miles of winter cross-country ski trails that morph into mountain bike trails (rentals available), as well as opportunities for novices to try their hand at fishing or paddling.

Pinkham Notch, moreover, offers year-round access to its spectacular heights. In winter SnowCoaches carry visitors (weather permitting) halfway up the Auto Road, and the AMC Visitors Center is the venue for workshops in winter sports and skills. Wildcat Ski Area offers some of New England's longest and most satisfying trails and boasts eye-level views from its slopes of spectacular Tuckerman Ravine, which becomes a ski mecca in its own right come April and May. Great Glen also draws cross-country skiers and snowshoers.

Just south of Pinkham Notch, Jackson is cradled in the high, horseshoe-shaped Wildcat River Valley. From Rt. 16, the first entrance to the village is through a covered bridge; beyond is a steepled church shouldering the shingled library. Ample village lodging includes the Wentworth Resort Hotel with its adjacent 18-hole golf course. Follow the stream uphill and you come to another nicely restored 19th-century survivor, the Eagle Mountain House. At the top of "the Loop" are newly renovated Whitneys Inn and Black Mountain, New England's only surviving ski hill (and there were many) to be opened behind an inn.

An incubator for alpine skiing in the 1930s (there were also rope tows behind the Wildcat Tavern and Thorn Hill), Jackson is better known today as a cross-country ski destination. The nonprofit Jackson Ski Touring Foundation, founded in 1972 when that sport was in its infancy, presently maintains a 137km trail system.

Thanks to careful zoning and a strong community spirit, the atmosphere in Jackson is relaxing for guests and residents alike.

GUIDANCE Jackson Area Chamber of Commerce (603-383-9356; 800-866-3334; jacksonnh.com), Box 304, Jackson village 03846. Information and reservation system.

The Appalachian Mountain Club Pinkham Notch Visitor Center (603-466-2721; outdoors.org) is a departure point for hiking and other ways of tuning in to this naturally spectacular area. Check out the daily weather information (ext. 773). Also see *To Do*.

GETTING THERE "**1**" **Concord Coach Lines** (800-639-3317; concordcoach lines.com) offers daily bus service from Boston and Logan Airport, with a flag stop on Rt. 16 in Jackson and at the Appalachian Mountain Club's Pinkham Notch Camp.

GETTING AROUND The **AMC Hiker Shuttle** (603-466-2727) operates daily early June–early Sept., then weekends and holidays until mid-Oct., 8–4, based at the Pinkham Notch Visitor Center and serving trailheads throughout the White Mountains. For details, see the "Mount Washington" section.

✳ To See

SCENIC DRIVES Pinkham Notch Scenic Area, Rt. 16, between Jackson and Gorham. Approaching from the Jackson end of the notch, Rt. 16 begins a long, gradual ascent, passing the beginnings of several hiking trails and a few pullouts adjacent to the Ellis River. Watch the ridge of the mountains on the western side, and gradually the huge Glen Boulder becomes silhouetted against the sky. This erratic was dragged to this seemingly precarious spot eons ago by a glacier. Situated at an elevation of about 3,700 feet, the boulder is a 1.5-mile, two-hour hike from the highway, a short but steep climb to tree line. At the top of the notch, the mountainside drops steeply to the east and allows a panoramic view south down the Ellis River Valley toward Conway and Mount Chocorua. Across this valley rises the long ridge of Wildcat Mountain. Just ahead is a parking lot for Glen Ellis Falls, one of the picturesque highlights of the notch. To see the falls, cross under the highway by the short tunnel, then walk 0.2 mile down a short trail to the base of the falls.

North along Rt. 16, as the highway skirts along the side of Mount Washington, are the **AMC Pinkham Notch Visitor Center**, then **Wildcat Mountain** (with summer and fall mountain ziplines and gondola rides) and the **Mount Washington Auto Road** at the Glen. Here is one of the most magnificent views in all the mountains. At left can be seen the summit of Mount Washington, although it doesn't appear to be the highest spot around. Rising clockwise above the **Great Gulf**—another glacial valley—are **Mounts Clay, Jefferson, Adams** (the state's second highest peak), and **Madison**. Rt. 16 continues north to Gorham, passing en route the WMNF Dolly Copp Campground and the entrance to Pinkham B (Dolly Copp) Rd., which connects to Rt. 2 at Randolph. Just north of Pinkham Notch, several hiking trails head east into the Carter Range. One, the Nineteen Mile Brook Trail (3.8 miles, two and a half hours), leads to the AMC Carter Notch Hut, another full-service facility. It is also open on a self-service, caretaker basis in winter.

Jackson Loop. This 5-mile circuit drive begins in Jackson village. Follow Rt. 16B at the schoolhouse, up the hill with views across the valley to Whitney's; then turn left for a couple of miles to Carter Notch Rd., where you turn left again, past the Eagle Mountain House and Jackson Falls, before reaching the village. For a variation on this drive, turn right at Whitney's, and right again at Black Mountain onto Dundee Rd., which changes to gravel now and again as it passes abandoned farms and mountain scenery en route to Intervale at Rt. 16A. Turn right and pick up Thorn Hill Rd. to return to Jackson.

WATERFALLS Glen Ellis Falls, On Rt. 16 look for the parking area 0.7 mile south of Pinkham Notch (2 miles south of Wildcat). It's also marked for the Glen Boulder and Wildcat Ridge Trails. Follow the tunnel under the highway. Turn right; it's 0.2 mile to the spot at which the Ellis River drops 64 feet to the basin below.

Crystal Cascade. Park at the AMC Pinkham Notch Camp (Rt. 16) and follow the Tuckerman Ravine Trail to the left of the Trading Post. The falls, 0.3 mile uphill, are two-tiered, dropping 60 feet and then 20 more at a spot where the river angles 90 degrees.

Thompson Falls. From the Wildcat Ski Area parking lot (Rt. 16) follow the "Way of Wildcat" nature trail 0.7 mile. This is a series of falls along Thompson Brook.

Jackson Falls, Carter Notch Rd. (off Rt. 16A), Jackson. See *Swimming*.

✳ To Do

The Appalachian Mountain Club Pinkham Notch Visitor Center (603-466-2721; outdoors.org). Opened in 1920 and expanded several times since, this complex (alias Pinkham Notch Camp) is the North Country headquarters for an organization of some 90,000 members (the main office is in Boston). Members receive the AMC's several publications and discounts on its many books, maps, hikes and workshops, and accommodations, which include a variety of family "camps" (inquire about **Cold River Camp** in Chatham) and **Joe Dodge Lodge** as well as at their eight high huts, each spaced a day's hike apart in the White Mountains (see *Hikers' Lodging* in "Mount Washington"). Everyone is, however, welcome to use AMC facilities and to participate in their programs. With its trained staff and large membership, the AMC is one of New England's strongest conservation voices, promoting the protection and enjoyment of the mountains, rivers, and trails throughout the Northeast.

In the **visitors center** a diorama of the Presidential Range presents an overview of the area's hiking trails. The center also sells hiking guidebooks and maps and posts the day's weather and trail conditions. Three daily meals (see *Eating Out*) are served up in the big open-timbered dining hall, which is also the venue for year-round free evening lectures on a broad range of topics (including slide shows on

MOUNT WASHINGTON AUTO ROAD AND GREAT GLEN TRAILS

(603-466-3988; mt-wash ington.com), Rt. 16, Pinkham Notch. The Auto Road is open daily, weather permitting, early May–mid-Oct., 7:30–6 most of the summer, with shorter hours earlier and later in the season; in winter, 8:30–3:15.

Courtesy, Mount Washington Auto Road

HORSE CAR MEETS AUTO ON THE MOUNT WASHINGTON CARRIAGE ROAD C. 1910

The Mount Washington Carriage Road opened in 1861, and for its first 50 years a 12-person wagon pulled by six horses carried passengers to the summit. arrival advent of the Cog Railroad in 1869 cut into business, but with the advent of the motorcar its popularity revived. The first motorized ascent in 1899 was by F. O. Stanley of Stanley Steamer fame. The 8-mile, graded road climbs steadily, without steep pitches but with an average grade of 12 percent, from the Glen to the summit. Although the road is narrow in spots and skirts some steep slopes, it has a remarkable safety record and annually carries some 100,000 visitors.

Most (but not all) passenger cars are permitted to make the climb to the summit. A one-and-a-half-hour guided tour in chauffeur-driven vans, "stages" to keep alive a historical tradition, is also offered. On the rainy June day that we took the stage, private vehicles were not permitted. Our driver narrated mountain facts and history as we climbed above the clouds; at a pull-out we watched a rainbow arching over the Great Gulf *beneath* us.

The **Great Glen Trails Outdoors Center** opened in 1995, serving as a spacious base lodge for both the Auto Road and **Great Glen Trails** (see *Biking* and *Cross-Country Skiing*). It stands near the site of the Glen House, first opened in 1852. Three increasingly grand versions of this hotel succumbed to fire, and the fourth closed in

PIERCE ARROWS AT THE STAGE OFFICE, 1920S

Courtesy, Mount Washington Auto Road

Courtesy, Mount Washington Auto Road

MOUNT WASHINGTON AUTO ROAD SNOWCOACH

the 1960s. At this writing construction is set to begin on the fifth rendition of this hotel, a full-service 80-room facility.

The wonder is that all this has been under the same ownership since 1906, perhaps explaining why—throughout the current operation—there's such a palpable sense of pride. The base lodge includes the **Glen View Café**, a cafeteria-style amenity with unexpectedly good soups, sandwiches, and specials and a first-rate sports shop. Downstairs a sports desk serves as rental and check-in point for winter cross-country skiers and summer mountain bikers. A real gem, the **Red Barn Museum** out back displays an amazing collection of vintage vehicles. These include an original 1870s Abbot-Downing Concord Coach and a 12-passenger Mountain Wagon, which was the original and signature transport on the Carriage Road. Also worth noting: a 1918 Pierce-Arrow from the '20s fleet, a 1938 Ford Woody Station Wagon, and a 1963 International Travelall.

Passenger-car rates in 2010: $23 for car and driver, $8 each additional passenger, $6 ages 5–12, includes an audio tour in English, French, or German. Guided tour: $29 adults, $25 seniors, $12 ages 5–12. $14 for motorcycle and driver. In winter the SnowCoaches—vans specially designed for the ascent—transports you up the Auto Road to just above tree line, with a view down into the Great Gulf Wilderness ($45 per adult, $30 per child).

FABYAN HOUSE STAGE IN THE RED BARN MUSEUM
Chris Tree

exploring the world's backcountry). In the neighboring Joe Dodge Lodge you'll find year-round workshops on outdoor skills, ranging from hiking, skiing, snowshoeing, woods crafts, and canoeing to bird study, photography, art, and writing. These vary in length from a few hours to a few days. This is also pickup point for the **Hiker Shuttle** (see *Getting Around*).

Note: Because AMC staffers often volunteer for mountain rescues, they are careful to give considered advice to hikers. The *AMC White Mountain Guide* has the most comprehensive trail information available for hikers, but also see Daniel Doan and Ruth Doan MacDougall's *50 Hikes in the White Mountains.*

AERIAL RIDES Wildcat Mountain Gondola Ride (603-466-3326; skiwildcat .com), Rt. 16, Pinkham Notch. In summer and fall (weekends Memorial Day weekend–mid-June, then daily through mid-Oct.) Wildcat's quad chair is replaced by a gondola that hoists visitors to the summit, with a viewing platform of Mount Washington and a trail along the ridge. **The Ziprider** with four cables is another way to take in the view, descending 2,100 feet over the trails, treetops, and Peabody River to a landing platform near the base lodge. Riders travel at speeds of up to 45 mph.

CANOEING/KAYAKING Golf Wentworth Resort Golf Club (603-383-9641; thewentworth.com), Jackson village. Eighteen holes, with pro shop, club and cart rentals, full lunch available. Call for tee times.

Eagle Mountain House (603-383-9111; 800-966-5779; eaglemt.com), Carter Notch Rd., Jackson. Among New Hampshire's prettiest nine-hole courses, rated 32 by the USGA, these links lie on the tumbling Wildcat River with elevated tees and great views.There's a small pro shop and driving range.

FISHING Great Glen Outdoor Center (603-466-2333; greatglentrails.com) offers an introduction, based at its pond; also guided canoe, driftboat, and wading trips to North Country waters. Open daily 9–5.

HIKING Mount Washington is crisscrossed with trails, but by far the most popular is the **Tuckerman Ravine Trail** (see "Mount Washington"), beginning at the AMC Pinkham Notch Camp on Rt. 16. We also recommend **Eagle Mountain Path** (1 mile, 50 minutes) beginning behind the Eagle Mountain House (see *Lodging*) in Jackson. **Black Mountain Ski Trail** (1.7 miles, an hour and 45 minutes) begins on Carter Notch Rd., 3.7 miles from the village. It leads to a cabin and a knob that offers a fine view of Mount Washington. **North Doublehead**, via the Doublehead Ski Trail, begins on Dundee Rd., 2.9 miles from the village, and follows an old ski trail to the WMNF Doublehead cabin on the wooded summit. A path leads to a good view east, and by using the Old Path and the New Path, you can make a roundtrip hike from Dundee Rd. over both North and South Doublehead and back to the road. To North Doublehead, 1.8 miles and an hour and 45 minutes hours; a roundtrip to both summits is about 4.3 miles and four hours. **Rocky Branch Trail** makes a loop from Jericho Rd. off Rt. 302 in Glen to Rt. 16 north of Dana Place. We suggest walking the Jericho Rd. end (turn off 302 in Glen and follow the road about 4.3 miles to the trailhead), which follows the brook for a couple of miles to a shelter. Allow two hours to make the roundtrip on a smooth trail. The Rocky Branch is one of the better trout-fishing brooks, and in spring it is prime wildflower country (look but don't pick!).

HORSEBACK RIDING Black Mountain Stables (603-383-4491), Rt. 16B. Memorial Day–Halloween. Trail rides geared to novices depart five times daily ($45). There are also pony and overnight rides.

MASSAGE AND YOGA Finding a local massage therapist is not a problem. According to Shana Myers, the first in Jackson a dozen years ago, there are now some 35 in the Mount Washington Valley. Note the full-service spas at the Thorn Hill Inn. Myers operates **Moondance Massage** (603-383-9377; moondancemassage.info), Rt. 16 across from the covered bridge. Inquire about joining a regularly scheduled yoga class.

MOUNTAIN BIKING Great Glen Trails Outdoor Center (603-466-2333; greatglentrails.com), Rt. 16, Pinkham Notch. In summer the 25-mile network of cross-country trails is smoothly graded, perfect for beginning to intermediate bikers and their families. Rentals include a special attachment that turns an adult bike into a tandem bike so small children can ride, too. Inquire about biking workshops.

PADDLING Great Glen Trails Outdoor Center (see above) offers canoeing and kayaking trips on the Androscoggin River and elsewhere north of the Notch.

SWIMMING ✔ At **Jackson Falls**, above Jackson village, the mountain-cool Wildcat River tumbles over rocky outcrops, forming several glorious swimming holes. **Rocky Branch Brook**, just off Rt. 302 in Glen, is another favorite spot. Watch for Jericho Rd.; follow it to the Rocky Branch Trailhead and walk about 50 yards back along the river toward Rt. 302.

✳ Winter Sports

CROSS-COUNTRY SKIING AND SNOWSHOEING ✔ **Jackson Ski Touring Foundation** (603-383-9355; 800-927-6697; jacksonxc.org), Rt. 16A, Jackson. This nonprofit organization promotes the sport of cross-country skiing and maintains some 148km of groomed (doubletrack) trails, the most extensive in the East. The trails range in elevation from 755 to 4,000 feet and from easy to difficult, so be sure to consult the map before heading off. The popular **Ellis River Trail** heads from the center north to Dana Place Inn and loops back through the woods or up along the Hall Trail and out along a ridge with great views. Even in snow droughts this section of the trails

SKIERS IN JACKSON VILLAGE
Thom Perkins. Jackson Ski Touring Foundation Photo

SNOW TUBING AT GREAT GLEN TRAILS
OUTDOOR CENTER

can be groomed to replicate fresh snowfall. Honest. We just tested it and were totally amazed. Our favorite is the **East Pasture Loop** with great views down East Branch Valley. Expert back-country skiers (again, conditions permitting) can also access the **Wildcat Valley Trail**, dropping down into the valley from the top of the Wildcat Ski Area's quad chair to that summit. Also check out The Wave. It's part of Jackson's FIS-approved competition trail system—one of only three fully certified FIS facilities in the United States. The touring foundation's center is on the golf course in the middle of the village and includes a family-friendly base lodge with retail and rental shop, also changing rooms with showers. Inquire about guided tours, clinics, and races. Trail fees and memberships pay for trail maintenance and improvements. $19 adult trail fee, $8 ages 10–15; $15 seniors. Rental pulk sleds are available to pull small children behind. There is an extensive system of separate snowshoeing trails.

Great Glen Trails Outdoor Center (603-466-2333; greatglentrails.com), Rt. 16, Pinkham Notch, Gorham 03581. Open daily 8:30–4:40. Located at the base of the Mount Washington Auto Road, 25km of wide trails groomed for skate skiing, diagonal stride, or snowshoeing, plus 26 miles of backcountry trails. Heated cabins with sundecks are spaced along the trail. A spacious base lodge offers a café, climbing wall, rentals, and ski shop. Lessons are offered. Snow tubing is also available. Experienced snowshoers, skiers, and telemarkers inquire about taking the SnowCoaches 4 miles up the Auto Road and skiing or snowshoeing down. Adult ski passes are $18; $12 junior and senior.

AMC Pinkham Notch Visitor Center (603-466-2727; outdoors.org). Many miles of ungroomed cross-country trails are found in Pinkham Notch. Ask advice at the AMC Visitors Center and pick up a copy of the AMC Winter Trails map detailing cross-country and snowshoeing trails in the area.

SNOWSHOEING Trails are available at all three centers described above; also on the **Tin Mountain Conservation Snowshoe Trails** (tinmountain.org), Tin Mine Rd., Albany.

Nestlenook Estate Resort (603-383-0845), 66 Dinsmore Rd., Jackson, offers rentals as well as a trail network (trail passes: $6).

DOWNHILL SKIING Wildcat Mountain (603-466-3326; lodging 800-255-6439; skiwildcat.com), Rt. 16, Pinkham Notch, Jackson. North-facing Wildcat gets and holds snow, and its 2,112-foot vertical drop makes for some of the longest continuous runs in the East. The 4,100-foot-high mountain faces Mount Washington's eastern slopes across Pinkham Notch, with spectacular views of Tuckerman

Ravine. Surrounded by national forest, it retains a "pure" feeling and enjoys a dedicated following. Lifts and grooming are thoroughly up to date. The Wildcat Trail, cut by the Civilian Conservation Corps in 1933, was ranked among the toughest racing trails in the United States, but Wildcat the ski area didn't open until 1957. It was founded by a small group of former ski racers who cut fall-line black diamond trails. While it continues to appeal to expert skiers (many regulars know off-piste routes down), it also offers "Polecat," a 2.75-mile run from the summit, gently canted in such a way as to nudge even the most nervous novice into step with gravity and that soaring sense of what it means to ski. It's also a favorite with telemarkers and skiers of every level. Longtime legendary manager Stan Judge designed several other intermediate trails, noteworthy for the way they curve naturally with the contours of the mountain, a rarity among modern ski trails. March can be glorious here, and Wildcat is usually the last New Hampshire ski area to close.

Vertical drop: 2,112 feet.

Lifts: One high-speed detachable quad, three triple chairs.

Trails and glades: 47 on 225 acres (25 percent novice, 45 percent intermediate, 30 percent expert).

Snowmaking: 90 percent coverage.

Facilties: Base lodge with ski shop, rentals, lockers, pub and snack bar, ski school.

For children: Lion's Den Kids' Ski & Snowboard School (ages 5–12), Lion Cubs ski & snow-play program (ages 3–5), Lion Cubs Nursery Sitting Service (ages 2 months–5 years).

Lift tickets: Any day: $65 adults, $55 teens, $39 juniors/seniors.

✦ **Black Mountain** (603-383-4490; 800-698-4490; snow phone 603-475-4669; blackmt.com), Rt. 16B, Jackson. A historic New Hampshire ski area, dating from the 1930s when Bill Whitney hooked 75 shovel handles to an overhead cable, the better to haul skiers up his hill. Now a haven for families in search of a small, quiet mountain. Trails off the 3,303-foot-high summit include several double diamonds.

Vertical drop: 1,100 feet.

Lifts: Double and triple chairlifts and a T-bar.

Trails: 40 trails and glades on 143 acres.

POWDER SKIING AT WILDCAT MOUNTAIN
Brooks Dodge-Wildcat Mountain

Snowmaking: 95 percent snowmaking.

Facilities: Base lodge with ski and snowboard school, rentals, and a connection (conditions permitting) to Jackson's 139km of cross-country trails. Dining and lodging at the base in Whitneys' Inn, also slope-side condominiums.

For children: Kids' programs and child care.

Lift tickets: $39 adults, $25 juniors/seniors on weekends; free ages 5 and under; weekdays $29 adults, $20 juniors/seniors; family pass $99 weekends, $79 midweek.

Also see Attitash Ski Area in the "North Conway Area," and Tuckerman Ravine in "Mount Washington."

ICE SKATING *&* A town-maintained ice-skating rink is located in the center of the village across from the grammar school, and **Nestlenook Estate Resort** (see below) has rentals and skating for a fee. The Wentworth resort, across from the library, has a rink open to the public as well as guests and rents skis.

SLEIGH RIDES *&* **Nestlenook Estate Resort** (603-383-9443; nestlenook farm.com), Dinsmore Rd., Jackson village. Daily except Fri.–Sat. and holidays, conditions permitting; 25 minutes takes you through the woods beside the Ellis River in a 25-person rustic sleigh or a smaller open sleigh. Wheels are added for summer rides.

WINTER WORKSHOPS **The AMC Pinkham Notch Visitor Center** (603-466-2727; outdoors.org) and Joe Dodge Lodge serve as a base for midweek and weekend workshops in cross-country skiing, telemarking, snowshoeing, winter camping, ice climbing, tracking, winter photography, and more.

✴ Lodging

RESORTS *&* **Wentworth–An Elegant Country Inn** (603-383-9700; 800-637-0013; thewentworth.com), Jackson village 03846. Dating back to the 1860s and accommodating 400 people at its height as a self-contained summer resort (with its own farm, electric plant, greenhouse, orchestra, and golf course), the 55-room Wentworth has been reborn as a smaller, friendly, comfortable, but still-grand inn. Over the years Swiss-born and -trained owner-manager Fritz Koeppel has transformed rooms one by one, adding bells and whistles like Jacuzzis, hot tubs, and gas fireplaces as well as air-conditioning and discreetly hidden cable flat-screen TVs, furnishing each in a different combination of reproduction antiques. Guest rooms are divided among the handsome three-story main building and several adjoining, neighboring annexes. In summer the long porch is lined with wicker rockers, decked in flowers, shaded by green-and-white-striped awnings. Guests can take advantage of the heated pool or walk to the river for a dip in the cool mountain water of the Wildcat River. The Wentworth's golf course is 18 holes; its clubhouse doubles as the winter lodge for the **Jackson Ski Touring Foundation**. Guests can also walk to tennis and to several lunch options "downtown." Breakfast and dinner are served in the hotel dining room, and food is very much a part of the experience (see *Dining Out*). Rooms are $194–354 including a four-course menu for two as well as breakfast; the

VIEW FROM THE PORCH AT EAGLE MOUNTAIN HOUSE

Chris Tree

B&B rate is $134–264. Inquire about renting one of the 14 two- and three-room condominiums that adjoin the property, overlooking the golf course.

✪ ⌒ 🐾 ⌀ ⁰₁⁰ **Eagle Mountain House** (603-383-9111; 800-966-5779; eaglemt.com), Carter Notch Rd., Jackson 03846. Open all year. Established in 1879, this "baby grand" White Mountains hotel in its present form with an immense veranda opened in 1916 and has been sensitively renovated. The ambience is gracious but not stiff, and the essentials are up to date. Rooms are furnished in country pine and cheery prints, 30 with queen beds and 30 with two doubles plus 30 suites (with a queen and foldout couch), all with private bath, phone, WiFi, and cable TV. We hated to leave our snug third-floor room (there's a lift) with its view up the valley. There is a nine-hole golf course (see *Golf*), lighted tennis courts, an exercise room with sauna and hot tub, and heated outdoor pool. Winter guests can step off onto the Jackson Touring Foundation's extensive trail system, but be forewarned:

It's a delightful downhill to the center, but you will want a ride back up. Unwind in the **Eagle Landing Pub**, where lunch is served. Breakfast, Sunday brunch, and dinner are in Highfields Tavern, the inn's dining room (see *Dining Out*). $129–189 per room in high seasons (summer, fall, and winter seasons), $189–229 per suite, but check out the many packages including

EAGLE MOUNTAIN HOUSE

Chris Tree

breakfast, dinner, skiing, golf, and more. Children 18 and under stay free in the same room with parent. Arrangements to bring pets must be confirmed in advance.

∞ ☻ ♪ "1" **Whitneys' Inn** (603-383-8916; 800-677-5737; whitneysinn.com), 357 Black Mountain Rd. (Rt. 16B), Jackson 03846. First opened as a summer boardinghouse in 1894, this became one of the country's first ski inns in the 1930s when Bill Whitney installed a motorized lift with shovel handles for skiers to grasp on their way up Black Mountain (see *Skiing*) just behind the inn. Now there's both alpine and cross-country skiing (Jackson Touring Foundation trails are easily accessible) all winter. The top-of-the-valley location is appealing in summer and fall when horseback-riding treks originate at the Black Mountain Stables. Since acquiring the inn in 2007 Don and Joyce Bilger have totally renovated the rambling main building main building with its 16 upstairs rooms and many common spaces. The rooms here have king beds and are freshly furnished in hickory, pine log, and farmhouse decors. Eight two-room family suites in Lift Line Lodge have a bedroom with a queen bed and a pullout in the living room with its stone (gas) fireplace and mini kitchen. Two-bedroom cottages also have fireplace and flat-screen cable TV. There are two pet-friendly cottages. The remodeled barn houses the Shovel Handle Pub (see *Eating Out*), a hot après-ski spot and popular as an informal dining spot year-round. In summer there are lawn games, a trout-stocked mountain pond with kayaks and a heated pool for swimming, and tennis and volleyball courts. The dinner menu (see *Dining Out*) changes seasonally. Rooms from $109 off-season, $139–289 per couple during peak periods, with a full breakfast served in spacious inn dining room. Reasonably priced ski packages.

INNS The Inn at Thorn Hill & Spa (603-383-4242; 603-383-6448; 800-289-8990; innatthornhill.com), Thorn Hill Rd., Jackson village 03846. Open all year. Long considered one of New Hampshire's most romantic inns, this 1895 mansion, designed by Stanford White, was completely rebuilt and upgraded after a fire in 2002 and offers "luxury with a view." Innkeepers Jim and Ibby Cooper took great pains to preserve the inn's Victorian character, retaining the gambrel roof, adding gables and a turret. The number of rooms was also increased and spa facilities added. All 16 rooms in the main inn now have Jacuzzi tub, fireplace, TV, and traditional decor. There are six more rooms in the Carriage House (four with Jacuzzi) plus three deluxe cottages, all with fireplace, Jacuzzi, and outside deck and/or screened porch. Common areas include an attractive bar and lounge that serves an à la carte menu and has a wide selection of wine by the glass. (The inn's wine cellar holds 2,500 bottles.) The main dining room seats 75 and has a view down the valley to the village and across the hills to Mount Washington. Dining nightly 6–9 (see *Dining Out*). Swim in the inn pool, have a restorative spa treatment, relax in the outdoor hot tub, or cross-country ski from the door. The village is a short walk down the hill. MAP $169–440 depending on season and accommodations; various package plans including ones for the spa.

Christmas Farm Inn & Spa (603-383-4313; 800-443-5837; christmasfarminn.com), P.O. Box CC, Rt. 16B, Jackson 03846. Among the oldest inns in Jackson, Christmas Farm offers a choice between traditional rooms and the Carriage House with luxury suites, a fitness center, and a full-service spa.

There are now 41 guest rooms and cottages. The main inn incorporated the original 1786 farmhouse (given as a Christmas present, hence the name) and adjacent saltbox. Each has nine rooms, and there are four loft suites in the nearby old barn. A two-room log cabin, a two-room sugarhouse (it looks like a dollhouse and is popular with honeymooners), and 5 two-bedroom cottages suitable for families are also scattered around the grounds; there are also 12 suites in the Carriage House, all with king-sized bed, whirlpool tub, gas fireplace, and either private deck or patio. B&B rates are $163–373, double occupancy. MAP and spa packages are available.

✦ **Wildcat Inn & Tavern** (603-383-4245; 800-228-4245; wildcattavern .com), Rt. 16A, Jackson village 03846. Open all year. Nothing fancy but if you like to be in the middle of everything, try this old favorite, the 1930s home of the Jackson Ski School. Walk to cross-country skiing, shopping, golf, or tennis; the tavern offers folk music on weekends. Rooms are cozy, with queen beds and small private bath, cable TV, and AC. Half a dozen suites have a small sitting room; there's also a two-bedroom cottage, "the Igloo." Beware rooms over the Tavern unless you are a night owl. Rates include morning coffee and juice, but for breakfast guests head next door to Yesteryears (see *Eating Out*). The restaurant is open nightly in summer, otherwise check (see *Dining Out*), and the tavern is the true village gathering place. Summer: $69–99 for rooms, $79–119 for suites; $149–229 for the Igloo. Winter: $70–159 for rooms, $69–109 for suites, $109–269 for the Igloo. Cheaper off-season. Many packages.

BED & BREAKFASTS "ʏ" **The Inn at Jackson** (603-383-4321; 800-289-

8600; innatjackson.com), Jackson village 03846. Open all year. This Stanford White–designed mansion is a couples-geared beauty overlooking the village. Innkeepers Don and Joyce Bilger have brought in professional decorators to brighten up the old inn while retaining its character. The dining room has been opened up by incorporating a former sunporch and has a panoramic view of the village and the mountains. There are 14 large, well-furnished rooms, all with private bath. Second-floor rooms are Victorian themed and have gas fireplace and tastefully recessed TV. Less expensive but quite cozy third-floor rooms are "lodge style" with wood-paneled walls. Amenities include a downstairs parlor with fireplace and overstuffed armchairs, a second-floor common room with Internet access, and an outdoor hot tub. Cross-country ski from the door; walk to lunch or dinner. A full breakfast is served with a choice of hot entrées. Children ages 8 and up are welcome. B&B $129–249. Inquire about packages.

✪ "ʏ" **The Inn at Ellis River** (800-233-8309; innatellisriver.com), 17 Harriman Rd., Box 656, Jackson 03846. Open all year. Off Rt. 16, beside its namesake river, this turn-of-the-20th-century farmhouse is a real find. Frank Baker and Lyn Norris-Baker have created a comfortable, special-occasion kind of place. There are 20 air-conditioned rooms with period furnishings, 18 with gas, electric, or wood-burning fireplaces, 9 with two-person Jacuzzi. Request a river view. There is a heated outdoor swimming pool with adjacent sauna, and a Jacuzzi overlooking the river. You can swim or fish in the river, relax in the gazebo, or cross-country ski. A full breakfast with two hot entrées and afternoon snacks are included in the rates, $119–189 for rooms without, $139 for those with fireplace, $180–299 for Jacuzzi rooms and suites. Not appropriate for children under 12 years.

⁰ɪ⁰ **Carter Notch Inn** (603-383-9630; 800-794-9434; carternotchinn.com), 163 Carter Notch Rd., Jackson 03846. Perched on a hillside overlooking the Wildcat River Valley beside Eagle Mountain House, this attractive B&B offers a wraparound front porch, a living room with a wood fire, seven air-conditioned guest rooms, and a hot tub on the back deck—not to mention plenty of old-time nostalgia. Brits Sally Carter and Dick Green vacationed in the area for many years before making the big move and are enthusiastic hosts. Rates are $99–250 and include a full country breakfast.

Snowflake Inn (603-383-8259; 888-383-1020; thesnowflakeinnjackson .com), Main St., Jackson village 03846. Jackson's newest inn is all about romance. The 20 "suites for two" all have gas fireplace and two-person Jacuzzi. Packages include "candles and petals" (call for details) and in-room massage. The yellow-clapboard inn is in the very middle of the village, with a spacious common area and a small, jet-fed indoor pool. $169–375, depending on room and season.

The Blake House (603-383-9057; blakehousebandb.com), 15 Blake House Dr. (off Rt. 16), Jackson 03846. Open all year. Sarah Blake Maynard's father built this place as a ski cabin in the 1930s, and it now offers four rooms with two shared baths. Set back from the highway and surrounded by white birches, this is a quiet, woodsy place frequented by hikers and skiers. One room has a king-sized bed, one has a double with a separate screened porch, others have twins. The guest living room has cozy chairs, TV, VCR, books, games, and a fireplace, while the dining room features a huge win-

dow overlooking the forest and the rushing Sand Hill Brook. Breakfast is an expanded continental offering with fresh fruit and breads, hot and cold cereals, and egg dishes featuring eggs from Sarah's chickens. $70–90 most of the year; $120 peak times.

⁰ɪ⁰ **Windy Hill Bed & Breakfast** (603-383-8917; 877-728-8927), P.O. Box 462, Black Mountain Rd., Jackson 03846. The town's most secluded lodging option, 2.5 miles up the valley from the village, a find for hikers and cross-country skiers. This is a farmhouse with three guest rooms, each with private bath, two accommodating couples and the third with an extra bed. $75–100 includes breakfast. In fall and winter dinner can be arranged with prior notice ($15–20). Vegetarian options at both meals.

OTHER 🐾 🐕 ♿ ⁰ɪ⁰ **The Lodge at Jackson Village** (603-383-0999; 800-233-5634; lodgeatjacksonvillage.com), P.O. Box 59, 153 White Mountain Hwy. (Rt. 16), Jackson 03846. Open all year. Inspired by the area's Colonial architecture, this 32-room motor lodge offers mountain views, air-conditioning, cable television, telephone, and refrigerator. Dana and Cathi Belcher

HIKERS SNACK AT THE AMC'S PINKHAM NOTCH CENTER

Chris Tree

pride themselves on offering "old fash-ioned hospitality with modern com-fort" as well as award-winning gardens. There's a pretty pool and gardens, ten-nis courts, an outdoor hot tub, and an 18-hole golf course/cross-country ski trails across the road. $129–199 per room during ski season, $149–209 in summer. More during foliage, less off-season.

🛶 ♿ **Appalachian Mountain Club Pinkham Notch Visitor Center** (603-466-2727; outdoors.org), Rt. 16, Pinkham Notch, Box 298, Gorham 03581. This is a full-service facility offering three all-you-can-eat meals, bunk beds, and shared baths. Knotty-pine-walled bunk rooms for two, three, and four people accommodate more than 100 guests in the Joe Dodge Lodge. A few family rooms have a dou-ble bed and three bunks. Handicapped accessible. Geared to outdoors people (hikers, skiers, and such), it is cheerful (quilts, curtains, and reading lights) and comfortable, with a library and a huge fireplace in the living room and a game room with a children's corner (educa-tional games and nature books). The main-lodge dining area is another gath-ering area. Free lectures nightly after dinner in July and August and Wed. and Sat. throughout winter. Families are encouraged. Open to AMC mem-bers and the general public. Reserva-tions are recommended. $50–60 for nonmember adults without meals; inquire about packages. For nonmem-bers breakfast is $11.50, trail lunch $9.50, and dinner $22. For information about the eight full-service mountain huts (only reached by walking) main-tained by the AMC in the White Mountain National Forest, see *Hiker's Lodging* in "Mount Washington."

Nordic Village Resort (603-383-9101; 800-472-5207; nordicvillage

.com), Rt. 16, Jackson 03846. This resort complex is a mix of condo clus-ters. Units feature fireplace, two-per-son Jacuzzi, and cooking facilities (ranging from token to full); facilities include indoor pools and four-season outdoor pools, tennis, and skiing (trails connect with the Jackson Touring Foundation system). Check the web-site for a wide choice of packages.

CAMPGROUNDS WMNF Dolly Copp Campground (603-466-3984; campsnh.com/dollycopp.htm), Rt. 16, Pinkham Notch, Gorham 03581. Open mid-May–first week in Oct.; camping fee is $18. Some of the 176 sites are available through the National Recre-ation Reservation Service (877-444-6777; reserveusa.com). There is a $10 charge for changing or canceling reser-vations. The reservation service oper-ates Mar.–Sept.

✳ Where to Eat

DINING OUT ✪ The Thompson House Eatery (603-383-9341), 193 Main St., Jackson village. Lunch 11:30–3.30, dinner 5:30–10 except Mon. Check off-season. Reservations accepted. The ambience in this 1790 eatery overlooking the golf course is casual, colorful, and comfortable. There's patio dining in summer and a glowing woodstove in winter, when it's the perfect place for a lunch break from cross-country skiing, with sun streaming in through stained glass. It's the food, however, that makes this the top choice with locals. Since 1977 chef-owner Larry Baima has been preparing locally sourced, distinctive, and imaginative combination sand-wiches, soups, salads, and dinner entrées. At dinner try the natural, boneless duck breast pan browned and served with smoked duck sausage, spinach, and fresh sage risotto, topped with homemade blood orange and sweet pepper marmalade. Entrées come with salad and fresh bread, $16.95–31.95. Lunch salads and sandwiches average $10.

Inn at Thorn Hill & Spa (603-383-4242; 603-383-6448; 800-289-8990; innatthornhill.com), Thorn Hill Rd., Jackson village. Open all year. Dining by reservation nightly 6–9. The menu, characterized as New England fusion cuisine, includes an award-winning wine list and changes biweekly. You might start with a goat cheese crêpe ($11), and dine on seafood risotto with mussels, shrimp, and calamari, served with grilled asparagus. Entrées $24–32. A lighter menu is served in the lounge.

Wentworth—An Elegant Country Inn (603-383-9700; 800-637-0013; thewentworth.com), Jackson village. Dinner served 6–9; reservations recommended. Jackets are not required, but jeans, T-shirts, and the like are considered inappropriate in this gracious dining room. Chef Brian Gaza came to the Wentworth from the upscale Boston Harbor Hotel and knows his craft. Appetizers might include coriander-crusted boneless wild boar ribs; entrée choices, beef short ribs braised in Pinot Noir, and homemade Asiago cheese tortello with melted leeks, spinach, and tomato concassé. Entrées $20–29. The extensive wine list has earned the *Wine Spectator* Award of Excellence.

Wildcat Inn (603-383-4245; wildcattavern.com), Jackson village. The inn dining room is open for dinner all year. Entrées might range from pasta primavera to filet mignon, $19.95–29.95. Also see Wildcat Tavern under *Eating Out.*

♪ **Highfields Tavern at Eagle Mountain House** (603-383-9111; eaglemt.com), Carter Notch Rd., Jackson. This is a classic old hotel dining room with paneling, chandeliers, and picture windows letting in the view—but it's also a comfortable place for families, with well-spaced tables and a reasonably priced menu ranging from linguine and meatballs to glazed duckling ($12–27). The Sunday champagne brunch served 10–1 is a Valley-wide favorite. $17.95 adults, $7.95 under age 12.

Also see **Libby's Bistro**, destination dining in Gorham, in "Northern White Mountains."

EATING OUT ✪ ♪ Shovel Handle Pub (800-677-5737 whitneysinn.com), Rt. 16B, Jackson. Housed in the inn's multilevel rustic barn at the base of Black Mountain, this has become one of the most popular places for evening comfort food and weekend music. Chef Seamus McGrath serves up a wide choice of comfort food, entrées like shepherd's pie, lasagna, and Bourbon Street marinated sirloin tips. Try the lobster orzo in a cream sauce with fennel and leeks. $13.95–19.93. Brews on tap. The children's menu is $6.95.

Wildcat Tavern (603-383-4245), Rt. 16A, Jackson village. The tavern itself (as opposed to the dining room) remains the town's ever-popular après-ski spot with its overstuffed couches and easy chairs by the fire as well as the long, inviting bar area. "Tavern Suppers" include baby back ribs and shepherd's pie, along with the signature 8-ounce Tavern Burger. From $7.95. Tuesday is Hoot Night when local musicians congregate.

♪ **The Shannon Door & Pub Restaurant** (603-383-4211; shannondoorpub.com). Rt. 16, Jackson village. A long-established Irish pub that's popular for après-ski in winter, open 4–9 for dinner, until 11 for pizza, burgers, also steak *au poivre* and Cajun beef tips, nightly specials and spirits week-

days, until midnight on weekends with live entertainment Thu.–Sun. Outside seating in summer, kid-friendly.

🖉 **Yesterdays** (603-383-4457), Main St., Jackson village. Open daily 6:15 AM–2 PM. Literally the heart of the village, decorated with blow-ups of vintage postcards. Breakfast all day and good for burgers and sandwiches. We lunched happily on eggplant and pepper soup with half a sandwich on crusty oatmeal bread.

🖉 **The Red Fox Bar & Grille** (603-383-4949; redfoxpub.com), Rt. 16, Jackson village. Open daily from 4 PM. Lunch on weekends. Jazz breakfast buffet Sundays (7:30–1). Children's movies and a playroom for small children during dining hours. A cheerful restaurant featuring Buffalo wings, baby back ribs, baked pesto bread, and a range of soups, sandwiches, salads, and burgers.

J-Town Deli (603-383-9106), 174 Main St., Jackson. Open 7 AM–6 PM, later in summer. Great sandwiches and pleasant back-of-the-store seating. Try a pesto-ranch veggie wrap or the soup of the day and half a sandwich, or the homemade quiche with house coleslaw. This is also the local source of wine, beer, and dinners to go.

As You Like It Café (603-383-6415), Rt. 16A, Jackson Village. Tucked into the same white-clapboard complex with the Jackson chamber of commerce, creative sandwiches on fresh-baked breads, soups, limited seating.

The AMC Pinkham Notch Visitor Center (603-466-2727), Rt. 16, Pinkham Notch. Check to see what the evening lecture is (Wed. and Sat. in winter, Sat. in summer). The big open-timbered dining hall with its long tables is the setting for an all-you-can-eat breakfast (6:30–8), lunch (11:30–1), and dinner (6 sharp, except Fri. when

it's a buffet 6:30–8). Breakfast and dinner are ample and frequently outstanding, served family-style. Lunch and snacks are available, too, from the **Black Moose Deli**.

✳ Selective Shopping

Ravenwood Curio Shoppe (603-383-8026), Jackson village. Larry Siebert took nine years building this fantastical, multistory shop on the site of a garage. He explains that the building couldn't exceed its footprint. Siebert continues to expand the sculpture garden, and the shop itself is filled with an eclectic selection of furnishings and gift items, all of them fairly unusual.

RAVENWOOD CURIO SHOPPE, JACKSON
William Davis

Beware: We came away with a lamp we certainly never needed.

White Mountain Puzzles (603-383-4346; puzzlemaps.com), made in Jackson, are available at the chamber of commerce and at Gallery for All Seasons in the Snowflake Inn.

Farmer's market (603-356-6406), summer Saturdays 9–noon in Jackson village: veggies, fruit, crafts.

✳ Special Events

Winter: **Cross-country skiing**, Jackson village. Throughout the ski season, weekend citizens' races are held, and often special international events use the Jackson trails.

Late January: **New Hampshire Snow Sculpture Competition**.

February: **Winter Wildquack duck race**, Black Mountain, Jackson. As spectators cheer, yellow rubber ducks slip slide and crash to the finish line in 10 heats. Participants can win up to $1,000. There's no charge to watch.

March: **Great Glen to Bretton Woods Adventure**, a 50km cross-country ski race.

Memorial Day weekend: **Wildquack River Festival**, Jackson village. Some 2,000 rubber duckies race down the river; first duck down wins $1,000. Rent your own for $5.

Early June: **Jackson Covered Bridge 10km**, Jackson village. One of the most demanding 10K road races in New England.

Mid-June: **Bikes Only Day**—motorcycles rule on the Mount Washington Auto Road.

✎ *Fourth of July:* **Family in the Park**, Jackson village. An old-fashioned Fourth of July celebration.

Mid-July: **Jackson Jazz Festival**, Black Mountain Ski Area.

Late August: **White Mountains Arts Festival** in Jackson Village. **Mount Washington Auto Road Bicycle Hillclimb. Zucchini Festival**.

Early September: **Apple Days Hospitality Tour**. **Mount Washington Bike Race** (603-466-3988), Mount Washington Auto Road, Pinkham Notch. This event attracts some of the top US racers.

October: **Return of the Pumpkin People** in Jackson: creative pumpkin sculptures.

November: **Traditionally Yours Holiday Celebration**.

Early December: A **Yankee swap**.

CRAWFORD NOTCH AND BRETTON WOODS

In 1771 Timothy Nash of Lancaster was tracking a moose over Cherry Mountain when he noticed a gap in the high range to the south and recalled Native American lore about a trail to the coast. Nash found his way through the "Notch" and all the way to Portsmouth, where he convinced Governor John Wentworth to grant him land at the head of the pass on condition he build a road through it. This trail was passable by 1775, and in 1790 Abel and Hannah Crawford traveled it to settle at present-day Fabyans in Bretton Woods. Two years later Hannah's father, Eleazer Rosebrook, brought his family to join them but, declaring he needed "more elbow room," Abel and his family moved 12 miles south to present-day Harts Location at the head of the notch. Both families maintained inns, and in 1819 Abel and his son Ethan Allen blazed the Crawford Path, the first footpath to the summit of Mount Washington. By 1840 summer visitors were making the trek on horseback.

Despite daunting difficulties—the gain of 1,623 feet in elevation in the 30 miles between North Conway and Fabyans and the required construction of the 80-foot-high, 500-foot-long Frankenstein Trestle and Willey Brook Bridge (100 feet high and 400 feet long)—the railroad began runs from Portland, Maine, to Fabyans in 1857. The Crawford House, opened in 1859 in Harts Location, was a prefab building, cut in nearby towns and hauled overland, then assembled in nine months on the spot, with neither pillars nor posts in its grand dining hall. In 1869 the world's first mountain-climbing cog railway opened, running from Fabyans up to the summit of Mount Washington. Eventually as many as 57 trains a day transported guests to hotels in and above Crawford Notch.

"Look at me gentlemen, . . . for I am the poor fool who built all this!" coal baron Joseph Stickney is reported to have exclaimed on the July day in 1902 when the Mount Washington Hotel first opened. It's noted that he "laughed heartily at his own folly." By and large the 200-room hotel has been lucky. Although Stickney died in 1903, it remained in his family until World War II and was then lavishly refurbished by the US government for the 1944 Bretton Woods Monetary Conference, which set the gold standard and created both the World Bank and the International Monetary Fund. During the ensuing decades it had its ups and downs. At this writing, fresh from another multimillion-dollar face-lift, the vintage diva has never looked better. From the Great Hall to guest rooms and baths to the entirely new Presidential Wing with its full-service spa, alterations have been subtle, sensitively enhancing the hotel's already considerable character.

In addition to the Mount Washington Resort, Crawford Notch lodgings include the Appalachian Mountain Club's full-service Highland Center on the site of the Crawford House, and Notchland, a small but special inn, said to mark the site of Abel's tavern in Harts Location.

Impressive as they are, all the human-made attractions past and present in Crawford Notch and the valley above it are dwarfed by natural beauty, a fact recognized by the state in 1912 when Crawford Notch State Park was established, easing access to several dramatic waterfalls and panoramic views.

GUIDANCE **Appalachian Mountain Club Highland Center** (603-466-2727; outdoors.org), Rt. 302, Crawford Notch. Open year-round, hiking information, maps, rental equipment, and workshops. See *Hikers' Lodging*.

Twin Mountain/Bretton Woods Chamber of Commerce (800-245-TWIN; twinmountain.org) produces a brochure and operates a summer information center at the junction of Rts. 2 and 302.

GETTING AROUND **The AMC Hiker Shuttle** (outdoors.org) operates June–mid-Oct. serving trailheads. It's suggested that you spot your car and take a van to the trailhead from which you intend to walk out.

For sights on the top of Mount Washington, see "Mount Washington."

APPALACHIAN MOUNTAIN CLUB HIGHLAND CENTER

Sarah Jan Shangraw, courtesy AMC

MOUNT WASHINGTON COG RAILWAY AND SKI TRAIN (603-278-5404; 800-922-8825; thecog.com), off Rt. 302, Bretton Woods. Operates daily Memorial Day week-end–Oct.; week-ends in May. Steam buffs may

THE COG DESCENDING

White Mountains Visitors Bureau

want to reserve space on the 9 AM train. Opened in 1869, this was the world's first mountain-climbing cog railway, and it remains one of the few places where you can observe steam locomotives at work.

At one time regular trains followed a spur line to the base station, where passengers boarded the cog railway directly for the summit. So unique and ambitious was the plan to build the railroad that its promoter, Sylvester Marsh, was told he might as well "build a railway to the moon." The eight little engines that could, each made for the purpose by this rail-road company, have boilers positioned at an angle because of the steep grade up the mountain. Spring through fall the three-hour roundtrip, which includes a 20-minute stop at the summit, features each engine pushing a single car up, then backing down in front of the car to provide braking. Unique cogwheels fit into slots between the rails to provide traction and braking. The average grade along the 3.25-mile track is 25 percent, but at Jacob's Ladder trestle it rises to 37.5 percent. Several switches permit ascend-ing and descending trains to pass en route. The base sta-tion, a short drive on a paved road from Rt. 302, includes a visitors center and museum, a restaurant, a gift shop, and an RV park. $62 adults, $57 ages 65 and over, $39 ages 4–12.

THE COG IN THE CLOUDS, BEGINNING ITS DESCENT FROM THE SUMMIT

Chris Tree

Bretton Woods chairlift, canopy tour, and mountain biking (603-278-4947; brettonwoods.com), Rt. 302 at the ski area. The canopy tour is open in winter as well as summer seasons. There really is nothing like flying through the sky with the Presidential Range in your face. The full, guided three-and-a-half-hour tour across a series of nine treetop ziplines ($110) requires a reservation, but the 20 minutes on the Willwaw Racing Zip is first come, first served ($15). In summer months the lift is also running; you'll find lift-serviced mountain biking and disk golf. The Top o' Quad restaurant (see *Eating Out*) at the top of the lift is a great place for lunch with a great view of both Mount Washingtons (hotel and mountain).

GOLF Omni Mount Washington Resort Golf Course (603-278-GOLF; omni mtwashington.com), Rt. 302, Bretton Woods. Open to the public early May–Nov. There are 27 holes of golf here on two historic, recently restored courses. The original nine-hole, par-35 Mount Pleasant Course opened in 1895. Two decades later Scotsman Donald Ross designed and supervised the construction of a second, 18-hole, par-71 course, restored in 2008 by architect Brian Silva. The clubhouse includes a pro shop and **The Grille** restaurant with an outdoor patio.

HIKING Many hiking trails cross and parallel the notch. One is the Appalachian Trail, which you can follow north to Maine or south to Georgia. Consult the *AMC White Mountain Guide* for details of the many trails. Below are some of our favorite, less ambitious alternatives.

Arethusa Falls Trail is a 1.5-mile, one-hour, easy-to-moderate walk to New Hampshire's most impressive and highest waterfall, at its best in spring and early summer when water is high. The well-marked trail begins on the southern side of Rt. 302 near the eastern entrance to Crawford Notch State Park.

✍ **Mount Willard Trail** begins at the AMC Crawford Notch Highland Center. An easy 1.4-mile, one-hour walk along a former carriage road leads to rocky ledges with a truly panoramic view down through Crawford Notch. The railroad station once served the old Crawford House, one of the earliest of the old hotels. It was closed in the 1970s and finally burned.

✍ **Saco Lake Trail** (0.4 mile, 15 minutes), across the street from the AMC Highland Center, the source of the river that flows through Crawford Notch, then on to Maine and the Atlantic Ocean. Behind the trail is Elephant Head, a rocky ridge shaped like a pachyderm.

Crawford Path, from Rt. 302 (opposite the Crawford House site) to

THE OMNI MOUNT WASHINGTON OFFERS 27 HOLES OF GOLF

Courtesy, Mount Washington Resort

Mount Washington Resort

HORSEBACK RIDING AT THE MOUNT WASHINGTON RESORT IS OPEN TO THE PUBLIC

Mount Washington, is the oldest hiking trail in the country, built in 1819 by the Crawford family and used as a bridle path in the 1870s. The path is a long 8.2-mile, six-hour walk. The **AMC Mizpah Spring Hut** is a 2.5-mile, two-hour walk over the well-worn trail.

Ammonoosuc Ravine Trail. See "Mount Washington."

HORSEBACK RIDING Omni Mount Washington Resort (603-278-1000), Rt. 302, Bretton Woods. Open to the public seasonally, the Omni Mount Washington's impressive Victorian-era stables offer unusually scenic trail rides, with guided group and individual trail rides for both beginner and advanced riders. The hotel also offers a horse-drawn carriage and sleigh rides.

SPA The Spa at the Omni Mount Washington Resort (603-278-4286) is open to the public as well as to guests Sun.–Thu. 9–7, Fri.–Sat. 9–9. The 25,000-square-foot, full-service spa opened in 2009 with 13 treatment rooms, a fitness studio, and an image center. Facilities include men's and women's locker rooms, relaxation lounges, steam, sauna, and an outdoor garden lounge with whirlpool. *Note:* Nonguests have use of the facilities only with purchase of a service.

✳ Winter Sports

DOWNHILL SKIING Bretton Woods Ski Area (603-278-5000; 800-232-2972; brettonwoods.com), Rt. 302, Bretton Woods. Although traditionally this ski area

VIEW OF MT. WASHINGTON FROM THE QUAD RESTAURANT AT BRETTON WOODS SKI AREA

Chris Tree

was considered more enjoyable than challenging, an aggressive expansion policy has added acres of expert terrain, including 30 acres of expert glade trails and 11 trails in Rosebrook Canyon. Arguably the state's largest ski area and one with a commanding view of Mount Washington.

Vertical drop: 1,500 feet.

Summit elevation: 3,100 feet.

Lifts: Nine, including two high-speed quads.

Trails and glades: 101; 33 percent novice, 34 percent intermediate, 33 percent expert. 434 aces of skiable terrain including 190 acres of glades.

Snowmaking: 92 percent of trails; annual snowfall of 200 inches.

Night skiing and snow*boarding:* Five trails, two lifts

For children: Ski and Snowboard School (ages 4–12; for snowboard, 6–12), Hobbit Ski & Snowplay Programs (ages 3–5), and Babes in the Woods (2 months–5 years).

Lift tickets: $66–74 adults, $53–60 teens, $40–46 juniors; seniors $25–74.

The multitiered, post-and-beam base lodge is nicely designed, and the Top o' Quad Restaurant (see *Eating Out*) offers a glorious view of Mount Washington. The entire mountain is open to snowboarding; four terrain parks are open for snowboarding and freestyle skiing. Riders will also enjoy bumps, jumps, bowls, and glades on West Mountain and in the Rosebrook Canyon area! The Alpine Rental Center offers half-day, full-day, and night equipment rentals. Inquire about the **Adaptive Skiing Program** for physically and developmentally challenged individuals (603-278-3398).

CROSS-COUNTRY SKIING ☙ **Bretton Woods Nordic Center** (603-278-5181; brettonwoods.com) at the Omni Mount Washington Hotel. Open to the public, a spacious, full-service center offers parking, a café, ski passes, and equipment sales and rentals for the 100km network (95km are tracked and groomed for both skating and diagonal stride and also open to snowshoers), one of the best in New England. Also 5km backcountry and 12km designated dog-friendly. Trails are mapped, marked, and divided into linked trail systems. The wooded, 5-mile Mountain Road trail on Mount Rosebrook can be accessed via the Bethlehem Express quad chair at Bretton Woods Ski Area. (A shuttle service operates back and forth.) There are gentler options past beaver ponds and forest glades, and several rest stops. Nordic daily trail passes are $17 adults, $14 ages 6–12 and over 65. The **AMC Highland Center at Crawford Notch** (see *Hikers' Lodging*) also rents equipment as well supplying it (free) to guests. The Bretton Woods cross-country ski network can also be accessed from there.

Backcountry skiing is popular in the **Zealand Valley**, off Rt. 302 between Bretton Woods and Twin Mountain. Well-equipped and -prepared skiers can schuss from Rt. 302 some 7 miles to the **AMC Zealand Falls Hut** (603-466-2727; outdoors.org), which is open all winter on a caretaker basis. Bring your own sleeping bag and food; use their cabin and cooking facilities. Telemark ski rentals available at the Bretton Woods Ski Area (see below).

SNOWSHOEING Snowshoes can be rented at Bretton Woods Ski Area, and a network of high-altitude trails is accessible from the Bethlehem Express Quad. You can download from the same chairliftused to access mountaintop trails. Adult snowshoe rental (ages 13–64) $15; all other ages $12. Single chairlift ride $7. Nordic trail pass required. Snowshoe rentals and terrain are also available at the Bretton Woods Nordic Center.

ICE SKATING AND SNOW TUBING Rent tubes at the Omni Mount Washington Resort's Stone Pillar Activities Center, located beside the Nordic Center. Tube rental costs $5 per hour. Ice skating is offered on an outdoor rink here; rentals a run $5 per hour for nonguests.

✳ Green Space

Crawford Notch State Park (603-374-2272), Rt. 302, Harts Location, 12 miles west of Bartlett. This 5,775-acre park is surrounded by, and predates, the White Mountain National Forest. The **Willey House Snack Bar, Visitors Center, and Gift Shop** (open daily, Memorial Day–Columbus Day weekend), housed in 1920s log buildings (originally a cabin colony), mark the site of an unusual mountain tragedy. In August 1826 a terrible rainstorm blew through the notch, frightening the Willey family, who operated a small inn. Hearing an avalanche sliding down the steep side of the mountain, the family and two employees ran from the inn— only to be swallowed up in the debris as the avalanche split above the inn, leaving it intact. All seven people died; the avalanche scar can still be seen on the mountain. This park was established in 1912 when the state purchased the virgin spruce forest to save it from loggers' axes. The park includes picnic tables, a waterfowl pond, and self-guided nature trail. Note the trails to Arethusa Fall (see *Hiking*); two more waterfalls, the **Silver** and **Flume Cascades**, can be seen from your vehicle at the top of the notch, where there is a parking lot and a scenic outlook. Also note small Saco Lake, just north of the park, headwaters for the Saco. For the **Dry Diver Campground** see *Camping*. **Eisenhower Memorial Wayside Park** is on Rt. 302, 2 miles west of Crawford Notch. A short walk leads to a magnificent view of Mounts Eisenhower, Monroe, Washington, Jefferson, Adams, and Madison. The tracks of the Mount Washington Cog Railway can be seen ascending the side of Washington, and sometimes smoke from one of the engines is visible.

✳ Lodging

INNS The Notchland Inn (603-374-6131; 800-866-6131; notchland.com), Rt. 302, Harts Location 03812. Open all year. This granite mansion was built by pioneering Boston photographer Samuel Bemis in 1862. An inn since the 1920s, it's set in 100 acres of woodland, surrounded in turn by national forest, projecting a true sense of isolation. The parlor, complete with unusual hearth, was designed by Arts & Crafts pioneer Gustav Stickley, and innkeepers Ed Butler and Les Schoof have a nonfussy, though respectful, attitude about this legacy. They offer seven exceptionally attractive and spacious guest rooms and five suites with sitting rooms. All feature wood-burning fireplaces; some also have private deck, skylight, and Jacuzzi. There's a music room with piano and stereo, a library, and, for summer guests, a sunroom with wicker furniture that overlooks the pond. The Saco River flows through the property (harboring fine swimming holes), and the Davis Path up Mount Crawford begins across the road. Notchland's two Bernese mountain dogs may accompany your hike. In winter snowshoes are available at a nominal rate; trails lead into the woods. Five-course dinners, served nightly at 7, draw raves (see *Dining Out*). A room with breakfast (two-night minimum required on many weekends) runs $195; $260 for a suite with river view; $245–310 during holiday and foliage seasons; for dinner add $35 per person; two- to five-night midweek packages are also available. $25 per extra person, $30 less single.

🐾 ✿ ✐ "♥" **The Bartlett Inn** (603-374-2353; 800-292-2353; bartlettinn.com), Rt. 302, Box 327, Bartlett 03812. Open all year. Just west of Bartlett village, this comfortable, simple inn appeals especially to hikers, Nordic skiers, and lovers of the outdoors. The innkeepers, Miriam Habert and Nick Jaques, are enthusiastic and knowledgeable about all kinds of outdoor recreation in the surrounding area, and they can direct guests to the best areas while they're cooking and serving the hearty breakfast that is included in room rates. Nordic skiers can ski directly from the inn onto the extensive trails of the Bear Notch cross-country ski area and return to soak in the inn's outdoor hot tub. The 15 rooms are divided between the main inn and the attached cottages, where pets are permitted. All rooms have private bath, and some have fireplace and kitchenette. $99–245 per couple. $15 per pet.

OTHER OPTIONS ❀ ✎ **The Lodge**, Rt. 302, Bretton Woods (603-278-1000; 800-258-0330; brettonwoods .com). This is good value. The 50 motel-style rooms are all large and pleasant with two double beds, TV, and private patio or balcony overlooking the Mount Washington Hotel and Presidential Range. Amenities include an indoor heated pool, Jacuzzi and sauna, and comfortable common rooms with fireplaces. The restaurant, **Darby's**, serves breakfast, lunch, and dinner. From $89 per night, including morning coffee.

✎ **The Townhomes** (603-278-1000; 800-258-0330; brettonwoods.com), Rt. 302, Bretton Woods. A variety of two-to five-bedroom condominiums with full kitchens, laundries, and fireplaced living rooms; includes access to the health and fitness center and the resort shuttle.

AMC HIKERS' LODGING ✪ 🐾 ✎ "🍴" **The AMC Highland Lodge at Crawford Notch** (603-466-2727; out doors.org). Opened in October 2003, this is the Appalachian Mountain

ZEALAND FALLS HUT

Club's most luxurious lodge. It's constructed, as you might expect, of energy-efficient materials and in a way to maximize heat, minimize fuel. Sheathed in natural clapboard and featuring attractive common spaces with mountain views, it accommodates 122 people in 15 rooms with private bath,

ZEALAND TRAIL IS A RELATIVELY EASY HIKE TO A HUT BY A WATERFALL AND WITH GREAT VIEWS

Chris Tree

Courtesy, Mount Washington Resort

OMNI MOUNT WASHINGTON HOTEL AT THE FOOT OF MOUNT WASHINGTON

RESORTS

Lodging at the Omni Mount Washington Resort at Bretton Woods (603-278-1000; 800-258-0330; omnimtwashington.com) includes the **Omni Bretton Arms Inn**, Rt. 302, Bretton Woods 03575.

❝ℸ❞ ✿ ♿ **The Omni Mount Washington Hotel**. Open year-round. Think *Titanic*: This 200-room, national historic landmark rises like a white cruise ship from a landlocked green sea, backed by New England's highest, frequently snow-capped mountains. The approach is up a mile-long drive, the veranda is vast, the lobby is high and columned, the dining room and its menu are immense (see *Dining Out*).

The hotel took two years and 250 Italian artisans to build, and its steel frame was considered state of the art when it opened. Henry Morgenthau Jr. and John Maynard Keynes were among the 700 delegates who gathered here for the Bretton Woods Monetary Conference of 1944. The roster of famous visitors includes Babe Ruth, Thomas Edison, Princess Margaret, and several US presidents. After nearly a century, however, the hotel was showing its age, and

19 bunk rooms with shared baths, and 2 large bunk rooms in the neighboring **Shapleigh Bunk House**. First-floor rooms are in the "Hardwoods," the second are on the "Boreal" level, and the top floor are "Alpine. " There's an inviting, many-windowed living room with a fireplace, a library, and a patio with a view of the notch. An impressive array of educational and outdoor programs is offered. There's also a children's discovery room. We visited in March and took advantage of the cross-country trails connecting with the Bretton Woods Nordic system. Here, as at the Pinkham Notch Visitor Center, three very good, full meals a day are served; both wine and beer are available. This is also a year-round information center for outdoor activi-

in 1991 it was auctioned off. Luckily the group of northern New Hampshire entrepreneurs who purchased it has restored it to its previous grandeur and even winterized it. The current owners, CNL Lifestyles, have again thoroughly renovated both public spaces and guest rooms, adding a spa and meeting space.

Tours are offered twice daily, and the public is welcome to attend various presentations on White Mountains cultural and natural history. Families are especially welcome here, with a number of two-room Family Suites joined by a common bath. **Kids' Club** offers daily and evening programs for ages 5–12, including hikes, visits with the golf pro and the chef, crafts, and various sports during the summer season. Other amenities include the granite-walled **Cave**, a former speakeasy lounge with nightly live entertainment; gift, clothing, flower, and sweet shops; heated indoor and outdoor pools; four red clay tennis courts; horseback riding; movies; hiking (the resort's own 1,250 acres are surrounded by White Mountain National Forest); 9- and 18-hole golf courses (see *Golf*); and the Bretton Woods Ski Area (see *Skiing*, as well as *Nordic Skiing* and *Snowshoeing*). The indoor pool is renovated and a whirlpool added and the new outdoor pool is open year-round. A full-service spa and a fitness studio with a complete range of Cybex and cardiovascular machines opened in 2009. In 2010 rates are $179–399 per couple EP, $219–349 B&B, and $339–559 MAP. The high end is for a three-bedroom, one-and-a-half-bath suite with a rooftop patio and Jacuzzi. Inquire about special-event and weekend packages. See the introduction to this section for more about the hotel's history.

🌸 🏨 **The Omni Bretton Arms Inn** (603-278-1000; 800-258-0330). A former annex of the Mount Washington Hotel, built in 1896, with 34 guest rooms, this is a more intimate and casual alternative to the grandeur of the main hotel, still with facilities for a small conference, a lounge with weekend entertainment, and dining (see *Dining Out*). Dogs are accepted in some rooms. From $179 B&B.

ties. A big plus: Outdoor gear, including backpacks, rain gear, fleece jackets, and hiking boots donated by L.L. Bean, is available free to guests and program participants. We strongly recommend spending a first night here before striking off to any of the high huts accessible from Crawford Notch. That way you can also take advantage of the gear room. Check the website for current programs. $59–174 per adult, $34–60 per child ages 12 and under, includes dinner and breakfast. In the neighboring Shapleigh Bunk House rates are $41–46 adult B&B, $63–69 with dinner. Prices quoted are for nonmembers. For membership details see *Appalachian Mountain Club* in "What's Where.

Zealand Falls Hut, an **Appalachian Mountain Club high hut** (603-466-2727; outdoors.org), off Rt. 302 at Zealand Rd. It's a glorious—especially in fall, given the mix of deciduous trees—mostly level 2.8 miles to the hut from the end of Zealand Rd. The view from the hut is down the notch to a neighboring waterfall you can cool off in. Overnight guests need to pack in bedclothes or a sleepimg bag and towels; meals, bunks, blankets, and educational programs are provided. In winter you must pack in your food but have full use of the kitchen, oven, stove, and cookware. The winter trip is a longer hike or ski, some 6.5 to 7 miles because Zealand Rd. is closed. Also see Mizpah Spring Hut in "Mount Washington."

CAMPGROUNDS 🐾 In Crawford Notch State Park, **Dry River Campground** (603-271-3628), open early May– early Dec., offers 35 wooded sites ($25 per site); flush toilets and showers.

White Mountain National Forest Campgrounds in Zealand Valley, 3 miles east of Twin Mountain off Rt. 302 on Zealand Rd. Open mid-May–mid-Oct. **Zealand Valley Campground** (first come, first served) has 11 grass pads, open sites, handicapped-access flush and vault toilets, fire ring, picnic tables, and pump water ($16). Off the same access **Sugarloaf I** with 29 sites and flush toilets ($18) and **Sugarloaf II** with 32 sites and vault toilets ($16) can both be reserved (877-444-6777).

Crawford Notch General Store and Campground (603-374-2779; craw fordnotchcamping.com), Rt. 302 south of Crawford Notch in Harts Location. The store, open all year, sells gas, groceries, and hiking and camping supplies; the campground has wooded sites and log camping cabins on the Saco River, as well as tables, fireplaces, and hot showers; open May–Oct.

✳ Where to Eat

DINING OUT The Omni Mount Washington Hotel Main Dining Room (800-314-1752; 800-258-0330), Rt. 302, Bretton Woods. Lavish breakfast buffet ($20 adults, $10 ages 5–12), and a dinner menu that changes nightly. Reservations are required. Dress for dinner in this historic room, originally designed as a circle so that no one ends up in a corner. Every night is an occasion with dancing, tuxedoed waiters, crystal chandeliers, and the full-blown elegance of another era. The menu is à la carte and averages $60 per person for three courses.

Bretton Arms Dining Room and Parlor (603-278-1000), Rt. 302, Bretton Woods. Open year-round for breakfast and dinner. Casually elegant dining room. Entrées $20–35.

⊘ **The Notchland Inn** (603-374-6131; 800-866-6131; notchland.com), Rt. 302, Harts Location. Open Wed.–Sun. Said to be part of Abel Crawford's original tavern, this dining room was moved down the road to the Notchland Inn in the 1920s. It overlooks gardens and a pond on one side, Mount Hope on the other. Although the chef creates a new menu nightly, there's always a choice of appetizers and soups, three entrées, and three desserts. You might begin with herbed biscuits and a spicy tomato soup, then a moist crabcake, followed by braised chicken thighs with a mixed greens salad, topped off with a caramel-apple tart. Allow at least two hours to dine. Generally for guests, the five-course dinners are also served in a single, 7 PM seating to the public, by reservation only. Prix fixe is $45 for nonguests, $48 on Fri. and Sat. The rate for guests is $38 per person all evenings.

EATING OUT **Stickney's** (603-278-10000) at the Omni Mount Washington Hotel. Lunch year-round, dinner buffet in selected seasons. Squirreled away on the hotel's lower level, this is a great casual, family-friendly spot for lunch, with patio dining in warm weather.

Fabyan's Station Restaurant and Lounge (603-278-2222), Rt. 302 at the junction of the access road to the Cog Railway, Bretton Woods. Lunch and dinner year-round in a restored railroad station. Pub menu in the lounge.

Top o' Quad Restaurant at Bretton Woods Ski Area. Open during ski and summer seasons, accessed by chairlift and worth the effort for lunch on a nice day for the fabulous view of the Mount Washington Hotel set against the Presidential Range.

The AMC Highland Center (603-466-2727; outdoors.org), Rt. 302 at Crawford Notch, offers three meals to the public as well as guests in the attractive dining room. Breakfast is buffet-style, lunch options include sandwiches, soup, and salad bar. Sat.–Thu. dinner is served family-style at 6 PM. On Fri., a dinner buffet is served 6–9. Beer and wine available.

THE WESTERN WHITES

INCLUDING THE WATERVILLE VALLEY REGION; LINCOLN AND NORTH WOODSTOCK; AND FRANCONIA AND NORTH OF THE NOTCHES

The heart of the Western Whites is Franconia Notch, a high pass between the granite walls of Cannon Mountain and Mount Lafayette. Here I-93 narrows and traffic slows as it enters Franconia Notch State Park. This "Franconia Notch Parkway" accesses easy strolls into the dramatic Flume Gorge and the Basin; the aerial tram to the top of Cannon Mountain and the beach at Echo Lake. Trails also lead to AMC huts and represent some of the White Mountains' most rewarding day hikes.

A footpath from Franconia Notch to the top of Mount Lafayette is said to have been blazed as early as 1825, the year the area's first hotel opened. By the 1880s it was served by a narrow-gauge railroad transporting patrons to several hotels here, including the 400-room Profile House. The nearby villages of Franconia, Bethlehem, and North Woodstock also had more than their share of the White Mountains' best 19th-century summer hotels.

The area's steep, heavily wooded mountains were as enticing to loggers as to tourists. While early conservationists fought to preserve the "notches" and "gorges," lumber companies built wilderness railways and employed small armies of men to clear-cut vast tracts. Legendary lumberman James E. Henry transformed the little outpost of Lincoln, with 110 residents in 1890, into a booming logging center of 1,278 by 1910. His J. E. Henry Company owned 115,000 acres of virgin timber along the East Branch of the Pemigewasset River, reducing much of it to pulp.

Ultimately the tourists won out over the loggers. The Society for the Protection of New Hampshire Forests (SPNHF) was formed, an outgrowth of the Appalachian Mountain Club (AMC), specifically to work for the passage of the 1911 Weeks Act, enabling legislation to found White Mountain National Forest.

This Pemigewasset ("Pemi") River area became part of the White Mountain National Forest in the mid-1930s. In 1959 a 35-mile east–west forest road through its heart, climbing to almost 3,000 feet on the flank of Mount Kancamagus, was opened as a scenic highway. It offers the national forest's most popular campsites and many hiking trails as well as several historic sites.

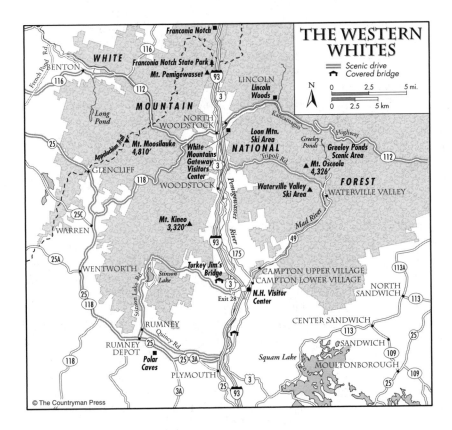

THE WESTERN WHITES

Scenic drive
Covered bridge

© The Countryman Press

The Pemi was still being logged in 1923 when Sherman Adams came to Lincoln to work for the Parker-Young Co., J. E. Henry's successor. Over the next 20 years Adams came to know the valley intimately, and when he returned to Lincoln in the 1960s after having served as New Hampshire's governor and President Eisenhower's chief of staff, he opened Loon Mountain Ski Area.

In that same month another public figure—young ex-Olympic skier Tom Corcoran—opened another ski area less than a dozen miles away (as the crow flies) in Waterville Valley. Up in Franconia Notch, state-run Cannon Mountain's aerial tramway and steep slopes had been attracting skiers since 1938, but these newcomers both represented something novel—rather than being just "ski areas," both were "ski resorts," spawning new communities.

Dictated by both the personalities of their founders and the lay of their land, Loon Mountain and Waterville Valley have, however, developed differently. Conservative Adams saw his business as running a ski area and left condominium development to others. Corcoran, fresh from Aspen, planned a self-contained, Rockies-style resort from the start. Loon's facilities, moreover, lined a narrow shelf of land above the Pemigewasset River on the edge of a mill town, whereas Waterville was in an isolated valley with two ski hills facing each other across 500 acres just waiting to be filled.

Loon Mountain and Waterville Valley are now both owned by national resort management companies and, thanks to their abundance of attractive, family-geared lodging, are as busy in summer as winter. Local summer-only family-geared attractions, most predating the region's ski era, increase the appeal of this region.

The "beaten track" through the Western Whites remains delightfully narrow. The quiet old resort villages of Bethlehem, Franconia, and Sugar Hill have changed little in many decades thanks to the persistence of locals and new arrivals who have worked side by side to preserve the area's heritage, and the Ammonoosuc Valley retains its distinctively remote feel. Farther south, the Baker River Valley offers another little-traveled, scenic byway through the mountains.

The full magnificence of the mountains themselves can only be appreciated by climbing (or riding) to their summits, but the beauty of their high, narrow notches and hidden valleys is accessible to all.

GUIDANCE The White Mountains Gateway Visitors Center (603-745-8720; 800-346-3687; visitwhitemountains.com). Open 8:30–5 daily, until 6 in summer. A walk-in facility (just off I-93 Exit 32, on the Lincoln–North Woodstock line) with restrooms, features displays on the history and nature of the area and has recently expanded to include a Forest Service information center, an outstanding source of lodging, dining, and general information for this entire area.

Ski New Hampshire Association (800-887-5464; skinh.com), based at the White Mountains Visitors Center in Lincoln (see above), is an information source for all the state's major ski areas.

Note: Chambers of commerce are also listed under *Guidance* within the three sections of this chapter, "The Waterville Valley Region," "Lincoln and North Woodstock" (covering the Loon Mountain area), and "Franconia and North of the Notches."

THE WATERVILLE VALLEY REGION

Waterville Valley itself is a 10-mile-deep cul-de-sac cut by one of New England's many Mad Rivers and circled by majestic mountains, many of them more than 4,000 feet tall.

In 1835 city folk began flocking to the town's sole lodging establishment for rest and relaxation, and by 1868 the green-shuttered inn was consistently booked. Families were attracted to the area to pursue more strenuous activities like hiking but also devoted themselves to prayer and Bible study in this inspiring wilderness. The original visitors and their progeny found the valley addictive and, in 1919, purchased the inn when it came up for sale. So principled were they that in 1928 they donated all but a few hundred of their 26,000 acres to the White Mountain National Forest. These same families founded and filled the ski clubs that fueled the inn's winter economy, beginning in 1935 when a few trails were etched on Snow's Mountain. In 1937 the Civilian Conservation Corps (CCC) cut a precipitous 1.5-mile trail down the southern shoulder of Mount Tecumseh, across the valley from Snow's.

Tom Corcoran, a prep school student from Exeter, dreamed of skiing the treacherous Tecumseh Trail and arrived at Waterville Valley in 1949 to pursue his goal. Corcoran continued downhill racing with Dartmouth's ski team, then the US Olympic ski team; after a stint with the Aspen Corporation he was ready to buy his own ski mountain. The Waterville Valley Inn was up for sale along with 425 acres—virtually all the town that wasn't in the national forest. Corcoran's Waterville Valley—complete with four chairlifts, a T-bar, even some snowmaking—opened for Christmas 1966. The inn burned that first season, but two new ski lodges were ready the following year, as were some condominiums, then as new to the eastern ski scene as snowmaking. Over the years Tom Corcoran developed Mount Tecumseh into a major ski mountain, added condo-style lodges and more than 500 condominiums, a pond, a sports center, a nine-hole golf course, and a year-round skating rink. Finally, at the center of the resort, he built a "Town Square": three interconnected, clapboard buildings four and a half stories high with traditional saltbox lines, softened by modern touches like an occasional round window and 100 dormers, a variation on the lines of an old White Mountain hotel.

In 1966 Waterville Valley was acquired by George Gillett Jr. and Booth Creek Holdings, which also owns two California resorts and Cranmore Mountain in North Conway. It continues to be an outstanding, self-contained, family-geared resort, a genuine value for families in its lively off-season—which lasts all summer with family-geared programs and special events.

The neighboring village of Campton offers a few friendly bed & breakfasts and restaurants. You'll find a surprisingly lively look to nearby Plymouth, thanks to Plymouth State University. The number and variety of hikes and scenic drives in this area keep area residents and tourists alike active throughout the year.

GUIDANCE Waterville Valley Region Chamber of Commerce (603-726-3804; 800-237-2307; watervillevalleyregion.com), just off I-93 Exit 28 in Campton. Open 9–5 daily. Restrooms, brochures, and phones. Here you can purchase snowmobile licenses and activity-specific guidebooks from the helpful staff.

Waterville Valley Resort Association: *winter*: waterville.com; *summer/fall*: visitwatervillevalley.com.

GETTING THERE *By bus:* **Concord Coach** (603-228-3300; 800-639-3317; concordcoachlines.com) from Boston's Logan Airport stops in Plymouth at Chase Street Market, 83 Main St.

By car: I-93 to Exit 28, then 11 miles up Rt. 49.

TOWN SQUARE AT WATERVILLE VALLEY

Waterville Valley

GETTING AROUND The Shuttle Connection in Lincoln (603-745-3140; 800-545-3140; theshuttleconnection.com) provides a 24-hour service among attractions, ski areas, airports, and bus terminals.

WV Cab Company (603-726-6536; wvcabco.com) provides taxi and limo service, noon–7 daily. Pets and bikes welcome.

MEDICAL EMERGENCY Dial 911.

✳ Towns and Villages

Plymouth (pop. 6,362; plymouthnh.org). From I-93, what you see of Plymouth are the high-rise dorms of Plymouth State University (plymouth.edu), a clue to the existence of shops and restaurants catering to the needs of more than 4,000 undergraduates and 2,000 graduate students. What you don't see from the highway is the region's appealing old commercial center. Its mills have produced mattresses, gloves, and shoe trees as well as lumber. The long-vanished Pemigewasset House, built by the president of the Boston, Concord & Montréal Railroad, was favored by Nathaniel Hawthorne, who was living in Plymouth before his death in 1864. Today the college campus forms the centerpiece for the town, and some good restaurants can be found within walking distance.

Rumney (pop. 1,474). A picture-perfect village with a classic common, Rumney is in the Baker Valley, just far enough off the beaten path to preserve its tranquility. The Mary Baker Eddy House, Quincy Bog, the Town Pound, and Stinson Lake are all described under *Scenic Drives*.

Warren (pop. 870). A white-clapboard village at the base of Mount Moosilauke, Warren has had more than its share of monuments. First there was the massive Morse Museum, built in the 1920s by a Warren native who made a fortune making shoes in Lowell, Massachusetts. It displayed exotica from his travels, as well as the world's largest private shoe collection. The Morse Museum was closed several years ago (even the mummies were sold off), but the Redstone Rocket booster with USA emblazoned on its side still towers bizarrely over the common. A local restaurant owner, we're told, brought it back from Huntsville, Alabama, and tried to give it to Derry, New Hampshire (home of astronaut Alan Shepard), which refused to take it. Warren, we understand, remains divided on whether it belongs there or not; the VFW post keeps it painted. Ask directions to the Dartmouth Outing Club cabin. From the cabin a former carriage road (to a former summit hotel) is one among a choice of hiking trails to the summit. Warren is off the beaten path but a scenic way between the Connecticut River and the mountains, so it's useful to note that it offers two eateries, **The Garlic Clove**, 17 Tarlton Rd., and **Calamity Jane's Restaurant** (603-764-5288) on Water St.

Wentworth (pop. 793). A picturesque, white wooden village with a triangular common, set above the Baker River.

✳ To See

COVERED BRIDGES Blair bridge. The easiest way to find this bridge is from I-93 Exit 27; at the bottom of the exit ramp, follow Blair Rd. to the blinking light, then go straight across.

Turkey Jim's bridge. At I-93 Exit 28, follow Rt. 49 west. After about 0.5 mile (as you cross over the metal bridge), look for a sign on your right for Branch Brook Campground. You must drive into the campground to see the bridge.

Bump bridge. At I-93 Exit 28, follow Rt. 49 east for about 0.5 mile. Turn right at the traffic lights and go over the dam. Turn right again onto Rt. 175 south. After 3 or 4 miles, you come to a sharp left turn; bear to the left and stay straight, down the dirt road. Take the first right, and the covered bridge is about 0.5 mile on your left.

FOR FAMILIES ❧ **Polar Caves** (603-536-1888; polarcaves.com), Rt. 25, 4 miles west of Plymouth. Open daily early May–mid-Oct., 9–5. Discovered by neighborhood children around 1900 and opened as a commercial attraction in 1922, this is an extensive property with a series of caves connected by passageways and walkways, with taped commentaries at stations along the way. The name refers to the cold air rising from the first "ice" cave, where the temperature in August averages 55 degrees. There's much here to learn about minerals and geology, much that's just fun, like a mining sluice and an extensive rock garden with contrasting hot and cool sections and formations for kids to crawl through. The complex includes picnic tables and a snack bar. $15 adults, $11 ages 4–10.

Also see **Waterville Valley Resort** for reasonably priced family-geared summer lodging and activities as well as skiing.

SCENIC DRIVES Rumney Loop. The easiest way to begin is from Rts. 25/3A west of Plymouth. Take Airport Rd., then go left on Quincy Rd. The sign for **Quincy Bog** (603-786-9465) should be just beyond Quincy State Forest, but if the sign is down, look for stone pillars flanking a small road to the right. One-tenth of a mile down this road, look for a left leading to the bog entrance, from which you can access trails and a viewing deck. This 40-acre peat bog is a place to find frogs in April and May, to see bog plant blooms in May and June, to hunt for salamanders and newts, and to bird-watch. The nature center here is open mid-June–mid-Aug. En route to the bog you pass the old **Rumney Town Pound**, an unusual, natural animal pen formed by gigantic boulders. Continue into Rumney, and then head out Main Street and follow it past the **Mary Baker Eddy House** (603-786-9943), home of the founder of Christian Science in the early 1860s (open May–Oct., Tue.–Sat. 10–5). Continue along isolated **Stinson Lake**, good fishing (trout, perch, pickerel) year-round. **Stinson Mountain Trail** is marked, beginning with a dirt road, then a left through the woods and a right at the brook, up through spruce and fir to the summit ledges. Great views. Continue east on this road out to West Campton and I-93 Exit 28.

The Baker River Valley. The Baker River charts a natural path from the base of Mount Moosilauke southeast through hilly woodland to the Pemigewasset River. It was known as the Asquamchumauke River until 1712, when a group of soldiers headed by Captain Thomas Baker of Northampton, Massachusetts, defeated a band of local Native Americans on the site that's presently Plymouth. Today Rt. 25 shadows the river, beginning as a commercial strip west of Plymouth but quickly improving. You pass the Polar Caves, Rumney, and continue on through Wentworth and Warren. To return to Waterville Valley, take mountainous Rt. 118 east to North Woodstock, then I-93 from Exit 32 to Exit 28.

WATERVILLE VALLEY RESORT

(800-GO-VALLEY; 800-468-2553; waterville.com), 1 Ski Area Rd., P.O. Box 540, Waterville Valley 03215. For summer/fall activities: visitwatervillevalley.com.

YEAR-ROUND

FITNESS CENTER **White Mountain Athletic Club** (603-236-8303; wmacwv.com), Valley Rd. Indoor tennis, racquetball, and squash courts, 25-meter indoor and outdoor swimming pools, jogging track, fitness evaluation facilities, Nautilus exercise equipment, aerobics, whirlpools, saunas and steam rooms, tanning booths, massage service, restaurant/lounge, and game room.

SUMMER

Rey Center & the Curious George Cottage (603-236-3308; thereycenter.org). Margret and Hans Rey, authors and illustrators of the popular Curious George books, spent many summers in Waterville Valley. The Reys were active members of the community and known for their passions—astronomy, natural history, photography, environmental action, animals, gardening, walking, bicycling, and children's experiential learning. In 1992 their home here was donated to the town and has become a multigenerational learning center. The Town of Waterville Valley Recreation Department (603-236-4695; watervillevalley.org) offers three drop-in **summer camp programs** for children ages 4–12, from late June through late Aug. Camps focus on outdoor exploration, cooking, games, crafts, and making new friends.

BOATING **Corcoran's Pond at Waterville Valley Resort** (603-236-4805). Paddleboat, canoe, and kayak rentals on 6 acres.

CHAIRLIFT RIDE at Snow's Mountain, operating daily from Memorial Day weekend, 10–5, weekends after Labor Day. Bring your mountain bike or hike down.

GOLF **Waterville Valley Resort** (603-236-4805; wvnh.com/golf.htm). A nine-hole "executive" course; rental carts.

ICE SKATING The town of Waterville Valley's indoor ice arena (603-236-4813) operates daily late June–mid-Apr. Hours vary due to hockey tournaments and lessons. Skate rentals available.

MOUNTAIN BIKING **Adventure Center** (603-236-4666). Daily July–Labor Day, weekends from Memorial Day and until Columbus Day. Lift-assisted biking to the 2,090-foot summit of Snow's Mountain. Rentals throughout the season.

SKATEBOARDING (wvskate.com). An outdoor skate park featuring a 10-foot-high half-pipe and street course, along with an outdoor dirt BMX track. Lessons, equipment rentals. Part of the Adventure Center (see above). Day, weekend, and weekly skate camps.

Waterville Valley Summer Camp (800-832-4242; wvsportscamp.com), Sports for a Lifetime Academy is a coed camp for children ages 8–14 in Waterville Valley. WVSC offers **one- and two-week overnight sessions** running Sun.–Sun., as well as a **day camp** Mon.–Fri.

SWIMMING Corcoran's Pond, with a sandy beach, is Waterville Valley Resort's principal summer swimming area.

White Mountain Athletic Club, Waterville Valley, offers an indoor pool. Several lodges also offer indoor pools.

✐ **Waterville Valley Tennis Center** (603-236-4840; wvtennis.com). Eighteen outdoor clay courts, two indoor courts at the White Mountain Athletic Club; clinics, round-robins. A junior tennis program for children 18 and under includes private lessons, drill sessions, and round-robins.

WINTER

DOWNHILL SKIING ✐ **Waterville Valley** (603-236-8311; snow report 603-236-4144; 800-468-2553). Billing itself as "Altitude without attitude," Waterville is a favorite with Boston skiers. It's just a seven-minute ride to the summit of Mount Tecumseh on the high-speed detachable quad, and the way down is via a choice of long, wide cruising trails like Upper Bobby's Run and Tippecanoe.

YOUNG SKIERS AT WATERVILLE VALLEY

Waterville Valley

SCHWENDI HÜTTE, WATERVILLE VALLEY

Waterville Valley

Mogul lovers will find plenty to please them on True Grit and Ciao, and beginners have their own area served by the Lower Meadows Double. Glades and terrain features all over the mountain; Little Slammer and Exhibition Park feature a street hubba and superpipe.

Vertical drop: 2,020 feet.

Lifts: Two high-speed detachable quad lifts, two triples, three doubles, five surface.

Trails: 52 on Mount Tecumseh.

Glades: Getting off the groomed trails and into the woods has become a popular alternative to traditional trail skiing. Skiers and riders can start learning this skill by maneuvering in and out of widely spaced trees on Waterville Valley's Greenhorn Glades, located at the top of Valley Run. Intermediate-level glades are nestled between the classic Old Tecumseh ski trail and Lower Tippy. The blue-square "Old T Trees" glades are a stepping-stone to tree skiing in the black-diamond Psyched Out and Sunnyside Terrain Parks.

Snowmaking: 100 percent.

Terrain parks: Freestyle skiers and snowboarders can progress at their own pace with a variety pack of parks. The Burton Progression Park is designed for entry-level park riders with features specifically built close to the ground. The Little Slammer Park offers 2 acres of small terrain features that include jumps, rails, and boxes. One of the top-rated parks in the East, Exhibition at the base of the mountain is serviced by its own Poma lift.

On-mountain eating facilities: **Schwendi Hütte** at the 4,000-foot summit is a rustic hideaway serving up homemade pastries and fondues by the fire. Stop by at 11 for out-of-the-oven chocolate chip cookies. In the base area check out T-Bars: Christie's creative oven-baked sandwiches like melted Brie on multigrain with sprouts, spinach, and tomato dressed in Parmesan vinaigrette; duck salad; and the Buffalo Soldier (bison burger topped with blue cheese and bacon) or Burton Burger (grilled venison topped with cheddar and grilled onion). Live après-ski entertainment on weekends. **Buckets, Bones & Brews** features pulled-pork sandwiches, sliders, shaved steak sandwiches, and curly fries to go with its buckets of ribs and wings. Serving beer on tap, wine, and a Sunday Bloody Mary bar. The heated deck is next to the White Peak Quad. Midmountain look for **Sunnyside Timberlodge** (an oasis with a hearth cafeteria, good soups, and deli sandwiches).

Ski school: Specializes in clinics for all ages and all abilities; also private lessons for all, including a Trail Along program that lets parents take part in their kids' snow time.

For children: There is a nursery for children from age 6 weeks. Kids Venture Kamps are for ages 3–12. Small children have their own hill, with its own lift and terrain garden. Also evening children's programs with the Town of Waterville Valley Recreation Department and Curious George Cottage.

Lift tickets: $67 adults, $57 ages 13–18, $43 ages 6–12; buy tickets 48 hours before at waterville.com and save $10—and the ticket is good all season. On Wed. it's $20 off tickets purchased online. Nonholiday Mon. and Fri. are twofers.

Senior discounts and perks: $43 a day, Mon.–Fri. nonholidays. Seniors can also enjoy special treatment by joining the Silver Streaks. There is an annual fee that offers preferred parking, separate lounge area, and après-ski events.

SKI TIPS The front side of the mountain gets the best morning sun. Be on the lift by 8 AM for untouched corduroy and before the weekend families arrive. First-track favorites are blue-square Tippecanoe and Tyler too, both wide, mellow cruisers back to the quad. Experts, be sure to check out double-black-diamond True Grit, steep but groomed on one half with the other half bumped up. There are many trails for intermediate skiers—including Oblivion, which runs from the top of the Sunnyside lift. Don't be deterred by the short, steep lip at the top. The trail levels out with lovely winding turns. When the trail ends, skiers can choose to follow Upper Valley Run down to the bottom, or take a lovely, quiet ride on the aptly named Stillness Trail.

LODGING TIPS Last-minute lodging deals are posted weekly on water-ville.com. Most ski-and-stay packages include access to the White Mountain Indoor Sports Center.

CROSS-COUNTRY SKIING Nordic at Waterville Valley (603-236-4666; 800-468-2553; waterville.com), in Town Square, Waterville Valley. Ski school, warming and waxing areas, rentals. More than 70km through the valley and surrounding national forest groomed for classical and skating; 35 additional kilometers are marked. The center's location in Town Square features a crackling fire and easy access, though there are too many condos to go by before you get up into the woods. Take a picnic and thermos with you and warm up by the stove in the Nordic Center Yurt on Bob's Lookout Trail on the north end of the trail system. Or drive to the edge of the White Mountain National Forest and ski directly off into the woods. Inquire about conditions on the Greeley Ponds Trail. Open daily 8:30–4. Skating as well as classic lessons are offered; also moonlight guided tours, weekly races, and telemark clinics. $19 adults, $14 ages 6–12, $14 seniors.

ICE SKATING Waterville Valley Ice Arena (603-236-4813; watervillevalley .org). A covered, hockey-sized ice-skating rink maintained throughout the year in Town Square. Complete with skate rentals, maintenance, and repairs.

SLEIGH RIDES Throughout the winter, horse-drawn sleigh rides depart afternoons and evenings from **Town Square**, Waterville Valley.

Tripoli Rd. (closed in winter). A shortcut from Waterville Valley to I-93 north: roughly 10 miles, paved and unpaved, up through Thornton Gap (a high pass between Mount Osceola and Mount Tecumseh) and over a high shoulder of 4,326-foot Mount Osceola. Begin on West Branch Rd. (a left before the Osceola Library); cross the one-lane bridge and turn right into the national forest. Note the Mount Osceola Trail 3 miles up the road. Continue through the Thornton Gap. Note trailheads for the Mount Tecumseh and East Pond trails.

Sandwich Notch Rd. (closed in winter). A steep, roughly 10-mile dirt road from Center Sandwich to Waterville, built 1 rod wide for $300 by the town of Sandwich in the late 18th century. Best attempted in a high, preferably four-wheel-drive vehicle. Be prepared to make way for any vehicle coming from the opposite direction. The road follows the Bearcamp River; stone walls tell of long-vanished farms. Center Sandwich offers a crafts center, museum, and dining (see "The Lake Winnipesaukee Area").

✳ To Do

BICYCLING See **Waterville Valley Resort** for bike rentals and lift-assisted mountain biking on Snow's Mountain, also cross-country trails and logging roads. Mountain bike clinics, special events.

BOATING **Ski Fanatics** (603-726-4327), Rt. 49 in Campton, rents kayaks and offers shuttle service 6 miles or farther up the Pemigewasset so you can paddle back down. **Branch Brook Campground** (603-726-7001), Rt. 49 in Campton, also offes canoe and kayak rentals.

Also see **Waterville Valley Resort**.

FISHING Stream fishing was one of the first lures of visitors to this valley, and the fish are still biting in **Russell Pond** (Tripoli Rd.) and all along the Mad River, stocked with trout each spring. **Campton Pond** (at the lights) is a popular fishing hole. **Perch Pond**, off Rt. 175 in Campton, is another popular spot, with boat access and a hiking trail around the pond.

GOLF **Owl's Nest Golf Club** (888-OWL-NEST; owlsnestgolf.com), Rt. 49, 1 mile west of Exit 28 off I-93, Campton. A par-72 championship, 18-hole course with four sets of tees on each hole, accommodating all skill levels. Restaurant (see *Dining Out*) and lounge.

Waterville Valley Resort (see the box) offers a nine-hole golf course built in 2006.

Sugar Shack Golf Range (603-726-8978), Rt. 175, Campton. A multipurpose activity center.

HIKING **Mount Osceola**. A 7-mile (roundtrip), four-and-a-half-hour hike beginning on Tripoli Rd. This road crests at the 2,300-foot-high Thornton Gap; the Mount Osceola Trail begins some 200 yards beyond. Follow an old tractor road up through many switchbacks and along Breadtray Ridge, then across a brook, up log steps, by another ridge to the summit ledges. This is the highest of the mountains circling Waterville Valley, and the view is spectacular.

Greeley Ponds Trail begins at the end of the old truck road, which is a left off Livermore Rd., just past the clearing known as Depot Camp. The trail crosses a wooden footbridge and follows the course of the river to Greeley Ponds between Mounts Osceola and Kancamagus. It's a gradual grade all the way to the upper pond and continues as a gradual ascent to the Kancamagus Highway.

Welch Mountain. Open ledge walking at a surprisingly low elevation overlooking the Mad River Valley. It's a challenging 4-mile roundtrip hike but well worth the sweat. According to local hiking guru Steve Smith, the broad sheets of granite offer views and blueberries in abundance. The panorama from the open summit includes Sandwich Mountain, Mount Tripyramid, Mount Tecumseh, and Mount Moosilauke. You can extend the hike into a loop by continuing over the slightly higher **Dickey Mountain** and its fine north viewpoint (the ledges on this hike may be slippery when wet). The trailhead for this loop is on Orris Rd., off Upper Mad River Rd. between Campton and Waterville Valley.

Also see **Waterville Valley Resort**.

HORSEBACK RIDING **Rocky Ridge Ranch** (603-726-8067), just off I-93 Exit 28 (south of the information center). Trail rides are offered year-round for beginners and intermediates, as is a two-hour "adventure ride."

ROCK CLIMBING The most popular spot for rock climbing is the area around Buffalo Rd., accessible from I-93 by taking Exit 26 and driving about 8 miles on

Rt. 25 until you reach Stinson Lake Rd.—essentially the town center of Rumney. From there, drive about a mile to a parking lot on the right. The Meadows, the cliffs you'll be scaling, lie directly above this parking area. **Tenney Mountain** also offers a summer rock climbing program.

SWIMMING On Rt. 49 look for **Smarts Brook Trail**—an easy mile's hike over logging and dirt roads to a swimming hole among the pools of a mountain brook. **Mirror Lake**, Mirror Lake Rd., Thornton is just north of Exit 29, Thornton.

✍ **Adventure Gorge Zip Line Canopy Tour** (888-289-1020; whitemountain exploration.com), Tenney Mountain, Plymouth. Open weekends mid-May–mid-June, daily through Labor Day. Reservations recommended. Tours begin at 9 AM, weather dependent. There's a chairlift to the summit, and you descend via cascades, waterfalls, and a walkway to base lodge. A "kids-only" version is also offered. Also see **Waterville Valley Resort**.

❋ Winter Sports

DOWNHILL SKIING Waterville Valley (see the box) is the big draw.

✍ **Tenney Mountain** (603-536-4100; 888-289-1020; tenneymtn.com), 151 Tenney Mountain Hwy., Plymouth. Open except Tue.,Wed. of nonholiday weeks. Honestly, we took a look at this ski area on an early-March day in 2010 when the other ski hills in this chapter were fully open and it looked like it had been closed for weeks. With a vertical drop of 1,450 feet, snowmaking on (theoretically) 85 percent of its 48 trails, two chairlifts (one a triple), and $50 adult weekend tickets, you would expect more. The tubing on a 110-foot-long slope accessible via platter lift is $14–19.

❋ Lodging

LODGES

In Waterville Valley

🍴 ✍ **Snowy Owl Inn** (603-236-8383; 800-766-9969; snowyowlinn.com), 41 Village Rd., Waterville Valley 03215. An attractive lodge with a central, three-story fieldstone hearth and a surrounding atrium supported by single log posts; there's a cupola you can sit in. A case can be made that this is the most innlike and romantic of the Waterville Valley lodges, but it's also a good place for families, thanks to the lower-level game rooms adjoining a pleasant breakfast room. There are indoor and outdoor pools as well. Of the 85 rooms, more than half have a wet bar, fridge, and whirlpool tub, and all have voice mail, dataports, and satellite television. A two-bedroom suite offers its own gas log fieldstone fireplace. Rates include a breakfast buffet. Inquire about when dinner is served in the **Owl's Roost Pub** and **Owl's Landing Restaurant**. $89–179 in summer, $119–219 for rooms, more for condo-style studios and suites per night, depending on room and season.

🍴 ✍ **Golden Eagle Lodge** (603-236-4551; 888-703-2453; goldeneagle lodge.com), 28 Packard's Rd., Waterville Valley 03215. Architect Graham Gund's imprint is all over this resort outpost. He first designed the Waterville Valley Town Square, then added this fieldstone- and shingle-sided hotel.

Both are a tribute to another era. With its sloping roofs and tall towers, the exterior of the Golden Eagle suggests a monumental, 19th-century mountain lodge, but the inside is totally in tune with today. Amenities include an indoor pool, whirlpools, and saunas. Roughly 90 of the one- and two-bedroom condo suites (all have a kitchen and eating area) are available for rent at $123–310, including resort fee; inquire about the many special packages.

✍ **Black Bear Lodge** (603-236-4501; 800-349-2327; black-bear-lodgenh .com), 3 Village Rd., Waterville Valley 03215. This comfortable and well-laid-out condo hotel, a three-minute walk from Town Square, offers 107 one-bedroom or loft suites that sleep four to six people. Each suite has a kitchen, dining area, sitting area with queen-sized bed and cable TV, and separate bedroom; indoor/outdoor pool, outdoor whirlpool, sauna, steam room, game room, and children's cinema on the lower level. Summer $135–185, winter $120–290.

🐾 ✍ **Best Western Silver Fox Inn** (603-236-8325; 888-236-3699; silver foxinn.com), 70 Packard's Rd., Waterville Valley 03215. If you're looking for a room rather than a suite, this is a lower-cost alternative. All 32 guest rooms are air-conditioned, with two double beds or one queen. Breakfast, afternoon wine and cheese, and free shuttle service are included. $110–120 summer, $120–150 winter; the inn also rents some 40 condos.

Valley Inn (603-236-8425; 800-343-0969), 17 Tecumseh Rd., Waterville Valley 03215. An attractive, 52-room lodge with an indoor/outdoor pool, whirlpool, saunas, exercise room, game room; the only valley lodging with its own dining room. All rooms have TV and phone, and some have kitchen unit, fireplace, sauna, or whirlpool bath. From $105 for a standard room off-season to $255 in ski season for a suite with a deck, kitchen facilities, fireplace, and whirlpool bath.

CONDOMINIUMS IN WATER-VILLE VALLEY Some 500 condominiums are scattered in clusters between the ski slopes and Town Square, but most are not in the rental pool. These represent a fabulous family value, especially in summer when rates begin at $184 for a family of four, including all summer activities. Also see waterville.com.

✍ **Village Condominiums** (603-236-8301; 800-532-6630; villagecondo .com), 8 Davos Way, Waterville Valley 03215. Privately owned two- to five-bedroom condominiums, each with a fully equipped kitchen, washer/dryer, color cable TV, fireplace with wood, private phone and entrance. On-site clubhouse amenities include a heated outdoor pool, saunas and showers, a large recreation room with Ping-Pong, a projection TV with DVD and VCR, and kitchen with access window to the pool. Two-bedroom units from $155, tax included.

Town Square Condos (888-462-9887; townsquarecondos.com), P.O. Box 344,

THE GOLDEN EAGLE AT WATERVILLE VALLEY
Kim Grant

Waterville Valley 03215. A favorite of families looking for spacious quarters, Town Square rents 32 three-bedroom, two-bath condos, and a small number of one-bedroom condos, all with full kitchen. Located on the third floor of Town Square itself, and convenient to shops, restaurants, a Nordic and bike center, and an ice arena. Adjacent to Corcoran's Pond. Access involves elevator plus steps—there are ski lockers located on the bottom floor. $145–285 summer/fall, $150–350 winter.

BED & BREAKFASTS

In Campton

Note that the village of Campton is just off I-93, 10 miles west of Waterville Valley.

⌀ 🐾 😺 ✎ "♈" **The Mountain-Fare Inn** (603-726-4283; mountainfareinn .com; mtnfareinn@cyberportal.net), 5 Old Waterville Rd., Campton 03223. Susan and Nick Preston run this B&B as smoothly as they do the slopes at Waterville Valley. Both high-powered coaches of competitive skiers (including US ski team members), the Prestons spend their off-slope time managing one of the most classic ski lodges around. Their 1840s village home and carriage house annex offer 10 sunny guest rooms, many with wide-pine floors and all furnished with bright fabrics and country antiques. All but one have a private bath. Common space includes an old-fashioned living room; a great game room with pool table, television, card tables, and woodstove; and a place to store and tune skis. There's also a sauna. Guests sit down together (or separately) to breakfast in the pleasant dining room, where a very full, buffet-style breakfast is set out. $105–150 high-season doubles; $98–140 low-season doubles. A great place for a family reunion or for a solo traveler. Pets possible.

"♈" **The Sunny Grange B&B** (603-726-5555; 877-726-5553; sunnygrange .com), 134 Rt. 175, Campton 03223. Situated at the intersection with Mad River Rd. on a triangular piece of land, this lovely yellow farmhouse built in 1811 is tastefully decorated, inviting, and relaxed. There are five rooms with private bath and access to the common areas that include fireplaces and gas-fired stoves. Two rooms are two-room suites with fireplace, Jacuzzi, and sitting area. Each room has telephone, air-conditioning, and TV/VCR combination. Innkeeper Tami Sullivan is a trained chef, and a full country breakfast is included in rates of $119–165, depending on the room and season.

😺 ✎ **The Campton Inn** (603-726-4449; 888-511-0790; peter@evp creative.com), Rt. 175 and Owl St., Campton 03223. A vintage-1835 multi-gabled village house offers a large living room with a woodstove and piano, and a pleasant screened porch. Five guest rooms, one with private bath, some designed for families. $95–115.

In Waterville Valley

Chester H. Pond Cottage (603-254-4654; chesterpondcottage.com), 33 Greeley Hill Rd., Waterville Valley 03215. One of the Valley's original 19th-century summer cottages, complete with belvedere tower. There is plenty of common space; the three guest rooms are spacious, all with gas fireplace, two with shared bath. It's off away from the condos, handy to Snow's Hill. $150 for shared bath, $200 for private (with Jacuzzi), including a full breakfast.

Elsewhere

😺 ✎ **The Common Man Inn & Spa** (603-536-2200; 866-843-2626; the cmaninn.com), Main St., turn right off I-93 Exit 26 in Plymouth. (Mail: P.O. Box 581, Ashland 03217.) An 1890s birch mill has been transformed with the sure touch that marks everything this locally based group touches. Each of the 37 themed rooms is different; all are equipped with wireless access, some with lofts, fireplace, deck, and Jacuzzi. From $109 for a queen-bedded room in low season to $252 for an Adirondack-style "camp" suite with all the bells and whistles in high season. Inquire about packages. Amenities include a restaurant, tavern, and full-service spa.

Federal House Inn (603-536-4644; 866-536-4644; federalhouseinnnh .com), junction of Rts. 27 and 25, Plymouth 03264. This classic vintage-1825 brick home has been expanded and renovated to hold two attractive guest rooms and three suites. Common space includes a library and living room with fireplace; amenities include an outside hot tub. Handy to Tenney Mountain. $129–189 includes a full breakfast. Inquire about dinner, offered by reservation for groups of more than six.

🐾 ✍ **Hilltop Acres** (603-764-5896), East Side and Buffalo Rd., Wentworth 03282. Open May–Oct. A pleasant old farmhouse with a large, pine-paneled rec room containing an antique piano, cable television, fireplace, and plenty of books. Rooms with private bath run $100; pets are welcome in the housekeeping cottage with fireplace and screened porch ($125 per night, $750 per week). Room rates include breakfast.

CAMPGROUNDS White Mountain National Forest. In the WMNF section of this chapter, check the **Campton**, **Russell Pond**, and **Waterville** sites.

Branch Brook Campground in Campton (603-726-7001) with large tent and trailer sites, play and lap

pools, a rec hall, and much more, and **Goose Hollow Campground** in Waterville Valley (603-726-2000), are privately owned alternatives.

✳ Where to Eat

DINING OUT William Tell (603-726-3618; williamtellnh.com), Rt. 49, Thornton. Open for dinner in winter and summer seasons except Mon., Tue.; Sun. brunch 11–3 and dinner all day. The lounge opens at 3. Under new management in 2009 but still serving the alpine specialties that its stucco-and-timber exterior evokes. This is one of the best-rated restaurants in the mountains. You can dine on Wiener schnitzel or sauerbraten but also on seafood bouillabaisse or rack of venison; entrées $17–32. Lighter fare always includes a burger, maybe a grilled beet and goat cheese sandwich.

✍ 🍺 **Foster's Boiler Room** (603-536-2764; thecman.com), I-93 Exit 26, 231 Main St. at the Common Man Inn & Spa, Plymouth. Open weekdays at 4, weekends at noon. Housed in a former birch mill, part of the Common Man family of restaurants. Great atmosphere and dependable fare ranging from burgers, pizza, and burgers to tenderloin steak; this big menu has something for everyone. Entrées $7.99–22.95.

The Sunset Room at Owl's Nest Golf Club (603-726-3076; owlsnest gold.com), junction of Rt. 49 and Owl St., Campton. Open daily for lunch and dinner. We've heard rave reviews for this attractive dining room with its views west over the mountains. The menu might include PEI mussels in a cilantro Dijon cream sauce, baby back ribs, and espresso-rubbed rib-eye steak. Entrées $18–25.

✍ **Wild Coyote Grill** (603-236-4919; wildcoyotegrill.com), Rt. 49, above the

White Mountain Athletic Club in Waterville Valley. Dinner nightly 5:30–close. Casually elegant, chef owned, and highly rated. Sean Stout's entrées might range from vegetable potpie and buffalo meat loaf to rack of lamb. A pub menu features salads and flatbread pizzas. Entrées $15–28.

✍ **Diamonds' Edge North** (603-236-2006; diamondsedgenorth.com), Town Square. Open daily for dinner, the upscale option in Town Square. A wide-ranging menu featuring pastas and steaks (entrées $13.50–19) with a "comfort food," a "burgers etc.," and a young adult menu also available.

EATING OUT

In Waterville Valley

Jugtown Sandwich Shop and Ice Cream Parlor (603-236-3669), the heart of Town Square. Open daily 9–4. An extensive deli featuring specialty sandwiches. There are some tables, but in warm-weather months you just step outside with salads and sandwiches to the tables in the square. Fresh bagels and breads baked daily. Sandwiches are served through late afternoon; ice cream all evening.

Waterville Valley Coffee Emporium (603-236-4021), Town Square. Open daily 6:30 AM–6 PM. Enjoy cappuccinos, lattes, smoothies, chai, breakfast waffles and omelets, afternoon tea, homemade pastries, and other treats while overlooking the pond and mountains.

In Campton

🍴 **Mad River Tavern & Restaurant** (603-726-4290; madtav.com), Rt. 49 (just off I-93, Exit 28). Open for dinner, lunch on weekends. Serving Fri. and Sat. until 11 PM. A homey atmosphere with an overstuffed couch, blackboard specials, and a large, varied menu. There's a wide choice of pastas

and breads as well as fish. We recommend the veal Oscar, lightly breaded and topped with lobster, asparagus, and béarnaise sauce. Burgers, sandwiches, salads, beer, and wine are also served. Appetizers $2–10; pasta $7–14; entrées $11–18. Lunch $4–7.

✍ **Sunset Grill** (603-726-3108), corner of Rts. 3 and 49. Open daily except Mon. 11:30 AM–10 PM, Sun. brunch 9–2. A funky, friendly roadhouse with good food: a wide selection of pastas and house specials ranging from calves' liver to buffalo steak; also burgers, chili, and Cajun dishes. Sunday brunch is a specialty, featuring lobster omelets and crêpes Florentine. Fifty brands of bottled beer. Live music Sat night; "Kids Menu."

The Stix Mountain Food & Spirits (603-726-8787), 18 Six Flags Rd., around the corner from the gas station just off I-93 Exit 28. Open 7–2, until 3 Sat., with beer and wine service beginning at 11. Rustic and very reasonably priced. Breakfasts feature omelets and offbeat egg dishes like smoky "Eggs in a Nest" (two eggs baked in a biscuit with melted cheddar and home fries). The lunch menu is far from dull. We can vouch for the gumbo soup with okra and shrimp.

In Plymouth

Biederman's Deli and Pub (603-536-3354), 83 Main St., under Chase Street Market. Open for lunch and dinner daily. A brick-walled, pubby spot claiming 180,000 combinations using Boar's Head meats and cheeses; also deli salads and bag lunches, a wide selection of beers. Inquire about comedy nights and live bands.

✍ **The Main Street Station** (603-536-7577), 105 Main St. Open Mon.–Sat. 7–3, Sun. 7–1. Diner buffs head for this vintage 1946 classic (Worcester Streamliner #793A) in the middle of Plymouth's Main St. Breakfasts are a gut-busting affair of eggs in all forms, pancakes, waffles, and French toast; better-than-average diner food and fast, friendly service.

Italian Farmhouse (603-536-4536), 331 Rt. 3, 2 miles south of Plymouth. It's also 4 miles north of I-93 Exit 24. Open for dinner nightly. Another Common Man creation, this old farmhouse is now a local favorite featuring fresh-baked Italian bread, fried calamari, stuffed veal, and brick-oven pizza. Mixed reviews.

The Country Cow Restaurant at Blair Bridge (603-536-1331), off I-93 Exit 27, Blair Rd., Campton. Lunch and dinner except Tue.; Sun. brunch. Early "Milking Hour" specials, 4:30–5:30. Chef owned, cheerful, reasonably priced pastas, salads, steaks, lighter items like a veggie bowl and burgers. Full liquor.

🖋 **George's Seafood & B-B-Que** (603-536-6330), 588 Tenney Mountain Hwy., Plymouth. Open for lunch and dinner. A cheerful family-owned and -geared restaurant specializing in lobster, seafood, and ribs—but there's plenty besides. Beer and wine, reasonable prices.

✷ Entertainment

Silver Cultural Arts Center at Plymouth State University (603-535-2787; plymouth.edu/silver), Main and Court Sts., Plymouth. Check the website for current concerts, theater, and live performances. This is the summer venue for the New Hampshire Music Festival (nhmf.org).

The Flying Monkey (603-536-2551), 39 S. Main St., Plymouth. Formerly the Plymouth Theater, a 1930s movie palace that's recently reopened after a major renovation. Now part of "The Common Man Family" (thecman

.com), it features live performances as well as films.

Shakespeare in the Valley (603-716-0098), Noon Peak Rd., Waterville Valley. July–Aug., lively presentations of "Shakespeare as Willy himself intended." Also some children's productions.

✷ Selective Shopping

CRAFTS SHOPS Artistic Roots Art Center (603-536-2750; artisticroots .com), 75 Main St., on the common, Plymouth. Open daily 10–6. This is a great crafts co-op representing 40 artists and artisans from many parts of the state, with a range of furniture, jewelry, pottery, cards, art, and more. Inquire about workshops and classes. The new cellar-level space is large enough to permit special performances and events such as Saturday Souperbowl: you eat the soup and take home the member-made bowl.

Shanware Pottery (603-786-9835; shanware.com), 1918 Rt. 25, Rumney. Open daily, varying hours. A working studio, gallery, and sculpture garden featuring functional stoneware pottery and porcelain: mugs, casseroles, chimes, dinnerware, planters, plus distinctive one-of-a-kind creations.

SPECIAL STORES

In Waterville Valley Town Square
Dreams and Visions (603-236-2020), 6 Village Rd. Books and gifts.

🖋 **Bookmonger and Toad Hall** (603-236-4544). Toys and games for children of all ages, paperbacks, games, CDs, magazines, general titles.

I Dream of Beading (603-236-4166). Make your own beaded jewelry.

Mountains of Chocolate (603-236-3301). Novelty, candies, and fine chocolates.

In Plymouth

Plymouth Book Exchange (603-536-2528), 91 Main St., Plymouth. A full-service bookstore, also office and art supplies, children's and audio books.

✳ Special Events

Easter Sunday: **Sunrise service** on Mount Tecumseh.

Memorial Day weekend: **Annual Chowderfest** at Waterville Valley.

Fourth of July: **Parade and fireworks** at Waterville Valley.

August: **Curious George Family Festival** (*early*), **Bluegrass Festival** (*late*), Waterville Valley. **Pemi Valley Bluegrass Festival** at Branch Brook Campground, Campton (603-716-7001). **White Mountain Boogie'n'Blues**, Thornton (nhblues.com).

September: **Waterville Valley Labor Day End of Summer Bash**.

Columbus Day weekend: **Fall Foliage Festival** at Waterville Valley.

November: **Ski trails open** midmonth at Waterville Valley; Northern Lights Celebration with **tree lighting** and fireworks, Thanksgiving weekend.

LINCOLN AND NORTH WOODSTOCK

North Woodstock is a sleepy village. Lincoln, a mile east, is one of New Hampshire's liveliest resort towns. Until relatively recently, the opposite was true. Around the turn of the 20th century, Lincoln boomed into existence as a company town with a company-owned school, store, hotel, hospital, and housing for hundreds of workers, all built by the legendary lumber baron J. E. Henry. It remained a smoke-belching "mill town" well into the 1970s.

North Woodstock, set against two dramatic notches—Kinsman and Franconia—boasted half a dozen large hotels, among them the Deer Park, accommodating 250 guests. Today Deer Park is still a familiar name, but only as one of the dozen major condominium complexes that have recently become synonymous with this area. With Loon Mountain as its centerpiece, the Lincoln-Woodstock area can now accommodate 18,000 visitors.

Loon Mountain was opened by former New Hampshire governor Sherman Adams (see "The Western Whites" introduction) in 1966 with a gondola, two chairlifts, an octagonal base lodge, and the then unheard-of policy of limiting lift-ticket sales. In 1973, I-93 reached Lincoln, depositing skiers 3 miles from the lifts. But it wasn't until the early 1980s that the town of Lincoln itself began to boom.

Three things happened at that time: All the land owned by the paper mill, which had closed in 1979, became available; Loon itself had grown into a substantial ski area; and a real estate boom was sweeping New Hampshire's lakes and mountains. Just south of Franconia Notch and surrounded by national forest, Lincoln was a developer's dream: relatively cheap land with no zoning. A heady few years ensued, and eventually zoning kicked in. Then came decades of permitting and reviews. Finally, under ownership by Michigan-based Boyne Resorts, Loon Mountain has opened its South Peak area with easy access from upscale new single family homes and luxury condos. It's also connected by a fast quad and several trails to the original Lincoln Peak area. The town now "sleeps" 13,000 visitors.

Summer is busier than winter, given the natural and family attractions—such as the **Annual New Hampshire Highland Games**, where thousands of people turn

Scottish for this annual salute to tartan, haggis, and bagpipes—as well as hiking, camping, and touring. In winter Loon is the only big draw. There's also skiing and snowshoeing off the Kancamagus.

GUIDANCE **White Mountains Gateway Visitors Center** (800-346-3687; visit whitemountains.com). Open daily 8:30–5, later in summer; just off I-93 Exit 32. This is one of New England's outstanding visitors centers, recently expanded to include superb displays on the area's resort history, the logging era, and the White Mountain National Forest. The tourism side is also staffed and helpful. Note the diorama of the entire White Mountains region.

Lincoln-Woodstock Chamber of Commerce (603-745-6621) maintains an office upstairs in the Village Shops (formerly the Mill Marketplace; open weekdays 9–5), as well as the website lincolnwoodstock.com.

GETTING THERE *By bus:* **Concord Coach** (800-639-3317; concordcoachlines .com) provides daily service to and from Concord, Manchester, and Boston, stopping at the Shell station on Rt. 112 in Lincoln.

By car: I-93 Exit 32 accesses both towns.

GETTING AROUND During ski season the Loon Mountain Shuttle services local lodging, making coming by bus a viable option.

The Shuttle Connection (603-745-3140; 800-648-4947; theshuttleconnection .com) serves local destinations and offers drop-offs for hikers as well service to Manchester and Logan Airports.

WHEN TO COME Weekends in summer, fall, and winter are all busy, and there's a hum to the place; we favor midweek in late September, early October, and during ski season.

MEDICAL EMERGENCY Call **911**. **LinWood Medical Center** (603-745-8136), Lincoln.

✳ To Do

AERIAL RIDES **Zip-Line Canopy Tour, Alpine Adventures** (603-745-9911; 888-745-9911; alpinezipline.com), 41 Main St., Lincoln. This was New England's first treetop canopy tour, now with six lines, from 80 to 600 feet and as high as 250 feet, including a suspension bridge over Barron Gorge. A Sky Rider tour sends you soaring then dropping 80 feet at 50 mph. $85 per ride.

Also see the **Loon Mountain Gondola Ride** in the Loon Mountain box, and **Cannon Mountain Aerial Tramway** in the Franconcia Notch State Park section of the next chapter.

BICYCLING **The Franconia Notch Recreation Trail** is a favorite route that runs 9 miles one way from the Flume Visitor Center to the trailhead for the Skookumchuck Trail on Rt. 3. *Note:* Rentals are available at Loon Mountain, which offers a shuttle to Echo Lake, where you can pick up the bike path. **Biking trail maps** of the WMNF are available at the White Mountains Gateway Visitors Center. Rentals are available from the **Loon Mountain Bike Center** (see the Loon Mountain box).

BOATING Outback Kayak (603-745-2002; outbackkayak.com), Main St., North Woodstock, rents kayaks and offers shuttles to upper (more rapids) and lower (easy) sections of the Pemi.

CAMPING For a list of public campgrounds along the Kancamagus Highway, see "White Mountain National Forest."

FOR FAMILIES *Indian Head*. Like the vanished Old Man of the Mountain, this craggy profile on Mount Pemigewasset, visible from Rt. 3, is an old local landmark. It is best seen from the Rt. 3 parking lot of the Indian Head Resort. The summit is accessible via the Mount Pemigewasset Trail, which starts off the Franconia Notch Recreation Trail just north of the Flume Visitors Center.

Clark's Trading Post (603-745-8913; clarkstradingpost.com), 110 Rt. 3, Lincoln. Open daily July–Labor Day, 9:30–6; weekends Memorial Day–June and Sept.–mid-Oct. One of the country's oldest theme parks, begun in the 1920s as a sled dog ranch (Florence Clark was the first woman to reach the summit of Mount Washington by dogsled). Still owned and managed by the Clark family, known for trained-bear shows (three times daily in July and August), also featuring a steam train and variety of steam-powered attractions, a haunted house, Avery's old-time garage and the 1890s fire station, a photo parlor, bumper boats, Merlin's Mystical Mansion, and a variety show. $18 ages 6–64, $7 ages 3–, $16 over 65.

& Lost River Gorge & Boulder Caves (603-745-8031; lostrivergorge.com), 1712 Lost River Rd. (Rt. 112), 7 miles west of North Woodstock. July–Aug. 9–6; May and June plus Sept.–mid-Oct., 9–5. This was the first acquisition of the Society for the Protection of New Hampshire Forests, purchased from a local timber company in 1912. The Nature Garden here is said to feature more than 300 varieties of native plants, and the glacial meltwater gorge is spectacular. Boardwalks thread a series of basins and caves, past rock formations with names like Guillotine Rock and Hall of Ships. Now maintained by the White Mountains Attractions, the complex includes a snack bar and gift shop. You can also pan for gemstones at the Lost River Mining Co. $15 adults, $11 ages 4–12.

CLARK'S TRADING POST

Hobo Railroad (603-745-2135; hoborr.com), Hobo Junction (just east of I-93), Rt. 112, Lincoln. Open Memorial Day–Halloween, daily July–Labor Day, otherwise weekends, and again on weekends from Thanksgiving to Christmas. A 15-mile roundtrip excursion along the Pemigewasset River in "dining coaches" with velour seats and tables. Optional lunch and snacks. $13 adults, $10 ages 3–12.

✔ **Hobo Hills Adventure Golf** (603-745-2125), Rt. 112, Lincoln. Late May–mid-Oct. Three acres of greens and putts through caves and waterfalls. $8 adults, $7 ages 4–12.

✔ **White Mountain Motorsports Park** (603-745-6727; whitemountainmotor sports.com), Rt. 3, Woodstock. Open late Apr.–mid-Oct. A 0.25-mile asphalt track with stock-car races every Saturday. $20 adults, $5 children.

✔ **The Whale's Tale Waterpark** (603-745-8810; whalestalewaterpark.net), Rt. 3, Lincoln. Open daily late June–Labor Day 10–6; weekends from Memorial Day. A 17-acre water park with a wave pool, speed and curvy slides, wading pool for small children, tube rentals. Rates are $30 per day, including tubes. Children under 3 and adults over 70, free.

Also see the Loon Mountain box.

FISHING The free Freshwater Fishing Guide is available at local information centers. Anglers frequent the East Branch of the Pemi, Russell Pond, and many mountain streams.

GOLF Jack O'Lantern Country Club (603-745-3636), Rt. 3, Woodstock. Eighteen-hole, par-70 course, instruction, rental clubs, golf carts, and pull carts. Also see the golf courses described in "Franconia" and the **Owl's Nest Golf Club** in the "Waterville Valley" section of this chapter.

HIKING *Note:* **Mountain Wanderer Map & Bookstore** (603-745-2594), 57 Rt. 112 in the middle of Lincoln, is a prime source of local hiking suggestions as well as maps and books. Owner Steve Smith edits the AMC's *White Mountain Guide*; his own book is *Wandering Through the White Mountains*.

Mount Moosilauke. The **Benton Trail** ascends the northwest flank of Mount Moosilauke at a steady, moderate grade. The trail begins in a parking area off Tunnel Brook Rd.; take Rt. 112 west from North Woodstock about 10 miles and drive 3 miles south on Tunnel Brook Rd. Other trails, the most popular being the **George Brook Trail**, begin at the Dartmouth Outing Club's **Ravine Lodge** (603-764-5858). Our favorite description of the view from the 4,802-foot summit is credited to clergyman and author Dr. Washington Gladden: "I give my preference to Moosilauke over every mountain whose top I have climbed. The view from Washington is vast, but vague; the view from Lafayette is notable, but it shows little of the sweet restfulness of the Connecticut Valley; on Moosilauke we get all forms of grandeur and all types of beauty."

For trails off the Kancamagus Scenic Byway, see "The White Mountains National Forest."

Greeley Ponds. This easy trail is 4.5 miles roundtrip, beginning on the Kancamagus Hwy., 9 miles east of Lincoln. As local hiking guru Steve Smith describes it: The trail climbs gradually to the high point of Mad River Notch, then dips down to Upper Greeley Pond, a deep tarn hemmed in by the cliff-studded slopes of Mount Osceola's East Peak and Mount Kancamagus. Half a mile farther you reach the south shore of boggy Lower Greeley Pond, where you can look north into the cleft of the notch.

Lincoln Woods Trail begins in the parking lot of the Lincoln Woods information center (warm drinks, restrooms, trail maps) on the Kancamagus Hwy. just east of Lincoln. The trail crosses the East Branch of the Pemigewasset via a suspension bridge and follows the river along the bed of the old logging railroad. It accesses several other relatively short trails leading to Black Pond and Franconia Falls, connecting with the **Wilderness Trail**, which in turn accesses several trails through the Pemigewasset Wilderness.

MOOSE-WATCHING Look for moose along Rt. 118 and the Kancamagus Scenic Byway (see *Scenic Drives*). **Pemi Valley Excursions** (603-745-2744), Rt. 112, Lincoln, offers morning and evening guided Moose Tours.

PICNICKING *Note:* See the Kancamagus National Scenic Byway, below. Also:

Beaver Pond, Rt. 112 west from North Woodstock in Kinsman Notch, beyond Lost River. A beautiful pond with a rock promontory for picnicking or sunning and a view of Mount Blue.

ROCK CLIMBING Pemi Valley Rock Gym (603-745-9800), Main St., Rt. 3 at Alpine Village, North Woodstock. Twenty-foot-high indoor rock climbing wall with beginner to advanced routes.

Also see the Loon Mountain box.

SCENIC DRIVES Kancamagus National Scenic Byway (Rt. 112). The 34.5-mile paved "Kanc" is open all year, weather conditions permitting. It's detailed in the previous "White Mountain National Forest" chapter, but you might want to stop at the **White Mountains Gateway Visitors Center** in Lincoln or at the **Lincoln Woods** information center/warming hut staffed year-round by national forest rangers. Pick up a map and guide to the highway and detailed sheets on specific trails and campgrounds. Most travelers drive this as part of **the White Mountains Trail**, turning north in Conway on Rt. 302 and following it through North Conway and Crawford Notch to Rt. 3 south to the **Franconia Notch Parkway**, the area's other prime scenic drive, detailed in the next chapter in the detailed section on Franconia Notch State Park.

Kinsman Notch. Rt. 112 west from North Woodstock is less traveled but as beautiful as the Kancamagus, climbing quickly into Kinsman Notch—past **Lost River** and **Beaver Pond**—crossing the Appalachian Trail. You can continue on by the Wildwood Campground to Mount Moosilauke or cut up Rt. 116 to Easton, Sugar Hill, and Franconia, and back down through Franconia Notch. Another option is to take the dirt Long Pond Road off Rt. 116 beyond Kinsman Notch, through the national forest to Long Pond, where there is a boat launch and, we're told, good fishing; also picnic sites. You can return to Rt. 116 or continue on to Rt. 25.

Tripoli Road. Pronounced *triple eye*, this shortcut from I-93 (Exit 31, Woodstock) to Waterville Valley accesses a number of hiking trails and campsites. It is also a fine foliage-season loop, returning to Woodstock via Rts. 49 and 175.

Rt. 118 west from North Woodstock climbs steeply through the national forest (there's a panoramic view near the top of the road), then down into the Baker River Valley. You may want to stop at the **Polar Caves** in Plymouth and cut back up I-93; or take Rt. 25 to Haverhill with its handsome old village center (just south of the junction of Rts. 25 and 10), returning via Rts. 116 and 112 through Kinsman Notch.

HORSEBACK RIDING See the Loon Mountain box and Franconia Stables in the next chapter.

SWIMMING *Swimming holes:* The **Lady's Bathtub**, in the Pemigewasset River, Lincoln. Deep and fringed with a little sand, accessible through the parking lot at Riverfront Condos. In North Woodstock the **Cascades** is a favorite dunking spot in the Pemi, especially good for small children, accessible from the park right behind Main Street. Other spots on the Pemi can be found along Rt. 175 in Woodstock. One is just across from the Tripoli Road–I-93 interchange.

Also see the **Whale's Tale Waterpark** under *For Families* and the Loon Mountain box.

TENNIS Indian Head Resort (603-745-8000). Outdoor tennis courts.

The Mountain Club Fitness Center (603-745-8111). Loon Mountain also offers outdoor courts.

✳ Winter Sports

CROSS-COUNTRY SKIING Lincoln Woods Trail. Off the Kancamagus just west of Lincoln, an inviting warming hut (warm drinks, restrooms) staffed by national forest rangers marks the entrance to an extensive trail system; the first 3 miles are groomed on both sides of the river.

Stop by the White Mountain National Forest desk in the White Mountains Gateway Visitors Center (see *Guidance*) and pick up detailed maps to and advice about trail networks farther along the "Kanc." These include the Lower and Upper Nanamocomuck Ski Trails, the Oliverian/Downes Brook Ski Trail, and the Greeley Ponds Trail.

Also see the Loon Mountain box.

DOWNHILL SKIING See the Loon Mountain box.

SNOWMOBILING Trail maps available locally detail the extensive local system. Guided tours and rentals are offered in Lincoln by **Alpine Adventures** (603-745-9911), 41 Main St., and **Outback Kayak** (603-745-2002), 112 Main St.

✳ Lodging
CONDO-STYLE RESORTS

In Lincoln
✦ Ẓ **The Mountain Club on Loon** (603-745-2244; 800-229-7829; mtnclub.com), 90 Loon Mountain Rd.,

Lincoln 03251. Forget the hassles of parking a mile away and lugging your gear to the slope. Any time of year, this

LOON MOUNTAIN RESORT

(603-745-8111; 800-229-LOON; loonmtn.com), Rt. 112, 2 miles east of I-93 Exit 32. Summer activities are offered late June–Columbus Day, from 9:30 AM. Ski season is late Nov.–mid-April. Year-round facilities include The Mountain Club on Loon, The Mountain Club Fitness Center, and Viaggio Spa.

IN SUMMER

🖊 **Aerial Ride Loon Mountain Gondola Skyride** (603-745-8111). Mid-June–Columbus Day, 9:30 –5:30. Ride in a four-passenger, enclosed gondola to the summit, where there's an observation tower and summit cafeteria. Here, too, a stairway leads through boulders and into glacially carved caves, on to hiking trails. On summer Sundays there's a nondenominational service at the summit, followed by brunch.

🖊 **Loon Mountain Adventure Center** (603-745-8111), Lincoln. Open late June–mid-Sept., offering mountain bike rentals and guided group tours. Shuttle service is offered to Echo Lake in Franconia Notch State Park. The 9-mile bike trail back through Franconia Park and then a few more miles to Loon is generally gently downhill. Serious bicyclists will also find guidance about trails accessible from the Kancamagus Hwy.

🖊 **Horseback Riding Loon Mountain** (603-745-8111). Summer trail rides for beginners and intermediates, also private tours. Must be 8 years old.

HORSEBACK RIDING AT LOON

Loon Mountain Resort

LOON MOUNTAIN SKIERS

SWIMMING **The Viaggio Spa at the Mountain Club** (603-745-2244), Rt. 112, Lincoln. Open 7 AM–10 PM daily. Indoor lap pool, outdoor pool in summer. Full spa service.

IN WINTER

DOWNHILL SKIING Known for long cruising trails and easy access, Loon is a nicely designed mountain, with dozens of intermediate trails streaking its face and a choice of steeply pitched trails, served by their own high-altitude East Basin high-speed detachable chair on North Peak. Beginners have the Kissing Cousins chair and slope to themselves, then graduate to a choice of equally isolated (from hot-rod skiers) runs in the West Basin.

The only hitch is that the main base area and West Basin are separated by a long, string-bean-shaped parking lot. The lay of the land dictates the strung-out shape of Loon's base facilities—along a narrow shelf above the Pemigewasset River, which in turn has cut this steep Upper Pemi Valley.

For **snowboarders** there's Little Sister, a first-of-its-kind Burton Progression Park. For thrillseekers, both boarders and freestyle skiers, there is award-winnng Loon Mountain Park.

Vertical drop: 2,100 feet (base 950 feet; summit 3,050 feet).

Lifts: Four-passenger gondola, three high-speed detachable quads, one quad, one triple, three double chairs, and three surface lifts.

Trails: 49—with 20 percent easiest, 64 percent more difficult, and 16 percent most difficult—plus 6 glades (26 miles total).

Snowmaking: 98 percent.

Facilities: Three base lodges, rental shop, terrain parks, **Superpipe** (425 feet), **tubing, indoor climbing wall**, midmountain lodge. Slope-side lodging at the 234-room **Mountain Club** includes condo units, indoor pool, game rooms, and restaurants; ice skating, cross-country skiing. No less than nine slope-side food sources include the **Summit Café** at the top of the gondola; **Camp III**, good for stews and baking near the NorthPeakExpress; the spacious **Cornerside Café** and **Hearthside Pub** in the Octagon Lodge; and a choice of basics in the Governor Adams Lodge as well as the new **Pemigewasset Base Camp** at the Lincoln Express Quad serving South Peak. For après-ski check out the **Paul Bunyan Room** on the top floor of the Octagon Lodge.

Ski and snowboard school: More than 200 instructors can teach ages 3–93, all abilities and all terrain.

For children: Loon Mountain Nursery for ages 6 weeks–6 years; P. K. Boo Bear Camp (3-year-olds), Kinder Bear Camp (4–6), Discovery Camp (7–12).

Lift tickets: $73 adults, $63 teens, $53 junior/seniors; those 80-plus and 5 and under ski free.

CROSS-COUNTRY SKIING 22km of trails, some winding partway up the mountain, others following the riverbed. Rentals, instruction, special events.

ICE SKATING Lighted outdoor rink near the main base lodge; rentals available.

VIEW FROM LOON MOUNTAIN

Loon Mountain Resort

is your best bet if you want to take full advantage of what Loon Mountain Resort offers. The 234-condo unit hotel has standard rooms with king beds, studio family rooms with cooking facilities, and 117 "suites"—two rooms with cooking facilities, dining, and lounging space. Facilities include a formal restaurant, informal tavern dining, and room service. A complete health club with indoor and outdoor pools, Jacuzzis, saunas, squash court, and steam rooms—plus the full-service spa. $125–292 in winter, from $89 summer/fall. Packages are available throughout the year.

🌿 ✏ **Lodge at Lincoln Station** (603-745-3441; 800-654-6188), P.O. Box 906, Lincoln 03251. Midway between town and mountain, with studios, one-bedrooms, and loft suites overlooking the river (be sure to request one) and a central "Great Room" with a hearth; also indoor and outdoor pools, a Jacuzzi, saunas, game room, and tennis courts. Rates in-season $75–110 for a hotel room, $100–130 for a studio, $130–199 for suites sleeping four to six people.

✏ **The Village of Loon Mountain** (603-745-3401; villageofloon.com), 94 Loon Mountain Rd., Lincoln 03251. Positioned directly across the road from Loon Mountain, nicely designed to blend into the hillside. Of the 650 units here, less than 100 are in the rental pool. Amenities include two indoor pools, 12 outdoor tennis courts (2 are flooded to form a skating rink in winter), a kids' game room with arcade, and table tennis. One-, two-, and three-bedroom units from $149, two-night minimum.

InnSeason Resorts South Mountain (603-745-9300; 866-873-2766; inn season.com), P.O. Box 1058, Lincoln 03251. Handy to the Village Shops and restaurants in a former mill and to Loon's new South Mountain base area, a choice of standard units, also one- and two-bedroom units. Amenities include indoor and outdoor pools, whirlpools, and an exercise room. $129–229.

INN ♿ "🍴" **The Woodstock Inn** (603-745-3951; 800-321-3985; woodstockinn nh.com), P.O. Box 118, Main St. (Rt. 3), North Woodstock 03262. Known for its microbrewery and its formal (on the glassed-in front porch) and informal dining (in Woodstock Station out back; see *Eating Out*), this long-popular establishment also offers 33 antiques-furnished rooms (31 with private bath) in the main inn and in three additional Victorian houses. All rooms have a phone and color TV; some have Jacuzzi, fireplace, and air-conditioning. $78–204 (high end is for a suite) per couple. Children free in the same room with parent but charged for breakfast.

BED & BREAKFAST 🌿 ✏ "🍴"
Wilderness Inn (603-745-3890; 888-777-7813; thewildernessinn.com), Rt. 3 and Courtney Rd., North Woodstock 03262. This 1912 Arts & Crafts–style house was well built by a lumbermill owner on the edge of the village, and within earshot of the Lost River. It's one of the most charming places to stay in the White Mountains, good for couples, singles, and families alike, depending on which room you pick. Each is themed for a country owners Rosanna and Michael Yarnell visited with their children during a year of traveling around the world. The New Zealand Room is good for a single or loving couple while the Italian Suite offers both the romance of a gas fire-place and whirlpool tub and bunk beds for the kids in the adjoining room. We particularly like the French Room with

its impressive four-poster and whirlpool tub, and the colorful Caribbean Cottage with its queen sleigh bed, whirlpool tub, and gas fireplace. There's an inviting living room with a wood-burning hearth and an enclosed sunporch on which breakfast is served from an extensive menu (see *Where to Eat*). All have private bath and TV. The cottage has air-conditioning and a deck. Rates are $95–175 in high season, $70–140 in low, and include a full breakfast.

MOTELS ✒ **Indian Head Resort** (603-745-8000; 800-343-8000; indian headresort.com), Lincoln 03251. First opened in the 1920s, gradually evolving to its present 98 motel rooms on three floors (no elevator) and cabins (with fireplaces but closed in winter). All units have 50-inch plasma HDTV. Indoor and outdoor heated pools, lake with pedal boats, tennis courts, game room, coffee shop, Laundromat, and dining room. Inquire about children's entertainment and special children's activities. $89–199.

Woodward's Resort (603-745-8141; 800-635-8968; woodwardsresort.com), Rt. 3, RR 1, Box 107, Lincoln 03251. An 85-unit complex that has grown gradually over the past 48 years, this resort is now open year-round, still managed by the Woodward family. Rooms are clean but plain, though extras like refrigerators and coffeemakers make you feel right at home. Recreational facilities include indoor and outdoor pools, an indoor racquetball court, a tennis court (you can rent racquets), and a pond used for winter ice skating (management provides skates). In summer there are also lawn games. The **Colonial Dining Room** serves breakfast daily, and dinner is served nightly in the **Open Hearth Dining Room**; there's also a lounge. $95–145.

Kancamagus Motor Lodge (603-745-3365; 800-346-4205; kancmotor lodge.com), Rt. 112, Lincoln. Family owned, with a nice feel to its 34 rooms with queen or two double beds, air-conditioning, steam showers and baths; some have balcony or sleeper sofa. Amenities include an indoor pool, a game room, a locally liked restaurant (Brittany's) serving breakfast and dinner (see *Eating Out*), and a sports bar. $99–149 in summer.

✴ Where to Eat

DINING OUT ✒ **Gypsy Café** (603-745-4395), 117 Main St. (Rt. 112), Lincoln. Open except Mon. and Tue. for lunch (11–4) and dinner (5–9). Fully licensed. Reservations suggested on weekends. The previous chef-owner established a stellar reputation for the varied menu, now maintained by Clare Duris and son Dan Duris now maintain. We can recommend the Gypsy Niçoise salad: grilled yellowfin tuna on greens with grilled asparagus. Lunch options include panini and grilled sandwiches as well as daily-made soups. Dinner choices include slow-cooked osso buco with a sweet tomato demiglaze, Thai red curry duck, and Jamaican jerk salmon. Lighter meals are also available at dinner. The Cuban flan (rich and creamy with a caramel topping) is a standout, and key lime pie is a specialty. The "Kids Menu" includes pizza and quesadillas. The colorful 10-table front dining room is backed by an attractive blue and blue-lit (smoke-free) bar specializing in margaritas; an enclosed side porch is warmed by a gas fireplace. $14.99–22.99.

The Common Man (603-745-3463; thecman.com), at the corner of Pollard Rd. and Main St., Lincoln. Open nightly except Thanksgiving and Christmas. The winning formula here is a limited menu stressing simplicity and fresh ingredients, from pasta primavera, to lobster and rock crab cakes, to prime rib and filet mignon plus a grill menu. There's a huge fireplace and the cozy lounge. Entrées $15–24.

The Mountain Club on Loon (603-745-6281), 90 Loon Mountain Rd., Lincoln. Open daily for dinner. This fairly formal restaurant features entrées that might range from portobello mushroom ravioli ($27) to lobster linguine ($34). Sides include truffled french fries ($7) and lentil fennel apple salad ($6).

Clement Room Grill at the Woodstock Inn (603-745-3951; woodstock innnh.com), Main St. (Rt. 3), North Woodstock. Open nightly 5:30–9:30. Set crisply with white linen tablecloths and fine china, the inn's formal dining room offers an à la carte menu including appetizers like ostrich quesadilla and pan-fried ravioli with red pepper pesto. Entrées range from chicken dishes to fillet Barcelona: a 9-ounce center-cut fillet butterflied and stuffed with sautéed scallops and crab and topped with hollandaise sauce ($13–24).

Ø **Gordi's Fish and Steak House** (603-745-6635), Rt. 112, Lincoln. Dinner is served daily 4–10 PM. The decor is glitzy Victorian mixed with photos of ski heroes past and present (Owner Gordi Eaton was a member of the 1950 and '64 US Olympic ski teams and coached Karen Budge, a member of the '68 team and now his wife). There are nightly specials like blackened tuna, stuffed pork with apple gravy, or salmon en papillote; standard menu items include fish-and-chips and other seafood. Beef lovers are well served with prime rib, filet mignon, or New York sirloin. Lighter meals include chicken done up a number of ways as well as pasta dishes—and you

can also make a meal of the salad bar. Thursday is an all-you-can-eat fish fry for $9.79; otherwise $12.99–23.

Café Lafayette Dinner Train (603-745-3500; nhdinnertrain.com), Rt. 112, North Woodstock. Late June–Labor Day: departures Tue., Thu., Sat., and Sun. at 5:30 in summer, at 5 in fall. Weekends in spring. A vintage-train ride. Rolling stock includes a restored 1924 coach with brass and stained glass, a tri-level 1952 domed observation car, and a 1953 café coach. Tables are geared to four; there's a surcharge for a private table for two (when seated with a guest, you are both on the same side of the table). Tickets include a two-hour ride and five-course meal. The typical menu might open with pâté, then proceed through sorbet to a choice of chicken, salmon, or pork dishes; dessert but not wine is included. $73–83 adults, $53–63 ages 6–11. Reservations recommended.

EATING OUT 🍴 *Ø* **Woodstock Station** (603-745-3951; woodstockinnnh .com), at the Woodstock Inn, Main St. (Rt. 3), North Woodstock. This railroad station was built in the late 1800s in Lincoln and continued to serve visitors—including skiers bound for Cannon Mountain—into the 1930s and 1940s. In 1984 it was sawed in half and moved to its present location at the rear of the Woodstock Inn. The old freight room is now the bar, and the passenger waiting room is the lower dining room. This large, eclectically furnished space, which now includes the Woodstock Inn brewery, is one of the liveliest dining spots in the North Country, and the menu boasts—count 'em—148 items: everything from frogs' legs to Peking ravioli, quesadillas and nachos and burritos (lots of Mexican), a wide choice of original sandwiches, pastas, baked scrod, ribs, and burgers, children's menu. Beverages fill four more pages of the menu and include a wide variety of imported and micro-brewed beers.

✐ **Fratello's Ristorate Italiano** (603-745-2022; fratellos.com), Village Shops, Main St. (Rt. 112), Lincoln. One in a New Hampshire chain of atmospheric, reasonably priced family restaurants. The menu is large, with plenty of pastas, pizzas, "antipasti," and "insalata" from which to choose along with classic veal and seafood entrées.

Texas Toast Eatery (745-9977), Village Shops, Rt. 112, Lincoln. Open daily for breakfast and lunch (7–2). Hidden away in the Village Shops (former Mill Marketplace), this pleasant café specializes in freshly made New England and southern comfort food prepared from scratch.

Brittany's Café (603-745-4899), Rt. 112, Lincoln. Open daily for breakfast and dinner. This pleasant dining room in the Kancamagus Motor Lodge is worth finding: good food, reasonable prices. The signature dishes are garlic steak and Chicken Brittany, but the choice is wide. The adjoining sports bar and pub, **CJ's Penalty Box**, is a popular gathering spot.

✐ **Peg's—A Family Restaurant** (603-745-2740), 99 Main St., North Woodstock. Open daily for breakfast and lunch. Roll up your sleeves alongside loggers and other local denizens in this plainly furnished but friendly room for rib-sticking breakfasts of eggs and steak, omelets, pancakes, and Belgian waffles. On a budget? Keep an eye out for the 99¢ breakfast specials. New England favorites like hot meat loaf, turkey, and roast beef sandwiches—not to mention burgers, hot dogs, western and eastern sandwiches—are all served with a smile and words of wisdom. Look for daily specials like American chop suey (macaroni, beef, and tomato

sauce baked together) or liver and onions served with mashed potatoes.

✿ ✐ **Truants Taverne** (603-745-2239), Main St., North Woodstock. Open daily 11:30 AM–10 PM. Hung over the river in a back-behind kind of space, part of an old mill yard. Polished pine tables and a large menu that's fun to read. For lunch choose from a wide selection of cleverly named burgers as well as soups, sandwiches on house-made honey wheat bread, and salads. Longtime Truants chef John Marro prides himself on fresh seafood and on using Black Angus beef. You'll also find Mexican dishes and a wide selection of beers. A good place.

Chieng Gardens (603-745-8612), Lincoln Square, Main St., Lincoln. A better-than-average Chinese restaurant with a large, reasonably priced menu and the best view (upstairs, facing the mountains) of any restaurant in Lincoln.

For breakfast

Wilderness Inn and Café (603-745-3890), Rt. 3 and Courtney Rd., North Woodstock. Serving mid-Feb.–mid-Sept. 8–10 AM. It's a short walk from downtown to this pleasant, hospitable guesthouse serving freshly ground coffee, homemade muffins, selected hot crêpes, and multiple choices of pancakes with homemade syrup, eggs, and omelets. Reservations appreciated.

The Woodstock Inn (603-745-3951; woodstockinnnh.com), Main St. (Rt. 3), North Woodstock. A wide range of waffles, omelets, and other memorable breakfast fare—like homemade red-flannel hash with poached egg and home fries, bagels and lox, and huevos rancheros.

Also see **Texas Toast**, **Brittany's Café**, and **Peg's**, above.

SNACKS Udderly Delicious Ice Cream Shop (603-745-6668), 121 Main St., Lincoln. Open daily in summer, closed Tue.,Wed. off-season. Bobby-Sue's ice cream is homemade in Freedom, New Hampshire, served in hand-dipped, chocolate-coated waffle cones in an ice cream parlor complete with black-and-white-tiled floor and cast-iron tables.

✳ Entertainment

🎭 **Papermill Theatre** (603-745-2141; papermilltheatre.org), at **North Country Center for the Arts** (603-745-6032), Village Shops, Main St., Lincoln. Professional summer theater with shows July and Aug. Mon.–Sat; musicals, comedy, classics, children's theater on Wed. and Sat.

Lincoln Cinemas 4 (603-745-6238), Lincoln Center North, Main St., Lincoln. Four screens.

Summer band concerts are held regularly on the common in North Woodstock.

White Mountain Music Festival (603-444-0309). The North Country Chamber Players perform at the Governor's Lodge at Loon Mountain, among other regional venues, in July and Aug.

✳ Selective Shopping

Note: Lincoln's Main St. (Rt. 112) is a string of independent shops, gas stations, fast-food chains, and several mini malls—Lincoln Center North, Lincoln Square Mall, and the largest, a converted paper mill that now houses several shops and restaurant. It's not an inviting place to walk—but it half hides some gems.

SPECIALTY SHOPS Mountain Wanderer Map and Bookstore (603-745-2594; mountainwanderer

.com), Main St., Lincoln. Not your ordinary bookstore, this is a prime source of hiking, biking, paddling, snowshoeing, and other outdoor recreation and travel tomes, plus New England maps and natural history; also USGS topographic maps, compasses, and White Mountain gifts. Owner Steve Smith is himself an avid hiker, snowshoer, and expert on area trails, the author of *Wandering Through the White Mountains* and *Snowshoe Hikes in the White Mountains*; coauthor of *The White Mountains* and *The 4,000 Footers of the White Mountains*. Check out the website for online orders and his frequently updated "Mountain Wanderer" blog.

Innisfree Bookshop (603-745-6107), Lincoln Square, Main St. (Rt. 112), Lincoln. The region's full-service bookstore, specializing in New England titles, White Mountain guides and trail maps, ski titles, field guides, and children's books and educational toys.

Pinestead Quilts (603-745-8640), 31 Main St., Lincoln. Quilt maker Kathleen Sherburn offers a great selection of locally made quilts, machine-pieced but with hand-tied, traditional designs. Also place mats, potholders, pillowcases, and table runners, plus fabrics, patterns, and other quilt-making supplies. The Sherburn family has operated Pinestead Farm Lodge (pinestead farmlodge.com) in Franconia since 1899.

SPORTING GOODS Lahouts (lahouts.com), New Hampshire North Country's version of L.L. Bean, maintains four shops along Main St. (Rt. 112) in Lincoln, all open daily. There's the original **Lahout's Country Clothing and Ski Shop, Inc.**, **Lahout's Discount Warehouse** (41 Main St.), the **Concept Shops**, and the big, serious emporium for climbing and other adventure equipment, **Lahouts North Face Summit Shop** farther along in the Lincoln Square Mall (165 Main). The first Lahouts opened in Littleton in 1922.

Rodgers Ski Outlet (603-745-6485), Main St., Lincoln. Open daily 7 AM–9 PM. "La who?" the competition may well ask if you mention Lahout's. More than 1,500 pairs of skis in stock at any time; tune-ups, rentals, repairs are the specialties. Billed as "northern New England's largest volume ski shop."

✳ Special Events

January: **Independence Day Weekend** at Loon Mountain, "celebrating Loon's independence from nature."

March: **Governor's Briefcase Race**.

June: **Old New England Day** in North Woodstock: antique cars, yard sales, live music.

July: **Fourth of July celebration**, Lincoln-Woodstock.

Labor Day: **Rubber Ducky Regatta** in North Woodstock. Live music, games in Cascade Park, thousands of ducks race down the Pemi River.

September: **The Annual New Hampshire Highland Games** in Lincoln is a huge celebration of all things Scottish.

October: **Oktoberfest** at Loon Mountain.

November: **Opening Weekend at Loon**.

FRANCONIA AND NORTH OF THE NOTCHES

Wrapped in forest and dominated by granite White Mountain peaks, the Franconia-Bethlehem area seems to be the distilled essence of northern New Hampshire. Northwest of this high, wooded country, the landscape changes suddenly, flattening around Littleton, the shopping town for this region. For views of both the Green Mountains and the White Mountains, follow this Ammonoosuc Valley south to Lisbon and Bath, then back up to Sugar Hill and Franconia on memorable back roads.

The town of Franconia alone packs into its 65 square miles more splendid scenic vistas and unusual natural attractions than many states can boast. Curiously, while annual visitors to Franconia Notch are said to outnumber New Hampshire residents, relatively few stray into the delightful neighboring valley just behind this wall of mountains.

Franconia and its small satellite towns of Sugar Hill and Easton have been catering to visitors for more than 150 years. Travelers were first attracted to Franconia Notch by its convenience as a north–south route through the mountains, but they were invariably impressed by the scenery. Not long after the War of Independence, a few inns and taverns appeared.

In the mid-19th century the railroad arrived, inaugurating a grand resort era. Such literary notables as Nathaniel Hawthorne, Washington Irving, John Greenleaf Whittier, and Henry Wadsworth Longfellow were all Franconia summer visitors whose enthusiastic accounts of the region fanned its fame. Hawthorne wrote a story about the (former) Old Man of the Mountain, "The Great Stone Face."

One of the most celebrated hotels in America in its day, and a symbol of the White Mountains' golden age, the 400-room Profile House stood in the heart of Franconia Notch. Besides elegant service in a rustic setting, the hotel offered its

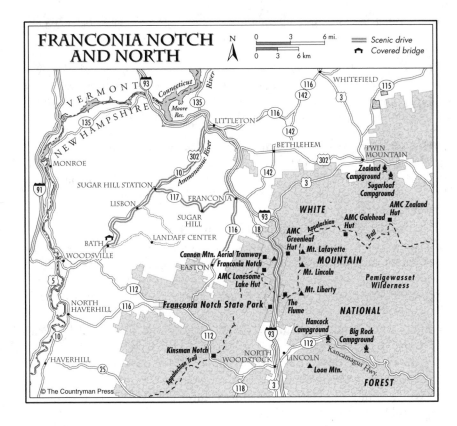

FRANCONIA NOTCH AND NORTH

guests a superb view of the Old Man. An institution for 70 years, Profile House burned down in 1923. Its site is now part of Franconia Notch State Park.

Grand hotels also appeared in Bethlehem, known for its pollen-free air. It became headquarters for the National Hay Fever Relief Association, which was founded here in the 1920s. At one time Bethlehem had 30 hotels ranging from simple to large and luxurious indeed. A 2-mile-long boardwalk invited guests to stroll.

Although many once-famous grand hotels closed their doors in the 1920s and 1930s, a few lasted until the 1950s, when railroad service to the White Mountains ended. Here and there traces of Bethlehem's glory days remain, such as the impressive fieldstone-and-shingle clubhouse (formerly The Casino) of the Maplewood Golf Course.

As the summer resort scene began to fade in the White Mountains, a winter season commenced. Americans discovered skiing. The Franconia area can claim a number of skiing firsts, among them the nation's first ski school, opened at Peckett's-on-Sugar-Hill in 1929, and this country's first aerial tramway (constructed in 1938), which ran to the summit of the state-owned Cannon Mountain. Cannon also hosted America's first racing trail in the 1920s and its first World Cup race in the 1960s. The New England Ski Museum is sited beside Cannon's tramway base station.

In 1945 a flamboyant Austrian aristocrat, Baron Hugo Von Pantz, founded Mittersill, a Tyrolean-style resort adjacent to Cannon. It attracted high-society types from New York and Boston. For a brief time Franconia was the New England's St. Moritz.

Times change. The current ski crowds head for Loon Mountain and Waterville Valley. Cannon still has its following, though, and the area offers extensive cross-country skiing. Inviting inns and bed & breakfasts are scattered throughout the folds of the valleys and gentler hills north and west of Franconia Notch.

GUIDANCE Littleton Area Chamber of Commerce (603-444-6561; littleton areachamber.com), 32 Main St., Box 105, Littleton 03561. There's an information center next to the post office on Main St., open Memorial Day–Columbus Day daily—but available by phone year-round. The website is excellent, covering the Franconia/Bethlehem areas.

Also see **golittleton.com** for current and community news.

Franconia Notch Chamber of Commerce (mid-May–Oct. 603-823-5661; otherwise 603-823-3450; franconianotch.org), P.O. Box 780, Franconia 03580. A downtown information booth in the middle of the village (Rt. 18, off I-93 Exit 28, is open mid-May–Oct., 10–5; another is open summer weekends at the Cannon Mountain tramway base station.

Bethlehem Information Center (603-869-3409; 888-845-1957; bethlehemwhite mtns.com). Open Memorial Day–Labor Day, 10–4. A walk-in information center in the middle of the village (junction of Rts. 302 and 142) displays souvenirs from the town's many vanished hotels.

The White Mountains Gateway Visitors Center (see "Lincoln and North Woodstock") also covers this area.

GETTING THERE *By bus:* **Concord Coach Lines** (800-639-3317; concord coachlines.com) has daily service from Boston to Franconia Village and Littleton.

By car: From north or south, take I-93 to Franconia Notch Parkway (Rt. 3). Rt. 302 is the major east–west route, running from I-91 at Wells River, Vermont, to Littleton and east through Bethlehem.

MEDICAL EMERGENCY Call **911**. **Littleton Regional Hospital** (603-444-9000), 600 St. Johnsbury Rd., Littleton, at Exit 43 off I-93.

✳ Villages

Bethlehem (pop. 2,200). Sited at 1,426 feet above sea level, "the highest township east of the Mississippi River," Bethlehem became a haven for hay fever sufferers early in the 1800s. Guests first came by stages from Concord; later there were three stations in town, with as many as 10 trains a day depositing guests at a total of 30 lodging establishments. Why the town's name was changed from Lloyd Hills to Bethlehem remains a bit of a mystery, though the moniker acquired new meaning beginning in 1919 with the founding of the Bethlehem Hebrew Congregation. During the 20th century the surviving hotels filled all summer with Hasidic Jews, most from Brooklyn. The hotels have now all but disappeared, but two golf courses survive and a large 19th-century summer "cottage" or two has turned into an inn. The village itself is once more a cluster of interesting shops and restaurants, its art deco **Colonial Theater** restored as an art house and venue for live performances. The **Rocks Estate** is a year-round resource.

Franconia (pop. 1,040) was named in 1782 for its resemblance to Germany's Franconia's Alps and is best known for its notch, mountains, and other dramatic natural features. The village itself clusters in the Gale River Valley west of Cannon Mountain. In the early 19th century a rich vein of iron ore was mined here; the **Franconia Iron Furnace**, just south of the junction of Rts. 116 and 117 (with interpretive panels), evokes the era. The **Franconia Heritage Museum** (603-823-5000; franconiaheritage.org), 553 Main St., is open May–Oct., Thu. and Sat. 1–4. Franconia College, a progressive 1960s institution housed in the former (long-gone) Forest Hills Hotel, closed in 1978, but a number of graduates still salt the local population of farmers and summer residents. **The Robert Frost Place** commemorates the poet's time in town (1915–1920). For more on Franconia's resort history, see the chapter introduction.

Sugar Hill (pop. 641). New Hampshire's youngest town, part of Lisbon—some 10 miles away and a very different community—until 1962. Set high on a ridge with views to Franconia Ridge and the Presidentials, this cluster of homes, inns, and churches is one of the state's prettiest communities. **Sugar Hill Historical Museum** (603-823-5336; franconianotch.org), Main St. (Rt. 117), Sugar Hill is an interesting little local museum with changing exhibits about aspects of the town from its pioneer settlement in 1780 until the present. Open June–Columbus Day, Fri. and Sat. 11–3.

Littleton (pop. 6,173). The spirited hub of northwestern New Hamsphire, Littleton offers an architecturally pleasing lineup of independently owned shops and restaurants along Main Street and 60 feet above the Ammonoosuc River. Look for parking behind the shops and steps leading down to the river, which drops 144 feet on its way through town and was once harnessed by no less than six dams to power mills. Amazingly, one of the oldest mills has survived and been restored. The 1798 **Littleton Gristmill** (603-444-3971; 888-284-7478; littletongristmill.com), 18 Mill St., is open year-round, grinding organic grains for pancake, muffin, and waffle mixes served up in the nearby **Littleton Diner**, a 1940s classic that's another must-stop. Sit by the waterwheel and watch it turned by the fastflowing river and cross the neighboring **covered footbridge** (vintage 2004) to the river walk on the opposite bank.

ST. MATHEW'S EPISCOPAL CHURCH, SUGAR HILL

Michael Hern

Chris Tree

DOWNTOWN LITTLETOWN

Along Main Street itself note the **Littleton Public Library** (603-444-5741), 92 Main St., with its handsome reading room and collection of White Mountain art; inquire about its collection of stereoscopic slides developed and produced by the famous Kilburn Brothers. The statue of **Pollyanna** beside its door commemorates her creator, Littleton-born Eleanor Hodgman Porter (1868–1920). Stop by the seasonal info center (see *Guidance*) beside the post office and pick up a map and pamphlet *Walking Tour*. Across the street is **Thayer's Inn**, which has been welcoming guests since 1850. The region's big-box stores cluster just west of town on Rt. 302.

Lisbon (pop. 1,587). An Ammonoosuc River town centered on woodworking mills, a nontouristy " small town with a big heart." You'll also find a small golf course, a couple of places to stay and to eat, and a big Memorial Day weekend Lilac Festival, honoring the state flower.

Landaff (pop. 376). Set well back into the hills east of Rt. 302, accessible from the village of Bath, this is one of New Hampshire's most photographed old hill towns. In Landaff Center the town hall commands a superb view of the hamlet. You can't help wondering what it would be if Dartmouth College had been sited here the way Governor John Wentworth suggested in 1770.

Bath (pop. 967). The village of Bath itself is known for its vintage-**1832 covered bridge** and for the neighboring 1804 **Old Brick Store**, billed as the country's oldest general store. A shorter covered bridge can be found on Rt. 112, spanning a branch of the Ammonoosuc River in the village of Swiftwater. **Upper Bath Village**, a few miles north of the store and covered bridge on Rt. 302, is a striking cluster of Federal-era brick homes set against surrounding fields.

✷ To See

The Robert Frost Place (603-823-5510; thefrostplace.org), Box 74, Ridge Rd., off Rt. 116, Franconia. Open weekends Memorial Day–July 4, then Wed.–Mon. 1–4 until Columbus Day; also inquire about evening poetry readings. Frost's home from 1915 to 1920, now a town-run museum on a "road less traveled by," attracts international visitors. Each year a resident poet spends the summer on the property imbibing views of the same unfolding hills and fields of lupine that inspired New England's best-known poet. The 1859 farmhouse and barn are the site of frequent poetry readings and workshops. The home contains rare editions of Frost's books, photos, and memorabilia, and a 20-minute slide presentation depicts his life and work in Franconia. A 0.5-mile nature trail behind the house is posted with 16 Frost poems. Admission $4 adults, $3 seniors, $2 ages 7–12.

Also see **Franconia Notch State Park** under *Green Space* and descriptions of Sugar Hill and Littleton under *Villages*.

Scenic Drives The Franconia Notch Parkway, the 10-mile segment of I-93 that's been downsized through Franconia Notch State Park (see the box), is one of the state's most scenic corridors.

Rt. 117 from Franconia village. This road winds steeply uphill to Sugar Hill. Take the short Sunset Hill Road for breathtaking mountain views, then continue down to Lisbon on Rt. 302/10 and turn north beside the Ammonoosuc River to Littleton, or turn south through Lisbon village to Bath, with its old country store and covered bridge.

Rt. 116 follows the valley between Franconia and Easton. Old farms and mountain scenery.

Rt. 142, the quick, old way from the middle of Franconia to the middle of Bethlehem, is steep, woodsy, and scenic, much better the long way around via I-93 and 302.

✷ To Do

AERIAL TRAM RIDES Cannon Mountain Aerial Tramway. See the Franconia Notch State Park box.

BICYCLING Franconia Notch Recreation Trail. An 8.9-mile-long bicycle/walking path, used in winter as a cross-country ski trail and snowmobile corridor, traverses the notch. **Franconia Sports Shop** (603-823-5241; franconiasports .com), Main St., Franconia. Offers half-day to five-day mountain bike rentals.

ROBERT FROST PLACE, FRANCONIA

Michael Hern

GREEN SPACE
FRANCONIA NOTCH STATE PARK

(603-823-8800; franconianotchstatepark.com). This 6,440-acre park lies between the Franconia and Kinsman mountain ranges in a 0.5-mile-wide high pass, or notch, that contains many of the White Mountains' most notable natural sights. Long used by the Pemigewasset tribe and discovered by white settlers before the Revolution, it remains the quickest route from northern Vermont and points west to Concord and Boston. It's currently a 10-mile-long segment of I-93 that's blessedly scaled back here to two lanes, the Franconia Notch Parkway, funneling traffic through with minimum scenic and environmental impact.

Franconia Notch was a major summer destination for a century. The present park includes the site of the former 400-room Profile House, named for the nearby "Old Man of the Mountain" stone profile. The hotel burned down in 1923, and the entire notch came up for sale for $400,000. It would have been acquired by logging interests had not the Society for the Protection of New England Forests (SPNHF) raised half the sale price and a Boston philanthropist supplied another $100,000. The remaining $100,000 was raised by women's clubs, schoolchildren, and small donors; the reservation became public in 1928. It is surrounded by the White Mountain National Forest, with trails maintained by the WMNF and Appalachian Mountain Club (AMC). Unfortunately the Old Man who saved the notch crumbled and fell in 2003.

The principal sights of the notch are all within the park and easily accessible from the parkway. Also see *Hiking*.

Sites are listed from south to north

THE GILMAN VISITORS CENTER AT THE FLUME GORGE, Exit 34A, open May–late Oct., 9–5, until 5:30 in July and Aug. Sited at the entrance to the Flume, this center provides information and shows a free 15-minute film about the park. It also has a snack bar, restrooms, and souvenir shop. Displays include a vintage-1874 Abbot & Downing 21-passenger (including 9 on top) Concord Coach, which carried the mail from Plymouth to the Profile House until 1911.

✎ THE FLUME GORGE (flumegorge.com). See above. $13 adults, $9 ages 6–12; under 5 free. (*Note:* A combination ticket with the Cannon Mountain Aerial Tramway is $24/$18.) A sheer-sided 700-foot-long, deep and narrow gorge—no more than 20 feet wide but up to 90 feet high—through which Flume Brook flows. It was discovered in 1808 by an avid local fisherman, 93-year-old "Aunt Jess" Guernsey. A system of staircases and boardwalks was constructed in the 19th century; now an updated network takes visitors through the Flume to Ridge Path, which leads to Liberty Cascade and on to **Sentinel Pine covered bridge,**

THE FLUME GORGE IN FRANCONIA STATE PARK

NH State Parks

overlooking a clear mountain pool. The Wildwood Path loops past giant boulders brought down by the glaciers and returns to the Flume entrance. Note also the **Flume covered bridge** here.

THE BASIN A pull-off is marked from the parkway both northbound and southbound. From the parking lot a paved path leads to Cascade Brook and a deep glacial pothole or natural pool almost 30 feet in diameter created over the eons by the churning action of water rushing down from the nearby waterfall. Follow marked trails to Cascade Brook and Kinsman Falls.

BOISE ROCK A marked northbound pullout. There's a spring right by the parking lot, and a short trail leads to this huge glacial boulder. Picnic tables offer views of the Cannon Cliffs and the rock climbers scaling them.

A VINTAGE POSTER IN THE NEW ENGLAND SKI MUSEUM

Courtesy, New England Ski Museum

LAFAYETTE CAMPGROUND (603-823-9513). Southbound access only. Ninety-seven campsites, $25 each, can be reserved a day in advance.

PROFILE LAKE was named for its site below the former Old Man of the Mountain. No swimming, but these headwaters of the Pemigewasset River are open to fly-fishing and said to be good for brook trout.

Off Exit 34B

CANNON MOUNTAIN, Parkway Exit 34B. Besides operating during ski season, the **Aerial Tramway** runs late May–Columbus Day, when autumn colors are usually at or near peak. A roundtrip tram ticket is $14 adults, $10 ages 6–12; free 5 and under. One-way tickets available. Inquire about the combination ticket with the Flume Gorge. One of New Hampshire's most popular ski areas and the site of America's first aerial tramway. The present tramway, which replaced the 1938 original in 1980, carries 80 passengers to the summit of the 4,180-foot-

CANNON MT. TRAMWAY IN FRANCONIA STATE PARK

NH State Parks

high mountain, where there is an observation tower and the panoramic Rim Trail. For winter information, see *Downhill Skiing*.

NEW ENGLAND SKI MUSEUM (603-823-7177; 800-639-4181; ski museum.org), Exit 34B off the Franconia Notch Parkway, beside the Cannon Mountain Aerial Tramway, Franconia. Open Memorial Day–Mar., daily 10–5. Free. This popular museum relates the history of skiing in New England and beyond. There's a combination of permanent and changing exhibits of skis, clothing, and equipment dating from the 19th century to the present, along with vintage still photos and film. Fabulous vintage ski posters are available in the shop and online.

THE OLD MAN OF THE MOUNTAIN MUSEUM AND HISTORIC SITE In 2003 the famous 40-foot-high rock formation high above Profile Lake—the state's official symbol—fell down. Too beloved to be forgotten, it is now memorialized in a small museum while fund-raising is undertaken for a more fitting memorial. There is also an ice cream stand here.

Off Exit 34C

SWIMMING/BOATING AT ECHO LAKE BEACH at the base of Cannon Mountain in Franconia State Park. Open June–Labor Day, 10–5:30. $4 adults, $2 ages 11 and under. At this 28-acre lake (elevation 1,931 feet), the mirror-like surface perfectly reflects Mount Lafayette and Cannon Mountain. You'll find picnic tables, a swimming beach, a snack bar, changing facilities, a boat-launching area, **canoe and paddleboat rentals** ($10 per hour), and seven sites for RV hookups.

BALD MOUNTAIN and **Artists Bluff**. See *Hiking*.

PICNICKING AT SUNSET BRIDGE Turn left instead of right at the stop sign and head over the bridge to the Governor Gallen Memorial area parking lot. Walk out onto the bridge for great views.

RECREATION TRAIL This 8.9-mile walking/biking/cross-country ski and snowmobile trail begins at the Flume and runs uphill to Cannon, then on 2 more miles to Rt. 3. Most people begin at the northern end, as it slopes gently downhill the whole way. See *Bicycling* in this section and in "Lincoln and North Woodstock" for bike rentals and shuttle service.

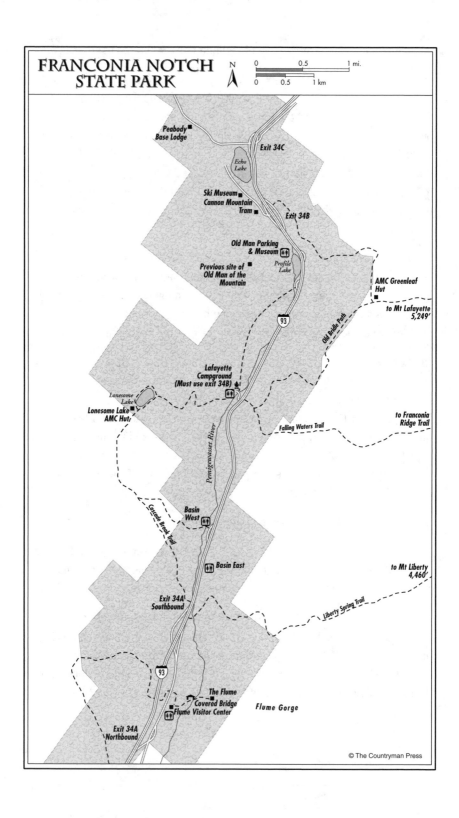

FRANCONIA NOTCH
STATE PARK

N

| 0 | 0.5 | 1 mi. |
| 0 | 0.5 | 1 km |

Peabody
Base Lodge

Exit 34C

Echo
Lake

Ski Museum
Cannon Mountain
Tram

Exit 34B

Old Man Parking
& Museum

Previous site of
Old Man of the
Mountain

Profile
Lake

AMC Greenleaf
Hut

to Mt Lafayette
5,249'

93

Old Bridle Path

Lafayette
Campground
(Must use exit 34B)

Lonesome
Lake

Lonesome Lake
AMC Hut

Falling Waters Trail

to Franconia
Ridge Trail

Pemigewasset River

Cascade Brook Trail

Basin
West

Basin East

to Mt Liberty
4,460'

Exit 34A
Southbound

Liberty Spring Trail

93

The Flume
Covered Bridge
Flume Visitor Center

Flume Gorge

Exit 34A
Northbound

© The Countryman Press

FISHING **Profile Lake**. See the Franconia Notch State Park box. Franconia Sports Shop (see above) sells fishing licenses.

GOLF **Maplewood Country Club and Hotel** (603-869-3335; 877-869-3335; maplewoodgolfresort.com), Main St. (Rt. 302), Bethlehem. An attractive, Donald Ross–designed 18-hole layout with a grand clubhouse, this par-72 course offers a challenge to all players. There's a pro shop, driving range, and unique par-6 hole. The course is so popular on weekends that carts are required of all players to speed up play.

Bethlehem Country Club (603-869-5745), Main St. (Rt. 302), Bethlehem. This par-70, Donald Ross–designed course in Bethlehem offers 18 pristine holes of golf; cart and club rentals are available. Check with your accommodation about package rates.

Lisbon Village Country Club (603-838-6004), Bishop Rd.,off Rt. 302, Lisbon. Nine holes.

Sunset Hill Golf Course (603-823-5522), Sugar Hill. This short nine-hole par-33 course sits atop Sunset Hill and gives players dramatic mountain views.

GLIDING **Franconia Inn** (603-823-5542; 800-473-5299; franconiainn.com; info@franconiainn.com), 1300 Easton Rd., Franconia 03580. Open mid-May–mid-Oct., daily except Wed. 9–5:45. Soar with an FAA-certified glider pilot for a sublime view of some of the continent's most sublime scenery. Fifteen-, 25-, or 35-minute rides range $60–100.

HIKING Franconia Notch offers some of the most rewarding short hikes in the White Mountains. They include:

Artist's Bluff and **Bald Mountain**. Both trails begin at the Echo Lake parking lot in Franconia Notch State Park (I-93, Exit 34C). Favored by 19th-century guests at the notch's former hotels, Bald Mountain is a short but rocky ascent with sweeping views. First you follow an old carriage road to a saddle between two summits, then branch left to Bald Mountain, right to Artist's Bluff. You should investigate both. The roundtrip is 1 or 1.8 miles.

Basin–Cascades Trail. Start at **the Basin** (see the Franconia Notch State Park box) and ascend along Cascade Brook leading to the Cascade Brook Trail.

⌀ **Lonesome Lake Trail**. From Lafayette Place on Rt. 3 in Franconia Notch, an old bridle path leads to a 14-acre lake that sits at an elevation of 2,734 feet and is warm enough in summer for swimming. The Appalachian Mountain Club's Lonesome Lake Hut offers overnight lodging and a variety of family-geared programs. Contact the AMC Pinkham Notch Camp (603-466-2727).

Mount Lafayette via the Old Bridle Path. This is a full day's hike, and you should pick up a detailed map before attempting it. After 2.9 miles you reach the AMC Greenleaf Hut (for lodging, phone 603-466-2727); the summit—with magnificent views—is another 1.1 miles. If the weather is good and your energy high, continue along the **Franconia Ridge Trail** south over Mount Lincoln to Little Haystack. This narrow, rocky route is spectacular, but there are steep drops on both sides of the trail. At Little Haystack turn right (west) onto the **Falling**

Waters Trail. This trail passes more waterfalls in 2.8 miles than any other trail in the mountains; it ends back at Lafayette Place.

Also note the **Rim Trail** from the Cannon Mountain Aerial Tramway.

Two **Appalachian Mountain Club high-mountain huts** (603-466-2727; out doors.org) are accessible from Franconia Notch. The 1.7-mile trail to **Lonesome Lake Hut**, sited at an elevation of 2,760 feet on a flank of Cannon Mountain, and the 2.5-mile hike to **Greenleaf Hut** at 4,200 feet on Mount Lafayette both begin here. Lonesome Lake is an easy hike for children, and there is swimming and fishing in the lake. This hut is open on a self-service basis (use of kitchen facilities) Jan.–late May and mid-Oct.–Dec.; Greenleaf is open self-service mid- to late May. Both are staffed June–mid-Oct., serving breakfast and dinner, furnishing pillows and wool blankets for their 48 bunks. For more about the AMC see "What's Where."

HORSEBACK RIDING Franconia Notch Stables (603-823-5542), Franconia Inn, Rt. 116, Franconia. Guided group and private rides, pony rides, lessons.

SWIMMING See the Franconia Notch State Park box for details about **Echo Lake Beach**.

✳ Winter Sports
CROSS-COUNTRY SKIING

In Franconia
Franconia Village Cross Country Ski Center (603-823-8078; 800-473-5299; franconiainn.com), Franconia Inn, Easton Valley Rd. (Rt. 116). This is the most extensive and best-maintained system in the region, with 65 kilometers of tracked trails; 5km are skate-groomed. Most are singletracks, winding through woods and across meadows in this 1,100-foot-high valley. The full-service ski shop offers rentals (skates and snowshoes, too). A skier's bag lunch is available weekends and holidays at the inn. Trail fee $12.

Sunset Hill House Touring Center (603-823-5522; 800-SUN-HILL), Sunset Hill Rd., Sugar Hill. Trails are tracked on the neighboring golf course and out across meadows. No ski shop.

In Franconia Notch
Lafayette Trails, Rt. 3, Franconia Notch. The **Notchway Trail** is the old Rt. 3 roadbed, accessed from Rt. 141 just east of I-93 Exit 36. It's identified by a metal sign with a skier symbol. The trail is 2.1 miles; side loops include the short **Bog Trail**, the more difficult **Scarface Trail** (1.2 miles), and the **Bickford Trail** (0.3 mile).

The Pemi Trail, Franconia Notch. Just over 6 miles long, this trail extends from Profile Lake to the Flume parking lot and is open to cross-country skiers, snow-shoers, and hikers. It can also be accessed from the Echo Lake, tramway, and Flume parking areas. Pick up a map at the information booth at the Cannon Mountain base lodge in Franconia Notch.

Beaver Brook Cross Country Trails begin at the Beaver Brook Wayside on Rt. 3 between Twin Mountain and Franconia Notch. The **Beaver Loop** is 2.3km, Badger is a more difficult 3.1km, and **Moose Watch** is classified as "most difficult," a total of 8.6km with some spectacular views. These trails are ungroomed and not regularly patrolled, so be sure not to ski alone.

In the White Mountain National Forest
For detailed trail maps, check with the **White Mountain Visitors Center** in Lincoln.

DOWNHILL SKIING/SNOW BOARDING Cannon Mountain (603-823-8800; snow conditions 603-823-7771; cannonmt.com), Franconia Parkway Exit 34B, Franconia. State-owned Cannon Mountain boasts some of the toughest trails in the East. It was the site of America's first racing trail in the 1920s, of its first aerial tramway in the '30s, and of its first World Cup race in the '60s—a clue, perhaps, to why Franconia's Bode Miller is now officially recognized as the most talented skier in the world, winning the 2005 World Cup and three medals, including a gold for the United States at the 2010 Winter Olympics. While its image remains "The Mountain That'll Burn Your Boots Off!," in reality many trails here have been softened—broadened and smoothed as well as carpeted with snowmaking.

Vertical drop: A whopping 2,146 feet.

Lifts: The present 80-passenger aerial tram dates from the 1980s. Lifts also include two regular-speed and one high-speed quad chairs, three triple chairs, Wonder Carpet, and rope tow.

Trails: 55. In addition to runs in Franconia Notch itself, more than a dozen intermediate and beginner runs meander down the mountain's gentler northern face to the Peabody Slopes base area. The only trails still "au naturel" are Taft Slalom (a remnant of that 1920s racing trail) and the Hardscrabbles—both of which command their own followings.

Snowmaking: 97 percent.

Features: Brookside Learning Center at the Peabody Slopes offers separate beginners' trails and several adult learning programs, a children's program for ages 3–13, and day care for those 6 weeks and up.

Facilities: Cafeteria and retail shop at the base of the tramway. The tram is a great

LOWER SKI SLOPES OF CANNON MOUNTAIN RISE BEHIND ECHO LAKE

Kim Grant

start for intermediate and expert skiers/riders. The Peabody Base Area also offers a ski shop, rentals, cafeteria, lounge, first aid, and deli.

Lift tickets: $66 adults, $50 ages 13–17, $40 juniors and seniors.

ICE CLIMBING Popular local sites include **Cannon Cliffs** (park at the south side of Profile Lake), **Artist Bluff** (Rt. 43 Exit 34C, north on Rt. 3/18 to park at Echo Lake), and **Eagle Cliff** (Rt. 93 Exit 34B; park at the tram parking lot and follow the Greenleaf Trail).

ICE SKATING The Franconia Inn offers ice skating to the public.

SLEIGH RIDES Both **The Rocks Estate** in Bethlehem (see *Green Space*) and the **Franconia Inn** (see *Lodging*) offer sleigh rides.

SNOWMOBILING In Franconia Notch the bike path serves in winter as a corridor connector for the 100-mile network of snowmobile trails in this area. For maps and other information, contact **Twin Mountain Snowmobile Club**, Box 179, Twin Mountain 03595; the **Trails Bureau** (603-271-3254, option 4); the **New Hampshire Division of Parks and Recreation** (603-271-2006); or the **New Hampshire Snowmobile Association** (603-224-8906). (Also see "Crawford Notch and Bretton Woods.")

SNOWSHOEING The Franconia/Kinsman area is a mecca for snowshoers. Popular treks begin at the Flume and Lonesome Lake in Franconia Notch State Park. Check with the Appalachian Mountain Club (outdoors.org) for details about trekking into their Lonesome Lake hut. Check with the Franconia Inn Village X-C Ski Center (franconiainn.com) for rentals and details about the Coppermine Trail and Bridal Veil Falls in the Easton Valley. *Showshoe Hikes in the White Mountains* by Steven D. Smith (Bondcliff Books) offers detailed descriptions of trails throughout this area.

The **Rocks Estate** in Bethlehem (see *Green Space*) is also webbed with good snowshoeing trails. Also see trails described under *Cross-Country Skiing*.

✳ Green Space

The Rocks Estate (603-444-6228; therocks.org), Rt. 302 off I-93 Exit 40, 0.25 mile on the right, Bethlehem. Owned by the Society for the Protection of New Hampshire Forests (forestsociety.org), this estate with huge barns is the northern headquarters for the state's largest and most active conservation organization. The estate's 1,200 acres are managed as a tree farm by the SPNHF; a large area is reserved as a Christmas tree plantation. Trees are sold during the annual Christmas tree celebration in December. Several nearby inns offer special package plans for lodging, meals, and a Christmas tree. Various conservation and family programs are held through the year. There's a self-guided nature trail that's great for snowshoeing, though it's a bit narrow and steep for cross-country skiing.

✐ **Bretzfelder Park** (603-444-6228; 603-869-2683; therocks.org), Prospect St., Bethlehem. This 77-acre site is managed as a community park, with a summer lecture series plus picnic tables, fishing, and a guided nature trail.

✳ Lodging

INNS

In Franconia/Sugar Hill

⊗ ♂ ⅃ ❝❞ **Franconia Inn** (603-823-5542; 800-473-5299; franconiainn.com; info@franconiainn.com), 1300 Easton Rd., Franconia 03580. The hospitable grande dame of the Franconia Notch region keeps you busy with four clay tennis courts, a heated swimming pool, guided horseback tours, bicycles, a croquet court, and a glider port, all on 107 acres in the heart of the Easton Valley. There's even a swimming hole. In winter the inn's well-groomed cross-country trail system with touring center is a big draw. Founded just after the Civil War, the inn has 30 guest rooms (including wheelchair-accessible accommodations on the first floor) and two family suites (two bedrooms sharing a bath), all furnished in traditional style. There are also four family suites and in the neighboring Kinsman Cottage, two family-geared units with full kitchens and a pullout in the living room. Common areas include an inviting oak-paneled library, a spacious living room with a fireplace, and two porches to catch sunrise and sunset. Two candlelit dining rooms provide casually elegant dining and spectacular views (see *Dining Out*). Downstairs there's a family-sized hot tub and the Rathskeller Lounge. $131–161 B&B for rooms, $186–211 for family suites and units. More during peak foliage and Christmas week; EP and MAP rates and package plans are also available.

⊗ **Sunset Hill House** (603-823-5522; 800-SUN-HILL; sunsethillhouse.com), 231 Sunset Hill Rd., Sugar Hill 03586. Open all year. The view of the White Mountains to the east is magnificent. The 1880s-era property, set atop a 1,700-foot ridge, was built as an annex for one of the area's grandest hotels. Still it's an imposing 21-room inn with its own 7-room annex. All of the traditionally furnished guest rooms come with comforters and coordinated fabrics, antique and reproduction furniture, and private baths. There's also a pair of two-room Jacuzzi and fireplace suites, and five other rooms with a choice of gas fireplace or Jacuzzi. All rooms have a phone, and local calls are free. Common areas include a TV room, a small bar, a heated pool, and a nine-hole golf course/cross-country skiing across the road. $100–399 B&B; rooms average $160. Also see *Dining Out*.

Lovett's Inn (603-823-7761; 800-356-3802; lovettsinn.com), by Lafayette Brook, 1474 Profile Rd. (Rt. 18), Franconia 03580. A tradition in these parts and still one of New Hampshire's outstanding inns, Lovett's was built in 1794 and is listed on the National Register of Historic Places. Since 1929 it has operated as an inn, securing a reputation with generations of guests for its warm hospitality, fine views, and excellent food (see *Dining Out*). Innkeepers Jim and Jan Freitas have upgraded all five rooms and suites in the original inn with antiques and renovated baths, CD player, and hair dryers. Our favorite is the Nicholas Powers Room, which has great views of Cannon Mountain as well as a single whirlpool tub ($205 B&B, $283 MAP). Additional cottages with fireplaces, several with Jacuzzi, are scattered around the grounds and are well appointed. There is also an outdoor pool and spa. Rooms range $135–270, suites and cottages $145–185; MAP rates also available. More during fall foliage.

❝❞ **Sugar Hill Inn** (603-823-5621; 800-548-4748); sugarhillinn.com, 116 Rt. 117, Franconia 03580. A much-expanded 1789 white-clapboard roadside farmhouse, set on manicured lawns with a pool, gardens, and woodland beyond. Owner Steve Allen is a graduate of the French Culinary Institute, and dining is important here. A four-course dinner is served Thu.–Mon. and open to the public by reservation ($52 per person). Rooms are handsome indeed, ranging from from $155 midweek for a classic room to $275 for a whirlpool suite and $345 for the dream cottage on summer weekends. Rates include full breakfast and tea.

BED & BREAKFASTS 🎗 🐾 🐾 "❡"
The Hilltop Inn (603-823-5695; 800-770-5695; hilltopinn.com), 9 Norton Lane, Sugar Hill 03586. Mike and Meri Hern chuckle when reminded that they are now senior innkeepers in these parts. Drawn to Franconia by progressive Franconia College (opened in the 1960s, closed in 1978), they pride themselves on the warmth and informality of this expansive 1895 Victorian B&B atop Sugar Hill. The six

guest rooms with full bath are each very individually furnished with period antiques. Beds are fitted with handmade quilts and a choice of cotton or English flannel sheets. On a winter morning we found it difficult to leave the breakfast table with its view of the lively bird feeder, after consuming too many strips of perfectly crisped bacon, along with quiche and a full fruit plate. The woodstove with its ring of rockers is another sticking point, as is the deck, especially if there's a sunset. Mike and Meri are, however, full of suggestions to get you out hiking or skiing (options include trails through their own more than 30 magical acres) and are well versed in area shops and restaurants. Rates run $110–140 per couple, $40 per extra person in the room; $135–195 during foliage season. Minimum two-night stay requested only on summer and foliage weekends. Pets are welcome for $10.

🎗 🐾 🐾 "❡" **Kinsman Lodge** (603-823-5686; 866-KINSMAN; kinsmanlodge

HILLTOP INN

Michael Hern

.com), 2165 Easton Rd. (Rt. 116), Franconia 03580. An 1850s lodge that's been in Sue Thompson's family since 1910. The nine bedrooms are bright and comfortable, sharing two full baths and one half-bath. There's a large, cheerful old-fashioned dining room, as well as a room with TV and gas fireplace and another with a wood-burning hearth. In summer there are also the rocking chairs on the front porch. $55 single, $95 double, full breakfast included. Pets and kids are graciously welcomed. Handy to great hiking trails.

🐾 ✎ **Pinestead Farm Lodge** (603-823-8121; pinesteadfarmlodge.com), 2059 Easton Rd. (Rt. 116), Franconia 03480. The Sherburn family has been welcoming rusticators to their rambling farmhouse since 1899, most recently with four "efficiency units": each with bedrooms sharing a fully equipped kitchen and bath. Beds feature quilts by Kathleen Sherburn, and guests receive a discount at her Pinestead Quilts shop in Lincoln. Bedrooms may also be rented individually, from $45 per night. Beloved by hikers and snowshoers, the lodge is handy to the Mount Kinsman, Coppermine, and Bridal Veil Falls Trails.

🐾 ✎ **The Homestead** (603-823-5564; thehomestead1802.com), on Rt. 117, Sugar Hill 03586. Sitting at the corner of Rt. 117 and Sunset Hill Rd. Run by the seventh generation of the Hayward family, who are currently struggling to keep it open. Antique furniture, books, and photographs fill the common rooms, making the atmosphere throughout pure, authentic nostalgia. Rooms in the neighboring Family Cottage all have private bath. $60–70 single, $80–95 with shared bath, $95–130 with private, slightly more in foliage season, full breakfast included. Chil-

dren 6 and under are free; $10 for pets.

In Bethlehem

INNS Adair Country Inn & Restaurant (603-444-2600; 888-444-2600; adairinn.com), 80 Guider Lane near the junction of I-93 and Rt. 302, Bethlehem 03574. Double front doors open onto a large center hall with a wide stairway leading to two floors with nine luxurious guest rooms, some with fireplace. All have private bath (three have two-person tub, and one has a whirlpool bath) with king or queen beds and are furnished with antiques or reproductions. Downstairs there are gracious dining and living rooms with fireplaces. The granite-walled basement is the inn's kick-back common area with a grand old pool table and lots of comfortable seating. Guests are welcome by reservation for dinner, generally served Thu.–Mon. (the three-course choice menu is $42 per person). The Rocks Estate with its wooded nature trails, good for cross-country skiing, is just down the road. The resident innkeeper provides afternoon tea and a full breakfast, included in the room rate: $195–375, depending on season and room.

🍷 🐾 ✎ ♿ "🍴" **Wayside Inn** (603-869-3364; 800-448-9557; thewaysideinn .com), 3738 Main St. (Rt. 302), Bethlehem 03574. Longtime Swiss innkeepers Victor and Kathe Hofmann have preserved this friendly old riverside inn, which dates in part to 1825. They offer 14 guest rooms furnished with traditional New England country pieces, and a dozen additional motel rooms with balcony, cable TV, refrigerator, and air-conditioning. There's a sandy beach by the river. Room rates of $88–168 include a full breakfast. MAP rates also available. Also see the Riverview Restaurant in *Dining Out*.

BED & BREAKFASTS Bear Mountain Lodge (888-869-2189; bearmountainlodge.net), 3249 Main St., Bethlehem 03574. Despite its address, this log home is a bit off the beaten track, set in 26 wooded acres. Michael and Carol Kerivan designed and built the lodge to be a B&B in 2005 with nine gust rooms, three with in-room Jacuzzi, all with cable TV/DVD player (movie collection available), AC, and ceiling fan. A soaring central "great room" has a soapstone woodstove and views of the Presidentials. $165–300 per couple (higher in foliage) includes a full breakfast, served at individual and group tables at 8:30 AM.

In Littleton

INNS The Beal House Inn & Restaurant (603-444-2661; bealhouseinn.com), 2 W. Main St., Littleton 03561. A rambling, vintage-1833 home at a busy intersection on the western edge of town. Under new ownership since 2009, the emphasis is on food (see *Dining Out*) but the three guest rooms and four two-room suites (with gas fireplace) are attractive; request one in the rear.

✿ "¶" **Thayer's Inn** (603-444-6469; 800-634-8179; thayersinn.com), 136 Main St., Littleton 03561. Open year-round. Located on busy Main Street, this classic, white-pillared, Greek Revival structure has been a beacon to weary travelers since it opened in 1843. The 34 rooms and suites have private bath, TV, and telephone, and all are air-conditioned. The two-bedroom suites are great for families. From $70 per couple, per room, through $160 for family suites (some kitchenettes), continental breakfast included.

In Lisbon

The Ammonoosuc Inn (603-838-6118; 888-546-6118; ammonoosucinn.com), 641 Bishop Rd., Lisbon 03585. Open year-round. A 19th-century expanded farmhouse set on a knoll, across the Ammonoosuc River from Rt. 302, surrounded by the nine holes of the Lisbon Village Country Club. Owners include French-trained chef Karen Melanie, and the focus here is on Melanie's Bistro (see *Dining Out*). Rooms range from country comfortable to a suite with Jacuzzi and fireplace ($139–210 B&B) and massage is offered in the new spa; check out golf and dining packages.

✿ "¶" **Blueberry Farm Bed and Breakfast** (603-838-5983; blueberryfarmbnb.com), 445 Rt. 302, Lisbon 03585. Margaret McKenna welcomes guests to the family's cheerful 1850 farmhouse, set on a hill above Rt. 302 west of town, with views of the Ammonoosuc River. The country kitchen with its vintage Glenwood woodstove forms the center of the house. There are two downstairs guest rooms with private bath (one with a Jacuzzi) and two on the second floor. $85 includes a full breakfast (no credit cards). Amenities include a pool. The McKennas annually harvest 1,200 bushels (four varieties) of blueberries between July and Sept.

∞ ✿ ✿ "¶" **Bishop Farm B&B and Cottages** (888-383-2474; bishopfarm.com), 33 Bishop Cutoff, Lisbon 03585. The big red barn for this handsome 1870s farmhouse is a landmark just off Rt. 302. Recently renovated by the Salter family, it offers seven nicely, crisply decorated guest rooms in the main house and six cottages (children and dogs welcome) with kitchenette. Rooms are $129–159, $239 for the suite; cottages are $139–169.

MOTELS ✿ ✿ ✿ "¶" **Gale River** (603-823-5655; 800-255-7989; galerivermotel.com), 1 Main St. (Rt. 18),

Franconia 03580. Now run by Kevin Johnson, the tidy Gale River Motel has 10 rooms and two cottages. Amenities include in-room coffeemaker, refriger-ator, TV, and telephone, plus a heated outdoor pool, whirlpool, and hot tub. Rates for a double, $55–120. Cottages, which sleep six, are $140–170, with a three-night minimum stay. Summer weekly cottage rental, $875. Children under 15 are free, but pets are $10 per night. In winter just four units are open for nightly rentals, as skiers rou-tinely rent the rest by the season.

✍ **Stonybrook Motel** (603-823-5800; 800-722-3552; stonybrookmotel.com), 1098 Profile Rd. (Rt. 18), Franconia 03480. A five-room lodge and 18-unit motel minutes from Cannon Moun-tain. Amenities include indoor and out-door pools and a game room with pool table. Doubles run $79–109 in the lodge, from $59 in the motel.

OTHER LODGING AMC Lonesome Lake Hut (outdoors.org). Set at 2,760 feet in elevation on a flank of Cannon Mountain, this westernmost "high hut" has been operated by the Appalachian Mountain Club since the park's cre-ation in 1929. It's open year-round, a favorite with winter snowshoers and climbers as well as summer families. It's about an hour's hike up from the road, with a view of the Franconia Range. It's open on a self-service basis fall, winter, and spring, full service with special programs for children during summer. Check the website for rates.

CAMPGROUNDS Lafayette Camp-ground (603-823-5563), a popular state park facility just off the parkway in the heart of Franconia Notch, has 97 wooded tent sites available on a first-come, first-served basis. A central lodge has showers and a small store with hiking and camping supplies.

Echo Lake in Franconia Notch also has 10 sites for RV hookups.

Local private campgrounds include **Fransted Family Campground** (603-823-5675; franstedcampground .com), Rt. 18, Franconia, with 65 wood-ed tent sites and 26 trailer sites; and **Apple Hill Campground** (603-869-2238; 800-284-2238), Rt. 142 North, Bethlehem, with 45 tent sites, 20 trailer hookups, a store, and a bathhouse.

✳ Where to Eat
DINING OUT

In Franconia/Sugar Hill

✍ ♿ **Franconia Inn** (603-823-5542; franconiainn.com), 1300 Easton Rd. Breakfast (7:30–9:30) and dinner (6–8:30) nightly, aside from mud and stick seasons when the inn is closed. Reservations advised. Long considered the local restaurant for elegant dining and special occasions, the Franconia Inn's two handsome candle- and hearth-lit dining rooms offer black-tie service and a mountain view. Cocktails are served in the cozy, paneled basement-level **Rathskeller Lounge**. Despite the elegant surroundings, children are warmly welcomed by the kid-oriented menu featuring a "mega-grilled" cheese sandwich and baked crispy chicken nuggets. And the kids can spend their (or your) quarters in the video game room while waiting for their meal. Entrées might include pan-roasted lamb, and roasted Long Island half duck served with almond cherry wild rice and kirsch. Appetizers such as lob-ster bisque (made with fresh lobster meat, sherry, and local dairy cream) and a vegetarian napoleon run $5–8; entrées, $20–27. Full liquor.

Lovett's by Lafayette Brook (603-823-7761; 800-356-3802; lovettsinn .com), 1741 Profile Rd. (Rt. 18),

Franconia. Dinner 5:30–9; reservations suggested. You can quaff predinner cocktails in the cozy lounge, then retire to one of three connecting open-beamed rooms to savor a memorable meal. Chef-owner Janet prepares a wide range of entrées that may include veal Genovese and chicken forestier. Full liquor. Entrées $16–28.

Sugar Hill Inn (603-823-5621; 800-548-4748; sugarhillinn.com), 116 Rt. 117, Franconia. Dinner, by reservation only, is served Thu.–Sun. during busy seasons. Dinner is a four-course culinary event with a prix fixe of $52 per person. Stay-and-dine packages are the house specialty. See *Lodging*.

Restaurant at Sunset Hill (603-823-5522; 800-SUN-HILL; sunsethillhouse .com), 231 Sunset Hill Rd., Sugar Hill. Dining by reservation only; also pub menu served daily in the tavern. Dine bathed in the sunset's afterglow as well as the glow of the candlelight and warmed by the fireplace in this nicely renovated old inn dining room with a view of the Presidential Range. The formal restaurant offers a five-course menu ($45); there's also a "children's table" ($35).

In Littleton

tim-bir alley restaurant (603-444-6143), 7 Main St. Open Wed.–Sun. 5–9. Reservations suggested. Chefs Timothy and Biruta Carr have an enthusiastic following. This attractive space with its 10 tables, wood floors, and brick walls is the setting for an eclectic menu that changes weekly. It's famed for homemade desserts—like a white chocolate, coconut, and ricotta strudel with dark chocolate sauce and mango-coconut compote. The chefs take great care to ensure that each meal looks as great as it tastes. Entrées $18.95–28.95.

Beal House Restaurant & Lounge (604-444-2661), 2 W. Main St. Open

Tue.–Sat. for lunch 11–2, dinner from 6, Sunday 10–9. Reservations advised. Since opening in 2009 the restaurant in this vintage inn has been busy. Chef Brian Coffey is well known in the state and specializes in organic, New England–sourced products. Lobster (about which he's written two cookbooks) is a specialty, and lobster potpie is usually on a menu that might include sautéed free-range chicken with oyster mushrooms, or braised shortribs of Angus beef with blackstrap molasses. There's an eclectic list of boutique wines. Piano music Thu.–Sat. Entrées $18–29; "small plates" $6–10.

Bailiwicks (603-444-7717; bailiwicks finerestaurant.com), Thayer's Inn, 111 Main St. Open daily: Thu.–Sat. for lunch 11:30–4, Sun.11–4; dinner nightly. Highly rated for its bar (big martini list) as well as contemporary cuisine and ambience. Entrées $19–30.

In Bethlehem

✪ ⟁ **Cold Mountain Café** (603-869-2500; coldmountaincafe.com), 2015 Main St. Open for lunch (11–3) and dinner 5:30–9, Sun. 10–2. Credit cards and reservations are not accepted but personal checks are. A colorful, laid-back ambience with changing local art on the walls and an eclectic blackboard menu attract devotees to this attractive small café (36 patrons max) in a row of shops. Ex–New Yorker Jack Foley's dinner menu might include sun-dried tomato and mascarpone ravioli served with polenta, chicken with tamari and Thai basil, or baked salmon with tamari-ginger glaze. Wine and beer are served. Inquire about music. Dinner entrées $13–20.

✂ ⟁ **The Riverview Restaurant at the Wayside Inn** (603-869-3364; the waysideinn.com), Rt. 302 at Pierce Bridge. Open nightly except Mon., spring–fall; Fri. and Sat. in winter 6–8 PM. Victor and Kathe Hofmann, the

European owners of this dining room at the Wayside Inn, emphasize Continental cuisine with candlelight and a river view. Specialties include Wiener schnitzel, veal Zurich (sliced veal with mushrooms in a light cream sauce), and venison Baden-Baden (with pears, red cabbage, chestnuts, and spaetzle). There's also a kids menu. Entrées $13.95–23.95.

In Lisbon

Melanie's Bistro at the Ammonoosuc Inn (603-838-6118; ammonoosucinn.com), 641 Bishop Rd. Open (except Tue.) for lunch and dinner seasonally. Marked from Rt. 302. Classically trained chef-owner Karen Melanie presides in the kitchen of this attractive country inn dining room. Choices might range from a burger and chicken potpie to filet mignon with caramelized onions Entrées $25–32.

EATING OUT

In Franconia/Sugar Hill

❍ ¹ **Wendles's Delicatessen Café + Then Some** (603-823-5141), middle of Main St., Franconia. Open daily in summer 7–4, closed Mon. in winter; Sun. 8–2. Wendy Manning has created a bright, informal, and comfortable gathering space with good food. We savored an egg and veggies breakfast sandwich and will be back for a "build your own sandwich," or maybe the green Thai curry chicken salad wrap.

Dutch Treat Restaurant (603-823-8851), 317 Main St. Open for all three meals. A dependable, family-owned restaurant with an adjoining lounge that broadcasts sporting events and classic movies.

Above the Notch View Restaurant and Tavern (603-823-8077), 729 Main St. at the Cannon Mountain View Motor Lodge. Open Wed.–Sun.

for breakfast and lunch; Sat. and Sun. for dinner, but check. Hours vary summer to winter and in between. The local hangout, with a surprisingly diverse dinner menu.

🦐 🍴 ♿ **Polly's Pancake Parlor** (603-823-5575; pollyspancakeparlor.com), 672 Rt. 117, Sugar Hill. Open weekends 7–2 mid-April, early May, late Oct.–Nov.; daily mid-May–mid-Oct., 7–2 weekdays, 7–3 weekends. A restaurant operated by members of the same family since 1938, this modest 1830s former carriage house overlooks the majestic Kinsman mountain range and serves standard lunch fare, but is widely known for its legendary pancakes (buckwheat, cornmeal, oatmeal, buttermilk, and whole wheat), waffles, and French toast drizzled with the locally harvested maple syrup—the sugar in Sugar Hill. There are also salad plates, homemade baked beans,

COLD MOUNTAIN CAFÉ IN BETHLEHEM IS WORTH A DETOUR

Chris Tree

Chris Tree

POLLY'S PANCAKE PARLOR IN SUGAR HILL
HAS BEEN FAMILY-OWNED SINCE 1938

sandwiches on home-baked bread, and pies. Thanks to Americana-themed restaurant guides and cultural detectives such as Charles Kuralt, Polly's has gained a national reputation for providing diners a glimpse into a passing era. Walls are decorated with antique tools found in family and neighbors' sheds as well as portraits of the family who have owned this farm, one way or another, since 1819. Expect fresh food and snappy service—just don't expect to be served one minute after the restaurant closes for the afternoon (and, believe us, it sure is disappointing to find a CLOSED sign and an empty parking lot at 3:05 PM). *Tip:* Reservations are accepted on nonholiday weekends; you can also call an hour before arrival and put your name on the list. Prices range $5–25.

In Bethlehem
Rosa Flamingo's (603-869-3111), Main St. Dinner nightly from 5. Lunch Fri.–Sun. Bar menu 4–11. Lunch Fri.–Sun. A peppy Italian menu includes standards like lasagna Bolognese, eggplant parmigiana, steaks, chops, and chicken. Locally famed for its pizza. Children's menu.

✪ "❡" **The Maia Papaya** (603-869-9900), 2015 Main St., next to the post office. Open Mon.–Thu. 7–3, Fri.–Sun. 7–5. An attractive café with a blackboard menu featuring organic, vegetarian breakfast sandwiches, soups, wraps, smoothies, and an espresso bar. On a drizzly day this was a bright, welcoming oasis with WiFi and interesting books to scan while sipping chai on the coach.

Also see **Cold Mountain Café** under *Dining Out*. It's open for lunch Mon.–Sat. 11–3:30, serving soups, salads, and sandwiches.

In Littleton
Littleton Diner (603-444-3994; littletondiner.com), 145 Main St. Open daily 6 AM–8 PM in winter, until 9 in summer. No credit cards. This vintage-1940s parlor-car diner sits staunchly on Main Street thumbing its weathered nose at the fast-food outlets down the road. Portions are large and there are genuine daily specials like meat loaf, pot roast, clam chowder, and roast pork dinner. Breakfast is served all day with pancakes made from flour stone ground at the nearby Littleton Grist Mill and a menu that includes steak and eggs. Your coffee cup is bottomless; pies are a specialty. Prices are reasonable.

"❡" **Miller's Café and Bakery** (603-444-2146; millerscafeandbakery.com), 16 Mill St. Open 11–2 daily (except Mon.) for lunch, from 8:30 AM for coffee. Sited by the Ammonoosuc beside the Littleton Gristmill, an attractive space with a riverside deck in warm weather. The blackboard menu lists imaginative grilled panini, pizzas, hot pita wraps, soups, quiche, and salads. We lunched happily on a half grilled Provence panini (filled with chicken, tomato, goat cheese, red peppers, and greens) with a Styrofoam cup of gingered carrot soup.

The Coffee Pot (603-444-5722), 30 Main St. Open weekdays 6:30 AM–4 PM, Sat. until 2, Sun. till noon. Jim and Jean McKenna have a loyal following for their reasonably priced breakfast (all day, every day) specials, which include chef's hash, designer omelets, and Belgian waffles. Very reasonably priced.

Topic of the Town (603-444-6721), 25 Main St. Open Mon. 5 AM–2 PM; Tue.–Sat. 5 AM–8 PM; Sun. 6 AM–3 PM. Locals gather here to discuss the events of the day and to enjoy simple food at modest prices. Friday night is the famous fish fry with free second helping. Full liquor license.

In Lisbon

Ammonoosuc Pub at the Ammonoosuc Inn (see *Dining Out*). Open Tue.–Sat., 5–9:30. Local brews are on tap, and the moderately priced menu features wild mushroom, asparagus, and goat cheese strudel; poached salmon; as well as burgers and sandwiches. Inquire about live music.

River Café (603-838-2815), 6 South St., Lisbon. Open daily 7–3; until 8 Mon., Fri., and Sat. A spiffy middle-of-town place featuring Boar's Head deli meats in sandwiches, very reasonably priced diner fare for dinner.

ICE CREAM **Bishop's Homemade Ice Cream Shoppe** (603-444-6039), 183 Cottage St. (off Rt. 302), Littleton. Open mid-Apr.–mid-Oct., noon–10. A destination in its own right. Try Bishop's Bash. Also flavored yogurts and sorbet, all made here. Eat inside or out.

Rennell's Ice Cream (603-869-5888), 2050 Main St., Bethlehem, next to the Colonial Theater. Open 1:30–8, Wed.–Sat. in winter, more days in summer. Rave reviews for this homemade ice cream with flavors like Moose Dream, Crawford Crunch, Pumpkin Pie, and Mountain Mash.

✳ Entertainment

North Country Chamber Players (603-444-0309), Sugar Hill. Mid July–mid-Aug., Sat. at 7 PM at the Sugar Hill Meeting House; Sun. 3 PM at various locations.

Colonial Theater (603-444-5907; bethlehemcolonial.org), 2050 Main St. (Rt. 302), Bethlehem. Open May–Oct. Billed as "oldest theatre in the US!", this restored art deco facility shows art films and stages live performances, movies nightly at 7:30.

Jax Jr. (603-5907), Main St., Littleton. First-run films.

Also see the **Weathervane Theatre** (weathervanetheatre.org) in "Northern White Mountains" and the Papermill Theatre (papermilltheatre.org) in "Lincoln and North Woodstock."

✳ Selective Shopping

In Bath

The Brick Store (800-964-2074; the brickstore.com), Rt. 302 in the village. Open year-round, daily until 9 PM. Billed as "America's oldest continuously operated General Store," the Brick Store is tourist geared with fudge, cheese, doughnuts, and much more.

In Bethlehem

Bethlehem Flower Farm (603-869-3131), Rt. 302. Open Wed.–Sun., Memorial Day–Labor Day. More than 10,000 daylilies grow in the fields, with the best array in early August during the farm's annual festival. The gift barn offers lots of gardening accessories, as well as a café for lunch and afternoon tea.

Women's Rural Economic Network (WREN) Gallery and Ovation, 2013 Main St. Fine art and crafts by more than 100 local craftspeople.

ANTIQUE STORES Bethlehem Village is all about antiques. We counted half a dozen varied stores within a mile.

In Franconia/Sugar Hill

Garnet Hill Firsts and Seconds Store (603-823-5917), 297 Main St., Franconia Village behind Wendle's Delicatessen. Open Fri.–Sun. Known for flannel sheets and housewares, also good for children's clothing.

Sugar Hill Sampler (603-823-8478) Rt. 117, Sugar Hill. Open mid-May–Christmas. A 1780s barn with a folksy pioneer museum and a large selection of candies, cheese, crafts, and antiques.

Harmans Cheese and Country Store (603-823-8000; harmanscheese .com), Rt. 117, Sugar Hill. The specialty is well-aged cheddar, but the store also stocks maple sugar products and gourmet items.

In Littleton

Lahout's: **Main Store** (603-444-5838), 127 Union St.; **Discount Warehouse** (603-444-0328); and **Northface Patagonia** (603-444-0915). Herbert Lahout, a Lebanese immigrant, opened his first store in Littleton's Grange Hall in 1920. Originally a dry-goods and grocery store, it was gradually expanded by the next generation to serve the needs of skiers at Cannon Mountain. Now with four stores in Lincoln, Lahout's claims to be "the oldest ski shop in America." It's good for a full range of clothing, especially sporting.

The Village Bookstore (603-444-5263; booksmusictoys.com), 81 Main St. Open daily. The largest and most complete bookstore (and one of the

THE COLONIAL THEATER IN BETHLEHEM

Chris Tree

state's best) north of the mountains. Also a superb selection of cards and educational toys.

League of NH Craftsmen (604-444-1099), 81 Main St. One of less than a dozen outlets for New Hampshire's premier crafts group: fine furniture and furnishings, glass, clothing, art, and more.

Chutters (603-444-5787; chutters .com), 43 Main St., Littleton. The longest candy counter in the world, according to the *Guinness Book of Records*.

Tannery Marketplace (603-444-1200), 111 Saranac St., behind the Littleton Diner by the Ammonoosuc River. A former tannery, now housing salvage, antiques, and artists' studios.

Littleton Stamp and Coin Company (603-444-5386), 253 Union St. A local business with a national reputation for selling and buying stamps and coins.

FotoFactory (603-444-5600), 53 Main St. An outstanding photo shop. We stopped by to get a passport photo and walked out with a first-rate digital camera and a sense of how to use it.

Littleton Co-op (603-444-2800), corner of Cottage St. and Rt. 302, I-93 Exit 41. Open 8–8. A big new addition to town in 2009, featuring local produce.

The Arts Gallery (603-838-2300), 28 Main St., Lisbon. Open Wed.–Sun. A volunteer-run gallery for the Ammonoosuc Region Arts Council with works in varied media; worth checking out.

Littleton Farmers Market is held summer Sundays 10–1 at the Littleton RiverWalk overlooking the majestic Ammonoosuc River, and is accessed through Riverglen Lane.

✳ Special Events

February: **Forest Festival** (603-444-6228; therocks.org), The Rocks Estate, Rt. 302, Bethlehem. A mid-February day in the woods with logging demonstrations plus snowshoeing and cross-country skiing. **Frostbite Follies**, a weeklong series of events around Franconia and Littleton, includes sleigh rides, ski movies, broom hockey, ski races, and community suppers.

April: **Maple Season Tours** (603-444-6228; therocks.org), The Rocks Estate, Rt. 302, Bethlehem. Early-April weekend features a workshop about maple trees; also learn about gathering sap and boiling it down to make maple syrup.

Late May: **Lilac Time Festival** is a down-home festival in Lisbon honoring the state flower; highlights include a golf tournament, parade, pancake breakfast, bands, and a dance.

June: **Fields of Lupine Festival** (603-823-5661; 800-237-9007), Franconia and Sugar Hill. Arts and crafts, concerts revolving around breathtaking hillside displays of blossoming lupine. **Wildflower Festival** (603-444-6228; therocks.org), The Rocks Estate, Rt. 302, Bethlehem. Guided walks, workshops, demonstrations, and a children's walk on a Sunday in early June.

July: **North Country Chamber Players**, Sugar Hill. Classical concerts Saturday at 8 PM in the Sugar Hill Meeting House.

August: **Day Lily Festival**, Bethlehem. **Horse Show**, Mittersill Resort, Franconia.

September: **Franconia Scramble**, Franconia. A 6.2-mile footrace over Franconia roads. **New England Boiled Dinner**, the Town House, Franconia. Corned beef and all the fixings. **Annual Antique Show and**

Sale, Sugar Hill Meeting House. Selected dealers of antiques and collectibles.

October: **Quilt Festival**, Franconia. **Durrell Methodist Church Bazaar**, Franconia, Saturday of Columbus Day weekend. **Crafts Fair**, elementary school, Bethlehem, Sunday of Columbus Day weekend. **The Halloween Tradition** (603-444-6228; therocks .org), The Rocks Estate, Rt. 302, Bethlehem. Ghosts and goblins haunt the estate in a program co-sponsored by local Boy and Girl Scouts; also apple bobbing, pumpkin carving, and ghost stories told around the fire.

Early December: **Oh! Christmas Tree** (603-444-6228; therocks.org), The Rocks Estate, Rt. 302, Bethlehem, weekends. Celebrate Christmas with wreath making, ornament making, and a hay-wagon tour of the Christmas tree plantation. Pick your own tree to cut. Tree sales daily in December.

The Great North Woods

7

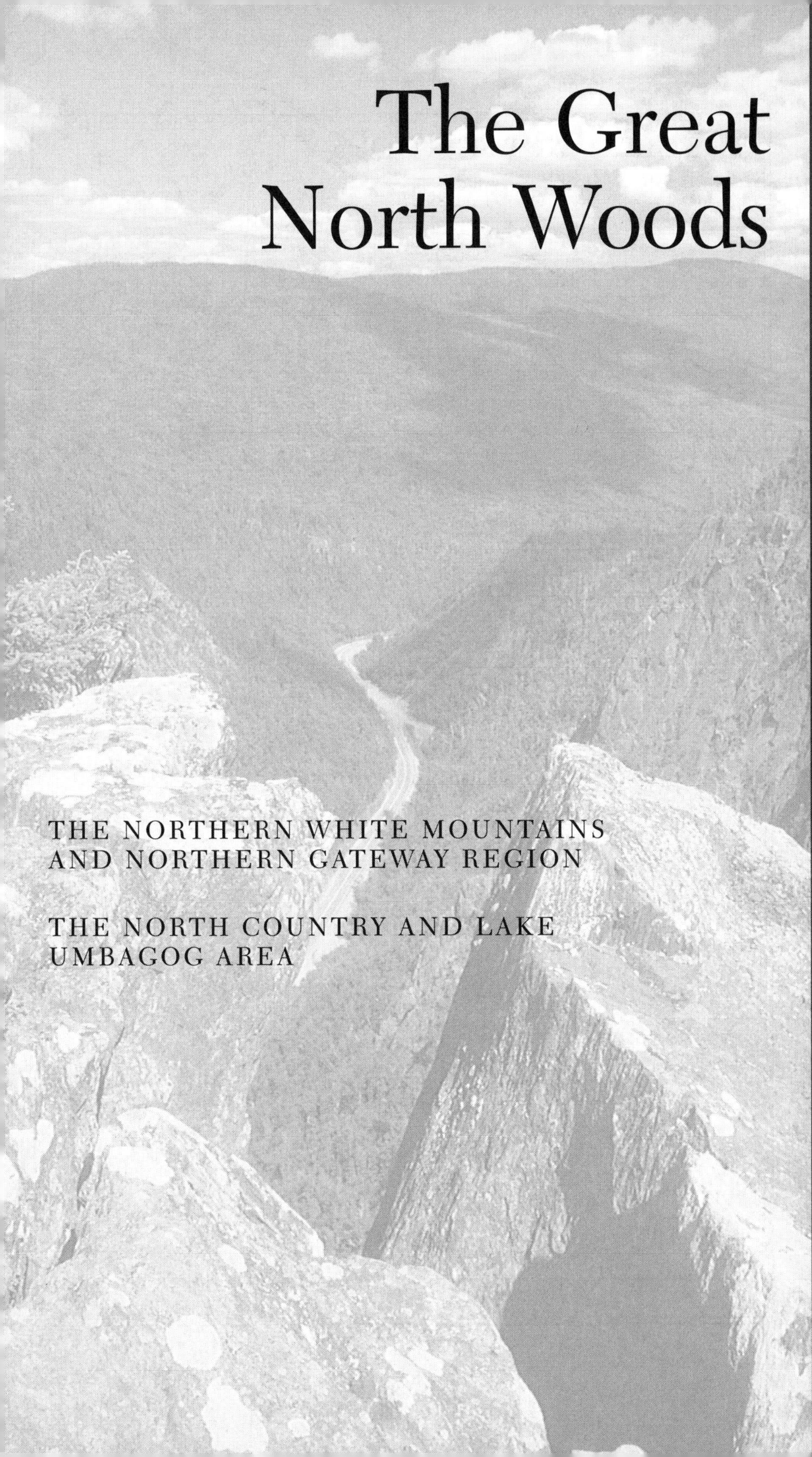

THE NORTHERN WHITE MOUNTAINS AND NORTHERN GATEWAY REGION

THE NORTH COUNTRY AND LAKE UMBAGOG AREA

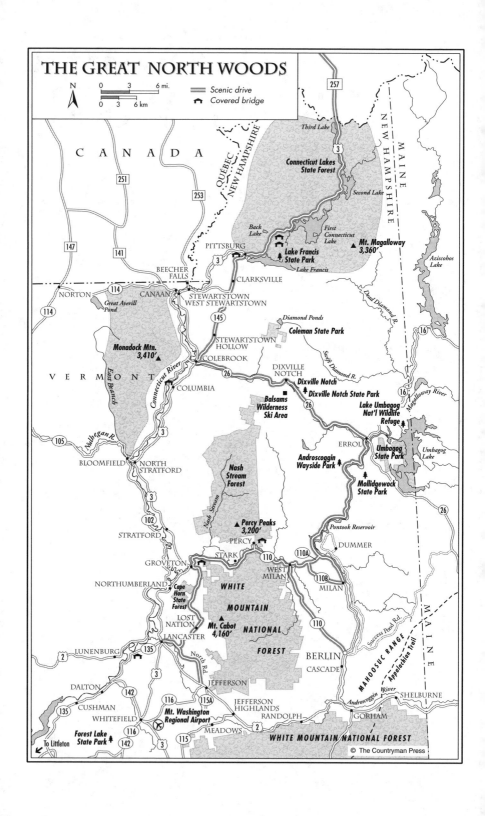

THE GREAT NORTH WOODS

N   0   3   6 mi.
0   3   6 km

Scenic drive
Covered bridge

257

C A N A D A

251

253

QUÉBEC
NEW HAMPSHIRE

Third Lake

Connecticut Lakes
State Forest

3

147

141

Second Lake

NEW HAMPSHIRE

MAINE

PITTSBURG

*Back
Lake*

*First
Connecticut
Lake*

▲ Mt. Magalloway
3,360'

*Aziscohos
Lake*

3

BEECHER
FALLS

Lake Francis
State Park

Lake Francis

CLARKSVILLE

Dead Diamond R.

NORTON

114

CANAAN

STEWARTSTOWN
WEST STEWARTSTOWN

*Great Averill
Pond*

145

Diamond Ponds

Coleman State Park

16

114

STEWARTSTOWN
HOLLOW

Monadock Mtn.
3,410' ▲

COLEBROOK

Swift Diamond R.

V E R M O N T

East Branch

26

COLUMBIA

DIXVILLE
NOTCH

Dixville Notch
Dixville Notch State Park

16

Connecticut River

Balsams
Wilderness
Ski Area

26

Lake Umbagog
Nat'l Wildlife
Refuge

Magalloway River

105

Nulhegan R.

BLOOMFIELD

NORTH
STRATFORD

3

Nash
Stream
Forest

Androscoggin
Wayside Park

ERROL

Umbagog
State Park

*Umbagog
Lake*

Mollidgewock
State Park

102

STRATFORD

Nash Stream

▲ Percy Peaks
3,200'

Pontook Reservoir

26

GROVETON

STARK

PERCY

110

110A

DUMMER

NORTHUMBERLAND

*Cape
Horn
State
Forest*

WEST
MILAN

110B

MILAN

LOST
NATION

WHITE

▲
Mt. Cabot
4,160'

MOUNTAIN

110

LUNENBURG

LANCASTER

135

North Rd.

NATIONAL

BERLIN

Success Pond Rd.

MAHOOSUC RANGE

Appalachian Trail

MAINE

2

FOREST

CASCADE

DALTON

142

135

CUSHMAN

WHITEFIELD

116

116A

115A

JEFFERSON

Mt. Washington
Regional Airport

JEFFERSON
HIGHLANDS

RANDOLPH

Androscoggin River

SHELBURNE

GORHAM

To Littleton

Forest Lake
State Park

116

142

3

115

MEADOWS

2

WHITE MOUNTAIN NATIONAL FOREST

© The Countryman Press

INTRODUCTION

New Hampshire's high hat—its least populated, narrowest, northernmost region—is actually larger than Rhode Island. It roughly coincides with 1,855-square-mile Coos County (pronounced *co-hos*), an Abenaki word for which we have read several meanings, including "place of white pines" and "crooked," perhaps referring to a river bend. The *Great North Woods* designation is relatively recent, coined to underscore the contrast between this region and the more heavily touristed sections of the White Mountains directly to its south. Towns are small and widely scattered. Most attractions are natural, not human-made.

Ironically, on road maps the Great North Woods shows up as gray, in contrast with the green of the White Mountain National Forest to the south. That's because, with the exception of an 800,000-acre WMNF tract and the vast Nash Stream State Forest, it is largely privately owned by paper and timber-management companies. For a century these have permitted recreational use while managing the woods for a continuous yield. Although most woodland has been cut more than once, the overall impression is one of wilderness. Unfortunately, this system of dual use is now threatened by global economics as paper companies sell off their forests. Still, there are some positive developments, such as the 171,500 acres of formerly commercial timberland around the Connecticut River headwaters that were secured by The Nature Conservancy and The Trust for Public Land, then transferred to the state. An additional 10,000 acres, the Vickie Bunnell Preserve in Columbia and Stratford, has also been conserved.

Coos County is home to fewer than 33,000 people and not many less than 6,000 moose. It's an area of broad forests, remote lakes, fast-running rivers, and rugged mountains. It's also the source of two of New England's mightiest rivers, the Connecticut and the Androscoggin. Early inhabitants are said to have traveled these rivers at least 8,500 years before the first white settlers arrived and set to chopping trees. Then, for more than a century, the rivers carried timber to mills, which were positioned at their steepest drops. Log runs on the Androscoggin continued into the 1960s.

In the 1850s railroads began exporting wood products and importing summer tourists. Local farmers were encouraged to take in guests, and huge hotels sprouted in the wilderness. By the 1950s, however, when passenger service from Portland ceased, all but a handful of the big old hotels had closed and travel patterns had shifted. In subsequent decades the interstates (I-93 on the west and I-95 on the east) steered travelers in other directions. New Hampshire's "North Country," as it's still commonly known, remained chiefly the preserve of serious outdoors-men—with two high-profile exceptions.

Both the Balsams Grand Resort Hotel up in Dixville Notch, and the Mountain View, recently resurrected atop a ridge near Whitefield, were gracious 19th-century summer hotels that now to attract guests year-round.

Less well known are the sporting camps and campgrounds at the very apex of the state. Similar to the rustic hunting and fishing lodges scattered widely across Maine's North Woods, here they cluster around lakes near the pristine source of the Connecticut River.

Camps and campgrounds are also gathered near the shore of beautiful Umbagog (*um-BAY-gog*) Lake to the east. From Umbagog the Androscoggin River flows south through a long, wooded valley, beloved by canoeists and anglers. Eventually it drops through the city of Berlin and, not far below in Gorham, turns abruptly east and heads into Maine.

Logistically (if not politically) the Great North Woods divides into a northern tier—the Connecticut Lakes, Dixville Notch, and the Umbagog Area—and a southern tier, the Connecticut and Androscoggin River Valleys, including towns along the two roads linking them.

The Great North Woods will never be a tourist destination in the Mount Washington Valley sense—not unless a new interstate slashes across it, once more changing traffic patterns. The region is, however, reawakening as a destination for birders and hikers as well as hunters and fishermen. Visitor services are increasing, and many seasonal lodging places now operate year-round, thanks to snowmobilers.

The 19th-century hotels were all geared to summer use only and, while Berlin's Nansen Ski Club (founded in 1872) claims to be the country's oldest ski club, this region, unlike the White Mountains to the south, was virtually unchanged by the alpine ski boom and cross-country ski boomlet. With New England's most reliable snow cover (equaled only by Maine's less accessible North Woods and Aroostook County), it is now a mecca for snowmobilers. Far fewer in number, but growing quickly, are snowshoers. Thanks to advances in equipment and clothing, average folks are discovering the beauty of winter woods, empty of all but animal tracks and sparkling with sun on snow.

The animal for which this region is best known is, of course, the moose. The Great North Woods is a moose mecca. The Annual North Country Moose Festival in late August is the event of the year, and the Gorham-based Moose Tours are a big attraction.

THE NORTHERN WHITE MOUNTAINS AND NORTHERN GATEWAY REGION

THE ANDROSCOGGIN AND CONNECTICUT RIVER VALLEYS, INCLUDING SHELBURNE, GORHAM, BERLIN, WHITEFIELD, JEFFERSON, AND LANCASTER

This easily accessible tier of the North Country is far less touristed than the landscape just to its south. It's also surprisingly varied.

The New Hampshire stretch of Rt. 2, which both defines the area's southern boundary and serves as its prime east–west highway, measures just 36 miles but links two very different north–south corridors carved by two major rivers, the Androscoggin and the Connecticut.

The Androscoggin rises in streams above Umbagog Lake, long a mecca for birders and anglers and now both a national wildlife refuge and a state park. Nearby Errol (pop. 303) serves as the hub for canoeing, fishing, and otherwise exploring both the lake and the wooded corridor along the Androscoggin as it courses south, shadowed by Rt. 16. The village, once a stop for rowdy log drivers, retains a frontier feel. At Berlin the river drops 200 feet in 3 miles, the obvious site for mills. By the 1890s Berlin boasted the world's largest paper mills, employing skilled workers representing no less than nine major ethnic groups. The Northern Forest Heritage Park on the northern fringe of town offers a sense of the rich past of the city and its woodlands, and also serves as departure point for river tours.

At Gorham, 6 miles south of Berlin, the Androscoggin River turns abruptly east. Gorham has been catering to tourists since 1851, when the Atlantic & St. Lawrence Railroad (now the Canadian National) began transporting them from Portland to the White Mountains via this direct, northern route, avoiding North Conway and more southerly White Mountains resorts. The old railroad station now houses a historical collection, as does the neighboring library; the 1858 four-story Gorham House, while no longer a hotel, still marks the center of town.

Gorham remains a prime crossroads. Main St. is a brief stretch of Rt. 2, on its way west to Burlington, Vermont, and east to Bangor, Maine. Here it meets Rt. 16, running south through the White Mountains and north into the northern forest. The Appalachian Trail passes through, too, on its way from Georgia to Maine. This explains the choice of reasonably priced good places to eat in town as well as the unusual number of good, family-owned motels. Gorham's hidden gem is Exchange St., an appealing mix of shops.

East of Gorham, Rt. 2 follows the Androscoggin River 10 miles to the Maine border, passing through an impressive corridor of birch trees that the town of Shelburne maintains as a memorial to their war dead. Across the river on the Maine line is Philbrook Farm, currently operated by the fifth generation of a family who responded to the state board of agriculture's 1860s pleas that local farmers take in guests.

West of Gorham, Rt. 2 traverses Randolph and Jefferson, century-old summer havens with exceptional panoramic views of the northern peaks of the Presidential Range. In Jefferson the memory of the Waumbek, one of the grandest of all the vanished White Mountain hotels, is preserved in its 18-hole golf course. The imposing 146-room Mountain View in nearby Whitefield has been luckier. After decades of decline and then closure, the 19th-century landmark is a grand resort once more.

If Rt. 2 continued due west, it would run into Whitefield (Rt. 116 forms the link). Instead it angles north, following the Israel River to Lancaster seat of Coos (*co-hos*) County, an inviting North Country town with a classic village square surrounded by shops, homes, and churches. Note the Great North Woods Welcome Center just off Main St.

Around the turn of the 20th century, when lumbering was at its peak in this area, it was Lancaster native John Wingate Weeks who sponsored the highly controversial bill resulting in the creation of the White Mountain National Forest. Weeks's former estate atop Mount Prospect, south of Lancaster, is now a state park, well worth a stop.

From Lancaster, Rt. 3 follows the Connecticut River north. The approach to Groveton is a tableau combining North Country history and the region's prime industry: Before the Wausau paper mill stands the Groveton covered bridge, and beside it is an old logging engine dating to the days when many miles of logging railroads webbed this area. Rising high in the background are the distinctive Percy Peaks, suggesting, perhaps, that the future of this area lies in its wilderness.

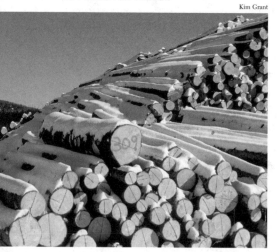

CUT LOGS FOR TIMBER

Kim Grant

Turn east on Rt. 110 from Groveton and continue 6 miles to tiny Stark village. Here a covered bridge stands by the Union Church, both built in the mid-19th century. During World War II, German prisoners of war were brought to a camp here to work in the woods. To complete a loop through this region, continue east on Rt. 110, through White Mountain National Forest. It also accesses the 40,000 acres that now form Nash Stream State Forest.

GUIDANCE Androscoggin Valley Chamber of Commerce (603-752-6060; 800-992-7480; northernwhitemtnchamber.org), 961 Main St., Box 298, Berlin 03570.

Great North Woods Gateway Welcome Center (603-788-3212; northerngate waychamber.org), 25 Park St. (off Main St. between the Lancaster Motor Inn and Sullivan's Drugstore), Lancaster. Open Memorial Day–Oct, Mon.–Fri. 11–3, Sat.–Sun. 10–2; shorter hours in shoulder seasons. Off-season contact the **Northern Gateway Regional Chamber** at 603-788-2530; 877-788-2530; northerngate waychamber.org.

A New Hampshire Information Center, Rt. 2 in Shelburne, with restrooms and picnic tables, is open year-round, Mon.–Thu. 9 AM–8 PM, Fri.–Sun. 9–9.

WMNF Androscoggin Ranger Station (603-466-2713), 2.5 miles south of Gorham on Rt. 16. Open daily 8–4:30. Good for year-round outdoor recreation info.

Seasonal information booths can be found on the town common in Gorham (603-466-3103; gorhamnewhampshire.com) and on the square in Whitefield.

GETTING THERE *By bus:* **Concord Trailways** (800-639-3317; concordtrailways .com) provides scheduled service from Boston to Gorham and Berlin daily.

MEDICAL EMERGENCY 911 works throughout this area.

Androscoggin Valley Hospital (603-752-2200; avhnh.org), 59 Page Hill Rd., Berlin.

Weeks Medical Center (603-788-4911; weeksmedical.org), 173 Middle St., Lancaster.

✴ To See

Berlin. Pick up the leaflet walking tour. As you may suspect, judging from the steep tilt of Berlin's streets, they were laid out on a map in Boston with no thought to the actual topography. Highlights include the Holy Resurrection Church (20 Petrograd St.) on Russian Hill—which contains Russian icons, reputedly a gift from Tsar Nicholas, but which, unfortunately, is not open on a regular basis. Cathedral-sized St. Ann's Church, serving the city's dominant French Canadian population, crowns the city's central hill. Inside is a 1907 Casavant Freres pipe organ with 1,763 pipes. The Berlin Public Library (603-752-5210), Main St., displays a collection of Native American stone implements, some dating back 7,000 years. Note the strong French Canadian influence here, because many residents are descended from Quebec immigrants who came to work in the woods and mills. French remains a second, or sometimes primary, language of many people, but the city retains evidence of a multitude of immigrant groups, including Germans, Irish, Italians, Russians, and Scandinavians. North of downtown, the Northern Forest Heritage Park (see the sidebar) gives more history of this area.

Weeks State Park (603-788-4004), Rt. 3, 2 miles south of Lancaster. This 446-acre mountaintop park is open year-round for outdoor recreation (the gated access road is open when either the park manager or fire lookout is on duty). In winter people walk, snowshoe, and ski the access road. The 3-mile Around the Loop Trail (rated "easy walking") is well maintained, and the 0.5-mile Nature Trail loop begins at the fire tower. The lodge/museum is usually open mid-June–Labor Day, Wed.–Sun., and weekends until Columbus Day. Not recommended for RVs, the narrow access road winds for 1.5 miles up the side of Mount Prospect, through stands of white birch and with two scenic lookouts overlooking the Connecticut River Valley. At the top is the summer home of Lancaster native John Sinclair Weeks (1860–1926) who, as a Massachusetts congressman, was responsible for the 1911 bill establishing the White Mountain National Forest and all national forests in the eastern United States. His son Sinclair was President Eisenhower's secretary of commerce.

Mount Prospect is only 2,059 feet in elevation but, true to its name, offers a spectacular 360-degree view—from the Presidentials to the Green Mountains and the Kilkenny Range. Weeks's ancestors, who farmed on this mountain, maintained a bridle path to the summit in the early 19th century, which was improved and served a hotel built at the peak in 1883. The hotel closed, but local residents continued to come to the summit. When Weeks bought much of the mountain, he upgraded the road for motor traffic and built the 87-foot-high fieldstone Mount Prospect Tower. His fanciful 1912 summer home, Mount Prospect Lodge, is pink stucco and houses the Lancaster Historical Society's collection of local birds, as well as displays on the White Mountains and on his own fascinating life. On summer Thursdays, 7 PM lectures (free) are sponsored by Friends of the Park here in the Great Hall. Subjects range from nature to history, music, and art. Inquire about naturalist-led bird and flower walks, occasional concerts, lectures and field trips, available for a nominal fee.

COVERED BRIDGES Mechanic Street bridge, Lancaster, built in 1862, spans the Israel River east of Rt. 2/3.

The Mount Orne bridge crosses the Connecticut River to Lunenburg, Vermont, 5 miles southwest of Lancaster off Rt. 135. Built in 1911, it's more than 266 feet long.

The Groveton bridge, just south of the Wausau paper mill on Rt. 3, is open to foot traffic. With a new bridge crossing the Upper Ammonoosuc, an antique locomotive, and the area's old mill stacks, the setting exemplifies the area's several eras of enterprise.

The Stark bridge, just off Rt. 110, east of Groveton. Built in 1862 with a much-modified Paddleford truss. The bridge and 1853 Union Church form a calendar-perfect scene.

FOR FAMILIES ✐ **Santa's Village** (603-586-4445; santasvillage.com), Rt. 2, Jefferson. Open from 9:30 AM (closing time varies) Memorial Day weekend; weekends until mid-June; daily through Labor Day; weekends until Columbus Day; then weekends again, featuring Christmas lights, Thanksgiving–mid-Dec. Santa and his elves, along with the reindeer, are in residence, and you can ride the Yule Log Flume, railroad, Ferris wheel, or roller coaster; watch the trained macaw show; see the animated Twelve Days of Christmas kiosk; and, of course, sit on Santa's lap. Food and gift shops. Check for admission fees. Ages 3 and under accompanied by an adult visit free as Santa's guest.

✐ **Six Gun City and Fort Splash Waterpark** (603-586-4592; sixguncity.com), Rt. 2, Jefferson. Open weekends mid-May–mid-June, then daily through Labor Day;

9:30–6 in summer, 10–5 in the shoulder seasons. Over the past 50 years this family-run attraction has evolved from a few false-fronted buildings to a variety of cowboy skits and frontier shows, combined with 35 western town buildings; an outstanding horse-drawn-vehicle museum (preserving coaches from the area's many vanished inns); miniature burros, horses, and other animals; 11 rides; and two waterslides plus a Gold Rush Express Runaway Roller Coaster. Food and gift shops. Admission includes unlimited rides, including go-carts, waterslides, laser tag, mini golf, and shows. Check for prices. Under 4 free, and free pass for another visit with first day's admission ticket.

HISTORICAL SOCIETIES **The Moffett House Museum** (603-752-4590), 119 High St., Berlin, open Tue.–Sat. noon–4 and Wed. evenings 6–8, is a Victorian house with exhibits on the history of Berlin and Coos County.

Gorham Historical Society (603-466-5338), Railroad St., Gorham. Open daily in July and August and through foliage and beyond as weather permits. The Railroad Station Museum contains displays on local history and especially railroading, tourism, and logging, while a nearby boxcar offers more on local railroading in the area.

Jefferson Historical Society (603-586-7021), Rt. 2 east of the Waumbek Golf Club, open Memorial Day weekend–Columbus Day, Tue., Thu., and Sat., 11–2. Housed in St. John's Methodist Church, displays include photos of the more than a dozen summer hotels for which Jefferson was once known. The largest and most famous was the Waumbek.

Wilder-Holton House (603-788-3004), 226 Main St., Lancaster 03584. The first two-story house built in Coos County (1780), once a stop on the Underground Railroad and now the museum of the Lancaster Historical Society. It's usually open Sun. in summer, more often depending on volunteers.

Groveton's Old Meeting House (603-636-2234), south of town on Rt. 3. This 1799 house with Northumberland Historical Society exhibits is open summer weekends but depends on volunteers.

RAILROAD STATION MUSEUM, GORHAM

Chris Tree

HISTORIC SITES AND MUSEUMS

Northern Forest Heritage Park (603-752-7202; northernforestheritage.org), Rt. 16, 961 Main St., Berlin. Open late May–mid-Oct., Mon.–Fri. 10–4 and off-season for special events. Sited on 10 riverside acres on the northern fringe of the city, the park celebrates the story of the working forest and the multi-cultural heritage of the region. A three-story clapboard Brown Paper Company boardinghouse, built in 1853 to house incoming employees, serves as an interpretive center and Artisans Gift Shop. In the reconstructed logging camp across the street on the river, costumed interpreters reenact life in the woods circa the 1880s through the 1920s. The town's paper industry started in 1877; 16 years later Berlin was manufacturing more than 125 tons a day, supplying newsprint for the *Boston Globe* and *New York Tribune*. With the arrival of the Cascade Mill (later the Brown Company) in 1904, "the city that trees built" produced 1,000 cords a day, all floated down the Androscoggin. You can leave here on a narrated river tour (aboard a pontoon boat), describing the way the river was used to float logs down to the mills. Just above Berlin (since World War I, pronounced *BURR-lin*) you see large pilings, once used to anchor booms that kept the logs moving swiftly to the mills. This is also the departure point for self-guided historical walking tours and for Moose Tours, with a pre-tour video on the habits and habitat of moose. The park's riverside amphitheater is the venue for a lively series of year-round events, including annual Great North Woods Lumberjack Championships in early October and periodic Lumberjack Dinners in the lumber camp cookhouse.

Northern Forest Heritage Park

MOOSE The local "Moose Alley" is Rt. 16 north from Berlin and the length of Rt. 110. Organized **Moose Tours** (603-466-3103; 877-986-6673) run from Memorial Day weekend through foliage season. Nightly two-and-a-half-hour moose-viewing van tours depart at dusk from the Gorham information center at the town common, 962 Main St., Gorham. Call for reservations.

Chris Tree

SCENIC DRIVES Rt. 16 North from Berlin to Errol. The 31 miles between Berlin and Errol twist and turn with the Androscoggin River.

WARNING SIGN AT THE BEGINNING OF MOOSE ALLEY, RT. 3 NORTH OF PITTSBURG

Four miles north of Berlin look for riverside **Nansen Wayside Park** with several picnic sites and a boat-launch ramp. Across the road you can see the 170-foot steel ski jump built by the Nansen Ski Club in 1936. For 50 years it was the largest ski jump in the East. North of Dummer, the **Thirteen-Mile Woods Scenic Area** is the most beautiful stretch of the river. At about the midpoint **Androscoggin Wayside Park** offers picnic tables on a bluff overlooking the river.

Pinkham B Rd. (formerly Dolly Copp Rd.) is a mostly unpaved wilderness road running from Dolly Copp Campground on Rt. 16, past the base of Mount Madison, to Rt. 2 at Randolph. Several hiking trails begin on this road. Not winter-maintained.

Jefferson Notch Rd. is a historic route beside the western edge of the Presidential Range. Not winter-maintained, this winding gravel road reaches the highest elevation point of any public through road in New Hampshire at Jefferson Notch: 3,008 feet. Drive with care, because snow and mud remain until late in spring and ice returns early in fall; it is best used in summer. The Caps Ridge Trail, at the 7-mile point on Jefferson Notch, offers the shortest route to any of the Presidential Range peaks: 2.5 miles to Mount Jefferson. From the north, Jefferson Notch Rd. leaves Valley Rd. (which connects Rts. 2 and 115) in Jefferson and runs south to the Cog Railway Base Station Rd. At that intersection, paved Mount Clinton Rd. continues on to the Crawford House site on Rt. 302.

Shelburne's **North Rd.** is a winding country byway with great views of the Presidential Range across the Androscoggin River. The road connects Lancaster with Jefferson and offers country views of the mountains, especially Mount Cabot and the Kilkenny Wilderness Area east of Lancaster. Just south of Lancaster, **Lost Nation Rd.** departs from North Rd. and runs north to Groveton. According to one tradition, this area was named by a traveling preacher who, when he could get only one person to attend church, likened the local folks to the lost tribes of Israel.

Rt. 110 and **Rt. 110A/110B** from Groveton to Milan and Berlin are picturesque in any season, but also try the secondary road parallel to Rt. 110 north of the Upper Ammonoosuc River. It runs from Groveton village through Percy and Stark to rejoin Rt. 110 just west of the 110–110A intersection.

Pleasant Valley Rd. is a loop beginning in downtown Lancaster's Middle St. (there's only one way to turn). Take the first left (past the medical center) onto Grange Rd. Follow Grange to a fork in the road and bear right onto Pleasant Valley to its junction with Garland Rd. Maps are available at Lancaster Town Hall (603-788-3391).

In Vermont. From South Lancaster you might cross the Connecticut on the covered bridge (Rt. 135) into Lunenburg, a beautiful village with views east to the mountains.

Also see **Weeks State Park** above.

✳ To Do

BIKING **Altitude 6288 Sports** (see *Selective Shopping*) in Gorham sells and services bikes and steers patrons toward innumerable trails and loops. **Moose Brook State Park** in Gorham and the **Nansen Ski Club Trails** north of Berlin are popular with mountain bikers.

BIRDING **Pondicherry National Wildlife Preserve** (see *Green Space*) in Whitefield with its Big and Little Cherry Ponds and extensive wetland is well known to New England birders. More than 234 species have been recorded here. It's also a haven for buterflies, dragonflies, and moose. The adjacent grasslands around the Whitefield Airport are also a prime birding area.

Also see **Weeks State Park** under *To See*.

CANOEING AND KAYAKING The **Androscoggin River** north of Berlin is one of the state's most popular canoeing waters. Paddlers are advised to check with the *AMC River Guide* or *Canoe Camping Vermont and New Hampshire Rivers* (Countryman Press). Pick up the AMC's *Androcoggin River Map and Guide.* East of Gorham you can paddle flatwater to Bethel and on to Rumford. See the next chapter for rentals in Errol. **Wild River Adventures** (207-824-2608), based in Bethel, Maine, rents canoes and kayaks, also offers shuttle and guide service, on the Androscoggin in Gorham.

MOUNTAIN BIKING AT MOOSE BROOK

NH State Parks

The **Connecticut River** from the Columbia bridge south to Moore Dam is beautiful paddling with many put-in places. See *Connecticut River* in "What's Where."

CAR RACING **Riverside Speedway** (603-636-2005), Brown Rd. (just off Rt. 3), Groveton. Phone for the schedule of weekend races. Sited on flats along the Connecticut River with 20 acres of field (camping permitted) and a 0.25-mile track with seating for 3,500 on the front stretch and another 5,000 in the pit area.

FISHING The Androscoggin River is a source of pickerel, bass, trout, and salmon. New Hampshire fishing licenses, required for adults, are sold online and at many stores throughout the region. Another recommended fishing spot is South Pond Recreation Area, off Rt. 110, West Milan. It has a picnic and swimming area. The Peabody River and Moose Brook are also frequented by anglers. See Great Glen Outdoor Center in "Jackson and Pinkham Notch" for fly-fishing programs. Also see the next chapter.

GOLF Androscoggin Valley Country Club (603-466-9468; pro shop 603-466-2641), Rt. 2, Gorham. Eighteen holes, bar and food service.

The Waumbek Golf Club (603-586-7777; playgolfne.com), Rts. 2 and 115A, Jefferson, is a championship 18-hole course overlooking the Presidential Range, built in 1895 to serve one of the region's largest 19th-century resort hotels. Food and beverages, plus pro shop and tennis, are available.

Mountain View Country Club (603-837-2100), Whitefield. Nine-hole course with a clubhouse offering tennis courts, a pool, and saunas, operated by the Mountain View. On a clear day the summit of Mount Washington seems but a long 2-iron shot away.

HIKING *Note:* This area offers some of New England's most spectacular hikes. Indeed, hikers represent a larger percentage of visitors here than in the Mount Washington Valley. In Gorham, **Altitude 6288** and several lodging places cater to through-hikers on the Appalachian Trail (it crosses Rt. 2 here). The following hikes just begin to suggest the quantity and quality of hikes accessible from this area in the Presidentials, as well as in the Moriah, Mahoosuc, and Kilkenny Ranges.

Presidential Range. The **Appalachian Mountain Club's Pinkham Notch Visitor Center** (603-466-2727; outdoors.org), 9 miles south of Gorham on Rt. 16, offers an overview of what's available on these northern and western slopes of the Presidential Range. If you're not familiar with the area, it's the place to begin. Since 1888 the AMC has also operated Madison Spring Hut, a full-service, summer-only facility at tree line between Mount Madison and mile-high Mount Adams.

For any White Mountain hiking, consult the *AMC White Mountain Guide* for details about trailheads, routes, distances, hiking time estimates, and special information. (Also see *50 Hikes in the White Mountains* or *50 More Hikes in New Hampshire,* both by Daniel Doan and Ruth Doan MacDougall, Countryman Press.) A map is vital here, since myriad trails interconnect on the northern side of the rugged Presidential Range peaks. There are three parking areas on Rt. 2 and another on Pinkham B (Dolly Copp)Rd., connecting Rts. 2 and 16, which are at the most popular trailheads for climbing the northern peaks of Madison, Adams, and Jefferson. Most of these trails lead above tree line and should be attempted only by properly equipped hikers. Winter weather conditions can occur above tree line any month of the year. Most of the trails to the summits are 4 to 5 miles in length and require four or five hours to reach the top. The lower portions of the trails pass through wooded areas along streams and are suitable for short walks.

Randolph Mountain Club (randolphmountainclub.org) maintains a 100-mile network of hiking trails, along with two cabins and two shelters for hikers high on the side of Mount Adams. Nominal overnight fees are charged. The cabins have cooking utensils and gas stoves in July and August, but hikers must supply their own food and bedding.

Pine Mountain is a less rigorous hike, yielding fine views of the Presidential Range. Off Pinkham B (Dolly Copp) Rd. (2.4 miles from Rt. 2 or 1.9 miles from Rt. 16), a private road that is open only to public foot traffic leads to the summit and connects to a loop trail. Estimated hiking time is two hours for a 3.4-mile roundtrip.

Mahoosuc Range. Stretching from Shelburne northeast to Grafton Notch in Maine, this rugged range offers some of the most difficult hiking on the Appalachian Trail (the mountains are not high, but the trails steeply ascend and descend the peaks). Many of the peaks—as well as rocky Mahoosuc Notch, where the ice stays in crevasses year-round—are most easily reached by Success Pond Rd., a logging road (sometimes rough) on the northern side of the mountains. In the middle of Berlin, turn east at the traffic lights across the river, through the log yard of the paper company, then travel up to 14 miles along the road to get to the various trailheads. Watch for logging trucks on this road. (See the *AMC White Mountain Guide* for hiking details.)

Waumbek and **Starr King Mountains**, north of Rt. 2 in Jefferson, are popular hikes. The climb is 3.8 miles and requires just over three hours to the top.

The Kilkenny District of the White Mountain National Forest is popular although the trails are not as well marked as in the mountains farther south. The Percy Peaks (2 miles, two hours), north of Stark, offer views across the North Country and are not likely to be crowded with other hikers. Check the *AMC White Mountain Guide* for directions to Cabot and the Percy Peaks.

The Cohos Trail (cohostrail.org) is described in the *The Cohos Trail* by Kim Nilsen (Nicolin Fields Publishing). This new trail links existing hiking paths, railbeds, and logging roads to form a continuous trail, accessible at many points along the way, running north–south through the region beginning in Bartlett and ending at the Canadian border in Pittsburg.

SWIMMING 🐾 ♿ **Forest Lake State Beach, Dalton** (603-837-9150), on a side road off Rt. 116 south of Whitefield. Open weekends from Memorial Day, daily late June–Labor Day. One of the original state parks dating from 1935, this 50-acre site has a 200-foot-long swimming beach, a bathhouse, and picnic sites. Handicapped accessible. Free.

Libby Pool, Rt. 16, Gorham. Facilities include a bathhouse, slide, and floats, but no lifeguards. Nominal admission.

South Pond Recreation Area in the White Mountain National Forest, off Rt. 110, West Milan. Open mid-June–Labor Day, this spot offers a long, sandy beach and picnic area. Fee.

✳ Winter Sports

CROSS-COUNTRY SKIING The **Mountain View Grand Resort and Spa** (mountainviewgrand.com) in Whitefield offers rentals and 27 kilometers of trails for both cross-country and snowshoeing. See *Lodging.*

The Nansen Ski Club (603-752-7968; 603-752-1650), arguably the country's oldest ski club (in 1872, when it was founded, you had to speak Norwegian to belong), maintains several miles of trails on the far side of the Androscoggin River from Rt. 16 in Milan. Trail maps are available at the clubhouse (with a woodstove) on the Success Loop Rd. off the East Milan Rd. (look for Nansen Ski Club signs on Rt. 16).

Cross-country ski rentals are available at **Great Glen Trails Outdoor Center** (greatglentrails.com; see "Jackson and Pinkham Notch"), which also offers 25km of trails groomed for traditional stride and skating (8 miles south of Gorham), and at **Bretton Woods Nordic Center** (brettonwoods.com; see "Crawford Notch and Bretton Woods") with its outstanding 100km network.

SNOWSHOEING Altitude 6288 Sports in Gorham (see *Selective Shopping*) rents as well as sells snowshoes, publishes a guide to local trails, and offers occasional evening tours. *Snowshoe Hikes in the White Mountains* by Stephen Smith details excellent hikes in this area.

SNOWMOBILING Hundreds of miles of trails web this area, connecting with Vermont and Maine systems. New Hampshire registration is necessary (call Fish and Game: 603-271-3422). Snowmobile rentals are available at Seven Dwarfs Motel (603-846-5535) in Twin Mountain and at Jefferson Notch Snowmobile Rentals (800-345-3833; jeffnotchmotel-cabins.com) on Rt. 2 in Randolph. On the New Hampshire Snowmobile Association (603-224-8906) website (nhsa.com), click on Coos County for the contact info for local clubs: the Lancaster Snowdrifters, Presidential Range Riders (Gorham), White Mountain Ridge Runners (Berlin), and Whitefield Sno-kings.

The nearest alpine skiing is less than 12 miles south of Gorham at Wildcat Mountain (skiwildcat.com; see "Jackson and Pinkham Notch") and at Bretton Woods (brettonwoods.com; see "Crawford Notch and Bretton Woods"), 4 miles south of Twin Mountain.

SNOWMOBILERS

LeRoy Anderson

✳ Green Space

White Mountain National Forest. For information about the sections in the Milan, Berlin, Gorham, and Shelburne areas, check with the WMNF Androscoggin Visitors Ranger Station south of Gorham on Rt. 16 (see *Guidance*).

Nash Stream State Forest (603-788-4157) is a 40,000-acre, undeveloped wilderness located in the towns of Odell, Stratford, Columbia, and Stark. Jointly managed by conservation groups and the Forest Service, it was rescued from sale to a developer back in 1988. It is open to day use for mountain biking, hunting, fishing, hiking, cross-country skiing, and snowmobiling. There is a seasonal, maintained gravel road off Rt. 110 (4 miles west of Groveton, turn north off Emerson Rd.).

Pondicherry National Wildlife Preserve, Airport Rd., Whitefield. This exceptional 5,500-acre preserve includes bogs (traversed by a 1.5-mile trail), fens, marshes, and Big and Little Cherry Ponds as well as streams and boreal forest. A mecca for bird-watchers, it's said to offer the greatest diversity for breeding birds in New Hampshire. Foot, canoe, and wheelchair access are planned for 2006.

Also see **Weeks State Park** under *To See* and see Milan Hill and Mollidgewock State Parks under *Campgrounds*.

MOUNTAINVIEW GRAND RESORT AND SPA   Chris Tree

RESORTS

🎿 ♿ **The Mountain View Grand Resort and Spa** (603-837-2100; 866-484-3843; mountainviewgrand.com), 101 Mountain View Rd., Whitefield 03598. Opened as an inn in 1865 after the Dodge family rescued some weary stagecoach travelers on a dark and stormy night, the original farmhouse eventually grew into a 200-room wooden summer hotel with golf course, tennis courts, and heated in-ground pool. After 1986 when it closed its doors, seemingly forever, the hotel went through a series of owners and restorations, including a $20 million makeover in 2002. In the past five years, new owners have added further amenities, including a health and wellness studio with personal trainer and yoga, a small movie theater, a family-oriented game room, a regulation-sized

INNS **The Spalding Inn** (603-837-2572, 800-368-8439), 199 Mountain View Rd., Whitefield 03598. Open year-round. This century-old estate—a seasonal resort since the 1920s—was once known for its lawn bowling (it hosted the US singles and doubles championships). More recently the rambling inn was acquired by Kris & Jason Hawes and Reanna & Grant Wilson, known as the Ghost Hunters. Along with romantic weekend escapes, the Haweses and Wilsons offer packages for paranormal buffs, who are invited to discover the inn's "hot spots." We've stayed there under previous ownership without noticing anything creepy so, ghost hunter or not, the 36-room inn remains a destination for those interested in the beauty of the mountain air and 360-degree views. There's HDTV and a billiards table in the pub; manicured lawns and perennial gardens outside. Rooms range $129–169 and include a continental breakfast.

croquet lawn, clay tennis courts, wedding terraces, a refurbished golf course, and a state-of-the-art meeting facility.

What has never changed is the spectacular panorama, which bursts on you only as you round the last curve of its driveway. Surrounding the massive yellow hotel, the Presidentials and seemingly all of the White Mountains appear to march across the horizon. The Mountain View now offers 145 rooms with private bath, featherbed, mahogany furniture, phone with Internet hookup, individual temperature control, and oversized TV. Amenities include twice-daily housekeeping and 24-hour room service. A spa with an infinity-edge soaking tub and a view that goes forever now occupies the Italian Revival–style central tower. Other amenities on the 1,700-acre site include a 9-hole golf course (there are plans to expand to 18 holes) with a clubhouse and elaborate landscaping, including waterfalls and flower gardens; an Olympic-sized outdoor pool at the clubhouse and indoor pool in the hotel; bike rentals, nature trails, full-service stables, a complimentary children's program, shuffleboard, paint ball, carriage rides, a fitness center, and tennis. There's also a new Mountain View Farm where guests can visit goats, sheep, pigs, llamas, alpacas, donkeys, and chickens. In winter there's ample cross-country skiing, ice skating, snowshoeing, sleigh rides, daily family activities, and connecting trails to interstate snowmobile corridors (snowmobile rentals). Dining options range from the informal Clubhouse Café and Tavern to award-winning dining (see *Dining Out*). Rates range through no less than nine categories of rooms, from $149–299 (low season) to $199–379 (high EP). Inquire about package plans.

Also see **The Balsams** in the next chapter.

Listed east to west along Rt. 2

♂ **Mt. Washington B&B** (603-466-2669; 877-466-2399; mtwashingtonbb.com), 421 Rt. 2, Shelburne 03581. At this classic 19th-century clapboard inn Mary Ann Mayer offers a hearty welcome and a choice of two-room suites with whirlpool tub, along with several rooms with private bath and family suites (well separated from the romantically themed rooms). The decor is a mix of antique and reproduction furniture. Rates, which include breakfast, range $140–165 for the suites, $120–125 for the rooms, a very full breakfast included.

🐾 ♂ ♿ "ĭ" **The Jefferson Inn** (603-586-7998; 800-729-7908; jeffersoninn.com), Rt. 2 (at the junction with Rt. 115A), Jefferson 03583. Open year-round. Eric and Gwen Higgins have reinvigorated this fine 1896 inn with its wraparound porch and view of the

🦆 🐾 ♂ **Philbrook Farm Inn** (603-466-3831; philbrookfarminn.com), 881 North Rd., Shelburne 03581. Open May 1–Oct. 31 and Dec. 26–Mar. 31. Back in 1861, when Susannah and Harvey Philbrook began hosting summer boarders, "guest farms" were as common as B&Bs are today. Sited as it is above a floodplain on the Androscoggin River and circled by magnificent mountains, this one prospered. Now on the National Register of Historic Places, it is said to be the country's oldest inn continuously operated by the same family.

"Every generation has added a piece," noted a member of the fifth generation to operate the inn that's now three stories high and rambles far from its original 1830s core. In the 1890s several summer "cottages" were built, each large enough to sleep a family of eight. Resort amenities now include an outdoor pool and lawn games plus nearby swimming holes and canoe launches. In winter there's snowshoeing and cross-country skiing.

While it's definitely not for the Jacuzzi set, this 18-room inn offers far more than firm mattresses and private baths. Guest rooms are comfortable as well as gracefully old-fashioned, curtained in organdy, papered in delicate flowers, and furnished with the kind of hand-me-downs for which many innkeepers would kill. The seasonal cottages range from one room to up to five bedrooms. All have a fireplace and living room.

Your hosts are Ann Leger and Larry Leger, direct descendants of the original Philbrooks. Parlors meander on and on, and everything in them has a story. Standing lamps in the living room turn out to be muskets (one from the War of 1812, the other from the Civil War); a closet is stuffed with jigsaw puzzles cut by grandfather Augustus. Ann recounts how people laughed when her grandparents paneled the large, handsome dining room in pine, considered junk wood at the time.

Dinner is served by reservation (6:30–7:30 PM). It's hearty New England

Presidential Range. The 11 rooms, all with private bath, include bright, inviting doubles and family suites accommodating up to five. The Monticello is the turret room with a four-poster and Jacuzzi. The Shaker Room boasts an allergy-free environment. Santa's Village is 1 mile down the road. A trail for nearby Starr King and Waumbek Mountains leaves from the inn, which is a favorite with hikers and bikers. Snowmobile trails also leave directly from the inn, and there are discount ski tickets available to Bretton Woods. Golfers will enjoy the 18-hole Waumbek Country Club course, the oldest in the state. Just across the street is a wonderful old spring-fed swimming pool with a beach for children. Rates are $90–190 (high end are suites), including afternoon tea and a full breakfast. Pet-friendly, wireless Internet, some ADA-accessible rooms.

Applebrook B&B (603-586-7713; 800-545-6504; applebrook.com), Rt. 115A, Box 178, Jefferson 03583.

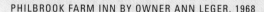

fare, usually soup and a roast with vegetables plus a relish tray (BYOB). Breakfast is memorable for the littlest, lightest of doughnuts, baked that morning.

Although no longer a working farm, the property is still 1,000 acres of fields and wooded trails, surrounded by White Mountain National Forest. It is part of a multifaceted conservation initiative to ensure that it remains as a legacy for future generations. A time warp outside as well as in, it's a difficult place to leave.

MAP rates include a full breakfast and single-entrée New England dinner with breads and pastries baked daily. Rates per couple are $130–150 MAP, $120–140 B&B; housekeeping cottages for up to eight people are $800 a week. Single rates also available. Pets are accepted in the cottages.

PHILBROOK FARM INN BY OWNER ANN LEGER, 1968

Open year-round, this rambling, pink Victorian inn is an informal, shoes-off kind of place that caters to groups and families. On our last visit, in the middle of a cold, cold afternoon, the pot-belly stove and big open view from the sitting room, along with the savory smells from the kitchen, lured us inside for a good read. But this is also a place for bicyclists, hikers, skiers, and families with happy children. There are nine rooms, all with private bath, plus three family suites. Two rooms have their own hot tub. There are cross-country/walking trails nearby. A full breakfast is included, and dinner is available to groups by advance reservation. The new innkeepers are Thomas and Joy McCorkhill; rates: $95–205.

Great Gully Lodge (603-466-2403; greatgullylodge.com), 328 Durand Rd., Randolph 03593. On a quiet road parallel to Rt. 2, this woodsy lodge boasts a wide front porch that overlooks a panoramic view of the Presidential Range, including Mount Adams's King Ravine, the "great gully" where reputedly winter's last vestige of snow appears in the form of the numeral 7. Over the years the original 1911 home has been completely redone by owners Dennis and Sara Tupick. Outside the door are 150 miles of hiking trails maintained by the Randolph Mountain Club. Inside are four bedrooms (two with private bath), each boasting its own entrance. The Adams suite offers a king bed, pull-out couch, fireplace, refrigerator, and balcony with mountain views. Rates range $80–125 with full breakfast.

Elsewhere

Stark Village Inn (603-636-2644), just across the covered bridge off Rt. 110, west of Milan or east of Groveton (mail: 16 Northside Rd., Stark 03582). Open year-round. Beautifully positioned beside a church and a covered bridge spanning the Upper Ammonoosuc River, this restored farmhouse is one of the most photographed scenes in the state. Innkeeper Nancy Spaulding offers old-fashioned comfort and plenty of knowledge about the area. The inn's three rooms (two with double beds and all with private bath and a full breakfast) are furnished in comfortable antiques. A long, rambling living room overlooks the river and is filled with books and magazines. Nearby you'll find trout fishing, hiking, bicycling, cross-country skiing, skating on the river, and snowmobiling. $50 a double room, $30 a single (plus tax).

MOTELS

In Gorham

Gorham, a former rail junction with several large hotels, is now a major highway junction with, we are told, some 600 motel rooms. We've checked out the following:

Town and Country Motor Inn (603-466-3315; 800-325-4386; townandcountryinn.com), 120 Rt. 2 (P.O. Box 20), Shelburne 03581. At the eastern edge of Gorham on the verge of the Shelburne Birches, the T&C offers 160 air-conditioned rooms with a restaurant, health club, indoor pool, whirlpool, and steam bath. It's been owned since 1956 by the Labnon family and is a favorite meeting place for area residents as well as a way stop for families and groups. Reasonable rates; inquire about golf, attractions, ski, and many more packages.

Royalty Inn (603-466-3312; 800-43-RELAX; royaltyinn.com), 130 Main St., Gorham 03581. Family geared and family run since 1956 by three generations of the King family, this middle-of-town motor inn offers indoor and outdoor heated pools, Jacuzzi and sauna, a fitness center, racquetball and basketball courts, a game room, and a restaurant. There are also 90 spacious guest rooms, some with kitchenette. $62–119, less off-season. Inquire about packages.

In Lancaster

☀ ✎ ⚲ **Coos Motor Inn** (603-788-3079; coosmotorinn.com), junction of Rts. 2 and 3, also on Snowmobile Trail 5 and Main St., Lancaster 03584. An attractive 41-room motel in the middle of town. Amenities include a 24-hour Laundromat and continental breakfast; air-conditioned rooms with two double beds, phone, and cable TV. $45–90; suites $85–150.

☀ ✎ ⚲ **Cabot Motor Inn & Restaurant** (603-788-3346; cabotmotorinn .com), 200 Portland St., Lancaster 03584. Located a mile east of downtown Lancaster on Rt. 2, a 55-room motor inn with an indoor pool, sauna, Jacuzzi, game and fitness room, and locally popular restaurant. All rooms have phone and cable TV. $59 in the older motel building across the road, $90 in the newer building.

☀ ⚲ **Lancaster Motor Inn** (603-788-4921; 800-834-3244; lancastermotor inn.com), 112 Main St., Lancaster 03584. You'll find 33 clean, comfortable, middle-of-town rooms, along with some efficiency and family units with sleep sofas. All have TV, VCR, free videos, Internet access, and phone; a continental breakfast is served. The motel caters to snowmobilers in winter and offers guided moose tours in-season. $59 per couple, $49 per single; slightly higher in summer; free under age 16.

CAMPGROUNDS White Mountains National Forest Dolly Copp Campground (603-466-2713, July–Labor Day), off Rt. 16, just south of Gorham 03581. Open mid-May–mid-Oct. With 176 sites, many of them available

through a toll-free reservation system (877-444-6777), this is one of the most popular campgrounds in the WMNF, attracting regulars year after year. The reservation service operates Mar.–Sept. (Mon.–Fri. noon–9, weekends noon–5). Reservations are accepted, but must be made at least seven days before arrival.

Two private campgrounds that come highly recommended are **Timberland Camping Area** (603-466-3872) and **White Birches Mountain Camping Park** (603-466-2022), both on Rt. 2 in Shelburne.

For details on reserving sites at the the following state-operated campgrounds, see nhparks.state.nh.us:

Milan Hill State Park, Rt. 110B (off Rt. 16), Milan. A small park with 24 primitive camping sites, picnic tables, and a playground. A fire tower atop the 1,737-foot-high hill offers sweeping views of the North Country and into Canada. Camping and day-use fees charged.

✎ **Mollidgewock State Park** (603-482-3373), Errol 03579. Open mid-May–Columbus Day. Located about 3 miles south of Errol village, in the Thirteen-Mile Woods Scenic Area. There are 42 somewhat primitive tent sites with picnic tables, fireplaces, water, and outhouses, but they are beside the river and perfect for fishing and canoeing. For reservations, call 603-271-3628.

☀ ✎ **Moose Brook State Park** (603-466-3860), Jimtown Rd., off Rt. 2, Gorham. Mid-May–mid-Oct. This small park has a large outdoor pool (known for its cold water), a small beach, 58 tent sites, a store, and showers. Camping and day-use fees charged.

In Vermont

Maidstone State Park (802-676-3930) in Brunswick. Open daily

Memorial Day–Labor Day. Easily accessible from North Stratford. Five miles south of Bloomfield on Rt. 102, then 5 miles on a dirt road, this is a forest of maple, beech, and hemlock around a large lake, with a beach, picnic area, rental boats, picnic shelter, hiking trails, and 83 campsites, including 37 lean-tos.

✴ Where to Eat

DINING OUT Libby's Bistro (603-466-5330), 111 Main St., Gorham. Open Wed.–Sat. 5:30–9 PM. Closed Apr. and Nov. Reservations recommended. Liz Jackson's appealing bistro, a series of warmly lit rooms in the vintage-1902 former Gorham Savings Bank, draws patrons from restaurant-rich North Conway (20 miles south) as well as from throughout the North Country. The half a dozen entrées change frequently, but you might begin with a creamy mushroom soup, garnished with truffles from Umbria, and move on to moist, seared ahi tuna, crusted with sesame and served with wasabi-laced mashed potatoes and crispy, light vegetables tempura. Don't make the mistake we did of dipping too heavily into the tapenade. Leave room for the restaurant's signature flourless baby chocolate cake. Jackson's skills were honed in cooking school and prepping for Julia Child's television shows, but she likes to point out that she is cooking just down the street from a diner her grandmother opened during the Depression. Her husband, Steve, who owns the nearby Altitudes sporting goods shop, shares both the cooking and hosting. Entrées $17–23. The **Salt Pub**, located in the restaurant's downstairs, opens at 4:30 Tue.–Sun. and offers draft beers, a full bar, and pub menu.

The Mountain View Grand Main Dining Room (603-837-2100), Mountain View Rd., Whitefield. Former Kennedy family chef Neil Connolly is master of this elegant AAA Four Diamond eatery, which is divided into three spaces, all with windows overlooking a magnificent mountain view. The menu is equally so with entrées that focus on such local game as venison and quail but also include New England trout with apples and walnuts for $25 all the way up to Wagyu beef with a blue cheese demiglaze for $43. Open in late fall and winter Thu.–Sat. 6–9, daily during holiday weeks and summer/fall. Also open daily for breakfast 7–11. For a more intimate setting and multicourse extravaganza, diners can reserve the chef's table in the 9,000-bottle wine cellar.

The Tavern at Mountain View Grand (603-837-2100), Mountain View Rd., Whitefield. A more casual but still sophisticated alternative to the main hotel dining room, the tavern offers such hearty New England classics as lobster Newburg, fish chowder, chicken potpie, Indian pudding, and Boston cream pie. Open daily 11–10 for lunch and dinner. Lunch ranges from $7 for a salad to twice that for New England pot roast; dinner entrées $14–28.

The 2 Kings Restaurant and Pub (603-837-2572; spaldinginn.com) at the Spalding Inn, 199 Mountain View Rd., Whitefield, is open for dinner Thu.–Sat. 5–10 PM, Sun. 4–9 PM. Pub grub is available noon–1 AM, Fri.–Sun. Entrées $12–20.

EATING OUT

In Gorham and Berlin
J's Corner Restaurant & Lounge (603-466-5132), 277 Main St., Gorham. Open Thu. 7 AM–9 PM, Fri. and Sat. till 10, Sun. 8 AM–9 PM, other days 11–9. A popular local spot with a big, reasonably priced menu. Fisher-

man's stew with garlic bread for $8.95 is a specialty.

Mr. Pizza Family Restaurant & Cracker Jack Lounge (603-466-5573), Rt. 2, Gorham. Open until 9 PM. This looks and feel like a chain, but it isn't—and judging from the number of vehicles always parked here, it's the local hot spot. The full menu ranges from burgers, salads, and pizza to surf and turf with a choice of salads; cocktails served.

The Moonbeam Cafe (603-466-5549), 19 Exchange St., Gorham Open all year, Wed.–Sun. 7–2; daily except Tue. in summer. The black bean and pumpkin soup is so delicious that the recipe is a secret. Breads (celery, onion, anadama, and the like) are baked daily, sandwiches tend to the unusual (like Oriental chicken salad with walnuts), and breakfast, featuring crêpes, is served all day. This is an attractive storefront space with pressed-tin walls and a mirrored credenza left over from its days as a barbershop. Not quick but worth the wait as everything is made to order.

Saladino's Italian Market and Restaurant (603-466-2520; saladinos italianmarket.com, 152 Main St., Gorham. Open Tue.–Thu. 10–6, Fri.–Sat. until 9 PM. A longtime local establishment with reasonably priced, traditional Italian pastas, salads, and pastries available all day in a clean, attractive atmosphere. Also has a small take-out counter with breads, meats, cheeses, biscotti, and more.

White Mountain Café and Wonderland Bookstore (603-466-2511; whitemountaincafe.com, 212 Main St., Gorham. Open daily 7–4. Pull up a chair or relax on the couch while sipping coffee, Italian soda, beer, or wine. There's also breakfast (homemade granola for $4.25), lunch, scrumptious pastries, wheat-free snacks, and a small but well-stocked bookstore.

Ingy's Ice Cream (603-752-7150), 10 Unity St., Berlin. Open May 1–foliage season. Cross the Cleveland Bridge and the huge ice cream cone atop the telephone pole means you've arrived. More than 50 hard-serve ice creams plus chicken salad and barbecue pulled pork. Ask about the Zamboni challenge.

The Northland Dairy Bar and Restaurant (603-752-6210), 1826 Riverside Dr., Berlin (Rt. 16, just north of the city). Open daily at 11 AM. Popular with canoeists and hikers, this clean, modern eatery overlooks the Androscoggin River and features fresh seafood, sandwiches, and its own fresh-made pies and ice cream.

In Jefferson, Lancaster, and Whitefield

Big Bear Family Restaurant in the Lancaster Motor Inn (603-788-4921; lancastermotorinn.com), 112 Main St. Open Wed.–Sat. 7–2 and 4–8:30. Papa-Bear-sized meals. Daily specials, homemade desserts, prime rib for $13.95.

Grandma's Kitchen Restaurant (603-837-2525), Rt. 3, 1 mile north of

MOONBEAM CAFÉ ON RAILROAD ST., GORHAM

Chris Tree

Whitefield. Opens weekdays at 6 AM, weekends at 7; closes Sun.–Wed. at 8 PM, other nights at 9. One of the best way stops along the entire length of Rt. 3: a screened porch, a U-shaped counter, immaculate, good for homemade chowders and pastries, open-faced sandwiches, and Grape-Nut pudding. Breakfast (served all day) includes superb omelets and steak or corned beef hash with eggs on toast. Dinner options include liver and onions and roast turkey with all the fixings ($9.95).

Scorpio's Pizza & Sports Pub (603-788-3660), 180 Main St., Lancaster. Open Sun. 11:45–9, Mon. 10:45–9, Thu.–Sat. 10:45–10. "Come in and watch the game," say the owners, and plenty of folks take them up on it. Pizza, calzones, Mexican, and more.

Lancaster SS Restaurant (603-788-2802), 70 Main St. Casual, family atmosphere with wooden booths, American and Chinese food. An upstairs pub has pool tables and entertainment.

Cabot Inn (603-788-3346), in the motel by that name, Rt. 2 west of downtown. Open 5 AM–8 PM. All the basics.

Common Ground Café (603-788-3773), 55 Main St. Open Sun.–Thu. 9–8, Fri. 9–3, closed Sat. An adjunct to Simon the Tanner sports and shoe store operated by the Twelve Tribes. Good for soups, sandwiches, and baked goods.

Water Wheel (603-586-4313), Rt. 2, Jefferson. Open daily June–Oct. 6–2, otherwise closed Tue. and Wed. Breakfast and lunch.

✳ Entertainment

Weathervane Theatre (603-837-9322; weathervanetheatre.org), Rt. 3, Whitefield. Open July and Aug. A widely respected repertory theater

(since 1966), housed in a converted barn featuring old favorites, musicals, comedies, and mysteries.

St. Kieran's Community Center for the Arts (603-752-1820; 603-752-2880), 162 Madison Ave., Berlin. Plays, concerts, and other live entertainment.

Royal Cinema I & II, Green Square, Rt. 16 north of downtown Berlin, shows first-run films.

Rialto Theater (603-788-2211), 80 Main St., Lancaster. Recently restored and reopened, a classic old downtown theater showing first-run films.

✳ Selective Shopping

ANTIQUES Israel River Trading Post (603-788-2880, 603-636-1771), 69 Main St., Lancaster. Open Tue.–Sat. 10–3. Antiques, auctions.

Potato Barn Antiques (603-636-2611; potatobarnantiques.com), Rt. 3, Northumberland, 4.5 miles north of the Lancaster Fairgrounds. Open Apr.–Dec., daily 9–5 except Tue. and Wed.; Jan.–Mar., Fri.–Sun. 10–4 Billed as the largest group shop in northern New Hampshire: two floors of vintage clothing, costume jewelry, china, paper, and White Mountain collectibles.

MAPLE PRODUCERS Bisson's Maple Sugar House (603-752-1298; bissonssugarhouse.com), 61 Cates Hill, accessible both from Gorham and Berlin. High on Cates Hill with panoramic views, this has been a family-operated business since 1921. The wood-fired evaporator is also used to make maple taffy ("tire"), butter, and sugar. Tours available in-season.

Burns Lake Farm (603-837-2501), 378 Littleton Rd., Whitefield. Syrup for sale and visitors always welcome. A taste of syrup and sap during the sugaring season.

Fuller's Sugarhouse (877-788-2719), 267 Main St., Lancaster. Open year-round. Dave and Patti Fuller operate a sugarhouse and country store selling maple products and local specialty items.

OUTDOOR EQUIPMENT AND SPORTS STORES

Altitude 6288 Sports, formerly Moriah Sports (603-466-5050), 101 Main St., Gorham. Open daily July 4–Labor Day, otherwise closed Sun. and Mon. A popular, long-established stop on the AT as well as with savvy hikers in general, the store takes its name from the height of Mount Washington. Owner Steve Jackson stocks a wide selection of backpacks, outdoor clothing, and gear; he sells and services bikes and offers maps and info. His selection of snowshoes (which he also rents) is wide. There's a brochure guide to local hiking and snowshoeing trails and occasional nighttime snowshoe treks. Cross-country skis are also sold. Check out the bargain basement.

Gorham Hardware & Sports Center (603-466-2312). A big, old-fashioned hardware store with plenty of things you may have forgotten if you are camping. Also a full line of sports equipment.

Simon the Tanner (603-788-4379; simonthetanner.com, 55 Main St., Lancaster. Open 9–8 Sun.–Thu., until 3 on Fri.; closed Sat. Rustic, wood-paneled store offering an extensive and sophisticated selection of name-brand shoes and casual clothing. Operated by the Twelve Tribes.

Also see LL Cote (llcote.com), central supply for the Lake Umbagog area, under *Selective Shopping* in the next chapter.

Other Old Mill Studio (603-837-8778), on the common, Whitefield. Open Wed.–Sat. 10–6, longer in summer. Tucked into a corner of the common overlooking the river, this gallery/shop represents well over 100 local artists and offers classes and stitching supplies.

Wonderland Book Store (603-466-2511), 212 Main St., Gorham. Open daily 7–4. A small but first-rate independent bookstore inside the White Mountain Café. Hiking books, maps, children's selections, and more.

Artisans Store at the Northern Forest Heritage Park (603-752-7202; northernforestheritage.org), 961 Main St., Berlin. Open May–Oct., Mon.–Fri. 9–4 and off-season for special events. This adjunct to the museum (see *To See*) is a wide but selective representation of artisans and craftspeople of the North Country.

Birds of a Feather (603-788-2552; birdsofafeathernh.net), 52 Main St., Lancaster. A collection of local artists producing handcrafted items ranging from baskets to jewelry, watercolors, and toys.

CMW Emporium (603-788-2421), 18 Middle St., Lancaster. Large selection of candles, toys, pottery, jewelry, soaps, Christmas items, and more.

Gateway Gallery & Gifts (603-466-9900), 36 Exchange St., Gorham. Open Wed.–Thu. 12:30–5, Fri. 10–5,

GORHAM HARDWARE & SPORTS CENTER

Chris Tree

Sat. till 4. A mix of vintage glassware and jewelry, art, White Mountain memorabilia, framed antique post-cards, and new photographs by owner Carla Lapierre.

✳ Special Events

January: **Winterfest** in Berlin/Gorham. Winter activities including children's sports, a Loggers' Dinner at the Northern Forest Heritage Park, sleigh rides and more.

Third weekend in March: **New Hampshire Maple Weekend**. The area's sugar shacks hold open house.

Late May–early October: **Moose Tours** daily from the Gorham Information Booth. **River Heritage Boat Tours**, daily (weather permitting) from

the Northern Forest Heritage Park in Berlin.

Last Sunday in June: **Old Time Fiddlers' Contest** (603-636-2106), Lancaster Fairgrounds, Lancaster. Bring a picnic lunch and a blanket or lawn chairs, and enjoy the music of dozens of fiddlers. Food available. Admission fee.

July–August: **Weathervane Theatre** in Whitefield.

June–October: **Lancaster Farmer's Market**, Sat. 9–noon. Local and organic produce, cheese, flowers, and much more.

Mid-June–mid-August: Tue.-evening **band concerts** on the Gorham Town Common.

July: **Berlin's Fourth of July Parade** with fireworks and duck races. **Lake Umbagog to the Ocean**—six days of canoeing, kayaking, and related events.

Early August: **Old Home Days** in the tiny towns of Milan and Stewartstown.

✍ *Labor Day weekend:* The **Lancaster Fair** is a real old-fashioned country fair. A large midway, food, and thrill rides plus 4-H animal judging, Grange exhibits, displays of vegetables and handcrafts, and ox and horse pulling. Admission fee; children under 12 free.

Late September: **Great North Woods Lumberjack Championships**, Northern Forest Heritage Park, Berlin. **International Road Forest Rally**, Northern Forest Heritage Park, Berlin. A form of NASCAR but in the woods.

THE NORTH COUNTRY AND LAKE UMBAGOG AREA

INCLUDING CONNECTICUT LAKES, DIXVILLE NOTCH, COLEBROOK, PITTSBURG, AND ERROL

Two destinations draw travelers to the top of New Hampshire: the Connecticut Lakes in Pittsburg and The Balsams in Dixville Notch.

In all there are four Connecticut Lakes, and below them Lake Francis (created in the 1930s). Each is successively larger and lower in elevation and connected by the nascent, stream-sized Connecticut River as it begins its journey down the length of New England. The lakes are strung along some 22 miles of Rt. 3 between the village of Pittsburg and the Canadian border, the stem of a backwoods system of timber company roads.

This magnificent semi-wilderness has been known for more than a century to anglers and hunters, sustained in recent winters by snowmobilers. Now word is spreading, thanks chiefly to its reputation as a moose mecca, promoted through the colorful North Country Moose Festival, held the last weekend before Labor Day. Visitors are discovering the area's exceptional bird life, its hiking and mountain bike trails, its wilderness cross-country and snowshoeing possibilities, and the expanses of quiet water so inviting to canoeists and kayakers. Lodging options are surprisingly varied and plentiful, ranging from classic lodges like the Glen and Tall Timber Lodge through rental camps to primitive and not-so-primitive campgrounds.

This entire Connecticut Lakes area lies within Pittsburg, New Hampshire's northernmost town and the largest in area east of the Mississippi. With more than 300 mostly wooded and watery square miles and a population of fewer than 1,000, Pittsburg retains a frontier atmosphere. Many residents work in the woods and spend their spare hours hunting and fishing, often displaying a spirit of independence that goes back to 1832 when portions of this town became an independent nation called the Indian Stream Republic. The name comes from a tributary of the Connecticut River, but the nation evolved when local settlers, disgruntled by boundary squabbling between Canada and the United States, solved the problem by seceding (at a town meeting) from both countries. They created their own stamps, coins, and government, but their independence lasted only a few years before the Webster-Ashburton Treaty in 1842 put the republic back in New Hampshire.

From Pittsburg two roads (Rts. 3 and 145), both exceptionally scenic, run south to bustling, friendly Colebrook, a crossroads shopping center (junction of east–west Rt. 26 from Errol as well as north–south Rt. 3 from Lancaster) for the Vermont communities of Canaan and Beecher Falls (site of Ethan Allen's huge furniture factory) as well as Columbia, Stewartstown, Errol, Pittsburg, Clarksville, and Dixville Notch.

Not so much a town as it is a place (since its tiny population is mostly connected with The Balsams resort), Dixville gets a moment of fame every four years when all 30 voters stay up past midnight to cast the first votes in the presidential election. The northernmost of New Hampshire's notches, Dixville is worth the ride just for views of this rugged, narrow pass surrounding The Balsams, the grandest of all New England's grand old hotels. It draws repeat winter- and summer-season patrons from every corner of the country, for a week at a time. It's been lucky in its ownership. In 1954, when it came up for auction, the hotel was acquired by Neil Tillotson, a descendant of Dixville Notch homesteaders. An inventor and inventive businessman, Tillotson (who died at age 102 in 2001) installed a rubber balloon factory in the former garage (still producing medical exam gloves). Even if you aren't a registered guest here, be sure to stop. The palatial resort—its dining rooms, golf courses, and 15,000-acre property webbed with hiking, mountain biking, and cross-country ski trails—welcomes visitors. The hotel's east wing, built in 1917, was the state's first multistory steel-frame-and-concrete structure. Lake Gloriette, though human-made, is perfectly suited to the setting. Nearby a Watchable Wildlife site boasts peregrine falcons.

Dixville Notch lies midway between Colebrook on the Connecticut River and Umbagog Lake, long a mecca for birders and anglers and now both a national

PITTSBURG INFORMATION CENTER

Chris Tree

wildlife refuge and a state park. Nearby Errol (pop. 303) serves as the hub for
canoeing, fishing, and otherwise exploring both the lake and the wooded corridor
along the Androscoggin River to the south.

GUIDANCE North Country Chamber of Commerce (603-237-8939; 800-698-
8939; northcountrychamber.org), P.O. Box 1, Colebrook 03576. Rt. 3, 1.5 miles
north of Colebrook. Open year-round daily. The chamber offices are in the **Great
North Woods Welcome Center**, open year-round daily 9–7, weekends 8–8. This
is an exceptional rest area stocked with information on the entire area, from Island
Pond, Vermont, on the west to Errol on the east. Other helpful websites: northnh
.com; ctrivertravel.net; nhconnlakes.com; greatnorthwoods.org.

Umbagog Area Chamber of Commerce (603-482-3906; umbagogchamber
commerce.com) is a year-round source of information with a seasonal booth that
also serves the Errol area.

Note: Pick up a current local map at a local store. We bought *Connecticut Lakes
Region Pittsburg, NH Road & Trail Guide*, printed in Colebrook, showing local
woods roads (which change each year) and pinpointing landmarks like Magalloway
Mountain and Garfield Falls. The *Colebrook Chronicle* (free) is an excellent way
of tuning in to the local scene, accessible online: colebrookchronicle.com. The
News and Sentinel, Inc., keeps you up to date on all so-called happenings and
upcoming events: colebrooknewsandsentinel.com.

GETTING AROUND *Crossing the border:* The US Customs and Immigration
Service maintains a point-of-entry station in Pittsburg on Rt. 3 at the international
border (819-656-2261), open 24 hours, seven days a week.

Note: Throughout this area, notably above the village of Pittsburg, moose are quite
common—especially at dusk when they are least visible to vehicles. Proceed slow-
ly.

MEDICAL EMERGENCY 911 works throughout the region.

Upper Connecticut Valley Hospital (603-237-4971), Corliss Lane (off Rt. 145),
Colebrook. This little, well-equipped hospital is the health care center for a large
area of northern New Hampshire, Quebec, Vermont, and Maine. At least one doctor has a private plane and makes house calls by air.

✳ To See

COVERED BRIDGES The **Columbia bridge** crosses the Connecticut River
south of Colebrook, linking Columbia village with Lemington, Vermont. Pittsburg
has three covered bridges: The **Pittsburg–Clarksville bridge**, 91 feet long, is off
Rt. 3, 0.25 mile east of Pittsburg village; **Happy Corner bridge**, 86 feet long, is
east of Rt. 3, 6 miles northeast of the village; **River Road bridge**, 57 feet long
and one of the state's smallest covered bridges, is 1 mile east of Rt. 3, 7 miles
northeast of the village.

**HISTORICAL SOCIETIES AND MUSEUMS Colebrook Area Historical
Society** (603-237-4470), Colebrook Town Hall, 2nd floor, 17 Bridge St. Open July
and Aug., Sat. 10–2. **Pittsburg Historical Society** (603-538-6342) maintains a

museum in the town hall that's open for the July 4 Old Home Day, Moose Festival in Aug., and 1–3 PM on Sat. in July and Aug. Town memorabilia aside, this museum displays a flag of the Indian Stream Republic and material relating to it. The Indian Stream School House on Tabor Rd. is listed on the National Register of Historic Places.

The Grave of Minik, Indian Stream Cemetery, Tabor Rd., Pittsburg. Minik came to the United States in 1897 with Admiral Robert Peary as one of six Eskimo "specimens" placed on exhibit at the Museum of Natural History in New York. When he returned to Greenland at the age of 18, he found himself a man without a country. Eventually he returned to Pittsburg, where he worked as a logger for a brief time before his death. He is buried here in the Afton Hall family lot. In 2005 a Danish film crew came to town to make a film based on this story.

In Canaan, Vermont, just over the bridge from West Stewartstown, the **Alice M. Ward Memorial Library**, open daily, houses the Canaan Historical Society's fascinating changing exhibits. The lovely yellow, Greek Revival building was built as a tavern in 1846 and said to have served for a while as the northernmost US stop on the Underground Railroad.

ABOUT MOOSE

Moose are the largest animal found in the wilds of New England. They grow to be 10 feet tall and average 1,000 pounds in weight. The largest member of the deer family, they have a large, protruding upper lip and a distinctive "bell" or "dewlap" dangling from their muzzle.

"Bull" (male) moose have long been prized for their antlers, which grow to a span of up to 6 feet. They are shed in January and grow again. Female moose ("cows") do not grow antlers, and their heads are lighter in color than the bull. All moose, however, are darker in spring than summer, grayer in winter.

Front hooves are longer than the rear, as are the legs, the better to cope with deep snow and water. In summer they favor wetlands and can usually be found near ponds or watery bogs. They also like salt and so tend to create and frequent "wallows," wet areas handy to road salt (the attraction of paved roads).

Moose are vegetarians, daily consuming more than 50 pounds of leaves, grass, and other greenery when they can find it. In winter their diet consists largely of bark and twigs. Mating season is mid-September until late October. Calves are born in early spring and weigh in at 30 pounds. They grow quickly but keep close to their mothers for an entire year. At best moose live 12 years.

When under attack, moose face their attacker and stand their ground—so it's natural for them to freeze when a car approaches head-on. It's best to stop and pull to the side of the road yourself.

The **Poore Family Homestead Historic Farm Museum** (603-237-5500; poore family.homestead.com), Rt. 145 halfway between Colebrook and Pittsburg, is generally open June–Sept., weekdays 11–1, weekends 11–3 or as posted, and for special events. The 1840s barn displays tools and daily household and farm equipment. The neighboring 1825 farmhouse on this 100-acre property is under restoration (suggested donation $4 per adult). Inquire about concerts and demonstrations.

MOOSE The local "Moose Alley" is Rt. 3 north from Pittsburg to the Canadian border. The annual North Country Moose Festival, held the last weekend in August, has become the region's biggest event, usually attracting more than 3,000 people, featuring a Moose Calling Contest, street fairs and dancing, barbecues, an antique car show, and a moose stew cook-off. Guided moose tours available; see "Northern White Mountains."

SCENIC DRIVES Rt. 3 north from Pittsburg. It's 22.5 miles from the village to the border, much of it through the Connecticut Lakes State Forest, a wooded corridor along both sides of Rt. 3, from the northern end of the First Connecticut

Moose are most numerous along roads early in the morning and again at dusk. Along "Moose Alleys" such as Rt. 3 north of Pittsburg and Rt. 16 north of Berlin, it's not unusual to see a dozen within that many miles, especially as the summer wears on and the animals become accustomed to "moose-watchers." Remember, however, that moose are wild animals. Don't try to see how close you can get.

While the area's first settlers reported seeing moose aplenty, they were hunted so aggressively (the tongue and nose were particularly prized as delicacies in 19th-century Boston) that they dwindled to a dozen or so in the entire state. The current count is around 9,500. New Hampshire's annual moose hunt is nine days, beginning the third Saturday in October.

WARNING The state records hundreds of often deadly collisions between moose and cars or trucks. The common road sign and bumper sticker reading BRAKE FOR MOOSE means just that. Be extremely wary at dusk when vision is difficult and moose are active.

Chris Tree

Lake to the Canadian border. Lake Francis comes into view in the village of Pittsburg itself. Look for the turnoff for Lake Francis State Park, a right after the left turn for Back Lake. First Connecticut Lake is next, sprinkled with lodges and cabins off the shore along Rt. 3 but uninterrupted forest on the far side. Note the lakeside picnic facilities. When you next see the Connecticut River itself, just south of the Second Connecticut Lake, it is a small stream. Note the Deer Mountain Campground next on your left, and finally the Third Connecticut Lake. Even in mid-August the light is northern here, and the sky seems very close. Third Lake is smaller than the others, with wooded mountains rolling away to the east and north.

Magnetic Hill in Chartierville, Quebec. Continue to the bottom of the hill north of the border on Rt. 3, then 0.25 mile and turn around. A sign instructs you (in French) to put your vehicle in neutral and hold on while your car is pulled backward uphill. It's one of those things that are impossible to describe.

Rt. 26 from Colebrook through Dixville Notch. East of Colebrook 7 miles, Fish Hatchery Rd. departs Rt. 26 north for the Diamond Ponds and Coleman State Park. The road is paved most of the way, but several gravel side roads wind over and around the hills of East Colebrook, and one continues on to Stewartstown Hollow and Rt. 145 (see below). Rt. 26 continues to climb gradually into Dixville Notch where the castlelike Balsams Grand Hotel rises above Lake Gloriette, backed in turn by craggy Abenaki Mountain. The road continues to climb by Table Rock and crests before spiraling down between sheer mountain walls. Note the picnic area on Flume Brook and, a bit farther west, the turnoff to the picnic area at Huntington Cascades. Rt. 26 continues 5 more miles to Errol, site of Umbagog Lake State Park. Rt. 26 south through Thirteen Mile Woods and the loop back via Rt. 110 to Rt. 3 takes you through uninterrupted timberlands.

Rt. 145 between Colebrook and Pittsburg is best driven from north to south for the sweeping view from Ben Young Hill. En route to and from Pittsburg, you will cross the 45th parallel, halfway between the North Pole and the equator. Dairy farms with red barns are impressive, dotting the hillsides and views. Beaver Brook Falls, just north of Colebrook on Rt. 145, is the local Niagara, with a picnic area maintained by the Kiwanis.

✳ To Do

BIKING Request or pick up a free map/guide, *Great North Woods Bicycle Routes* (nhbikeped.com), from the North Country Chamber of Commerce. Actually this is a no-brainer if you want to stick to paved roads; for mountain bikers there are miles and miles of woodland roads. **Tall Timber Lodge** (603-538-6651) rents mountain bikes.

BIRDING A splendid, free *Connecticut River Birding Trail/Northern Section* map/guide is available from local lodges and by contacting the Connecticut River Birding Trail (802-291-9100, ext.107; birdtrail.org), 104 Railroad Row, White River Junction, VT 05001.

BOATING, INCLUDING CANOEING AND KAYAKING Several lodges keep paddleboats moored on more than one lake for use by guests. **Pathfinder Tours** (603-538-7001) based at Timberland Lodge on First Connecticut Lake rents kayaks and also offers guided tours on the lakes and the Connecticut River. **Tall**

NH State Parks

KAYAKING LAKE FRANCIS

Timber Lodge rents kayaks for use on Back Lake, and **Lopstick Lodge** does the same for First Connecticut Lake as well as the Connecticut and Androscoggin Rivers. **The Balsams** offers kayak instruction on Lake Gloriette, kayaking on Mud Pond, and guided tours on Umbagog Lake.

On Lake Umbagog

Northern Waters Outfitters (summer 603-482-3817; winter 603-447-2177; beoutside.com) in Errol village has rentals, instruction, guided trips, and other canoeing information. They also coordinate flatwater kayak trips on the Magalloway River and Lake Umbagog and offer whitewater rafting, wildlife pontoon boat cruises, and tubing.

Umbagog Outfitters (603-356-3292), Box 268, Errol 03579. Offers guided flatwater and whitewater kayak tours and instruction on Lake Umbagog and nearby rivers.

On the **Connecticut River** paddlers put in at the Vermont end of the Canaan–West Stewartstown bridge off Rt. 3. The only difficult rapids (Class II) in this area are below Columbia. They run for about 7.5 miles and cannot be navigated when the water is low. Paddlers are advised to check the *AMC River Guide: Vermont and New Hampshire* (AMC Books) and two free guides: *Explorations Along the Connecticut River Byway of New Hampshire and Vermont*, a detailed guide available from the Connecticut River Joint Commissions (ctrivertravel.net), and *Canoeing on the Connecticut River.* See *Connecticut River* in "What's Where."

FISHING Fishing is what this area is about: Operators of most lodges, motels, and campgrounds depend for their livelihoods on seekers of trout and salmon. The several Connecticut Lakes; Lake Francis; Back Lake; Hall, Indian, and Perry Streams; and the Connecticut River provide miles of shoreline and hundreds of acres of world-class fishing: trophy brook trout, giant browns, and landlocked salmon for both fly- and spin-fishermen. The 2.5-mile "Trophy Stretch" of the Connecticut

River (good throughout the summer because of dam releases) is fly-fishing only. The trout season opens Jan. 1 on streams and rivers, on the fourth Sat. in Apr.–Oct. 15 for lakes, but the best fishing months are May, June, and early fall. Most of the lodges provide guides, sell licenses, sell or rent tackle, rent boats, and will give fishing information. The North Country Chamber of Commerce publishes a pamphlet guide listing local ponds, rivers, and rules.

Lopstick Outfitters and Guide Service (800-538-6659; lopstick.com), 45 Stewart Young Rd., First Connecticut Lake, Pittsburg. Orvis-endorsed fly-fishing outfitter, driftboat fishing. Offers beginner casting instruction in a 14-foot-deep, spring-fed trout pond on the premises.

Master of the Androscoggin (207-364-2506; mountainranger.com). Mountain ranger and registered New Hampshire and Maine Guide Sandy MacGregor offers fishing, guide service, and intimate riverside dining on the Androscoggin in his 17-foot handcrafted wooden driftboat.

Osprey Fishing Adventures (603-922-3800; ospreyfishingadventures.com), P.O. Box 121, Colebrook 03576. Mid-June–Labor Day. The first fishing guide on this uppermost stretch of the Connecticut River, Ken Hastings is a biologist who teaches at Colebrook Academy in the "off-season." His one- and three-day fly-fishing trips use a special 14-foot, three-person MacKenzie-style driftboat and include the guide, fly-fishing instruction if requested, and lunch. Both Connecticut and Androscoggin River trips are tailored to meet clients' abilities.

Tall Timber Lodge (800-83-LODGE; talltimber.com) offers boat rentals and sells a wide selection of flies. Inquire about fly-fishing school.

TNT Guide Service (603-752-9688, 603-723-6736; tntguide.org), 481 Enman Hill Rd., Berlin. Provides boats and guide service for various outdoor activities. Party boat holds up to 15 people.

For fishing in the Upper Androscoggin Valley see the previous chapter. **LL Cote**, a sporting goods store in Errol, is the source of fishing tips as well as equipment for Umbagog Lake area (see *Selective Shopping*).

GOLF Panorama Golf Course (603-255-4961), part of The Balsams resort, Dixville Notch. This 18-hole, par-72 course, rolling over beautiful mountain slopes, was designed by Donald Ross in 1912. The lower nine-hole Coashaukee course is great for novices. Pro shop, lessons, and cart rentals; tee times are required.

Colebrook Country Club (603-237-5566; colebrookcountryclub.com), Rt. 26, east of Colebrook village. A nine-hole, par-36 course that has a wide following.

HIKING Fourth Connecticut Lake: The Source. A small sign just north of the US Customs Station marks the start of the 0.5-mile trail to the 78.1-acre watershed surrounding the pond-sized Fourth Connecticut Lake. Owned and maintained by the New Hampshire Chapter of The Nature Conservancy, it's a surprisingly rugged trail, and you should allow two hours to adequately enjoy the roundtrip. (In 2005 the trail and bridge systems around the lake were generally improved.) The first 15 minutes are the steepest and well worth the effort as you scramble back and forth along the ridge between Canadian and American rocks, with views into the Oz-like Quebec Valley that lies just north, a pastoral mix of farms and woods around the village of Chartierville. At 0.1 mile the Conservancy's trail turns south from the international boundary, and you follow it 0.1 mile to the north end of the lake. The 2.5-acre pond lies in a wooded hollow at 2,670 feet in elevation. According to The Nature Conservancy's pamphlet guide, it's a "northern acidic mountain tarn, a remnant from the post-glacial tundra ecosystem and unusual in New Hampshire." A 0.5-mile path circles the pond, and you can step back and forth across the stream that marks the first few feet of the river's 410-mile course. The actual outlet varies, determined by resident beavers. The entire loop is 1.7 miles.

Monadnock Mountain. Overlooking Colebrook from the Vermont side of the river is Monadnock Mountain, which rises steeply and offers a nice view from the summit fire tower. From Colebrook cross the Connecticut to Rt. 102 in Vermont and turn right. Park in the sand/gravel pit by the marked signs on the left. The trail leads to a former (but safe-to-climb) fire tower.

Table Rock in Dixville Notch. Take Rt. 26 east 10 miles from Colebrook. There's a trailhead parking area on the right, behind the sign ENTERING DIXVILLE NOTCH STATE PARK. This cliff is less than 10 feet wide at its narrowest point; the vertical drop is 700 feet. The view is fabulous, but be careful! The trail is steep and rocky and should not be attempted when wet.

Mount Magalloway (2 miles, one and a half hours)—at 3,360 feet, the highest peak in this neck of the woods—offers access to a fire tower. From First Connecticut Lake Dam, turn right just past Coon Brook onto a gravel road and follow LOOKOUT TOWER signs. Two trails, the Coot and the Bobcat, lead to the summit. Coot is quicker, but Bobcat is less strenuous. Bobcat is the recommended way down. *Note:* Logging trucks have right-of-way on this road.

HUNTING Contact the listed lodges or New Hampshire Fish & Game (603-271-3211; wildlife.state.nh.us).

SWIMMING **First Connecticut Lake** has a sandy beach and picnic area; watch for signs on Rt. 3. On **Back Lake** a slide and sand beach are good for young children. **Garfield Falls** is also a local swimming hole. Ask locally about access to this beauty spot: a 40-foot drop in the East Branch of the Dead Diamond River with pools below.

WHITE-WATER RAFTING **Northern Waters Outfitters** (603-482-3817; beoutside.com), based in Errol, offers rafting on the Magalloway, Rapid, and Androscoggin Rivers to take advantage of timed releases, usually the last two weekends in July and first in August. The Magalloway is a beginner-level trip, but the rapid is advanced.

✳ Winter Sports

CROSS-COUNTRY SKIING **The Balsams Grand Resort Hotel** (800-255-0600; in New Hampshire 800-255-0800), Rt. 26, Dixville Notch. This 95km network is one of New England's best-kept secrets. Elevations range from 1,480 feet at Lake Gloriette in front of the hotel to 2,686 feet at the summit of Keyser Mountain. The majority of the 35 trails generally can be skied even when far more famous White Mountain touring centers are brown or icy. Most trails are double-track and packed for skating, but a few remain narrow and ungroomed. Our favorite is Canal Trail, a 2km corridor between tall balsams, following the turn-of-the-20th-century canal that still channels water from Mud Pond (where there's a warming hut) to the hotel. Rentals, lessons. Trail fee; free to guests.

DOWNHILL SKIING **The Balsams Wilderness** (800-255-0600; in New Hampshire, 800-255-0800), Rt. 26, Dixville Notch. The most remote ski area in New Hampshire, with abundant natural snow, rare lift lines, and a country-club rather than commercial-ski-area feel. Geared to guests at the resort.

Vertical drop: 1,000 feet.

Lifts: Four: one double chair, two triple chairs, one surface.

Trails: 16.

Facilities: Ski school, rentals, restaurant, child care.

Rates: Free to inn guests, otherwise $40 per adult on weekends, $35 weekdays; $30 per junior weekends, $25 weekdays.

SNOWMOBILING More than 200 miles of groomed trails are maintained by the **Pittsburg Ridge Runners** (603-538-1142; pittsburgridgerunners.org) alone, one of a dozen North County clubs, linking with trail systems in Maine, Vermont, and Quebec. From the Pittsburg lodges and Colebrook motels, the snowmobiler can head off after breakfast and have lunch in Maine or Canada, then return to the lodge for dinner. For maps and other information, contact the **New Hampshire Snowmobile Association** (603-224-8906; nhsa.com).

Pathfinder Sno-Tours (603-538-7001) offers tours with your own or a rental snowmobile. Rentals are also offered by **Pittsburg Motor Sports** (586-7123), **Lopstick Snowmobile Rentals** (603-538-6659; 800-538-6659), **LL Cote** (800-287-7700), and **Tall Timber Lodge** (800-835-6343).

The Umbagog Snowmobile Association (603-482-7669; umbagogsnowmobile .com) based in Errol maintains trails and offers maps for that area.

TRACKING **Paul Piwarunas** (603-538-0356) is one of several New Hampshire–registered guides who offers winter tracking in the Pittsburg area.

✳ Green Space

🐾 **Coleman State Park** (603-538-6707; off-season 603-538-6707). Primarily in Stewartstown but accessed from Rt. 26, 12 miles east of Colebrook. Excellent trout fishing in Little Diamond Pond; small boats are permitted but speed is restricted. Pets are permitted. The park marks the terminus of the 55-mile Androscoggin Trail from Berlin.

Lake Umbagog National Wildlife Refuge (603-482-3415), Rt. 16 (5.5 miles north of Errol village), mail: P.O. Box 240, Errol 03579. Umbagog (pronounced *um-BAY-gog*) is said to mean "clear water" in the Abenaki tongue. This 10-mile-long (with more than 50 miles of shoreline and many islands) largely undeveloped lake, with some 15,000 surrounding acres now declared a national wildlife refuge, is one of the finest wild areas in New England. It's home to nesting bald eagles, sharing the skies with ospreys, loons, and varied waterfowl. Moose amble the shorelines, and the fishing is great. The northern end of the lake is the most interesting, especially in the extensive freshwater marshes where the Androscoggin and

Magalloway Rivers meet. Contact the refuge headquarters for detailed canoe and kayaking routes.

Umbagog Lake State Park (603-482-7795; nhstateparks.org), Rt. 26, south of Errol, offers boat rentals (canoes, kayaks, rowboats, and motorboats), boat launch, 35 campsites with water and electrical hookups, three cabins, and 34 remote campsites around the lake, accessible only by boat. There's a beach area for swimming. $3 adults, $1 ages 6–11.

Nash Stream State Forest (603-788-4157) is a 40,000-acre, undeveloped wilderness located in the towns of Odell, Stratford, Columbia, and Stark. Jointly managed by conservation groups and the Forest Serice, it was rescued from sale to a developer back in 1988. It is open to day use for mountain biking, hunting, fishing, hiking, cross-country skiing, and snowmobiling. There is a seasonal, maintained gravel road off Rt. 110 (4 miles west of Groveton, turn north off Emerson Rd.).

Johnson Memorial Forest (860-642-7283). The trailhead with a user register and posted trail map is on Rt. 3, just above Pittsburg village, across from the fire/safety complex. With 2.5 miles of loop trails, this is a great place for birding.

✳ Lodging

INNS 🐾 🎣 **The Glen** (603-538-6500; 800-445-GLEN; theglen.org), 118 Glen Rd., First Connecticut Lake, Pittsburg 03592. Open early May–mid-Oct. Since 1962 this former private estate (vintage 1904) has been catering to hunters, anglers, and vacationers. Novices to the Great North Woods will feel at home here, thanks to longtime innkeeper Betty Falton. She's been around more than half a century and is so naturally hospitable that everyone immediately feels like family—the kind of family who appreciates the area's excellent birding ("more species of birds than anywhere else in New Hampshire") and moose-watching, mountain biking, and canoeing as well as fishing. Roughly 70 percent of the patrons return, and more than half are, of course, here to fish (staff will serve your catch at one of the three home-cooked meals), but there's no pressure to do anything; just tuning in to the inn's 160-acre lakeside property can absorb a week. The main lodge, with its large stone fireplace and long porch, offers six rooms with twins and doubles with private bath. Seven cab-

ins, some accommodating up to seven people, are scattered along the lake; the two up behind the lodge also have water views. Boats and motors for rent. Rates include all three meals (lunches are boxed): $102–133 per person plus 9 percent tax and 15 percent gratuity, discounts for seven days or more; children 4–16 are one-half adult rates. Pets are permitted in the cabins.

🍴 **The Inn at Bear Tree** (603-538-9995; beartreecabins.com), 3329 N. Main St. (Rt. 3), Pittsburg 03592. This restored 1800s homestead boasts all the amenities of home, including four well-furnished rooms with cozy quilts, private baths, HDTV, and WiFi. Rates range from $70 for "The Cabin," which has a shared bath, to $145 for the Magalloway Suite, big enough for a family with a queen bed and sleep couch. Downstairs is Murphy's Steakhouse, some of the best dining in the area (see *Dining Out*). The owners also offer a variety of other lodging, including log cabins both lakeside and woodland.

SPORTING LODGES 🐾 🎣 **Tall Timber Lodge** (603-538-6651; 800-835-

6343; talltimber.com), 609 Beach Rd., Back Lake, off Rt. 3, Pittsburg 03592. Open year-round. Founded in 1946 and owned by the Caron family since 1982, this is New Hampshire's top sporting camp. With guide services, a tackle shop, and a fly-fishing school, it's a base for novices as well as seasoned fishers. Guests are also encouraged to try kayaking (rental kayaks), mountain biking (rental mountain bikes), and sledding (rental snowmobiles). Cross-country skiing, hiking, boating, and birding venues are researched by the staff, who all seem to have the same last name. Judy, Cindy, Tom, and

THE BALSAMS GRAND RESORT HOTEL   Chris Tree

RESORT

✒ **The Balsams Grand Resort Hotel** (800-255-0600; in New Hampshire 800-255-0800; thebalsams.com), Rt. 26, Dixville Notch 03576. Open year-round. Set beneath the jagged peaks of Dixville Notch, this rambling hostelry is one of this country's outstanding survivors from the era of the grand resort. First opened in 1866 with 25 rooms, The Balsams now offers more than 200 guest rooms and a staff of more than 300. After a few years with a national management company, the hotel recently restored its traditional "innkeeper" approach with Jeff McIver, a member of the old Balsams corps, returning as president and general manager. McIver's love of the place shows; he and the staff warmly welcome both returning and new guests as if they were old friends.

Outside, 15,000 acres of mostly wilderness celebrate nature's grandeur; inside, refined elegance reigns. In the evening gentlemen still don jackets and ladies, their best attire. Even the children—of whom there are usually a number—seem to sense what's expected of them in this opulent world of intricately carved teak, ginger jars, potted palms, and endless carpeting. Youngsters find their way (via an ornate, vintage-1912 Otis elevator) to the library with its tiers of books and piles of puzzles. Some never make it to the pool tables, TV, or

David Caron operate the lodge and, happily, each seems to have a different area of expertise. In the lodge itself are eight air-conditioned rooms (four with private bath) that share their own upstairs common room with wet bar. The 25 two- to four-bedroom cabins, most lakefront, range from rustically comfortable 1940s "camps" to house-sized retreats with cathedral ceiling, stone fireplace, two-person Jacuzzi, color television, and a wall of glass overlooking the lake. Cabin and cottage rates run $150–400 in high season (Dec. 24–Mar. 12 and May 20–Columbus Day weekend), less off-season and game rooms. For adults there is evening music in the Wilderness Lounge, the ballroom, and during dinner.

Dinner is the big event of the day. At 6 PM promptly, the leaded-glass doors of the dining room slide open and guests begin strolling in to eye samples of each dish on the menu—appetizers through desserts—all exhibited on a specially designed, two-tiered table topped by silver candelabra.

Over the last few years all guest rooms have been totally renovated, from plumbing and windows to flower-patterned wallpaper, and their number has been reduced as rooms were merged to create sitting areas and new, larger bathrooms. Closets remain deep and sizable, and the windows are still curtained in organdy, the better to let in the amazing view.

In summer there is the championship 18-hole, par-72 Panorama Golf Course as well as hiking, biking, tennis on both clay and deco-turf hard courts, and boating and swimming in Lake Gloriette. The options of horseback riding, whitewater rafting, and guided kayaking as well as pontoon cruises on nearby Lake Umbagog have recently been added. In addition, a daily summer camp and babysitting are offered.

Winter brings sleigh rides and skiing on the resort's own 16-trail ski hill and 95 kilometers of high-elevation, dependably snow-covered trails. Snowshoeing is on an entirely separate, superb 45km network. Snowmobilers also find direct access to the area's extensive trail system. One way or another you can steep yourself in the magnificence of these mountains.

For the past half century, the dozen or so voters of Dixville Notch have used the hotel's Ballot Room to cast their votes in private voting booths; thus, Dixville Notch is the "First in the Nation" to report the results of the presidential election. Vintage political photos and memorabilia make this a must-see for political and history buffs.

Rates are on a per-person, per-diem basis and range $125–269, plus tax and service, depending on day and room. Winter rates are MAP with free skiing; in summer, it's either all meals or just breakfast and dinner. Children, ages 5–16, are $77.50 in winter, $97.50 in summer; under 4 free. Inquire about special packages and theme weekends.

LeRoy Anderson

LODGING ON THE ANDROSCOGGIN, ERROL

by the week. Lodge rooms are $65–105 (single rates also available). Children under 16 are free; those 6–16 are prorated by age. The Rainbow Grille (see *Dining Out*) is open nightly in-season, and breakfast is served daily. Inquire about a variety of packages.

☀ ☙ Lopstick Lodge and Cabins (800-538-6659; lopstick.com), Rt. 3 at the First Connecticut Lake, 45 Stewart Young Rd., Pittsburg 03592. She's a fly-fishing and small-game guide; he's a professional photographer; together they offer a wide variety of housekeeping cabins, from vintage one-, two-, and three-bedrooms to more than a dozen built or renovated recently and featuring Jacuzzi and gas fireplace. Most overlook First Connecticut, but three are beside Perry Stream; the most luxurious (three bedrooms) is on Back Lake. $85–300 per cabin in summer. Snowmobile ride-and-stay packages available in winter. Also see *Fishing*.

Powder Horn Lodge and Cabins (866-538-6300; powderhorncabins .com), 545 Beach Rd., Pittsburg 03592. Seven cabins and two homes fully furnished and heated; one with a hot tub, most with fireplaces, and all with cable TV, VCR/DVD, and wireless Internet. Prices range $40–60/person per night, depending on season. Boat rentals. Children under 6 free.

Ramblewood Cabins & Campgrounds (603-538-6948; 877-RAMBLEWOOD; ramblewoodcabins.com), 59 Ramblewood Rd., Pittsburg 03592. Strung along the First Connecticut Lake (and Rt. 3), these attractive modern cabins, some Lincoln Log–style and almost all log brown, appear to be unusually nicely designed and furnished, some with docks. $80–180 per couple plus $45 per additional adult in summer, slightly more in winter. Inquire about cross-country trails.

In the Lake Umbagog area
150 Main Street, Lodging on the Androscoggin (603-482-3150; 603-482-3884; lodgingontheandroscoggin .com), 142 Main St., Errol 03579. Open all year. Although this clean and pleasant nine-room house fronts Main St., out back there's a river view with pastures, horses, and even the occasional eagle. There's also a well-equipped kitchen, dining room, parlor, and three private guest rooms, each with its own bath. Rates $75–85 or $240/night for the whole house.

♥ ♂ ♿ Magalloway River Inn (603-482-9883; magriverinn.com), 3331 Dam Rd. (Rt. 16), Wentworth Location, Errol 03579. Unfortunately the namesake 19th-century inn burned down in 2002, but Granite State natives Bob and Suzanne Senter have replaced it with five cozy cabins, each with a kitchen/living room combo and sleep sofa as well as bedroom; one is handicapped accessible. $75–85 per couple, $10 per extra person, $5 per pet.

The Errol Motel (603-482-3256; errol-motel.com), P.O. Box 328, Rt. 26, Errol 03579. Open year-round; under new ownership since 2008. There are six recently renovated rooms and three housekeeping units. Snowmobile trails from the motel connect with all local trails; this is also a popular place for kayakers and fishermen. Rates are $57 per person, $67 per couple, $77 for three. Housekeeping units begin at $77; add $10 per person. Free wireless access and satellite TV. Three rooms are pet friendly.

Worth crossing the Connecticut River

♥ ♂ Quimby Country (802-822-5533; quimbycountry.com), P.O. Box 20, Averill, VT 05901, 10 miles east of Stewartstown, N.H.). As northeast as you can get in Vermont's Northeast Kingdom. This 1,050-acre resort is a 19th-century lodge and grouping of 20 cabins overlooking 70-acre Forest Lake. It is also 0.25 mile from 1,200-acre Great Averill Pond, 4 miles from 400-acre Little Averill, and surrounded by its own woodland, which, in turn, is surrounded by more woodland, much of it now conservation land. Begun as a fishing lodge in 1894, Quimby Country evolved into a family-oriented resort under the proprietorship of Hortense Quimby, attracting a large following in the process. Fearful that the place

might change when it came up for sale upon Miss Quimby's death, a number of regular guests formed a corporation and bought it. When the place is in full operation, late June–late August, it's about families and returnees. Rates are $145–167 per adult, $65–96 per child depending on age and week, with all three meals and a supervised children's program geared to ages 6–15 that includes swimming, hiking, overnight camping, and rainy-day activities. Reasonable rates during spring fishing season (May 10–June 27), and again Aug. 30–foliage season when cottages are available on a housekeeping basis and it's quiet enough to hear the leaves fall. This is a great place for birders, walkers, good conversation, and family reunions.

COLEBROOK MOTELS Colebrook motels include the **Northern Comfort** (603-237-4440); the **Colebrook Country Club and Motel** (603-237-5566), which also has a dining room and a lounge; and the **Colebrook House** (603-237-5521; 800-626-7331), a small village hotel with motel section, lounge, and dining room.

CAMPGROUNDS Coleman State Park (603-237-4560) is in Stewartstown, but it is most easily reached from Rt. 26 east of Colebrook. Open May–mid-Oct. There are 30 tent-camping sites, a recreation building, and picnic tables. Fishing is good in the Diamond Ponds and surrounding streams. Reservations are on a first-come basis. Fee charged.

Lake Francis State Park (603-538-6965), off Rt. 3 on River Rd., 7 miles north of Pittsburg village. Open mid-May–Columbus Day. This small park beside the 2,000-acre, human-made lake has 45 primitive campsites, a boat-launching ramp, showers, laundry, flush toilets, picnic area, and an information center open 8–8. A popular camping site for anglers and canoeists. No reservations. Fee charged.

Deer Mountain Campground (603-538-6955), Rt. 3, 5.5 miles south of the Canadian border. State run, no electricity, spring for water, earth toilets, 22 primitive sites.

Paradise Point Cottages on Lake Umbagog (603-482-3834; paradise pointcottages.com), Rt. 26, 8 miles north of Errol next to the public boat landing. Open year round. Five one-bedroom and 2 two-bedroom housekeeping cottages, each with its own dock, on the shores of Lake Umbagog. Refrigerator, stove, microwave, pots and pans provided; also TV sets with cable. Bring your own linens and towels. Rates $95–110 per couple; $15 each additional person.

👣 🐾 Umbagog Lake State Park (603-482-7795), Rt. 26, Errol. Mid-May–mid-Sept. Formerly a private campground, this park now offers a store, boat rentals, showers, laundry facilities, housekeeping cabins, and 38 campsites as well as 30 primitive sites accessible only by boat (rentals available). Campers must bring tents and food; there are picnic tables and fireplaces. See **Lake Umbagog National Wildlife Refuge** under *Green Space*.

Note: There are also half a dozen private campgrounds in the area.

✳ Where to Eat

DINING OUT **The Balsams** (603-255-0800; 800-255-0800; thebalsams.com), Rt. 16, Dixville Notch. The Grand Dining Room is open nightly 6–8 for a memorable meal where men and women still dress the part of elegant diners (jackets required). For nonguests, dining room reservations are requested for the $59, five-course

dinner with music and dancing. Breakfast ($24), much less formal in terms of dress but not service or selection, is served 8–10. The resort also operates a more casual **Tavern**, open from 11:30 AM with dinner served until 9 PM, drinks until closing. The **Panorama Grille**, open 11:30–3 in summer, offers a view of three states and two countries, as well as an excellent, reasonably priced menu. Check the resort's website for current menus.

Quimby Country (802-822-5533; quimbycountry.com), P.O. Box 20, Averill, Vt., 10 miles east of Stewartstown, N.H. Open last week of June–last week in Aug., serving a very full breakfast ($15) and a generous delicious dinner (BYOB) featuring fresh local produce, on-premises daily baking, and a limited menu as well as weekly lobster bakes ($30 for dinner, plus gratuity).

The Glen (603-538-6500), marked from Rt. 3 on First Lake. Open mid-May–mid-Oct. By reservation, space permitting. When you call, check what's for dinner. It's a blackboard menu and includes everything from juice to dessert. $20–27 per person; add 15 percent gratuity (BYOB). See *Lodging*.

Murphy's Steakhouse (603-538-9995; beartreecabins.com, 3329 N. Main St. (Rt. 3), Pittsburg. Open Wed.–Sun. 8–11 for breakfast, 11–2 for lunch, and 5–9 for dinner. Since John and Georgie Lyons redid this historic home a few years ago, this comfortable but sophisticated restaurant has become a mecca for some of the best dining in northern New Hampshire. Along with beamed ceilings, wide-board floors, candlelight, and crystal, there's a big-city-type menu that includes grilled bruschetta ($7) and pulled pork with chipotle barbecue sauce ($9) for lunch, and everything from creamy mushroom risotto ($18) to Angus strip steak *au poivre*

($28) to osso buco ($29) for dinner. Breakfasts range $4.50–7. With three days' notice, you and the culinary-trained chefs can even plan your own four-course "Chef's Table" menu.

❖ **Rainbow Grille at Tall Timber Lodge** (603-538-9556; 800-83-LODGE); rainbowgrille.com, 6091 Beach Rd., Back Lake, Pittsburg. Dinner nightly 5:30–8, Fri. and Sat. until 9. Request a table as close as you can get to windows, overlooking the lake in this lakeside lodge. The house specialty is rainbow trout encrusted with hazelnut flour, pan-fried in lemon butter; also baby back ribs and an extensive selection of Black Angus beef. Entrées $15.99–23.99, market price for some steaks and fish. Includes soup or salad. Children's menu and full bar. There's also a reasonably priced tavern menu. Reservations suggested.

❖ **Indian Stream Cantina & Steakhouse** (603-538-9996), Rt. 3, 2 miles south of Pittsburg village. Open daily for lunch and dinner—but check. There's a bar side and an attractive dining side. The specialty is prime rib ($19.95 for 16 ounces, $15.95 for 12 ounces), but most entrées are under $15 (with salad, starch, and rolls). The lunch menu (burgers, wraps, et cetera) is available all day, along with quesadillas and a full range of Tex-Mex. Known for its frosted Bloody Marys.

EATING OUT ❧ *❖* **Bessie's Diner** (603-266-3310), 166 Gale St., Canaan. Open weekdays from 6 AM, Sat. from 7, and Sun. from 8; closes at 8 every night. Admittedly we're suckers for cheap and friendly, but this place is so pleasant and wholesome—ditto for the food—that we can't rave enough. The menu includes burgers, 30 different kinds of sandwiches. We recommend "The Gobbler": turkey, cream cheese,

cranberry, and lettuce! Open-faced bagel-wiches (try the Grump-Fish), subs, and wraps. Poutines (Quebec-style french fries with gravy and cheese curds) are a specialty; a wide array of dinner choices average $6.75. Service is fast and friendly. Wine and beer. "Cow Licks," an ice cream window, operates summers.

Happy Corner Café (603-538-1144), Rt. 3 Pittsburg. Open Sun.–Thu. 6:30 AM–8 PM, Fri. and Sat. until 9 PM. Sharing the parking lot with Young's, the big supply source for this backcountry, this is a cheerful place specializing in big breakfasts—the usual choices plus biscuits with sausage, gravy, eggs, and home fries ($4.95)—soups (always French onion), sandwiches, pastas, and chicken. Wine and beer served.

Dube's Pittstop and Village Café (603-538-9944), 1564 Main St., Pittsburg village. The café in this general store is open most of the time for food, most days 5:30 AM–noon for table service. Hours vary with season. Burgers, omelets, ice cream, pizza, subs, and more, but the baking is the big thing here, known locally for cookies and whoopee pies.

The Spa Restaurant (603-246-3039), West Stewartstown. Open Mon. and Tue. 3:30 AM–8 PM, Thu. until 9 PM, Fri. and Sat. until 10 PM, Sun. 5 AM–8 PM. This is a big, locally popular place with breakfast specialties that include homemade rolled crêpes ($4.75) and corned beef hash with a poached egg. The lunch and dinner menus are both large. Dinner runs from pizzas through king crab legs and lobster tail.

Wilderness Restaurant (603-237-8779), Main St., Colebrook. Open 3:30 AM–9 PM daily. All down-home cooking; lounge and entertainment on weekends.

LE RENDEZ VOUS CAFE, COLEBROOK

LeRoy Anderson

Le Rendez Vous Café (603-237-5150), 121 Main St. (corner of Bridge). Open daily except Sun. and Mon. 8–5:30. Parisian pastries, cut Belgian chocolates, and a café full of armchairs and inviting corners make this authentic boulangerie seem almost like an apparition on Colebrook's Main Street. Combine your coffee and apple-cranberry-walnut torte with soup or quiche to make a meal. Friday is the big bread day; choices include French baguettes, wheat, Polish, dark rye, and fougasse (herbed), not to mention real croissants and a variety of flavored madeleines. They also sell top-quality ingredients to make your own. Locals loved what the Parisian owners did to this former bank building so much that they rallied the State Department to keep them from being sent back to France.

In Errol

Nothern Exposure (603-482-3468), junction of Rts. 16 and 26. Open weekdays 6 AM–7 PM, Sat. from 5, Sun. 6. Pub opens Thu.–Sat. at 3 PM. On a snowy Sunday in January we waited more than an hour to even place our order here—not because the staff members weren't friendly and efficient, but because this also happens to be at the junction of two major snowmobile trails. Winter weekdays and snowmobile season aside, no problem. This is a popular local gathering place any day, with a downstairs pub.

✳ Selective Shopping

Le Rendez Vous Café (see above), outstanding breads, chocolates, munchies, and quality cooking ingredients.

Fiddleheads Distinctive Gifts (603-237-9302; fiddleheadsusa.com, 110 Main St., Colebrook. Bennington and other pottery, jewelry, photography, gift baskets, and more with an emphasis on items from the USA, Canada. and the Fair Trade Federation.

Creative Natives (603-237-5541), 117 Main St. A gallery of locally crafted items and collectibles.

The Copper Leaf Gift Shop (603-237-5318; copperleafstore.com), 232 Rt. 3 north of Colebrook. Open Mon.–Fri. 9–5, Sat. 10–4. A green warehouse with a retail store showcasing gifty items from the Far East, also manufactures its own art glass.

Young's Store (603-538-6616), Rt. 3, Pittsburg. Everything you can think of needing, way beyond where you thought you'd find it: a huge store with a wide choice of meats, groceries, sporting goods, hunting and fishing licenses, boat and snowmobile registration, diesel and gas, liquor, hardware, and pizza to go. When they say "We sell generally everything," they mean it.

LL Cote (603-482-7777; llcote.com), 25 Main St., Errol. Home of a stuffed white moose and an albino porcupine, this is *the place* for gear and info. The largest establishment in town even before its 2004 expansion, Luc and Louise "Coty's" is now 50,000 square feet filled with guns, fishing tackle and flies, bows and arrows, clothing, ATVs, snowmobiles, hardware, and much more, including a foot-and-a-half-long beef bone for your dog. Needless to say, this is information central for fishermen and for supplying northern forest camps and campers for hundreds of surrounding miles. Also rents canoes and kayaks; inquire about snowmobile rentals. Open daily, even Christmas; the convenience and hardware side 6 AM–7 PM, sporting goods 8–5.

✳ Special Events

February: **Pittsburg-Colebrook Winter Carnival**, Kiwanis Club. Activities and events daily during the week of February school vacation.

March: **Sno-Deo** in Colebrook.

June: **Blessing of the Bikes**, Shrine of Our Lady of Grace, Rt. 3 south of Colebrook. The shrine was built some 50 years ago to serve the motoring public.

The festival, held the weekend after Father's Day, attracts thousands of bicyclists and an ever-increasing number of RVs, snowmobiles, and antique cars.

Fourth of July: **Fourth of July celebrations**. Fireworks at dusk at Murphy Dam, Lake Francis, also barbecue, live music, airplane rides. Parade and barbecue in Colebook.

Late July: **Logfest** in Stewartstown (logfest.com).

Third Sunday of August: **Pittsburg Old Home Day**.

Last weekend before Labor Day: **Annual North Country Moose Festival** (603-237-8939; moosefestival .com), Pittsburg, Colebrook, and Errol, New Hampshire, and Canaan, Vermont. By far the biggest annual event in the North Country, this is a region-wide celebration of the popular moose with parades, barbecues, dances, auto shows, arts-and-crafts exhibits, and sales.

September: **Annual Fiddler's Contest**, Lancaster Fairgrounds.

INDEX